THE
DEMOCRATIC DEBATE

An Introduction to American Politics

Fourth Edition

Bruce Miroff
State University of New York–Albany

Raymond Seidelman
Sarah Lawrence College

Todd Swanstrom
Saint Louis University

HOUGHTON MIFFLIN COMPANY   Boston   New York

Publisher: Charles Hartford
Associate Editor: Christina Lembo
Editorial Assistant: Kristen Craib
Senior Project Editor: Margaret Park Bridges
Senior Manufacturing Coordinator: Renee Ostrowski
Executive Marketing Manager: Nicola Poser
Marketing Associate: Kathleen Mellon

Cover image: © Harold Burch, Harold Burch Design, NYC

Acknowledgments

Excerpts in Chapter 7 from Matt Bai, "The Multilevel Marketing of the President,"
New York Times Magazine, April 25, 2004, © 2004 Matt Bai. Reprinted by permission.

Printed in the U.S.A.

Library of Congress Control Number: 2003110190

Instructor's exam copy:
ISBN 13: 978-0-618-73029-2
ISBN 10: 0-618-73029-X

For orders, use student text ISBNs:
ISBN 13: 978-0-618-43679-8
ISBN 10: 0-618-43679-0

123456789-CRS-10 09 08 07 06

BRIEF CONTENTS

CONTENTS

PART TWO
PARTICIPATION

PART THREE
INSTITUTIONS

PART FOUR
POLICY

PREFACE

The Democratic Debate reflects our dissatisfaction with existing American politics texts. Most mainstream texts claim to be objective descriptions of American politics. In fact, they present a consensus interpretation that supports the status quo and deadens students' critical sensibilities. Worse, they often make politics seem distant and boring, as if the important debates are over. We are also dissatisfied with the left-wing point-of-view texts that first emerged in the 1960s. These books raise critical issues and challenge the status quo, but after using them, we noticed that they did little to counter student cynicism about politics. Most of these texts argue that American political institutions are corrupted by the structures of global capitalism. After documenting the economic forces that overwhelm democracy, the authors often turn around in the last chapter and call for radical change. As teachers, we felt the unintended effect was to reconfirm student cynicism about all politics, even the democratic kind.

When we wrote the first edition of *The Democratic Debate* we were convinced that many students and professors were looking for a different kind of textbook—one that covered the conventional topics in American politics but in an unconventional way. Instead of taking our critical standard from European socialism or utopian democratic theory, we wrote a point-of-view text that draws its standard from the homegrown traditions of participatory democracy in America. These traditions are rich and deep, stretching from the Anti-federalist critics of the Constitution to the Populists, the progressive unions, the civil rights movement, and more recent struggles, including the women's rights, gay rights, environmental, fair-trade, and peace movements. The positive response to the first three editions has convinced us that our initial intuition was right.

THE CURRENT SITUATION

For mainstream texts, contemporary American politics are only the latest incarnation of politics "as usual." In this new edition of *The Democratic Debate*, we begin with the premise that American politics are not "as usual" today. American democracy faces unusual—indeed critical—challenges.

On August 29, 2005, Hurricane Katrina slammed into the Gulf Coast of Alabama, Mississippi, and Louisiana with devastating effect. The hurricane exposed disturbing facts about American democracy at the start of the twenty-first century: the class and racial bias of the American political system and the neglect of public investments needed to protect the nation from natural disasters. In New Orleans the surging waters broke through the levees, flooding most neighborhoods and threatening the city's very existence. The poor, most of whom are black, suffered the most. Lacking cars to flee and often living on the lowest, least attractive land, many were trapped by rising floodwaters and later victimized by roving gangs. Government help arrived too late for many. The political isolation of the poor and minorities was undoubtedly a factor in the government's sluggish response to their plight. Hurricane Katrina also exposed a shameful neglect of the public infrastructure needed to protect our citizens. After decades of politicians attacking government as the problem, not the solution, and with massive resources committed to the war in Iraq, a federal government led by President George W. Bush was not prepared to deal with a major natural catastrophe.

Popular democracy today is threatened by the enormous consolidation of presidential power under George W. Bush. Taking advantage of the mood of fear created by the terrorist attacks of 9/11, Bush has asserted novel presidential controls over American liberties and sought to prevent the courts from reviewing his actions. Enshrouding his administration in secrecy, he manipulated public opinion to begin a war in Iraq. While the public is focused on disturbing events abroad, he has moved behind the scenes to benefit his business supporters at the expense of the environment and the safety of workers. With a disciplined Republican majority in Congress giving him enthusiastic support, Bush's expansion of power at the expense of popular democracy has not been subjected to the checks and balances that are supposed to keep American politics anchored to moderation and fairness.

Conventional texts often assert that American elections represent the "median," or middle, voter and that the mobilization of one set of interests is "balanced," in pluralist fashion, by the mobilization of opposing interests. These assertions are belied by the facts. Even though voting turnout improved to 59 percent in the 2004 election, Bush still won with less than one-third of the eligible electorate. Moreover, the poor and working classes are seriously underrepresented in the active electorate, as are the young and minorities. Many citizens are withdrawing from voting because they fear, with good reason, that elections are determined by big campaign contributions, not by ordinary voters. Those big contributions flow to the Democratic Party as well as to the Republicans. Increasingly, a handful of large corporations control the mass media. Corporations and wealthy elites are able to not only influence Congress and the presidency but also to set the very agenda of politics—to determine what we talk about in the first place. Not surprisingly, Bush's massive tax cuts went overwhelmingly to the rich, who are able to use their burgeoning wealth to further corrupt the political process in a vicious circle of rising economic and political inequality.

But what about the argument that the Republican majority represents ordinary Americans, especially Evangelical Christians, who have too long been disenfranchised in the political process? Undoubtedly, the Christian Right has vigorously asserted cultural positions on issues like abortion, pornography, euthanasia, and prayer in public schools that elites had previously ignored. Unlike any other mass movement in American history, however, the Christian Right has formed a strategic alliance with wealthy corporate elites. We would not go so far as to say that Evangelical Christians have been duped by wealthy elites, but it is clear that the Christian Right has won mostly symbolic victories, whereas corporations and wealthy elites have realized tremendous material gains, often at the expense of the very working- and middle-class Christians who gave them the electoral majority. Despite all of its popular democratic trappings and deeply felt cultural issues, the Christian Right, far from representing outsiders, has now become a powerful faction in the ruling coalition, representing issues, such as restrictions on immigrant rights and free speech and support for an imperialistic foreign policy, that are far from democratic.

Although we are realistic about the current threats to American democracy, in the long run we are optimistic about the prospects for popular democracy. Past periods of elite rule and conservative reaction have been followed by democratic upsurge and reform. The Gilded Age of the late nineteenth century, for example, was followed by the populist and progressive movements that extended well into the twentieth century. The silent 1950s were followed by the civil rights and other social movements of the 1960s and 1970s. Over the long run, the trend is toward greater democracy, not less. Over and over again, democratic rights have been extended to new groups, including women, African Americans, young people, Native Americans, gays, and those with disabilities. We are confident that, as before, democratic mobilization from below will curtail the current threat to our democratic rights. We already see stirrings in the form of politically progressive unions, faith-based community organizing, and the anti-sweatshop, fair trade, and peace movements.

THEMATIC FRAMEWORK

Students can easily become overwhelmed and confused by the sheer volume of facts presented in most textbooks on American politics. They need a framework to make sense of the facts. We have developed a simple yet powerful framework for analyzing American politics. In *The Democratic Debate* the facts of American politics are organized around the theme of democracy. Specifically, each chapter examines the debate between what we call elite democracy and popular democracy, showing how that debate has impacted the particular institutions, process, or policy covered in the chapter. The overall goal is to assess the prospects and possibilities for the extension of democracy in the United States.

Our thematic framework leads us to treat the conventional topics of American politics very differently from other textbooks. Many texts, for example, treat the framers as a brilliant group of men who gave the country a Constitution that created a consensus about democracy that has persisted to this day. Because they lost the debate on the Constitution, the Anti-federalists are viewed by most textbooks as backward-looking opponents of progress who were relegated to the dustbin of history. *The Democratic Debate* is the only major American politics text to take the arguments of the Anti-federalists seriously. In our view, the founding period did not end debate but began a debate about American democracy between the tradition of elite democracy, as founded by the Federalists, and popular democracy, as founded by the Anti-federalists. To emphasize that point, we have included an Anti-federalist paper in the Appendix of the book.

Although the basics of the democratic debate were laid down at the founding, both the elite and popular democratic positions have evolved over the years. We define *elite democracy* as a system in which elites acquire the power to rule by a free competition for the people's votes; between elections the elites are given substantial autonomy to govern as they see fit. Elites stress that inequalities of power and economic resources are justified if they reflect real differences in ability, knowledge, and ambition. Over the years, the elite justification for rule has been buttressed by their claims of knowledge and expertise in an increasingly technically complex, dangerous, and competitive world.

We define *popular democracy* as a system of government in which people participate as much as possible in making the decisions that affect their lives. Popular democracy does not just mean majority rule, however, because it requires rules of the game that ensure basic equality, tolerance, and respect for individual rights. That's why the Constitution cannot be changed just with a majority vote. Although elites have successfully used claims of expertise to buttress their rule, popular democrats have not been without resources. Since the first ten amendments to the Constitution were added, partly at the insistence of the Anti-federalists, popular democrats have succeeded in amending the Constitution in a more democratic direction, including winning the vote for women and African Americans. The inclusionary logic of democracy, based on the language of equal rights and equal participation, has been used to revive the spirit of protest that began the American Revolution and to build popular democratic movements throughout American history.

In addition to organizing the facts of American politics, the theme of the democratic debate helps students to become personally engaged in the material. The book challenges students to examine their own beliefs about democracy. At the most basic level, the democratic debate revolves around different conceptions of human nature. Elite democrats view most people as private and self-interested; with the exception of a well-educated elite, they argue, people are not well suited to make public policy decisions. Popular democrats, on the other hand, view people as political beings by nature; once involved in democratic participation, they are capable of transcending their narrow parochial interests and becoming responsible, public-spirited citizens. *The Democratic Debate* challenges students to devise their own democratic philosophy based on their view of human nature.

One final point: Although we make every effort to present both sides of the democratic debate, we make no pretense of impartiality. In the pages ahead, we develop a popular democratic critique of American politics. Our values are clear. We constantly ask the question: How is it possible to increase democratic participation in American politics and create a more democratic society?

New to the Fourth Edition

The fourth edition has retained the most successful features of the previous three editions while adding extensive discussions of new developments in both popular and elite politics. Highlights among the new developments and controversies covered in the fourth edition include:

- Full coverage of the 2004 election
- The new Republican Party machine
- Republican and corporate influence on news media coverage and formats
- Impact of new campaign finance laws
- The Tom DeLay Congress and the politics of partisan polarization
- Bush's consolidation of presidential power
- The "Wal-Martization" of the American economy and the new inequality
- The power of money in interest group politics: AstroTurf lobbying
- Bush's stealth deregulation and its damage to the environment and worker safety
- Gay marriage and the culture wars
- The Christian Right as a new kind of mass movement
- The battle over Social Security
- Bush's doctrine of "preventive war" and its application in Iraq

Organization of the Book

The Democratic Debate covers all the conventional topics treated in mainstream texts. One of the main purposes of a textbook, we believe, is to cover all the important institutions and processes of American politics that should be addressed in an introductory course, thus freeing the instructor to lecture on themes of particular interest that supplement the text. We do not sacrifice coverage to develop the theme but rather use the theme to draw the reader along, examining the essential facts and concepts that are covered in other texts.

We also discuss a number of unconventional topics that are not covered in most mainstream texts. We feel, for example, that a book with democracy as its central theme must have a chapter on nonvoting, probably the most serious flaw in American democracy. Chapter 5, "Where Have All the Voters Gone?" examines why so many Americans don't vote and how voters might be mobilized. Chapter 3 examines the political economy, showing why corporations cannot be viewed as just another interest group, and Chapter 10 explores mass movements—their history, tactics, and importance to American democracy.

The book is organized in four parts. Part One deals with the foundational rules and structures of American politics. After a short introductory chapter that lays out the theme of the democratic debate, we go on to examine the Revolution and the struggle over the Constitution. In this book, the chapter on the founding is not just of historical interest in explaining the Constitution, as it is in most texts, but instead, it defines the basic contours of the democratic debate that have persisted to this day. Chapter 3 analyzes the political economy, showing how the private system of wealth formation affects the public system of democratic governance. Part One concludes with a chapter on public opinion and political culture.

Part Two covers the basic processes of participation in American politics. As befits a book that is focused on the issue of democracy, this section is longer than in most texts, spanning six chapters. Part Two is designed to acquaint students with the basic patterns of participation and the literature in political science that helps explain why some people are well represented in the political system and others are not. In the absence of strong political parties, we argue, other institutions, such as the mass media and interest groups, take over important political functions, with questionable effects for democracy. While fully documenting the phenomenon of nonvoting and other obstacles that lie in the path of democratic participation, Part Two ends on a hopeful note by examining the ability of mass protest movements to level the playing field of American politics.

Part Three covers the basic institutions of American politics—Congress, the presidency, bureaucracy, the courts, and the system of federalism. In Chapter 2, we showed how the original Constitution set up institutions that were highly elitist in nature, with the House of Representatives the only institution directly elected by the people. Since then, democratic struggles have made the major institutions more responsive to popular pressure, although they still contain many elitist elements. A theme of Part Three is that institutions have an independent effect on political outcomes and on the democratic debate.

Part Four explores the democratic debate further by looking at three policy areas: civil rights and civil liberties, economic and social policy, and foreign policy. The democratic debate concerns not just processes and rules but the distribution of rights, resources, and services. Part Four examines contemporary public policy debates through the lens of democracy, concentrating on a question usually ignored by policy analysts: Does a particular policy enhance or undermine democratic participation?

Special Features

We have included a number of special features to help students learn from the book and deepen their understanding, but we have tried not to clutter the text with too many distractions from the central theme.

To give students a road map through the book, we have included an outline at the beginning of each chapter. Important terms are boldfaced, listed at the end of the chapter, and defined in the glossary. As a guide to further reading, an annotated bibliography follows each chapter, as well as a list of Internet resources.

A boxed feature called "A Closer Look" provides students with vivid examples of the democratic debate. "Making a Difference" boxes profile extraordi-

nary individuals and groups, famous and not so famous, who have made a difference in popular democratic struggles. We also include "New Ideas," short descriptions of practical reforms that have been proposed to further the goals and
values of popular democracy.

We have illustrated our book with cartoons instead of photographs. We think
that the cartoons we have selected are eye-opening as well as funny.

TEACHING AND LEARNING AIDS: FOR INSTRUCTORS

A new, more comprehensive ancillary package accompanies the fourth edition
of *The Democratic Debate*. Available resources for instructors include the following items:

- *Instructor's Resource Manual.* Written by Leah Murray of Weber State University, Utah, this manual provides chapter summaries, ideas for lectures,
  and innovative classroom exercises.
- *Test Items.* Also written by Leah Murray, the test bank contains multiple
  choice, identification, and essay questions.
- *PowerPoint Slides.* These text-specific PowerPoint slides include chapter
  outlines and figures from the fourth edition.

You can access this content in three ways:

- Log on to the text's new ONLINE TEACHING CENTER at
  http://college.hmco.com/pic/TheDemocraticDebate4e. This site contains all of the instructor resources listed above except test items, and it
  also includes the content from the student site (see below).
- Contact your Houghton Mifflin sales representative for a free copy of
  the text's ClassPrep CD-ROM with HM Testing. This disk contains all of
  the instructor resources listed above, and it also includes the HM Testing
  electronic test generation program.
- Contact your Houghton Mifflin sales representative for a free Blackboard
  or WebCT course cartridge to accompany this text. The cartridge contains all of the instructor resources listed above, plus general suggestions
  for teaching online, online homework on selected topics, and a link to
  student material at the ONLINE STUDY CENTER.

TEACHING AND LEARNING AIDS: FOR STUDENTS

Students can access the text's new ONLINE STUDY CENTER (OSC) at
http://college.hmco.com/pic/TheDemocraticDebate4e. Site content includes
chapter outlines, ACE self-tests, flashcards, a glossary, primary source documents, and annotated Web links.

DEBATING DEMOCRACY: A READER IN AMERICAN POLITICS

We note with pride that we also publish a reader called *Debating Democracy*, building on themes in our text. Each chapter in the reader features a debate between two opposing sides on an important issue for democracy, such as the new media, the USA Patriot Act, presidential leadership, and economic inequality. The enthusiastic reception of *Debating Democracy* has made it clear that it can be used in conjunction with any American politics text. It works especially well, however, as a companion volume to *The Democratic Debate*. The two books, when purchased together, are available at a discount. Contact your Houghton Mifflin representative.

ACKNOWLEDGMENTS

Like democracy itself, this text has benefited from the participation of many people. We were fortunate to have a series of dedicated professionals to guide this project over the years at Houghton Mifflin: Gregory Tobin, Margaret Seawell, Jean Woy, Janet Young, Tracy Patruno, Fran Gay, and Katherine Meisenheimer. We especially want to acknowledge the work of our editor for the first edition, Ann West, who improved the book immeasurably with her suggestions. Naomi Kornhauser helped select appealing cartoons and photos for the first edition. Our editors for the second edition, Ann Torbert and Melissa Mashburn, did an excellent job working under extremely tight deadlines. Mary Dougherty, our editor for the third edition, also gave us wise guidance and support. Christina Lembo was a careful and attentive editor for the fourth edition, and Nancy Benjamin at Books By Design did an excellent job of handling the day-to-day production.

Our friends and colleagues Walter Balk, Susan Christopherson, Peter Dreier, Marty Edelman, Anne Hildreth, and Steve Wasby provided insightful feedback on a number of chapters. A number of graduate students at SUNY Albany, including Martin Shaffer, David Filbert, Christopher Price, Yong-Hoo Sohn, and Paul Alexander, helped us with research on the text. At Saint Louis University, Mamoun Benmammoun provided valuable research assistance. Michael Gizzi and Lance Denning wrote the original glossary and assisted with the research. Paul Goggi updated tables and wrote drafts of several boxes.

At Sarah Lawrence, students Joni Ang, Asia Friedman, and David G. Hill provided outstanding research assistance for the second edition. Amanda Slagle, Claire Landiss, and Brooke DeRenzis provided indispensable help with research and with the themes and writing of many feature boxes for the third edition. Laura Ann Pechacek was a great help in preparing the fourth edition. The staff of the Esther Raushenbush Library—especially Charling Fagan, Bill Haines, David Nicholls, Judy Kicinski, and Barbara Hickey—showed how patient librarians can be with impatient scholars. Grants from the Julie and Ruediger

Flik Travel Fund and the Hewlett-Mellon Fellowship Fund helped provide the time needed to meet publishing deadlines.

The book benefited greatly from the comments of many political scientists across the country. Fortunately, these outside reviewers did not spare us in their criticisms, and although we squirmed, the book was ultimately much better because of their efforts. Our thanks go to Gordon Alexandre, Glendale Community College; Stephen Amburg, University of Texas–San Antonio; Theodore S. Arrington, University of North Carolina at Charlotte; Judith A. Baer, Texas A & M University; Horace Bartilow Jr., University of Kentucky; Gerald Berk, University of Oregon; Jim Bromeland, Winona State University; John P. Burke, University of Vermont; Michael John Burton, Ohio University; Richard Bush, Southern Illinois University; Allan J. Cigler, University of Kansas; Sue Davis, University of Delaware; Jeffrey Edwards, Roosevelt University; Henry Flores, St. Mary's University; Dennis J. Goldford, Drake University; Richard Herrera, Arizona State University; Herbert Hirsch, Virginia Commonwealth University; Steven Hoffman, University of St. Thomas; James Hogan, Seattle University; Kenneth Kennedy, College of San Mateo; Robert Kerstein, University of Tampa; Dr. Virginia G. McClamm, City College of San Francisco; James Meader, Augustana College; Jerome O'Callaghan, State University of New York at Cortland; Mark P. Petracca, University of California, Irvine; George Pippin, Jones County Junior College; Jerry Pubantz, Salem College; Ted Radke, Contra Costa Community College; Leonard Ritt, Northern Arizona University; John S. Robey, University of Texas–Brownsville; Pamela H. Rodgers, University of Wisconsin–La Crosse; John Squibb, Lincoln Land Community College; M. Elliot Vittes, University of Central Florida; and Mitchell Weiss, Charles S. Mott Community College.

Finally, we want to thank our families for their love, support, and patience: Melinda, Nick, Anna, Fay, Eva, Rosa, Katie, Jessica, Madeleine, and Eleanore.

B. M., R. S., T. S.

ABOUT THE AUTHORS

Bruce Miroff (Ph.D. University of California, Berkeley, 1974) is professor of political science at the State University of New York–Albany, and is the past president of the Presidency Research Group of the American Political Science Association. He is the author of *Pragmatic Illusions: The Presidential Politics of John F. Kennedy* and *Icons of Democracy: American Leaders as Heroes, Aristocrats, Dissenters, and Democrats*, as well as numerous articles on the presidency, American political theory, and American political development. Along with Seidelman and Swanstrom, he is co-editor of *Debating Democracy: A Reader in American Politics*, also published by Houghton Mifflin.

Raymond Seidelman (Ph.D. Cornell University, 1979) is a professor of politics and the Sara Exley Yates Professor of Teaching Excellence at Sarah Lawrence College in Yonkers, New York. Seidelman is the author of *Disenchanted Realists: Political Science and the American Crisis*, and the co-editor (with James Farr) of *Discipline and History: Political Science in the United States*. He instructs courses in American electoral politics, the mass media, and urban and suburban history and politics. He has taught in China and South Korea and lectured extensively in many East Asian countries.

Todd Swanstrom (Ph.D. Princeton University, 1981) teaches in the Department of Public Policy at Saint Louis University. Specializing in urban politics and public policy, he is the author of *The Crisis of Growth Politics: Cleveland, Kucinich, and the Challenge of Urban Populism* and co-author of *City Politics: The Political Economy of Urban America* (5th edition, 2006) and *Place Matters: Metropolitics for the Twenty-First Century* (2nd edition, 2005). Recently, he collaborated with a group of political scientists in writing *Democracy at Risk: How Political Choices Undermine Civic Participation, and What We Can Do About It.*

Introduction
The Democratic Debate

> Men, by their constitutions, are naturally divided into two parties: 1. Those who fear and distrust the people, and wish to draw all powers from them into the hands of the higher classes. 2. Those who identify themselves with the people, have confidence in them, cherish and consider them as the most honest and safe, although not the most wise, depository of the public interests. . . . The appellation of Aristocrats and Democrats is the true one, expressing the essence of all.
>
> Thomas Jefferson, *Writings*, vol. XVI, p. 73

Most Americans view the United States as a model democracy. Sure, there are flaws in our government, but most people agree that the foundation for a democratic society was secured by the Constitution and later laws. The great debates about the rules of the game are settled. Consider elections. The consensus view is that we gradually progressed over history to free and fair elections. We began as a nation that excluded African Americans, women, and people without property from voting. But property requirements were struck down early in the nineteenth century, women got the vote with the adoption of the Nineteenth Amendment in 1920, and African Americans finally won full voting rights with the passage of the civil rights laws of the 1960s. We now have universal suffrage. Democracy is complete.

In the pages ahead, we will argue that American democracy is far from complete. We are still debating the fundamental rules of the game about how far democracy should be extended. If anyone believed that there was a national consensus about the rules of the democratic game, this illusion should have been punctured by the 2000 presidential election.[1]

In this election, Al Gore received over a half million more votes than did George W. Bush, yet Bush "won" because he got more votes in the Electoral College. The Electoral College was written into the Constitution because the framers did not trust ordinary citizens to elect a president. As a result, four times in American history (1824, 1876, 1888, 2000) the winning presidential candidate actually received fewer votes than his opponent. In addition, the Electoral College gives disproportionate influence to small, rural states over large, urban states. Each New York electoral vote represents 550,000 people, but each South Dakota electoral vote represents only 232,000 people. Many have called for scrapping the Electoral College as a violation of "one-person, one vote."

The controversy over counting votes in Florida also exposed flaws in our elections. Methods of casting ballots varied in different counties; as a result, in some counties many more ballots were invalidated than in other counties. The counties that used punch-card systems, a method that produces high error rates,

were mostly those with large poor and minority populations. In part, this was because punch-card systems are cheaper than optical scanners or mechanical voting machines.

To ensure that every vote was counted, the Florida Supreme Court ordered a manual recount of ballots. At the last minute, the U.S. Supreme Court stepped in and stopped the recount. In *Bush v. Gore*, a divided court, led by Republican-appointed justices, violated its prior commitments to judicial restraint and states rights to effectively give the election to Bush. The reasoning of the majority was that the recount violated the constitutional guarantee of equal protection because it used different standards in different counties. What the Court failed to note, however, is that without a recount votes in different counties would still be counted differently. In a stinging dissent, Justice John Paul Stevens charged that the decision would harm "the nation's confidence in the judge as an impartial guardian of the rule of law."

Besides the serious flaws exposed by the cliffhanger 2000 presidential election, consider the following damning facts about American elections:[2]

- Despite an election that was too close to call right up to election day and that had the most expensive get-out-the-vote drives in history, the turnout in the 2004 presidential election was only 59 percent, about the same as 1956 when a popular incumbent (Dwight Eisenhower) won handily.
- In 2004 just 2 percent of House incumbents lost reelection; with congressional districts drawn by the parties to protect incumbents, voters have little reason to go to the polls.
- Since the mid-1970s the percentage of adolescents who see themselves as working on a political campaign has declined by half.
- Despite an increase in voting by eighteen- to twenty-four-year-olds in 2004, their turnout still remained below 50 percent.
- According to surveys, 90 percent of citizens with annual incomes above $75,000 say they voted, compared to less than 50 percent for those who earned less than $15,000.
- Many states bar ex-felons from voting, even after they have completed their prison sentence. As a result, according to one estimate, 7.5 percent of African American males are denied the right to vote.

These facts demonstrate that when it comes to elections, the United States has an incomplete democracy. At best, American democracy is a work in progress. The struggle for democracy is never ending. In the pages ahead, we will introduce you to the democratic debate in the United States.

WHAT IS DEMOCRACY?

The central idea of democracy is quite simple. Democracy originated in the fifth century BCE in the small city-states of Greece. The word *democracy* comes from the Greek words *demos*, meaning "the people," and *kratein*, meaning "to rule." Therefore, democracy means simply "rule by the people." Defined as "rule by the people," democracy, Americans agree, is the best form of government. Americans disagree, however, about what democracy means in practice and how far democratic decision making should be extended.

One of the fundamental disagreements is over who is best suited for democratic decision making—the masses or political elites. *Elites* are small groups of people who possess extraordinary amounts of power. Throughout history, advocates of elite rule have argued that ruling is too difficult for ordinary citizens. Elites dominate many political systems—including communist, aristocratic, and even formally democratic ones. Elitism comes in various forms, with claims to rule based on different criteria. A totalitarian regime, for instance, is ruled by an elite few with unlimited power to control the daily lives of the citizens; a theocracy is a system run by religious elites. Although these are among the most extreme forms of elitism, even U.S. democracy is seen by some as controlled by a group of highly educated and wealthy elites. This was C. Wright Mills's central argument in *The Power Elite* (1956). Today, many Americans would support citizens being represented by a well-heeled and well-educated few who are presumably best qualified to make important decisions.

Few Americans are classical elitists, however; a strong democratic impulse pervades American culture and politics. Anyone who argued that family genes, religious training, or even wealth automatically qualified a person to rule would not be taken seriously in the United States. Americans believe in the democratic principle that political power should ultimately stem from the people. Americans also agree on certain basic principles of democratic government, including the importance of a written constitution, representative institutions, and basic rights such as freedom of speech and press. Throughout American history, political movements have risen to extend democratic citizenship to blacks, women, and other excluded groups. Political equality is a strong value in American politics.

A deep elitist strain, however, also pervades our politics. Americans believe in rule by the people, for example, but we still cede power over war and peace to an executive elite on the grounds that "the president knows best." Americans generally support elitism not because they believe elites are inherently superior to the common people, but because they believe elites have the specialized knowledge and experience to make the best decisions. In a technologically complex and dangerous world, democracy must often defer to specialized expertise, whether in government or in private corporations. Democracy is a fine ideal, many people argue, but to be realistic and effective, "the people" must cede much of their decision-making power to elites.

The thesis of this text is simple: American politics is characterized by a fundamental conflict between elite democracy and popular democracy. **Elite democracy** is a political system in which elites acquire power by a free and fair competition for the people's votes.[3] Once elected, elites are given the freedom to rule as they see fit. If the people do not like the results, they can vote these elites out at the next election and put different elites into office. Under elite democracy, the people are not expected to participate in the day-to-day affairs of governing.

Popular democracy has its roots in **direct democracy**, in which all citizens gather in one place to vote on important matters. In the Greek city-states, where democracy originated 2,500 years ago, democracy meant face-to-face debate and decision making by all citizens, with offices rotating among the citizens. Some examples of direct democracy still exist in the United States, such as the New England town meeting, where all town citizens gather in one hall to debate and decide important issues.

Popular democracy is the adaptation of direct democracy to a large country with a modern economy and society. **Popular democracy** can be defined as a political system in which the people are involved as much as possible in making the decisions that affect their lives.[4] Popular democrats maintain that ordinary citizens should be closely involved in governing and that, in the long run, they will govern more wisely than elites. In a large country, popular democrats admit, everyone cannot meet in one place to make decisions. Political representatives are needed, but they should remain as close as possible to the people who elected them, accurately reflecting their values and interests. Between elections, citizens should be involved in political affairs, holding representatives accountable and making sure that experts, who are necessary in a complex modern society, serve the needs of the people and not the needs of elites.

It is crucial to recognize that popular democracy is not the same as majority rule. Ironically, majorities have often supported elite rule and undemocratic values. Ordinary citizens, for example, often defer to corporate elites in the private marketplace, and for much of American history a majority opposed giving full civil rights to African Americans and women. Popular democrats believe that basic rights, such as freedom of speech and freedom of religion, should not be subject to a vote, to the whims of the majority. The question of whether the rights guaranteed to all citizens should extend beyond basic civil liberties to include positive rights that would require action by government, such as the right to health care or a roof over one's head, is at the heart of the democratic debate today. (We examine the question of whether citizens should have the right to welfare or a job in Chapter 17.) Although majority rule should be limited by basic rights, and majorities often make mistakes, popular democrats still believe that for most issues, most of the time, majority rule is best. The greatest threat to democratic values comes from minority elites, not from majorities.

At the heart of American politics lies an essential tension between two different conceptions of democracy. We are not the first to present a conflict interpretation of American politics. Marxists have long focused on the "contradictions" of capitalism, particularly the conflict between workers and capitalists. Although class inequalities have often caused deep divisions in American politics, we believe that the enduring conflict has been between elite democracy and popular democracy. The United States does have a radical political tradition, but it is rooted in homegrown ideas of popular democracy rather than in European socialism.

As we flesh out the principles of elite and popular democracy that serve as the framework of this text, we begin in the 1780s, the founding period when the U.S. Constitution was written and approved.

ORIGINS OF THE DEMOCRATIC DEBATE: THE FOUNDING

Normally, the founding period is treated as a celebration of the American consensus on democracy as embodied in the Constitution. As Chapter 2 shows, however, the U.S. Constitution was born in conflict, not in consensus. The ratification of the Constitution did not end debate but began a new debate about the meaning of democracy. The terms of this debate, which were laid down over two hundred years ago, continue to influence American politics to this day.

Our Constitution was not written by lofty statesmen who offered their eternal truths to a grateful nation. The men who wrote the Constitution were practical politicians with pressing political objectives. The framers distrusted popular democracy, especially the power of the majority. (Read James Madison's *Federalist No. 10* in the Appendix.) The supporters of the Constitution in the late 1780s, known as **Federalists**, were the founders of elite democracy in the United States. The Constitution they wrote and ratified was mixed, containing elements of both elitism and democracy. The original Constitution placed severe limits on majority rule and contained many elitist elements; neither the president nor senators, for example, were to be elected directly by the people. (In the original Constitution, senators were chosen by state legislatures and presidents were elected by an elite, the Electoral College, appointed under procedures chosen by the state legislatures.)

The ratification of the Constitution was bitterly opposed by a group known as the **Anti-federalists**. The Anti-federalists were the founders of popular democracy in the United States.[5] The Anti-federalists denounced the proposed Constitution as a betrayal of the democratic spirit of 1776 and the American Revolution itself. The new Constitution, they protested, took too much power away from the states and localities and gave it to the central government. In the long run, they charged, the Constitution would erode the face-to-face participation necessary for a healthy democracy. The Anti-federalists were not a marginal group; many state conventions ratified the Constitution by only the narrowest of margins.

Federalists and Anti-federalists disagreed about the most basic questions of human nature, society, and politics (see Chapter 2). In the eyes of the Federalists, the mass of Americans were passionate and selfish creatures. In a small republic where simple majority rule prevailed, nothing would stop this mass from taking away the rights or the property of the minority. But in a national republic, where the majority could not rule directly, minority rights would be protected. Elite representatives, likely to be drawn from the wisest and most virtuous segment of society, would rise above selfish conflicts and pursue the common good. Should these elites themselves go astray, other elites would check them through the ingenious constitutional system of checks and balances.

Anti-federalists had more faith in the common people. They believed that most people could be educated into civic virtue, overcoming their selfish inclinations and learning to pursue the common good. They wanted representatives who would not claim superiority over the masses, but who would faithfully reflect ordinary citizens' grievances and aspirations. To the Anti-federalists, the main threat to democracy came not from majorities but from selfish and powerful elites. Instead of elites checking elites, they wanted ordinary citizens to check elites and hold them accountable. The best way to protect against the tyranny of an aristocratic elite was to have the people participate directly in political decisions.

The original debate between Federalists and Anti-federalists had its limitations. In contemporary terms, neither the Federalists nor the Anti-federalists were true democrats. Many on both sides owned slaves, for example, and neither advocated citizenship rights for women, African Americans, or Native Americans. Both Federalists and Anti-federalists supported property qualifications for voting.

Although the Federalists and Anti-federalists were limited by the prejudices of their times, they laid down the basic principles of the democratic debate that have animated American politics to the present. Even though the principles have remained the same, the debate between elite and popular democrats has evolved dramatically in response to the changes in American society over the past two centuries. Understanding this evolution is necessary to understand the contemporary democratic debate.

Evolution of Popular Democracy: The Logic of Inclusion

The Anti-federalists are frequently viewed as losers who had little impact on American politics. This is false. Although the Anti-federalists lost the initial struggle over the Constitution, their perspective has had a tremendous influence on American politics.

If the founding document of elite democracy is the Constitution of 1787, the founding document of popular democracy is the Declaration of Independence of 1776. With its bold statement that "all men are created equal" and are "endowed by their Creator with certain unalienable Rights," the Declaration laid down the basic principles of popular democracy. The Declaration of Independence proclaimed a radical idea: If the government violates people's rights, they have a right "to alter or abolish it." This "Spirit of '76"—based on political equality, rights, and rebellion—has inspired popular democrats ever since.

The democratic faith of Americans, as expressed in the Declaration of Independence, has given popular democrats an ideological advantage and has frequently placed elite democrats on the defensive. In 1791, for example, two years after the Constitution was ratified, the first ten amendments—the Bill of Rights—were added, mostly at the insistence of the Anti-federalists, who wanted to ensure protection of their political rights. (Chapter 16 discusses the importance of civil rights and civil liberties for popular democracy.) Nearly all the amendments to the Constitution since then have moved it in a popular democratic direction, including the Fifteenth Amendment, which extended the legal right to vote to African Americans in 1870; the Seventeenth Amendment, which required the direct election of senators in 1913; the Nineteenth Amendment, which extended the right to vote to women in 1920; and the Twenty-sixth Amendment, which gave the vote to eighteen- to twenty-year-olds in 1971.

Popular democratic influence, however, has not been limited to amending the Constitution. It has also affected how we interpret the Constitution. Elected in 1800, Thomas Jefferson, who shared many of the beliefs of the Anti-federalists, can be viewed as our nation's first popular democratic president. As such, Jefferson could have proposed writing a new constitution. Instead, he decided to infuse democratic content into the Constitution of 1789 by expanding the participation of common people in governmental decision making. Jefferson supported a narrow interpretation of the powers of the federal government, preferring that as many decisions as possible be made by state and local governments that were closer to the people. Jefferson's attempt to read popular democratic views into the Constitution was pivotal in American history and helps explain why Americans love the Constitution but disagree so vehemently about how to interpret it.

Although politicians like Jefferson, at the top of the political system, sometimes championed popular democracy, more often such impulses came from ordinary citizens. Throughout American history, popular democrats have mobilized the masses to expand democratic decision making. Periods of elite dominance have given way to periods of mass participation and popular democratic upsurge, such as the 1890s, the 1930s, and the 1960s.[6] During the last period, the civil rights, feminist, environmental, and neighborhood organizing movements, among others, challenged the power of entrenched elites and forged landmark legislation such as the 1964 Civil Rights Act and the 1970 Environmental Protection Act.

In mobilizing people for mass movements, popular democrats have appealed to the ideas of political equality and rights found in the Declaration of Independence. In 1848, for example, Elizabeth Cady Stanton used the language of the Declaration of Independence to write a women's declaration of independence. Her Declaration of Sentiments is considered the founding document of the women's rights movement, which won the right to vote in 1920 and flowered into a modern feminist movement in the 1960s. In the 1950s and 1960s, Martin Luther King Jr. used the popular democratic language of rights and equality to energize the civil rights movement and appeal successfully to a broad white audience. The civil rights movement, examined in Chapter 10, shows how protest politics goes beyond electoral politics and uses the techniques of direct action to empower the powerless.

EVOLUTION OF ELITE DEMOCRACY: THE LOGIC OF EXPERTISE

Elite democrats have not stood still while popular democrats pushed for extending democracy. Throughout American history, elite democrats have been immensely resourceful, devising new arguments for limiting democracy. In the early years of the republic, many openly defended elite values. However, the democratization of American values soon rendered such naked appeals to elitism illegitimate. Elitism is no longer defended on the grounds that elites are inherently superior to the masses or that certain people are destined to rule. In contemporary American society, elites profess democratic values but maintain that elite rule is necessary in many spheres of modern society. Elite democrats would not admit they are elitist; they would simply say they are realistic.

The elite democratic position cannot be easily dismissed. When we ride on an airplane, for example, we do not take a vote to see how high the plane will fly or who will serve as pilot. Everyone acknowledges that democratic decision making must defer to rule by experts, or technical elites, in particular situations. But where do we draw the line? Elite democrats believe that in a rapidly changing, technologically complex, and dangerous world more and more power must be ceded to elites—elites whose power is justified not by birth or wealth but by their knowledge, expertise, and experience. Democracy is viewed as a kind of luxury that we cannot "afford" too much of, especially given our desire for economic growth and the necessity to compete with other nations for economic, political, and military advantage.

The elite democratic position has evolved over the years, especially in response to changing economic conditions. At the time of the debate over the Constitution, few private corporations existed; those that did were small and family owned. By the late nineteenth century, huge railroad and industrial corporations controlled national markets and employed thousands of workers. These private corporations were run in a top-down fashion by wealthy elites. Elite democrats argued that the owners of capital should be free to run corporations as they saw fit. Corporations would be held accountable by market competition; by giving free rein to the corporations, government would encourage economic growth that would, in the long run, benefit everyone. This argument for elite autonomy based on free market capitalism has continued into the present period of multinational corporations. Chapter 3 examines the argument for free market capitalism that is so important for contemporary elite democrats, as well as the popular democratic response that corporations exert power over the marketplace and thus must be held democratically accountable.

In the late nineteenth century, a popular democratic movement called *populism* emerged, challenging the control of corporate elites over the economy. In the crucial election of 1896, however, the populist candidate, William Jennings Bryan, was defeated by the candidate of big business, William McKinley. Drawing on huge corporate contributions, McKinley is credited with having pioneered the first modern campaign using mass-media techniques of persuasion. McKinley's victory ushered in a long period of weak party competition and declining voter turnout. Chapters 6, 7, and 8 document the power that money can exert over the electoral process when parties decline and their functions are taken over by the mass media.

In the political struggles produced by economic changes, elite democrats and popular democrats have reversed some of their original positions. One of the most important shifts concerns whether power should be centralized in the national government or decentralized into the states and localities. At the time of the founding of this country, elite democrats like Alexander Hamilton favored a strong national government, whereas popular democrats wanted states and localities to retain most powers. The rise of powerful corporations, which helped to spawn tremendous inequalities in the private economy, caused popular democrats to reverse their position and favor expanded powers for the federal government. Beginning with President Franklin Roosevelt's New Deal, popular democrats have increasingly turned to the federal government as a counterweight to the power of private corporations and as a way of ensuring action on behalf of the disadvantaged.

Present-day elite democrats often appeal to the popular democratic value of states' rights or local control in order to defend elite privileges. The principle of states' rights was used for many years to prevent the federal government from intervening to guarantee African Americans the right to vote. The need to expand the powers of the federal government, however, has placed popular democrats on the horns of a dilemma. Although an expanded federal government is necessary to address inequalities and curb the powers of entrenched elites, the result, too often, is a government removed from popular democratic participation. Chapter 15 examines this dilemma of federalism.

Although elite and popular democrats have nearly switched positions in domestic policy, in foreign policy elites continue to favor decision making by the few, whereas popular democrats remain suspicious of centralized power and its potential for elite tyranny. In the twentieth century, many have argued that trends in this country and in the world justify concentrating power in the hands of experienced elites. These trends include the increasing complexity of social relations, the mobility of capital in an international economy, and the so-called global war on terrorism. Just as the Anti-federalists feared, presidents have gained substantial powers at the expense of Congress, which is often viewed as too slow to act effectively in the modern world. In particular, the Cold War

"We can't come to an agreement about how to fix your car, Mr. Simons. Sometimes that's the way things happen in a democracy."

against communism was used to justify the creation of what we call in Chapter 18 the "national security state"—a shadow government, led by an elite in the executive branch, with substantial power over American foreign policy and little congressional oversight. Popular support for the national security state demonstrates that elitism has not been supported only by elites; ironically, elitism has often enjoyed widespread popular backing.

Summarizing the Democratic Debate

Americans supposedly agree that democracy is the right way to make decisions. Everyone who runs for elected office uses the myths, symbols, and rhetoric of democracy to win votes. According to the consensus view of American politics, there are no more burning debates about the rules of the game. If Americans disagree, it is over specific policies, not the rules of the game.

This consensus view of American politics fundamentally distorts reality. Americans do disagree about the rules of the game. In particular, Americans disagree about the meaning of democracy and how far democratic decision making should be extended into the economy and society. This text argues for a conflict, not a consensus, approach to American politics. American politics is best understood as embodying an essential tension, or conflict, between two different conceptions of democracy: elite democracy and popular democracy. The differences between these two approaches can be summarized in six points.

ELITE DEMOCRACY

1. With the exception of an educated, largely white male elite, most people are uninterested in politics and uninformed about issues; most people are more interested in their own private lives than in politics.

2. When the masses do get involved in politics, they tend to be highly emotional and intolerant; the main threat to democracy comes from the masses, not from elites.

POPULAR DEMOCRACY

1. People are naturally inclined to participate in the decisions that affect their lives; if they don't participate, something must be wrong with the democratic system.

2. Through democratic participation people can overcome their parochial interests and become public-spirited citizens. When their powers and privileges are threatened, elites often respond by curtailing democracy; the main threat to democracy comes from selfish elites, not from ordinary citizens.

ELITE DEMOCRACY	**POPULAR DEMOCRACY**
3. Democracy basically means free and fair elections in which elites acquire the power to rule by competing for people's votes.	3. Democracy means more than fair elections; it means the participation of ordinary citizens in the decisions that affect their lives in an atmosphere of tolerance and trust.
4. The main goal of democracy should be to protect the rights of individuals to pursue their own interests, especially the acquisition of property. Because of varying talents and ambitions, democracies must tolerate substantial inequality.	4. The main goal of democracy should be to strengthen community; inequalities that divide the community should be minimized.
5. Political representatives should filter the views of the people through their superior expertise, intelligence, and temperament.	5. Representatives should stay as close to their constituents as possible, accurately reflecting their views in the political system.
6. Reforms in America almost always come about gradually, through the actions of elites.	6. Meaningful reforms in American politics have almost always come about because of political pressure from below by ordinary citizens.

INTERPRETING POLITICAL FACTS: THE PROBLEM OF PARTICIPATION

It is easy to become confused by the complexity of American politics. Magazines, newspapers, radio, and TV bombard us with facts about political negotiations in Congress, interest group bargaining, maneuverings of the political parties, the state of the economy and its effect on political fortunes, key decisions by the Supreme Court, and the actions of foreign countries. The sheer volume of political facts threatens to overwhelm our ability to comprehend them. Students of American politics need an organizing framework to make sense of these facts—to identify patterns, decide which facts are important, and evaluate political outcomes.

The ideas of elite and popular democracy can serve as an interpretive framework to help us make sense of American politics. To understand how this framework is used in the text, we apply it here to one example: the different ways that people interpret basic facts about political participation in American politics (a topic covered in Chapter 5).

The facts of political participation in the United States are well known. Voting is the most common political act, yet only about 59 percent of the eligible electorate voted in the most recent presidential election; the turnout rate in off-year congressional elections is only about one-third.

Although these facts are straightforward, making sense of them is more difficult. For example, how do we assess the simple fact that about half of the eligible electorate normally votes in presidential elections? Is the glass half full or half empty? What you see depends as much on your interpretation of the facts as on the facts themselves.

For elite democrats, the glass of democratic participation is half full. According to this view, the fact that only about half the people participate in elections is a sign of a healthy democracy. People are not inclined to participate in politics; most prefer to spend their time in private pursuits: making a living, raising children, watching TV. The fact that many people do not participate in politics is a sign of satisfaction. After all, nothing is stopping them from voting — legal barriers to voting (property qualifications, poll taxes, literacy tests) have been eliminated. If the masses of nonvoters felt their interests were threatened by government, they could mobilize their slack resources, including the vote, and influence the system. Moreover, because we know that nonvoters tend to be less educated, we should be happy that many do not participate in politics. As *Newsweek* columnist George Will put it, "The reasonable assumption about electorates is: smaller is smarter."[7]

Popular democrats contest the elite democratic interpretation of the facts of participation on every count. For them, the glass of democratic participation is at least half empty. They see low levels of political participation as a sign of a sick democracy. Popular democrats believe that people are naturally inclined to participate in the governance of their societies. When they don't participate, something must be wrong. Although there are no legal barriers preventing Americans from participating in the political process, popular democrats argue, many people feel so alienated from politics that they view their own participation as meaningless. They see the decisive role of money in elections and conclude that ordinary citizens have little influence. Moreover, when they see the limited choices on the ballot, they think that it doesn't matter who wins. In short, those who fail to participate in politics are not satisfied; they are *discouraged*.

Who is right? As the example of participation shows, political facts do not speak for themselves. The same facts can be seen from radically different perspectives. Interpreting the facts of American politics is like viewing a Gestalt drawing (Figure 1.1); what you see depends on how you look at it. Do you see a vase or two faces? You can see one or the other, but you cannot see both at the same time. As with the Gestalt diagram, we must interpret the facts of American politics to give them meaning. Elite and popular views of democracy are the two frameworks we will use to interpret the facts of American politics.

There is an important difference, however, between interpreting the Gestalt diagram and interpreting political facts. What you see in the Gestalt diagram does not affect anyone's interest. In politics, interpretations of the facts are hotly

FIGURE 1.1

Gestalt Drawing

contested because they directly affect people's interests. Consider the different interpretations of nonvoting. If nonvoting is an expression of satisfaction, then the system is legitimate—those in power are viewed as having the right to rule. On the other hand, if nonvoting is an expression of alienation, then the government loses legitimacy and political protests outside of normal channels, such as street demonstrations and civil disobedience, are justified. Our interpretations of political facts shape our evaluations of right and wrong, and what should and should not be done.

Conclusion: Joining the Democratic Debate

We must end this introduction with a warning: The authors of this text are not neutral observers of the democratic debate. Although we present both sides, we defend popular democracy and develop a popular democratic critique of American politics. We do so to redress an imbalance that is unconsciously embedded in most treatments of American politics, both in scholarly texts and in the mass media.

Finally, we invite readers not to accept our bias but to critically examine their own views toward democracy. In short, we invite you to join the democratic debate.

KEY TERMS	elite democracy	Federalist
	direct democracy	Anti-federalist
	popular democracy	

INTERNET RESOURCES

▓ Center for Democracy and Citizenship
www.publicwork.org

Located at the University of Minnesota's Hubert H. Humphrey Institute of Public Affairs, the Center for Democracy and Citizenship offers information about various citizenship projects as well as information about the center's own publications; it also provides links to other sites on citizenship.

▓ Institute for the Study of Civic Values
www.libertynet.org/edcivic

This website of a nonprofit Philadelphia organization provides classic articles and lectures on American democratic values, as well as information on civic values projects.

▓ Democracy Now!
www.democracynow.org

Democracy Now! is an independent news program aired on over 300 stations in North America that covers people and perspectives rarely heard in the corporate-sponsored media.

SUGGESTED READINGS

Robert A. Dahl, *Democracy and Its Critics*. New Haven, Conn.: Yale University Press, 1989. In a sweeping defense of democracy, Dahl argues here that democratic decision making should be extended into all areas of the society and economy.

Stephen Macedo et al. *Democracy at Risk: How Political Choices Undermine Citizen Participation, and What We Can Do About It*. Washington, D.C.: Brookings Institution Press, 2006. A synthesis of what political scientists know about the obstacles to greater civic participation, with concrete proposals for correcting these flaws.

Frances Moore Lappé, *Rediscovering America's Values*. New York: Ballantine Books, 1989. Written as a dialogue between two points of view that correspond roughly to elite and popular democracy, the book synthesizes a great deal of information on American value conflicts.

Bruce Miroff, Raymond Seidelman, and Todd Swanstrom, eds., *Debating Democracy: A Reader in American Politics*, 5th ed. Boston: Houghton Mifflin, 2005. Designed to accompany *The Democratic Debate*, this reader has eighteen chapters with sharply contrasting arguments about central questions facing American democracy.

C. Wright Mills, *The Power Elite*. New York: Oxford University Press, 1956. The classic statement that America is ruled by a small elite who occupy the command posts at the top of the economy, the polity, and the military.

The Revolution and the Constitution
Origins of the Democratic Debate

When modern American politicians hope to establish their noble aspirations and to provide their policies with the sanction of higher authority, they invariably turn to the founders of the republic—even to those whose ideas seem very different from their own. Proclaiming a new national beginning after the dark days of Watergate, President Gerald Ford, a conservative, quoted radical Thomas Paine on our revolutionary beginnings. President Bill Clinton, an advocate of an activist national government, was fond of citing Thomas Jefferson, who favored local action and feared national power. Republicans or Democrats, conservatives or liberals, American political leaders speak in hushed tones of the founders as our political saints.

Ford and Clinton drew on assumptions that most Americans hold: that the founders agreed among themselves about the fundamental premises of politics and government; that they believed in the same kind of democracy that we profess; and that they were above the desires for power and wealth that seem to drive most present-day political leaders. All of these assumptions are essentially false. The founders of the republic did not agree among themselves; they argued vehemently about fundamental issues of human nature, society, and government. Many were skeptical about democracy and its values, and held to an elitist conception of government that no contemporary American politician would dare to profess openly. Struggles over power and wealth were as central to their politics as to our own.

This chapter demonstrates that the American political system was born not in consensus but in conflict. American political life at the time of our founding was characterized by a debate between popular and elite democracy—a debate that has driven our politics ever since. The two sides differed on six basic political issues:

1. Human nature

2. The proper scale of political life

3. Representation

4. Separation of powers and checks and balances

5. The purpose of government

6. Stability and change

Popular democratic answers to these questions produced a hopeful brand of politics that extended self-government to ordinary citizens. Elite democratic answers left ultimate sovereignty to the people but placed actual governance in the hands of a political and economic elite.

The story of the American founding that this chapter tells unfolded in three stages. It began as Americans cast off their colonial past and launched a bold experiment in republican politics. The hopeful political spirit of 1776 was expressed in the philosophy of the Declaration of Independence, the original state constitutions, and the Articles of Confederation. Popular democratic answers to the six basic questions of politics prevailed during the revolutionary upsurge.

But this revolutionary beginning gradually became caught up in economic conflict and political controversy. In the second stage, a conservative and propertied elite, unhappy with the emerging popular democracy, developed an alternative political philosophy that answered the six basic questions very differently. These men produced a national constitution in 1787 that reflected the new brand of elite democracy.

In the concluding stage of the story, the ratification of the new constitution provoked a fundamental and wide-ranging debate between elite democrats and popular democrats. Their conflicting answers to the six basic questions were fully developed in the ratification debate. Pages 32–40 of this chapter present the climax of the story—and an essential key for an understanding of the whole book.

The story of the American founding does not produce a final victory for either elite democrats or popular democrats. In studying the Revolution and the Constitution, we witness the origins of the democratic debate. Particularly in the argument over the new Constitution, which pitted Federalists against Anti-federalists, the democratic debate was launched with a depth and passion that still echo in today's politics.

FROM COLONIALS TO REVOLUTIONARIES

In 1763 the idea that the American colonies of Great Britain would declare their independence, start a revolution, and shape a political system unlike any then known would have seemed absurd. In the first place, the colonists enjoyed their status as outposts of a glorious empire. England, their "mother country," was nurturing and permissive. The colonies flourished economically and possessed a considerable degree of liberty and self-government under the relatively lax British administration. Second, the colonists not only thought of themselves as English people but also resembled them in many respects. Historian Gordon Wood has written that colonial America was, like Britain, a "monarchical" society, hierarchical in character and dominated by a small elite of "gentlemen."[1] Americans felt a strong allegiance to the king and liked to celebrate his birthday with rousing toasts.

Beneath the surface, however, elements of a distinct American identity were detectable. Immigrants from many European countries — Scots, French Protestants, Germans, and others — made the colonies far more heterogeneous than their "mother country." Economic development brought increasing numbers of American farmers into international commerce. Politics in many colonies took on a more popular and competitive character than was to be found back in Britain. And the emerging American brand of religious freedom gave the colonists a spiritual diversity found nowhere else in the world. Even as they continued to think of themselves as English, Americans were becoming a separate people.[2]

By 1763, the British had defeated the French and Spanish in the Seven Years' War and established their dominance in the New World. They needed revenues to pay off the debts incurred in this war. As beneficiaries of the British efforts, the American colonists seemed the obvious targets for new taxation. However, this assumption proved to be disastrous for the British. Colonial America responded to the first British tax levies, the Sugar Act and the Stamp Act, with spirited resistance. While American writers denounced taxes imposed by a Parliament in which the colonies were not represented, American "patriots" formed organizations known as the Sons of Liberty and mobbed stamp-tax collectors until they resigned their royal commissions.

For the next decade, a political dynamic developed that led the Americans toward independence. When the British eased their attempts at taxation, peace returned. But every time they tried to reassert their authority, the American

After listening to a reading of the Declaration of Independence, a New York crowd of soldiers and civilians pulls down a statue of King George III. The picture dramatizes the overthrow of monarchism (rule by one) by republicanism (popular rule).

Library of Congress

spirit of resistance grew stronger. It was not that Americans rushed eagerly into revolutionary politics; even the leaders of the patriot forces continued to swear allegiance to the (unwritten) British constitution and to claim that they were only seeking to preserve the rights of all Englishmen. Yet the increasingly bitter conflict wore away old loyalties and crystallized an independent American identity.[3]

Two events epitomized the colonists' growing radicalism. One was the famous Boston Tea Party in 1773, where Boston patriots, disguised as Indians, dumped a shipload of tea into the harbor in protest of a tax on the beverage. Notable here was the colonists' militancy, their reliance on direct popular action to redress a grievance. A second event was the fiery rhetoric of the most widely read pamphlet calling on Americans to declare their independence: Thomas Paine's *Common Sense*, published early in 1776. Paine poured scorn on a monarch whom Americans had customarily revered. By sending his troops to enforce his taxes with bayonets, wrote Paine, George III deserved to be called the "Royal Brute of Britain." Monarchy itself, Paine thundered, was a crime; if we could trace the origins of kings, he wrote, "we should find the first of them nothing better than the principal ruffian of some restless gang. . . ."[4] A decade of resistance and protest had undermined much of the hierarchical thinking of colonial Americans; reading Tom Paine, many of them became filled with a bold and hopeful spirit that was ready to launch a grand revolutionary experiment in popular democracy.

The Birth of Republicanism

To understand this revolutionary experiment, we need to look beneath questions of taxation and representation. Contemporary historians have identified a deeper level of thought that transformed loyal colonials into defiant revolutionaries. This body of thought shaped the political activities of Americans and infused them with the revolutionary "Spirit of '76." The name historians have given to this body of thought is **republicanism**. (The republicanism of the Revolution should not be confused with the ideas of the Republican Party, formed in the 1850s.[5])

What were the central ideas of republican ideology, and how did they shape the thinking of the American revolutionaries? We focus on four interrelated ideas: liberty versus power, legislatures versus executives, virtue, and the small republic.

Liberty versus Power. Eighteenth-century republicans saw the struggle between liberty and power as the core of political life. *Power* meant dominion or control. Although necessary for the maintenance of order, power's natural tendency was to exceed legitimate boundaries and to invade the sphere of liberty. By *liberty*, republicans meant both private liberty—such as property rights—and public liberty—the right of the people to have a collective say in government. This view of politics made the actions of the British government especially frightening to the American colonists. The taxes imposed by London, the flood of new royal officials to rule over the colonists, and the troops eventually sent to America to support both were viewed not as limited measures but as steps in a comprehensive plot to reduce Americans to servility.

Legislatures versus Executives. Republican theory identified power largely with executives. Executives were entrusted with enforcing the laws, but they had a natural inclination to arbitrary rule and self-aggrandizement. Thus, executives were seen as the most likely threats to liberty. Legislatures, on the other hand, were the most likely defenders of liberty. Closer to the people, mirroring the people's desires, cherishing the people's liberties, the legislature was the natural adversary of the executive. This view helped Americans make sense of their quarrel with Britain. Executives—the royal governors appointed by London, the ministers of the King, and ultimately George III himself—were assailing American liberty; American colonial legislatures and later the Continental Congresses were championing it.

Virtue of the American People. Why were republicans so optimistic about the people and their representatives in the legislature? Might not the people, under some circumstances, also prove dangerous? Republicans conceded that liberty could go too far and become anarchy. But they hoped for a people characterized by virtue rather than lawlessness. By *virtue*, they meant the willingness of individuals to subordinate their private interests to the common good. Virtue was a passion for the public good superior to all private passions. Americans believed that the British effort to introduce tyranny into the colonies showed that the British government and even the British people had become corrupt; selfishness had destroyed their traditional commitment to liberty. But America—peopled by those who had fled the Old World in search of liberty—was a land where virtue still resided.

The Small Republic. What conditions encouraged virtue? As good republicans, the American revolutionaries stressed such things as simplicity and frugality. But the single most important condition necessary for republican virtue was the small republic. In a large republic, diverse economic interests and dissimilar ways of life would produce factional conflicts, encouraging selfishness and eroding virtue. In a small republic, however, a genuine common interest could be found, for the people would be more homogeneous and united. To the Americans of 1776, the British empire proved how a large republic became hostile to liberty and the common good. The revolutionaries' goal was not to build a large republic of their own but small republics that would nurture virtue and the public good. Their principal political efforts were focused on the governments of the thirteen new states, not on the national government.

Thus, the revolutionary assumptions of 1776 were the danger of power and the need to safeguard liberty, the threat of executives and the confidence in legislatures, the hope for a virtuous people, and the stress on small republics and political decentralization. On the basis of these popular democratic assumptions, Americans began shaping their own independent governments in 1776. However, each of these assumptions would be challenged in the decade that followed and debated at length in the struggle over the Constitution.

The Spirit of '76

The American Revolution exploded in 1776 with political energy and creativity. The institutions it first shaped were soon replaced by others, but the ideals it espoused were to form the base of America's democratic creed. Both the successes and the failures of revolutionary creativity are evident in the Declaration of Independence, the constitutions of the new states, and the Articles of Confederation.

The Declaration of Independence. When the Second Continental Congress finally decided that the moment had arrived for the decisive break between America and Britain, it appointed a small committee to prepare a justification for such revolutionary action. This committee of five wisely turned to its best writer, the young Thomas Jefferson of Virginia. The **Declaration of Independence**, the document that Jefferson drafted and that the Congress adopted with some revisions on July 4, 1776, has become, along with the Constitution, the most hallowed of all American political texts. Its opening words are very familiar, so familiar that we usually do not read them with the care and reflection they deserve.

> When in the course of human events, it becomes necessary for one people to dissolve the political bands which have connected them with another, and to assume among the powers of the earth the separate and equal station to which the Laws of Nature and of Nature's God entitle them, a decent respect to the opinions of mankind requires that they should declare the causes which impel them to the separation.
>
> We hold these truths to be self-evident, that all men are created equal, that they are endowed by their Creator with certain unalienable rights, that among these are life, liberty, and the pursuit of happiness. That to secure these rights, governments are instituted among men, deriving their just powers from the consent of the governed. That whenever any form of government becomes destructive of these ends, it is the right of the people to alter or to abolish it, and to institute new government, laying its foundation on such principles and organizing its powers in such form, as to them shall seem most likely to effect their safety and happiness.

Scholars argue about the sources of Jefferson's ideas in the Declaration of Independence. The most common view is that he was influenced by an English philosopher, John Locke. Several of Locke's central themes are evident in the Declaration: that the primary objective of government is the protection of life, liberty, and property, and that all legitimate political authority derives from the consent of the governed and can be taken away from rulers who betray the will of the people. Locke's ideas are considered central to the political philosophy of liberalism.

If Locke's liberal philosophy is found in the Declaration, the democratic Jefferson gives it a more revolutionary interpretation than the English philosopher intended. The Declaration of Independence establishes equality as the basis for American political thought and makes "life, liberty, and the pursuit of happiness" universal rights. It dethrones government as a higher power and renders it subject to the consent of the people. In its argument, and even in its form, it transforms the nature of political life, supplanting the commands of a king with the discussion and persuasion suitable to a free people.[6]

Like most great documents, the Declaration of Independence bears the marks and limits of its time. Its words about equality and rights were not meant to include women or African Americans. The American revolutionaries used universal terms but restricted them in practice to white males. Still, the Declaration created a standard to which later popular democrats would appeal in efforts to include those who had originally been excluded from its promises. Battling the spread of slavery, Abraham Lincoln grounded his opposition on the words of the Declaration, proclaiming in 1859 that the "principles of Jefferson are the definitions and axioms of free society."[7] Feminist and African-American movements for emancipation have also rested their cases on the Declaration of Independence.[8]

The Revolutionary State Constitutions. The revolutionary ideas of 1776 were also embodied in the first state constitutions. In 1776, ten states established new constitutions to replace their old colonial charters. These constitutions reflected both the struggle with Britain and the core ideas of republicanism. They provided popular democratic answers to the basic questions at issue in the democratic debate—answers that would be rejected a decade later by the elite who drafted the U.S. Constitution.

Three features of the new constitutions were noteworthy: the inclusion of a bill of rights, the weakening of executive power, and the enhancement of legislative power.[9] After years of fighting against British invasions of their rights, Americans wanted to make it clear that these rights were sacred and inviolable, beyond the reach even of the governments that they themselves were establishing. So most of the new constitutions contained a bill of rights; several, including Virginia's influential one, began their constitutions with such declarations.

Colonial experience and republican theory had identified executive power as the chief threat to liberty. Therefore, the revolutionary constitution makers sought to guard against the return of executive despotism. Revolutionary executives were, intentionally, weak executives. In the first state constitutions, executives were chosen by the legislature and held office for a term of only one year. They were stripped of the executive powers traditionally exercised by the British monarch and were left with only modest duties of law enforcement.

The revolutionary mistrust of executives did not extend to legislatures. In the eyes of the constitution writers of 1776, the legislature was not likely to threaten liberty because it would be close to the people, even an embodiment of the people. Legislators were expected to act as mirrors of the people's views and interests. American revolutionaries were not, however, completely optimistic about legislative politics. The bills of rights they wrote were designed to limit what the legislatures could do. Equally important, the revolutionaries attempted to make the state legislature, particularly the more popular lower house, genuinely representative. This required annual elections so that legislators would frequently be returned to live among the people and feel the effects of the laws they had passed. It also required a large and equal representation so that all areas of a state would be fairly reflected in the deliberations of the legislature.

The Articles of Confederation. The states, not the nation, were seen as the centers of political life in 1776. More than a holdover from colonial experience, the primacy of the states reflected the belief that republics were workable only in a small territory. Consequently, the first American system of national government was a confederation, a loose association of states that agreed to join in a compact for common ends (especially foreign relations and the conduct of war). In a confederation, the individual units remain sovereign, so each state had supreme power within its borders. The **Articles of Confederation**, adopted by the Continental Congress in 1777 but not finally approved by all thirteen states until 1781, put little power in the hands of a centralized authority.

Congress under the Articles of Confederation was an assembly of delegates from the states, each of which had one vote. It had the authority to levy taxes

A CLOSER LOOK

A Revolutionary Experiment in Popular Democracy

All of the state constitutions written in 1776 reflected the revolutionary desire to restrict the power of rulers and to place government more directly in the hands of the people. No state carried this impulse further than Pennsylvania. The Pennsylvania Constitution of 1776 was the boldest revolutionary experiment in popular democracy.

In most states, the struggle for independence created a coalition between the social and economic elite and "common" folk. In Pennsylvania, however, the elite clung to the hope of reconciliation with Britain. Encouraged by champions of independence in the Continental Congress, middle-class and working-class Pennsylvanians—small merchants, shopkeepers, and artisans—shouldered aside this elite. Aiming to shift political control to the people and to prevent wealthy "gentlemen" from resuming their traditional rule, they drafted a constitution whose character was, for its day, remarkably democratic.

The principal institution in the new government was a unicameral (one-house) legislature. Pennsylvania democrats saw no need for an "upper" house, which would be dominated in any case by the elite. To ensure that this legislature would represent all the people, the constitution established the easiest suffrage requirement in any of the states. To ensure that it did what the people wanted (and did not become a new elite with interests of its own), it provided for annual elections and prohibited any representative for serving for more than four years out of every seven. Even more fearful of executive despotism than constitution writers in the other states, popular democrats in Pennsylvania eliminated the office of governor, putting in its place an Executive Council of twelve, elected directly by the people and holding very limited powers.

Critics complained that this simple form of government placed no checks on the power of the unicameral legislature. Defenders of the constitution responded that it was designed to make the people themselves the check. The constitution made government in Pennsylvania more open to public knowledge and involvement than in any other state. It required that the doors of the legislature be open for public attendance and votes be published weekly for public scrutiny. Once the legislature passed a bill, it could not become law until the next session, allowing the people time to consider it and, if they chose, to reject it through their election of new representatives.

Was this popular democratic experiment in government workable? What makes the question hard to answer is that the experiment never had a clear trial. Opponents of the constitution, many from the old social and economic elite, fought from the beginning to obstruct and overturn it. Their powerful resistance gained ground as the revolutionary spirit of 1776 faded. In 1790, Pennsylvania adopted a new constitution, setting up a government similar to those in other states, and ended its revolutionary experiment in popular democracy.

Sources: The Pennsylvania Constitution of 1776; David Hawke, *In the Midst of a Revolution* (Philadelphia: University of Pennsylvania Press, 1961); Gordon S. Wood, *The Creation of the American Republic, 1776–1787* (New York: W. W. Norton, 1972).

and raise troops but had to requisition each state to supply its assigned quota; should a state fail to meet its duty, the central government could do little about it. The suspicion of the states toward national authority was displayed most dramatically in the provision of the Articles of Confederation regarding amendments: No alterations in the Articles could be made until the legislature of *every* state agreed to them.

That this first national authority was not a real central government was evident in its fundamental differences from the first state governments. The national government could not tax the people directly. There was no provision in the Articles for either an executive or a judiciary. All of this government's limited and closely watched powers were left in the hands of the Congress.

The deficiencies of the Articles of Confederation became apparent once it was put into practice. Supporters of the 1787 Constitution based their strongest arguments on the inadequacy of the Articles of Confederation to meet America's need for an effective national government. Alexander Hamilton, in particular, heaped scorn on the Articles of Confederation as weak and futile, and his sarcasm has shaped the way later generations have regarded them. Yet it should be remembered that the Articles of Confederation were not designed to create a strong national government. The framers of the Articles, adhering to the revolutionary spirit of '76, believed that local liberty—and not national power— was the true source of republican strength and virtue.

FROM REVOLUTION TO CONSTITUTION

What happened to the political institutions established by the American revolutionaries? Why did the spirit of '76, the hopeful experiment in liberty and virtue, give way to a more somber spirit a decade later, as reflected in the Constitution and in the arguments that upheld it? To answer these questions, we must look at the years between the Declaration of Independence and the Constitution, some of the most fateful years in American history.

In 1776 the American revolutionary cause attracted a broad coalition. The struggle for independence and self-government united wealthy merchants, slave-owning planters, and lawyers with yeoman farmers, urban artisans, and unskilled laborers. But during the war for independence, and even more in the years immediately following the war, major economic and social tensions emerged in the revolutionary coalition. Revolutionary unity broke down, and with the new economic and social divisions came divisions over both government policies and fundamental matters of political philosophy. The result was a sense of crisis in the new American republic that engendered a move to reconstitute American politics on a different basis than that of 1776.

Economic and social tensions in the revolutionary coalition that had begun during the war with England grew much worse after the fighting stopped. A short-lived boom in imports from England produced a depression that spread from commercial areas to the countryside. As prices for both manufactured and agricultural goods fell, money became scarce, especially specie or "hard money" (gold and silver). Hardest hit during this depression were the small farmers, who constituted the majority of Americans at the time. With falling prices and a shortage of specie, farmers could not pay off their creditors. Because many states were levying taxes to pay off wartime debts, the farmers also faced demands for payments from the tax collector. The combination of debt and taxes threatened many small farmers with foreclosure—the loss of their tools, livestock, or land. Some faced prison, for in this period one could be jailed for a failure to pay debts.

Not surprisingly, small farmers faced with such dire losses became the main source of political agitation in the mid-1780s. They wanted their state legislatures to relieve their distress. They petitioned for "stay laws" to postpone foreclosures and "tender laws" to allow payment of debts and taxes in agricultural commodities. Most of all, they sought paper money—a new and inflated currency that would make paying their debts and taxes easier.

In some states, legislators were not responsive to these demands. In Massachusetts, the failure of the legislature to do anything about the plight of the rural majority led to an explosion. The counties in the western part of the state repeatedly petitioned for relief, but the legislature, dominated by the merchants and moneylenders of the coastal cities, ignored them. By the fall of 1786, conditions were ripe for rebellion. Under the leadership of Daniel Shays, a former revolutionary army officer, farmers in the western counties banded together to close down the local courts and prevent further foreclosures. When Shays and his followers marched on the state armory in Springfield, they were dispersed by the state militia. **Shays's Rebellion**, as this event came to be called, was hardly a revolution; it was a disorganized campaign by desperate farmers who felt they were losing everything that the American Revolution had promised them.

To the more conservative and propertied American republicans, Shays's Rebellion was a disturbing yet familiar phenomenon. Just as republican theory had warned that power, if not properly checked, led to despotism, so it had also maintained that liberty, if not properly contained by power, led to lawlessness. But in the 1780s, what most troubled the conservative and the propertied was not the people's rebellions against the state governments. Rather, they were troubled that the majority of the state governments, with their strong legislatures and weak executives, *were* responding to popular grievances. For example, seven states passed paper money legislation; stay and tender laws were also put into effect. Attempts by the agrarian majority to alter contractual obligations and to interfere with what conservatives defined as the sacred rights of property were now obtaining the force of state law.[10]

Why were the legislatures in the majority of the states so responsive to mass grievances? One reason was the popular democratic nature of these revolutionary governments. With annual elections and with large and equal representation, the legislatures were quick to grant their constituents' requests. A second reason was the character of the representatives themselves. Before the Revolution, colonial assemblies had been dominated by an upper class of merchants, lawyers, and large landowners. But the Revolution had brought new men into politics from the middle class, and the composition of the legislatures had changed. Now, when yeoman farmers petitioned their state legislatures, they were heard in many states by people like themselves.[11]

To conservative and propertied republicans, the new state laws (such as paper money legislation) and the new state legislators called into question the assumptions about politics that had been shared by all republicans in 1776. These men, looking fearfully at developments in the states, no longer believed the core ideas of 1776. In their eyes, power was no longer the problem; liberty was. Executives were no longer the major threat; legislatures were. Shays's rebels and debtors seeking paper money aroused concern about the virtue of the American people. The turmoil in the states seemed to invalidate the capacity of a small republic to arrive at a common good. Condemning the "Vices of the Political System of the United States," the young James Madison, soon to play the leading role at the Constitutional Convention, placed them at the doorstep of "the representative bodies" and "the people themselves." To Madison, the heroes of 1776 had become the culprits of 1787.[12]

The Constitutional Convention of 1787 assembled largely in response to these developments in the states. The delegates who came to Philadelphia agreed that efforts in the states to block what was happening had been unsuccessful. They also agreed that the weak national government under the Articles of Confederation, with its dedication to state sovereignty, provided no recourse. If they hoped to restore stability and protect property, the answer was in a new set of national institutions. These delegates were still republicans, but they no longer hoped to base the American republic on the virtue or public spirit of the people. As they saw it, if republicanism was to survive in America—without subverting either order or property—only a proper constitution could save it.

THE CONSTITUTIONAL CONVENTION

The Constitutional Convention of 1787 was a lengthy affair, lasting from May 25 to September 17. For nearly four months of a sweltering Philadelphia summer, fifty-five delegates from twelve states (Rhode Island refused to send a delegation) orated, debated, and negotiated the creation of a new American political system. Their proceedings were secret, and our knowledge of what took place rests mainly on notes of several delegates—particularly James Madison. In considering the Constitutional Convention, we focus on the creation of a strong national government, the shaping of new national institutions, and the political values that guided the delegates.[13]

A Strong National Government

Forging a new national government was a complex process whose eventual outcome no one really anticipated. Most of the principal figures at Philadelphia—the delegates who took leading roles—wanted a far stronger national government than the Articles of Confederation provided. But the actual features of this government would emerge only gradually through the debates, votes, and compromises of four months.

As the debates commenced, the delegates were subject to conflicting pulls. On one hand, these mostly propertied and conservative men were representatives of the tradition we call elite democracy, and they were eager to end the upsurge of popular democracy that had been manifested in paper money legislation and Shays's Rebellion. Furthermore, they hoped that a lofty new national government, elevated high above local democracy, would be dominated by people like themselves rather than by the more ordinary folks who had gained prominence in the state legislatures. On the other hand, they knew that whatever they might consider the best plan of government, the new Constitution would have to obtain the approval of the American people. Frequent references were made during the proceedings to the values or "genius" of the American people, which could not be ignored or overridden. As historian Alfred Young has observed, the leading figures at the convention were "accommodating conservatives" who "made democratic concessions to achieve conservative ends."[14]

The initial agenda for the convention was set by the **Virginia Plan**, introduced on May 29 by that state's governor, Edmund Randolph, but principally the handiwork of James Madison. Where the Articles of Confederation had been based on the sovereignty of the states, the Virginia Plan made national government primary and reduced the states to a subordinate position. It envisioned the United States as a large republic—the kind of centralized political order that the American revolutionaries had opposed as inconsistent with liberty. Under the Virginia Plan, representation for each state in *both* houses of the bicameral legislature was to be based on either taxes paid to the national government or the number of free inhabitants—provisions that would favor the large states. The provision that most strongly indicated how authority was to be shifted from the state governments to the national government was one crafted by Madison that empowered the national legislature to veto state legislation.

Although the Virginia Plan dominated the initial debate, it leaned so far in the direction of the large states that the smaller states took alarm. On June 15 they countered with an alternative framework, introduced by William Paterson of New Jersey and thus known as the **New Jersey Plan**. The New Jersey Plan was essentially a reform of the Articles of Confederation rather than a wholly new constitutional order. It retained from the Articles a unicameral legislature in which each state would have equal representation. It strengthened the Articles by bestowing on Congress greater powers over revenues and commerce and by establishing a plural executive and a national judiciary. The New Jersey Plan never had enough support to gain serious consideration, but the concerns of the small states that it raised had to be addressed if the convention was to arrive at sufficient agreement to present a new constitution to the nation.

The quarrel between large and small states over representation was finally settled through a compromise proposed by the delegation from Connecticut and known as the Connecticut Compromise, or **Great Compromise**. Under the terms of this compromise, the House of Representatives would be apportioned according to the populations of the various states, whereas each state would have two members in the Senate. Senators would be selected by their state's legislature. The origination of revenue acts would be an exclusive right of the House. Through this compromise, the large states had the dominant position in the House and a more favorable position with regard to taxation, yet the small states were well protected by their equal representation in the Senate.

The delegates who were most eager to build national power at the expense of the states had to make compromises that pained them. Equal representation for the states in the Senate was one blow to the "nationalist" position; another was the defeat of Madison's plan for a national veto power over state legislation. Rather than drawing clear lines of national dominance and state subordination, the constitution that began to emerge by midsummer drew uncertain boundaries between national and state powers. The Constitution of the United States is celebrated for creating a novel system of **federalism**, under which power is divided between the central government and the states. Alexander Hamilton and especially James Madison applauded the virtues of this federalism in *The Federalist Papers*, considered later in this chapter. The irony is that this system of federalism was not what Hamilton, Madison, or their allies wanted. If they had not needed to compromise on representation and had not lost on the veto over state laws, we would have had a far more centralized government.

National Institutions

The Articles of Confederation had provided only a single legislative branch. But the Constitutional Convention intended to create a more complex government, possessing a bicameral legislature, a national executive, and a national judiciary. Molding these institutions and determining the appropriate relationships between them occupied much of the convention's time. In framing new national institutions, most of the delegates rejected the assumption that had dominated constitution making a decade earlier: that the legislature—the branch closest to the people—should be entrusted with the most power. Recent actions of the state legislatures had soured most of the men at Philadelphia toward the virtues of the people's representatives and made them look more favorably at traditional organs of power.

The Legislature. The House of Representatives proved to be the least complicated of the institutions to fashion. The delegates were clear that this branch would directly reflect the people's opinions and interests. But they were also clear that a legislative body so closely representing popular democratic sentiments would need strong checks. The House was seen as the most democratic part of the new system—and for that very reason the part most feared and constrained.

The nature and shape of the second legislative body, the Senate, occasioned greater controversy. Many delegates envisioned the Senate as an elite assemblage, a forum where the nation's economic, political, and intellectual aristocrats would constrain the more democratic House and supply wisdom and stability to the process of lawmaking. Those who wanted a cool, deliberative, elite legislative body fought hard against making the Senate a forum for state interests. Madison bitterly opposed the Great Compromise, saying it would turn the Senate into a copy of the inept Congress under the Articles of Confederation. Yet even though the Senate that emerged, with its special protection for the small states, fell short of the elite national body that Madison and his allies urged, it was viewed by all as more selective, conservative, and stable than the House. As a consequence, it was given deliberative functions and prerogatives denied to the House: Senate consent was required for treaties and for presidential nominations to the executive branch and the judiciary.

The Executive. If the fashioning of a Senate gave the convention its share of pains, the shaping of the executive was a continual headache, not relieved until the closing days of the proceedings. The Virginia Plan had left open the question of whether the United States would have a single or a plural executive. To some delegates, the idea of a single man exercising executive powers over so vast a country as the United States conjured a disturbing likeness with the king of Great Britain. Thus, when James Wilson of Pennsylvania proposed on June 1 that "the Executive consist of a single person" who would provide "energy, dispatch, and responsibility to the office," Madison's notes observe "a considerable pause ensuing." Attacking Wilson's proposal, Governor Randolph of Virginia claimed that a single or "unitary" executive would be the "fetus of monarchy" and suggested instead that the executive consist of three men.[15]

After vigorous debate, Wilson's proposal for a unitary executive carried, but another of his proposals—election of this executive by popular vote—failed. For most of the remainder of the convention, the prevailing view was that the national executive should be selected by Congress. But the convention was moving, gradually and fitfully, to strengthen the executive office. Revolutionary fears of executive power were waning, especially among conservative and propertied republicans; a more favorable view of executives as pillars of order and stability was gaining ground. The willingness of the delegates to create the kind of powerful American executive that would have been unthinkable in 1776 was furthered by the universal assumption that George Washington would be the first president. The final key decision of the convention on the executive—selection by electors rather than by Congress—added greatly to executive independence and strength.

The Judiciary. The third branch of the new national government provoked surprisingly little debate. Given the suspicions of the smaller states, one of the few contested issues involved the relation between federal courts below the Supreme Court and the courts in the states. The idea of "judicial review"—that federal courts have the authority to judge a law by the standard of the Constitution and to declare it null and void should it be found incompatible—was not stated in the Constitution but was discussed by the delegates. Although they did not agree universally on the subject, their comments about judicial review suggest that most delegates did assume that the federal courts would have this authority.

Values, Fears, and Issues

The Constitution was gradually shaped by the convention as institutions were formed, their powers defined, and their relationships to one another determined. In this process a number of values, fears, and issues drove the work of the framers. The next sections consider the interrelationship of one value, property, one fear, democracy, and one issue, slavery, in the development of the Constitution.

Property. Ever since historian Charles Beard charged in 1913 that the Constitution of the United States was written for the direct economic benefit of its framers, a debate has ensued about the role of property in the Constitutional Convention.[16] Although Beard's specific arguments about the framers' personal economic gains have been successfully refuted by other historians, considerable evidence remains in the record of the convention debates that the general protection of property was an objective for many of the framers. The new national government was designed to make property far more secure than it had been under the state constitutions. The convention bestowed on the national government new powers that holders of substantial property desired, such as the means to pay off public debts, disproportionately held by the wealthy. Equally important, it prohibited the state governments from coining money, issuing paper money, or "impairing the obligations of contracts," thus putting an end to the popular democratic efforts of the 1780s to aid the many at the expense of the few.

The "Threat" of Democracy. In the eyes of most of the framers, democracy was the chief threat to property. When the framers talked about democracy, they usually meant the lower house of the legislature, where the people's interests and feelings were directly represented. Some delegates assailed democracy on the grounds that the people were ignorant, subject to fits of passion, and prone to pursuing their own economic interests at the expense of a minority of the most industrious, successful, and propertied citizens. Others feared the people less because of their inherent flaws than because they were so easily duped by demagogues, selfish leaders who stoked the flames of popular passion to gain power. Given this perspective, it is not surprising that the delegates aimed many of the checks and balances they were writing into the constitution at democracy. Only the House of Representatives would be directly democratic, and it would be restrained by the Senate, president, and judiciary, all of which would be selected in an elite rather than a popular fashion.

Slavery. The delegates at Philadelphia concurred on the importance of promoting property and averting the dangers of democracy. But they were sharply divided on another issue: slavery.

Four positions on slavery were advanced during the debates. Some northern delegates opposed giving slavery any protection in the Constitution on economic grounds; if slaves were property, why should this form of property alone gain special safeguards? Other delegates—from both northern states and the upper South—denounced the institution itself on moral grounds. Against these two positions, delegates from South Carolina and Georgia insisted that slavery was indispensable to their economies and repeatedly warned the convention that if slavery was not given special protection, their states would not join the Union. The fourth and ultimately decisive view was put forward by delegates from New England, who expressed dislike for slavery but suggested that the convention should not meddle with this topic and should accept the compromises necessary to keep the most southerly states in the Union. In accordance with this position, slavery was given three special safeguards in the Constitution: (1) to apportion direct taxes and representation in the House, slaves would count as three-fifths of free persons, thereby enlarging southern representation; (2) the slave trade could not be banned for at least twenty years; and (3) fugitive slaves would be returned to their owners.

The framers of the Constitution compromised in this case for the sake of harmony and union, justifying their moral lapse with the belief that slavery would gradually die out without any forceful effort against it. The Civil War would show this pious hope to have been their greatest error. Remarkably, one delegate uttered a chilling prophecy of just such a catastrophe as the Civil War. In words that foreshadowed Abraham Lincoln's Second Inaugural Address at the close of the Civil War, George Mason of Virginia, an opponent of slavery (and soon to become an opponent of the Constitution itself), warned his fellow delegates that "by an inevitable chain of causes and effects providence punishes national sins by national calamities."[17]

The full text of the Constitution is in the Appendix at the end of the book. Table 2.1 summarizes the features of the Preamble and the seven articles. The final article stated that ratification by conventions in nine of the thirteen original states would be sufficient to put the Constitution into effect. It began one of the most important contests in American history—a political and philosophical struggle to determine nothing less than the basis on which all subsequent American political life would be conducted. It is to this debate that we now turn.

Ratification Struggle and the Democratic Debate

Most contemporary Americans assume that the greatness of the Constitution under which we have lived for two hundred years must have been obvious from the start. In reality, the ratification of the Constitution required a long and sometimes bitter struggle whose outcome was by no means certain. Although some states ratified the Constitution swiftly and with little dissent, in a number of the larger states the contest was close. In Massachusetts, the vote in the ratifying convention was 187 to 168 in favor of the Constitution. Virginia ratified by the narrow margin of 89 to 79; New York endorsed the Constitution by a vote of 30 to 27.[18]

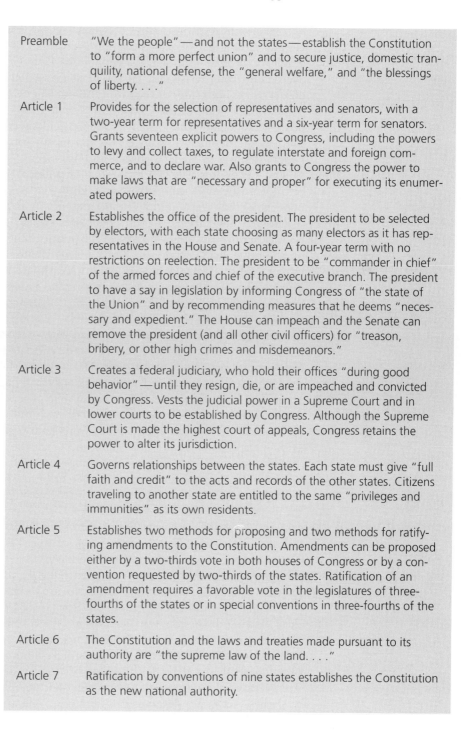

TABLE 2.1

Preamble and Articles of the Constitution

Preamble	"We the people"—and not the states—establish the Constitution to "form a more perfect union" and to secure justice, domestic tranquility, national defense, the "general welfare," and "the blessings of liberty. . . ."
Article 1	Provides for the selection of representatives and senators, with a two-year term for representatives and a six-year term for senators. Grants seventeen explicit powers to Congress, including the powers to levy and collect taxes, to regulate interstate and foreign commerce, and to declare war. Also grants to Congress the power to make laws that are "necessary and proper" for executing its enumerated powers.
Article 2	Establishes the office of the president. The president to be selected by electors, with each state choosing as many electors as it has representatives in the House and Senate. A four-year term with no restrictions on reelection. The president to be "commander in chief" of the armed forces and chief of the executive branch. The president to have a say in legislation by informing Congress of "the state of the Union" and by recommending measures that he deems "necessary and expedient." The House can impeach and the Senate can remove the president (and all other civil officers) for "treason, bribery, or other high crimes and misdemeanors."
Article 3	Creates a federal judiciary, who hold their offices "during good behavior"—until they resign, die, or are impeached and convicted by Congress. Vests the judicial power in a Supreme Court and in lower courts to be established by Congress. Although the Supreme Court is made the highest court of appeals, Congress retains the power to alter its jurisdiction.
Article 4	Governs relationships between the states. Each state must give "full faith and credit" to the acts and records of the other states. Citizens traveling to another state are entitled to the same "privileges and immunities" as its own residents.
Article 5	Establishes two methods for proposing and two methods for ratifying amendments to the Constitution. Amendments can be proposed either by a two-thirds vote in both houses of Congress or by a convention requested by two-thirds of the states. Ratification of an amendment requires a favorable vote in the legislatures of three-fourths of the states or in special conventions in three-fourths of the states.
Article 6	The Constitution and the laws and treaties made pursuant to its authority are "the supreme law of the land. . . ."
Article 7	Ratification by conventions of nine states establishes the Constitution as the new national authority.

The closeness of these votes becomes less surprising when we recall that the Constitution largely reversed the political verdict of 1776 by ending the revolutionary experiment in state-based popular democracy. Its supporters had to overcome strong resistance. Historian Saul Cornell notes that "Contemporary observers on both sides of the ratification debate were struck by the intensity of popular opposition to the Constitution."[19] If the Constitution was a defeat for popular democracy and a victory for an elite democracy (moderated by concessions to the democratic spirit), how did its supporters, who called themselves Federalists, win in the face of such opposition?

The Federalists enjoyed a number of political advantages over opponents of the Constitution, who came to be known as Anti-federalists. Perhaps most important, they were united around a common and positive program. With a solution in hand to the nation's distresses (which they often exaggerated for rhetorical purposes), they possessed the political initiative. The Anti-federalists, on the other hand, could not agree among themselves either about what was wrong with the Constitution or about what should take its place. The Federalists also had an advantage in disseminating their ideas. Based largely in the cities and supported by most of the wealthy, they had better access to newspapers than the Anti-federalists.

The Federalist cause was also blessed with exceptional intellectual talent. A majority of the distinguished, learned, and articulate men in America argued for the ratification of the Constitution. Among them, none presented the case for the Constitution so brilliantly as Alexander Hamilton, James Madison, and John Jay in *The Federalist Papers*. These eighty-five papers laid out the arguments for the new constitutional order so profoundly that they transcended their immediate aim and became the most famous American work of political theory. (Some of their arguments are presented later in this chapter.)

Although a number of able writers opposed the Constitution, no single Anti-federalist writing was comparable to *The Federalist Papers*. Moreover, the Anti-federalists can be said to have lost the intellectual debate because their side lost the political contest. *The Federalist Papers* thus overshadowed Anti-federalist thought. Yet both sides were important in the debate over the Constitution. As political theorist Herbert J. Storing has written, "If . . . the foundation of the American polity was laid by the Federalists, the Anti-Federalist reservations echo through American history; and it is in the dialogue, not merely in the Federalist victory, that the country's principles are to be discovered."[20]

The dialogue that Storing mentions is what we call the democratic debate. In the following discussion, we pay equal attention to both voices in the debate—Federalist and Anti-federalist, elite democrat and popular democrat. We consider six issues on which the two sides differed: human nature, the proper scale of political life, the character of representation, separation of powers and checks and balances, the purpose of government, and stability and change. The debate over these six issues deserves careful study. The arguments between the elite democratic position and the popular democratic position recur throughout this book; they form the essence of the democratic debate.

Human Nature: Its Dangers and Its Possibilities

The basic issue of the democratic debate is human nature. The Federalists held a pessimistic view of human nature. In the most famous of *The Federalist Papers*, number 10 (printed in full in the Appendix at the end of the book), James Madison wrote that people were "much more disposed to vex and oppress each other than to cooperate for their common good."[21] Alexander Hamilton's view of human nature was even bleaker: Men, he wrote, are "ambitious, vindictive, and rapacious."[22] Although Madison could also write that "there are other qualities in human nature which justify a certain portion of esteem and confidence,"[23] the Federalist view was that good government could not be founded on the idea of goodness in its participants.

Any goodness in human nature, the Federalists believed, was most likely to be found in elites. Madison argued that the new national government would bring to power the relatively few citizens who were both wise and public spirited. Hamilton claimed that his favorite institution, the presidency, would be filled by men "preeminent for ability and virtue."[24] The Federalists recognized that the dangerous qualities in human nature might also show up in the governing elite. But their greater fear was the raw human nature of the masses. The history of experiments in popular democracy had, in the eyes of the Federalists, demonstrated that most ordinary people were prone to passion, selfishness, and disorder. To the Federalists, any attempt by the people to assemble and debate affairs in a face-to-face or direct democracy would inevitably degenerate into mob rule.

The Anti-federalists were not naive optimists who held a rosy view of human nature. They, too, wrote vividly of the ambition and greed that could disfigure the human character. Yet they differed profoundly from the Federalists on where virtue and vice were most likely to be found. Ordinary individuals, most Anti-federalist writers believed, had modest aspirations; they wanted to live a life of comfort, decency, and dignity. Moreover, whatever natural tendencies existed toward selfishness and quarreling could be counteracted through instruction in morality and religion. Virtue could be taught by republican institutions, laws, and customs, and it would grow as citizens participated in the politics of their communities.[25]

The Anti-federalists feared human nature among elites. Power, they claimed, was intoxicating, especially when the connection between governors and citizens grew distant and the instruments for abuse and corruption were nearby. Human nature at its worst was not a lawless people, the Anti-federalist Patrick Henry of Virginia proclaimed. Rather, it was "the tyranny of rulers."[26]

Scale of Political Life

From this initial difference between Federalists and Anti-federalists over human nature flowed a further difference over the proper scale of political life.

Federalists favored a large republic (national government); Anti-federalists favored small republics (state governments).

In the view of the Federalists, the small republic brought out the worst in human nature. In the face-to-face political space of the small republic, a majority of selfish but like-minded individuals would form a "faction" or political group and try to oppress a minority, such as those who owned large amounts of property or those who held unorthodox religious beliefs. Irrational and violent passion would spread among this majority like an infectious disease, and politics in the small republic would degenerate into turbulence, injustice, and misery.

But in the large republic, the Federalists claimed, the selfish passions of the people could not have this unhappy result. There would be so much diversity in the large republic that a powerful and unjust majority faction was unlikely to form. James Madison explained the logic of the large republic: "Extend the sphere and you take in a greater variety of parties and interests; you make it less probable that a majority of the whole will have a common motive to invade the rights of other citizens; or if such a common motive exists, it will be more difficult for all who feel it to discover their own strength and to act in unison with each other."[27]

Given their view of human nature, the Anti-federalists favored the small republic and feared the large republic. The Anti-federalists saw the small republic as the home of liberty rather than oppression. It was only in the small republic, they argued, that citizens were close enough to their representatives in government to have confidence in them and to hold them accountable for their actions. Further, only in the small republic could citizens participate in political affairs and, through the practice of active citizenship, develop a broader and less selfish understanding of the common good.[28]

The Anti-federalists saw the large republic as bringing out the worst in human nature. Above all, they mistrusted the national elites on whom the Federalists were banking their hopes. As a New York Anti-federalist who used the pseudonym of Brutus (killer of the tyrant Caesar, who had destroyed the Roman republic) put it, "In so extensive a republic, the great officers of government would soon become above the control of the people, and abuse their power to the purpose of aggrandizing themselves, and oppressing them."[29]

Representation

Federalist and Anti-federalist understandings of representation also followed from their differing views of human nature. Because ordinary people were prone, the Federalists believed, to selfish, factional, and even violent passions, the task of the elected representative was to filter out these bad impulses and seek the people's true welfare. In a large republic, James Madison argued in *Federalist No. 10*, the process of representation would "refine and enlarge the public views by passing them through the medium of a chosen body of citizens, whose wisdom may best discern the true interest of their country and whose patriotism and love of justice will be least likely to sacrifice it to temporary or partial considerations."[30] The Federalist claim was that representatives, as a distinctive elite, would both know better and do better than the people themselves.

The Anti-federalists denied that representatives should act the part of the people's superiors. Representatives, they argued, should not filter out what the people wanted; they should mirror the people's exact hopes and goals. In the words of New York Anti-federalist Melancton Smith, "The idea that naturally suggests itself to our minds when we speak of representatives is that they resemble those they represent; they should be a true picture of the people; possess the knowledge of their circumstances and their wants; sympathize in all their distresses, and be disposed to seek their true interests."[31]

Separation of Powers and Checks and Balances

Although the Federalists entertained high hopes for a talented and virtuous elite to run the new national government, they were aware that concentrated power could be abused. Their remedy was to separate the powers of government into three branches—legislative, executive, and judicial—each of which would have the constitutional weapons to check the others. Thus, the president could check the legislature with his veto, the Senate could check the executive with its power over appointments, and the judiciary could check the other two branches by its authority over the meaning of the Constitution and the laws. Members of each branch were expected to defend their rightful powers against the others, James Madison explained, less out of virtue than out of a regard for their own interests. To guard against an oppressive concentration of powers within government, he wrote in one of his most famous sentences, "ambition must be made to counteract ambition."[32]

However, the Federalists did not see all branches as equally dangerous. They worried most about the popular democratic body, the House of Representatives. The more elite institutions were expected to hold the House in check and thereby ensure wiser and more stable governance. Madison and Hamilton preferred institutions that were more remote than the House from the pressures of popular democracy. Madison described the Senate as a select body that would provide cool deliberation even in the heat of passionate political controversies. Hamilton placed his greatest hopes on the presidency. Perhaps his most famous sentence in *The Federalist Papers* proclaims, "Energy in the executive is a leading character in the definition of good government."[33]

The Anti-federalists viewed the institutions of government in a different light. Some preferred a simpler structure of government than that provided in the Constitution, arguing that its complex arrangement of conflicting powers would leave the people confused about whom to hold accountable for abuses. However, the more common Anti-federalist perspective accepted the idea of separation of powers and checks and balances but complained that the Constitution was checking the wrong people. It was not the democratic House that needed most closely to be watched, but rather the elite branches. Patrick Henry thus warned that Hamilton's energetic executive "squints toward monarchy."[34] Anti-federalist writers also denounced the constitutional alliance between a monarchical president and an aristocratic Senate in making treaties and appointing civil officers, judges, and ambassadors.

Purpose of Government

What was the purpose of government? Both Federalists and Anti-federalists agreed that government must protect and promote the liberty of the people. Yet they meant different things by *liberty*. To James Madison, liberty was primarily a private possession—private property or private convictions. Liberty in this sense needed to be protected from oppressive majorities that would take away property or force the same religious faith on everyone. If liberty was protected, individuals would, Madison believed, succeed or fail in accordance with their own abilities. A free society would inevitably be marked by a substantial amount of economic inequality that resulted from the natural differences between people, and such a society was therefore just.[35]

Alexander Hamilton thought of liberty in slightly different terms—as the freedom to acquire greater property and power. He wanted a powerful national government that would promote the economic growth and develop the military potential of the United States. The purpose of government was to steer the United States in the direction of national greatness. In the right hands, he suggested in *The Federalist Papers*, this bold young nation "might make herself the admiration and envy of the world."[36] Hamilton's vision of a prosperous and mighty America was beyond the sight of most of his fellow Federalists. But he shared with them the idea that inequality in wealth and power inevitably accompanied liberty.

To the Anti-federalists, liberty was equally precious. But they emphasized the political rights of the people as much as the people's right to property. Understood in this way, liberty was endangered less by oppressive majorities than by oppressive rulers. The most common Anti-federalist complaint against the Constitution—that it contained no bill of rights to safeguard the people against government oppression—is considered in the next section.

The Anti-federalists also disagreed with the Federalists about how liberty related to economic life and national defense. Although desiring a prosperous America, they hoped for a simpler and more egalitarian society than the Federalists. If wealth became highly unequal and Americans began desiring luxurious goods, they feared, the republic would lose its anchorage in the civic virtue of the people. The public good would be neglected once Americans cared only about getting rich. Anti-federalists also worried about the rise of a powerful military that might be used by rulers for domestic tyranny or foreign aggression.

The Anti-federalist view of the purpose of government looked back to the vision of popular democracy that had fired the hopes of American revolutionaries in 1776. Their protest against turning America away from its original democratic dream and making it more like the undemocratic governments of Europe was eloquently expressed by Patrick Henry:

If we admit this consolidated government it will be because we like a great splendid one. Some way or other we must be a great and mighty empire; we must have an army, and a navy, and a number of things. When the American spirit was in its youth, the language of America was different. Liberty, Sir, was then the primary object.[37]

Stability and Change

The final critical area of difference between the Federalists and the Anti-federalists involved their perspectives on stability and change in American politics. Responding to the upsurge of popular democracy in the Revolution and its aftermath, Federalists looked for sources of stability in a new constitutional system. Their chief answer to the danger of radical economic and social change through popular democracy lay in the complex mechanisms of the Constitution itself. In the vastness and diversity of a large republic, majorities desiring radical change were unlikely to form; should they overcome the problem of distance and gain power in the democratic branch—the House of Representatives—the more elite branches would check their progress and protect the status quo. Federalists were not averse to all change—witness Hamilton's program for economic development—but they wanted change guided by an elite.

Among the Federalists, James Madison was particularly insightful in recognizing a more profound basis for stability. He saw that if the Constitution could prevail over its initial opposition, its status as the foundation of American politics would eventually cease to be questioned. It would gain "that veneration which time bestows on everything, and without which perhaps the wisest and freest governments would not possess the requisite stability."[38] Madison foresaw that Americans would come to love the Constitution. Forgetting the original debate over it, they would revere the document—and the ideas—produced by the winning side.

What the Federalists desired as stability looked to the Anti-federalists like the most dangerous form of change: political corruption and decay. The Anti-federalists were not worried that the people would become unruly; they feared that the people would become apathetic about public affairs. Under the new constitutional order, they predicted, arrogance and corruption would grow among ruling elites, while the people would become preoccupied with the scramble for riches. Unless ordinary citizens were called to remember their political rights and to exercise them, liberty was sure to be lost.

The Anti-federalist view continued the spirit of protest and resistance that had marked the American Revolution. No one expressed this spirit so strongly during this period as Thomas Jefferson. Strictly speaking, Jefferson was neither Federalist nor Anti-federalist; as the American minister to France during the years in which the Constitution was written and debated, he stood at a distance from the conflict over it. Yet his support for popular protest, expressed in letters to friends in America, dramatically opposes the Federalist dread of popular action. Whereas the Federalists reacted in horror to Shays's Rebellion as a signpost of impending anarchy, Jefferson wrote to Madison that "I hold it that a little rebellion now and then is a good thing, and as necessary in the political world as

TABLE 2.2	Issue	Federalists	Anti-federalists
Differences Between the Federalists and Anti-federalists	Human nature	Ordinary people basically selfish; capacity for virtue greater among elites	Ordinary people moderately ambitious and capable of virtue; dangerous ambitions found among elites
	Scale of political life	Favored a large republic (national government)	Favored a small republic (state governments)
	Role of representatives	To refine the public views	To mirror the people's hopes and goals
	Separation of powers	Favored checks and balances, with particular eye on the House of Representatives	Believed in checks and balances, with particular eye on the president and Senate
	Purpose of government	To protect liberty, especially private rights; expected inequality as just result	To protect liberty, especially political rights; sought to prevent large inequalities that threatened values of a republic
	Stability and change	Stability found in complexity of Constitution and in public reverence for it	Feared political decay and corruption; favored spirit of protest embodied in the Revolution

storms in the physical."[39] Jefferson, like the Anti-federalists, believed that only an alert and active citizenry could preserve the democratic values of the American Revolution (see Table 2.2).

THE BILL OF RIGHTS

When farmers in the back country of South Carolina heard that their state had ratified the Constitution, they "had a coffin painted black, which borne in funeral procession, was solemnly buried, as an emblem of the dissolution and interment of public liberty."[40] Such Anti-federalist fears—that the Constitution would become a monstrous mechanism for oppressing the people—strike us today as absurdly exaggerated. Yet in one crucial respect, the fears of the Anti-federalists were fortunate and productive. Without them, we would not have gained the Bill of Rights.

Among the Anti-federalists' objections to the Constitution, none was as frequently voiced, as popularly received, and as compelling in force as the complaint that the Constitution lacked guarantees of the people's basic liberties. Most of the state constitutions, Anti-federalist writers and debaters pointed out, expressly protected the fundamental personal and political rights of the people against arbitrary and invasive government. Yet this new national constitution contained no such guarantees of liberty. Anti-federalists at the state ratifying conventions thus began to propose various amendments to the new Constitution as safeguards of the people's fundamental rights.

Some Federalists resisted the call for amendments, fearing that they would weaken the new political system. But the more moderate supporters of the Constitution increasingly recognized that amendments that guaranteed the rights of the people would conciliate opponents of the Constitution and thus give the new system a better chance to survive and flourish. The leader of these moderates was James Madison. To win election to the House of Representatives, Madison had pledged to the voters in his district that he would introduce amendments in the first Congress. Fulfilling his promise, he became the principal drafter and legislative champion of what became the Bill of Rights. The greatest thinker in the American tradition of elite democracy thus became one of the greatest contributors to the American tradition of popular democracy.[41]

The Bill of Rights adds to the original Constitution a commitment to the personal and political liberties of the people. It safeguards the rights of religious conscience, free speech, a free press, and political activity; it protects the people against an invasion of their homes and papers by an intrusive government; it guarantees a fair trial and a freedom from excessive punishment. If the Constitution proved to be the great charter of American government, the Bill of Rights was the great charter of American liberty. It stands as an enduring testament to the vision and values of the Anti-federalists. Today, when Americans think of the U.S. Constitution, the Bill of Rights seems as much a part of its original composition as the seven articles drafted at the Philadelphia convention of 1787. The original democratic debate had made the Constitution a better — and a more democratic — document.

CONCLUSION: BEGINNING THE DEMOCRATIC DEBATE

The ratification of the Constitution was a victory for elite democrats in the original democratic debate. Not only did this victory lie in the creation of lofty national institutions in which elites would control most of the offices, but even more, it lay in the impediments to popular democracy that the constitutional system established. The growing size of the national republic tended, as Madison had argued, to fragment potential popular democratic movements and encourage in their place the narrower struggles of interest group politics. The complexity of national institutions tended to stalemate democratic energies for social change. The remoteness of national institutions tended to undermine the civic virtue nourished in local, face-to-face political participation.

Elite democrats also won a philosophical victory in 1787. Embodied in many of the clauses of the Constitution and brilliantly argued in the pages of *The Federalist Papers*, the premises of elite democracy have come down to Americans with the sanctity of the highest political authority.

Yet the victory of the Federalists, the original elite democrats, was far from complete. Historian Saul Cornell observes that the "ideas of the Anti-Federalists, the Other Founders of the American constitutional tradition, continue to provoke, inspire, and complicate our understanding of what the Constitution means."[42] When Americans today discuss the Constitution, their assumptions about the document's democratic character reflect many of the Anti-federalists' central arguments.

Popular democrats thus were not really vanquished in the era of the American founding. Later generations of popular democrats have looked back to the founding for authority and inspiration—though to the Revolution more than to the Constitution. The American tradition of popular democratic protest and struggle finds its roots in the Sons of Liberty, the Boston Tea Party, and the revolutionary war militia. The popular democratic vision of equality and self-government rests on the opening paragraphs of the Declaration of Independence. Echoing the revolutionaries of 1776 (and the Anti-federalists as well), popular democrats balance their fears of remote and unaccountable power with hopes for democratic community and public-spirited citizens.

Today's popular democrats not only can claim the revolutionary heritage, but they can also point to concessions obtained from elite democrats in the constitutional system itself. The framers of the Constitution had to include elements of popular democracy in order to win ratification. Subsequent to ratification, popular democrats won an even larger victory when the Bill of Rights was added to the Constitution. Later amendments have also made the Constitution more compatible with popular democracy. The Thirteenth, Fourteenth, and Fifteenth Amendments, products of the Civil War and Reconstruction era, established the rights of African Americans to participate in the American political system. The Nineteenth Amendment established women's right to suffrage. Products of long struggles by popular democratic movements, these amendments opened doors that the founders had kept shut. They established the equal right—although not the equal chance—of all Americans to exercise the political rights and enjoy the political rewards that had originally been reserved for white males alone.

The Revolution and Constitution engendered a great democratic debate, but they did not resolve it for all time. Throughout this text, we point out how the democratic debate continues to flourish in American politics. For example, should large corporations be regarded as the indispensable engines of economic growth, or should we instead discourage concentrated economic power and favor smaller economic enterprises and a more equal distribution of economic resources? Do contemporary elections foster civic virtue or bury it under a blizzard of media spectacles financed by elite money? Is the modern president the "energetic executive" that Alexander Hamilton applauded or the arrogant "monarch" that Patrick Henry dreaded? In these and many other forms, the democratic debate still animates American politics. As we study its contemporary expressions, we need to recall the fundamental terms of the debate set down by the founders of the American Republic.

KEY TERMS

republicanism
Declaration of Independence
Articles of Confederation
Shays's Rebellion

Virginia Plan
New Jersey Plan
Great Compromise
federalism

INTERNET RESOURCES

▪ Founding Fathers Website
www.foundingfathers.info/federalistpapers
This site contains the complete text of *The Federalist Papers*, as well as other important documents from the founding period.

SUGGESTED READINGS

Saul Cornell, *The Other Founders: Anti-Federalism and the Dissenting Tradition in America, 1788–1828*. Chapel Hill: University of North Carolina Press, 1999. The most thorough study of the Anti-federalists, emphasizing both their diversity and their subsequent influence on the American political tradition.

Ralph Ketcham, ed., *The Anti-Federalist Papers*. New York: New American Library, 1986. An anthology of the leading Anti-federalist critics of the Constitution.

Richard K. Matthews, *If Men Were Angels: James Madison and the Heartless Empire of Reason*. Lawrence: University Press of Kansas, 1995. A provocative analysis of Madison as an elite democratic theorist.

Jack N. Rakove, *Original Meanings: Politics and Ideas in the Making of the Constitution*. New York: Alfred A. Knopf, 1996. A wide-ranging yet subtle examination of the Constitutional Convention and the major ideas that it produced.

Clinton Rossiter, ed., *The Federalist Papers*. New York: New American Library, 1961. Hamilton's and Madison's brilliant defense of the Constitution—and the foremost work in the history of American political thought.

Gordon S. Wood, *The Creation of the American Republic, 1776–1787*. New York: W. W. Norton, 1972. The leading work on the transformation of American political thought from the popular democracy of the Revolution to the elite democracy of the Constitution.

The American Political Economy

In the summer of 2000, Barbara Ehrenreich traveled to Minneapolis as part of a journalistic experiment to see if a single, unskilled woman could make ends meet in today's labor market.[1] Posing as a recently divorced homemaker entering the labor force after several years as a stay-at-home mom, Ehrenreich allowed herself one concession in her experiment: a working automobile that was paid for. Minneapolis had a tight labor market that summer, and after submitting to a demeaning drug test, Ehrenreich quickly landed a $7 an hour job at Wal-Mart. Sorting clothes in the women's section, she found the work surprisingly demanding—and her fellow workers surprisingly devoted to Wal-Mart.

Try as she might, however, Ehrenreich could not find an apartment she could afford on her Wal-Mart wages. The best she could find was a $245 a week room at a motel a twenty-minute drive from the store. The room smelled of mouse droppings and lacked air conditioning and screens on the windows. (Minnesota summers can be surprisingly hot.) One day, raw sewage backed up through the drains and flooded her room. Admitting defeat, Ehrenreich later acknowledged that she might have been able to make it in Minneapolis if she had been willing to live in a $19 a night "dormitory." But the fact is, she showed that a single woman cannot live on $7 an hour with any semblance of dignity or safety.[2]

Ehrenreich's story illustrates a basic fact about the current American political economy: a single person—let alone an entire family—cannot exist on the low-wage, service-sector jobs available today. And Wal-Mart epitomizes this trend. In 2002 Wal-Mart surpassed General Motors as the largest U.S. company. In 1997 the *Wall Street Journal* contrasted the average wage of a GM assembly-line worker ($19/hour) with the average at Wal-Mart ($7.50/hour). When benefits, such as health insurance, are included, the GM wage jumps to $44 an hour, while the Wal-Mart wage increases to only $10 an hour.[3] Wal-Mart can be considered a mirror that reflects the changing American political economy. A closer look at Wal-Mart reveals the strength of American capitalism when it comes to "delivering the goods," but it also highlights the burdens our political economy places on workers and the way it distorts the democratic process.

WAL-MART: THE FUTURE POLITICAL ECONOMY?

With 20 million shoppers visiting its stores daily and annual sales topping $250 billion, Wal-Mart has become the most successful retailer in history. The basic reason for its phenomenal growth is that Wal-Mart has focused like a laser on one and only one goal: lowering prices. And Wal-Mart has been remarkably successful at achieving this goal, saving American consumers billions of dollars each year. When it enters a product category, Wal-Mart typically undercuts the competition by 10 percent or more. With 70 percent of its shoppers being blue collar, unemployed, or elderly, Wal-Mart caters to lower-income groups, concentrating its stores in small towns or working-class suburbs.[4] Consumers love Wal-Mart because it saves them time in shopping and provides them with incredible deals and friendly service. And Wal-Mart prides itself on customer service. Employees who find themselves within ten feet of a customer are supposed to smile and offer assistance. The firm is known for offering advancement opportunities to noncollege graduates and a stock option plan to all employees.

But there are also many costs, often hidden, to Wal-Mart's remarkable success. Wal-Mart can offer very low prices because it pays very low wages. In the early twentieth century, Henry Ford paid his workers handsomely so they could afford to buy his cars. Sam Walton, the charismatic founder of Wal-Mart who died in 1992, basically turned Ford's approach on its head: Wal-Mart pays its workers very little so the only place they can afford to shop is Wal-Mart. The average Wal-Mart wage in the United States is $9.64 an hour, close to half of what workers earn in unionized chains such as Costco. By hiring professional union busters and firing union supporters—even though that is illegal—Wal-Mart has ensured that no U.S. store is unionized. Its health care benefits are meager, and, mostly as a result of low wages and high turnover, less than one out of fifty Wal-Mart workers ever accumulates as much as $50,000 in Wal-Mart stock.[5]

Although Wal-Mart treats its women customers well, it often treats its women employees poorly. A remarkable 11 percent of all women workers in the U.S. work for Wal-Mart. In 2001 the average female Wal-Mart employee earned $5,000 less annually than the average male employee's salary, even if they both had the same position. Women make up 72 percent of the chain's hourly workforce but only 34 percent of its salaried managers.[6]

The other key to Wal-Mart's low prices is that its products are made with cheap overseas labor. Wal-Mart is a prime example of the globalization of American businesses. Although it exudes patriotism with its "Made in America" slogan, 85 percent of Wal-Mart's products are made overseas. (Ironically, Sam Walton's autobiography is titled *Made in America*.[7]) Its biggest overseas supplier is China. (In her book *Selling Women Short*, Liza Featherstone states, "If Wal-Mart were a country, it would be China's fifth largest export market."[8] Unions are illegal in China, and workers are forced to endure deplorable working conditions. Wal-Mart has a code of conduct concerning working conditions for its suppliers, but like most retailers, it does little to monitor and enforce the code. Apparel workers in Guatemala work fifty-four hours a week, and many are paid less than the country's minimum wage of $2.80 a day. Also, there is evidence that Wal-Mart has imported products made with prison labor in China.[9] In relying on products produced in Third World sweatshops, the company is not much different from most American retailers. With its huge volume, however,

Mike Keefe, The Denver Post.

Wal-Mart has more leverage to force its suppliers to lower their prices, thus putting downward pressure on wages.

How does Wal-Mart get away with paying near poverty-level wages? Part of the answer is that the taxpayers are forced to pick up the tab. Documents show that Wal-Mart encourages its workers to apply for food stamps and other social welfare benefits. One study by a Democratic congressman found that each Wal-Mart that employs 200 people costs taxpayers $420,750 per year in public assistance.[10] Wal-Mart also pits communities against one another to garner tax breaks and other subsidies from local governments. These governments, hungry for sales and property taxes, are put in the perverse position of subsidizing the largest corporation in the world in order to drive down wages in the local economy, giving new meaning to the term **corporate welfare**.

Finally, Wal-Mart stores erode local civic life. When a Wal-Mart moves into an area, it takes business away from small stores in town centers, and family-owned businesses are often forced to close. These small businesses support Little Leagues and Kiwanis clubs. Wal-Mart, on the other hand, donates very little to charity, although it makes sure its generosity is widely publicized.[11] In addition, Wal-Mart requires its managers to work seventy to eighty hours per week, leaving little time for civic commitments. The old mixed-use town square where people would gather for conversation and major civic events is now replaced by a huge, windowless box surrounded by a sea of asphalt.

Wal-Mart likes to portray itself as a popular democratic institution that caters to working-class individuals and communities. (One of its Three Basic Beliefs is "Respect the individual.") Its founder, Sam Walton, drove a pickup truck all his life and abhorred those who flaunted their wealth. Beneath the populist rhetoric, however, is an elitist and hierarchical institution. Wal-Mart has become so big it can dictate terms to suppliers as well as entire communities. The free market claim that individual workers have an equal voice in negotiating wages and working conditions with the largest corporation in the world is simply absurd. Corporations as large as Wal-Mart do not support popular democracy; they contradict it.

Does Wal-Mart represent the future of American political economy? The country's rule of law and popular democratic resistance to elites make this unlikely. As a result of workers' struggles during the Great Depression, in 1938 Congress passed the Fair Labor Standards Act, which established a minimum wage and overtime pay for weekends and more than forty hours of work per week. Wal-Mart has been successfully sued several times for not paying overtime when it was justified. (Lacking such laws, workers in Third World countries are forced to work fifty and sixty hours per week with no extra pay.)

The Equal Employment Opportunity Commission (EEOC), established in 1964 through the struggles of the civil rights movement, prohibits job discrimination on the basis of race, gender, age, religion, or disability. As a result of data that Wal-Mart was required to submit to the EEOC, a federal judge agreed to certify a lawsuit brought by 1.6 million current and former women employees alleging discrimination by Wal-Mart (*Dukes v. Wal-Mart Stores, Inc.*), the largest class-action civil rights lawsuit in history. As a result of the suit, Wal-Mart has improved its treatment of women employees. And in communities around the nation, local activists are challenging Wal-Mart's demands for tax subsidies and zoning changes, often successfully.[12]

There is no question that Wal-Mart is a remarkably efficient and successful corporation, but it did not achieve this success solely through its own efforts in the private market. Without the massive government expenditures on streets and highways, Wal-Mart would be lacking both the goods and the customers that make it so profitable. Wal-Mart's growth is rooted in dedicated working-class employees and social welfare policies that help them to make ends meet. Because Wal-Mart depends on society, it must in turn be responsible to society. The company should be judged not only on its efficiency and prices but on its contribution to a democratic society based on equal rights and respect for the individual.

THE DEMOCRATIC DEBATE ON THE POLITICAL ECONOMY

Unlike most American politics textbooks, we do not treat large corporations, like Wal-Mart, as just another interest group. With their global reach and control over investment and people's livelihoods, the contemporary corporation possesses levers of power that no other group can duplicate. Charles Lindblom calls this the **"privileged position of business."**[13] To understand American politics, it is necessary to study not just the rules of the political game but also the rules of political economy. Economic rules are as important as political rules, such as those in the U.S. Constitution, when it comes to understanding how power really works in American society.

Throughout our history, Americans have engaged in heated debates about how our economy should be organized, who should make key decisions, and what effects the economy has on the quality of democratic life. These debates have not been between advocates of communism—government ownership of the means of production—and free market capitalism. Even Americans who are critical of the economic system have shunned state ownership of factories and advocated that private goods and services be produced and distributed by markets, not by governments. Within the American consensus about markets, however, there have been important lines of division.

Most Americans agree that government should not interfere with private transactions in the market as long as they do not harm other people. But market transactions have all sorts of effects on society, affecting the air we breathe, the revenue for local governments, and the health of our citizens. Everyone agrees that some public goods, like highways and clean air, must be provided by government, but there is much disagreement about how much to spend on these public goods. In short, determining where to draw the line between the private sector and government has always been a hotly contested issue in American politics. Debates about the proper relationship between governments and markets often focus on how to make a more efficient and productive economy, but they also hinge on how to make a better democracy, and that is our main concern in this chapter. How far should democratic decision making be extended into the American economy? Should government help those who cannot succeed in the private market, or should the primary goal be to spur investment and growth? What kind of political economy will produce strong social institutions and communities that promote democratic decision making and participation?

The example of Wal-Mart shows the two faces of modern American capitalism. As an engine of prosperity and innovation, American capitalism delivers a dazzling array of goods and services. At the same time, it imposes tremendous costs not only on individuals but on the political system as well. The modern U.S. economy has three characteristics that raise troubling questions for American democracy: unaccountable corporate power, growing inequality, and the erosion of civil society.

Unaccountable Corporate Power. Huge corporations, owned and run by a small elite, control vast resources and make decisions that affect the lives of millions. Can these corporations use their power over the private economy to influence government priorities and undermine democratic decision making? Are there any forces in the economy itself that check corporate power? Do citizens have the resources to hold corporations accountable for their actions?

Growing Inequality. Even though the American capitalist system generates tremendous wealth, the fruits of the economy are unequally distributed. Indeed, economic inequality in the United States has grown worse in the last three decades and is now much greater than in any other advanced capitalist democracy. Do economic inequalities translate into political inequalities? What happens to democracy when the middle class shrinks and the gap between the rich and the poor widens?

Erosion of Civil Society. Americans are working harder today in an increasingly competitive and insecure economy. Women have entered the workforce in large numbers, and employees of both sexes are working longer hours. The issue for democracy is basic: At what point does participation in the competitive market economy take away from participation in politics and from the institutions of civil society, such as churches and community organizations, that are essential for a healthy democracy?

Free Markets: The Elite Democratic View

Elite and popular democrats take dramatically different perspectives on American political economy. To elite democrats, American capitalism reflects human nature: The masses of ordinary citizens are oriented toward private pursuits and want minimal government interference in their lives. For elite democrats, the economy does not present much of a problem for democracy. Indeed, choice in the marketplace virtually defines what democracy is. Popular democrats, on the other hand, stress that people are naturally inclined to participate in the decisions that influence their lives. If the private economy stimulates private pursuits at the expense of civic commitments, that is a problem. Moreover, rising levels of economic inequality threaten our democratic system. For popular democrats, consumer choice is not enough; economic power must be held accountable by an organized citizenry.

In the elite democratic view, markets maximize freedom and minimize power. Unlike government, with its laws, police, and bureaucracy, markets don't force people to do anything. Whether at a yard sale or a global financial transaction, no one has to buy or sell unless they want to. The genius of economic markets (at least in theory) is that if every individual pursues his or her selfish interest, the result is the greatest good for the greatest number. A modern market economy is less interested in the motives of the participants than in the overall beneficial results. In this view, Wal-Mart, even though its goal is to maximize profits, is a stunning success because it offers people more choices at lower costs.

Elite democrats use the language of democratic politics to explain how the free market works. Terms like consumer "sovereignty" are employed to suggest that markets are driven by the wants and needs of individuals who "vote" with their dollars. From this point of view, citizens do not need to be involved directly in controlling corporations. Instead, they are held accountable by consumers who either buy or don't buy their products. Similarly, the market, like American government under the Constitution, has its own automatic "checks and balances." If a corporation performs inefficiently or charges excessively high prices, then it will be challenged by entrepreneurs willing to supply superior goods to consumers at lower prices.[14]

Modern elite democrats do not contend that markets always work perfectly or that they can be completely self-regulating. They acknowledge that government should play an important, if limited, role in the marketplace, setting the rules that ensure fair and honest competition and intervening when the market breaks down, as during a depression. Government should supply public goods that the market cannot easily provide, such as clean air, military protection, dams, and highways. And it should take care of those who, through no fault of their own, can't compete in the marketplace: the aged, children, and the disabled. Beyond these policies, elite democrats argue, government should stay out of the way of the market.

One thing government definitely should *not* do, from the elite democratic perspective, is to meddle with economic inequalities. Most inequalities fairly reflect varying individual abilities and effort and help to make the economy function efficiently. Inequalities provide the incentives to ensure that the most important and difficult tasks in society are performed by the most motivated and talented people. Few have the talent to be brain surgeons, software engineers, or entrepreneurs. If these people make vastly more money than the average worker, it is because they are fulfilling the demands of the marketplace. If unskilled work produced a comfortable income, individuals would have no incentive to work harder and learn new skills. Attempting to rectify economic inequality, government would retard economic growth, eventually leaving the poor—the very people who were supposed to benefit from redistribution—even poorer.[15]

According to elite democrats, the market reflects human nature: People are basically self-interested and competitive. We need to build democracy on the way people really are, not on some utopian ideal of virtuous citizens. People do not want to spend endless hours in democratic meetings; they would much rather spend their time earning more money or enjoying their family. What citizens want is the better goods and services, not more meetings.

Although most people are interested in private pursuits, because of their education and experience, a tiny elite is deeply interested in politics. Ordinary citizens do not need to be directly involved in running either private corporations or governments in order to hold these elites accountable. Just as consumers hold corporations accountable through the marketplace, citizens hold political elites accountable through periodic elections.

If the market disrupts people's lives—plant closings, job relocations, increased pressures on workers' time—these are the unavoidable side effects, say elite democrats, of a free and prosperous economy. Modern corporate capitalism offers the average person an abundance of choices—more and better goods and services than ever before. Everyone, regardless of race, religion, or gender, has access to the objects of consumption through which they can fulfill their hearts' desires. What could be more democratic than that?[16]

The Popular Democratic Perspective

Popular democrats do not disagree with elite democrats about the importance of markets and private property. If economic exchanges are purely private and do not harm anyone, they should be allowed to proceed without interference from government and politics. The problem is that in the real world of corporate capitalism the power of corporations to decide what goods will be produced and how and where they will be produced has massive effects on society. Too often, corporations use their power and wealth to tilt the playing field of democratic politics in their favor. The principle of market economics is that economic decision making should be strictly separated from political decision making. Instead, economic and political decision making are increasingly intertwined in a system that gives tremendous political advantages to those who control economic wealth.

Popular democrats support free markets; they just don't think that free markets exist in many areas of the American economy. Small businesses do engage in free market competition. Think of restaurants or dry cleaners in your hometown. Small businesses cannot control prices, manipulate consumer demand through advertising, or obtain huge tax breaks from local governments by threatening to leave. Large corporations, on the other hand, shape the market as much as the market shapes them. Instead of individuals cooperating and competing in the free market, popular democrats see large organizations and wealthy individuals doing most of the voluntary cooperating and deciding. The rest of the population of wage workers are generally compelled to take the kinds of jobs offered to them and to obey the rules of a marketplace over which they have little say. Elite democrats argue that free markets and small government disperse power. Yet the campaign contributions and lobbying power of huge corporations like Wal-Mart hardly separate and disperse political and economic power. What is notable is the close link between economic and political power.

The amount of inequality in the present American economy is excessive, popular democrats argue. To be sure, a certain amount of inequality is necessary to motivate people to perform unpleasant and demanding tasks. Because people have different talents, skills, and willingness to work long hours, incomes will always be unequal. But the amount of inequality today far exceeds what is necessary to motivate people to work. More importantly, it does not fairly reflect people's contributions to the productive process. Thus, massive economic inequality is hardly efficient from a democratic standpoint. It wastes human talent and potential, erodes social trust and community bonds, and spurs crime and drug use as many, despite their struggles, fall into poverty and hardship in our affluent society. For popular democrats, a certain amount of economic inequality is inevitable but not extremes of wealth that invade and corrupt the political process.

Popular democrats also have problems with the messages that free market capitalism sends to citizens. Corporate advertising floods the airwaves, fills magazines, and is even infiltrating elementary school classrooms. Corporations give free educational materials to schools—on the condition that students are forced to watch ads. Far from cultivating the virtues necessary for democratic citizenship, modern **corporate capitalism** often confuses greed and envy with virtue. Slick ads teach that life can be fulfilled by consuming goods, not by participating in society. For popular democrats, corporate capitalism accentuates the acquisitive side of human nature at the expense of our social or political side.

The market economy does not accomplish this just through advertising but by turning most everything we need as a society into things that are bought and sold. And most of the things that are produced are designed to maximize profits. That is why plastic surgeons, who make the super-rich look attractive, proliferate, but solutions to the problems of AIDS and obesity, diseases that disproportionately afflict the poor, get much less attention. Markets produce private cars in abundance but tear up mass transit systems that move people quickly, safely, and with far less pollution. Markets produce luxury condos and gated communities for the affluent, but ghettos and homelessness abound in inner cities. If we care as much for justice as we do for consumer goods, say popular democrats, then we have to humanize our economy by letting in the fresh air of democratic participation.[17]

Finally, popular democrats warn that market capitalism is prone to crisis and even self-destruction. In the 1930s, the unregulated economy collapsed, leaving a quarter of the U.S. workforce unemployed. In the late 1990s, an unanticipated Asian financial crisis nearly plunged the global economy into turmoil and recession. History teaches us that we are not immune from big—even massive—downturns. In this view, the public interest is too important to be left to the uncontrolled forces of market capitalism.

In short, popular democrats view modern capitalism with a great deal more skepticism than elite democrats. Purely private choices in the marketplace should be protected from governmental interference, but when concentrations of economic power invade and distort the political process, they must be checked by government. In recent decades, the celebration of markets and suspicion of government have drowned out the more participatory and egalitarian voices that have reverberated throughout American history. Popular democrats have always maintained that concentrations of economic power must be held in check by a mobilized citizenry. In order to check concentrations of corporate power, big government will often be necessary, but it should be a government accountable to the people. Democratic accountability will not be accomplished by a consumer mentality in which citizens choose every few years which set of elites will run the government. As much as possible, citizens must be directly involved in making the decisions that affect their lives.

Most commentary in the mass media, and even in scholarly journals, celebrates American capitalism and underplays the obstacles it puts in the path of advancing democracy. In what follows we try to right the balance by developing a popular democratic critique of the American political economy that points in the direction of democratic reforms.

UNACCOUNTABLE CORPORATE POWER

In the booming 1990s Enron seemed to be a model American corporation. For five years in a row (1996–2001) *Fortune* magazine named Enron as the most innovative U.S. company. Enron did not just dominate markets—it created them, devising new ways to trade in "futures," essentially ways to bid on what the price at some point in the future will be of gas, bandwidth, or a range of other commodities. (Enron even devised a way to trade on weather futures.) Dealing in a dizzying array of commodities Enron grew rapidly into a global giant, becoming the seventh largest company in the United States by 2000 with revenues of $101 billion. In 2001 Enron collapsed, exposing a system whereby top executives of large corporations, accountable to no one, can line their pockets at the expense of consumers and workers. Far from being servants of consumers, many corporate executives more closely resemble pirates or gang bosses.

It turns out that Enron's soaring stock price was based on fraud. The company had created over 2,800 phony off-shore subsidiaries that were used to hide debt and inflate profits. In addition, the company created secret partnerships, run by top executives, into which they had channeled hundreds of millions of dollars. When Enron's fraudulent accounting practices were revealed to the world, the stock price collapsed, falling from a high of $90 a share to 36 cents. Over $60 billion in shareholder value disappeared overnight, with Enron becoming the largest bankruptcy in American history. What really angered the 4,000 employees who lost their jobs, however, is that twenty-nine top executives, knowing the company was in danger, cashed in their stock—according to one lawsuit to the tune of $1.1 billion. Meanwhile, employees who owned Enron stock in their 401(k) retirement plans were explicitly forbidden to sell their stock. Many lost their entire retirement savings.

Workers were not the only ones gouged by Enron. New evidence shows that Enron played a key role in California's energy crisis that resulted in rolling blackouts during 2000 and 2001, costing California consumers billions of dollars. After lobbying successfully for deregulation of electricity, Enron exploited that situation by creating artificial shortages of electricity in California and other states. Concocting trading schemes with code names like "Ricochet" and "Death Star," Enron was able to manipulate energy prices. To get out from under price ceilings for electricity produced in California, for example, Enron would buy electricity generated in California, export it out of state, and then reimport it at higher prices. Audiotapes of Enron traders show them conspiring to temporarily shut down a Las Vegas power plant. The next day a half a million homes and businesses in California lost power. Traders gloated about inflating costs for "Grandma Millie" in California.[18]

As bad as it is, Enron is only the tip of the iceberg of unaccountable corporate power. After it was revealed that telecommunications giant WorldCom had inflated profits by roughly $11 billion, President Bush gave a speech saying that the corporate scandals were the fault of a few bad apples. The main response of Congress to the spate of corporate scandals was passage of the Sarbanes-Oxley Act that reformed corporate accounting practices. The act initiated long overdue reforms in accounting practices, such as requiring CEOs to personally certify their company's financial reports. But the underlying problem of corporate abuse of power cannot be solved by new accounting methods. The basic problem is that corporations have extraordinary political power that enables them to bend and twist the laws to their advantage. Until they are brought under democratic control, corporate abuse of power will be an everyday occurrence.

The Evolution of the Modern Corporation

When the American republic was founded, the democratic debate revolved around how to form and control governmental power. The Constitution was silent about concentrations of economic power. With the important exception of plantation slavery, the early republic contained few economic institutions that needed to be checked. Great inequalities of income and wealth existed, even among the population of free white males. Yet there also was a great degree of economic independence. The early economy was local. People grew crops and produced commodities within the web of small communities and cities. Most owned some land, or at least their own tools, and if they worked for wages, they did so in small shops alongside their bosses. If an individual did not want to work for someone else, he could move to the frontier, where free land was available. Corporations were chartered by state governments, which set strict limits on what businesses they could enter, their level of indebtedness, and even where they could do business.

Over the last century and a half, the modern corporation's rise has transformed the simple capitalism of the eighteenth century into modern corporate capitalism. In both eras, the means by which goods are produced—land, tools, workshops, factories, and stores—are in private hands. In both, entrepreneurs invest according to the profit motive. In both epochs, contracts between buyers and producers are essential and protected by law. In both eras, **market competition** drives the system. Yet corporate capitalism is no longer an economy based on small farms, artisans, local markets, and the checks on corporate power imposed by vigilant state governments.

After the Civil War, railroads became the nation's first big businesses, and corporations began to acquire monopoly power that threatened democracy.[19] In blatant violation of state incorporation laws, for example, John D. Rockefeller set up Standard Oil of Ohio, which placed controlling interest of the stock of supposedly competing companies in a trust run by a single board of directors. The Standard Oil Trust enabled Rockefeller to control 95 percent of all refined oil shipments in the nation. Trusts were soon organized in other industries: the Cotton Oil Trust in 1884 and the Whiskey Trust, the Sugar Trust, and the Lead Trust in 1887. In 1892 the Supreme Court of Ohio ruled that the Standard Oil Trust was "organized for a purpose contrary to the policy of our laws" and was therefore "void." Standard Oil, however, simply refused to obey the ruling, and in 1898 the Ohio attorney general brought a contempt citation to revoke Standard Oil's charter.

Playing one state against another, Standard Oil found an easy way out. In the 1890s New Jersey, which came to be known as "The Traitor State," passed new state incorporation laws that legalized trusts and basically gave up all pretense of holding corporations accountable through their charters. Standard Oil simply moved to New Jersey, as did other corporations, and soon incorporation fees flooded the state's coffers. Led by Delaware, other states followed suit, and since that time state incorporation laws have been toothless. Once it is incorporated in one state a corporation can do business across the nation because the Constitution (ART. IV) requires states to give "Full Faith and Credit" to the laws of other states. (We examine further how corporations have taken advantage of federalism in Chapter 15.)

Corporate capitalism has developed today into a very impersonal system, in which capital, stock, and currency traders seek the maximum possible return through the constant movement of all these on a global scale. In this system, most people work for wages, and the investor community tends to seek the cheapest and most productive labor available anywhere in the world. As a result, corporations often dwarf the power of governments, democratic or not (see Figure 3.1). The general store of 1787 and the General Electric of today may both be "capitalist," but huge corporations like GE create hierarchies and concentrations of power on a scale utterly alien to the merchant and farmer economy.[20] Corporate capitalism borrows from the rhetoric of individual freedom and enterprise that characterized early American capitalism, but beneath its rhetorical cover lies concentrated power that would have astounded the founding generation.

Corporate Organization: Special Privileges

The modern multinational corporation is often viewed as simply a series of individual contracts that are the natural outgrowth of the marketplace. In fact, the

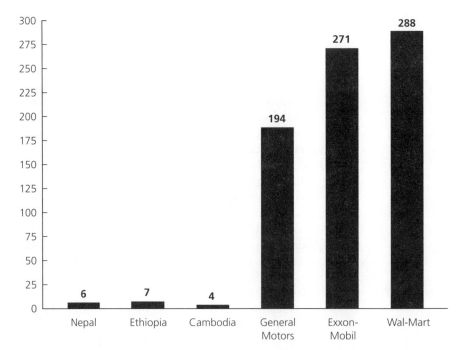

FIGURE 3.1

Worldwide Sales of the Three Largest U.S. Companies (2004) Compared to the Gross National Income of Developing Countries (2002) (in billions of $ U.S.)

Source: Fortune magazine ranking of the top 500 publicly traded U.S. companies; U.S. Bureau of the Census, *Statistical Abstract of the United States 2004–2005* (Washington, D.C.: U.S. Government Printing Office, 2004), p. 852.

modern corporation is a powerful institution that has been given huge grants of power by state governments (see Chapter 15), the federal government (see Chapter 17), and Supreme Court decisions (see Chapter 14). As developed in American law, the modern corporation has three legal characteristics that set it apart from the mom-and-pop grocery store

1. *Joint stock ownership.* Corporations pool the resources of a number of investors, called stockholders. The stock can be freely bought and sold. The owners of any company can, in short, change on a daily basis.

2. *Limited liability.* Corporations can attract investment more freely because no single owner is financially responsible for more than his or her own investment.

3. *Continuous legal identity.* Corporations do not dissolve with the death of any owner. Like the Energizer bunny, they just keep going, no matter what.

The law has established that corporations are like artificial persons. But these persons are giants who can traverse the globe in a few steps. And unlike real persons, these artificial persons have the best of both worlds: They have all the *rights* of real individuals but few of the *responsibilities*. In a seminal Supreme Court decision, *Santa Clara County v. Southern Pacific Railroad* (1886), the court declared that private corporations are "persons" for constitutional purposes. Thus, corporations have the right under the Fourteenth Amendment to "equal protection." Since then courts have given corporations eleven separate rights that we normally think of as reserved for persons under the U.S. Constitution.[21]

Unlike real people, however, corporations never die unless they want to, and no individual person is responsible for corporate actions. In contrast to individual citizens, corporations are not born with rights; they are licensed and, in effect, created by governments. There is an even greater difference: Corporations are composed of individuals in a hierarchy. With certain restrictions, the people who work for this abstract machine can be hired and fired at will and, within the limits of law, can be made to pursue the corporation's real interest: profits for stockholders. Even though corporations possess a wide array of rights, ironically, when individuals go to work for a corporation, they check their constitutional rights at the door. Your employer has the right to search your person, require you take a drug test, and stop you from speaking or handing out literature. As Barbara Ehrenreich, the woman discussed earlier who tried to make ends meet in a low-wage job, states:

> When you enter the low-wage workplace—in many of the medium-wage workplaces as well—you check your civil liberties at the door. . . . We can hardly pride ourselves on being the world's preeminent democracy, after all, if large numbers of citizens spend half their waking hours in what amounts, in plain terms, to a dictatorship.[22]

With a rigid hierarchy of CEOs, managers, vice presidents, and an entire chain of command down to the worst-paid laborer, corporations are hardly democratic institutions. Yet they exist as the central institutions of our economy. According to political scientist Charles Lindblom, "The corporation fits oddly into democratic theory and vision. Indeed, it does not fit."[23]

The Myth of Shareholder Democracy

According to economic theory, corporations are held accountable to their owners, the shareholders. In theory, the shareholders elect the board of directors, who in turn hire management. Because so many people own stock today, the system is said to be legitimated by **shareholder democracy**—or "people's capitalism." There are two fundamental problems with shareholder democracy: First, the ownership of stock is much less widespread than generally believed, and second, even those who do own stock have very little control over corporations, which are run by a self-selected oligarchy of top executives.

In 1999, for the first time in our history, about half of all U.S. households owned some stock, but this also means, of course, that almost as many people owned no stock at all. Among those who do own stock the distribution is heavily skewed toward those at the top. The richest 1 percent of households held on average $3.6 million in stocks; the bottom 40 percent average only $1,800 in stocks. The top 10 percent own over 75 percent of all stock market holdings.[24] The idea that a diverse nation of shareholders holds corporate power in check is

M. Wuerker.

highly questionable because the richest 5 percent of Americans own about half of all stock. Moreover, owning small amounts of stock hardly gives individual investors much power: Banks, insurance companies, and mutual fund and pension managers generally decide when stocks are to be bought and sold. Workers who own stock through their pension funds hardly have much control over corporate behavior.[25]

Even if you individually own some stock, however, your ability to influence corporate policy is almost nil. The annual shareholders' meeting is supposed to be an exercise in democracy, albeit with each share, not each person, representing one vote. In theory the shareholders choose the managers of the corporation and set broad policy, but in reality management tightly controls shareholder meetings. Usually management is able to get enough proxy votes to control the meeting. The election of the board of directors resembles elections under Soviet communism, with voters having only one slate to choose from, handpicked by management.

As noted earlier, state incorporation statutes completely gutted shareholder democracy. In 1934, however, Congress passed the Securities and Exchange Act that set up a commission to oversee all corporations that publicly trade stock on Wall Street. In 1942 the Securities and Exchange Commission (SEC) established the shareholder proposal rule that enables shareholders to submit resolutions to the SEC. Management must allow any proposal approved by the SEC to be introduced at the next shareholder meeting. Management can strictly limit debate, however, and very few resolutions are ever passed. For years several orders of Catholic nuns and groups of Protestant churches have introduced resolutions at shareholder meetings of military contractors, asking them to limit sales to countries with aggressive histories or where they would fall into the hands of child soldiers. Their resolutions have lost every time. "Sometimes," said Sister Mary Ann of the Sisters of Loretto in St. Louis, "it feels like I'm the only one concerned."[26] Nevertheless, these shareholder resolutions do create publicity for their cause, and in recent years management has agreed to sit down with them and talk about their concerns.

From the viewpoint of popular democracy, boards of directors of private corporations should not just represent shareholders but all the stakeholders that are affected by corporate policies, including workers, consumers, and the communities in which the corporation is located.[27] But as we have seen, even the much more modest idea of shareholder democracy is a myth. Corporations are controlled by executive oligarchies that rule in a top-down fashion. Most shareholders go along with this on the grounds that management elites know best how to maximize the profits of the corporation. In general, management does aim at maximizing profits, but often management acts to line its own pockets at great risk to the shareholders, as we saw in the case of Enron. Increasingly, soaring executive pay, which we examine later, has become an issue exposing conflicts between shareholders and top management.

Do Markets Check Corporate Power?

Even though private corporations are highly undemocratic institutions, run in top-down manner by an elite of managers, defenders of corporate capitalism argue that they are ultimately accountable to ordinary consumers through the marketplace. Citizens may have little direct control over corporations, but they have indirect control through the dollars they spend. In effect, consumers have delegated the production process to corporate elites, but the end goals of that process, the specific commodities produced, are determined by the consumers when they vote with their dollars. To respond to everchanging consumer preferences, companies must be free from governmental interference. Any corporation that engaged in lengthy democratic consultations with shareholders, workers, consumers, and governments would soon be left in the dust in the competitive race.

Popular democrats agree that companies must compete and respond to consumers. Yet just how they respond reveals how much discretion and unaccountable power they really have. Markets are justified by their "informality" and by the freedom of both producers and consumers, and are often contrasted to the "deadening bureaucratic hand" of government. But there is a great deal of bureaucracy inside corporations, which allocate huge amounts of resources inside the corporation according to a centralized plan, not the market. Ironically, modern corporations do precisely what free market economists don't like about government: They engage in **economic planning** by trying to dominate markets and control their environment.[28] Corporate managers must decide long in advance what to do with their investments—where to build factories, what workers to hire, and how much to pay the CEO. None of these decisions is dictated by the market.[29]

It seems as though consumer demand determines what items are produced, but this isn't strictly true. The advertising and marketing industries discovered long ago that consumer demand does not grow by itself but must be created and manipulated. Most advertising is designed not to inform you about the product but to create demand for the product or establish brand identities. Spending on advertising in 2004 was projected to reach an astounding $266.4 billion (up from $33.3 billion in 1976). The average American is exposed to a mind-numbing 100 commercial messages each waking hour.[30] By celebrating the upper-class lifestyle, ads encourage us to consume beyond our needs. One study found that each additional hour of television watched per week caused consumption to go up by $208 per year (or savings to go down by that amount).[31]

The Challenge of Globalization

In the 1950s and 1960s it seemed as though American capitalism had reached a peak of stability and growth. During this period a few hundred large and seemingly stable American corporations dominated trade, production, and banking. The "Big Three" automakers (Ford, General Motors, and Chrysler) dominated auto sales, and General Electric and Westinghouse controlled the electrical equipment and machine tool industry. These corporations had achieved **oligopoly** power, where a handful of firms could dominate a market and control production. This had advantages for unions because when they were successful at organizing an industry, the corporation could pass the wage concessions on to the consumers in the form of higher prices, without fear that competitors would move in to undercut them.[32]

The easy life of corporate oligopoly did not last long. Beginning in earnest in the 1960s Japanese and West European companies in high-technology manufacturing and East Asian companies in textiles, shoes, toys, foodstuffs, and home appliances invaded the American market with a vengeance. They undercut American-produced commodities in price and often in quality as well. Japanese cars achieved reliability records that far exceeded American-built cars. The very existence of American corporations was suddenly threatened by the new global competition, and American corporations responded in three basic ways.

Going Global. "If you can't beat 'em, join 'em" was the chief response of American corporations to their competitors. In search of larger profits and cheaper labor, companies with old-fashioned brand names like General Electric, General Motors, Ford, and RCA built new plants abroad, invested heavily in foreign corporations, replaced manufacturing at home with goods built abroad, or sold their own brand names to foreign companies. Much the same thing has been happening to "foreign" companies as well, as they dispersed their factories, started joint ventures, and shared technology. Taken together, these changes mean that most companies are transnational. They have shed their national characteristics because their capital, their production, and their marketing have what Richard Barnet has called a "global reach."[33] By the mid-1990s, these global companies had become so large that 40 percent of U.S. exports and half of our imports were actually goods that big global companies bought from and sold to one another.[34]

The globalization of corporations represents new challenges for democratic accountability. As the example of Wal-Mart shows, globalization has brought advantages to consumers in the form of lower prices as production has moved to low-wage countries. But for U.S. manufacturing workers—the backbone of the middle class in the 1940s, 1950s, and 1960s—the formation of the global corporation has generally been bad news. In the 1980s the United States lost over 1.3 million manufacturing jobs, devastating such towns as Youngstown, Ohio, and Schenectady, New York. Job growth has instead shifted to service workers, that broad swath of workers from hamburger flippers to paralegal assistants who make far less than manufacturing workers on average.[35]

The U.S. government has promoted globalization by signing on to international trade agreements that lower tariffs and other barriers to world trade. The most prominent of these is the World Trade Organization (WTO) with 130 members worldwide and the North American Free Trade Agreement (NAFTA), a trade agreement involving the United States, Mexico, and Canada. Free trade has many benefits for consumers and potentially even for workers, but truly free trade requires more than just cutting tariffs (taxes on imported goods). For example, does free trade exist if one country sells more cheaply by allowing child labor and arresting workers who even talk about joining a union? Critics also charge that international trade agreements give new rights to corporations that undermine the sovereignty of nations to protect workers and the environment. Under NAFTA, a U.S. waste disposal company, Metalclad, sued the Mexican government for stopping the construction of a waste dump because it would have polluted the local water supply. Arguing that this regulation interfered with its ability to compete in the global marketplace, a NAFTA tribunal awarded Metalclad $16.7 million from the Mexican government.

The fact is, international trade organizations are undemocratic bodies. They operate behind closed doors with little transparency, using economic jargon to create an aura of technical rationality to suppress democratic debate. In Chapter 10 we discuss the international mass movement that has emerged in opposition to globalization. Contrary to the way they are often portrayed by the mass media, global activists are not against free trade but are against the power of multinational corporations to undermine workers' rights and the environment.

Leaner and Meaner. A second corporate strategy has been to make companies leaner and meaner. An idea of what this means comes from the following: While the sales of the 500 biggest world companies have increased tenfold in the last twenty years, the number of employees of these firms has stayed about the same.[36] Part of this is due to higher productivity, as people who work with more skill and more sophisticated machines make more goods in less time. But it is partly a result of massive **downsizing**, as companies lay off workers to streamline and cheapen their operations. Between 1979 and 1999, over 50 million Americans lost their jobs as companies like ATT and IBM restructured their operations.[37]

What happened to the downsized workers? Most have found new jobs, but ones that pay less and have fewer benefits. That's often because the big companies have **outsourced** their operations by contracting out to smaller companies tasks they used to do "in house." Outsourcing has shaped a whole new subeconomy made up of part-time and temporary workers who lack the job stability and benefits of the more privileged sectors of the new economy. Silicon Valley's Sun Microsystems is a good example: Sun pays high wages to its skilled employees but outsources its cafeteria, janitorial services, and a host of "back office" functions to other companies that pay low wages. It is no accident, therefore, that Manpower, Inc., a company employing "temps," is now the largest private employer in the United States. In David Korten's words, "The giants are shedding people but not control over money, markets, or technology."[38]

The Casino Economy. Economist Susan Strange has coined the term **casino economy** to characterize the third corporate response to global competition.[39] Companies insecure about the new marketplace are often acquired by others, merged, dismantled, and then rearranged in order to gain increasing predictability and control over a volatile market. During the twelve Reagan/Bush years (1981–1993), the Justice Department approved 80,000 mergers. In the first six years of the Clinton presidency, it approved 160,000 mergers. The total amount of money spent on mergers and acquisitions reached a peak of $3.44 billion in 2000.[40] After a lull in the first years of the new century, mergers picked up again in 2005 when Procter & Gamble announced that it would purchase Gillette for $55 billion in stock, making it the largest consumer products business in the world, and SBC announced it was buying up AT&T for $16 billion.[41] Not since the period 1885–1910, when industrial titans such as J. P. Morgan and John D. Rockefeller created industrial behemoths like U.S. Steel and Standard Oil, has corporate America been reshaped by merger activity as broad and as deep as that taking place in recent decades.

While the global corporate casino is highly competitive, it is also becoming highly oligopolistic in many sectors, acquiring power over markets and governments. In short, the world's casino economy is becoming more like Monte Carlo and less like Las Vegas. The casino economy also features an astonishing explosion in the global finance industry: the banks and other institutions that trade and speculate in national currencies, stocks, bonds, and other forms of "bets" like "futures" and derivatives. The volume of trades is staggering: Over $1.2 trillion a day changes hands in the world's currency markets, and a mind-boggling $2 trillion is exchanged daily on the financial markets.

The casino economy is often justified as the inevitable partner of a global economy held together by rapid technological innovation. Yet, like the other two features of the new globalized corporate economy, it can be seen in a different light as well. Global financial markets generally evade the control of any single government or group of governments; if the world's financial elites don't like the policies being pursued by a democratic government, they can simply withdraw their investments and cash. In a democracy, government is accountable to an electorate made up of the adult citizenry, but in the new global economy, financial institutions are accountable only to a much narrower group: investors.

Labor Unions: Can They Control Corporate Power?

Many Americans assume that labor unions today serve as an effective counterweight to the power of large corporations. But this image of unions is badly outdated. During the New Deal, the **Wagner Act** of 1935 guaranteed workers the rights to organize unions and bargain collectively. Union membership soared, reaching a peak of 31.8 percent of the nonagricultural workforce in 1955. Union contracts negotiated with management often gave workers certain rights within the corporation—for example, to take work breaks and to refuse overtime work. Yet even at their peak, unions provided only a limited countervailing force to the power of corporate managers. As bread-and-butter organizations, concerned mostly with obtaining higher wages and better fringe benefits for their members, unions have largely conceded control over investment decisions and production methods to corporations.[42]

More important, as Figure 3.2 shows, union presence in the U.S. workforce has been declining since the 1950s. Today, only 13 percent of American workers belong to a union, one of the lowest rates among all the capitalist democracies. With a declining proportion of the workforce in unions, the bargaining strength of unions has deteriorated rapidly. Hanging over their heads has been the threat of corporate flight, automation, downsizing, and outsourcing. All these factors discourage workers from complaining, even though they have valid grievances.

Since the 1980s there has been growing support for unions among workers. By 2002, 50 percent of nonunion workers said they preferred to be represented by a union.[43] If most workers want to join a union, then, what prevents them? A major obstacle is the way the protections of labor law have eroded in the hands of administrators appointed by probusiness Republican presidents. Since the election of Ronald Reagan in 1980, people who want to unionize have been deprived of many of the legal protections their forebears once had.[44] It is illegal for companies to fire workers simply for supporting a union, but they do it anyway, knowing that at worst the courts will force them to pay back wages many years later. By then, the union drive will probably have been defeated.[45] Unions invested $44 million in the 2004 presidential election in a failed effort to defeat President Bush, but, as Figure 3.3 shows, unions don't come close to matching the contributions of corporations.

Part of the weakness of labor unions must be attributed to the unions themselves. Too often they have been undemocratic, bureaucratic, and parochial. In 1995 an insurgency in the American Federation of Labor/Congress of Industrial

Membership in Labor Unions, 1900–2004

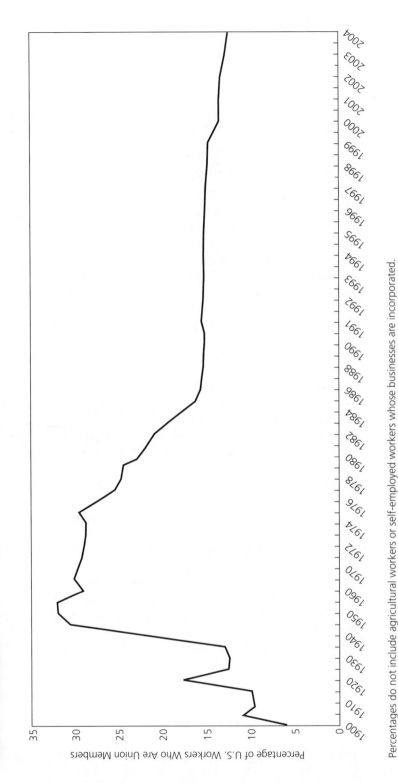

Percentages do not include agricultural workers or self-employed workers whose businesses are incorporated.

Sources: Harold W. Stanley and Richard G. Niemi, *Vital Statistics on American Politics, 1999–2000* (Washington, D.C.: Congressional Quarterly Press, 2000), p. 401; Bureau of Labor Statistics, Union Members Summary, Press Release, January 18, 2001; U.S. Bureau of the Census, *Statistical Abstract of the United States 2004–2005* (Washington, D.C.: U.S. Government Printing Office), p. 419; Bureau of Labor Statistics, Union Members in 2004, Press Release, January 27, 2005.

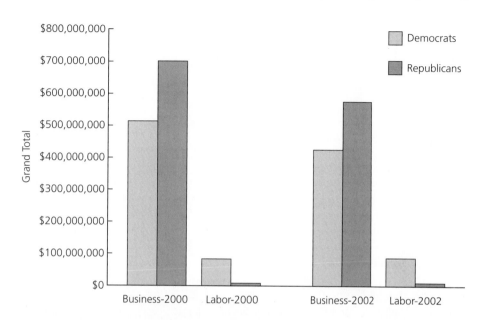

FIGURE 3.3

Campaign Contributions by Unions and Corporations in 2000 and 2002 Election Cycles

Source: The Center for Responsive Politics. Reprinted by permission.

Organizations (AFL-CIO) toppled the organization's conservative and bureaucratic leadership and installed a new president, John Sweeney, who poured millions of additional dollars into defeating antilabor legislators and organizing the unorganized (with only moderate success). In 2005 four unions, representing about 4.5 million of the AFL-CIO's 13 million members, pulled out of the AFL-CIO and formed their own labor coalition in order to put even more resources into organizing the unorganized. The split could weaken the labor movement, but it could also spur greater efforts to bridge gender and racial gaps by concentrating on organizing women, African Americans, Hispanics, and Asian Americans. In 1997 United Parcel Service (UPS) workers conducted the first victorious national work stoppage in twenty years, ensuring that the shipping giant would hire more full-time workers and contribute to a union-directed pension fund. As Robert Reich, former secretary of labor, observed, "Organized labor is an aging, doddering prizefighter still relishing trophies earned decades ago. But it's the only fighter in that corner of the ring. There's no other countervailing political force against the overriding power of business and finance."[46]

THE PROBLEM OF RISING INEQUALITY

A political economy composed of hierarchical corporations and a largely pro-business government limits the ability of citizens to control the forces that shape

MAKING A DIFFERENCE

Unions and the New Economy

Graciela Diaz never dreamed where she would end up when she illegally crossed the border from Mexico into the United States in 1991. Eventually, she won U.S. citizenship, but life was very tough at first. She began by working in a sweatshop in Los Angeles, earning about $30 a day. Three years later she met her future husband, Manuel, who persuaded her to move to Las Vegas where he had heard life was better. She began by taking back-breaking housekeeping jobs at various hotels, but her luck changed when she landed a unionized job at the La Salsa restaurant. After passing the course at the union's Culinary Training Academy, she was promoted to waitress, with wages and tips totaling about $20 an hour and generous health insurance. Meanwhile, Manuel landed a unionized construction job that paid $23.66 an hour, with substantial overtime. Now they own their own home and have big ambitions for their daughter, Cecilia: college and maybe law or architecture school.

The story of the Diazes is the story of the American Dream, but for many people, the American Dream is receding as dead-end, low-wage jobs lock them in poverty. For those with popular democratic institutions on their side, like progressive unions, however, the American Dream is very much alive.

Progressive unions, like those to which the Diazes belong, have had to change in order to survive. Consider the following: Las Vegas, with 1 million residents, is America's fastest-growing big city. Some call it the "Pittsburgh of the Twenty-first Century" because of the large numbers of workers in new factories there. But instead of making steel, today's workers make the beds, clean the toilets, shuffle the cards, and dig the ditches that make for a new service economy. In Las Vegas, service jobs mean gaming jobs.

All over America, but especially in Las Vegas, the new face of this service workforce is increasingly female, often Hispanic, African American, Asian American, and young. But until recently, organized labor has primarily been composed of male workers in declining manufacturing industries, such as autos and steel. That's one reason why union membership has been declining and, with it, the wages, working conditions, and job security of millions of new service workers.

For a long time, the leadership of American unions didn't pay much attention to organizing new workers. But back in 1994, the Culinary Workers Union, Local 226, began to fight for recognition at the MGM Grand Hotel—with 2,000 rooms, Las

their lives. Yet many reason that the loss of control is worth it if economic prosperity is secured for large numbers of Americans. Indeed, the United States now has one of the most productive and prosperous economies in the world. Americans consume more than ever before. The problem, however, is that the United States also has the greatest inequality—the gap between the rich and poor—of any developed nation. Besides signaling that the economic system is not working for many people, severe inequalities threaten the health of our democracy.

Vegas's biggest. MGM, like many companies, had wanted to outsource many of its restaurant jobs to subcontractors who paid their workers low wages and provided no medical insurance. After three years of struggle with MGM, the 4,000 workers won management recognition of their union and also a contract that paid a living wage and provided important benefits.

Can the Las Vegas model of multiracial, aggressive union organizing be successful elsewhere? The Justice for Janitors campaign in Los Angeles was a huge success, and in 1997 United Parcel Service workers won a historic new contract that turned many part-time workers into full-time employees. But there have also been many failures. Long strikes at Caterpillar, Inc., and against Detroit newspapers were eventually lost because companies could so easily hire replacement workers. Autoworkers, machinists, and flight attendants have often lost ground when companies have insisted that they will outsource or move abroad if unions demand too much.

Clearly, unions have begun to reform themselves internally, shaking up rigid bureaucracies to make them more responsive to the members. The leadership has been revamped to include more women and people of color—those with the lowest wages in the U.S. workforce. The AFL-CIO has urged all the member unions to spend up to 15 percent of their dues on new organizing activities. Unless unions make organizing a top priority, they will not be able to maintain their present members, let alone grow. Above all, they must shift away from business unionism, which focuses only on better wages for the members, to embrace social movement unionism where unions form alliances with environmentalist, civil rights, and consumer groups. One new labor strategy has been to reach out to students through "Union Summer," where college students work with union organizers on boycotts, strikes, and political campaigns.

Unions can be successful. Culinary Local 226, the one that Graciela Diaz joined, grew from 18,000 members in the late 1980s to over 48,000 today. And since becoming one of the most unionized cities in the nation, Las Vegas has prospered, contradicting corporate claims that unions choke off economic growth. Speaking of his unionized workers, the chairman of the MGM Mirage, which owns the largest hotel in the world in Las Vegas, said that happy workers make for happy customers. "Is it perfect? No. But it's as good as I've seen anywhere."

Sources: Steven Greenhouse, "Local 226, 'the Culinary,' Makes Las Vegas the Land of the Living Wage," *New York Times*, June 3, 2004; Steven Greenhouse, "American Dreamers: The Lure of Las Vegas," *New York Times*, June 3, 2004; Margaret Levi, "Organizing Power: The Prospects for an American Labor Movement," *Perspectives on Politics*, Vol. 1, No. 1, March 2003, pp. 45–68.

Historically, American society has been held together by an implicit social contract: "If you work hard, you will get ahead." Economic prosperity, Americans believe, benefits everybody. In President Kennedy's memorable words: "A rising tide lifts all boats." As Figure 3.4 shows, between 1947 and 1973, this was true: Those in the bottom 20 percent of the income range saw their incomes rise faster than those above them.

After 1973, however, the trend toward greater income equality reversed itself (Figure 3.4, bottom). Between 1973 and 2000, those in the bottom 20 percent

FIGURE 3.4

Family Income Growth by Quintile, 1947–2000

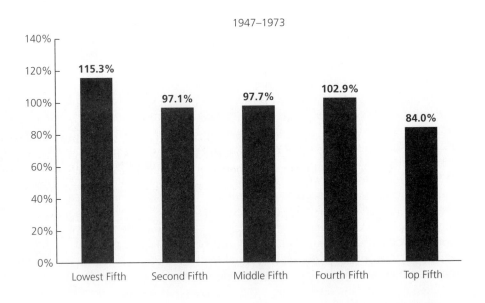

1947–1973

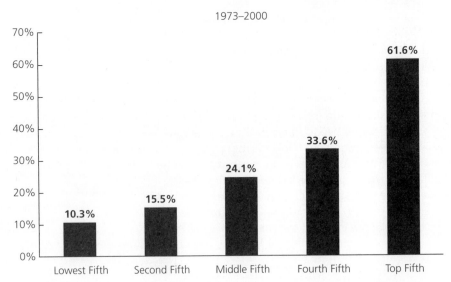

1973–2000

Source: Reprinted from Lawrence Mishel, Jared Bernstein, and Sylvia Allegretto, *The State of Working America, 2004/2005*. Copyright © 2005 by Cornell University. Used by permission of the publisher, Cornell University Press.

(families making less than $25,636 in 2000) enjoyed a modest 10.3 percent growth in income (all figures are controlled for inflation), whereas those in the top 20 percent (families making over $97,460) enjoyed a whopping 61.6 percent increase. (The top 1 percent enjoyed a stunning 184 percent real income gain between 1979 and 2000.) The share of total family income of the bottom 80 percent of families actually fell during this period; only the top 20 percent, what Robert Reich calls the "**fortunate fifth**," enjoyed an increase.[47] Those at the very top did especially well. Between 1979 and 2000, the top 1 percent of families saw their share of total income increase from 9.3 to 17.8 percent; at the same time, the bottom 20 percent saw their share of total income fall from 5.8 to 4.0 percent. As the gap between the rich and the poor widened, the middle class shrank. Between 1969 and 2002, the proportion of families making between $25,000 and $75,000 (in 2002 dollars) fell from 63.4 percent to 47.8 percent. As Table 3.1 shows, the United States has the greatest income inequality (measured by the ratio between the incomes of families at the ninetieth percentile with those at the tenth percentile) among all advanced industrial countries.

If income inequality has reached levels not seen since the Gilded Age of the nineteenth century, the figures for wealth are even more skewed. (*Wealth* is defined as people's assets in homes, stocks, bank accounts, or other possessions, minus what they owe to creditors). **Wealth inequality** has always been pronounced in America. In the 1950s and 1960s, wealth inequality remained fairly steady; a rising economic tide lifted most boats. Since the 1980s, however,

TABLE 3.1 Earnings Inequality	Country (Year)	Ratio of 90th to 10th Percentile
	United States (2000)	5.5
	United Kingdom (1999)	4.6
	Italy (2000)	4.5
	Australia (1997)	4.3
	Ireland (1996)	4.3
	Japan (1992)	4.2
	Canada (1998)	4.1
	Spain (1990)	4.0
	Switzerland (1992)	3.6
	France (1994)	3.5
	Austria (1997)	3.4
	Belgium (1997)	3.2
	Germany (2000)	3.2
	Netherlands (1999)	3.0
	Sweden (2000)	3.0
	Denmark (1992)	2.9
	Finland (2000)	2.9
	Norway (2000)	2.8

Source: Timothy Smeeding, *Public Policy and Economic Inequality: The United States in Comparative Perspective*, unpublished draft (2004); as reported in Lawrence Mishel, Jared Bernstein, and Sylvia Allegretto, *The State of Working America 2004/2005*. Copyright © 2005 by Cornell University. Used by permission of the publisher, Cornell University Press.

economic tides have only lifted the yachts, while swamping the small craft. The top 1 percent earned 14.8 percent of total income in 2001, but they owned 33.4 percent of all wealth (the value of assets minus debts), averaging over $12.7 million. By contrast, the bottom 80 percent of all households held only 15.6 percent of wealth. Between 1989 and 2001 the top 1 percent of households grew in wealth by an average of $2.8 million, whereas the assets of the middle 20 percent of households grew only marginally (from $63,900 to $75,000). (For most middle-class families their main source of wealth is their home.) Meanwhile, the poorest one-fifth improved slightly but still finished 2001 on average $8,200 in debt.

Are Inequalities Fair?

Defenders of corporate capitalism do not deny that inequalities are widening, but they argue that this is nothing to worry about. Inequalities are justified if they represent different levels of ability, skill, work, and risk. Ultimately, you are rewarded based on how much you contribute to production. Those who risk their fortunes in order to invest in a new product or a new business should be rewarded handsomely because they are the ones who bring progress and new wealth to society. As we discussed earlier, the high salaries of brain surgeons may be necessary in order to attract qualified people to perform this highly demanding and skilled function. If government programs redistributed wealth and income from the rich to the poor, this would undermine the incentives that make our economy so dynamic and productive.

The evidence shows that rising inequality cannot be explained by people's contribution to production. The reason why American workers are lagging farther behind the rich is not because they are lazy. In fact, Americans work more hours than workers in just about every other industrialized nation—and thus have much shorter vacations. Since enactment of welfare reform in 1996, welfare rolls have fallen by more than half. It also is not the case that American workers are not productive. In fact, the data show that they are among the most productive workers in the world. The problem is that their incomes have not kept pace with their growth in productivity. Before 1973 the incomes of American workers kept pace with the growth in productivity, but since then incomes have grown at about one-third the rate of economic productivity. The problem is essentially a political one: How does a society distribute its rewards? Increasingly, in the United States, the answer has more to do with your wealth and power, not with your willingness to work. As Felix Rohatyn, a Wall Street investment banker, put it, "What is occurring is a huge transfer of wealth from lower-skilled middle-class American workers to the owners of capital assets."[48]

Another problem with the productivity explanation of rising inequality is that the people whose incomes have surged the most are not research scientists, brain surgeons, innovative inventors, or others who have played major roles in the innovation that drives the American economy. Much of the wealth has gone to **paper entrepreneurs**, people who reap huge salaries from Wall Street investments, mergers, acquisitions, and other such deals. One example of the

Clay Bennet / © 2003 The Christian Science Monitor (www.csmonitor.com).

"rewards" of "jobs well done" can be seen in the compensation received by **chief executive officers** (CEOs) of U.S. corporations.

In 1996, General Electric agreed to a deal with its CEO, Jack Welch, that gave him lifetime access to the "perquisites and benefits" of his office. These benefits included, among other things, access to GE aircraft for personal as well as business use, a New York City apartment that rented for $50,000 a month, unrestricted access to a chauffeured limousine, a Mercedes Benz, free services of professional estate and tax advisors, a personal assistant, a bodyguard, and installation and maintenance of security systems in three of his homes. All of this was in addition to his salary, which totaled $123 million in 2000, his last full year at GE. The SEC ruled in 2004 that GE had violated the securities laws by failing to fully disclose to the stockholders the costs of this arrangement.

Jack Welch may be one of the worst cases of secret sweetheart deals for CEOs, but at least Welch was a successful CEO. CEO pay has soared no matter how well the corporation does. According to *Fortune* magazine, between 1970 and 1999 the average annual pay of the top 100 CEOs increased from 39 times the pay of an average worker to 1,000 times the pay of ordinary workers.[49] During the 1990s CEO pay rose by 571 percent, far outpacing average worker pay, which increased by only 37 percent. If the minimum wage had increased at the same rate, it would have reached $25.50 an hour by the end of the decade. Instead, it remained stuck at $5.15 an hour.[50] CEO pay has little relationship to performance. According to the *Financial Times*, the top executives and directors at the twenty-five largest companies that went bankrupt between January 2001 and July 2002 made off with $3.3 billion in compensation. At the same time, their companies were going bankrupt, 100,000 workers lost their jobs, and investors lost hundreds of millions of dollars.[51] In only one country in the world (Switzerland) are CEOs paid even half of what American CEOs make.[52]

If there is not a direct relationship between CEO salaries and profits, there is even less between unequal pay and long-term corporate health. A 1992 study of corporations with the highest levels of pay inequality found that they produced products of lower quality and that their workers were more demoralized and less productive than less unequal firms. As workers become less secure in salaries and jobs, they become less trusting of their bosses and less committed to their companies. Workers spend much of their mental energy looking for other jobs or finding innovative ways to give the appearance that they are devoted, while denying the company their full efforts.

How can U.S. companies get away with paying huge salaries to executives who do not even perform well? The answer is corporate governance. CEO compensation is determined by the corporate board of directors, which is largely under the control of management. Earning on average $20,000 per meeting, directors seem happy to rubber-stamp management's requests. In many ways, the leaders of large corporations set their own salaries—a situation fraught with conflicts of interest if not outright corruption.

The Political Effects of Economic Inequalities

Despite the great successes of American capitalism, the U.S. poverty rate is the highest among the developed countries of Western Europe, East Asia, and Canada. In 2003 the poverty rate was 12.5 percent, with almost one out of five children living below the poverty line. (The poverty threshold for a single individual was $9,393 that year.) However, government studies of poverty greatly underestimate the number of people who are poor.[53] One study found that the actual cost of a "bare bones" budget in New York City was five times the poverty level.[54] If a more realistic standard for poverty was used, 25 percent or more of the population would be classified as poor.

Defenders of corporate capitalism argue that we should not be concerned with inequality; the only thing we should be concerned with is whether those at the bottom are able to consume more than they did before.[55] From the viewpoint of sheer consumption, those at the bottom of American society are doing better than ever. Indeed, the consumption of the poor in American society would place them at the very top in many Third World countries. (The generally recognized poverty cutoff in Third World countries is one dollar a day.) But the fact is that poverty is not just a matter of inadequate consumption; it is about living a life with dignity and being able to participate fully in the society. In fact, it is much more difficult to be poor in an affluent society than in a society where most people are poor like you. In American society the rich bid up the cost of living, especially for housing and education.[56] American life is structured so that almost everyone needs to own a car to be a fully functioning member of society.

(A car costs a minimum of about $6,000 a year.) Moreover, inequality pulls down our quality of life. It is a major reason why the United States has significantly higher crime rates and lower average life expectancy than other advanced industrial countries.[57] An inegalitarian society produces feelings of resentment and inadequacy in the poor.

Philosophers from Aristotle to Thomas Jefferson have stressed that tremendous inequalities are dangerous to democracy. A healthy democracy needs a strong middle class that can function as a moderating force between the potentially divisive demands of the rich and the poor. Great inequalities undermine social solidarity—the idea that we are all basically in the same boat. Rising inequality makes blatant class legislation—laws that benefit one group at the expense of another—more likely. A huge gap between the rich and the poor makes it possible for the rich to dominate, even buy off, the poor. If the gap between the rich and the poor continues to widen, it is unlikely that even a carefully crafted campaign finance reform law will protect elections from the corrupting influence of concentrated wealth. One study found that rich constituents have almost three times as much influence over the voting patterns of their U.S. senators than poor constituents.[58] As a recent Task Force of the American Political Science Association said, "Citizens with lower or moderate incomes speak with a whisper that is lost on the ears of the inattentive government officials, while the advantaged roar with a clarity and consistency that policymakers readily hear and routinely follow."[59]

Democracies can tolerate economic inequalities. What democracies cannot tolerate is when wealth is used to acquire political power and then that political power is used to acquire more wealth, setting in motion a vicious circle that violates democratic principles of justice and fairness.[60] As we will see in Chapters 6–9, the wealthy can turn their money into political influence that often drowns out the voices of the less privileged. The bias of American public policies against the poor and in favor of the upper class is examined in Chapter 17.

Economic inequalities disadvantage the poor in the political system in many different ways. One way is by economic segregation.[61] In most American metropolitan areas, suburbs enact exclusionary zoning regulations to keep out the poor. Zoning laws forbid the construction of apartment buildings, for example, or require single-family homes to be built on large two- or three-acre lots. Poor people, especially minorities, are prevented from moving closer to where the jobs are, thus hurting their job prospects. In addition, the poor are relegated to central cities and inner-ring suburbs with weak tax bases and expensive service needs. As a result, participation in local government is less meaningful because the resources just aren't there. Rich suburban districts can spend up to twice as much per student as poor school districts. With education being so important to success in our high-tech economy, these educational inequalities have profound effects on economic inequalities.[62]

Economic inequalities bias the political system in other ways. The poor do not participate at the same rate that the middle class and the rich do. They lack the money to contribute to campaigns, and most lower-paid workers don't acquire the skills on the job that aid political participation, such as how to run a meeting or find information. The result is what a major study of civic participation called "participatory distortion."[63]

In short, the wider the income gap, the wider the gap in political representation. The result is a political system that violates the popular democratic principle of political equality.

The Prism of Race and Gender

Corporate capitalism may generate huge inequalities between income groups. Yet it has had a particularly big impact on women, African Americans, and Latinos (see Figure 3.5). Most people in these groups are not poor, but they bear, if for somewhat different reasons, a disproportionate share of poverty's burdens. Moreover, each group lags behind in wage levels, even when they work at jobs comparable to white males.

Since the late 1970s, women have made fairly large wage gains relative to men. In 2004 working women earned just over 80 percent of what men did—up from just 62 percent twenty-five years ago. Unfortunately, part of the reason for the reduction in the gap is that men have been more vulnerable to layoffs and have seen their earnings stagnate.[64] Black families saw their incomes improve significantly relative to whites in the 1990s, but when the labor market softened

FIGURE 3.5

Ratio of Black and Hispanic to White Median Family Income, 1947–2003

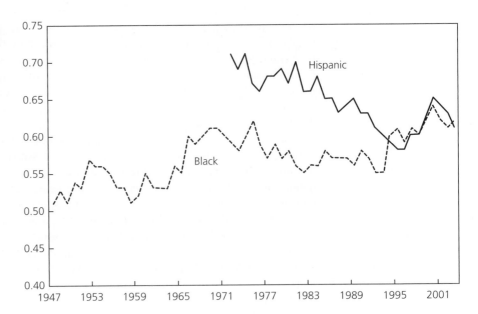

Source: "Ratio of Black and Hispanic to White Median Family Income, 1947–2003," from U.S. Bureau of the Census data. Reprinted from Lawrence Mishel, Jared Bernstein, and Sylvia Allegretto, *The State of Working America 2004–2005*. Copyright © 2005 by Cornell University. Reprinted with permission of the publisher, Cornell University Press.

in 2001, the gap widened again. In 2003, black and Hispanic family incomes were still less than 62 percent of white family income. Hispanics have actually fallen significantly relative to whites in the past thirty years.

What factors account for these economic inequalities? It isn't that blacks and Hispanics are not working hard. In fact, black and Hispanic middle-income families with children increased the number of hours they worked significantly between 1979 and 1998, and both work many more hours, on average, than do white families.[65] Defenders of corporate capitalism respond that these inequalities fairly reflect differences in education and skill. Besides, economic growth will take care of the problem in the long run.

Both explanations are flawed, however. Economic growth has not changed the ratio of white to black and Latino earning levels, and a large gap between men and women still remains. Moreover, all three groups have made great strides in educational and skill levels since the 1970s. If skills and education were rewarded equally in the marketplace, then the racial and income gap should be closing for African Americans and Latinos. Instead, it is widening for Latinos and not improving much for blacks.

African Americans have been especially disadvantaged in the marketplace, despite generally rising education and skill levels. For African Americans with college degrees or high school degrees in the 1980s and 1990s, earnings were 17 percent less than whites with similar education. Working-class blacks have been disproportionately harmed by a number of other factors. The decline in union membership, combined with the downsizing of many manufacturing industries, caused much pain. Jobs are moving to the suburbs, but discrimination in housing markets often leaves African Americans stuck in central cities, unable to reach the new jobs. And, finally, outright racism persists in the job market. An Urban Institute study sent testers of both races with equal qualifications and similar ages to apply for the same 476 jobs in the Washington, D.C., metro area. The study concluded that "discrimination against blacks appears to be highest in types of jobs offering the highest wages and future income potential."[66]

For women, the gap should have closed much more rapidly than it has. The market often pays women less when they have the same qualifications as men. Even in the highly skilled professions of law and computer programming, women receive about 20 percent less in their paychecks than men do. In other, less-high-status jobs, gender discrimination is equally acute. Secretaries, elementary school teachers, and registered nurses, occupations where women predominate, require comparable education and involve as much responsibility as carpenters, truck drivers, and high school teachers, occupations dominated by men. Yet there are big disparities again, up to 20 percent in how the two sets of jobs are compensated.[67]

Given the patterns of gender and racial inequality just detailed, it isn't surprising that the poorest group in American society is women of color, especially African-American and Latino women with children. Although women of color are in the workforce just as much as white women, their wages equaled only 86 percent of that of white women, a group whose wages already lag behind those of white men.

POLITICAL ECONOMY AND CIVIL SOCIETY

Democratic theorists have long recognized that a healthy democracy requires a strong civil society.[68] **Civil society** encompasses the voluntary associations that lie between the private realm of the family and the public sphere of politics. Alexis de Tocqueville, the French democratic theorist who visited the United States in the 1830s, argued that the great strength of American democracy lay precisely in the character of its voluntary associations. Voluntary associations, from food banks to labor unions, from Boys and Girls Clubs to arts associations, act like informal schools, enabling citizens to develop the civic skills that are necessary to participate effectively in a democracy. Civic associations can help to take the rough edges off of American individualism, with its tendency to worship individual wealth and competitiveness. Such associations help people realize that they are part of a community and that a meaningful life is found not in possessions but in building a shared life with others.

Since the days of Tocqueville, Americans have continued to be joiners. A 1990 national survey found that 79 percent of Americans were affiliated with at least one organization. Americans are still more likely to be members of voluntary associations than are citizens in other democratic countries.[69] On the other hand, evidence is mounting that civil society in the United States has deteriorated in the past thirty years. Robert Putnam titled his book on this issue *Bowling Alone* for good reason. Even though Americans are bowling more than ever, because of the rapid decline of bowling leagues, more people are doing it alone rather than as part of a group. Putnam surveys a wide range of data to document the decline of associations of all types, including the League of Women Voters, which is down 61 percent in its membership rate (actual members per eligible members) since its peak in 1965, and parent–teacher associations (PTAs), down 60 percent from their peak in 1966.[70]

The decline of civil society is a major cause of the decline in civic participation. Putnam documents that despite increases in education, since peaking in the 1960s, Americans have become 15 to 20 percent less likely to be interested in politics, 35 percent less likely to attend public meetings, and roughly 40 percent less engaged in party politics.[71] Even though voter turnout increased to 59 percent in the hotly contested 2004 presidential election, voter turnout is still much lower than its modern peak in the 1960 presidential election. (See Chapter 5.)

The deterioration in civil society is clearly related to changes in the economy. Putnam shows that there is a strong correlation between equality of income in states and an index of social capital. States that are more egalitarian have stronger civil societies, with citizens joining more associations and participating more in politics.[72] Ironically, the associational life of some people is harmed by having too little work, while for others the problem is too much work. The poor are increasingly concentrated with other poor people in so-called "underclass" neighborhoods that suffer from severe social problems, including high crime rates, drug abuse, and family breakdown. Lacking strong institutions and voluntary associations, underclass residents experience social isolation and deep feelings of powerlessness and despair. According to William Julius Wilson, the underclass has formed primarily because of the loss of industrial jobs that helped corporations regain their profits and "competitiveness."[73] Unable to support a family, some black males withdraw from the world of work, as well as civil society, and enter the underground economy. Single women, who are left to care for the children, are often too busy or fearful to participate in voluntary associations, though churches are still vibrant in many black ghettos.

Economic pressures to withdraw from associational life affect the working poor as well. In general, the poor are underrepresented in voluntary associations. Only 52 percent of the poor are involved in a nonpolitical organization, compared to 89 percent of the rich.[74] The economic pressure to work overtime and "moonlight," instead of being involved in voluntary associations, has increased.

The middle class has not emerged unscathed from the corrosive effects of the economy on civil society. During the 1950s and 1960s, middle-class households didn't generally suffer from the threats of downsizing, declining wages and salaries, or constant insecurities about how to balance work life with raising a family and participating in civic life. Many families could achieve homeowner status with only one wage earner, usually the male, in the workforce. Most of all, most families could expect to have stable job prospects and thus could make solid plans for their children's future. Yet the last twenty years has witnessed increased middle-class insecurity on all these counts. In 1996, nearly three-quarters of American households had a "close encounter" with a layoff. One in ten Americans said that a lost job had brought on "a major crisis in their lives." Workers with above-average educational levels felt the pinch, too, as layoffs for those with some college education began to outnumber layoffs for people with only high school diplomas.[75]

In the past, women who stayed home or worked part-time were a backbone of civic organizations, such as the League of Women Voters and the school PTA. Since the 1960s, many women have sought equality with men by entering the workforce and building their own professional careers. But for many women, working full-time was not a choice but an economic necessity. Survey research shows that three-quarters of women who work full-time do so to meet financial pressures, not to gain personal fulfillment. And it is precisely women who work full-time out of necessity (the largest, fastest-growing group) who are least inclined to be involved in the community.[76]

For many families, economic pressures create a "time crunch" in which taking time off from work to care for a young child or an aging parent just isn't economically possible. The corporate workplace is generally indifferent to the needs of both fathers and mothers, who find it hard to take time off to take a sick child to the doctor, much less participate in civic life. The phenomenon of "latchkey children" is less the product of immoral parents than it is of a political economy that pays less money for more work. Under these circumstances, it is not difficult to understand why many parents arrive home exhausted, "too busy" to participate in voluntary associations.[77] One of the best ways to improve the health of civil society would be to make it easier for women (and men) to work part-time if they wished. But this is not the direction that most corporations are moving in.

NEW IDEAS

Slowing (or Stopping) the Inequality Express

In the summer of 2001, Congress passed a $1.35 trillion tax cut over ten years. Smaller in size and less regressive than the one originally proposed by President Bush, the tax cut nevertheless benefits the rich much more than the middle class or the poor. Those at the bottom will receive a few hundred dollars in tax relief the first year while the 400 top earners in the country will average over $1 million.

Many people think there is very little the government can do to address rising inequalities because they are caused by the operations of the free market (globalization, immigration, the surge in the stock market, and so on). Some economists argue that if the government tries to reduce inequalities, it will undermine growth by reducing the rewards of working hard or taking risks to invest.

In fact, inequalities are not the result of the automatic workings of a free market economy. Policies shape the market, and we can enact policies that will reduce inequalities without undermining economic performance. Below are a few of the ways government could slow, or even stop, growing inequality.

1. *Make work pay.* Most people are not poor because they refuse to work but because the jobs they have do not pay enough. One way to address this is to raise the minimum wage. At $5.15 an hour in 2005, the minimum wage has not kept pace with inflation and is now worth 35 percent less than it was in 1968. Recognizing the inadequacy of the federal minimum wage, many states have enacted their own higher minimum wages, and 123 cities have passed "living wage" laws, with most applying only to firms with city contracts. Research shows that states that have raised the minimum wage have suffered no employment declines.

Anybody who works full-time should not have to live in poverty. This is the logic behind the Earned Income Tax Credit (EITC). Begun in 1975, the EITC provides a tax credit to low-wage workers, especially those with children, to move above the poverty line. In 1999 the EITC moved about 4.8 million people out of poverty. The EITC should be expanded and combined with a universal child credit that would be available to all taxpayers with children.

Indeed, the economic pressures on free time have negatively affected participation in civil society for all classes, even the fortunate fifth. A main culprit is the work demands of "lean and mean" corporations. In 1998 the average American middle-income family with children was working 560 more hours, or 14 full-time weeks of work, than in 1979.[78] Because their husbands still do relatively little of the housework, employed mothers average about 65 hours of work a week on the job and at home.[79] With this kind of harried schedule, it is not surprising that many women have withdrawn from participation in voluntary associations.

The growth of multinational corporations with few local loyalties has also hurt civil society. When a Wal-Mart takes over for local hardware and grocery stores, the new owners are much less likely to sponsor a Little League team or get involved in local community life or politics. Downsizing and outsourcing

2. *Empower labor.* One of the best ways to lessen inequality would be to give workers a better chance to form unions and bargain collectively for their wages. This would require Congress to reform the labor laws that presently allow companies to fire workers who support a union at little risk to the company.

3. *Promote asset ownership.* One of the most exciting recent ideas to attack inequality is to help those at the bottom acquire assets—to make everyone a capitalist. Most poor Americans have not benefited from rising stock prices or rising home prices because they have not been able to get into the game. One approach that has already been tried on a small scale is to set up Individual Development Accounts (IDAs) in which the government matches savings by low-income households. The money can be used for such things as education or starting a business. One of the more radical ideas is to create a stakeholder society: Young adults at age eighteen would receive an $80,000 "stake" that they could use similarly to an IDA.

4. *Tax wealth.* Unlike other developed countries, the United States does not tax wealth directly. A small tax on millionaires, as little as one-half of one percent, would affect only a small percentage of households but would generate billions of dollars for the federal treasury. (The recent repeal of the estate tax has exactly the opposite effect, enabling the wealthiest 2 percent of estates to avoid all taxes and creating an undemocratic class of superwealthy based on inherited wealth.)

5. *Reform campaign financing.* Probably the most important action that could be taken to slow rising income inequality would be serious campaign finance reform. Presently the rich are getting richer, and they are using their money to buy politicians. Does anyone doubt that campaign contributions had a great deal to do with the recent tax cuts for the rich and the repeal of the estate tax?

Rising economic inequality is not inevitable; something can be done about it. Popular democrats agree with the old saying that money is like manure: If you let it pile up in one place, it stinks to high heaven, but if you spread it around, it makes things grow.

Sources: Todd Schafer and Jeff Faux, eds., *Reclaiming Prosperity: A Blueprint for Progressive Economic Reform* (Armonk, N.Y.: M. E. Sharpe, 1996); Michael Sherraden, *Assets and the Poor: A New American Welfare Policy* (Armonk, N.Y.: M. E. Sharpe, 1991); Bruce A. Ackerman and Anne Alstott, *The Stakeholder Society* (New Haven, Conn.: Yale University Press, 1999); *The American Prospect*, Special Issue on Making Work Pay (June 19–July 3, 2000).

may have made some large corporations more efficient, but their effects on community life and participation can be devastating. Consider the case of Dayton, Ohio, a city that suffered from 50,000 layoffs in the 1980s. Civic leaders noticed a rapid decline in membership in churches, social service organizations, and even the Boy Scouts. According to a Dayton mother of three, the community is being pulled apart:

> Many of these kids I see are on their fifth or sixth move because the company keeps saying, "We're not making enough money; we need to downsize more. . . ." It really hurts the child's ability to develop those long-term commitments. It's devastating to the sense of community.[80]

The decline of civil society has been especially severe among the young. A survey has been conducted each year since 1966 of college freshmen documenting declining interest in politics and community involvement. Taken just before the hotly contested 2004 presidential election, the survey reported that 34.3 percent of freshman feel it is important or essential to "keep up to date with political affairs." This marks a substantial increase from the low point in 2000 at 28.1 percent, but it is still way behind the high point in 1966 when 60.3 percent said it was important to keep up with political affairs.[81] Clearly, a major cause of the declining interest in politics has been a rise of materialistic values, with the number of freshman reporting that "being very well off financially" was either "essential" or "very important" soaring since the 1960s.

The causes of rising materialism and declining political engagement are complex. One cause is clearly economic insecurity.[82] More generally, consumerism has permeated American life to the extent that it is driving out social and political commitments. Americans are now exposed to an average of 100 commercial messages every waking hour.[83] Have you seen any ads lately trying to persuade you to participate in local politics as a way to become more prestigious or sexually attractive? Americans now spend three to four times as much time shopping as do Western Europeans.[84] Following the tragedy of September 11, President Bush said that one of the best things citizens could do was to go shopping. As Cornel West put it: "The fundamentalism of the market puts a premium on the activities of buying and selling, consuming and taking, promoting and advertising, and devalues community, compassionate charity, and improvement of the general quality of life."[85]

Finally, it is not just that civic commitments and involvements have declined but that the organizations have changed as well. Tocqueville was enamored with voluntary associations because they had the potential to bridge the divides between citizens of different regions, ethnicities, and occupational backgrounds. But the modern political economy separates people into segregated groups that have little interaction with one another. Increasingly, the professional class is less oriented to membership in local associations and more oriented to national networks through which they can advance their careers.[86] What is lacking is not just community involvements but community involvements that can bridge the many economic, racial, and religious divisions that bedevil American society.

CONCLUSION: CHOOSING DEMOCRACY *AND* PROSPERITY

Elite democrats would have us believe that a prosperous economy requires a limited democracy. Democratic decision making is slow and inefficient. Corporations should be run in a top-down fashion by managerial elites, held accountable by consumers, who vote with their dollars on which products and services they want. Ever since James Madison warned in *Federalist No. 10* that "pure democracy" was incompatible with the "rights of property," elite democrats have warned that too much democracy could lead to the leveling of wealth and income, eliminating the incentives to work hard and invest that fuel economic prosperity.

Throughout American history, ordinary citizens have ignored these warnings, struggling to shape the political economy to democratic ends. During the Progressive period in the early twentieth century, popular democrats succeeded in passing the 26th Amendment to the Constitution (1913), which allowed for a progressive income tax and a tax on large estates (1916). During the New Deal of the 1930s, the right of workers to join a union was safeguarded by the Wagner Act (1935), and that same year unemployment insurance and Social Security were created to protect workers against loss of income due to layoffs and old age. In the 1960s and 1970s, two important institutions were created to protect the environment and worker safety: the Environmental Protection Agency (1970) and the Occupational Safety and Health Administration (1971).

In each case, elites predicted dire economic consequences if these popular democratic reforms were passed. In fact, there is no convincing evidence that these reforms significantly harmed the economy's ability to grow or to produce new wealth. Indeed, greater equality benefits the economy by stimulating consumer spending and giving workers greater motivation to work hard. There is no steep trade-off between equality and economic efficiency and growth. We *can* have both.

KEY TERMS

corporate welfare
privileged position of business
corporate capitalism
market competition
shareholder democracy
economic planning
oligopoly
downsizing

outsourcing
casino economy
Wagner Act
fortunate fifth
wealth inequality
paper entrepreneur
chief executive officer (CEO)
civil society

INTERNET RESOURCES

■ The Economic Policy Institute
www.epi.org
The best site for extensive data and analyses of current economic policy issues and for studies of income and wealth trends. The EPI is nonpartisan but is funded in part by labor unions.

■ The Heritage Foundation
www.heritage.org
Economic news and policy analyses from the premier right-wing think tank. Good links to other conservative foundations and public policy lobbies.

■ Center on Budget and Policy Priorities
www.cbpp.org
Reports on policy issues from a liberal think tank that concentrates on low- and middle-income citizens.

The Cato Institute
www.cato.org
Speeches, research, and opinion from the leading libertarian think tank in the United States. Provides economic data and opinion supportive of privatization of now-public functions, from environmental protection to schools.

SUGGESTED READINGS

Milton Friedman, *Capitalism and Freedom*. Chicago: University of Chicago Press, 1962. The now-classic defense of the positive relationship between economic markets and political freedom.

William Greider, *One World, Ready or Not*. New York: Anchor/Doubleday, 1997. A provocative account of economic globalization, showing how transnational corporations affect labor and consumption and weaken democratic governments.

Juliet B. Schor, *The Overworked American*. New York: Basic Books, 1992. An economist examines how business and government urge Americans to work long hours in order to consume more products, with dire effects on private and public life, families, and individuals.

David K. Shipler, *The Working Poor: Invisible in America*. New York: Alfred A. Knopf, 2004; and Barbara Ehrenreich, *Nickel and Dimed: On (Not) Getting By in America*. New York: Henry Holt, 2001. Hardheaded but passionate exposés demonstrating that hard, honest work does not enable many Americans to escape from poverty.

CHAPTER

4 Public Opinion and Political Culture
Can the People Be Fooled?

Ordinary people's beliefs and expressions about politics and policies are called **public opinion**. Today, public opinion seems to reign supreme. Dozens of polling organizations investigate and report minute changes in its mood, while social movements and interest groups compete to gain its attention and support. Political candidates and their organizations track it, while think tanks, lobbyists, and advertisers try to shape it. In a democratic society where the public's thoughts and beliefs should matter, all this is hardly surprising. Yet this apparent respect for public opinion is tinged with fear. It may disguise a deep elite skepticism about the public's capacity to understand, reason, or judge public policies. Beneath the constant monitoring is the worry that unless public opinion is carefully contained and properly educated, it may surge out of control. From the perspectives of elites in politics and business, the public may be dangerous, ignorant, or stupid—or a potent combination of all three.

Public opinion and the democratic debate

Skepticism about the inherent ignorance and passions of the public has long characterized elite democratic views. More than two centuries ago, Alexander Hamilton called public opinion "a great beast" prone to "sudden breezes of passion." In the 1920s, the first systematic student of public opinion, Walter Lippmann, observed that the public was "a bewildered herd" driven by "manufactured images." More recently, one prominent student of contemporary public opinion argued that on many important questions the public is so ill-informed and indifferent that opinions might just as well be decided by a coin toss.[1]

These days, elite doubts about the public are rarely voiced so bluntly, lest the public be offended by the insults. Still, skeptics have plenty of evidence to validate their doubts. Despite rising levels of formal education, most Americans are ignorant of key political facts. A majority cannot identify the chief justice of the United States, and even fewer can name their representative in the House. It is even worse when it comes to foreign matters: In 2004, the majority of Americans didn't know that weapons of mass destruction had never been found in Iraq, and most Americans couldn't locate Iraq or Afghanistan on a world map.[2]

Popular ignorance is one problem, but another is that public opinion is sometimes irrationally volatile or downright inconsistent. In the late 1990s, against all pundits' expectations, President Bill Clinton's performance ratings actually improved after his sexual escapades and less-than-candid behavior were revealed. More recently, George W. Bush's popularity ratings soared in the aftermath of 9/11, only to plunge in 2004. Despite this disapproval, he won the 2004 election.

Given these outwardly strange results, it is no wonder that elite democrats have voiced concern about how much public opinion does matter and how much it really should matter as an independent force. The billions of dollars spent to influence public opinion and to understand its workings may be used, in this sense, not so much to test public opinion but to manage and control what elites see as its potential excesses. Political scientist Ben Ginsberg calls this modern apparatus of public opinion management a huge elite effort to create a "captive public."[3]

But *is* the public "captive" and is public opinion as ignorant and volatile as some claim? According to popular democratic views of public opinion, which have an equally long history, the answer is no. Men like Jefferson saw public opinion as the fount of republican government, and Lincoln's belief that you "can fool some of the people some of the time, most of the people some of the time, but not all the people all the time" lives on as well. In the 1920s, philosopher John Dewey argued that both government and corporate propaganda did indeed pose a problem for democracy. Ordinary people would have a difficult time separating fact from fiction when the media, government, and corporations were all centralized and information became an elite resource alone. Yet Dewey argued that ordinary citizens and their deliberations were not the problem. Rather, democratic debate was the antidote to private and public propaganda. Ordinary people had to live with the consequences of war, inequality, and injustice in ways that expert elites usually didn't. As a consequence, the challenge for democrats would be to build strong communities and free spaces where people could talk, debate, learn, and interact. In this way, a strong civil society that promoted citizen discussion, development, and action would fulfill the promise of democracy. For popular democrats like Dewey, public opinion should be freed to do more, not less.[4]

The Vietnam War era provides one of the best examples of the emergence of the kind of active and informed public opinion that popular democrats like Dewey had in mind. At the war's beginnings, and in the early stages of U.S. troop involvement, most Americans didn't know many details about the war. Popular majorities, egged on by government propaganda and media complicity, initially supported U.S. engagement as the patriotic thing to do. Yet this was in part because the public was deprived of essential facts about the nature of U.S. involvement. The public, quite simply, had not thought much about the matter. As the war progressed, public opposition grew in tandem with new facts that revealed a pattern of government dishonesty, half-truths, and propaganda about the war's origins and its tragic consequences. As public discussion about the war broadened, and as an extensive antiwar movement arose to protest it, informed public opinion had a chance to mature. As it did, and as media coverage of the war expanded beyond cheerleading for the government, the public turned against the war and the politicians who had originated it and began to question elite assumptions about what was at stake in Vietnam. In popular democratic terms, public opinion played a key role in exposing, and then curbing, elite delusions about the Vietnam War's "progress."[5] Yet what is obvious here is that the democratic debate about public opinion raises fundamental questions about contemporary political life. If the public is as ignorant, fickle, and dangerous as elite democrats believe, then the manipulation and control of public opinion by "responsible" elites can be justified. If, on the contrary, these same elites in both government and corporations possess the means to seize control of democratic politics through intimidation and propaganda, then popular democratic ideas stressing the independent and intelligent democratic role of public opinion can be supported.

Just how government, the media, and large corporations try to control public opinion is discussed at length in Chapter 6. In this chapter we address two questions: Is the public as ignorant and irrational as many elites believe? From what experiences and sources do people derive their opinions? To answer these questions, we first look at whether ordinary Americans profess democratic beliefs about how government should operate. Second, we explain how different interpretations of common beliefs emerge and then explore the question of polarization in U.S. public opinion. Are Americans as divided as recent elections suggest? Third, we ask if Americans think consistently about public policies, and then we inquire about the circumstances that shape public opinion and how it changes. Finally, we turn briefly to the subject of public opinion's independence and effectiveness when it is measured by polls and polling organizations. The ongoing "war on terrorism" and the U.S. invasion in Iraq provide current tests of public opinion's knowledge and wisdom, and in this chapter we use them as prime examples.

AMERICAN POLITICAL CULTURE

As a multiracial, multicultural nation of immigrants, the United States' survival as a nation depends on the quality and scope of its democratic, political understandings. Common values of toleration, mutual respect, and national community must work to forge bonds among people of diverse races, national origins, religions, cultures, and political views. When these fail, the darkest dimensions of American politics emerge, whether in the form of African-American slavery and racism's legacy, the subjugation of Native Americans, or the demonization of nonconformist dissent as unpatriotic and "un-American." Our history suggests that the association between democratic values and nationhood hasn't been steady or easy. Alternatively, the brightest moments in U.S. history are those times when more and more people become included in the expanding democratic promise of American life.

What do citizens today understand about what it means to be an American? The set of common rituals, stories, symbols, and habits that Americans share might be called American **political culture**. Political culture is not just a set of abstract values; it is more like a common political language that we all speak. When we talk and act, we may disagree, but we do so using common, shared reference points. As such, a democratic political culture is broad enough to include both sides in the democratic debate and other values as well. Despite differences, the tradition of American political protest and dissent—embodied in the civil rights, labor, peace, and feminist movements—has something in common with the ideas of those who oppose many of the specific goals of political protest and dissent. The important point is that people share a common language, even if they disagree. Table 4.1 details some of the essential elements of our common political culture.

Patriotism, Democracy, and the National Community

As described in Chapter 2, democracy became an honored idea in the United States soon after the founding debates. Even in periods of crisis and upheaval (such as the 1960s), public support for the basic forms and procedures of democratic government has remained overwhelming and widespread. Today, the common language of democracy still stands as the essence of American political culture.

TABLE 4.1	**At least eight in ten Americans agree to the following:**
The Essentials of American Political Culture	1. Free speech should be granted to everyone regardless of how intolerant they are of other people's opinions.
	2. Freedom to worship as one pleases applies to all religious groups, regardless of how extreme their beliefs are.
	3. The private enterprise system is generally a fair and efficient system.
	4. A party that wins an election should respect the rights of opposition parties to criticize the way things are being run.
	5. Forcing people to testify against themselves in court is never justified.
	6. Our elected officials would badly misuse their power if they weren't watched and guided by the voters.
	7. A minority family that wants to move into a particular neighborhood shouldn't have to check with anyone before doing so.
	8. Everyone in America should have equal opportunities to get ahead.
	9. Children should have equal educational opportunities.

Source: Adapted and reprinted by permission of the publisher from *American Ethos* by Herbert McCloskey and John Zaller (Cambridge, Mass.: Harvard University Press). Copyright © 1984 by the Twentieth Century Fund.

The vast majority of Americans agree, at least in the abstract, on many fundamental tenets of democratic life. The ideas that public officials should be chosen by majority vote in regular elections and that minorities and individuals maintain rights to freedom of speech, press, expression, and religion are supported by more than nine in ten citizens. The idea that defects in the American system should and can be changed through legal processes and not through violence is also supported. Not surprisingly, the Constitution and the Bill of Rights receive similarly high levels of popular support.

Belief in democratic values is accompanied by extraordinarily high levels of expressed patriotism. More than nine in ten citizens profess pride in being an American—an attribute that crosses the divides of race, class, religion, region, and gender. A similar consensus extends to the "special" character of U.S. institutions and society, with overwhelming popular support for the belief that America has a "destiny" to set a democratic example for other nations and to "expand freedom for more and more people." The national community's image is thus strongly positive for most Americans and is often experienced symbolically as reverence for the flag, for our great public buildings such as the Capitol, Washington Monument, and Lincoln Memorial, and for U.S. holidays such as the Fourth of July and Thanksgiving. Nearly three in four Americans believe that "our system of government is the best possible system."[6]

Elites have often sought to use patriotism as a way of repressing dissent as "un-American." Occasionally, most especially in the 1960s, some protestors played into this idea by criticizing not only major institutions but "America" itself, as if it were a monolith. In large measure, however, dissenters from dominant policies and practices are just as prone to profess patriotic motives as anybody else. The U.S. flag was on display just as much at the massive antiwar demonstrations in 2003 as it was at any pro-Bush rally. Thus, while professions of faith in democracy and patriotism may seem vague and not very meaningful, or alternatively as ratifications of the status quo, it is significant that Americans express more of a consensus about such matters than the citizens of nearly any other country. Dissent and its opposite are equal parts of the American tradition.

Individualism and Liberty

Foreign observers since the beginning of the republic until today have observed that American culture is distinctively individualistic. In contrast to most of the world, Americans don't generally think of their society as having an existence separate from the individuals who make it up. Americans tend to think of society as composed of independent persons, each striving for unique goals in life. Individuals are thought to be the authors of their own destinies, endowed with the capacity—even the duty—to define beliefs, thoughts, and aspirations for themselves.

Thus, individualism is often associated with the idea that U.S. citizens are born with rights to liberty and freedom. No institution, including the family and especially the government, can arbitrarily command us to think, speak, or act in a way that we choose not to. For this reason, American political culture favors limits on government power in order to preserve liberty of individual thought and action. Government can violate an individual's liberty, Americans tend to believe, only in protection of the rights of others. Even then, government coercion can occur only after strict procedures are followed. Public support for freedom and liberty, especially of speech and religion, is virtually universal in surveys taken since the 1930s.

To whom should the rights of liberty extend? The idea that all "men" are created equal is as old as the Declaration of Independence. Through a bloody Civil War and numerous movements for equal rights, formal political equality has been extended to all U.S. citizens, regardless of race or gender. Formal political equality does not mean that all people are born with equal talents, capacities, or intelligence. It does mean that when it comes to civil and political rights—to the vote, to free speech, to association, to a fair trial, and to religion—citizens should be treated in the same way before the law. Again, more than 85 percent of Americans support such an idea of political equality. Large majorities of Americans also believe that such basic human rights should stretch to everyone across the globe.[7]

Community: A Country of Joiners

Except for survivalists and the Lone Ranger, Americans live in neighborhoods, families, and workplaces, where rugged individualism is neither possible nor desirable. When we care for sick relatives, work with others on a common project, vote, or attend a demonstration, Americans express interdependence and reliance on community and the larger society for support. Even in the 1830s, the French aristocrat Alexis de Tocqueville wrote that American individualists tempered their isolation by joining numerous associations and groups.

When Americans think of community, the key element is that we join groups voluntarily and that we're not forced by birth to believe certain ideas and participate in certain associations. Voluntary and civic efforts at the local level are the most valued. There may be no more prized symbol of American community than the small town or dense, friendly urban neighborhood and its intimate, face-to-face relationships among friends and families. The New England town meeting with its equality of participation and absence of hierarchy may be the model of government that many Americans most admire.

The reality, though, is that most of us no longer live in small towns, and the opportunities for face-to-face contact with others are much more restricted in a society of suburban sprawl and constant mobility. Yet the power of American community is often evident today in the attempt to reproduce its virtues in cities and suburbs and their various neighborhoods. While Americans today are often pushed and pulled by competing work, family, and community obligations, they continue to regard their attachments to others as most important. Organized religion and churchgoing remain more popular in America than in other rich countries, as do associations that help the needy, aid local schools, or organize community events like youth sports leagues and community cleanups.

Americans also join many associations of a more self-interested nature. State and national clubs and associations that bring together people of common lifestyles, political beliefs, or economic interests are more common in the United States than in any other country. Thus, even in a country that prizes liberty, more than eight in ten Americans today say that the pursuit of the public good should be of equal or greater priority than individual freedom alone. At least in the abstract, Americans still think of themselves as a nation of joiners and participants, although as we shall see in Chapter 5 this tradition of participation is in great jeopardy today.[8]

Political and Economic Equality

Not surprisingly, a culture that values individualism is also inclined to have generally favorable beliefs about private property, especially if it is acquired through individual work and effort. Massive popular assent to the idea that the private enterprise system is generally fair has consistently been recorded in surveys.

Yet in the political culture, favorable views of property ownership are generally associated with the broader social and political goals that it supposedly helps to further. Thomas Jefferson believed that a nation of independent farmers would instill resistance to arbitrary authority, and Alexander Hamilton believed that property ownership would build the nation's power and wealth. For most Americans today, owning property, especially in small or moderate amounts, is seen as a badge of achievement and a mark of character. Even most Americans who own neither a home nor a business seem to share in the political culture of property ownership—they aspire to own their own homes or start their own businesses, even though many have difficulty doing either. Most Americans rank small business entrepreneurs as one of the most respected groups in U.S. society.

Widespread cultural support for private property doesn't mean, however, that most Americans favor large gaps in either wealth or income. Neither does the public support certain key features and consequences of the corporate capitalist system. In fact, in some ways cultural beliefs in property ownership are accompanied by ideas that ownership should be diffused throughout the population and not concentrated in a few hands: Everyone should have *some* property, but no one should have so much that it deprives others of it. Thus, as we saw in Chapter 3, support for private property and the free enterprise system stops short of assent for many of the practices and power of private corporations.

Still, in comparison with the views of people in other wealthy countries, Americans are remarkable for how little they believe in **equality of condition**—leveling incomes and wealth so that nobody is either very rich or very poor. Instead of equality of condition, Americans generally support the vaguer idea of **equality of opportunity**. This belief embodies the idea that all people should begin their lives with an equal chance to succeed or fail on their own merits. In recent years, overt racial and gender discrimination, once accepted by many Americans, has given way to the widespread idea that discrimination should not prevent people from getting an education, working at a job, or buying a home. Of course, verbal assent to such ideas is very different from practicing them or promoting them in your own neighborhood and workplace. And equality of opportunity, like much in American political culture, can mean very different things to different people. For some, it means that government should help people start out with equal educational resources or compensate for disadvantages they experience because of poverty. For others, it simply is the right to succeed or fail on the basis of individual achievement alone, without government help.[9]

INTERPRETING DIVIDES WITHIN THE POLITICAL CULTURE

If U.S. public opinion is built on quicksand because people are basically naive, uninformed, and bereft of basic democratic values, then the republic is in serious trouble. It would be torn apart from its foundation by the slightest stress. Alternatively, people could easily become the instruments of propaganda, easily swayed by whatever point of view was sold to them by those in power. Is the existence of a broad, if vague, democratic political culture sufficient to allay these doubts? It may very well be true that most Americans don't know all the players and all the facts about particular issues. But ordinary Americans do share a common vocabulary, and they reason from something like the same principles about politics.

At least when it comes to these basics of political culture, the agreement is somewhat exceptional compared to many other nations. Few of us are monarchists or believe that the Bill of Rights should be suspended when dissenters emerge, that citizenship should be for whites only, or that a state religion ought to be put in place. Most of us want to believe in the civic ethics and symbols of American democracy and the broad outlines of a democratic system. While this may seem unremarkable, it isn't: Many democracies, when faced with an election as disputed as the 2000 (and even the 2004) presidential election might have plunged into turmoil or even civil war. Maybe this would have been understandable. Yet the norms of U.S. political culture are often strong enough to withstand, and perhaps even correct, massive democratic irregularities, or at least we would hope so given American political culture (see Chapter 6).[10]

The really important question might be this: How far does this political culture extend? Most periods of U.S. history have also been filled with conflict and often bitter divisions. This includes our own times: We might speak the same language, but that doesn't mean we say the same things. In the following section, we will examine three cases of divides within public opinion. Each case reveals deep fractures between elite and popular democratic views of democracy and of public opinion. Each shows that the apparent consensus in our political culture nonetheless leads to serious divisions when it comes to public evaluations of how well, or poorly, our economic and political institutions live up to common, if variously defined, democratic ideals. Each demands that readers consider this essential question: Are the opinions of the mass public a problem for American democratic politics? Or, rather, is the problem a democracy under threat from elite attempts to control it?

Civil Liberties and Political Tolerance

Ordinary people may profess support for civil liberties in the abstract, but what about in practice? For the last forty years, some studies have found that rhetorical support for civil liberties simply doesn't translate into popular toleration for cultural and political minorities. These studies conclude that ordinary Americans are intolerant of people who are culturally, politically, and racially different from the majority, or from whatever group that is considered as such. In contrast, highly educated and affluent people alone are said to be more tolerant, expressing much firmer support of the Bill of Rights and its guarantee of free speech, religion, and nonconformity. In political science, the ironic idea that the uneducated masses are really quite authoritarian, whereas elites are the real defenders of democratic values has been labeled **democratic elitism**.

Public intolerance seemed to run particularly high at the Cold War's beginnings, the so-called McCarthy era of the late 1940s and early 1950s. One study conducted during the era found levels of popular support of only 37 percent for freedom of speech by atheists and only 27 percent for communists. Only 6 percent believed that communists should be allowed to teach in colleges. Again, support for freedom of speech rose proportionately with level of education: Among "opinion leaders," levels of toleration were almost half again as high as they were for those with only high school diplomas.[11] In recent history, the notion of a split between "democratic" elites and "extremist" masses does not stand up well. It is true that elites often tell pollsters that they are tolerant, whereas a higher proportion of ordinary citizens say they are willing to restrict the speech of certain groups. Yet in practice, ordinary people have not been the instigators or even the participants in most of the acts of recent political repression. Even during the mass hysteria of the McCarthy era of the early 1950s, surveys revealed that the public was not as concerned about communism in the United States as governmental leaders were. In an important study, political scientist James Gibson found no evidence that the mass public favored repression of American communists. Rather, Gibson discovered that political elites in state governments were likely to push repressive legislation even when they weren't urged to do so by the public.[12]

A similar pattern was evident in the 1960s and 1970s. At that time, it was the federal government and some state and local political agencies that initiated secret plans of repression against antiwar activists, the Black Panthers, and the Native American movement. The COINTELPRO (short for Counter-Intelligence and Propaganda) program during the Nixon years deployed federal

© 2005 Tom Tomorrow.

agents from the FBI and CIA as plants in numerous political organizations. In the most visible episode, agents of the Nixon campaign (many former CIA operatives) in 1972 broke into the headquarters of the Democratic Party at the Watergate Hotel.

All of these operations were conducted secretly and were not subject to public debate. Thus, they could hardly have been caused, or even supported, by a tyrannical majority or a bewildered herd motivated by breezes of passion against political and cultural minorities. In fact, public opinion polls taken at the time recorded widespread public opposition to such measures when they were revealed. Rather than underscoring the dangers of popular democracy and uncontrolled public opinion, these episodes of repression seem to show that the chief dangers to democracy emerge when political elites monopolize information, spy on citizens, and narrow the range of discussion.[13]

What about now, in the aftermath of 9/11 and amidst widespread fear of Islamist inspired terrorism? Since September 11, 2001, the Bush administration and Congress have passed a number of measures that give new authority to various government agencies and provide guarantees of secrecy to their actions. Under the USA Patriot Act, the FBI can secretly monitor both Internet communications and library records. It can also search homes without notifying the occupants, and without their being present if they are suspected of terrorist activity. Since 9/11, the Bush administration has also proclaimed that citizens suspected of terrorist acts can be held without access to counsel and without charges, and that noncitizens can be held indefinitely if they are suspected of aiding terrorism. The Bush administration has created a new category—"enemy combatants"—under which it can hold hundreds of prisoners in Guantanamo Bay, Cuba, and elsewhere without charge or trial and, initially, without access to legal counsel. And, most notably, it has authorized the use of what some see as torture, in Abu Ghraib prison in Iraq and through the CIA, by claiming that the Geneva Conventions on torture do not apply to the present war. Through the "extraordinary rendition" program, the CIA has whisked away uncharged "suspects" to friendly countries like Egypt and Jordan for interrogations, knowing full well that such countries would torture these suspects in violation of U.S. law.

Has public opinion supported these measures? Initially after 9/11, public opinion provided wide support for government "antiterrorism" measures. Respondents claimed they were willing to give up many civil liberties to prevent future terrorist acts. But over time, this support has diminished, and now there is even widespread hostility toward many of these measures. By 2003, a slim majority opposed the preceding provisions of the USA Patriot Act, and a whopping eight in ten opposed the idea that Americans detained under suspicion of terrorist acts should have no right to legal counsel or a speedy trial. When it came to torture at Abu Ghraib or elsewhere, the public had turned against the government position. Fifty-one percent blamed government higher-ups for the torture scandals at Abu Ghraib, and an overwhelming 92 percent said that detainees—"illegal combatants" in the Bush administration's terms—had a right to a hearing and access to inspection of their condition by the Red Cross (a right presently denied by government policy).[14]

Two lessons can be learned from these experiences. First, during crisis periods elites have unrivaled ability to shape public opinion. But, second, citizens need to know what government officials are doing before they can make a judgment. Once they do know, however, they must deliberate, discuss, and listen to diverse opinions about government policies. In the case of post-9/11 and Iraq War government policies, most Americans provided broad support for "antiterrorism measures," but once they fully understood what these measures were, support declined. As knowledge grew, so too did divisions in public opinion, to the point where government policies even became unpopular.

The preceding cases reveal that public opinion can change radically but only gradually and over time. When the public is continually exposed to different points of view and new information, they learn, reflect, and, over months or years, often change their opinions. Table 4.2 shows that Americans are still sharply divided about the rights of specific political and cultural minorities, yet it also reveals growing support for increased tolerance since the 1950s. People who lived through the McCarthy era remain less tolerant of cultural and political nonconformists than did younger people who came of age during and after the civil rights, feminist, and antiwar movements of the 1960s and 1970s. However, even in the former group, the trend is toward greater tolerance. In the 1990s and early 2000s, toleration for the rights of gays and lesbians, and even popular support for special protections to prevent job and housing discrimination against them, has grown, especially among young people but also among self-proclaimed conservatives. And, while this is not included in Table 4.2, there are indications today that the initial hostility toward immigrants present after 9/11 has withered, becoming replaced by more nuanced and tolerant views.[15]

So to sum up, is the mass public likely to be intolerant, whereas elites uphold democratic norms? The answer is: when the nation is thought to be in crises abroad, public opinion will, at the beginning, back up almost anything the government does. However, almost never does the public initiate repressive measures, or even call for war as an immediate response; it is governmental elites and opinion makers that usually initiate these responses. And, over time and as events unfold and more facts about the consequences of policies are known, public opinion divides and even opposes many of the government's policies.

National Security: The Iraq War

High levels of patriotism—the belief that America has a unique mission in the world—and the nearly universal reverence for the symbols of U.S. nationhood might suggest that public opinion about American national security issues would spark few divisions. This is supported by other relevant facts: Most Americans have little direct knowledge about foreign countries and are almost entirely dependent on the government and the media for interpretations and information about situations abroad. Moreover, in times of crises that involve the world outside the United States, it might be natural for Americans to support the commander-in-chief and the military in just about whatever they do. Since the

TABLE 4.2		1954	1972	1998	2002
Public Tolerance for Advocates of Unpopular Ideas, 1954–2002	**Person Should Be Allowed to Make a Speech**				
	An admitted communist	28	52	67	69
	Someone against churches and religion	38	65	75	77
	Admitted homosexual	*	62	81	83
	Someone who believes that blacks are genetically inferior	*	61	62	63
	Person Should Be Allowed to Teach in College				
	An admitted communist	6	39	57	60
	Someone against churches and religion	12	40	58	60
	Admitted homosexual	*	50	74	78
	Someone who believes that blacks are genetically inferior	*	41	46	52
	Person's Book Should Remain in Library				
	An admitted communist	29	53	67	69
	Someone against churches and religion	37	60	70	73
	Admitted homosexual	*	55	70	75
	Someone who believes that blacks are genetically inferior	*	62	63	66

Sources: 1954 data from Samuel Stouffer, *Communism, Conformity, and Civil Liberties* (New York: Wiley, 1954); 1972 and 1998 data from the General Social Survey; 2002 data from Richard Niemi and Harold Stanley, *Vital Statistics of American Politics* (Washington, D.C.: Congressional Quarterly Press, 2004), pp. 156–58.
*Question not asked in 1954.

September 11 attacks, terrorism and national security have been the public's top priority, and many believe that this alone accounted for President Bush's 2004 reelection. For some, this may seem heartening—a nation "united" in confrontation with a threat from abroad seems healthy. But for popular democrats, it poses dangerous questions: placing all the emphasis on the foreign threat may disguise mistakes, provide new opportunities to silence critical voices and hide uncomfortable facts, and create new instruments to manipulate public opinion through the concentration of executive power.

The beginnings and progress of the Iraq War are thus an instructive test for the existence of democratic public opinion in a period of crisis. Has widespread belief in nationalism, combined with the "crisis" features above, prevented debate and disagreements from emerging? Figure 4.1 shows a time line charting

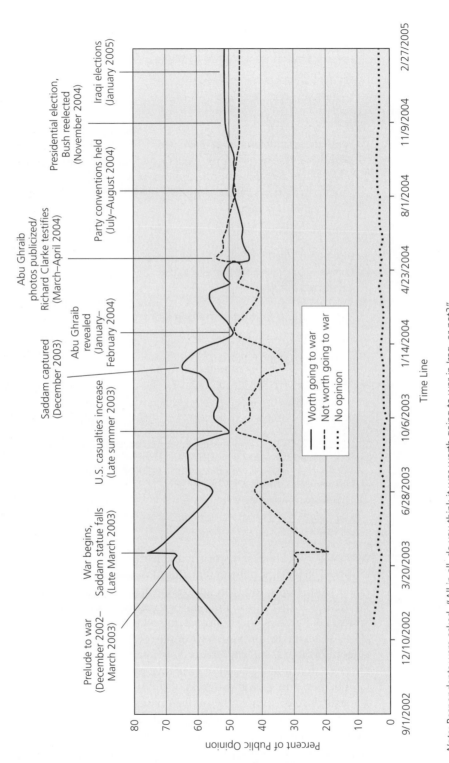

FIGURE 4.1 Public Opinion on the Iraq War, 2002–2005

Note: Respondents were asked, "All in all, do you think it was worth going to war in Iraq, or not?"

Source: CNN, *USA Today*, Gallup Poll. January 3, 2003–February 7, 2005. (*Polling Report.* 2004. pollingreport.com/iraq.htm. September 2004.)

the public's agreement or disagreement with the question "All in all, do you think it was worth going to war in Iraq, or not?" The figure indicates the important events and revelations that occurred from the war's prelude until the first Iraqi parliamentary elections in January 2005.

Before the war began in March 2003, the Bush administration had built its case based on numerous rationales. Later, however, all of them turned out to be false. Congress had seemingly authorized the war months before, and Colin Powell and numerous government officials had made the very public case that the Iraqi regime was hiding weapons of mass destruction, that it was close to producing an atomic weapon, and that it was in clear violation of U.N. Security Council resolutions demanding full disclosure of each. This case was more or less accepted as uncontroversial by the mainstream media, which devoted much more discussion to the question of whether the U.S. should go to war with or without explicit U.N. Security Council approval. More controversially, some administration officials, including Vice President Cheney, alleged that Iraq had ties with Al Qaeda and even possibly to the September 11 attacks and that Saddam Hussein had the ability to dispatch automated drones to bomb nearby nations. Not surprisingly, on the eve of war, more than two-thirds of Americans supported these rationales, whereas one-third opposed the rush into war. The largest antiwar demonstrations in the nation's history (and the world's) took place in February 2003. When the war started, and especially after early victories, Americans were firmly behind it; by April 2003, supporters outnumbered dissenters by over 3 to 1. Since then, however, support has narrowed, and since mid-2004, Americans have been divided about equally on support for the war, and by mid-2005 had swung decisively against it. Why did this happen? Initially, the chief reason for doubt seemed to be the growing insurgency, a phenomenon the Bush administration had not predicted. Then came the gradual revelations that neither atomic weapons facilities nor weapons of mass destruction had been found. Then in May 2004 photographs of tortured prisoners from Abu Ghraib prison were released, the 9/11 Commission reported that Saddam had no ties to Al Qaeda or the 9/11 attacks, and even Bush admitted that there had never been WMD. Temporary upticks in the war's waning popularity occurred only a few times: once when Saddam was captured in December 2003 and another after the Iraqi elections in January 2005.

This maturation of public opinion can be viewed in a positive way because it demonstrated that public opinion can be an independent judge of events as new facts are revealed and more deliberations take place, rather than simply an echo of statements by political and media elites. Yet there are other, less comforting conclusions: Surveys conducted in October 2004 showed that even after all these revelations, over half of Americans still believed that WMD had been found. One-quarter still believed that Saddam's connections to Al Qaeda had been verified. Almost all such respondents continued to support the war effort for these factually inaccurate reasons. Nearly eight in ten supporters of President Bush believed this, while only one-fifth of Kerry supporters did. The persistence of these misperceptions of reality in the mass public raise disturbing questions: apparently, some of the people can be fooled all the time.

What do these apparently strong divisions about the validity of the Iraq War reveal? On the one hand, the early and overwhelming support for the war demonstrates the enormous capacity to shape public opinion in crisis and war conditions when American troops are deployed abroad. During this period, official claims dominated the airwaves, media scrutiny of the claims was low, and public support followed. Yet as the public learned new facts, and after the subject was thrust into the public agenda by both the antiwar movements and the early candidates in the presidential election, opinions began to diverge. Finally, as at least some mainstream media sources began to investigate the Bush administration's claims and found them false, public support began to decline further. In short, as the public had the time and opportunity to learn, reflect on, and uncover new information, a substantial percentage of the public responded reasonably and rationally to events. The result was a nearly equal division about the war. We deal with this issue in much greater depth in Chapter 6, where the media's role in providing information about the war is discussed.[16]

Economic Elites and Power

Americans may ratify the general outlines of the capitalist system, but beneath the consensus, do they really believe that the economy's rules are fair? The sense that *corporate* America is out of touch has been extended with the decline in middle-class economic security and the rise in economic inequality since the early 1970s (see Chapter 3). While the economy grew at a consistent and rather rapid rate from 1993 until the century's end, much of this growth was not distributed equally. Only after 1997 did some of the growth spread to the middle class and the working poor, but after 2001, the increases in wealth and income began to disappear. Thus, although most Americans approved of the economic growth and voiced widespread support for the free enterprise system in the abstract, these opinions cannot be mistaken for confidence in corporate America, economic globalization, or the new economy.

Throughout the 1990s, surveys showed that over half of Americans believed that the American Dream of increased social mobility, home ownership, and education and job opportunities was a goal that fewer people could realize in today's economy. By large margins, the public blamed the job losses suffered in the U.S. economy on the policies of big corporations and of political and corporate elites. Not surprisingly, by large majorities the public felt that too much economic and political power is concentrated in the hands of big business and that corporations don't usually balance the pursuit of profit with protecting the public interest. More than ever since polling began, Democrats and independents state that corporations make too much profit, whereas Republicans are evenly split on this issue. Stricter environmental regulation of business practices is seen as particularly crucial, winning the support of over 80 percent of Americans in most surveys.[17]

Alongside the core belief that people who work hard can get ahead, most Americans nonetheless divide when it comes to the belief that equal opportunity really exists in today's economy. A small majority believes that most people don't have an equal chance to succeed in life, and up to one-third of Americans in 2002 told pollsters that they identified themselves with other Americans who weren't "making it" in today's economy. A majority also said that the major cause of poverty was the absence of equal opportunity. Many jobs, including teaching, nursing, and restaurant work, are seen as socially worthy but grossly underrewarded. In contrast, according to one exhaustive study, the "average person believes that much wealth is inherited and that the wealthy receive income greatly disproportionate to their roles' contributions to society." Before welfare was ended as an entitlement in 1997, Americans were prone to make a distinction between "undeserving," and "deserving" poor people. But since then, that distinction has been blurred. Today, more Americans—especially Democrats and independents—believe that the government should guarantee a minimal standard of living to each of its citizens, even if it means budget deficits or higher taxes. In this group, the majority supports increased government aid for medical care, food, housing subsidies, government measures to raise wages and require employee benefits, and increased spending on education.

Americans also remain torn over the benefits of globalization and pro-corporate trade agreements. In their broad survey of the political views of the working class, Ruy Teixeria and Joel Rogers write of the "new insecurity" felt by working-class Americans. By large majorities, ordinary Americans worry about the insecurities provoked by the new "flexible" corporation. For many it means decreasing health insurance coverage, loss of retirement pensions, no job security, and a radical increase in work hours. While Americans welcome globalization as an idea with great potential, "they are convinced . . . that globalization today is primarily benefiting business and that trade policy making is driven by business interests." Consequently, Americans are split over trade policy: middle- and low-income Americans believe that protecting jobs and improving the global environment ought to be the chief goals of trade policy. Upper-income citizens are more interested in promoting U.S. business and helping the economy grow, without regulations on trade.[18]

Although U.S. political culture does provide support for the basic outlines of the capitalist system—more than that of any other rich country—public opinion is divided when it comes to assessing the consequences of our brand of capitalism for the lives of ordinary people. Public attitudes about corporate power and corporate-friendly tax and regulatory public policies suggest deep divisions about the levels of class inequality that exist and government responses to them.

IDEOLOGIES AND PUBLIC OPINION

Great turbulence lies under the placid surface of U.S. political culture. Do Americans reason in systematic ways about politics and governmental activity, linking their beliefs about one issue with their views about another?

Specific world views that are used to form opinions about political issues are called political **ideologies**. Ideologies usually originate with intellectuals and activists; today the term has a more negative connotation, as "ideological" is seen as rigid and intolerant dogmas that ignore facts and enforce conformity. Ideologies can do both, but they don't by necessity do either.

Instead, they can simply be coherent and consistent ways of seeing what's valuable and worthwhile and how to achieve it. In political history, ideologies have often taken root in social and economic groups that forge broad political goals.

In Europe, politics has long been divided along broad ideological lines among socialists, communists, aristocratic conservatives, greens, religious advocates, economic liberals, and even neofascists and monarchists. At least since the 1950s, scholars have claimed that these large differences don't divide Americans. While there is some truth to that claim, it would be a mistake to see American political culture as a bland consensus bereft of difference.[19]

A Conservative Tide?

In place of the apparently larger ideological gulfs of European politics, American public opinion and politics have long been portrayed as divided over the lesser differences separating contemporary liberalism from conservatism. These are notoriously slippery terms that have peculiar American definitions and changing meanings even when they are defined. At minimum, modern **liberalism** features a strong belief in equality and in a government role in reducing racial, class, and gender inequities. Liberals promote government action to regulate some of the negative consequences of the corporate capitalist economy, and they defend the civil rights of cultural and political nonconformists as well as ethnic and racial minorities. In contrast, **conservative** ideology resists governmental spending programs that retard "natural" inequalities based on merit and achievement, resists governmental regulation that interferes with business growth and profit making, and calls for precise standards for private conduct, such as banning abortion and discouraging homosexuality. During the Cold War, liberals were thought to be less likely to use military force and conservatives more likely to do so, but this has hardly always been the case. At most but not always, American liberals favor diplomatic and multilateral means over the rapid use of military force, whereas conservatives are more prone to trust military, often unilateral, solutions first.

American liberalism and conservatism share much in common despite important differences. During the Cold War, both liberals and conservatives backed the national security state and the projection of America as the supreme world power. Both have come to agree that programs like Social Security and Medicare, once considered unabashedly liberal, ought to exist in some form. In recent years, liberals and conservatives also agree that running continuous federal budget deficits is a bad idea, even though in practice conservative presidents Reagan, George H. W. Bush, and George W. Bush have run the biggest deficits in U.S. history, while the "liberal" Clinton balanced federal spending and expenditures. Most importantly, both support the broad outlines of the American capitalist system and the private ownership of land, technology, factories, assets, and many other services that are public in other nations.[20]

For a long time, pollsters have been asking Americans whether they see themselves as liberals, conservatives, or moderates. The responses are summarized in Figure 4.2. These results can and have been interpreted as confirmation of growing support for conservative public policies, the Republican party, business, and what is loosely called "moral values." After all, self-proclaimed conservatives do outnumber liberals, and the percentage of people who identify with liberalism has declined slightly in the last decades. Combined with the election victories of conservative Republicans in the 1980s, 1990s, and the 2004 elections, this interpretation makes sense, at least at first glance.

Yet there are strong reasons to doubt a conservative ideological trend in public opinion. When other surveys probe further, they have found that a quarter of the public declines to identify with any ideological label. Of the three-quarters who do identify themselves as liberals, moderates, or conservatives, almost 40 percent choose the moderate label. Moreover, among people who label themselves conservatives, there is some, but not much, consistency about how they define what the term means or how it applies to specific public policies. For example, one-third of self-declared conservatives agree with two ideas considered "liberal": that "the government should provide more services even if it means an increase in spending" and that "abortion is a matter of choice." In 1994 a whopping 65 percent of proclaimed conservatives believed that the United States "should spend less on defense," and even under the Bush presidency there are doubts about the president's policies regarding the Patriot Act, tax cuts, Social Security, and the use of the U.S. military to promote what the president calls

FIGURE 4.2

Liberals and Conservatives in U.S. Public Opinion: 1976–2004

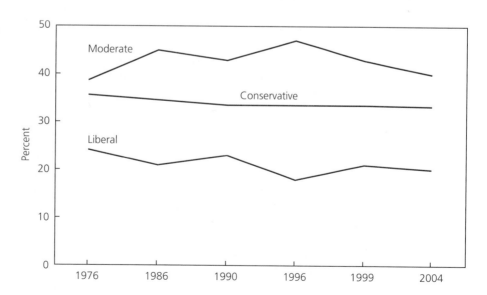

Source: Robert Erikson and Kent Tedin, *Public Opinion* (New York: Longman, 2001); Harris Interactive, 2004.

"freedom" abroad. Since the Bush presidency began, liberals are somewhat more consistent than conservatives appear to be in their definition of and support for generally recognized liberal policies and politicians. Still, all in all, even as identification with liberalism has waned and with conservatism has grown, the public's views of social and economic issues and policies have not changed all that much, or at least not as much as changes in policies, politicians, and institutions would suggest.[21]

Because there is confusion about the two terms among most citizens, and because there are so many self-proclaimed moderates, it might be thought that many people are centrists with views that are somewhere in between the two ideologies. But it turns out that people who say they are moderates don't necessarily have consistent or similar views, either. For example, many moderates favor government health insurance guarantees (a liberal position) but also strongly favor the death penalty for murder (a supposedly conservative position). Being a moderate doesn't mean that one is "in the middle"; it may mean instead that people simultaneously hold strongly conservative views about some matters and liberal views about others. Perhaps the easiest conclusion is that, for the most part, most Americans just don't think about politics in consistent ideological terms. Although most people understand something about what liberalism and conservatism mean, they largely don't use these terms themselves when they give their answers to survey questions.

Given all this complexity, it might be tempting to give up on these ideological labels altogether. However, there is some evidence that in very recent years conservatives and liberals are becoming more consistent and that this divide is captured in partisan terms as clear splits between partisan Republicans and Democrats. (For more on the parties, see Chapter 7.) Since 9/11, the Iraq War, and the Bush presidency, conservatives favor an aggressive foreign policy exporting "freedom," with a strong military taking unilateral action to combat terrorism, while liberals and most moderates favor diplomatic cooperation with allies and the U.N. first, and military action only as a second or last resort. Conservative Republicans are increasingly probusiness and oppose business regulation, favor tax-cuts, and oppose both legalized abortion and the rights of gays to marry, and most significantly favor the Iraq War. Liberals in recent years have increasingly favored opposite policies, providing even more support than they did in the past for a strong safety net, business regulation, and a diplomatic, cooperative U.S. approach to international affairs. Still, the proportion of conservatives, liberals, and moderates has not really changed in this decade.[22]

The reason to partially retain these ideological labels is that they do matter inside the Washington Beltway, among the elected officials, intellectuals, campaign consultants, lobbyists, and activists most involved in policy debates. Here, conservatives have made substantial gains, not only in terms of numbers of elected officials, but in terms of the power of rightwing think-tanks, mass media, and lobbies (see Chapter 7). In the end, though, most citizens seem unmoved by strictly ideological appeals to liberal or conservative doctrines, and even political leaders who are otherwise ideological themselves seem to understand this. Deemed the most liberal senator by the Republicans, John Kerry refused to campaign as one. And George Bush, arguably the most conservative president since Herbert Hoover, cast even his most radical proposal—for the transformation of Social Security as an entitlement—as a mere "reform" of the program first implemented by that liberal icon, President Franklin D. Roosevelt.

Beyond Liberalism and Conservatism: New Ideologies

At the very least, current conservatives and liberals are redefining the meaning of these doctrines. In terms of public opinion, we can draw two possible conclusions about the role of these ideological divisions. One is that most people just don't think very systematically, consistently, or coherently about politics, tending to cherry-pick positions without much consistency. This view confirms elite democratic expectations by blaming the people for their muddled and contradictory views. Facing a supposedly fickle public with inconsistent opinions, elites rightly reserve to themselves the real ideological debate and decisions. But there is an alternative, popular democratic explanation of the same phenomena: It is that ordinary people do bring systematic beliefs to real politics. It just so happens that their systematic beliefs have increasingly little to do with the liberal–conservative split so important inside the Beltway. People may think systematically but don't share elite definitions of what ideology is.

In *Why Americans Hate Politics*, journalist E. J. Dionne argues that both contemporary liberalism and conservatism distort and misrepresent what are systematic beliefs held by most ordinary Americans. Public opinion, Dionne states, was once less a set of abstract ideologies or random choices than an expression of the positive, concrete identities forged through debates and discussions in city neighborhoods, small towns, workplaces, schools, and families. Today, elites ignore these community contexts, preferring instead to appeal to citizens' fears and cynicism through broad and largely meaningless clichés or code words like "family values," "freedom and liberty," or "national strength." Is there really anyone in America who opposes values, strength, and liberty as political values? Of course not; as the question becomes not whether one favors "freedom" but what is meant by it. According to Dionne, elite ideologues pose "false choices . . . that make it extremely difficult for the obvious preferences of the American people to express themselves. . . . We are encouraging an either/or politics based on ideological preconceptions rather than a both/and politics based on ideas."[23]

What are these ideas and preferences of ordinary Americans? Dionne is reluctant to put a new ideological label on them. But other analysts have referred to a deeply ingrained **populist** and **communitarian** strain in American public opinion. Populist beliefs are particularly strong in the middle and working classes. They include hostility to all concentrations of economic and political power and a belief that institutions work best when they are simple, understandable, and accountable to the basic needs of people who work hard and play by the rules. At the same time, there is some resistance to forms of cultural nonconformity and a defensiveness about middle-class values, and a heightened belief that religious and ethical questions ought to be more important in political dialogue and public policies. Most Americans, according to Dionne, don't believe that either government or corporate America today operates according to such principles. They don't believe that enough people, rich and poor, really do play by the rules and take personal responsibility for their actions. And they don't believe that exclusively liberal or conservative ideas will help to resolve the central problems of U.S. society.[24]

Whether or not Dionne is entirely right, his argument raises an important issue. Most people may very well think systematically about politics. But the existing elite divisions between traditional conservatism and liberalism don't capture their perceptions, and most "populists" lack the organizations and power to articulate their opinions in a way that would allow such perceptions to become more articulate. If Americans do indeed think systematically about politics, where do their views come from?

WHERE DOES PUBLIC OPINION ORIGINATE?

Public opinion isn't formed out of thin air. We are not born with a ready-made political culture, a distinct political ideology, or precise ideas about human nature, the individual, equality, or democratic government. Opinions develop through a complex interaction among people's life experiences—in their families, at school, at church, at work, at leisure—and their experiences as American citizens, men or women, members of racial groups or of distinct religious or ethnic communities. Public opinion is also forged in response to national and international events—scandals, economic depressions, and most recently the post-9/11 climate—and people's collective and individual experiences of each of them. The formation of individual opinions is thus a lifelong process, often involving choice, change, and learning.

Chapter 6 discusses the mass media's impact on people's specific opinions. Here we concentrate on the broader views of politics and public life and how they are shaped.

Political Socialization

Basic views of the political and social order and of other people are formed quite early in life through a process called **political socialization**. In the impressionable years through age eighteen, basic political orientations concerning race, class, ideology, nationhood, and democracy are formed. Most of these orientations help to form specific opinions later on in adulthood. However, most children and adolescents lack opinions about specific government actions and policies.

The family is an important shaper of people's opinions later in life. Through parents and relatives, children learn basic orientations toward neighbors, strangers, the world of work, school, and government. The learning that happens may be indirect: Observing a parent or a relative struggling with tax forms or a period of unemployment probably has important but subtle effects on later political attitudes. Religious life may teach forms of morality that are later applied by children to their views about other races, groups, and believers. Family also has an important, but not decisive, influence in the later choice of a political party. Six in ten adult Americans develop the same allegiances to a political party (or nonallegiance, in the case of independents) as their parents.

However, there is reason to believe that the political views of parents do less to shape the political views of the young than they once did. Due to new patterns of increased work and lengthy commuting, many parents nowadays have less time to spend with their children, and consequently exert less influence on future political orientations. In many families, politics has never been much of a discussion topic anyway, and the increased role of media in the lifestyles of the young may further erode parental influence.[25]

Schooling is the second shaper of political orientations, especially of the broad features of political culture. For most people, schools provide the initial exposure to people of different races, creeds, and religions. Grade-school children learn basic civic rituals such as the Pledge of Allegiance and are introduced to highly favorable renditions of U.S. history, complete with biographies of national heroes and heroines. Science and social studies curricula currently teach students about environmental questions and geography. In recent years, multicultural curricula have been designed to teach that America is a land of racial and ethnic diversity. Political socialization in schools also helps to reproduce the social order. For example, numerous studies confirm that noncollege-bound students are treated very differently by teachers and school authorities, reinforcing their working-class status. Often, the treatment is subtle: Routines and regimens in different schools resemble the kind of workplace environment that teachers believe their students will face.

Schooling's specific effects on the political views of precollege-age children are unclear. What is clear is that schools help instill the core beliefs of the American creed. By the time people reach their twenties, many of their political preferences are already formed.

Yet schooling is not always just a way of transmitting the status quo or core political values. People learn from direct experience and are not just passive receptacles of authority. Events—depressions, wars, social protest, and cultural change—have a deep impact on each generation. These **generational effects** can have profound consequences on later politics. People who were adolescents or in their twenties during the onset of the Great Depression broke with their elders and for a long time were the most loyal Democrats in the electorate. Baby boomers, especially those that attended college in the 1960s, broke with many of the views about race, culture, and politics of their parents' generation. While they have become slightly more conservative as they've aged, the experience of many of the participants in social movements continues to strongly shape their current political orientations.[26]

What about young people today? In his massive study of U.S. civic life, Robert Putnam reports that Generation X (those who reached the age of eighteen between the mid-1970s and the mid-1990s) were socialized by their baby-boomer parents, television, and other factors to have a "personal and individualistic view of politics. They came of age in an era that celebrated personal goods and private initiative over shared public concerns." More materialistic, X'ers are less likely to trust other people, contribute money or volunteer time to charity or advocacy work, or engage in political discussions and actions. However, the situation may be changing for Generation Y—people of college age and in their twenties today. In the late 1990s, surveys of college freshmen began to detect an upsurge in political interest among eighteen-year-olds, and the 2004 election witnessed an upsurge in political interest and activity by many young people, especially college students. Y'ers are also more engaged in direct volunteer and advocacy work than their immediate predecessors and are much more concerned with question of economic equity and security, environmental causes, and civil liberties. Such data indicate how it is that change is possible—although the core values of each generation may be in place by the age of eighteen, the specific responses people make to politics are altered through learning and events.[27]

Social Differences and Public Opinion

Political socialization occurs in families and schools. But what seems to matter even more are people's identities and their perceived place in the social hierarchy. Shared conditions, histories, and experiences generate opinion similarities and divisions. How the political world is perceived to work is very much linked to people's social class, race, gender, and religion.

Social Class Differences. Since the advent of democratic governments in many Western countries, class difference has often been the major dividing line both in public opinion and in politics. Scholars and activists disagree about the definition of social class. Is class simply a group with higher or lower income and wealth? Or is it a broader term that includes collective experiences concerning where and how people work, how they are educated, how much schooling they have, and how much control they have over their own lives?

Chapter 3 presents evidence supporting the broader definition of social class. What the upper classes of owners, managers, and many professionals do with their money and how they use their power in economic and political institutions have enormous effects on democracy, culture, and the life chances of others in society. The majority of citizens neither own nor control these institutions. That important fact influences the way they think about politics and other aspects of life. Indeed, it would be surprising if social class did not have effects on people's opinions and political orientations, especially since wealth and income inequality is so pronounced in modern America.[28]

Class matters in public opinion, too, although not as much as one would think given the growing class inequalities in U.S. society. People with incomes below the median, who have not completed college, and who labor in nonprofessional blue- or white-collar jobs feel more vulnerable in the new global corporate economy than do wealthy professionals and managers. They are more likely to favor governmental programs that create jobs, raise the minimum wage, establish standards of occupational safety and health, and prevent corporate downsizing and workplace shutdowns. They are more dissatisfied with conditions in the workplace and are generally in favor of measures that promote universal medical insurance, government aid to education, and tax rates based on the ability to pay. People with incomes and levels of formal education below the median are more concerned about high unemployment than about high inflation. They are also more likely to think favorably about labor unions and unfavorably about corporate behavior than are people with the highest incomes. The gap between working-class and upper-class respondents is particularly large when it comes to support for government-run programs to guarantee universal health care; pensions, including Social Security; and unemployment insurance. In Table 4.3, some of the major differences are displayed.[29]

Class divides American public opinion. Yet it just doesn't make as much of a difference in opinions as it does in many other wealthy capitalist countries. Working-class people elsewhere might be surprised at the relatively high numbers of low-income Americans who oppose many measures that would redistribute wealth and power downward and limit corporate behavior. If American wage earners don't always think like a class, the upper classes generally do. Among owners and managers, there is scant support for measures to redistribute wealth and income.

While opinion divisions about economic equality are less pronounced in America than elsewhere, the classes are very much divided in two areas: Upper-class Americans have a strong sense that their participation in politics matters, and they have high levels of political efficacy. They also place more trust and confidence in the rules of the political system. The contrast with poor and working-class Americans is extreme. These groups have much lower political efficacy; they believe that their participation doesn't make much of a difference, and they tend to have much less trust in politicians and economic institutions. In Chapter 5, we explore further this class gap. Significant variations in voter turnout and political power result from the class divide.[30]

TABLE 4.3

Class Differences in U.S. Public Opinion

Wanting to spend more on	Working Class (%)	Middle Class (%)	Upper Class (%)
Health Care	70	65	49
Education	73	68	70
Retirement Benefits	59	42	27
The Homeless	76	71	59
The Poor	62	51	35
Child Care	57	47	44
Unemployment Assistance	43	28	35

Source: Adapted from Robert Erikson and Kent Tedin, *American Public Opinion*, 6th edition (Boston: Allyn and Bacon, 2001), pp. 84, 172.

Racial Differences. The prominence of racial divisions is one reason that American public opinion is less divided by social class than it is elsewhere. Low-income and vulnerable Americans of all races have often been separated from one another through the elite promotion of racial divisions as a way of blocking working-class solidarity. Historically, the prominence of race divisions in the United States has served to dilute class consciousness, especially among some relatively privileged white wage-earners.

Nearly thirty years after the civil rights revolution, some progress has been made in narrowing racial divisions in public opinion. However, whites and African Americans differ on many, though not all, important political questions. Although the divisions between whites of European origin, Latinos, and Asian Americans are also significant, the black–white split remains more pronounced than any other in public opinion.[31]

Most prominent is division about the nature of, and remedies for, racial discrimination. At one level, great strides have been made over the last three or four decades. On questions concerning equal treatment of blacks and whites in the major public spheres of life, public opinion registers a strong and steady movement of white attitudes from denial to affirmation of racial equality. Today, less than 5 percent of whites favor racial segregation in neighborhoods, workplaces, schools, or other public facilities. Whites reject racist organizations like the Ku Klux Klan in numbers as high as African Americans do, and 95 percent of whites say they would vote for qualified African Americans for the presidency and lesser offices. Very few whites say they oppose sending their own children to schools where black children attend, working in the same office as blacks, or eating in the same restaurants.

Although both whites and blacks oppose segregation in principle, significant differences remain about the sources and remedies for racial discrimination, and the degree to which it exists. About three-quarters of whites think that African Americans are more likely than whites to prefer living on welfare. In addition, overwhelming white opposition to segregation should not be read as unqualified support for integration. Whites almost unanimously find no problem with schools, neighborhoods, and workplaces where some blacks are present. White support for integration decreases when blacks equal or outnumber whites, especially in residential neighborhoods.[32]

Moreover, although big majorities of whites oppose discrimination and support general laws that do so, only a small plurality support specific governmental measures that compel integration in the workplace or in neighborhoods. Most whites are particularly opposed to so-called "race-targeted" programs such as Affirmative Action. Only one-fifth to one-quarter of white adults favor preferential admissions for African-American college applicants, and only one-tenth support preferences for blacks in hiring and promotion.

The views of African Americans about such matters are far different. Most African Americans (61 percent versus 31 percent among whites) from painful personal experience, believe that racial discrimination is an everyday occurrence, not a historical curiosity. The racial gap between whites and blacks is as large as 50 percent when it comes to views about race-targeted programs. Yet it is worth noting that support for such programs has even diminished somewhat among African Americans in the last twenty years. Apparently, more blacks now believe either that government hasn't been very effective or that measures to redress past racial discrimination are no longer necessary.

Apart from opinions about race and race relations, African Americans and whites differ most in their opinions about policies to reduce economic inequalities and, most recently, about the validity of the Iraq invasion and ensuing U.S. occupation. African Americans of all incomes are much more likely to believe that many features of the U.S. political economy are unjust not only for people of their own race, but for many whites and other racial minorities as well. Unique in the American population, high-income African Americans express opinions about economic equality that are remarkably similar to those of low-income blacks. They're even as likely as low-income whites to challenge economic inequalities. However, in terms of support for egalitarian public policies that stress greater government benefits, Latinos surpass African Americans. (See Table 4.4.) The majority of Latinos and African Americans oppose the Iraq War, whereas whites support it by a slender margin (see Table 4.4.)[33]

Given these opinion differences and similarities, how important is race as a dividing line in public opinion? One aspiration of popular democrats has been to bridge racial gaps through greater sharing of the nation's economic resources. Yet many poor and working-class whites may be less supportive of such goals

TABLE 4.4

Opinions of Whites, African Americans, and Latinos (of any race) on Various Issues

	Non-Latino Whites (%)	African Americans (%)	Latinos (%)
Prefer high taxes to support government with more services to low taxes and fewer services	35	43	60
Government rather than private organizations does best job in providing services to people in need	31	36	52
Government should see that people have good jobs and standard of living	42	76	*
Iraq War increases U.S. national security	54	22	44

Sources: Pew Hispanic Center and Kaiser Family Foundation, 2002 National Survey of Latinos; Steven Tuch and Lee Sigelman, "Race, Class, and Black-White Differences," in Narrander and Wilcox, *Understanding Public Opinion* (Washington, D.C.: Congressional Quarterly Press, 1996) pp. 48–49; Washington Post/Univision/TRPI Election Survey of Latinos, 2004; Joint Center for Political and Economic Studies, Focus, November–December, 2004.

* Not surveyed separately.

because they associate some government poverty programs with favoritism toward blacks. However, when it comes to social programs that seem to benefit people of all races, low-income whites, blacks, and Latinos often do express similar views.[34]

Gender Differences. Since the early 1970s, the **gender gap** in public opinion and in voting behavior (see Chapter 7) has sparked a massive amount of commentary. In the 2000 election, the difference between men and women in presidential preference was nearly 20 percent, while in 2004 it had narrowed somewhat to only 8 percent. The birth of the contemporary feminist movement clearly has something to do with now rather long-standing opinion differences based on gender. But much research indicates that the increasing economic independence of women and the perceived economic vulnerability of both genders have also widened the gap. The changing role of parenting has also contributed to the gap, as men and women have developed different expectations about their obligations to children, home, and the workplace. The gender gap is thus not only about women changing their opinions but about change in men's views of the world as well.

Perhaps surprisingly, the gender gap is least evident in opinions about gender equality and women's rights. Majorities of both men and women favor the right to legal abortions in many circumstances and oppose abortion on demand by narrow margins. Nor were there differences between men and women over the proposed Equal Rights Amendment (ERA) in the 1970s and 1980s. Although the amendment failed, similar majorities of both sexes supported it. The opinions of men and women do differ on some feminist issues, however: Women express more support for Affirmative Action, equal pay in the workplace, and legislation regarding sexual harassment.

The gender gap widens over policies on the use of force and violence by the military, the state, criminals, or in the family. Women are much more likely to oppose the use of military force, whether it is in Iraq, Somalia, Haiti, Bosnia, or Kosovo. A bare majority of women are in favor of the death penalty, but they are less supportive of it than men. Women favor gun control by margins of 10 to 15 percent over men. A majority of women, but a minority of men, believe that spanking a child is always wrong.

Women are also somewhat more likely to favor increased support for the weaker members of society, whether they be the ill, the elderly, the homeless, the working poor, or, most particularly, children. They are more inclined than men to favor higher governmental spending for education, the environment, health care, and social welfare. And they are more likely to favor laws that curb the use of pornography.

Significant differences exist among women as well. Single, working women tend to be much more "liberal" and "populist" in their political views than are married women who don't work outside the home. The former provide almost bloc support for Democratic candidates, for instance, while married women are just about evenly divided in their partisan preferences. On a whole number of measures, single women favor equalitarian public policies and are much more likely to support the right to choose, equality for gays and lesbians, and equality in the workplace.[35]

Religious Differences. After the 2004 election, some commentators argued that the "moral values" divide in U.S. society had worked to the advantage of George Bush and the Republicans. Others were more skeptical; Democratic voters see themselves as just as "moral" as GOP supporters.

This much, however, is sure: Views both stemming from religious beliefs and about religion's public role are becoming increasingly important divides in U.S. public opinion and in political discourse. An astounding three-quarters of the American population claim that religion is "very" or "somewhat" important in their lives; nearly half of American adults say that they pray every day; and over 40 percent say they go to religious services weekly. This is a much higher percentage than any other developed democracy, and there is evidence to suggest that people see their religious beliefs as more important than did the public ten years ago. Only 10 percent of Americans profess no religious faith at all. There has also been a slight uptick in the numbers of people who are either evangelical or "born-again" Christians, now about one in five American adults. The U.S. contains a greater religious diversity of religious faiths than ever, and many are more devout than ever. Still, the numbers of people who profess no religious faith and who don't attend church services is also rising. While all these trends are important, it is equally significant that even with the changes the basic religious affiliations of Americans are not radically different than twenty years ago.

One trend, however, is notable: For evangelical white Protestants and their secular and non-churchgoing opposites, religious beliefs (or the absence of them) appear to shape their ideological and political orientations more than at any other time since pollsters have asked these questions in the last twenty years. Increasingly, white evangelical Protestants are more closely linked to the Republicans and identify themselves as political conservatives, while seculars and those who attend church only occasionally are increasingly Democratic and identify with liberal positions on many social issues. Opposition to abortion, pornography, and gay marriage, and advocacy of faith-based social policies and school and public displays of religiosity are of intense interest to evangelicals, while "seculars" are more likely to be pro-choice, against media censorship, and favorable toward legalization of gay marriage. Catholics and mainline Protestants are generally in between these poles or do not consider these issues as particularly relevant to their political orientations.[36]

When it comes to economic issues, white fundamentalist and evangelical Protestants are more likely to take conservative positions as well. They register much greater resistance to domestic spending on health care and to income and wealth redistribution than do mainline Protestants, their black fundamentalist cousins, Catholics, and Jews. Evangelical Christianity is one case where religion has most decidedly acted to reduce class divisions in public opinion, largely because divisions of opinion about morality are generally deemed more important than economic questions. As a result, even low-income white evangelical Protestants have provided majority support for conservative politicians and policies.

Still, the relationship of growing evangelical Christianity with a general conservative trend in public opinion is less than clear. Catholics seem the most torn over questions of traditional family values and toleration, but they show little movement toward the positions or voting patterns of evangelical Christians. Catholics remain generally more liberal on both cultural and economic questions than are evangelical Protestants. For almost all those who are not evangelical Christians, the important point may be that the Christian Right's cultural agenda is just less important to them than other political questions.[37] The extreme views of many evangelical white Protestants can, however, be overstated. Even evangelical Protestants are considerably more tolerant of some aspects of gay rights than they were only fifteen years ago. White fundamentalists strongly oppose gay marriage but are more divided about civil unions. Fully 40 percent believe that a public school teacher's sexual orientation is no cause for dismissal.

However Americans feel about one another and whatever their views about politics, the divisions detailed here contradict the idea that most Americans decide on public issues by simply flipping a coin. Americans are united about many questions, but their gender, class, and race do result in rational and fairly consistent differences about preferred lifestyles, policies, and political ideas. In real life, Americans live as members of groups and communities, not as isolated individuals. Thus, the differences they reveal are long-standing and persistent, not driven by sudden and irrational shifts in mood. What changes we do see— from the emergence of more racially tolerant attitudes among the white population to divides between men and women on various issues—seem to emerge slowly. Far from the bewildered herd of elite democratic fears, the public and its opinions tend to follow the lines of power and inequality in American society.

How public opinion is organized: polls

No matter how rational and rooted it may be, public opinion goes unheard if it is not expressed and is powerless if it is not organized. But who does the organizing? If opinion is organized only by elites, or if the information available to the public is narrow and limited, then public opinion is merely an echo, not an independent voice. On the other hand, if the public has the means to get together, deliberate, and share a wide variety of information, then it fulfills the promise of popular democracy. In Chapters 6, 7, 8, 9, and 10 the important roles of the mass media, political parties, electoral campaigns, interest groups, and social movements are discussed with these questions in mind. Here we discuss the most obvious way in which public opinion is measured and even shaped: polling.

The Potential Tyranny of Polls

These days, polls are the most obvious way in which separate individuals are brought together to form a public. Even the most casual observer of American culture soon discovers that ours is a poll-driven society. The public's opinions on everything from the softness of toilet paper to the quality of marriages is tested; candidates and campaigns change their strategies, and sometimes even how they dress and what they do on vacation, on the basis of polls and surveys. This book uses surveys, as well. A reasonable question, then, is whether polls express or distort public opinion.

George Gallup, the founder of systematic public opinion polling, wrote in 1940 that his invention "means that the nation is literally in one great room. . . . After one hundred and fifty years, we return to the town meeting. This time the whole nation is within the doors." Like many of his successors, Gallup assumed that good surveys are simply a scientific tool to discover what the public really thinks and wants. Most surveys conducted by academics and by reputable national organizations such as the Gallup Organization or the CBS/New York Times poll strive to use neutral and professional methods. Much care is taken to conform to widely accepted standards of sampling, question wording, and answer coding.

To be sure, not all polls nowadays conform to such rigorous standards. Many advocacy polls and push polls, sponsored by interest groups and political candidates, ask loaded questions in order to achieve influence over the person being surveyed or push a larger political agenda in the paid or unpaid media. But for the polling industry, professional standards serve to undermine the credibility of such surveys. From this perspective, the chief problem with polling is limited to its abuses, not its uses.

Yet there may be a broader problem with surveys that goes beyond their scientific rigor. The very act of asking certain questions of separate and distinct individuals and then aggregating all the responses creates public opinion where it otherwise wouldn't exist. In short, polling organizes the public in a particular way that it wouldn't on its own. As such, polling is not only a way of recording opinions but of shaping what's on the political agenda.

What effects might such agenda setting have? Gallup talked of polling as if it were a town meeting. But asking individuals their views from a questionnaire is not at all the same as a meeting. The people interviewed in a typical opinion survey don't know one another, haven't talked with one another, and thus do not necessarily share what Susan Herbst calls a "coherent group identity." They can't listen to others or participate in a debate before they answer, nor can they control how their responses are recorded and used. Nor do people who are surveyed have control over which questions are asked. In most polls, they have no way of telling the sponsors that they think the questions being asked are not the right ones or that the situation is more complex than the surveys allow. Consequently, they can't give the open-ended and qualified answers that constitute independent and thoughtful public opinion in a supposedly democratic society.[38]

Therefore, insofar as polls organize opinion by standing in for the real discussion that is characteristic of the democratic debate, they can be deceptive and manipulative. They become useful to elites in their competition for advantage or, as in advocacy polls, for the interests that have the money and clout to

NEW IDEAS

Can the Public Deliberate? Fishkin's Big Idea

Ordinary polls are supposed to tell us what the public is thinking. Yet when people answer pollsters' questions, they often don't have time to think, nor will they necessarily be paying much attention. Most of all, they don't get to talk to anyone else or read anything before they respond. That's why some academics think that polling is a pseudoscience.

Yet what if people did have time to think and converse? A Stanford University political scientist, James Fishkin, has tested this idea through what he calls a "deliberative poll." The idea is simple: Take a national poll based on a representative sample of the entire U.S. population. Ask about many issues. Then bring a scientific sample of voters to one place, and hold weekly discussions together. Let them question experts, read carefully prepared materials on the issues, and talk among themselves with a neutral moderator present. Make sure that everyone has a chance to talk and ask questions. Then survey them again. After they'd become more informed, would their opinions be any different than they were before?

Throughout the 1990s Fishkin supervised several deliberative polls. In 2004, his own research center and PBS cooperated in both online meetings and in face-to-face encounters in seventeen cities for an hour and fifteen minutes every week for five weeks. The general results? For one, people became much more tolerant of one another. Racial, ethnic, and regional stereotypes broke down. The welfare mother, the truck driver, and the business executive ceased to be abstractions and became human. Generally, people didn't switch their views entirely, but moved towards commonsense solutions to policies and criticisms of the crude stereotypes served up by the media and by politicians.

In the 2004 experiment, the knowledge of participants increased substantially from that of mass public in the control group. While only about half the mass public knew that Iraq had no direct involvement in 9/11, that John Kerry had voted for a resolution authorizing the Iraq War, or that India was the major destination of white-collar jobs outsourced from the U.S., more than three-quarters

finance them. By asking a particular question and not another, polls may artificially increase what scholars call the salience, or priority, of what they do ask, and may reduce a strongly felt minority opinion to a marginal one.

One good example of such uses is the fate of the "Contract with America," the centerpiece of the GOP's platform in the 1994 congressional elections. Supposedly crafted by Republican pollsters, the "Contract" was a ten-point program calling for a balanced budget, term limits for officeholders, lower capital gains taxes, and other such measures. According to GOP pollsters, all the measures were "supported by at least six in ten Americans." According to reporter Frank Greve, however, that just wasn't true: The pollsters had concocted a number of biased and loaded questions, tested them with a few focus groups, asked some of them separately to a sample of Americans, and then pronounced knew these facts after the deliberative poll was taken.

Participants changed their views about a number of issues. Before the deliberative poll, participants believed by a margin of 14 percent that the Iraq War had strengthened national security, while afterward support for this position was about even. Bush's effort to make his first-term tax cuts permanent was supported by a margin of 10 percent before the deliberative poll but afterward was about even because some worried much more about the long-term effects of the budget deficits.

Other deliberative polls had similarly interesting results. In previous deliberative polls, participants emerged from the discussion favoring more government spending on health care, education, and child care, and favored an increase in the minimum wage. But they also favored stricter laws about divorce and efforts to make deadbeat dads pay child support. People came "to the realization that many people weren't making it," Fishkin said. Most of all, participants gained interest in politics and a renewed respect for its possibilities.

Fishkin and fellow political scientist Bruce Ackerman from Yale have proposed making deliberative polls an important and more frequently used practice in U.S. politics, both to increase citizen knowledge and temper the often dubious results of "normal" polls that don't allow people to think or talk before they respond. In their book *Deliberation Day*, they argue that with an investment of only several billion dollars, millions of citizens could be brought together in election years to discuss, debate, and educate themselves before they vote: "Deliberation makes a difference" they argue. Deliberation day could correspond with Presidents' Day and add civic meaning to the holiday. Expensive? "When it comes to citizenship development, we spend almost nothing" they argue. Besides, "Deliberation day will require presidents to rethink their relationship to the steady stream of polling data, and in ways that promote a more reflective relation to the public good."

Sources: Bruce Ackerman and James Fishkin, "Righting the Ship of Democracy," *Legal Affairs*, January–February 2004; Bruce Ackerman and James Fishkin, *Deliberation Day* (New Haven: Yale University Press, 2005); "Online Deliberative Poll Gives Picture of Informed Public Opinion," Center for Deliberative Democracy, Stanford University, October 2004; Steve Berg, "Reaching Common Ground on Volatile Issues," *Minneapolis Star Tribune*, January 26, 1996, p. A1.

that Americans supported the Contract in its entirety. As the Republicans were to learn in 1995, while polling had rocketed the Contract to prominence, it hardly guaranteed its success once these measures were subject to public discussion and scrutiny. Most of the Contract's measures went down to defeat in 1995 and 1996.[39]

When it taps into short-lived changes and immediate dramatic events, polling may only record spasms of mood and not the deeper considerations of the mass public. For that reason, in this book we use long-term trends from the most professional polling organizations in the hopes that these are more accurate. In the "New Ideas" feature box, we detail a different kind of survey, called a **deliberative poll**, which underscores both the democratic potential, as well as the limits, of modern polling.

Conclusion: the sensible public

Elite democracy thrives not on active but on passive public opinion; popular democracy thrives on an active and informed citizenry. U.S. public opinion is not always right, is frequently ill informed about policy details, and is especially subject to "sudden breezes of passion" when aroused by dramatic and rapid presidential acts abroad. Yet there is little evidence to support the elite democratic view of the public as a bewildered herd. Most of the public holds coherent beliefs, many of which are rooted in institutions such as families and schools, as well as in personal and collective experiences. Moreover, public opinion responds to new information and new events by modifying its views, albeit slowly. Public opinion reveals its best qualities when it is free to organize and is exposed to many sources of information about politics. Unfortunately, the workings of elite democracy make the organization and expression of public opinion more difficult than it ought to be. In future chapters of this book, we explain some of the struggles to organize public opinion and the work of the media, interest groups, parties, and social movements in this regard.

Public opinion is sometimes described as a sleeping giant. On a whole host of matters explored in this chapter, public opinion sometimes plays a crucial role in determining public policies and sometimes, probably the majority of cases, it is simply ignored or its meaning is twisted in actual political debate. On important occasions, the giant rouses itself slowly, discovers its own energy and power, and swings into action. The civil rights, women's, and antiwar movements of the 1960s at first faced formidable barriers. Participants were told that they were out of the mainstream, that their views were rejected by most Americans, that people didn't care. For a while, elites could simply ignore these movements. With patience, time, and discussion, each movement came to organize public opinion, carving out for itself a limited public space where its ideas could be disseminated. Yet important trends in public opinion—take, for instance the widespread public belief that health care should be a right or the idea that government has an obligation to ensure that people have enough to eat and a place to live—are simply outside elite political discussion. Just how loud or silent public opinion becomes depends on how it is organized, and just how it is organized has much to do with the power of elite and popular democracy

KEY TERMS

public opinion	conservatism
political culture	populism
equality of condition	communitarianism
equality of opportunity	political socialization
democratic elitism	generational effects
ideology	gender gap
liberalism	deliberative poll

INTERNET RESOURCES

▦ Public Agenda
www.publicagenda.org
An outstanding source for all kinds of polling data, along with helpful assessments about how to critically analyze surveys.

▦ Pew Research Center for the People and the Press
www.people-press.org
Independent opinion research group that conducts surveys about popular perceptions of the media, public policy issues, and public figures. Known also for its in-depth analyses of electoral divisions.

▦ Gallup Poll
www.gallup.com
The site of the United States' oldest continuing polling organization, with up-to-date surveys on contemporary issues.

SUGGESTED READINGS

Robert Erikson and Kent Tedin, *American Public Opinion*, 6th ed. Boston: Allyn and Bacon, 2001. An exhaustive and comprehensive account of the social science findings on the subject.

Susan Herbst, *Reading Public Opinion: How Political Actors View the Democratic Process*. Chicago: University of Chicago Press, 1998. A fascinating account of how elites misread and misinterpret public opinion, mistaking it for what the media and key interest groups assert.

Susan Herbst, Carroll Glynn, Garrett O'Keefe, Robert Shapiro, and Mark Lindeman, *Public Opinion*. Boulder: Westview Press, 2002. Provides historically and theoretically rich essays about the nature of U.S. public opinion, with substantial discussion of the role, possibilities, and limits of democratic deliberation.

Walter Lippmann, *The Phantom Public*. New York: Harcourt Brace Jovanovich, 1925. A classic work on the emergence of modern public opinion and the problems it presents.

CHAPTER

5

Where Have All the Voters Gone?

In early 2005, occupied Iraq held its first election since Saddam Hussein had been ousted from power. Utterly new to voting and beset by an insurgency against the election in three of its major provinces, Iraqis turned out at a rate of 58 percent. While this result seemed heartening in light of the circumstances, many observers warned that with more than four in ten eligible citizens absent from the polls, the political legitimacy of the new Iraqi government was in jeopardy.

Three months before, Americans went to the polls in the most expensive and most bitterly fought election in recent history. There was no civil war, the country was not under occupation, and the U.S.'s electoral machinery had been in place for over two centuries. After Election Day, commentators trumpeted that the election was among the most participatory in our recent history, as turnout did rise. Still, what's remarkable is this: the 2004 U.S. presidential election brought to the polls about the same proportion of eligible voters as in beleaguered Iraq. In the world's "model" democracy, more than four in ten eligible voters don't vote, and millions of others are not even eligible due to other restrictions.

Is nonvoting a problem? In this chapter, evidence is presented that links the phenomenon of nonvoting to many practices and beliefs associated with elite democracy and rule. Many of these practices emerged as ongoing controversies in the exceptional election of 2000. It was the first in over a century where the popular vote winner was denied the presidency and where voter registration and the counting of votes were hotly contested.

Yet despite its peculiarities, the 2000 election was not an exception. It just helped to bring into public consciousness countless features of U.S. elections that, either new or old, have served to discourage and retard widespread citizen participation and encourage nonvoting. These practices range from "winner-take-all elections," to electoral districts that prevent candidate and party competition, to the act of registration itself and the sometimes disturbing behavior of local elections officials, who in the United States exercise tremendous power and can disenfranchise thousands by their actions. To some, these practices can be seen as separate and unrelated accidents or just outmoded vestiges of a less-than-glorious past. To others, though, they fit into a larger story, sustaining the idea that a big electorate is feared by the powerful. Subtly or clearly, widespread political participation is seen as a danger rather than an asset.

In this chapter, we attempt to solve a mystery: Why do many people experience overwhelming obstacles to voting when it is enshrined as the key feature of our democracy? Why don't more people vote? Who benefits and who is hurt when massive numbers of people either stay away from the polls or whose votes aren't counted?

In Chapters 7 and 8, we address these questions in the specific context of the organization of political parties and contemporary campaigns. Here, however, we address this essential puzzle. In both 2000 and 2004, much attention was paid to how votes are counted. Yet why is it that with all the turmoil, there was little mention of a long-standing fact? Half of Florida's—and the nation's—eligible citizens didn't even show up at the polls in 2000. In off-year congressional elections, like in 1998, only a little more than one-third of eligible citizens voted. In 2004, turnout improved, and the vote count seemed largely honest. Yet more than four in ten people still didn't show at the polls. How come?

The nonvoting mystery deepens when a few other facts are noted: Nonvoting has generally increased even though Americans are more educated than they were forty years ago. Nonvoting has also risen even though overtly racist barriers to registration were toppled in the 1960s and even though it is generally easier to register to vote now than it was four decades ago.

In this chapter we attempt to solve the mystery of nonvoting by examining both elite and popular democratic explanations for low participation in this most basic of democratic acts. If we solve this mystery, then it may help to answer other questions as well. If Americans came to the polls in larger numbers, what might change about our polity and economy? Who benefits and who loses from low turnout in elections? What could be done to change the situation? As the most glaring defect of contemporary U.S. democracy, massive nonvoting needs to be explained through the lens of popular and elite democracy.

THE MYSTERIOUS FACTS ABOUT NONVOTING

First, the facts about nonvoting need to be set out. As Figure 5.1 shows, voter turnout in America declined sharply in the early twentieth century, recovered somewhat with the onset of the Great Depression up until 1960, and declined again for thirty-two years thereafter. Since 1992, it has risen and dipped, with the 2004 election representing a perhaps significant jump upward. The twists and turns can't disguise an undeniable fact: Americans vote in smaller numbers than they once did, and the situation isn't getting much better over time.

Figure 5.1 deals only with presidential elections. Generally, they provoke the highest turnout of any contests. Off-year congressional and state races have much lower turnout rates. Figure 5.2 displays participation rates for recent off-year elections.

FIGURE 5.1   **Voter Turnout in Presidential Elections, 1884–2004**

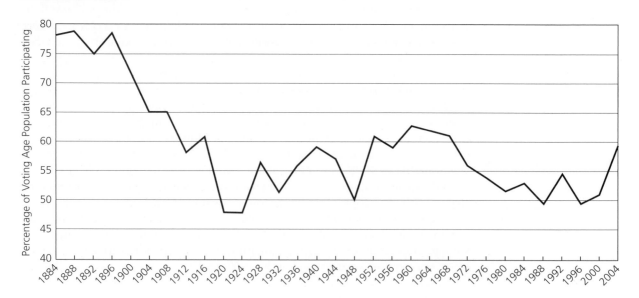

Sources: For 1860–1928: Bureau of the Census, *Historical Statistics of the United States, Colonial Times to 1970*, part 2, 1071; 1932–1944: *Statistical Abstract of the United States, 1992*, 517; 1948–2000: Michael P. McDonald and Samuel L. Popkin, "The Myth of the Vanishing Voter," *American Political Science Review* 95 (December 2001): table 1, 966. For 2004, Committee for the Study of the American Electorate, November 11, 2004, adjusted to voting age population as denominator.

Note: Turnout in this graph is percentage of voting age population.

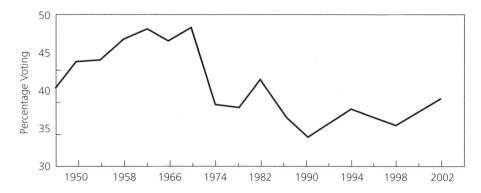

Sources: Federal Election Commission; George Mason University, United States Election Project. Data are based on voting age population.

Party primaries held to nominate candidates for public office draw even fewer voters. In the highly contested 1992 presidential primaries, 32.5 million voters, or less than one-sixth of the voting-age population, turned out to nominate the major party candidates. In 1996, party primary voting was even lower, dropping to 14 million for the highly competitive Republican primaries. In the 2004 Democratic primaries, one of the most contested in recent times, only 15.7 million voters came to the polls, a small fraction of the eventual vote for nominee John Kerry in the November general election.[1]

Local elections for mayor, city council, school boards, and the like are usually not held at the same time as state and national elections. For that reason, participation rates are generally the lowest of the low. More typically, about 10 percent to 25 percent of the voting-age population comes to the polls in the big city elections of Los Angeles, New York, Houston, and elsewhere.

The enormous size of the nonvoting population casts doubt on the "mandates" so often claimed by newly elected presidents and members of Congress. In 1992 and 1996, President Clinton defeated his opponents by convincing margins but in both years never received the votes of more than one in four adult citizens. Clinton's total is far less than the proportion received by 1936 Republican presidential nominee Alf Landon, who was crushed by Franklin Roosevelt in a historic victory. In 1994, Republicans took over Congress and claimed the people's support for the Contract with America. Yet the revolutionary Republicans received the votes of less than one-fifth of the voting-age population—hardly a mandate for long-term change. George W. Bush, who didn't even receive a plurality among those who did vote, has an even weaker claim to a mandate when it is observed that he received the support of less than one-quarter of U.S. adults in 2000 and less than one-third in 2004.

What sorts of people do and do not vote? The U.S. Census Bureau provides some interesting answers to this question in its post-election reports. Table 5.1 looks at the 2000 presidential election, comparing the voting participation rates of those Americans *most* likely to vote with those *least* likely to vote.

Four major social characteristics capture the vast social divide between those who vote the most and the least: age, income, race, and education.

People of non-European descent, with less formal schooling, and who are younger and poorer than the norm tend to vote the least in America. Voting participation among Latinos has recently increased but is still much lower than the general population. (See the "Making a Difference" feature box in this chapter.) Among African Americans there have been notable increases in 1984, 1988, and again in 2000, but blacks still lag somewhat behind whites in national participation rates. Asian-American voting rates have risen in some cases but still don't come close to equaling rates for Caucasians.

Yet race, ethnicity, education, and income aren't the whole story. Since 1960, almost *all* varieties of Americans, including highly educated and wealthy whites, vote less. And the most dramatic decline in voting turnout is among America's "new" working class—people who work in service occupations like the retail trades or as hospital orderlies, janitors, secretaries, and the fast-food industry. Below, more will be said about why this group, so increasingly numerous in the population, is declining among the active electorate.

TABLE 5.1				
Which Groups Vote the Most and Which the Least? The 2000 Presidential Election	**Groups Most Likely to Vote**	**Percent Turnout**	**Groups Least Likely to Vote**	**Percent Turnout**
	+$75,000 annual income	70.1	<$15,000 annual income	35.1
	People with advanced degrees	76.4	No high school diploma	34.0
	People ages 65–74	67.7	People ages 18–24	31.6
	Homeowners	60.2	Renters	39.3
	People currently employed	65.9	Unemployed	35.3
	Non-Hispanic whites	56.0	Hispanics	40.6
	Married, living with spouse	63.2	Never married	39.5
	Five years at same address	67.9	Less than one year at same address	38.0

Percentages are of voting eligible citizens, adjusted to reflect average overreporting by respondents sampled (–4.5%).

Author's note: Census data on the 2004 election will be released in February 2006.

Source: U.S. Census Bureau, "Voting and Registration in the Election of 2000: Population Characteristics," February 2002.

To sum up, people of all races, educational levels, ages, and income are voting less, and many are voting much less. At the same time, the huge gap between races, generations, educational levels, and social classes remains.

All this translates into some quite odd disparities within metropolitan areas, between inner cities and outer suburbs. In America's central cities, neither the Democrats, Republicans, nor independents are a majority—the "party of nonvoters" is. In Bedford Stuyvesant, Brooklyn, 90,000 voters elected Major Owens to Congress in 2004, even though there were more than 350,000 potentially eligible citizens. Less than thirty miles away, in the northern suburbs of much wealthier and whiter Westchester, Putnam, and Dutchess counties, 238,000 voters from a potential 400,000 elected a conservative Republican to office in the same year.[2] The overall decline of voting participation nationwide also disguises some important differences between regions. Generally, Southern states have witnessed a rise in voting participation since 1960, mostly due to the civil rights movement and the enfranchisement of millions of African-American voters. It is the northeastern, midwestern, and western states that have experienced quite steep drops.

What is remarkable is that voter turnout has not always been so low. Over a hundred years ago, in 1888, voting turnout was at its highest in the republic's history. Although high turnout was sometimes due to illegal and corrupt practices, like paying people to vote, there is still no question that citizens voted in greater numbers regardless of their race, education, social class, or age than they do these days. (In 1888, women couldn't vote.) Since 1888, the proportion of nonvoters and voters has fluctuated, but it has never come very close to the earlier standard. Clearly, one's social class, age, race, and educational level have not always made a difference. A century ago, many very rich people worried because they voted proportionally less than the poor. Yet for some reason all these characteristics matter much more than previously.[3] Some say that the decline in voting is associated with the increasing modernization of our country and the general prosperity of the American people. As people become more satisfied with private life, they are said to have fewer reasons to get excited about politics. With the temptations of consumer items, the pressures of work and raising a family, and the diversions of vacations and the mass media, many people just don't have the time or enough reasons to go out and vote.

Yet it seems curious that those who have the fewest reasons to be satisfied— people with low incomes or insecure jobs and the unemployed—are the most likely to stay away from the polls, while those with high levels of income and education turn out in fairly large, though also declining, numbers. It also seems strange that other very modern and wealthy countries like Japan, Sweden, France, and Germany have much higher participation rates than does the United States. While the U.S. government may pursue policies that stress its unique role as an exporter of "freedom" and "democracy" abroad, the prominence of American nonvoting is sobering. As Table 5.2 shows, the United States in fact ranks next to last in voting participation in comparison with other advanced industrial democracies and even is close to last among all countries that hold democratic elections.

TABLE 5.2

Voter Turnout (in percentage) in the World's Wealthiest Democracies, National Presidential or Parliamentary Elections, 1996–2001

Belgium	83.2	Japan	59.0
Australia	81.8	United Kingdom	57.6
Italy	77.0	Canada	54.6
Germany	75.3	**United States (2000)**	51.0
Norway	73.0	Switzerland	34.9
France	72.3		

Source: The International Institute for Democracy and Electoral Assistance, www.idea.int.

ELITE DEMOCRATIC THEORIES OF NONVOTING

There is clearly something peculiar and even mysterious about the current voting participation rates of Americans. Historically, we have had higher participation rates, and the United States once led the world in its enfranchisement of large numbers of citizens. At least if history and foreign experience are any guide, the currently high rates of American nonvoting are apparently not "natural." How, then, can nonvoting on such a massive scale be explained?

There are many schools of thought about why so many Americans fail to vote and even more about this situation's implications. They follow the lines established by the elite and popular democratic currents in American political life.

Nonvoting: Why Worry?

For elite democrats, nonvoting is generally not a problem of the political system but of the people in it. Some people lack the interest that is necessary for politics, others the knowledge to participate. Some are just too busy with personal affairs, while others get easily confused by all the complexity. In short, many people might just not be smart enough to participate in politics.

A rather crude example of this position was a poster of one pro-Bush protestor in Palm Beach, Florida, during the 2000 post-election recount. In that county, up to 25,000 elderly citizens confronted a confusing ballot and mistakenly punched the hole for Pat Buchanan, the Reform Party candidate. Trying to correct their mistake, they punched another hole for Al Gore and thus became nonvoters, as their votes were discarded by election officials. One opinion of this whole process was portrayed on the poster: "If you're too stupid to read a ballot, you're too stupid to vote."

ABC commentator and columnist George Will has captured the essentials of a more sophisticated elite democratic argument. "The fundamental human right," Will claims, is not to the vote, but to "good government." To Will, there is no necessary relationship among good government, American democracy, and high rates of voting participation. Why, Will asks, should people who are more interested in watching TV soap operas be urged to vote at all, and why should we be sad if they don't? Will argues that higher voter turnout could be dangerous for democracy. Many people who now don't vote are ignorant and ill informed, and bringing them to the polls would only worsen matters. Will also fears the passions of a highly mobilized but generally ignorant citizenry. As evidence, he recalls Germany's Weimar Republic of the 1920s. Germans turned out in high numbers, but the ultimate result was extraordinary polarization, the kind of extreme divisions that led to Nazi Party victories.[4]

Few elite democratic explanations are as blunt as Will's. For instance, scholarly studies emphasize the psychology of nonvoters in order to understand their abstention. Many studies confirm Will's views: Nonvoters are less interested in political issues, don't follow campaigns all that closely, and are less likely to believe that their participation will make a difference. Moreover, nonvoters usually have less formal education than do voters. All in all, nonvoters therefore lack **political efficacy**—the idea that they can have an impact if they do participate. Instead of just noticing that there is a relationship between all these factors and nonvoting, these writers argue that one tends to cause the other.

Nonvoting can thus be seen as a natural product of a person's individual attributes: Because of their lack of formal schooling, nonvoters can't figure out complex political issues, get contradictory bits of information, and can't even figure out how to register or where to vote. For most, the argument goes, voting just isn't worth the effort.[5]

Nonvoters: A Crisis in Morals?

In recent years, elite democratic intellectuals have developed a related explanation for both nonvoting and what they see as corrosive forces at work in popular culture. While embracing the preceding explanations, they place the blame on the "swollen government" produced by misguided New Dealers, 1960s liberals, and the culture of dependency on government both are said to have created. Government, and especially the welfare state, has assumed too many of the functions once left to **civil society**—individuals, communities, churches, charities, and businesses that operate independently of government and that nurture self-sufficiency and community. The result is that people get lazy and expect government to do for them what they once did for themselves. Government welfare payments and other forms of aid sap the independence that once prompted people to join community groups and get involved in the kinds of local activities that lead to voting and other forms of political participation. In this account, nonvoting is just one symptom of a larger breakdown in social norms and values that used to keep order and hold the country together. To *U.S. News & World Report* editor Michael Barone, participation will increase when America becomes "lightly governed, because government leaves to voluntary associations many kinds of social functions that elsewhere and at other times have been performed by the state."[6]

Blaming Nonvoters

The logical consequence of elite democratic thinking about nonvoting is that uneducated people may vote and we ought to even encourage them to do so. But if they don't, it is understandable and no real cause for alarm or dismay—in fact, it may even have some hidden blessings. From this perspective, nonvoting cannot really be blamed on defects in the dominant political and economic arrangements.

Scholars and commentators of the elite democratic school share many of the same assumptions about human nature with the earlier approaches pioneered by the Federalists. Then and now, elite democrats start with the premise that if ordinary people participate in politics, they are likely to be only interested in eroding liberty and engendering tyranny—the participation of the ignorant is not altogether welcome. Yet if people don't participate, they are blamed for their apathy or, more recently, overdependence on government aid. Given the natural differences in talents and interests, some people are just more interested in politics than others. And it may be just as well that more affluent and educated people are more likely to vote and participate in public affairs. After all, they are more attuned to the subtleties of political issues. In Will's words, "Thought must be given to generating a satisfactory (let us not flinch from the phrase) governing class. That there must be a class is, I think, beyond peradventure." Nonvoting is thus not a problem, because it allows such a "governing class" to form.[7]

POPULAR DEMOCRATS AND NONVOTING

While elite democrats worry when too many unqualified people come to the polls, popular democrats are concerned that the promise of democracy is being shortchanged by both new and old ways in which active citizenship is repressed and discouraged. From this perspective, nonvoting is not an attribute of abstract human nature and the supposed deficient psychology of ordinary citizens. Rather, it is a product of laws, procedures, and practices that limit voter choice and place formidable obstacles in the face of active citizens. The American historical record is full of frank attempts to limit the kinds of people who vote and to limit the choices of those who do vote and thus suppress voter interest and organization. More often than not, racial, ethnic, and class divisions and inequality in the United States have translated into laws that make it difficult for ordinary citizens to organize themselves and vote. Sometimes these obstacles have been overcome, and an expanding electorate has resulted.

While it might be comforting to believe that most of the formal legal impediments to registration and voting have been removed, nonvoting remains high in America because, in the words of historian Alexander Keyssar, "Democracy is not a fixed set of rules and institutions but rather a permanent project that demands ongoing effort and vigilance on the part of any nation's citizenry."

Keyssar's words may be as relevant now as they were throughout most of U.S. history. Below, we examine what might be called the **structural obstacles** that impede voting.[8]

The Registration Problem

Almost alone among the citizens of Western nations, each American is personally responsible for the sometimes complicated process of registering to vote. Most of us just take for granted that we are responsible for locating the local board of elections, finding a registration form online, and completing it correctly. When we move, as Americans often do, we are responsible for reregistering if we want to vote again and then locating the right voting place on Election Day. If we don't vote in one presidential election, we're often responsible for reregistering, too. If we are not home on Election Day, it's up to us to apply for an absentee ballot or, in some states, vote on another day.[9]

The system of modern personal registration is a descendant of a dark and undemocratic past. It is one of the vestiges of frank attempts to "purify" the electorate by removing "undesirable" elements. From the 1890s onward through the mid-1960s, white elites in the South used personal registration laws and much more draconian laws to prevent African Americans from voting. **Jim Crow laws** mandated strict segregation between the races. In terms of voting, blacks were subjected to such measures as poll taxes and highly discretionary "literacy tests" administered by segregationist county officials, and often to outright terror and intimidation. The result was an almost total elimination of blacks from the electorate of southern states; only the civil rights movement broke the back of Jim Crow. In the North, registration laws were introduced in many northern cities to prevent voter fraud. But the motive was also less honorable: Registration laws and other means were used to "cleanse" the electorate of urban immigrants and working-class voters by subjecting the process to state control; potential voters would often be purged from the rolls if they didn't vote in a single election, and registration forms were often invalidated for minor errors, or none at all.[10]

Jim Crow is now gone (see below for why), and registration has been made easier by the Voting Rights Act of 1965 and subsequent legislation. Still, the American system of **personal registration** favors those who aren't intimidated by the sometimes cumbersome and time-consuming registration process. To make things more complicated, each state and sometimes particular counties often have different forms and procedures for registering, and thousands of these counties often apply quite onerous and particular criteria to make things difficult for potential voters. In one Florida county in 2004, thousands were disenfranchised because they had not checked a box on the form verifying their U.S. citizenship, even though elsewhere on the form they'd already signed an affidavit to that effect. In some areas and states, voter registration forms in which an "i" is not dotted or a "t" is not crossed are still invalidated by elections officials.

In most other countries, the situation is quite different, and higher voter turnout is the result. National governments are responsible for making sure that citizens are registered and that they can vote. In Britain and Canada, officials monitor who has moved and who has not for the purpose of keeping voter lists up to date. In Italy, registration is not even an issue, because the possession of a national identity card is enough. And in Belgium and Australia, minor penalties are exacted on those who do not vote.

There is no doubt that duplicating these methods in the United States would raise levels of voting participation. We know that the vast majority of people in the United States who are registered to vote actually *do* vote, so making registration a governmental responsibility would boost turnout. Voter registration was originally part of an effort to depress turnout, so it makes sense that doing away with the system would boost voting levels.

Analysts agree that changing registration laws and voting procedures (by changing Election Day to a Sunday, allowing registration on election day as six states already do, or establishing Internet voting, as Oregon has) would probably raise American turnout. At the national level and in most states, though, Republicans have generally resisted registration reform, whereas many, but hardly all, Democrats have generally favored it for partisan reasons. Republicans tend to believe that easing registration requirements would bring to the polls more Democrats, who still predominate among low-income citizens.[11]

With Republican George Bush's defeat in 1992, Congress finally passed and President Clinton signed a watered-down version of the so-called "motor voter" bill. It mandated that registration forms and voter assistance be available in motor vehicle and other government offices and that mail-in registration be allowed in all states. In order to get majority support, the original provision calling for the *automatic* registration of all people who apply for drivers' licenses or public assistance was dropped. The new law produced a modest but important rise in voter registration; an estimated 11 million registrants were added to the national electorate by the 1996 election, and registration surged again before the 2000 and 2004 elections, partly as a result of the 2002 Help America Vote Act (HAVA). Among other reforms, HAVA urged, but did not require states to establish uniform standards for registration lists.

By itself, increased registration didn't lead to increased turnout. In 2000 and especially 2004, concerted campaigns to register and then turn out new voters, did seem to be linked to slightly higher turnout rates.

As a one-shot solution for massive nonvoting, registration reform has some advantages but also some limitations. Taken together, most analysts say that a combination of *all* the measures, including automatic registration, would probably boost actual voter turnout by only about 5 percent to 10 percent. There would be bigger turnout, and in close elections like the 2000 and 2004 contests, the changes could make a huge difference in the results. Even so, the most optimistic predictions about voter registration would only bring turnout back to what it was in 1960, a year when registration laws were quite tough. Under the most radical proposals, 10 or 15 million more people would come to the polls in future elections. While this is a very significant number, it would still mean that American turnout rates in the twenty-first century would be lower than in the nineteenth century, with affluent and better-educated voters still dominant.[12]

Registration reform would help increase voter turnout. But it is only a partial solution to the mystery, because voter turnout in the United States outside the South has been declining *even as* easier registration procedures have been introduced in most states and by the federal government. After all, voter turnout today is far lower than in 1940 and 1960, years when voter registration was much more complicated and blatantly racist. The fact remains that other explanations are needed to explain why, in the face of so much attention to the difficulties of personal registration, voting turnout continues to be so low.[13]

What National Election?

During the dramatic recount of Florida's votes after the 2000 election, Katherine Harris, the Republican secretary of state of Florida, became a well-known and controversial figure. Harris, now a Republican congresswoman from Florida, served as a co-chair of the Bush–Cheney election effort and at the same time as the official in charge of administering Florida's election laws. It was Harris's office that had directed the controversial—many would say grotesquely unfair—process by which voter registration lists were compiled, election workers trained (or not), and the vote count supervised in all of Florida's counties. Among other problematic acts, she'd hired a private company to list and help disenfranchise Florida's felons, who were legally disenfranchised by state law. Unfortunately (or by design), the company delivered a list that struck from the voting rolls not only former felons but everyone who had the same name as any felon. By coincidence or design, Harris's action probably disenfranchised over 40,000 registered voters in November, the vast majority of them African American or Hispanic and likely to vote Democratic had they been registered. To many observers, Harris's actions cost the Democrats the election in Florida and thus determined that Bush would become the next president by Supreme Court ruling.[14]

Vilified and praised, depending on one's politics, Harris was nonetheless hardly exceptional. In the U.S., the officials in states and counties administer election laws. Virtually all of them are partisan officials, chosen not because of their expertise or competence, with a direct or indirect stake in the outcome of the elections they supervise. No doubt, most of these officials try to conduct elections "fairly," and their actions can be tested in state courts. Still, when state and county officials are given free rein to interpret and administer a varied and complex set of state laws at their own discretion, distortions and abuses are bound to develop in many locales, and fraud is as well. In the past, "Jim Crow" was administered by hundreds of local elections officials tied to the segregationist and lily-white Southern Democratic parties. They used their discretion to make it impossible for black citizens to register. Nowadays, with the discretion that such officials possess, they can decide on registration procedures, they can decide the location of polling places, on how many voting machines are available and their reliability, and they supervise the counting of votes (and those controversial "hanging chads").

The result is a crazy quilt of different ballot designs, dissimilar voting machines, and different registration forms and counting procedures. In closely

fought contests, what these officials do really matters. As mentioned above, Katherine Harris hired an outside consulting firm that struck thousands of citizens from the voting rolls because they had the same names as convicted felons, probably changing the election result in the process. In Palm Beach County, a Democratic county official designed the infamous "butterfly ballot" that led thousands to cast more than one vote for president, and thus "spoil" their ballots. In 2004, the secretaries of state overseeing elections in three battleground states were co-chairs of the Bush campaign.

This process promotes nonvoting by undermining popular trust in the procedures, even in the absence of outright fraud. Election officials are largely unaccountable if they provide untrained election workers or inadequate voting machines in electoral precincts of their political opponents, as routinely happens in many of America's biggest cities. And in both the 2000 and 2004 elections, the maze of different practices implemented by local officials certainly produced questionable practices—long lines in heavily Democratic Cleveland, Ohio, and untrained electoral officials in thousands of precincts throughout the country.[15]

What Right to Vote?

The discretion and partisanship of thousands of elections officials is made possible by the silence of the U.S. Constitution on the most crucial democratic right, the right to vote itself. There is no explicit guarantee of the right to vote in the country's primary document, and as a result elections laws—with the exception of the Voting Rights Act—are left to the states. That's why in the historic December 2000 Supreme Court decision of *Bush v. Gore*, ultraconservative Justice Antonin Scalia could remind Americans that the right to select electors who in turn selected the president was not given to the people directly but to the states and their legislatures. As political theorist Ronald Dworkin has written, "The Constitution's design was rooted in an elitism which is no longer tolerable" because "the point of elections is to determine and reflect the people's will." Without such an explicit right, the conduct and administration of federal elections will continue to be characterized by a multiplicity of questionable practices puzzling to interested citizens. Among the most egregious are the maze of distinctive laws that serve to disenfranchise an estimated 4 million former felons, who have served their time but are still denied the franchise. So too were the votes of 2 to 4 million people whose votes were "spoiled" due to nonfunctioning voting machines or confusing ballot design.[16]

The Electoral College: Your Vote Doesn't Matter

As Americans learned in 2000, the Constitution's silence about the right to vote is compounded by its disdain for direct popular election of the nation's Chief Executive. The president is elected through the Electoral College system, which requires a majority of the 540 electors chosen by the states and their electoral procedures. In Chapter 7, we'll explain the Electoral College in more detail. Here, what is important was made crystal clear by Election 2004: The campaign for president was limited to twenty so-called "battleground" states where the candidates appeared, the campaign ads were run, and the party and other organizations mobilizing the vote worked. If you voted in Texas, California, New York, or twenty-seven other states deemed "safe" for either Bush or Kerry, then you and your interests were pretty much ignored by both campaigns. Not surprisingly, turnout increases in the battleground states exceeded the safe states by a margin of 2–1.[17]

Winner-Take-All Elections

With just a few exceptions, American elections are won by the candidates who receive one vote more than their opponents. To win any representation, a candidate or a new political party must defeat candidates of the two established parties. As a consequence, many voters and potential voters are in effect limited to the two choices presented by the two established parties and their candidates. That's the reason why Ralph Nader and his Green Party voters were blamed for handing the election to George Bush in 2000. The "winner-take-all-the-power" method also applies to the Electoral College—receive a plurality of the vote in any state and you get all the electoral votes of that state (two exceptions are Maine and Nebraska, which apportion electoral votes by congressional district).

Even if you win one-fifth of the popular vote, as did Ross Perot in 1992, you get no votes in the Electoral College at all.

While this way of conducting elections may seem normal to most Americans, it is not the practice in many other countries, which provide for some means to effectively widen voter choice and thereby maximize voter participation and power. Some have **proportional representation** systems, where seats in the legislature are apportioned on the basis of the percentage of the vote received by a political party. Others have two-round or "instant" runoff systems, where voters choose a first and a second preference, and the two top candidates then face off until one gets a plurality. Such systems, unlike our own, encourage voter participation by promoting parties and candidates that reflect all points of view and groups in the citizenry.

Noncompetitive Elections

When Americans vote for the supposedly most representative body of the federal government, the House of Representatives, they generally vote in electoral districts carefully crafted by state legislators intent on preserving the status quo. The redistricting of House seats has produced, in effect, a representative body that is fixed in advance and not subject to voter choice. Ninety-eight percent of all U.S. House incumbents won reelection in 2004, and of that number 95 percent were won by noncompetitive margins. Only a tiny proportion of House elections represented genuine competition between candidates. "Orphaned" voters—those stuck as permanent minorities within rigged legislative districts have few incentives to organize, and potential voters have few reasons to come to the polls if the outcome is virtually fixed in advance.

The practices just discussed are only the tip of the non-voting iceberg. Take, for instance, the problems new immigrants face when they try to become U.S. citizens. Between 2000 and 2004, Latino immigration to the U.S. has swollen, but participation rates have not kept pace for the simple reason that undocumented workers and even long-term legal residents face huge obstacles to the acquisition of citizenship and voting rights. One half of total U.S. population growth between 2000 and 2004 was due to Latino immigrants, but Latinos accounted for only one-tenth of the increase in the number of votes cast in 2004.[18]

Taken together, American institutions and practices present both formal and informal obstacles to both voters and potential voters. Yet would it make a difference if some of these practices were changed? And would it really bring out new voters? In part, these are chicken-and-egg questions. We do know that in other countries with different rules, levels of participation are indeed higher, sometimes *much* higher. The "New Ideas" box summarizes some of the major changes proposed by groups and advocates interested in solving the mystery of nonvoting.

At the same time, the structural obstacles discussed above have a long historical lineage in the United States. The Electoral College, the winner-take-all voting system, local control of elections, and other features that depress turnout have all been in place for over two centuries, though other phenomena, such as

NEW IDEAS

Making Votes Count

Better voting machines and clearer ballot design might help election officials count ballots more efficiently. Yet can't more be done to encourage voter participation and increase voter power? Many reforms have been proposed since Election 2000. Here are some of the most provocative.

Increasing Voter Registration and Turnout

- *Same-day voter registration.* In most countries, governments are responsible for compiling eligible lists of voters, and there is no requirement for individual registration. As a first step to reform, why not allow citizens the right to register as they vote? Five of the six states that now do this have the highest voter turnout in the country.
- *Automatic voter registration.* When people get a driver's license, graduate from high school, pay their taxes, buy stamps, or file a change-of-address form in the post office, they are in contact with government. Why not register all such people automatically?
- *Enfranchise people who have served their time.* The United States imprisons a higher percentage of its population than anywhere else in the world, and after felons have served their time, they still can't vote. There are an estimated 4 million former prisoners in the United States, and they are disproportionately African-American and Latino men. If they've served their time, why not let them vote?
- *How about "Democracy Days"?* In almost all wealthy democracies, Election Day is either a holiday or takes place on the weekend so that people don't have to choose between going to work and citizenship. Why not establish "Democracy Days"—two days of balloting scheduled to coincide with Veterans Day, a national holiday in November?

Enriching Democratic Choice

- *Reapportion the Electoral College, and establish proportional representation.* In the United States, winner-take-all elections mean that voters on the "losing" side receive no representation. At the presidential level, this means that all of Florida's twenty-five electoral votes went to George Bush, even though Al Gore got only 527 fewer ballots. House districts are often gerrymandered to the disadvantage of racial and cultural minorities, meaning that they will never be able to elect their own representative. Why not establish a proportional system for the Electoral College and proportional representation for Congress and for state legislatures so that a vote of 10 percent for a political party means 10 percent of the seats?
- *Cross-endorsements and fusion voting.* In most states, candidates can't be endorsed by more than one political party. This discourages third parties and voter choice because it means that voters can't express preference for a candidate and another preference for a party. Why not encourage more choice by allowing third parties to endorse dominant-party candidates?
- *Instant runoff voting.* Voters who don't like the major party candidates often don't vote, because they feel that voting for a third party candidate would be wasting their vote. Why not allow voters to express rank order preference for two candidates when they vote? After the votes are tabulated, the candidate with the most preference votes would be the victor.

Sources: Lani Guinier, "What We Must Overcome," *American Prospect*, March 12–26, 2001; Burt Neuborne, "Reclaiming Democracy," *American Prospect*, March 12–26, 2001; Stephen Hill and Rob Richie, "America: In Search of Electoral Standards," www.TomPaine.com, December 21, 2004.

partisan redistricting to assure safe seats, are more recent. Still, perhaps the mystery of nonvoting is not solved by reference to our institutions alone. There remains the central fact that voter turnout has sometimes been much, much higher, even within these legal and institutional constraints.

Grassroots Politics Matters

The fact that American institutions, laws, and political culture do little to encourage widespread voting may not be the only explanation for massive nonvoting. Even if some or all these constraints on participation were removed, perhaps voter turnout would still be relatively low. One reason may be the class and age biases that are so evident in the nonvoter/voter divide. For popular democrats, what is particularly worrisome is that the kinds of people who don't vote are often those who are the most vulnerable to elite power, whether it be exercised through government or through control of the corporate economy. The majority of nonvoters tend to be the least able to secure decent education for their children, and the least likely to have secure job prospects, and are the most powerless when it comes to control over the other major forces that shape their lives. Their powerlessness seems both confirmed and compounded by their political inactivity. If large proportions of low- to middle-income people stay home on Election Day, policies are decided on by people who are wealthier, less racially diverse, and older than the general American adult population. Elite democratic thinkers don't see this as much of a problem because they believe that current nonvoters are often uneducated and unmotivated. For popular democrats, however, a major question is this: If changing registration laws and other practices wouldn't bring many of these nonvoters to the polls, what would?

One response comes from U.S. history. Historically, voter turnout rises when people with little political power form strong social and community groups that lead to their collective power and to politics. For example, in the 1880s and 1890s the farmers of the Great Plains and rural South were economically poor and relatively uneducated—on the whole much more so than today's working class nonvoters. According to elite democratic ideas about nonvoting, "ignorant" and even illiterate farmers shouldn't have been active in politics at all. Yet over time, due to a strong network of religious and civic associations, they formed "farmers alliances" to purchase and market their farm produce and to pool their resources to gain cheaper credit than distant banks provided. The alliances were originally nonpolitical and nonpartisan, and they provided a framework for otherwise isolated farm families to meet, socialize, talk, and have a good time. But the alliances eventually evolved into Populism, one of the strongest political and social movements in U.S. history. Throughout the 1890s and into the early twentieth century, the Populist Party and its allies turned farmers and rural people into active voters, boosting participation in local elections to historic highs.

A more recent and telling example contradicting elite democratic ideas about nonvoters is provided by the southern civil rights movements of the 1950s and 1960s. During this period, African Americans organized themselves against the system of white domination and Jim Crow laws that had been in force since the turn of the century. Aided by a strong community of churches and by white and black students and supporters from the North, southern blacks took on the system of racial apartheid through boycotts, sit-ins, marches, and prayer vigils.

People who had previously thought that politics was not for them joined the civil rights movement in the 1950s and 1960s. One of them, Fannie Lou Hamer, had worked as a servant for a white plantation owner in Mississippi all her adult life. Before the civil rights movement had begun, she had thought little about politics. But after she talked to a civil rights organizer and attended some meetings, she decided to try and register to vote. After three attempts and a beating, she passed the highly biased literacy test administered by a hostile white county official. When she got back to the plantation, she told her boss what she had done. For registering to vote, he fired her. Ms. Hamer went on to become a full-time political organizer and a leader of the Mississippi Freedom Democratic Party. In 1964 her party challenged the "regular" lily-white Democratic Party of Mississippi, prompting a civil rights revolution in the national Democratic Party's rules.

Hamer's experience was not very different from hundreds of thousands of others in the South. Civil rights activists urged people to vote, a process that before that time had been almost impossible for African Americans. People not only registered to vote—often at great personal risk—but they did so as one act in a much larger political drama in which they were the protagonists. Registering and voting became important parts of a much larger experiment in the political empowerment of ordinary people through shared struggle for political and social equality. During this drama, many people changed in ways similar to Fannie Lou Hamer. If you had asked the African-American farmers and workers of the South in 1950 to state their political opinions, they might have just shrugged their shoulders and said that politics and voting were for white people and that it was safer to not get involved. But the advance of democracy in the South changed people like Hamer: She learned that what she was experiencing on the plantation was not only her reality but that of millions of others. More importantly, she learned that it could be changed, that one didn't have to be white or have a lot of schooling to be an active, intelligent citizen and to make a difference.

Under pressure from this movement, Congress passed and President Johnson signed the **Voting Rights Act of 1965**. The act swept away the racist legal impediments to registration and voting by blacks that had been in force for nearly ninety years. Federal inspectors were sent to the South to supervise the registration of black voters. Literacy tests, poll taxes, and all the other Jim Crow mechanisms were dismembered. In Mississippi, the partial removal of these barriers made a tremendous difference, as thousands of blacks registered and voted for the first time. But it is interesting to note that even before the passage of the Voting Rights Act, people like Fannie Lou Hamer had won some of these rights themselves. Hostile registration laws and the barriers posed by racist election officials were a barrier to popular democracy and to voting. Yet forming a social movement and a vibrant local democracy was just as important to the civil rights movement as the Voting Rights Act itself. People, in short, had gained the sense that popular democracy was possible and that exercising the right to vote had personal meaning.[19]

We will never know what would have happened in the South if registration laws had been magically removed by the federal government without a strong political movement urging it to do so. Yet we do know that in other places where registration laws were made more accommodating but where there was not a strong democratic movement present, a torrent of people did not come to the polls after registration was made easier. Before 1965, New York City had low turnouts in the black community, too, though not nearly as low as Mississippi. But New York did not have a "Freedom Democratic Party" in every neighborhood, either. For many reasons, African Americans in New York City were not very well organized politically in the early 1960s. Because of the low level of black participation in New York, federal inspection of registration and election procedures was ordered there, too. But black turnout in New York City hardly increased at all; in fact, it began to decline in the early 1970s and rose only in the 1980s, when Jesse Jackson's crusade for the presidency sparked a wide variety of political activism.[20] Only when the civil rights movement established a strong connection between popular democracy and voting did registration—and voting—really increase. In short, while nonvoting is partly the result of laws and practices that discourage voting, it is probably just as much the result of the powerlessness of the groups who make up the majority of nonvoters. Conversely, when grassroots social organizations and groups grow among ordinary people, so too does voting strength and power. And such power may be indispensable to electoral reform.

Nonvoting and Civil Society's Decline

What about nonvoting and its rise in recent years? There is substantial evidence to suggest that associational life, and thus voting participation, is declining among many ordinary Americans. Political scientist Robert Putnam has used a whimsical example to explain the dilemma of our own times: "Americans are bowling today more than ever before . . . but bowling in organized leagues has plummeted." The broader social and political significance of this decline, Putnam says, "lies in the social interactions and even occasionally civic conversations over pizza that bowlers now forego."[21]

According to Putnam, ordinary people are just not as likely to engage in the activities that their ancestors in the Populist Party and the civil rights movement once did. While some dispute Putnam's arguments, there does seem to be a consensus that associational life has declined among many low- and middle-income people. The consequences reveal much about the reasons for the rise in nonvoting among poor and middle-income people. Quite simply, there are new features of the modern economy, culture, and politics that make it difficult for grassroots politics and political participation to develop. (See Chapter 3.) From this perspective, nonvoting is less a product of ignorant and uninformed citizens than it is of an economy and political system that make it harder for ordinary people to get together, talk, act, and vote. Our politics, economy, and culture

America's Epidemic of Too Little Sleep ④
— how it works

ALARM GOES OFF, JOE GETS UP EARLY.

...GOES TO WORK WHERE HE DOES TWICE WHAT HE USED TO DO.

CORPORATION HE WORKS FOR CHALKS UP RECORD PROFITS.

CORPORATION DONATES RECORD AMOUNT TO POLITICIANS.

JOE TRIES TO FOLLOW WHAT THEY'RE DOING IN WASHINGTON.

WASHINGTON PRETENDS TO REFORM CAMPAIGN FINANCING.

SO JOE HAS TO GET A SECOND JOB, COMPLAINS.

WASHINGTON REPEALS A FEW MORE WORKER PROTECTIONS.

PRICE OF COFFEE— JUST WENT UP.

present new obstacles to full-scale democratic participation, and massive non-voting is less about ignorant people than it is about the power of elite democracy to control the political agenda.

One key support for this idea comes from the yellow pages of any big-city phone book. Under the heading "Associations" is listed an apparently democratic array of groups from doctors, lawyers, and realtors to chambers of commerce and sports clubs. In the biggest cities and especially in Washington, D.C., associations of everyone from soybean and corn dealers to financial experts and scientists and associations of different kinds of college professors might even be listed.

Apparently, civil society is quite strong—Americans are still "joiners." Yet *who* joins modern associations, which ones count, and the kind of "participation" undertaken by the joiners have surely changed. Modern associational life is biased, just like the act of voting, toward the affluent and educated. In phone books, there are few listings for organizations of janitors, daycare workers, home health aides, or restaurant workers. The farmers' and workers' associations mentioned above were made up of individuals with little economic or political clout and with few resources besides their numbers, their time, and their ability to organize and educate themselves. They were based on face-to-face conversations and relationships. In contrast, many of today's associations tend to be organized from the top down, are managed by professionals, and are composed mostly of middle- and upper-class people. Rather than encouraging widespread talk and grassroots organization, many of our political associations are composed of members who never meet or meet only in chat rooms online. Such **mail order politics** means that credit cards and checkbooks stand in for face-to-face conversations between ordinary people. As a result, paid professionals "do" politics "for" others in Washington. "Mail order politics," one exhaustive study concludes, means that political activism "largely remains the province of those with higher incomes and better education" and that "money is fast replacing time as the most valuable commodity in political campaigns."[22]

The affluent possess other kinds of resources that the nonaffluent don't have. A prime advantage is access to, and mastery of, the modern media of telecommunications and computer technology—now a necessity to be an informed citizen. In cyberspace, professionals can network and chat across the miles. At home, the affluent can afford computers and online services, e-mail, faxes, and cell phones. Such technology promotes political participation by easing quick communication and networking with those of like minds. Yet even as the affluent find new ways to associate, they can also wall themselves off from the problems of the broader society and polity. After all, the biggest boom in modern housing is "gated communities" where well-off people no longer have to share public services like parks, libraries, and even a police force with the broader public. Former secretary of labor and political economist Robert Reich calls this phenomenon the "secession of the successful." No wonder, then, that a prominent study of political participation finds that "when it comes to political participation, class matters profoundly in American politics."[23]

Meanwhile, the situation is far different for the **new working class**—people like the janitors, "temps," and Wal-Mart workers we discuss in Chapter 3. Here, the affluents' disproportionate access to technology results in a *digital divide*—the new working class is simply less likely to have a home or office computer or access to the Internet. They face low wages, long hours, tiresome commutes, job instability, and uncertain prospects for future mobility. Many of them don't have the middle-income wages or access to the fringe benefits and educational opportunities that America's older workforce once had. Such broader changes in work patterns are accompanied by changes in consumption, family, and residence patterns that make it difficult for these people to get together. The new working class lives in homes that are often dispersed in sprawling suburbs that make close contact with colleagues more difficult. They shop in supermarkets, Wal-Marts, and strip malls, where the business is strictly consumption, not informal talk and chatter. Disproportionately made up of women, the young, and people of color, the new workers generally aren't unionized either.

It is precisely among this fast-growing part of the population that voter turnout and political organization seem to have declined the most since the 1960s. Neither registration difficulties, apathy, nor stupidity really account for low voter turnout among these groups. The new difficulties faced by ordinary people do. Instead of participation, nonvoters seem to react by "tuning out" politics, less from apathy but from a sense of resignation, impotence, and a lack of time. Nonvoting is one such response, a "silent vote of no confidence" by millions of people to politics in its present form.[24]

Perhaps we have a tentative solution to the mystery of nonvoting. Neither our unequal economy nor our elite democracy makes it very easy for many citizens to participate in politics. As a result, what politicians talk about gets redefined in ways that tilt to the concerns of the affluent and educated and away from the themes and language that appeal to ordinary citizens. Like Fannie Lou Hamer in the 1950s, modern citizens with few resources to participate in politics understandably come to believe that "politics is for someone else."[25]

Is such a situation permanent in American politics? Could popular democracy be revived on a large scale? Elite democratic explanations of nonvoting tend to neglect the rich historical experiences of grassroots democracy and the contemporary changes that have helped to isolate ordinary people from politics. In America, formal education, income, and age do indeed correlate with high participation in elections more than ever. Yet these are less causes of nonvoting than they are symptoms of elite democracy.

MOBILIZING NONVOTERS: WOULD IT MAKE A DIFFERENCE?

What difference would it make if nonvoters came to the polls in large numbers? At least in part, Election 2004 helps to address these issues, as turnout increased by 6 percent, the most in decades. Yet this turnout surge, large as it was, could be but a short-term response to one of the most contested elections of modern times. And despite the large increase, it is no larger than the temporary surge in new voting in 1992, after which voting levels precipitously declined. We shall see if the long term trend is reversed only in 2006 and 2008.

Another way to address the question of nonvoting is to look at surveys that have been conducted over time, designed to investigate the views of nonvoters about political issues and their attitudes toward government. Such surveys have to be viewed with caution, though, because they try to predict the political actions of people who are not now very politically active. It may well be that any event or experience that would bring lots of nonvoters to the polls would also change their political perspectives, much as the civil rights movement did for African Americans. After all, the social movement that brought Fannie Lou Hamer from resignation to political activism made her a different person. So too is it likely that the process of making today's nonvoters into voters would change what nonvoters believe and do. Nevertheless, surveys *are* worth considering as snapshots of nonvoters as they are today, and as the survey researchers see them through the questions they are asked.

Very few, perhaps as few as one in eight nonvoters, are committed in principle to not voting. By large majorities, current nonvoters tell pollsters that voting is an important right and a civic duty that they may and should undertake sometime in the future. In recent years, younger people are less likely to have this sense of civic duty than do older nonvoters. Still, there are many nonvoters who apparently feel a little guilty about not going to the polls, so much so that about 5 percent more people report voting than actually do vote. Moreover, nonvoters are no more alienated and cynical about government than are voters—at least in surveys taken in 1996 and 2000, about 70 percent of both groups expressed high levels of distrust in government, believing that government is run for the "benefit of a few big interests." Like most voters, they are turned off by negative campaigning and by what seems like interminable electoral campaigns, during which they tend to lose interest. At first glance, it would seem that nonvoters have no special attitudes about politics that sharply distinguish them from voters.[26]

Except one. There is an important distinction between how nonvoters and voters think about their own power in politics. Nonvoters tend to believe that their participation wouldn't matter. They lack a sense of political efficacy and a belief that their vote could matter either for the result or for the fundamentals of public policy. For this reason, majorities of nonvoters don't think that elections decide anything important to them or that the parties present meaningful and competing philosophies of government. In Chapter 4 we noted that high political efficacy is a trait most often found today among affluent and highly educated citizens, and least found among the new working class. So it should not be surprising that working- and middle-class nonvoters share these characteristics as well.[27] More extensive evidence about the contrasting political beliefs of voters and nonvoters is provided by other surveys. Back in the 1980s, two researchers found that disproportionate numbers of nonvoters were economic "populists" hostile to the existing distribution of power and wealth. Conversely, this study, by William Maddox and Stuart Lilie, found that the groups friendliest to corporate and business power were overrepresented in the American electorate. Such findings are at least partly confirmed in a newer study, which finds that "waitress moms and technician dads"—people with stagnant wages and difficult circumstances in the new service economy—are increasingly disenchanted with electoral politics and are the most likely to drop out. Such nonvoters feel left out; one reason may be that the Democratic Party no longer speaks very well to the needs and interests of people left behind in the new economy, and neither do the Republicans.[28] (See Chapter 8.)

With their resentments of economic inequality and their prevalence in the American population, populists could trace the future of a new American politics. What could bring them in large numbers back into the electorate? And if they came back, what kind of politics might they bring?

The social makeup and opinions of many nonvoters suggest that there are powerful grievances and energies that could be tapped. In the "Making a Difference" box, the story of one such effort is told. What is clear is that if the new energies are to be used in a democratic way, then face-to-face, grassroots politics and organizations have to be rebuilt as well. Nothing less than the repair of the social and political organizations of the American citizenry is the solution to the "problem" of nonvoting.

How might the democratic debate and the political agenda change if nonvoters started to come to the polls in large numbers? Many have long argued that the Democratic Party would gain because its strongest supporters are among the working class and racial and ethnic minorities—the groups in U.S. society whose turnout is much below the median. Still other analysts argue that the corporate financial backing of both major parties makes them uninterested in mobilizing large numbers of nonvoters. After all, such a large influx of voters might threaten corporate interests and power. Still others have suggested that only new political parties, like the Greens or the Reform Party, could move large numbers of nonvoters into activity.

In Chapter 7 we discuss these arguments about how well or poorly the two major parties organize nonvoters and around what issues. Here, we discuss three examples of recent mobilization of nonvoters by the Christian Right, the American labor union movement, and among young voters. Each example sheds light on what it might take to organize nonvoters and what the effects of such an attempt could be. If there is a lesson to be learned, it is this: When nonvoters are appealed to directly by organizations that address their concerns, they do get organized and they do vote, even when it is difficult to do so. When nonvoters start to vote, the political agenda does indeed change. For better or for worse, the actual divisions in American society and opinion get expressed in electoral campaigns.

The Christian Right

Popular democrats often think of new voters as concerned with inequality in the new economy. Yet the so-called Christian Right indicates that turning nonvoters into voters is not the monopoly of people of color, labor, or other liberal causes. The Christian Right has organized new voters through its ability to create strong face-to-face communities where common values and lifestyles are formed. The Christian Right has forged an array of institutions that don't seem political: home schooling leagues, Christian radio and TV stations, bookstores, Christian rock music groups and concerts, and a number of potent national institutions like the Christian Coalition, Focus on the Family, and the Christian Broadcasting Network.

This strong—some would say insulated—culture has promoted an effective mobilization strategy based on opposition to abortion and gay marriage, advocacy for prayer in public schools and religious symbols in public places and, in 2004, sponsorship of state referenda banning gay marriage. Since 1987, the percentage of self-proclaimed evangelical and born-again Christians has increased only marginally, from 20 to 23 percent of American adults. Yet their political unity and power inside the Republican Party has been built on the ability to register and then intensively bring to the polls higher and higher proportions of disciplined believers. Ostensibly nonpartisan, the Christian Right organizes primarily within the Republican Party. In the 1980s, only one-fifth of the Republican vote were evangelical Christians, but by 2004 their percentage of the GOP vote was a whopping 36 percent.

Just how many new voters has the Christian Right organized? Before 2004, the high tide of the movement was the 1994 congressional elections, where the Christian Right distributed an estimated 50 million voter guides by mail, door

MAKING A DIFFERENCE

Mobilizing Latinos to Vote

Are nonvoters just turned off by politics and thus unlikely to ever participate? The 2000 census confirmed that Latinos are the fastest-growing segment of the U.S. population. Their numbers now equal those of African Americans, and in the last decade the Latino population has grown in virtually every U.S. state, with California, Texas, Florida, and New York in the lead.

Historically, Latino voting rates have been very low because many are recent immigrants and are ineligible to vote because they are not citizens. But in many states, Latino participation rates have increased in the last decades from very low levels. A record 6 million Latinos voted in the 2000 election, 1 million more than in 1996, and a further million were registered and voted in 2004. Latinos now constitute a record 6 percent of the electorate but 13 percent of the population. The increase was most dramatic in Southern California, where Latino voter participation has even outpaced the increase in the adult Latino population. What accounts for the dramatic rise, and what long-term effects might it have for the nation as a whole?

The upsurge has resulted from both long- and short-term factors. More Latinos have become citizens in recent years, boosting their eligibility to vote. Yet equally important has been the slow and steady growth of strong community organizations in the barrios and neighborhoods of big cities like Los Angeles and the working-class Latino suburbs of L.A. and Orange County. Back in the 1970s and 1980s, activist Willie Velazquez began the Southwest Voter Registration Project (SWVRP). A veteran leader of the farmworker union, Velazquez cajoled and prodded his fellow Mexican Americans both to vote and to run for office. He succeeded in reaching potential voters by stressing the practical results of democratic politics. "The revolution started when we got Mexican American candidates saying, 'Vote for me and I'll pave your streets,'" Velazquez once said. The SWVRP also launched legal challenges to ban gerrymandering of electoral districts against Latino candidates. The results: In the 1970s and 1980s, Latinos gained increasing representation in city and county governments and the state legislature.

Velazquez spurred more ambitious efforts by a new generation of Latino activists in the 1990s and early 2000s. A decade ago, a coalition of community groups launched an ambitious campaign to register and get to the polls over 1 million new voters. In California, this effort was spurred by a number of anti-immigrant initiatives placed on the state ballot by GOP governor Pete Wilson. Although these initiatives passed narrowly, it brought many new Latino voters and recently naturalized immigrants to the polls in opposition to it.

In 1998 and 2000, Latino voter participation jumped for yet another reason. Building on their strength in the Latino communities, the trade unions of Los Angeles launched important organizing drives. Especially effective was a 2000 strike by

to door, and in church parking lots. Over 4 million activists helped distribute the guides, all of which targeted selected incumbent House Democrats as "anti-family." This degree of mobilization worked, especially in an election where turnout among other groups was low. While only a little more than one-third of the eligible electorate turned out in 1994, 25 percent of the voters were white thousands of janitors, mostly Latinos who made no more than the minimum wage, that paralyzed the city but drew widespread public support. The "Justice for Janitors" strike was successful, and unions pledged to use their new power in political struggles as well. Between 1998 and 2000, the Latino vote in L.A. County alone grew by over 100,000—a 50-percent increase in just two years. With a lot of effort and a list of union-backed white and Latino candidates, the Latino vote came out as well. Reversing historic patterns, Latinos in Los Angeles voted in higher proportions than non-Latinos.

What kind of political issues has Latino mobilization brought to California politics? Most important, Latinos have forged effective coalitions with progressive African Americans and whites and secured large majorities in the state legislatures for the Democratic Party. California has a minimum wage $1.60 higher than the federal wage. Latinos, unionists, and progressives, led by the Los Angeles County example, now has twenty-three cities and counties that have passed living-wage ordinances. By large majorities, Latino voters believe that increased health coverage, stricter gun-control laws, and better education are the top priorities.

California's Latinos vote three to one for Democratic candidates over Republicans, and their rising participation was decisive in defeating four GOP House incumbents in 2000, and another GOP incumbent in 2004. In 2004, John Kerry's large victory margin in California was assured due to the Latino vote.

What's next? Can the Democrats count on the solid support of Latinos? Nationwide, some exit polls after the 2004 election indicated that George W. Bush made substantial gains among Latinos. Yet closer inspection reveals that these samples were inaccurate and that the Latino vote favored Kerry and the Democrats by a solid 61 to 39 percent margin. While the Latino vote helped the Democrats carry states like Wisconsin and Michigan, the Democrats still lost crucial states like New Mexico, Nevada, and Florida, where Latino turnout was not particularly high. There's some sense that Latinos, especially in California, will not be quiet supporters of just any Democratic candidate. Instead, Democrats must deliver on issues of concern to low- and middle-income people of all kinds. Moreover, there's still much work to do. The good news is that more Latinos voted in 2004 than ever. The job ahead is to organize new Latino voters politically in states besides California, where their numbers could spell the crucial difference in future U.S. elections. To do that is made more difficult by the large numbers of non-citizens in the soaring U.S. Latino population.

Willie Velazquez, the founder of SWVRP, died in 1988. But some measure of his achievements came when President Clinton posthumously awarded him the Presidential Medal of Freedom, the nation's highest civilian honor.

Sources: Tomas Rivera Institute of Public Policy, "California Latino Voter Survey," January 2000; Matt Barrett and Nathan Woods, "Voting Patterns and the Growth of the Latino Electorate"; Antonio Olivo, "Voting Project Uses Carnivals," *Los Angeles Times*, December 18, 2000, p. B3; Harold Meyerson, "A Tale of Two Cities," American Prospect, June 7, 2004; David Leal, Matt Barreto, Jongho Lee, and Rodolfo O. de la Garza, "The Latino Vote in the 2004 Election," PS, January 2005; Roberto Suro, Richard Fry, and Jeffrey Passel, "Hispanics and the 2004 Election," Pew Hispanic Center (www.pewhispanic.org).

evangelicals, constituting an astonishing one-third of all Republican voters. The margin of victory for conservative Republicans who defeated Democrats in 1994 was slim but was made possible by this kind of grassroots activism.

Before the 2004 election, Bush political adviser Karl Rove had argued that a permanent GOP majority could only be gained if 4 million new evangelical voters were mobilized and brought to the polls. While the exact numbers are controversial, Christian evangelical leaders claimed that they'd achieved that goal and given President Bush his 2004 victory through intense mobilization of Christian congregations in the rural areas of key battleground states like Ohio and Florida. What is certainly true is that the strong social networks of evangelical, mostly white Christians not only mobilized millions of new voters but also increased their cohesiveness. President Bush was the preference of 78 percent of white evangelicals in 2004, up 10 percent from his 2000 proportion.

The Christian Right's capacity to mobilize even more nonvoters may be limited by the fact that its vote numbers have grown even while the proportion of evangelicals in the population hasn't—at some point there's just no one left to bring to the polls. Yet whatever one may think of the political positions of the Christian Right, its activities indicate that low voter turnout is hardly "natural." The Christian Right tends to organize people of median incomes and median education, not the poor or the highly affluent. Yet as a social movement, it demonstrates that politics can be made to matter to large numbers of people —voting becomes less an isolated act than it does a form of group expression.[29]

The Labor Movement: Mobilizing in the New Economy

In Chapter 3 we discuss the ways in which the new economy has led to affluence for some but much harder lives for most others. In this chapter we've seen that young people with less schooling and lower incomes are the least likely to vote. In fact, there seems to be a direct link between the growth of low-wage work in our economy and depressed voter turnout. Yet there is an important qualification to this argument: It would appear that low-wage work and less education by themselves don't lead to nonvoting. When such workers are engaged in active unions that represent their interests, voting participation rises, sometimes dramatically. Moreover, when unionized workers vote in greater numbers, the political agenda changes and politicians—mostly Democratic officeholders— are put under pressure to address issues of economic justice and inequality.

Recent elections since 1998 provide evidence for this argument. In 1998 and 2000, the AFL-CIO and its more militant and powerful unions, including the SEIU (Service Employees International Union) launched aggressive campaigns to register new voters in "union households"—families where there's at least one union member. They also tried new strategies: Instead of just running TV ads, the unions enlisted already active members and retiree volunteers in face-to-face efforts to increase the power of the union vote. Meanwhile, many of the unions, especially those that were the most aggressive in organizing new workplaces, committed more of their struggles to electoral politics.

In both 1998 and 2000, these efforts generally paid off. Over 500,000 union members were registered to vote in those two election years. Most important, the proportion of voters who were members of union households nearly doubled, from a low of 13 percent in the 1980s to 26 percent of the vote in 2000.

Much like the Christian Right, union households constituted a higher percentage of the voting population than they did of the general adult population. And the increased labor vote went heavily, although not exclusively Democratic, providing a 2–1 margin for the Democrats and Al Gore's candidacy in 2000.

In cities where the union movement was most active, union mobilization made a huge difference in local races for the state legislature, city council, and mayor. Los Angeles is a case in point. Under the leadership of Los Angeles County Federation of Labor director Miguel Contreras, unions organized new voters and directed their support to aggressive, prolabor candidates—some of them union members themselves. By combining aggressive union organizing of janitors and other service workers in L.A., and winning the battle of public opinion in the city, L.A.'s unions translated their growing power in the labor market into political power at the ballot box. In one congressional district, a complacent incumbent was replaced by a prolabor challenger in the Democratic primary. In another assembly district where the vote total had been only 14,000 in previous elections, union efforts boosted the totals by an additional 9,000 and resulted in the election of a union activist to the State Assembly.[30]

In the 2004 elections, organized labor delivered again, although there efforts were generally offset by the countermobilization of the Christian Right (discussed above). The AFL-CIO spent over $45 million on the election, and big and active unions like the SEIU spent even more: $65 million. The unions enlisted over 225,000 volunteers, and that wasn't counting union members who worked in "affiliated" 527 groups like Americans Coming Together (see Chapter 8 for more about 527 groups). Most of the effort was devoted to the registration and organization of new voters, this time not only in union households but also among nonunion low-wage workers. Generally, these efforts were a success; in an election where turnout rose by 6 percent, so too did union household turnout keep pace. About 3 million new voters from union household families voted, many of them in key states like Ohio and Florida. In absolute numbers, the labor vote at 27 million was higher than it had ever been, despite the fact that organized labor was a much smaller share of the workforce than in many years.

The only problem, of course, was that union efforts to organize more workers for the Democratic cause was offset by Republican countermobilization, boosting turnout but again resulting in a narrow GOP victory. In the words of political scientist John Green, "It's not that the Democrats failed to do a great job. They did do a good job, and their get-out-the-vote effort was astounding in terms of resources and people—but not as efficient as it could have been. Their basic problem is that the Republicans did a great job too."[31]

The Youth Vote, 2004

Generally, nonvoters are not only poorer than voters but are also younger. In elections since 1972—the first where 18-year-olds could vote—the youth vote has been remarkably small, on average nearly 10 percent below the already low turnout rate of people older than 30. From an elite democratic perspective, young people were said by some to be selfish, cynical, or just too involved with the pursuit of their own pleasure to vote. Observers cited numerous surveys to demonstrate that young people were both less interested and less informed about politics than older voters.

In 2004, dozens of youth groups were formed to change that situation. Some of them were prompted by resistance to the Iraq War, others were nonpartisan, and still others were formed among the Christian right. On many college campuses, opposition to the Iraq War and to the Bush administration sparked new levels of activism. For Christian evangelicals, young voters and their political preferences were in the process of formation, and thus were also a prime target.

In large part, Election 2004 demonstrated that young people are not an inherently apolitical and cynical mass, preordained to reject politics. As in the two cases above, the key to what turned out to be an increased turnout of 9 percent (from 42 percent to 51 percent participating) were two key variables. Young people had to be persuaded to vote for a reason provided by someone they trusted, and they had to have issues that concerned them as a group. In 2004, both of these factors acted to raise turnout by over 5 million among people aged eighteen to twenty-nine. In part, the Iraq War and strong pro and con views of President Bush and his policies served as an important catalyst to this significant increase. In general, young people displayed much more interest in news stories and election coverage in 2004 than they did in 2000, albeit through new means such as the Internet. They paid much more attention to the conventions and the debates, and reported significantly higher numbers of conversations about politics than they had in 2000 or 1996. Important, too, was a reduction in youth cynicism: Young voters were actually less "disgusted with politics," and fewer young people than older reported that they found political issues too complex to understand. More young people, however, reported difficulties in registering and voting than did older people.

The 2004 election may or may not be the start of a new surge of increased voter participation by young voters. According to surveys, the key to the 5-million-vote increase among the young was whether they had been personally contacted about voting in the election. More than half of the young said that they voted because friends and family had encouraged them to participate in the election. They were less likely to say that they had been contacted by an advocacy organization or a political party asking them to vote, probably because fewer young people have fixed addresses or home telephone numbers.

The wave of new and young citizens who came to the polls in 2004 largely voted Democratic; John Kerry chalked up a 9 percent margin among the young, the highest percentage received by a Democratic presidential candidate in memory. But most of the new votes came from the mobilization of people who had either graduated from or attended college. For young people who had never attended college—an important bloc of nonvoters—very little changed. Despite their generally progressive views about business power, race, and sexuality, they were largely unaffected by registration and voting drives.[32]

CONCLUSION: WHO'S AFRAID OF NONVOTERS?

The Christian Right's successes and the resurgence of union influence in 1998, 2000, and 2004 are important signs that declining turnout is hardly inevitable. Mobilizing nonvoters widens the democratic debate to include concerns not often voiced. This is especially true with the political potential of union mobilization efforts because there is every indication that in the new economy, labor unions could expand, especially among groups that don't vote in high percentages now. If the issue of economic inequality and the distribution of economic resources is not now front and center in our electoral debates, there is every reason to believe that most nonvoters would be attracted by such a debate. Yet which comes first? Must nonvoters become voters and force new issues on the agenda? Or must the agenda first be changed so that nonvoters become interested in politics?

The answer is uncertain and remains so for future elections. Yet this much is clear: If America's limited electorate is expanded, so too will be the political agenda and most likely the level of polarization in American politics. As limited but important efforts have been made to expand the electorate, so too have new issues and increased conflict resulted. Despite the renewed differences in ideology, this much is also clear: Nonvoters are brought to action not by abstract appeals for them to vote but by concrete issues and by face-to-face grassroots organizations that connect what government does to people's daily lives. To make this connection, today's nonvoters need friends, families, and acquaintances to make the connection. Americans need a stronger and more democratic civil society in which it becomes clear that their individual fate is tied to that of others. While the results of such democratization may not be what we desire, they do at least in part return politics to the people.

Nonvoters are not likely to show up at the polls by appeals to duty and civic virtue alone. Nor will easing registration and voting requirements by themselves accomplish much, though both would certainly help somewhat. Rather, turnout decline is likely to be reversed only through a combination of factors. The most important, perhaps, is that the parties and groups that organize voters return to person-to-person, grassroots organizing. The second and equally important rule is that the collective interest of nonvoters be combined with those who do vote in new ways and new coalitions. The Christian Right has made elections matter for its constituency. But there are compelling reasons to believe that there is a much larger potential for turnout increase when those workers in the service economy get organized in unions and that this will lead to increased political participation. The case studies we saw in this chapter and the feature box on Latino voters demonstrate that when people get organized socially and economically, they are likely to turn to democratic elections.

For the present, though, it is enough to say that nonvoting is so central to present-day American politics that no discussion of democracy can start without confronting it. To solve the mystery of nonvoting, we've turned to the rich history of grassroots democracy in America. Massive nonvoting, far from a function of the "natural" ignorance or apathy of ordinary citizens, is a symptom and product of elite democracy. Nonvoting serves elite democracy by limiting political debate to the issues and alternatives most relevant to the affluent. Far from the indifference of citizens to political participation, today's high levels of nonvoting reveal the indifference of elite democratic institutions to the extension of democracy.

In the short term, a massive reentry of nonvoters into electoral politics is unlikely. Nor would a fully participating electorate magically solve all the nation's problems if it should occur. This is perhaps the point: Nonvoting is just not a bothersome blemish on an otherwise democratic system but one of the key foundations of elite democratic dominance. The elements of popular democracy that remain in our system suggest that mobilizing nonvoters would change what we talk about. It would widen debate to include the concerns and interests of millions who fare poorly in the new global economy. The media would have to respond to new groups and their concerns. The best, as well as the worst elements, in American politics would stir electoral debate.

Who's afraid of nonvoters who might become voters? In the nineteenth century, opponents of participation hardly disguised their elitism. Today, elitism is more subtle. The global political economy has helped to promote nonparticipation and nonvoting by fragmenting and dividing people with common interests. It makes it harder, though not impossible, for grassroots activism to start. The actions of elite politicians, interests, and institutions also have an important role in sustaining nonvoting. Concluding an exhaustive study of participation in political life, two scholars remark that "participation in electoral politics rises when political parties contact, when competitive election campaigns stimulate, when social movements inspire. . . ." How true. The problem is that our political institutions seem to do little to contact or stimulate social movements. From an elite democratic perspective, organizing takes time, money, and energy better devoted to influencing people who already do vote. And after all, elected officials have achieved their power within the *existing* electorate. So why bother with troublesome and unpredictable nonvoters and their demands?[33]

What are the prospects for a return to a fuller democratic debate? Even as elite democrats worry about too much democracy, there is every reason to believe that the problem is that there is too little. There is certainly no shortage of grievances that could bring nonvoters back into fuller participation. In future chapters we explore at greater length the dilemmas and opportunities that popular democracy faces in a world of media, parties, campaigns, and interest groups.

KEY TERMS   political efficacy   proportional representation
                 civil society   Voting Rights Act of 1965
                 structural obstacles   mail order politics
                 Jim Crow laws   new working class
                 personal registration

**INTERNET
RESOURCES**

■ National Research Commission on Elections and Voting,
Social Science Research Council
http://election04.ssrc.org
This site is a gateway to virtually all participation data and analysis of the 2004
election.

■ FairVote: The Center for Voting and Democracy
www.fairvote.org
Headed by former Independent presidential candidate John Anderson, this
research and advocacy organization here provides dozens of proposals for
improvement of U.S. electoral processes.

■ Demos: A Network for Ideas and Action
www.demos-usa.org
Research and advocacy group studying ways in which U.S. electoral design
depresses voter participation.

**SUGGESTED
READINGS**

John Keyssar, *The Right to Vote: The Contested History of Democracy in the United
  States*. New York: Basic Books, 2000. A noted historian makes an exhaustive
  historical case for the idea that expanding suffrage has required continuous
  popular pressure.
Thomas Patterson, *The Vanishing Voter*. Cambridge: Harvard University Press,
  2003. An exhaustive survey of nonvoters and a work that argues that negative campaigning and drawn-out election seasons discourage voting.
Frances Fox Piven and Richard Cloward, *Why Americans Don't Vote*. New York:
  Pantheon, 1987. Two scholars make a compelling argument about why
  increased voter registration is the key to increasing voter turnout and to fundamental political change.
Steven Rosenstone and John Mark Hansen, *Mobilization, Participation, and
  Democracy in America*. New York: Macmillan, 1993. An exhaustive study of
  electoral and other forms of political participation, and an attempt to explain
  their fluctuation.
Sidney Verba, Kay Schlozman, and Henry Brady, *Voice and Equality*. Cambridge: Harvard University Press, 1998. A magisterial work on the relationship between economic inequality, political participation, and political
  equality.

The Media
Who Sets the Political Agenda?

You've read this book's first five chapters. Many of you may not have strong opinions about the Constitution, and it may be difficult to get worked up over some of the recent trends in public opinion. Yet if you are breathing, standing, and alive in the early twenty-first century, it's our bet that the subject of this chapter will be different. The mass media, and the news media as a part of it, is hardly an abstraction for most of us. You can love the media or hate it. You can love parts of it, hate others, and try to ignore the rest. Yet in one way or another you probably have an idea about how and why the media does what it does and its effects on you and others. Controversy is inescapable, because whatever we say here—in *this* particular medium of a book—we all understand one another (or not) through the media channels we use.

So we begin with an interpretive puzzle about politics and the media. Beginning with this example no doubt reveals some of our biases, but we think they are defensible ones. Like the news media, we could have picked another story to tell, for there are lots of them out there. Yet also like the news media, we have a certain power. We're writing this book, so we set the agenda just like any other media source. We can't tell you what to think. Yet we can, at least for a little while, tell you what to think *about* and, by omission, what isn't important. In many ways, that's the message in this chapter about the power of the mass media.

So here is our puzzle: In 2004, the United States witnessed one of the most important elections in modern times. Turnout soared, and levels of activism exploded. To say the least, the presidential contest got lots of attention. George W. Bush was reelected. Four billion dollars was spent by the Democrats and Republicans and their allies on the campaigns, and $600 million was spent on presidential TV ads alone. George Bush and John Kerry had three televised debates. One of the biggest issues at stake was President Bush's conduct in the war on terrorism and in the war he initiated in Iraq. During the long campaign, the American news media produced literally hundreds of thousands of accounts of the dramatic campaign in the print and broadcasting media.

In a nationwide survey conducted just before the election, University of Maryland researchers discovered that nearly three-quarters of Bush supporters believed that weapons of mass destruction had been found in Iraq. A nearly similar percentage reported the view that Saddam Hussein's regime had supplied support to Osama bin Laden's Al Qaeda. Two-thirds believed that Bush supported the Kyoto treaty on global warming, the International Criminal Court, and the international treaty banning land mines. Big majorities of Bush voters believed that people around the world supported the Iraq War, including most Muslims in the Middle East.[1]

Do you see anything strange about this picture? Well, yes: If this survey is right—and no one has really contested its findings—there is a problem here for democracy *and* the media. The view of reality shared by most Bush supporters just isn't factually correct. Bush didn't support the Kyoto treaty, the International Criminal Court, or the treaty banning land mines. No weapons of mass destruction had been found in Iraq, and an administration official had testified to Congress to that effect. And the highly respected 9/11 Commission had reported no substantial connection between Saddam and Al Qaeda, a view that even Vice President Dick Cheney, one of the original purveyors of this claim, seemed to accept. Virtually every survey of world opinion showed massive opposition to the invasion in all but a few countries on the planet. While there might be many reasons to support President Bush, to do so on the basis of this kind of false information would seem to be something of a problem.

How would you interpret this finding? One way might be to say that people didn't care much about these matters and they voted for Bush anyway. The problem is that the same survey found that people did care; they said that if weapons of mass destruction hadn't been found, it might make a difference in their opinions. A second proposition might be that people weren't paying attention to all the public disclosures or to the news. Maybe—but other surveys reported that Bush supporters showed at least as much interest in the news as Kerry supporters and, if anything, possessed equal amounts of formal education as well as interest in news reports. The survey's results thus can't be explained by saying that Bush supporters were generally apathetic or uninterested. A third idea, the favorite of these University of Maryland pollsters, is that people believe what they want to believe: Because people liked Bush, they adjusted their beliefs about weapons of mass destruction into a frame that allowed them to continue to like him, regardless of what was actually being reported or the facts.

There is, however, a fourth interpretation. The people who believed these things were paying attention to news and to the campaign. But whatever they watched, read, or heard on the vast expanse of the mass media simply didn't report or mistakenly reported all these important stories. While the media had apparently been quite effective when it reported the Bush administration's justifications for the war, many outlets just hadn't been very effective reporting on how those rationales proved to be incorrect. Apparently, whatever these Bush supporters saw or read ignored the Bush administration's positions regarding the Kyoto and land mine treaties and the International Criminal Court. Something in the media, or at least large parts of it, had conveyed the altogether false impression that the world, except for maybe France and Germany, supported President Bush's actions in Iraq.

As it turns out, many Bush supporters did indeed get their information from news outlets that ignored, underreported, buried, or in some cases simply distorted the news about weapons of mass destruction and the absence of an Al Qaeda connection. Mostly, it was not outright lies that were the problem. The media most used by Bush supporters tended to specialize in stories that simply underreported the facts that University of Maryland researchers asked about. The deluge of campaign reports were about other matters, such as Senator Kerry's war record, whether or not the country was safe under Bush, or the issue of gay marriage. Bush himself, while briefly acknowledging that WMD hadn't been found, didn't talk about it much and slowly shifted his rationales for the Iraq War. John Kerry, because he had voted as a senator to authorize the president's march to war, hardly highlighted the WMD issue but rather talked about Bush's supposed mistakes after the war had begun.

Thus, while most of the mainstream media had reported these stories, some, like the Fox Network and radio talk shows, gave them little air time.[2] Our point is not that Bush voters are stupid or that they were deliberately duped. Rather, we are raising other, less strictly partisan questions about the role of the current news media and its relationship to democracy. Is our media system designed to produce relevant knowledge and diverse perspectives to inform the citizenry? Does the media system provide people with ways to separate facts from propaganda launched by the powerful? Does the media system serve, as the framers hoped when they wrote the First Amendment, as a watchdog on the powerful? In a democracy of nearly 300 million people, few of us can have direct, personal knowledge of the rationales provided by the powerful for their actions except through the mass media. If despite the avalanche of words, images, and commentaries and the billions of dollars spent on Election 2004 many people didn't know these basic facts, then these questions are surely relevant. Just what *is* amiss with the news media is the subject of this chapter.

THE DEMOCRATIC DEBATE AND THE MASS MEDIA

In the abstract, elite and popular democrats alike support the mass media's freedom, independence, and essential role in democratic life. The concept of a vast public arena in which ideas and diverse information are exchanged freely appeals to all. Yet here the consensus ends; elite and popular democrats differ about who and what controls today's media marketplace, who should control it, and with what effects. They agree that something is wrong but can't agree on what or why. Indeed, there is profound conflict about the main features of our media system, whether we have a "system" in the first place, and whether it is a free marketplace at all.

For elite democrats, the existing mass media system embodies the virtues of a free marketplace. Media producers enter the market, invest capital in media products, compete with others, and sell their products to consumers. When they are successful, profits are made and consumers are satisfied. Because consumers fulfill their wants by preferring some media companies and products over others, the whole media system is considered to be free. For elite democrats, the key to the media system is that it remain privately owned and thus free; the public interest is served when private producers compete for the consumer's attention. To preserve this freedom, government or other types of meddling in the rights of the private producers must be minimized. This doesn't mean there's no room for people who don't particularly care about making profits; if they can operate without the profit motive, that's fine. Just as in the political economy, government may have some role in preventing monopolies and in regulating the market system to make sure no one has an unfair advantage, but to maintain the independence and proper functioning of each, maximum autonomy of the capitalist marketplace should be preserved. The news media marketplace, in this sense, is like any other market.

To be sure, elite democrats can be critics of the mass media. Some are concerned when the mass media defy established authority, or tweak dominant cultural values, or spread what some might call indecency. Ironically, such criticisms are often couched in terms of the media's "elitism" and control by the rich and educated. People who have few problems with corporations owning the media do have serious concerns about some of the people the owners employ, who are often accused of berating mainstream values to make a cheap buck or satisfy the darker cravings of the immoral. The news media can go too far by peddling "unhealthy programming," criticizing American foreign policy abroad, or exposing Janet Jackson's breasts. Strangely, though, these critiques are never linked to doubts about the private and commercialized character of the media system.

In our own times, the major support for elite democrats' equation of the commercial media with maximum freedom is usually associated with what is often called the media revolution. Innovative telecommunications, said to be a product of healthy market competition, have greatly expanded people's access to all kinds of information, facts, opinions, and images. The media revolution features greater choice, increased interaction, and healthy competition. The possibility of greater public knowledge and enriched debate is claimed to be a result. With close to 2000 cable and satellite channels, 1,600 daily newspapers, 14,000 magazines, billions of websites and postings, and a new generation of bloggers, the face of media and the sources and definition of the news media have been transformed.[3]

Thus, to its boosters, the media has never been more democratic: No longer are passive consumers limited to a few national TV programs and stodgy newspapers. Media citizens today can actively ferret out information, create their own blog, and screen out ads from their 200-channel satellite television sets. Communication is faster and cheaper; over three-quarters of the public go online every week, and growing numbers of people turn to the Internet for news and information, as well as to shop and be entertained.[4]

From this perspective, the mistaken perceptions of Bush voters might be unfortunate, but they are a product of the free choice of media consumers. In a free market system, you can't force people to be correctly informed, as this would impose an orthodoxy.

So why call this "elite" democratic at all? Popular democrats are also interested in a marketplace of ideas and believe that the technological revolution presents some profound possibilities for democracy. Yet they doubt that a profit-driven and commercialized media landscape is really a marketplace, that citizens exercise free choice, and that the range of ideas is diverse and broad. This is especially true when it comes to the news media. While the telecommunications revolution could have great promise, popular democrats look at the ways it has been hijacked by concentrated private power and ever-larger media corporations in the profit-driven current system. While there are thousands of print, broadcast, and Internet outlets, nearly all of them have a commercial purpose. They are not so much in the business of selling products to consumers as of marketing and shaping consumers to be delivered to the advertisers and commercial interests that pay the media's bills and make money for stockholders.

More important, the increasing number of outlets may be impressive, but the number of owners has become more concentrated than at any time in U.S. history. Across the news media spectrum—from newspapers to the Internet— about twenty corporations control the vast bulk of what Americans actually read, see, and hear on the radio, television, in newspapers, and online. Concentrated private power in the media industry contradicts the image of a marketplace of small producers in which all can participate. Far from resembling a friendly farmers' market or a chaotic bazaar, the media marketplace is more like a rigid hierarchy of competing bureaucracies with their own distinctive interests. Far from being apolitical, these media companies are completely intertwined with

corporate capitalism at home and abroad, so much so that a company like Disney or General Electric may not only own ABC and NBC but interests in nuclear weapons and theme parks, as well as publishing and sports teams.

For popular democrats, a commercial media marketplace dominated by a few giants hardly promotes the political independence said to be the chief virtue of a free market. Like other industries, media corporations employ an army of lobbyists and deliver ample campaign contributions to politicians. They seek favorable tax breaks, subsidies, and regulations that restrict rather than enlarge the marketplace of ideas. Far from being independent actors free of governmental control, the news media has become powerfully intertwined with political elites and codependent on the powers that be. And if there's one thing that unites media corporations, it is their opposition to noncommercial, truly democratic media. Favored by government licenses and hidden subsidies and tax breaks, media corporations crush truly independent media sources and channels by controlling the "public airwaves." Even on the free spaces of the Internet, the dwindling number of Internet providers lead consumers to ads, news, and shopping sites brought to consumers by corporate America.

From this perspective, no wonder many Bush supporters didn't know the basic facts about the Iraq invasion or Bush's policy views. The commercial media system has few reasons to offend the powerful, and every reason to concentrate on those stories that please advertisers and attract consumers. These days, it has a tendency to fragment and ghettoize audiences in such a way as to undermine informed citizenship. The commercially propelled media marketplace is more like a gated community than a public square. It is entirely possible to watch a hundred corporate controlled channels and still encounter a filtered and structured reality that somehow doesn't get around to airing political basics. There is the illusion of choice but not the substance. And the billions that went to paid political advertising only demonstrated the power of the privileged: If neither Bush nor Kerry cared about politicizing the issue of WMDs or Saddam's ties to Al Qaeda, this is a news story that didn't matter and didn't get attention.

The most important questions concern the media's role in the democratic debate and their definition and portrayal of political life. Has the growth in media power fulfilled the hopes of those, like Jefferson, who assumed that it would be an instrument of democratic rule? Or do the media squelch active democratic citizenship, mistaking the sheer number of media outlets for political diversity and debate? Although sometimes critical of specific individuals in power, do the media nonetheless act to protect the profits and interests of an exclusive media system more concerned with the bottom line than the free exchange of information?

MEDIA POWER AND U.S. HISTORY

Two fundamental historical developments help to answer these questions. First, commercial media have grown in American life but have done so by crowding out other ways of getting information and sharing and debating ideas about politics and the nation. While the family, the school, the local community, the tavern, the church, and the political party used to be the chief sources and arenas for political knowledge and conversation, most of what Americans know and think today about politics comes from TV, radio, magazines, newspapers, and established sources on the World Wide Web. Second, media power and influence have followed the same tendencies rampant in the global political economy, which are outlined in Chapter 3. Political communications in America have almost never been owned or operated by government officials. However, over time, the character of "private ownership" of the media has changed, passing from local newspapers with individual owners to global corporations with direct economic interests in influencing public policy and politics according to their owners' interests. How did the present situation come about? Do these trends make any difference for our marketplace of ideas?

Newspapers

Today we'd think it odd if *USA Today* or the *Los Angeles Times* mixed its detailed weather reports and sports coverage with political philosophy essays on current topics. Yet New York City's *Independent Journal* printed the entire text of the *Federalist* in 1787 and 1788. That newspaper's role was hardly novel: From the Revolution to the Civil War, U.S. newspapers served as the premier vehicle of political communication. Making money was a secondary concern to the broader role of newspapers as instruments of partisan debates and attacks. In sharp contrast to today, newspapers were locally owned—they represented the democratic debate in towns, villages, and small cities of the early republic.[5] After the Civil War, the strictly partisan press began to be challenged by a new generation of owners. These press barons wanted to make money and achieve personal political influence, and they therefore sought the highest possible circulation in the big cities. While politics was hardly ignored, the definition of news was expanded, and it became a commodity to be manufactured, bought, and sold. William Randolph Hearst and Joseph Pulitzer helped to pioneer **yellow journalism** (named for the Yellow Kid, a cartoon character), which attracted readers with sensationalized accounts of crimes and scandals. The Sulzberger family took a contrary approach with the *New York Times*. The *Times* promoted the new doctrine of journalistic objectivity and professionalism, but its commercial aim was to sell papers to a growing middle class of urban professionals.[6]

During the twentieth century, titans like Hearst, Pulitzer, and Sulzberger were generally replaced by the cool and impersonal calculation of the corporate boardroom. With increasing momentum after World War II, formerly independent dailies in cities and towns were merged or eliminated. Newspaper "chains"—among them Gannett, Knight–Ridder, Scripps, the New York Times Company, and the Hearst Corporation itself—have absorbed most of the nation's dailies. The result has been a diminishing role for hard-hitting, independently owned local newspapers and the effective end of competition among newspapers in most metropolitan areas.[7]

Newspaper readership declined in the 1980s and 1990s, and today many struggle to expand readership by including new sections on lifestyle issues like cooking, entertainment, and fashion trends. Today, only about one-quarter of adults under forty-nine read a daily newspaper regularly—bad news for the once vibrant newspaper business. While most newspaper chains are still highly profitable, some argue that that this is so only because they have cut costs by standardizing news coverage and giving short shrift to many important, especially local, stories. At the same time, national newspapers like the *Washington Post*, *New York Times*, *Los Angeles Times*, and *Wall Street Journal* have sometimes enlarged their staffs and coverage of many international events and remain powerful shapers of elite opinion.[8]

Radio and Television

Newspaper ownership consolidated partly because of the competition from radio in the 1930s, network television in the 1950s, and now cable and satellite TV and the Internet. In radio's early days in the 1920s, stations were often owned by not-for-profit organizations, and the ownership was local. But the passage of the Federal Communications Act in 1933 promoted corporate ownership and the end of not-for-profit dominance on the radio. The Radio Corporation of America (RCA) quickly became the industry leader. Its new network featured little political news, concentrating instead on entertainment programming ranging from music to soap operas and comedies. World War II changed that, with the new CBS Radio Network and its reporter in war-torn London, Edward R. Murrow, leading the way.

Born from RCA, NBC, along with CBS and ABC, dominated early television, the revolutionary new medium of the 1950s. Yet much like radio in its early days, TV in its childhood was not particularly news oriented. As a result, the news divisions of the major networks were relatively free of the profit imperative. The news divisions of the networks were supposed to provide prestige to the network's image, not rake in huge amounts of cash. Though underfunded, the news divisions of the TV networks sometimes produced outstanding and even risky independent and professional news and documentaries.[9]

The real growth and expansion of TV news as the most watched and thus most profitable form of news coverage occurred only in the 1960s. Technological advances expanded the popular appeal of the evening television news. Hand-held cameras, satellite transmission, and videotape meant that TV journalism could move out of studios and newsreels and go where the live action was at home or abroad. Television news anchors like Walter Cronkite and David Brinkley became trusted celebrities, while the networks discovered that their news divisions could make a profit by drawing large audiences.[10]

The 1960s provided plenty of lively political events for the media to cover or even to create. The televised presidential debate between Richard Nixon and John Kennedy in 1960 began the trend. After that date, television became the premier medium of influence for politicians, and the coverage of presidential campaigns from their inception to the November election became the most important source of images and impressions. In turn, politicians began to treat television as the most important means of communication with voters.

For good or ill, for twenty years the network news did create a national audience and something like a public conversation around common issues like Watergate, the Vietnam War, and the civil rights movement. Today, that centrality has withered. These days, the audience for television news is much more fragmented into niche markets and infotainment formats like those of *20/20* and the *Today* show. The nightly 6:30 network news programs still remain the largest single sources of national news, with about 35 million viewers each night. Yet that number is down significantly from its high point of nearly half the adult population. The network news audience today has an average age of sixty years old, and less than one-fifth of young adults watch network news regularly. The decline in network news was perhaps prompted by declining network budgets for news and documentary but also by the rise of "new news" formats and "niche marketing" to specialized audiences. Cable television news, pioneered by CNN, first challenged the networks. By the 1990s and the turn of the new century, the Fox News Channel, MSNBC, and even C-Span featured "all news all the time" formats, gaining specialized audiences. Cable television also pioneered programs like *Crossfire*. Cheap to make and short on hard news, they featured the rise of what some call the "punditocracy." But most of all, "news" is no longer the purview of journalists alone. Shows like Oprah Winfrey's, Jay Leno's, and David Letterman's, and more recently Jon Stewart's *Daily Show*, mix parody, entertainment, and political commentary outside of news formats. For many young people, they are the major source of "news" coverage.[11]

The Internet and Broadband Communication

If the novel formats for news are transforming the old media, by 2005 one-third of U.S. adults were getting news from the Internet at least three times a week. The young and the affluent are particularly likely to consult the Web for news, but the new medium is making steady inroads among other groups as well. For the Internet's boosters, this kind of growth only underscored the power of the new medium. Media companies quickly invested millions in websites that served as promotion vehicles for their TV, newspaper, and film offerings. Most looked to the near future, where digital television and broadband communication would bring together cable television, telephone, and Internet services in one hookup. Today, virtually every advocacy and research group has its own website.[12]

The growth of online news sources also accompanies a widespread redefinition of what "news" is. The Web may have millions of sites, but most individual Americans don't consult more than a fraction of them. Service providers like America Online lead users to "preferred" links. Search engines like Yahoo! do the same thing. Not surprisingly, therefore, Web users are led to headlines, sports, and weather that come from the major media corporations. The most popular news sites are about weather, the stock markets, and sports. For most, but hardly all, Internet users, political news thus appears as nothing more than a headline, followed by a brief story if one clicks on the "link." Thus, far from enriching the news mix, the World Wide Web may actually encourage shortened attention spans and a redefinition of news away from politics and public policies. One important study reports that "Americans are losing the news habit, fewer people say they enjoy following (traditional) news, and fully half pay attention to national news only when something important is happening."[13] (See Table 6.1.)

Diverse Marketplace or Vast Wasteland?

In theory, the media revolution has made a broader range of new sources available to more people than at any other time in human history. Some talked of a **virtual democracy**, an era marked by instant communication between people and between citizens and powerful institutions.

At the same time, the new media spark fragmentation. As already noted, the digital divide separates people by their degree of access to the new technology, with whites, the affluent, and men at a profound advantage. But the media revolution creates other distinctions by eroding the breadth of the public square and public agenda. Media consumers can choose between hundreds of profit-making commercial outlets, but few have any political content whatever, and still others

TABLE 6.1

Changing Trends in
News Consumption,
1993–2004

Regularly watch . . .	1993 %	1996 %	1998 %	2000 %	2002 %	2004 %
Local TV news	77	65	64	56	57	59
Nightly network news	60	42	38	30	32	34
Network TV magazines	52	36	37	31	24	22
Network morning news	—	—	23	20	22	22
Cable (in detail)						
Fox News Channel	—	—	17	17	22	25
CNN	35	26	23	21	25	22
MSNBC	—	—	8	11	15	11
CNBC	—	—	12	13	13	10
C-SPAN	11	6	4	4	5	5
Other sources						
Newspaper[1]	58	50	48	47	41	42
Radio[1]	47	44	49	43	41	40
Online news[2]	—	2[3]	13	23	25	29

[1]Figures based on use "yesterday," from February 1994.
[2]Online news at least three days per week
[3]From June 1995

Source: Pew Research Center for the People and the Press, April–May 2004. Reprinted by permission.

appeal only to specialized tastes. The network news's dominance, whatever its problems, at least provided a common political vocabulary and set of reference points for most Americans. Produced by professional journalists partly shielded from the commercial interests of parent companies, the network news at least contained some recognized standards of reporting. The mass media today may be a marketplace, but it may not be free, insofar as public life and dialogue are tuned out.[14]

The average American still interacts with some form of media over eight hours each day, and over 100 million people daily hear some news via radio, TV, newspapers, or cyberspace. Taken together the news media remain extraordinarily powerful. The important question is how people understand what they read, see, and hear in the news media sources they watch. Back in the 1940s, researchers found that most people balanced what they heard through the news media with other influences: from friends, coworkers, family members, and local members of interest groups and political parties. In the 1970s, scholars found that the media did little to change political opinions, as people tuned out news stories they didn't care about or disagreed with and remained quite skeptical about what they saw and heard.[15]

Today, it is comforting to believe that what the news media convey is balanced by a rich civil society and popular skepticism. But media influence and power may be exercised in subtler ways. With the decline of political parties, trade unions, and many public associations, the mass media assume an increasingly important power as the commanding—even only—source of political information and talk. The modern news media are **agenda setters**. While the mass media may not tell us exactly what to think, they do tell us what to think about, and they determine the means of interaction with others. Out of the apparent chaos of newsworthy items, they select the stories and choose the narratives. When the media omit or "bury" a story, it is, in effect, censored and largely marginalized in public life. By setting the political agenda, the news media can shape, limit, or expand it. That's why the subject of the news media remains important. Which institutions and people define the agendas of the news media? Whose voice is reflected, and what kind of politics is bypassed or distorted?[16]

CORPORATE OWNERSHIP AND CONTROL

As we've seen above, the bulk of the American mass media has long been owned by profit-seeking private institutions and individuals. While there remains an important nonprofit sector in print and broadcasting that will be discussed below, the important fact is that for elite democrats in particular, competition in the private marketplace is supposed to promote free speech and the public interest.

Yet the most dramatic changes in American news media history are prompted by the ever-increasing **concentration of ownership** in the media business, combined with the giant size and diverse activities of the corporations that control the production of news as part of vast private entertainment empires. Gone are the fierce partisans, press barons, or even colorful media moguls of the nineteenth and twentieth centuries. Disappearing are the decentralized and disparate newspapers and individually owned radio and television stations that once dotted the landscape. In a free market, there are supposed to be extensive competition and easy entry for new producers of goods. But the new markets are hardly free and open to new voices because they are oligopolies in which a few firms dominate many markets and whose power prevent more competition.

The trend toward concentration became a revolution in the last twenty years. In the 1980s, General Electric absorbed NBC. In the 1990s, ABC and its parent company, CapCities, was gobbled up by Disney, Inc. CBS is now owned by Viacom, and Time-Warner, the biggest media corporation on the planet, first bought Ted Turner's CNN and then sold itself to the world's largest Internet provider, America Online. Rupert Murdoch's News Corporation, Sony, and German-based Bertelsmann round out the list of media giants.[17]

Each has consolidated holdings that span traditional television, cable television, satellite transmission, radio, newspapers, magazines, movies, book publishing, and music. Each news division is linked, through parent corporations, to industries like coal and gold mining, international nuclear power and armaments industries, chemicals and their disposal, medical services and research, worldwide finance and investment banks, theme parks, and housing developments. Mark Crispin Miller calls this new order the **national entertainment state**. Figure 6.1 provides a list of the partial holdings of just one of these megacorporations, Time Warner.

Figure 6.1 doesn't include the struggle for corporate mergers and consolidation in the telecommunications industry, where competition today seems to be headed toward new concentration tomorrow. Here, the same giant corporations are fighting it out for the rights to control broadband and other technologies that will promote the consolidation of the cable, television, Internet, and other industries. If events unfold as predicted, a new media system will emerge where a few corporations will produce the programming, news, and films and distribute their products through digital television, the Internet, and entertainment "multiplexes" that they own.

Viacom/CBS is a good example of such **vertical integration**, where firms control both the development of media content and its distribution through dozens of marketing conduits. With $27 billion in sales, here's a company that can produce a film at Paramount, air it on its cable station Showtime, play a related music video on MTV, market it on Nickelodeon or on its own CBS network, sell it as a paperback through Simon and Schuster, advertise it on its thirty-five local TV stations and 175 radio stations, show it at its movie theaters around the world, and advertise it on its highway billboards or through its chain of DVD stores.[18]

Concentration of ownership in the Big Five (News Corporation, Viacom, GE, Disney, and Time Warner) has sent shock waves through other media industries. "Second tier" companies such as Clear Channel, the New York Times Company, and Gannett tend to be the major players in a single media industry. Gannett, Inc., publisher of *USA Today*, expanded its holdings to become the largest publisher of suburban newspapers. In radio, Clear Channel, known for organizing pro–Iraq War demonstrations, competes with Viacom's Infinity network. Together, both now do more business and reach more audiences than the rest of the radio industry combined.[19]

Corporate Censorship?

What are the effects of megacorporate ownership on the news media? Don't bite the hand that feeds you may be one lesson for working journalists and editors. Stories critical of the global corporate economy's treatment of labor and the environment were never dominant in American media. Today, they are even less likely to even get started when editors know that their livelihoods and fates depend on companies with widespread interests in everything from nuclear waste disposal to disposable diapers. One blatant example of the costs of the megacorporate takeover occurred after Disney's purchase of ABC. Back before the Disney buyout, ABC's *Prime Time Live* ran several stories on the Disney Corporation, tracing the often negative effects of its theme parks on surrounding

FIGURE 6.1   The AOL-Time Warner Empire (a partial listing of holdings)

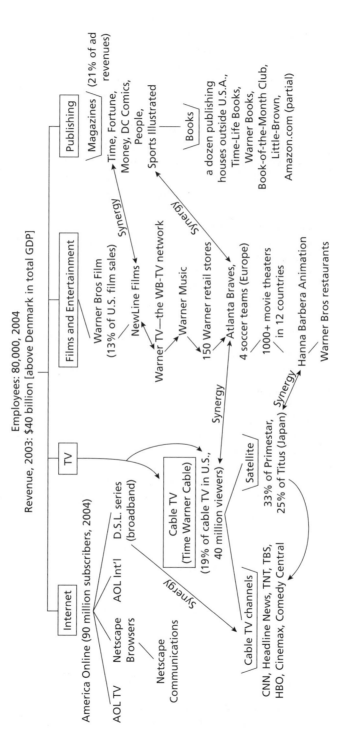

Employees: 80,000, 2004
Revenue, 2003: $40 billion [above Denmark in total GDP]

Internet

America Online (90 million subscribers, 2004)

AOL TV   Netscape   AOL Int'l   D.S.L. series
          Browsers   (broadband)

Netscape
Communications

Synergy

TV

Cable TV channels

CNN, Headline News, TNT, TBS,
HBO, Cinemax, Comedy Central

Cable TV
(Time Warner Cable)
(19% of cable TV in U.S.,
40 million viewers)

Synergy

Satellite

33% of Primestar,
25% of Titus (Japan)

Synergy

Films and Entertainment

Warner Bros Film
(13% of U.S. film sales)

NewLine Films

Warner TV—the WB-TV network

Warner Music

150 Warner retail stores

Atlanta Braves,
4 soccer teams (Europe)

1000+ movie theaters
in 12 countries

Hanna Barbera Animation

Warner Bros restaurants

Synergy

Synergy

Publishing

Magazines / (21% of ad
              revenues)

Time, Fortune,
Money, DC Comics,
People,
Sports Illustrated

Books

a dozen publishing
houses outside U.S.A.,
Time-Life Books,
Warner Books,
Book-of-the-Month Club,
Little-Brown,
Amazon.com (partial)

Source: Columbia Journalism Review, "Who Owns What?" (www.cjr.org); www.timewarner.com.

communities. After the merger, observers noted that ABC news programs tended to highlight Disney movies and products; its *World News with Peter Jennings* even buried a story dealing with pedophilia and sexual harassment at Orlando's Disney World.

More frequent than outright censorship of stories is media silence on a whole host of newsworthy and politically charged topics. Through this process, stories offensive to the media corporation's interests and other big business interests aren't squelched, because they are never produced in the first place. For a quarter of a century, journalism professors and media watchers have been compiling a list of major developments ignored by the mainstream media. "Project Censored's" list of unreported but crucial stories reads like a list of corporate abuses: the association of oil companies with domestic terrorism abroad, the rising tide of workplace injuries, the profiteering of drug companies in the United States and abroad, and the growth of wealth and income inequality led the "noncovered" stories list. Censored, or ignored, were the media mergers themselves and the ambitious legislative agenda of the National Association of Broadcasters (NAB), the industry's major trade association.[20]

The silence may be most deafening when it comes to coverage of organized labor and the kinds of new inequalities and struggles spawned by the corporate-controlled global economy. Although there are well over a thousand business reporters on the United States' major dailies, fewer than ten full-time reporters cover the labor movement for the mainstream mass media. Forty years ago, virtually every major newspaper and most networks had a full-time reporter assigned to American labor.

When not ignored, labor challenges to the global corporate order are covered as hostile and violent occasions in which unruly young demonstrators confront beleaguered police. The commercial media's coverage of the 1999 and 2000 demonstrations in Seattle and Washington, D.C., against the policies of the International Monetary Fund (IMF) and World Trade Organization (WTO) are cases in point. One study found that demonstrators were generally stereotyped as "lawless anarchists," even though all but a tiny minority of both demonstrations were peaceful and there were few arrests that led to formal charges. The same study found that both TV and newspaper coverage scorned or ignored protestors' claims, and TV in particular usually excluded protestors and their spokespersons from voicing their views. Police, IMF, and WTO public relations spokespeople, in contrast, were given more than three-quarters of the quotations and citations. All this is hardly surprising, because the media giants have a global reach and a direct material stake in relaxing trade rules, enforcing copyright protection, and producing international programming and news—all measures opposed specifically by the protestors.[21]

Commercialism and the News

In the olden days, when media companies were smaller and less driven by the effort to maximize profits at all costs, there were some social and cultural barriers that balanced the pursuit of profits with the search for quality and even prestige. Today's megacorporations, however, are more impersonal organizations single-mindedly concerned with the bottom line. As such, their prime motive of corporations is to attract the widest and richest possible audience. By acquiring viewers, networks can market them to advertisers, which provide the bulk of the revenues and the profits. Advertising revenue, after all, is the prime source of a media corporation's profit.

The power of advertisers need not be direct to have effects. Obviously, the richer the audience base the more likely they are to be able to buy products advertised through the mass media, and the more companies can charge for advertising. In news programming, the search for **upscale demographics** and higher revenues may bias both the definition and content of news. Stories that attract the more affluent are favored, while those that appeal to the working poor or the unemployed may be important but tend to get neglected. One obvious example of such bias toward the affluent is the proliferation of programs and newspaper space about business and the stock market. Every newspaper has a business section, and most TV and radio stations run stock market reports. Rarer are stories that appeal to or are about the lives of the working poor, such as what it is like to live on the minimum wage. Put simply, business news draws affluent readers and, thus, advertising.[22]

The drive for greater profits has caused other, much greater distortions. In the main, it has led news organizations to cut costs by cutting reporters and news bureaus, using outsourced reporters, and creating "synergy" by using the same reporters in their diverse print, TV, and radio operations. In the last fifteen years, the number of broadcast reporters in Washington has been halved, and foreign bureau stations have been cut back even more as news divisions of the megacorporations cut costs by using fewer journalists to serve TV, radio, and Internet venues. The result is that news is often reported from single sources, and much foreign news is left unreported or is covered only by the wire services, themselves reduced to the corporate-owned Reuters and the Associated Press. *CBS News*, once the flagship and standard of professional TV journalism, assigns one reporter to cover all of East Asia, and the number of reporters assigned to the entire African continent by the "Big Five" numbers less than six.

Here at home, harried journalists complain that they lack the time and resources to concentrate on important stories and, as a result, are more apt to rely on official sources and the packages handed to them by public relations spokespeople. For instance, in 2002 Democrats criticized Vice President Dick Cheney for his previous leadership of Halliburton, now the biggest private contractor operating in Iraq. The multibillion-dollar company hadn't paid federal taxes while Cheney was CEO. Yet the press simply reported the Democrats' attacks and Cheney's denial without investigating the story and determining who was telling the truth. The story was dropped, a casualty of cost-cutting and perhaps political pressures. On the other hand, stories that are cheap to cover and incur no political risk take precedence: Accidents, natural disasters, and dramatic crimes fit the bill on the local news. Nationally, reporters increasingly rely on reporting official sources and what they are saying because it is simply more economical to do so.[23]

What are the specific political effects of advertisers, who, after all, provide the bulk of revenues and profits to the megacorporations? Many observers have noted a continual erosion of what used to be the wall separating the business operation of a media corporation from the newsroom and professional journalism. The most blatant example is to use the news to promote the direct commercial interests of the parent corporation. *ABC World News Tonight* devoted headline coverage to the Olympics, the purview of ABC Sports and the Disney Corporation. More disturbing might be the behavior of the *Des Moines Register*, which offered its reporters' services to the newspaper's biggest advertisers to develop special sections in which their products and companies were mentioned. Perhaps the most egregious of all was the behavior of dozens of "business correspondents" who happily plugged "hot" stocks before the stock market's 2001 decline because they were being paid by advertisers on their "business news" programs. Celebrity journalists can also make big bucks by shilling for major advertisers, as CBS and PBS correspondent Charlie Rose did when he appeared as the master of ceremonies for the annual Coca-Cola Company shareholders meeting.[24]

Is the Internet an Alternative?

There is, of course, the Internet—the vanguard of the media revolution. Here, it is still possible, at least in theory, for anyone to launch a media site at low expense and reach an audience. Political activists all over the world have used the Internet to increase communication. Yet the democratic and deconcentrated character of the Internet is also threatened by megacorporations and their need to control it for increased profits. In its short life span, the World Wide Web has become more and more a multistop shopping mall, where the big companies compete to provide the ads, the promotions, the programming, and the brand names to dominate the search engines and service-providing business. Increasingly, most people will get their Internet hookups through broadband communication, which will be linked to telephones and cable TV transmissions. Companies like AOL Time Warner are trying to position themselves to control which sites can and can't be transmitted through broadband. Promising open access, AOL Time Warner at the same time aims to protect itself against so-called "unallied content"—news and views that don't originate from its own production and distribution networks. As Douglas Rushkoff, once a young booster of the Internet, now argues, "The slow but steady process by which the Internet was surrendered to commercial use falls somewhere in between a real conspiracy and an inevitable, natural shift. . . . It is a place to do business or one to avoid altogether. . . ."[25]

The fight for public access and control of cyberspace is hardly over. Even the AOL Time Warner merger, approved in early 2001, was accompanied by some provisions that ensured that other Internet services couldn't be shut out of the megagiant's sites. The struggle between commercial and public uses of cyberspace may in fact be the central issue in the democratic debate about the mass media.[26]

Government Influence on the Media

The new media corporations justify their power in the name of the free market-place and technological efficiency. Ironically, though, corporate power in the marketplace is made possible only by very friendly government policies. While the classic defense of elite democracy is that it is technologically efficient and in-dependent of political control, commercial media depends on federal power in dozens of ways. In areas where profits can be boosted, corporations have been cozy with big government, and there has been a price: The media have often been the arm of and not the check on abusive practices of government elites.

Disinformation and Intimidation

Private ownership of the mass media has hardly ever guaranteed independence from government officials or policies. This is particularly true when America goes to war or intervenes abroad. From the Spanish–American War through Vietnam, conflicts in Central America, and the Persian Gulf War, the mass media have often worked hand in hand with government officials and policies. During World War I and World War II, the private media helped boost popular support and suppress dissent. In both wars, government's efforts to suppress dis-sent were either supported or initiated by the U.S. major media companies. No major daily, for instance, ever expressed doubt even about the incarceration of Japanese Americans during World War II.

More recent is the sad record of media/government collusion during the Cold War. Throughout its history during the Cold War, the CIA organized "dis-information" campaigns to plant fabricated or trumped-up stories that confused and discredited domestic critics and foreign opponents of U.S. government interests. In the 1980s, for example, CIA director William Casey successfully disseminated false information about the supposed connections between Nica-ragua's Sandinistas and the drug trade.[27]

Government disinformation thus isn't new. But since September 11, and most especially during the prelude to the Iraq War when Bush's policies were being debated, it has reached new heights. The heart of President Bush's case for war rested on the idea that Saddam Hussein's Iraq was hiding weapons of mass destruction, including a potential nuclear arsenal and substantial stores of bio-logical and chemical weapons. There is "no doubt," Vice President Cheney declared in August 2002, that Saddam "has weapons of mass destruction" and has "resumed his efforts to acquire nuclear weapons." The administration ar-gued that Iraq had acquired a particular type of uranium called yellow-cake from Niger and had bought aluminum tubes necessary to make nuclear wea-pons. In his speech to the United Nations, Secretary of State Colin Powell pointed to pictures showing mobile biological weapons labs in Iraq. Later, after the war had begun, the administration and the Pentagon alleged that weapons of mass destruction were about to be found.

For the most part, the American media bought into these claims, including the elite media of the *New York Times*, *Washington Post*, CNN, and other outlets.

As it has turned out, however, none of these claims turned out to be true. For many observers, the administration's claims were not innocent errors but planned distortions and disinformation precisely designed to be broadcast by the media. The Pentagon had established an "Office of Special Plans" to find data that supported the administration's claims about Iraq. In the CIA, many intelligence analysts had dissented from the administration's case, but Vice President Cheney and CIA director Tenet had only used the conclusions of highly suspect Iraqi defectors and ignored the rest when it reported to Congress, the press, and the American people. According to John Walcott of Knight-Ridder newspapers, one of the few media outlets that had reported dissent from the administration's position within the bureaucracy, "In the case of Iraq," the political appointees "really closed ranks. So if you relied exclusively on traditional news sources, you would not have heard the things we heard." Conscious deception or unconscious misinformation, the case for the Iraq War well represents the dangers present in our existing media system.

Disinformation is one problem. The Bush administration has developed a more disturbing practice: employing government agents posing as reporters, who then deliver their "news" to receptive local TV stations who air it during their news broadcasts. In early 2005, the *New York Times* revealed that over $274 million of government money had been devoted to such "fake news" about subjects from Bush's education policies to the status of women in Afghanistan. On air, these stories were never labeled as derived from government sources. In content, all of them praised government policies and programs. The outlets most prone to air such stories were local affiliates of the networks, whose news operations had been cut back in order to boost profit margins.

Last but hardly least is the long history of government and federal court efforts to force reporters to reveal their anonymous and confidential sources. Such sources have provided the public with information about government and corporate misdeeds and lying in hundreds of cases. Back in the 1960s and 1970s, government prosecutors and politicians threatened reporters with jail time if they didn't reveal who'd "blown the whistle" by revealing secret and embarrassing government documents on matters ranging from the Vietnam War to the Watergate scandal. In 2005, *New York Times* reporter Judith Miller was jailed when she refused to reveal whom she talked to in her investigation of the White House's outing of a CIA agent whose husband, diplomat Joseph Wilson, had discredited the Bush administration's claims about nuclear weapons in Iraq. Miller had investigated the story but had never even written an article about it. Another reporter ordered to testify, Matt Cooper of *Time* magazine, was let free when Time Warner released Cooper's notes to the government. To many, this was a direct attack on press freedom and a signal that the government wouldn't tolerate whistle-blowers.[28]

The Revolving Door

Government influence over the news is not always so direct or deceptive. A subtler example of government influence these days is the **revolving door**. Quite often, independent journalists are picked to be government officials, and government officials find new and distinguished careers as reporters "covering" the institutions they recently left. When government "insiders" become working journalists, and vice-versa, the wall of separation between media and political authority may be weakened, and the incentive for reporters to file objective stories is greatly lessened.

"Celebrity" journalists are particularly prone to be beneficiaries of the revolving door. George Will soared to journalistic fame with ABC and through a widely syndicated column, but in 1980 he coached Ronald Reagan for his debate with Jimmy Carter. Employed by ABC at the time, Will later praised Reagan's debate performance in front of the TV cameras. (After his dual role of coach and commentator was revealed, Will apologized.) Ted Koppel touts his friendship with former Nixon national security adviser and secretary of state Henry Kissinger, who once offered him a job as press spokesperson for the Nixon State Department. And there is always George Stephanopoulos and William Kristol. Both parlayed government service into lucrative contracts with major networks.

The media's independence might be most compromised when it comes to the choice of "experts" on national news programs. Here, the revolving door spins the fastest. Most experts chosen tend to be fellow insiders, former government officials, academics associated with Washington think tanks closely tied to the federal government, or officials themselves. *Chicago Tribune* columnist Clarence Page has labeled this phenomenon the **Rolodex syndrome**. When a dramatic story appears, the news media all seem to call on a similar guest list of former government officials recast as journalists or neutral experts. In the Bush administration, the Rolodex syndrome has evolved into a more blatant attempt to actually pay journalists to toe the administration's line as "neutral" experts. In early 2005, two prominent pundits were found to be on the payroll of a public relations firm hired by the Bush administration. They had been paid hundreds of thousands of dollars to be advocates of Bush's domestic policies.[29]

Government Regulation of Broadcasting: Who Owns the Airwaves?

Why are the commercial news media so receptive to government claims? If the private marketplace hardly guarantees an independent media, what might? Corporate control of the mass media is hardly inevitable or the product of a free marketplace but of government policy that favors it. After all, the people of the United States are the official owners of the airwaves. Licenses for all TV and radio stations are lent to the likes of Rupert Murdoch and Sumner Redstone in return for their promise to serve the public interest as trustees. Since 1934, the power to regulate and license has been vested in the Federal Communications Commission (FCC), a body whose members are appointed by the president and approved by Congress.

Through the FCC, government thus possesses an enormous power to shape (or retard) public access to the airwaves. Historically, labor, consumer, and other citizens groups have pressed government for a media system where public access and even publicly owned, noncommercial broadcasting were promoted. Indeed, the statute establishing the FCC commands it to prevent monopolies, promote competition, and ensure that a wide diversity of news and views is disseminated. Yet the 1934 act provided few concrete provisions that defined public access or control and said nothing at all about public broadcasting.

Since the 1930s, periods in which popular democratic movements have been strong are also periods where the mass media's commercialism has given way to increased public access and diversity in both ownership and programming. The 1930s and 1960s are notable for important legislation regarding the broadcast media. In the 1960s, media activists also carved out limited public space for National Public Radio and the Public Broadcasting Service, then partly funded through tax dollars. Both were meant to be free of overt commercial influence.

From the 1940s through the early 1980s, the FCC did impose some obligations and rules on private broadcasters using the public airwaves. Stations were required to reserve part of their programming for public affairs. If stations aired advertisements for one political candidate, they were required to supply the same opportunity to others. (Communists were excluded.) The Fairness Rule required broadcasters to provide reasonable time to opposing views on controversial topics. Other provisions required that stations provide some time for public affairs topics. Monopolies in local markets were prohibited, as no single corporation could own local newspapers, television stations, and radio stations.

Yet over time and with increasing frequency since the Reagan presidency, most of the regulations and laws that promoted public access to the airwaves were gutted by Congress or the FCC or ruled unconstitutional by the federal courts. Through its powerful lobbying arm, the National Association of Broadcasters (NAB), the media industry led the charge against regulation and, with a few exceptions, has generally succeeded on all fronts. In the 1980s, the FCC's staff and budget were cut, making it difficult for the regulators to monitor television and radio companies. License renewals for TV and radio stations every eight years no longer required hearings and could be done by mail. The Fairness Rule was eliminated, and the obligation to broadcast public affairs programming was ended.

One important barrier to corporate media was FCC restrictions on ownership; companies could not own newspapers, TV stations, and radio stations in the same market. In the 1990s, the corporate media took aim at some of these restrictions. In the mid-1990s, the development of new broadcast technologies combined with increased competition among corporate giants in cable television, telephone, and networks. These developments led to new pressure on the government to "update" broadcasting regulations. The result was that the **Telecommunications Act of 1996** passed with substantial bipartisan support in the Senate and House. The ostensible goal of the bill's supporters was to further "competition" by breaking down the existing walls that prevented one industry from entering the market of another. For the bill's supporters, the act was supposed to stimulate a new "Information Age" of heightened competition and technological innovation.

Yet the decade since the act's passage has featured the opposite of increased competition. Indeed, the act has promoted the most massive concentration of corporate media power in U.S. history. The new law also gutted remaining restrictions that once prevented telephone, cable, television, and radio companies from competing in one another's markets. At the same time, it also allows them to combine in yet larger megacompanies that control communications in entire markets. Perhaps the most disturbing aspect of the bill has been the FCC's interpretation of it. Soon, television will be transmitted through a "digital spectrum," a new technology that will allow hundreds of new TV channels to transmit over the airwaves. In theory, the public owns the digital spectrum just as it owns the other airwaves. Yet by late 1997, the government was giving away the digital spectrum (with a market value of $70 billion) to the corporate megagiants that already controlled the TV airwaves. It was quite a present: Corporations like Rupert Murdoch's News Corporation and the Disney Corporation may use the new airwaves and cyberspace to make as much money as they want, without any obligation to broadcast news or public service programming, or even provide debating time to political candidates. The scale of corporate welfare even offended conservatives like columnist William Safire, who branded the giveaway a "ripoff on a scale vaster than dreamed of yesteryear's robber barons."[30]

In 2003, media industries came back for more, and under then FCC chairman Michael Powell they had an ever-friendlier advocate. Powell led an effort to relax its rules even further by allowing one company to own TV stations, radio stations, and newspapers in one "media market" or community. Under the new "rules" it would be possible for a single company to control the majority of media outlets in a city. For the first time in four decades, however, a broad-based coalition formed to overturn the FCC's decision. The "Making a Difference" feature box details how this new media reform movement finally drew the line against even more media oligopolies.[31]

Making (and Creating) the News

We've traced the story of increasing corporate control, but it's a little more difficult to understand how average journalists are affected by corporate ownership.

Media Bias: Which Way Does It Go?

Perhaps journalists are independent and willful enough to ignore or defy their corporate owners. Many certainly have good intentions and professional training. One prominent school of thought sees most working journalists as biased toward liberals and prone to grind ideological axes against big corporations and traditional family values. In recent years, conservative Republicans and even some Democrats have led spirited attacks on the television news media for supposed liberal biases. Ironically, the attacks have become more vehement as frankly conservative media outlets from talk radio to Fox News have grown in numbers and influence and as supposedly liberal outlets like National Public

MAKING A DIFFERENCE

The Media Revolution of 2003

Start a real national debate about the role of media corporations and what they own? Get millions of people to write letters and e-mails, even though you have no paid advertising and the entire media industry and its lobbying arm opposes you? Overturn a determined and powerful majority on the arcane Federal Communications Commission about a matter that is hard for the public to understand? The odds seemed impossibly long, even if you were an optimist. Yet that is just what a growing movement for media reform did in 2003. How did it happen?

When Bush appointee Michael Powell assumed the chairmanship of the FCC in 2002, implementing his procorporate ideas seemed like a slam dunk. Powell was the son of the esteemed Colin Powell. Republicans had majorities in both houses of Congress, controlled the White House, and had a conservative majority on the FCC itself. With the backing of President Bush and congressional Republican leaders, Powell had been appointed to strip the remaining regulations governing media ownership. "I don't see why we have to tell companies they have to eat their vegetables before they get their dessert," Powell opined. "Monopoly is not illegal by itself in the United States. The public interest works with letting the market work its magic." By late 2002, Powell and his colleagues proposed a closed-door process that would dismantle the last

federal ownership limits. Supported by the corporate media's lobbying arm and by all of the country's major media owners, the deregulation Powell proposed would allow a single company to own all the major media—cable, television, radio, newspapers—in the nation's metropolitan media markets. Powell claimed that the issue of media ownership was moot—an issue that had been surpassed by a media revolution and the Internet. Besides, a federal court had ordered the FCC to show reasons why media concentration might be harmful to information diversity. Powell could find no reasons.

That's when the opposition got its act together. It started small: The Media Access Project and Center for Digital Democracy had been working on bolstering, not stripping, media ownership rules for years. This time they pushed for open public hearings on Powell's proposal. They were joined by a courageous FCC commissioner, Michael Copps, who said that he'd have public meetings throughout the country even if Powell didn't attend. As Copps took his hearings across the country, the organizers were astounded by the turnout; the mainstream media had done nothing to cover these events. Yet the press coverage of the Iraq War—so friendly to all the administration's claims—had activated the growing antiwar movement to care about media issues. Many antiwar activists contacted the activist online group Moveon.org, which

---

Radio and the Public Broadcasting System have become more dependent on corporate "underwriting" for funding. Such charges virtually ignore all the conservative effects of corporate ownership that we've outlined above, resting the case for the liberal media on the assumption that journalists are not only liberal but are in complete control of their own stories and work routines quite apart from what the corporations who employ them claim. Nonetheless, it is still important to ask: Are journalists more "liberal"?

in turn distributed news of the ownership controversy over its 1-million-member website.

The FCC was deluged with over 750,000 e-mails opposing Powell's proposals, and so was Congress. Groups like Common Cause, who had never been active in media policy issues before, declared it the most important issue of the year. They were joined by organizations of journalists like the Newspaper Guild and the National Association of Black Journalists. But the media reform movement had to broaden beyond its liberal base, and it did. Alliances were made with evangelical Christian groups and even the National Rifle Association, who believed that local control of the airwaves was more important for their cause than centralized corporate ownership. The battle moved to Congress; Republican senators like John McCain and Trent Lott joined the battle, and so did almost all the Democrats in both houses. Public opinion polls revealed that the ownership battle had achieved increasing public visibility, with people overwhelmingly against the FCC proposal.

Although under increasing political pressure, Chairman Powell had been meeting and strategizing with his powerful friends in the big media lobby, the National Association of Broadcasters. They apparently gave him courage to persist, and in June 2003, Powell forced a favorable 3–2 vote in the FCC. The deregulation measures were poised to go into effect. The House of Representatives, however, was deluged with opposition letters and e-mails, more than at any time in its history about a media issue. Only the delaying tactics of the Republican leadership prevented it from coming to the floor for a vote. After a complicated series of maneuvers by the Bush administration, the Senate wrangled over counterproposals but ultimately voted down the new (de)regulatory policy. The last card, however, could be played in federal court, which had the power as final judge. A year later, in June 2004, a federal court rejected the FCC's new regulation and ordered the FCC to come up with a reason to justify why further media concentration would be in the public interest.

What lessons can be learned from this successful battle? To be sure, the victory did little to roll back an already highly centralized media system. Still, it did stop it from moving forward, and in the process it forged a broad and diverse coalition that put media regulation on the political agenda. Media scholar and activist Robert McChesney commented, "The challenge for those who support democratic media, and a democratic solution to the problem of the media, is to harness this energy and not allow it to dissipate. But the most important struggle is simply to convince people that the media are political forces than can be shaped, not natural ones to be endured."

Sources: Robert McChesney, *The Problem of the Media: U.S. Communication Politics in the Twenty-first Century* (New York: Monthly Review Press, 2004); Neil Hickey, "Media Monopoly: Behind the Mergers Q & A," *Columbia Journalism Review* (May–June 2003); "About the FCC June 2 Vote," Free Press (www.freepress.net/rules); Robert Siegel, "Federal Appeals Court Tosses Out FCC Regulations," *All Things Considered*, June 24, 2004.

The chief surveys of journalists do indicate that they are somewhat more likely than the public at large to vote for Democrats for president, and they are likely to be more "liberal" about social issues like abortion, gay marriage, and the death penalty. At the same time, journalists are more "conservative" than the public about issues such as taxation, Social Security, corporate regulation, and trade policies. Most journalists identify themselves as centrists, and their views actually are fairly similar to other professionals with similar educational and class backgrounds. Only 14 percent think that being "an adversary of business" is important in their careers. "Providing analyses of complex problems" and "getting news to the public quickly" rank more highly as professional values. Even the self-proclaimed "liberals" among the journalists define themselves as "not bound by doctrines or committed to a point of view in advance."[32]

With the important exception of celebrity journalists like Diane Sawyer, Brian Williams, or Wolf Blitzer and those who write for the most prestigious publications, most reporters' salaries average less than those of teachers and college professors. African Americans, Latinos, Asian Americans, and especially women have made employment gains in journalism over the last two decades. Still, the vast majority of journalists, much like those in other professions, are white males from upper-income families with graduate degrees. Often, as James Fallows demonstrated in his study about journalists and their coverage of "free trade" disputes, the Washington "press displays . . . an instinctive sympathy with the interests of the educated elite. The press chose the college-boy side of the argument—apparently without realizing that it was choosing sides." None of these characteristics support the idea that journalists are somehow biased against established interests and institutions, much less given to radical critiques of the American social, economic, or political order.[33]

Professional Standards

But even if liberals did predominate among journalists, the new work routines imposed by the companies that employ them combine with traditional professional standards to create a far different bias. Most journalists have nothing like the celebrity status or seven- and eight-figure salaries of the most famous anchors of network and cable news programs. For the average reporter, making the news is about the much less dramatic daily business of gathering facts, making phone calls, attending meetings and press conferences, and meeting deadlines. For news editors who supervise reporters, making the news is about assigning reporters to particular stories, ensuring that reporters' stories live up to professional standards, and making decisions about which stories will appear and where.

From inside any large or small news organization, blatant pressures from parent corporations, advertisers, the FBI, or the CIA may seem pretty remote. News media professionals point to how stories exposing corporate and government misdeeds—like Watergate in the 1970s, the savings and loan debacle of the 1980s, or the Lewinsky/Clinton scandal of the 1990s—have been unearthed by and through adherence by news organizations to high-minded standards of journalistic professionalism.

For journalists, professional standards are supposed to produce a firewall between the business interests of media corporations and what journalists actually do. Reporters are taught to be *objective*, in that they remove from their stories their own ideological point of view and let the facts speak for themselves and the chips fall where they may. As they seek *balance*, they report the diverse views of different spokespersons when a dispute arises. And, as news organizations compete to better inform the American public, they seek to create that wide "marketplace of ideas" that is supposed to be the major justification for media competition and press freedom in the first place.

These standards are no doubt professed by most reporters, producers, and editors, including the celebrities. Most are sincere in their attempts to uphold them, but the structure of modern news organizations makes it difficult. Objectivity and balance are difficult to maintain in a world where elite institutions have an advantage over ordinary citizens when it comes to both influencing what journalists see and defining the limits of "respectable" debate for news stories. And objectivity and balance, even if achievable, are supposed to work within organizational rules and constraints that define them in particular ways.

The Problem of Source Bias

News doesn't happen everywhere. Issues, facts, and events become news only when editors and reporters decide to make them so. And to report the news, journalists must be present where something happens. Thus, the "beats" chosen by news organizations often determine how news is defined and which sources are and aren't consulted. The vast majority of American political reporting comes from Washington, D.C., the White House, Congress, the Justice Department, the Pentagon, and other governmental agencies, which are the major "beats" of political reporters. Government agencies and institutions, as well as interest groups that can afford it, have thus become not only the major objects of political reporting but are the important sources for most political news. There is certainly no lack of government and corporate press relations personnel to "inform" and influence the press. In Washington alone, an army of 13,000 federal employees generates publicity for several thousand correspondents; the Pentagon's public relations budget alone far exceeds $3 billion annually.

Despite enormous resources and news bureaus, even the more prestigious media fall victim to **source bias**. It is understandable that the doings in Washington make news. But a natural corollary of the process is that Washington reporters mostly report what they hear in Washington from their sources. Day after day, reporters travel between press briefings issued by private and public organizations that spend millions on creating favorable public images for the people and institutions they represent. Thus, "balance" is sought within the quite restricted and establishment realm of the Washington world of think tanks, government agencies, and monied interests that have the wherewithal to establish themselves as newsmakers and legitimate sources. And almost all the sources upon which journalists rely for their information have a very direct, often personal stake in what is reported. Moreover, they have press relations bureaucracies in place to influence the press, and journalists come to rely on such staff to provide them access to the interviews, background information, and inside scoops necessary to get the job done. The result, Robert Entman has claimed, is that "the news largely consists of information supplied by sources who support democracy in the abstract, but must in specific encounters with the press subordinate that ideal to the protection of their own political interests."[34]

Given the establishment connection, it is difficult to see how journalistic objectivity can operate in practice. Some Washington beats—especially the White House, State Department, the Pentagon, and offices of the major congressional leaders—serve as the chief sources for hundreds of reporters. The press releases, interviews, and press conferences emanating from these sources by themselves make news. Even if false, what is said by the presidential press secretary must be reported. For "balance" or a response, yet another governmental official, probably from the opposing political party, is quoted. If the "legitimate" opposition doesn't oppose, as most Democrats didn't during the prelude to the Iraq War, then the issue is dropped. Beyond the pale are those groups without extensive clout or without Washington offices and the resources to employ press officers. These include most of the grassroots groups in American society that can't afford to employ the media experts, lawyers, and lobbyists that government and corporate America can. In the last decades, corporate wealth and the political right have also joined together to fund ever-more-important think tanks, precisely because they serve as prime "sources" and experts for journalists.[35]

Again, the Iraq War's conduct forms the most momentous case study of source bias. In this most dramatic of recent U.S. acts, reporters were "embedded" with U.S. troops, but their reports were censored if they offended "secrecy" criteria. The rest of the U.S. press corps either reported from Washington or from reports issued by the "Coalition Media Center" located outside of Iraq in the desert kingdom of Qatar. Briefings were held at a large conference center, behind a stage built with tax dollars at a cost of a quarter of a million dollars by a former Republican consultant employed by Bush's 2000 campaign. Michael Massing reported that "so stingy is Centecom with information that, at the daily briefings, the questions asked were often more revealing than the answers given." Inquiring reporters were told to "phone the office and leave your request with the officer on duty. If you're lucky, someone will come out and speak to you." The Coalition Media Center was in a position of power because busy reporters had to file daily stories. Massing reports that it was therefore unsurprising that the huge U.S. press corps, most of whom didn't speak Arabic and had no experience in the Middle East, "mostly recounted tales of American bravery and derring-do" supplied to them by the "Media Center."[36]

Experienced reporters could be subject to source bias, too: The *New York Times*'s Judith Miller (discussed above in another context) filed a breathless page-one story about an Iraqi scientist who purported to know where a huge stash of weapons of mass destruction was buried. The source, supplied by the Pentagon's favorite Iraqi in exile, Ahmad Chalabi, was never named by Miller so as to conform with the Pentagon's strictures. The story was used as evidence by the Bush administration that their claims about hidden WMD were about to be vindicated. As it turned out, Miller and the *Times* had been misled. So too had the reporters in hundreds of other less famous news stories where reporters had trusted sources provided by the military. In Iraq War reportage, source bias was endemic, not an aberration, as it extended to stories essential to the war's public support, from the story of Jessica Lynch to the existence of mobile biological weapons. What may be an aberration, however, was the depth of the *Times*'s editor's apologies for the error—an apology not matched by many other news organizations that had run similarly erroneous stories.[37]

In these ways, media reporting often reflects not "reality" but how the different representatives of the status quo construe it. Professor Lance Bennett comments, "Cooperation between reporters and officials is so routine that officials rarely have to employ intimidation tactics."[38]

McNews

The concentration on similar sources does not mean that all news is reported in exactly the same way. Television news specializes in the dramatic and the immediate, and it is more likely to cover one-time events and the activities of famous people and celebrities. In contrast, the print media tend to report on institutions, issues, and policies more extensively and in most cases provide stories with more information and factual support than does television. With the exception of National Public Radio and a few other sources, like the Pacifica Radio Network, radio news consists of short bulletins and little depth. Internet news tends to come as headlines, and the major sites link the user to transcribed TV or newspaper stories or to more extensive databases. In recent years, bloggers and nonestablished sources like Internet gossip columnists have entered the media picture, pressuring media organizations with stories that they'd have otherwise been unlikely to cover.

Yet despite these important contrasts, what is remarkable about "news products" is not how different they are but how similar they have become. Modern news organizations work according to routines and draw from other media sources that tend to "standardize" how the media define and report news. Many newspapers, as well as the networks, rely on the wire services of the Associated Press for their stories. And the New York Times Company and other media giants supply articles that are often picked up by smaller newspapers. To save money, local news stations—now more than ever owned by media conglomerates—often depend on their parent networks to lead them to important national stories. Moreover, to gain increased ratings, networks have turned to mixing news with entertainment—"infotainment."

As we've said, the corporate pressure to cut costs might be the chief culprit for "McNews." TV coverage is geared toward predictable, low-cost sites. Camera crews and reporters must generally be prepared in advance to "cover" speeches, hearings, floods, or the travels of politicians. Thus, those institutions and organizations that can preplan their events for the TV cameras are at an advantage over "spontaneous" events. Besides Washington, D.C., news beats are likely to include, in order of importance, New York City, Los Angeles, and Chicago, and these days perhaps Atlanta or Houston. News happening outside the reach of the national news bureaus stationed in such cities is likely to get much less attention. For local stations, the situation is even more driven by commercial pressures. Quite simply, local news stations find it cheaper and more profitable to cover sensational crimes, feature stories, weather, and sports. "Investigative journalism is just too expensive," explained one student of the subject.[39]

Although print and TV reporters do compete for stories, they also cooperate in a phenomenon known as **pack journalism**. Most of the time, reporters who are covering everything from political campaigns to presidential trips travel together, receive the same press kits, attend the same press conferences, and face the same requirements to file a story by the deadline. In these interactions, they acquire a collective sense of where the "story" does and doesn't lie. As Timothy Crouse said in his study of the 1972 presidential race, reporters "arrive at their answers just as independently as a class of honest seventh graders using the same geometry text."[40]

The result is a remarkably similar "spin" on a story and a strong consensus, forged by what the pack sees and hears. Journalists create **media frames**, or ideas about what should be emphasized and what deemphasized in their depictions. The problem is that what they see and hear is extremely limited by the nature of the "beat" itself and often by the public relations talents employed by the organization and persons being covered. Reporting on the 2000 presidential race, the *Washington Post*'s Dana Milbank told how the pack would assemble at the site of the each presidential debate, where they'd all sit in a room and watch the event together, only to interview the same "spinmeisters" of each candidate after the "show" was over. In 2004, a similar phenomenon occurred: Press coverage of Democratic candidate Howard Dean's "scream" ended his candidacy, most likely because the "pack" came to a consensus that Dean was mistake prone and possibly unstable. Yet later it turned out that Dean's shouting had much to do with the high level of noise in the room; he was trying to whip up his supporters and struggling to be heard.[41]

Conversely, where the pack "isn't" defines a news "nonevent." Back in October 2002, Washington witnessed one of the biggest antiwar demonstrations in U.S. history. Yet few seasoned reporters were assigned; the *New York Times* even misreported the story so badly that it had to apologize a week later. Unless there is predicted violence, protests lack a journalistic "pack" to give them coverage.[42] The biggest stories are often missed by hundreds of journalists assigned to cover conventional institutions and politicians. We've already mentioned the most important recent lapse: the utter falsity of the Bush administration's claims about weapons of mass destruction. But in the past, the exposure of major scandals like Watergate in the 1970s and the Iran–Contra scandal in the 1980s was hardly due to the huge numbers of reporters stationed at the Nixon or Reagan White House. The pack ignored—or remained ignorant of—both stories until well after the events had occurred.

Producing McNews doesn't mean that all news media say the same thing. Much like fast food chains, McNews can feature a seemingly broad fare even though it all assembled with the same factory-like techniques. Lending color and excitement and the appearance of diversity to newscasting has been pioneered by Fox, the upstart in the cable news business. While Fox' news-gathering techniques are essentially the same, what it does do is blatantly attempt to mirror public emotions rather than balance them with diverse information. Fox personnel can refer on air to Osama bin Laden or Saddam Hussein as a monster, play triumphal music as U.S. troops paraded toward Baghdad, and set up entertaining talking head formats in which pundits square off against each other. Substantive and expensive to produce stories can be bypassed or buried in the effort to entertain. What changes are the performance and format, all designed to increase audience share. The important news becomes the entertaining news that can find a niche market.[43]

Companies usually justify "McNews" by saying that news, like any other product, is simply a response to what media consumers want. This is an interesting rationale, for it seems to mean that news is not a set of objective or even real events but a planned and packaged contrivance manufactured for attractive sale to advertisers and consumers. Also, it may very well be that people watch McNews because it is the only available choice presented to them on the news menu. Media surveys of "consumers" rarely ask people what they really want or need to learn about public affairs. They instead confine their questions to choices between such weighty matters as the clothing styles and studio decorations most favored by listeners, or whether they like or dislike U.S. flags on the anchor's lapels. More expensive, perhaps riskier, alternative ways of defining and reporting the news are just not considered as options.[44]

Silence of the Lambs:
Journalists, Politicians, and Campaigns

Political campaigns are perhaps the most important moments when a full democratic debate could be possible. Politicians have to compete actively for popular support. Their records, speeches, and persons are scrutinized. They must answer questions continually about what they have done and what they will do. Or, at least, campaigns present those possibilities. How have the media performed in covering campaigns?

Although framed by radically different political contexts and issues, the 2000 and 2004 election campaigns both present clear tests of major trends in news journalism. While there are important changes in 2004, here it is worth noting the similarities and continuities in media coverage in these two election campaigns. (An extended discussion of these differences can be found in Chapters 7 and 8.) Source bias, the commercial impulse, and pack journalism are embodied in a unique campaign media form, **horse race journalism**.

The term captures the penchant of campaign media to cover the personalities, strategies, tactics, and drama of the presidential race. Media frames are created that allow journalists to judge the ups and downs of the race in terms of who is ahead, who's behind, and why the candidate's performance and the strategies and tactics of campaign consultants are or are not effective. The voters appear in polls, which in turn feed the media frame about how well or poorly the candidates are performing. Excluded from horse race coverage are the historical contexts in which the elections occur—the campaign appears as a topsy-turvy and unpredictable struggle between personalities locked in bitter competition. Issue differences are give short shrift, and so are the reasons why political and economic interests might support with their money one party and candidate or the other. Little is said about how the electoral outcome might affect ordinary voters and the world, but quite a bit is said about how candidates have committed gaffes, appeared stiff, or possessed momentum.

It is incontestable that horse race journalism has come to predominate in campaign news. In 2000, even the prestigious *Washington Post* and *New York Times* devoted more than two-thirds of all their campaign stories to campaign strategy, tactics, polling, and the all-important question of "who's ahead today." The situation was even more extreme with TV news and other print outlets. In 2004, a cross-media study by Columbia University's Project for Excellence in Journalism found even more horse race coverage than in 2000, despite the fact that the country and the parties were divided more than ever along issue and ideological differences. In 2004, just 13 percent of all campaign stories discussed issues and the partisan divide, and only one-fifth of the stories talked at all about how campaign news affected citizens via their policy implications. While newspapers did slightly better than broadcast journalism in these studies, an astounding two-thirds of stories were about "political internals" and "candidate performance."[45]

Partisans in both 2000 and 2004 claimed that the media were biased against their favorite, and they based their attacks on the media on its ideological biases. But horse race journalism creates a much more potent bias toward framing and

TOLES © 2004 The Washington Post. Reprinted with permission of UNIVERSAL PRESS SYNDICATE. All rights reserved.

then judging the character and performance of the candidate. In 2000, studies indicate that Bush was favored in news stories because Gore was framed as a cold and arrogant policy wonk, while Bush appeared to be an engaging and down-home populist. At least, that was the media judgment after their debates. In 2004, studies indicate more favorable news stories about candidate Kerry than Bush, largely because in their debate performances Bush was judged to be uncomfortable and defensive, whereas Kerry appeared competent and in control. While few remember what any of the candidates said, handicapping the horse race allows endless commentary by pundits and journalists. Perhaps this is why in the last two elections candidates and what they say have been reduced to eight-second sound bites on most TV news programs, even as journalists have increased their talking time sixfold over what it had once been in the 1970s.[46]

What might be some of the effects of horse race journalism's predominance on U.S. politics? Along with those just mentioned, here are a few more.

1. Dependent as it is on performance and strategy, horse race journalism relies on scoops and insider information. In this way, what campaign strategists are doing, saying, and leaking creates a momentous source bias. Voters' voices are reduced to focus groups and poll numbers.

2. The horse race emphasis excludes alternative voices and social movements. If the emphasis is on who is going to win, why cover people with few prospects? Ralph Nader and other third-party candidates learned this in both 2000 and 2004. Nader never thought he was going to win, but he wanted to get his critical message out. The press ignored him, except when he became a factor in 2000 in the "win-loss" media frame. Then he was depicted not for what he said but as a "spoiler." In 2004, he was virtually ignored altogether.

3. Personalization and dramatization depoliticizes and discredits citizen action and thus can serve to depress citizen participation. If campaigns are just about the jabs and punches of candidates in the political ring, campaign news becomes a jumble of discordant and confusing technical commentaries that mean little to the ordinary, noninsider voter. The result: withdrawal of many citizens from elections and voting as a kind of game which is either incomprehensible, unmanageable, or boring.[47]

Some argue that campaign journalism is the way it is because that's what "consumers" (voters) want. Yet both public opinion polls and TV ratings indicate that the media rendition of politics as a game turns off most citizens. Voters gave both the 2000 and 2004 campaign press barely acceptable grades; a majority of those who did vote said they thought they knew enough to make an intelligent choice. But perhaps the notable grade on the media comes from its inability or unwillingness to report matters from the standpoint of ordinary citizens. This has implications: As we'll see in Chapter 8, after President Bush was reelected in 2004, he claimed a "mandate" for the privatization of Social Security. Voters recoiled. Apparently they had meant no such thing. It didn't help that Social Security issues constituted less than 1 percent of campaign stories in 2004.

Ultimately, whether it is in the media's coverage of campaigns or battles in political institutions, the mass media seem to reserve to themselves the task of shaping the political agenda. Unfortunately, the agenda they set often bolsters elite democracy by confining citizens to the role of passive spectators and consumers in an election that is supposed to be theirs.

Conclusion: Democratizing the Mass Media

The features of corporate-run media and the commercial pressures besetting the newsroom today bolster elite democracy. If popular democracy is to remain alive in the United States, then the decisions now made about who owns and operates the media must be subject to a wider democratic debate. Is a democratic media possible, and what might it look like? As we saw above, a growing and broad media reform movement has had some recent successes. In the "New Ideas" box, we describe some of this movement's major proposals.

If the broad goals of democratic media reform are to be met, hope is also provided by a central fact. Despite all the powers of commercial media, large numbers of Americans, and especially young people, have tuned out the mainstream media and created alternative forms of communication. Declining numbers of TV watchers may represent a silent vote of no confidence in the likes of Disney and Rupert Murdoch. In recent years, this has led to an explosion of an alternative media. Some of it has built on the rich tradition of the alternative press, embodied in magazines like the *Nation* and in cultural forms like hip-hop and rock music.

There is also the rise of "fake news"—Jon Stewart's *The Daily Show* reaches millions of viewers with its sharp and humorous barbs skewering the mainstream media, and Stewart himself launched meaningful criticisms of his "serious" counterparts. Interestingly, Stewart's audience was found to be not only young but more knowledgeable about campaign issues than those who followed them in newspapers and on cable television. The most important role of alternative media is to break stories and pioneer cultural and political trends that most corporate media shun or ignore. In journalism itself, rebellion is also alive, fueled by awareness that traditions of investigative journalism are in danger from the profit-making demands of big media. Whether in journalism's Newspaper Guild or in the searing investigations of *The New Yorker*'s Seymour Hersh, the search for an independent journalism that connects to citizens continues.

Perhaps the Internet and the new forms it has spawned are the most lively. The blogosphere, for instance, presents the possibility of "new news." Since 2000, bloggers have exposed many of the distortions of mainstream news media, from the myths about who toppled Saddam Hussein's statue in Baghdad's square to the existence of so-called independent journalists who were paid substantial funds to support the Bush administration's agenda. In 2004, bloggers provided new energies to the campaigns of Howard Dean and, later, Bush and Kerry's campaigns. Blogging, though, also has its limitations: One study of blogs during

NEW IDEAS

What Would Media Democracy Look Like?

The new media reform movement has grown by leaps and bounds in the last few years, propelled by its ability to defeat a powerful FCC chairman and one of the richest lobbies in Washington: the National Association of Broadcasters (NAB). But besides playing defense, what would a democratic media system look like? Here are some of the ideas, gleaned from discussions at the National Conference on Media Reform.

- *Let noncommercial TV and radio flourish.* Why should costly and valuable TV and radio licenses be handed out to commercial outlets when America has a viable civil society of community groups, church congregations, and labor, environmental, and other associations? One starting point is to build up nonprofit media of all kinds. In radio, low-power FM would allow thousands of small stations owned by community groups to flourish. In TV, allow towns and cities to own their own stations, since there's plenty of room on the digital spectrum.

- *Revive and democratize public broadcasting.* Once strong and now weak, PBS and NPR lack the resources and power to compete with megacorporations and have become dependent on them for grants and gifts. Build up these entities by linking them to community radio and television stations, and provide them with the wherewithal to produce their own nonprofit programming, including news. A good start might be allowing taxpayers to check off up to $100 on their tax returns. The proceeds could go to public broadcasting.

- *Remember public interest regulation?* The U.S.'s airwaves officially belong to the public, but megacorporations now use them as if they were private property. At the very least, insist on regulations that promote commercial free broadcasting. Why not give each station their licenses for only eighteen hours a day, reserving the rest for public service programming? For the rest of the time, bring back requirements that limit advertising time and promote public debate, especially during election campaigns.

- *The Internet: Make it a freeway, not a toll road.* In Philadelphia and other cities, governments are fighting with telecommunications companies about who will provide Internet access to the millions who don't have it. Why should companies have the right to charge for Internet access if it can be provided by cities and communities? Of course, community-owned Internet access will fail if it can't provide the content that makes it interesting and provocative. Build a network of free, noncommercial Internet providers that privilege the work and sites of a wide range of community groups, from religious congregations to labor.

- *Break up the media oligopolies.* Why allow seven gargantuan companies to control most of what we see and hear? In America's past, antitrust laws provided the means to prevent concentrated private power. But in recent years, antitrust laws on the books haven't been used when it comes to the media industry. Start using those laws now to break up the largest firms and restore some semblance of competition.

Does all this sound like pie-in-the-sky? Perhaps, but only if one believes that corporate power has become so overwhelming that the public has no chance to check it. Corporate power now is sustained by government action; democratic electorates do have the power to change it through what they do. For democratic media activists, the time is now.

Sources: FreePress, "Activist Kit," www.Freepress.net; Robert McChesney, *Rich Media Poor Democracy* (New York: The New Press, 2001), final chapter; Elaine Kamarck and Joseph Nye, Jr., *Democracy.com* (Hollis, N.H.: Hollis Publishing, 1999).

the 2004 election campaign found that most of the popular blogs were just more sharply partisan renditions of the "horse race" already provided by the mainstream news media. One important and open question about all these forms is central: Will they feed on the tendency toward the individualization of news, or will they counter them? University of Chicago law professor Cass Sunstein writes of the dangers of a "Daily Me," in which people only read the news they want and filter out all alternate voices. Only time will tell if the new Internet forms create or limit a truly democratic public space.[48]

So all is not lost. Epitaphs for the popular democratic character of the mass media are not yet really appropriate. The media can and sometimes do reflect and enrich the democratic debate. For popular democrats, prompting the media to live up to their full democratic potential remains the central task.

KEY TERMS

yellow journalism
virtual democracy
agenda setters
concentration of ownership
national entertainment state
vertical integration
upscale demographics

revolving door
Rolodex syndrome
Telecommunications Act of 1996
source bias
pack journalism
media frames
horse race journalism

INTERNET RESOURCES

■ Media Matters for America
www.mediamatters.org
A major media "watchdog" group, specializing in unearthing distortions and omissions in the mainstream news media.

■ Free Press
www.freepress.net
Chief website of the broad coalition fighting for democratic, commercial-free media. Extensive commentary and archives about corporate ownership trends and alternative proposals.

■ Columbia Journalism Review
www.cjr.org
The site of the most prestigious magazine of contemporary U.S. journalism, it provides news about trends in media coverage and extensive archives and blogs from journalism students.

SUGGESTED READINGS

W. Lance Bennett, *News: The Politics of Illusion*. New York: Longman, 2005. The most comprehensive and vivid textbook covering all aspects of the trends and history of news organizations, with a heavy emphasis on how commercialism creates systematic bias.

Kathleen Hall Jamieson and Paul Waldman, *The Press Effect: Politicians, Journalists, and the Stories that Shape the Political World*. New York: Oxford University Press, 2003. An intelligent study of how media frames develop and distort, with special case studies of 9/11 and the 2000 election.

Robert McChesney, *The Problem of the Media: U.S. Communications Politics in the 21st Century*. New York: Monthly Review Press, 2004. A critical and scholarly account of both new and old developments that threaten public access to the airwaves. McChesney is one of the leading advocates of democratic media reform.

Douglas Rushkoff, *Coercion: Why We Listen to What "They" Say*. New York: Riverhead Books, 1999. A wild ride through the history of corporate efforts to commercialize media technology, written by one of the Internet's original boosters.

CHAPTER

U.S. Parties
Who Has a Voice?

Dateline: Kansas, 1892

The People's Party rally began with a long procession from town to the grove. Each Alliance and People's Party club member carried an appropriate banner. For two days, over a thousand people heard speeches, listened to band music, and sang songs. Nearly everybody, men, women, and children, wore the same kind of badge. "Equal rights to all, special privileges to none" was the favorite.

Dateline: California, 2004

As chairman, president and chief executive of Safeway Inc., the world's eleventh largest grocery chain, Steven Burd is the nexus of a wide network of subordinates and suppliers, as well as friends in corporate suites. . . . At two

Bush fundraising events in California last month, Burd filled ten tables with Safeway suppliers, including rice farmers, strawberry growers, and a cheese manufacturer, plus representatives of Breyers ice cream, Sunkist produce, and Del Monte canned goods, who paid $2,000 to hear Bush talk. Each donor wrote a four-digit "solicitor tracking code" assigned to Burd on his check so that the Safeway CEO will receive credit from Bush campaign officials and they can keep a running tally of his efforts. The possible rewards, depending on how much money he can bring in, include cocktails with campaign architect Karl Rove, dinner with Commerce Secretary Donald L. Evans, and photo opportunities and sessions with the president.[1]

More than a century apart, these two campaign reports show that American party politics and electioneering are about the business of gaining loyal supporters and staging often spectacular events. Yet despite similarities, these accounts also signify enormous changes that have transformed our political parties and the meaning of elections.

Return for a moment to 1892. Kansas farmers rallied under the banner of a political party, the "people's party," or Populists. Their loyalty to the Populist Party went beyond just voting for it. Their massive, open-air rally was not only support for a political candidate but also a community festival. A thousand farmers, most probably with little schooling, put up with two days of political speechmaking. By their presence and patience, Populists testified to their intense devotion to their cause. The banners they brought testified to the larger Populist goals: economic equality and an end to Wall Street misdeeds. Blending a community festival with serious political discussion, the party politics of the nineteenth century was a collective effort.

For these Populists, or even for their Democratic and Republican counterparts in 1892, the fundraising events of 2004 might be a shock. While the political parties today still stage rallies, most of what parties do to win votes requires enormous amounts of money to pay for the marketing, consultants, polls, ads, and get-out-the-vote drives run by the parties. Safeway's Mr. Burd, as well the company's suppliers, were less committed to a crusade than to their quite precise economic self-interest. Their support supplied access to some of the top officials of the land, and they could be sure that "bundling" together their contributions would make their voices heard. Many of the donors were not even Republicans but representatives of interest groups who gave to both parties.

These contrasting events capture the themes of this chapter. Much has changed about what political parties mean to people, how candidates present themselves to voters, and what the parties do. Today, they raise more money than ever. The parties increasingly recruit, train, and finance candidates, and partisan debates and rancor pervade Washington politics. Many observers of the 2004 election saw it as a sure revival of grassroots activism, as turnout climbed by about 6 percent and the nation's states were divided neatly into red and blue zones. For many, the parties are thus strong and vibrant democratic political instruments.

Yet, like most political words, much depends on what is meant by "strong" and "democratic." The parties might be well organized at the top, but they are often dominated by fundraisers, consultants, pollsters, and marketers. For many citizens, parties have weak or negative images and seem like distant and disconnected warring tribes. Although grassroots activism in the 2004 election increased dramatically, that was only after a long period of nearly three decades that has seen consistent declines. Both parties do have intense partisans, but most voters, and the 40 percent of the citizenry who don't vote, aren't real participants. For all the money and resources of both parties, they fail to inspire the activism of many, if not most, Americans. From this perspective, our two-party system may lead to hyperorganization at the top, but energy at the bottom is either missing or is based on a narrow segment of the population.

In this chapter, we explore the basic features of our party system. In Chapter 8, we detail the related story of how candidates and parties raise money for the campaigns. Here, though, the central question is: Do our parties today help to expand democracy by increasing the quantity, quality, and equality of participation and voting in U.S. elections? Or in their present form, do they serve to limit all three?

WHY POLITICAL PARTIES ARE IMPORTANT

We make no apologies: We are enthusiastic advocates of political parties that organize and mobilize people to become active in democratic politics. And so are most political scientists, regardless of their differences on other matters. Why is this the case? What makes parties in democratic countries different from other political organizations like social movements, interest groups, or debating societies?

Although parties do many of the same things as these organizations, they have a very special role in a democracy: They bring together individual citizens around democratic elections and voting, the most egalitarian of all political acts. While the vote of a single individual rarely makes a big difference in an election, blocs of voters can and do. Thus, parties can transform a relatively meaningless single vote into a representative collective voice. As individuals, ordinary people don't have much money, can't lobby, and have few personal connections. Through parties, ordinary voters can level the political playing field because their votes, as opposed to the lobbying power and connections of the affluent, are what matter. Parties can also provide a public, democratic space where people can converse, debate, and finally come to some agreement.

Parties naturally want to win as many votes as they can, if only because more votes mean more elected officials for them. So it would seem that parties generally would want to increase the turnout of their supporters, thereby boosting overall voter participation. Mobilizing maximum support usually requires parties to build *coalitions* among religions, regions, classes, races, and other social differences in American public opinion. Effective coalitions slowly alter the narrow claims of groups and individuals, turning them into a vision of the public interest through compromise and discussion. This *party philosophy* becomes important as a way of holding together different kinds of voters and forming an identity that endures over time.

In theory, parties can mean a lot for keeping elected officials accountable to their voters and conscious of a national vision. When parties are strong, they can *recruit and nominate* candidates and help them campaign for public office. You don't necessarily have to be rich to run and win political office in a strong party system because parties can supply you with the volunteers and resources to do so. When they are strong, parties also ensure that there is some minimal political similarity between people who run on the party's ballot line. By forming distinctive identities, parties can present clear choices to voters. As they compete, parties clarify these choices by accentuating their ideological and policy differences.

Strongly democratic political parties promote the *accountability* of elected officials to the voters who elected them. As we saw in Chapters 1 and 2, elite democrats have for a long time wanted to free officeholders from the supposed "whims and passions" of voters. In contrast, strong political parties can discipline elected officials by making sure that there is a correspondence between what elected officials do and the *party platforms* on which they campaigned.[2]

WHY AMERICAN PARTIES ARE UNIQUE

What parties *can* do to support an expansive democracy is pretty abstract. Scholars of American politics have coined the term **responsible parties** to summarize their potentially democratic virtues, yet they have also long observed a gap between theory and practice. For most of American political history, our parties haven't performed the functions all that well.

Listing the ideal virtues of parties is useful, however, because it allows questions to be asked about how well parties serve elite or popular currents of democracy. For example, have America's major parties organized some voters, while excluding or ignoring others? Do they really provide the electorate with a space to debate policies and philosophies? Do Republicans and Democrats really reflect the wide differences and commonalities of the American citizenry? Or do they squelch popular participation and distort the real issues when it comes to organizing voters and then govern as they please when in power? Asking such questions leads to a bigger one: Do American parties work to retard or further political participation in politics?

Our two major parties have complex histories. Next, we trace their uniqueness compared to political parties elsewhere in the democratic world.[3]

Age and the Weight of Tradition

Americans often think of their nation as young. Yet the Republican and Democratic parties are extremely old. Born in the 1790s and energized by Andrew

Jackson in the 1820s, the Democratic Party is one of the oldest political parties in the world. The Republicans are younger but can still trace their origins to the 1840s and 1850s and the battles to limit slavery's expansion.

The fact that our two major parties are old might be a sign of their ability to adjust. But it might also be a sign of their ability to exclude competition and reject innovation. Both parties began organizing voters around issues that have little relevance to the twenty-first century. Both parties were up and running before the country spanned the continent. They predate the formation of great cities or leafy suburbs, an industrial working class, African-American emancipation, the Great Depression, and the new global economy. The GOP and the Democrats were competing before the modern corporation existed and before the United States was a great world power.[4]

Their longevity is an achievement, but it also makes them quite unwieldy instruments of rapid electoral change. Samuel Huntington has commented that "our parties resemble a massive geological formation composed of different strata, each representing a constituency or group added to the party in one political era and then subordinated to new strata produced in subsequent political eras." Our parties have noble traditions, but also bad habits hard to break. Only a century after the Civil War ended did the Democratic Party squarely address the question of its own segregationist history. Both parties today have only begun to adjust to the new waves of immigration from Latin America and Asia. And some would argue that neither party has ever effectively represented working-class voters, perhaps because both were born around very different conflicts in the pre-industrial era. Many people remain loyal to parties out of habit alone, not because of their platforms or their vision of the future. As a result, both parties can be tradition-bound and quite conservative institutions that persist despite big changes in the culture and economy.[5]

Political Parties as Local Organizations

The age of American parties suggests the supreme role of tradition in American elections. But there is something else: Reflecting their nineteenth-century beginnings and the impact of American federalism, parties are still organized and oriented toward controlling powerful offices in particular states, regions, and locales. Only very recently have they fully organized as national parties (see below), and some say they still struggle to achieve a coherent national agenda and identity. More often, at the national level both parties have often been quite loose coalitions of state and local groups that have had little in common but their desire to nominate a winning presidential candidate.

Take as an example the different social groups that supported the Republicans and Democrats in the less than memorable election of 1920. In the Republican bastion of upstate New York, the GOP appeared as a party of small-town, native-born Protestant farmers and shopkeepers. Yet in New York City and Boston, Republicanism meant the party of big business and of the up-and-coming urban professional middle class. In the South, the descendants of African-American slaves and a few dissenting whites were the only Republicans to be found. Looking backward, the 1920 Democrats are even harder to comprehend. The new Irish and Italian immigrants of New York and Boston called themselves Democrats. But so too did Protestant plantation owners and businessmen of the South. Such variety sparked some perplexing contradictions within party ranks: The 1920 Democratic Convention featured bitter debates about whether to support or condemn the Ku Klux Klan. One segment of the party—Irish Catholic Democrats—were victims of the Klan, while many of its southern and Midwestern loyalists were its founders and supporters.[6]

Ideological Fuzziness

The local origins and complex social diversity of American parties present a big contrast to their distant European cousins. Western European political parties originally organized national identities around strong political ideologies. Generally, European parties were born out of the class tensions accompanying the Industrial Revolution. They developed comprehensive party platforms. The first European "mass" parties were critical of industrial capitalism and tried to advance democracy by campaigning for the mass suffrage. They thrived on grassroots organization, forming party "sections" and "branches" in factories and city neighborhoods. Clearer about whom they wanted to organize than were Democrats or Republicans, Europe's mass parties thrived on activism and voter mobilization. More often than not, the upper- and middle-class parties that formed to compete with labor, socialist, and social democratic parties had to form similarly strong national identities.[7]

Although the U.S. has had many third parties, including a Socialist Party once able to win 6 percent of the national vote, America's two oldest parties have never been organized around the issue of social and economic inequalities exclusively. For that reason, they've also rarely built strong national organizations with a party press, newspaper, or local volunteer organizations. Until very recently, both national parties maintained only a skeletal national staff and headquarters. In 1972, employees of Richard Nixon's reelection campaign burglarized the headquarters of the Democratic National Committee in the Watergate complex in Washington. From a foreign perspective, what they found was puzzling. The national center of the "biggest and oldest" political party in the world was far smaller than the Safeway Supermarket downstairs and the luxury co-op apartments and hotel rooms above.

Today, we are apt to think of Republicans and Democrats as highly polarized. Yet historically and comparatively, the two parties are not ideologically so distinct. Both parties agree about many of the central questions that have divided parties elsewhere. Democrats and Republicans both support capitalism and a powerful international role for the United States but oppose the redistribution of wealth. Both support a very limited role for government in planning the national economy. As their rather general names imply, "Democrats" and "Republicans" are broad designations that offend nobody. In short, our dominant parties have often, though not always, blurred social differences and ideological distinctions, even when conflicts exist in U.S. society. Although it may be hard to believe after recent elections, the range of partisan disagreement is quite limited in comparative and historical terms.[8]

Why Only Two Parties?

All of these factors contribute to the most obvious fact about American political parties: Mostly, it has been Democrats and Republicans winning elective offices for the last 150 years (with some very notable exceptions—see below). This **dominant two-party system** is a great rarity elsewhere in the world. What accounts for it?

Some say Americans don't have many political differences, so smaller, more ideological parties just don't get off the ground. Yet a two-party system is sustained not because there is a strong popular consensus and few divisions but rather because the two parties tend to blunt conflicts and possess enormous structural and legal advantages that their long occupation of power has built. Far from expanding democratic choice and representation, the two-party system has often crushed both, and at a high cost to participation.[9]

The largest instrument sustaining party duopoly is unknown to most Americans because it is taken for granted, and it is not an issue dividing the two parties. In Chapter 5, we wrote of the **single-member** or **winner-take-all electoral system** and its effect on voter turnout. Here, in a different context, we note how it serves to perpetuate the two-party system by making it highly unlikely that smaller groups seeking representation will receive any. In systems using **proportional representation**, third parties receive substantial representation.[10]

Getting a third party on the ballot is no picnic either. Each state has different requirements, but for the most part, new political parties and candidates have to spend most of their scarce resources just fulfilling the peculiar rules of each state, even as established parties usually have permanent ballot positions. New parties wind up spending most of their resources just in fulfilling these rules and then lack the ability to compete in the ensuing election. Third parties often occupy poor ballot positions as well, making it hard for inexperienced voters to locate them on the ballot.

Historically, third parties have been helped when they ran some of their own candidates exclusively but also endorsed the candidates of other parties if they agreed with them. In New York City in the 1930s, such a process made the legendary Fiorello La Guardia mayor, supported by parties as diverse as the Republicans and the American Labor Party. Today, New York State still allows this "fusion" ballot, and it has resulted in the growth of the Working Families Party, backed by New York labor unions. But in two thirds of the states, this "fusion" idea has been declared illegal by legislatures controlled by the two major parties. A 1997 Supreme Court ruling found the state prohibitions against fusion to be constitutional, effectively institutionalizing the two-party system in most states.[11]

After 2000, most Americans are familiar with the antidemocratic features of the **Electoral College system** used only to elect presidents (see Chapter 5). To the surprise of most foreigners, and to many Americans, it is possible for a presidential candidate to win the Electoral College vote and the presidency, while losing the national popular vote. In the "New Ideas" box, we explain this antiquated institution. In addition to its other antidemocratic features, the Electoral College makes unlikely any serious challengers to the national parties and their presidential candidates. To get any electoral votes in any state, you'd have to actually defeat the two major party candidates; if not, you get no electoral votes. In 1992, Ross Perot received an impressive 19 percent of the popular vote but zero electoral votes, and in 2000 Ralph Nader ran at close to 10 percent in the polls until worried Democrats were brought back into the fold by the age-old "don't waste your vote" argument. Nader wound up with 2.7 percent of the total. Whatever the Electoral College's merits, it helps to sustain the two-party duopoly of presidential contests.[12]

Last but hardly least is **gerrymandering**, the practice of redrawing district outlines to favor one outcome over another. Gerrymandering has a long pedigree from the earliest days of the republic, but it has become virtually institutionalized in the last thirty years. It is a precise science whereby legislators and parties draw district lines to their own advantage. The modern impetus was the Supreme Court's "one–person, one–vote" *Baker v. Carr* ruling of the early 1960s. This required states to redraw federal and state legislative districts every ten years to reflect population shifts. While a worthy goal, the result recently has been "incumbency protection acts" across the nation. State legislatures are charged with the duty of redistricting, and they've generally used their power to ensure that the status quo and existing party balance is preserved. In 2004, only 2 percent of House incumbents lost their seats, a record unsurpassed even by the Soviet Union's former parliament. In California's 2004 state legislative and congressional elections, not a single seat changed parties in over 153 separate legislative elections. However, in recent years gerrymandering has become even more combative and blatantly partisan. Texas Republicans, urged on by House Majority Leader Tom DeLay, forced an unusual second reapportionment act through Texas government after they won big majorities in the 2002 election. The goal was to gerrymander five Democratic House members out of their seats by carving up their urban districts into pieces dominated by rural, pro-GOP voters. DeLay's maneuver worked, rewarding the national GOP with a four-seat gain in the state's House delegation in 2004. In this climate, where two-party competition is even difficult, third-party challenges are completely swamped.[13]

Third Parties and Popular Democracy

The effect of all these measures is to institutionalize the two-party system and reduce the kind of lively competition that might expand voter interest, turnout, and representation. Despite all these obstacles, third parties have played important roles in U.S. history and continue to do so today. Third parties have often served to shake up the dominant two-party system by trying to organize new voters and issues into politics. Third parties can be "wake-up calls" for a complacent and stagnant two-party system.

NEW IDEAS

Flunking Out of the Electoral College

Would any contemporary politician publicly defend the idea that one person's vote should be worth more than another's? Not really, even though there's less than a majority who'd vote to rid the nation of the one political institution that thoroughly embodies that principle. That's the Electoral College: An institution born in a compromise at the Constitutional Convention, it's had both dramatic and subtle effects on U.S. politics ever since.

Here's how it works: Each state gets one electoral vote for each of its senators and for each member it has in the House of Representatives (D.C. gets three electoral votes, even though it has no congressional representation). The states themselves decide how the electoral votes are to be allocated. All but two states, Maine and Nebraska, allocate all the electoral votes to the popular vote winner of that state. Maine and Nebraska give two electoral votes to the statewide winner but then divide the other electors by who wins each congressional district. The electors themselves are almost always partisans who are pledged to vote for their party's candidate. (Sometimes in U.S. his-

tory, an elector has voted for someone else, but it's never made a difference in the outcome.) After the election, the electors meet in their state capitals, cast their votes, and then in early January, Congress certifies the result. The candidate with 271 electoral votes — a majority — wins the presidency.

The Electoral College is frankly undemocratic. Because of the way electors are allocated, a Wyoming voter has nearly four times the power of a California voter. States with small populations are grotesquely overrepresented. Then there's the problem of the "unit rule" — a one-vote plurality wins all the electoral votes of a single state, effectively throwing out all the other votes. In Florida in 2000, Bush's contested 512-vote plurality won him all of Florida's electoral votes — and the election. In 2004, had John Kerry and George W. Bush traded a mere 60,000 votes in Ohio, Kerry would have taken the White House. Like his predecessor, he'd have won the Electoral College but not the popular vote.

There's more: Since the presidential race is about the Electoral College and not the popular vote, presidential campaigns ignore voters in states

On the political right, third parties interested in preserving states' rights and racial segregation won presidential electoral votes in 1948, 1960, and 1968, reflecting a "white backlash" against the growing civil rights proposals of the national Democratic Party. More important, perhaps, have been farmer–labor parties like the Populists in the 1890s, the Progressives in 1924, and the Socialist Party, which won 6 percent of the presidential vote in 1912 and many local offices in the early twentieth century. The goals of these parties have been broad, in the fullest expansive traditions of popular democracy. The abolition of child labor, the progressive income tax, the direct election of U.S. senators, and women's suffrage were all reforms first pressed by these "left" parties.

In the last decade, two new parties have emerged that contest what they see as the undemocratic, elite character of the Republicans and Democrats. In 1992 where they are sure to win or lose, and devote all their time and attention to the "battleground states." In 2004, this means that California, Texas, New York, and Illinois—all with high minority populations and big cities—got almost no attention at all, while tiny Nevada and tinier New Hampshire got lots. Finally, there's the Electoral College and the two-party duopoly: The system makes it virtually impossible for third parties to run effective presidential candidates, because they'd have to win on their first try to receive any representation at all.

So what keeps the Electoral College going? Historically, it was the power of the southern slave states and later the power of the segregationist South that sustained the system. In the South, blacks in slavery weren't counted as voters, and later were prevented from voting. Yet they were counted to allocate electoral votes to each state. This was the case up to the time of the civil rights movement, as blacks were largely disenfranchised by Jim Crow laws. In 1969, the country came close to getting rid of the College, only to be blocked by a filibuster led by South Carolina's Strom Thurmond in the Senate. Today, the Electoral College lock held by the GOP in the South may preclude congressional support for eliminating the Electoral College. GOP members of Congress would have to vote for a constitutional amendment that might weaken

their party's lock on the electoral vote in Southern states and in the small states of the Mountain West and Great Plains. Two-thirds of the state legislatures would have to pass any constitutional amendment—an unlikely event indeed in states that hope to maximize the advantages given by the Electoral College's operation.

Still, since 2000 the call for the college's abolition has grown. Will the movement build up enough momentum? Perhaps, but it is difficult to maintain popular enthusiasm to change an institution that becomes visible only once every four years. Perhaps little Maine and Nebraska have the more practical idea: States, after all, are free to make their electoral votes proportional by congressional district or even to allocate the electoral votes according to the proportion of the vote each candidate receives. If all states had adopted these practices in 2000, Al Gore might have been now enjoying his second presidential term.

Sources: George Edwards, *Why the Electoral College Is Bad for America* (New Haven, Conn.: Yale University Press, 2004); Alexander Keyssar, "The Electoral College Flunks," *New York Review of Books*, March 24, 2005; and Jack Rakove, *The Unfinished Election of 2000* (New York: Basic Books, 2001).

and 1996, the Reform Party was formed. Initially a vehicle for multimillionaire Ross Perot, the Reform Party was a strong opponent of federal budget deficits, corporate-sponsored international trade agreements, and the corruption by money and lobbying of Washington politics. Perot received 19 percent and 8 percent of the presidential vote in 1992 and 1996, respectively, enough to gain federal public financing. But the party broke apart in 2000, divided over the candidacy of former Republican conservative Pat Buchanan.

A somewhat similar fate has befallen the Green Party, a loose national confederation of state organizations dedicated to progressive environmental and economic policies. The Green Party is a force in many European countries, and in the United States it holds a number of local elective offices. Its national presidential candidate in 2000, Ralph Nader, received 2.7 percent of the national vote. But in 2004, the Greens divided and didn't nominate Nader, who went on to a doomed independent candidacy. Despite many loyal activists, Libertarians and various Labor parties have suffered the same fate.

The problem of American third parties is not that they lack potential popular support. But they are hardly ever on a level playing field with the two major parties, and they face a seemingly permanent "chicken-or-egg" dilemma. The legal mechanisms controlled by the two major parties mean that many potential supporters don't want to "waste" their vote by voting for a party with few prospects of electoral victory. Yet any challenge to single-member districts, the Electoral College, ballot access requirements, or gerrymandering is precluded by the fact that third parties lack powerful elected officials because of the present rules. For the existing laws and practices to change, third parties need the political and legislative power that they now so sorely lack.[14]

Agents of Change—Sometimes

The vast democratic potential of political parties has often been compromised by their unique history in the United States. Often, they've acted as elite democratic devices, holding onto their power at the cost of laws and practices that serve to depress participation and representation by large numbers of people. There is no major party in America that is specifically tied to advancing the interests of average wage earners or defending them from the power of large corporations. The "localism" of American parties means they've often ignored or even suppressed conflicts and debates about national and international issues in favor of defending the power structures in the areas where they've been dominant. The old age of American parties makes them often resistant to social changes, whether it be the drive for women's suffrage, the civil rights struggle, or gay and lesbian rights. To some elite democrats, the two-party system may be preferable to a multiparty one because it brings stability, but at the cost of limiting dissent and activism to factional struggles contained within the Democrats or Republicans. As a result, the discontented may give up on elections, stay home, or take to the streets. For elite democrats, all this distinctiveness makes the dominant two-party system into a virtue that preserves elite power and resists change. Giovanni Sartori, a prominent scholar of political parties, has praised them precisely for their ability to "control society."[15]

Yet it would be a mistake to dismiss the two major parties as elite democratic instruments all the time. At crucial moments, they've been indispensable agents responding to, and sometimes even promoting, massive political change. The democratic debate within and about our political parties has been most heated before and immediately after what scholars call **critical**, or **realigning, elections**. Table 7.1 lists these important electoral moments. In the past 210 years, these have been rare events but of much importance. Walter Dean Burnham, the foremost student of realigning elections, has called them "America's surrogate for revolution."[16]

			Partisan
Election	**Party System**	**Big Issues**	**Consequences**
1800 (Jefferson)	*First*: Democratic-Republicans over Federalists	"Privilege"; agrarian v. urban interests; power of national government	Repudiation of Federalist Party
1828 (Jackson)	*Second*: Democrats over Whigs	Democracy of common man; state v. federal power	First mass-party system; introduction of patronage; Democratic predominance
1860 (Lincoln)	*Third*: Republicans over Democrats	Slavery; states' rights; North v. South	Republicans as party of Union; growth of urban machines; the Solid Democratic South
1896 (McKinley)	*Fourth*: Republicans over Democrats and Populists	National depression; industrialized North v. agrarian South and West; monopolies v. "the People"	Republicans as party of modern business prosperity; decline of party competition; Jim Crow in South
1932 (Roosevelt)	*Fifth*: Democrats over Republicans	Depression; social rights; government responsibility for economy	Democrats as party of equality and prosperity; mobilization in North; Solid South persists
1968 (Nixon)	*Sixth*: Partisan dealignment or gradual GOP ascendancy?	Law and order; economic decline; American strength as world power; "moral values," wedge issues	Party decomposition at grassroots; breakup of Democratic South; Republican gains

TABLE 7.1

Realigning Elections and Their Consequences

What happens during these important realigning periods? They are usually prompted by a crisis that the existing party alignments cannot contain. In the nineteenth century, new parties were born or achieved power for the first time, as with Andrew Jackson's 1828 Democratic victory and Abraham Lincoln's 1860 Republican ascendancy. In others, like 1896 and 1932, the parties kept their names but succeeded by altering their philosophies and appealing to new parts of the electorate with changed platforms and appeals. Critical elections can shake up the electorate's existing political allegiances, as the parties respond and react to new social movements and groups seeking redress through elections. In a critical election, new voters come to the polls. After such events, new dominant **party regimes** are built in which a majority party enacts big policy and institutional changes, while the opposition more or less succumbs to its dominance or retreats to the states and locales where it remains strong.

The two "realigning elections" with the most impact on today's politics are the 1896 and 1932 contests.

The System of 1896

Held in the aftermath of a severe economic depression, the 1896 election featured two contrasting visions of the nation's past and future. The first, crystallized in the Populist and Democratic presidential candidacy of the Nebraskan William Jennings Bryan, recalled the anti-federalist and popular democratic vision of the early republic. Bryan, and most especially his followers, claimed that the growing power of banks, trusts, and corporations was strangling a democracy of small farmers, merchants, and laborers. The Republican nominee, William McKinley, ran the first modern campaign, spending $3.5 million in a crusade promising corporate-led prosperity.

The 1896 contest split the nation's regions, with the West and South siding with Bryan and his Populist/Democratic coalition, and the densely populated Northeast and Midwest backing the GOP. Here, McKinley's campaign money helped win the election by a narrow margin of 3 percent. With an 80 percent turnout, the 1896 election was a dramatic and polarizing struggle about American political identity.

The result was the **system of 1896**, thirty-six years of mostly continuous Republican national dominance of both Congress and the White House. For present politics, the system of 1896 had profound and ironic effects. Born in an election that mobilized and stimulated the electorate, the leaders of the victorious GOP and defeated Democrats ironically went on to suppress political participation and debate in the regions they each controlled.

In their midwestern and northeastern strongholds, the GOP and their allies effectively disenfranchised industrial workers and immigrants whose loyalty to the GOP was either tenuous or nonexistent. They did so by imposing difficult personal registration laws and disenfranchising immigrants and the poor through literacy tests. In the South, the system of 1896 was much more brutal. Here, the potential voters to be controlled were poor, black, or both—the people who had supplied the mass support for the Populist Party in the 1890s. The region's factory owners and big landowners moved successfully to take over the Democratic Party. While race had long been a useful instrument to divide the poor in the South, the new elites instituted segregation through **Jim Crow laws**. In elections, the Democrats instituted all-white primaries, poll taxes, literacy tests, and outright violence against those who protested. (See Chapter 5.)

Intended or not, the system of 1896's legacy were dramatic declines in voter turnout and the emergence of a huge class and race gap between ordinary citizens and the Southern Democratic party, and industrial workers and the affluent Republicans in the northern and midwestern states. The most important states became one-party kingdoms. By 1924, twenty-eight years after McKinley's election, only 30 percent of the working-class voters of industrial Pittsburgh, Chicago, and Philadelphia were showing up at the polls. In Democratic-dominated Virginia, less than one-quarter of the adult citizenry voted, and less than 2 percent of the African-American citizenry did. With a demobilized electorate, the GOP could hold onto power at the national level, while the Democrats exerted iron control of their southern bastions and a few northeastern cities. Overall, the system of 1896's effect was to produce a party system friendly to corporate power in the North and white-owned plantations in the South.[17]

1932: Rise of the New Deal Democrats

With low turnout and outright repression as key ingredients, the system of 1896 strains to be called democratic at all. One-party rule in many northern states and throughout the South meant that the new social movements that developed among industrial workers, farmers, and feminists achieved only limited electoral influence.

Relying as it did on probusiness prosperity and profound social inequality, the system of 1896 was shaken by the collapse of the business system in 1929, the year the Great Depression began. Under Republican Herbert Hoover, by 1930 one-quarter of the American workforce was unemployed, life savings disappeared as banks failed, and the entire financial system was on the brink of total collapse. Under these pressures, a new voter realignment occurred—at least in the industrialized North and West. In the elections of 1932 and 1936, the revived Democrats and Franklin Roosevelt swept to large majorities in Congress and occupied the White House. With their developing philosophy of active government dedicated to promote prosperity and some degree of economic justice, the Democrats forged a new dominant party by drawing in new voters, especially in the North.

The **New Deal Democratic coalition** was based on the new electoral mobilization of northern industrial workers, small farmers, working-class Catholics, and the unemployed in a reformed Democratic Party. Senators and House members from the highly industrialized states and depressed rural areas provided the impetus for reforms that made the federal government responsible for the national economy and for providing a minimal but important standard of living for all. New Deal legislation created government jobs, allowed the growth of the union movement, and established a minimum wage and the Social Security system. The Democrats and Franklin Roosevelt posed as a party opposed to the "economic royalists" who hoarded the country's wealth. By the 1940 election, the U.S. electorate and parties were more divided by social class than probably at any time before or since. Low-income voters in the North generally backed the Democrats, and they voted in large numbers. Middle- and upper-class voters moved to support the now-minority Republicans, as voter turnout surged on both sides. By emphasizing economic justice as the central issue of U.S. politics, the realigned New Deal party system fed off of renewed voter participation.

Yet voter turnout in national elections during the New Deal never reached the high levels of the 1896 election. The grand limitation of the New Deal system was racism. In the solidly Democratic South, the 1896 system largely persisted, and blacks and many poor whites remained disenfranchised. Some southern Democrats arose to challenge the old elites of the Democratic Party and made direct appeals to tenant farmers and industrial workers. Yet not even these "reform" southern Democrats—Louisiana's Huey Long is the most famous—at their most radical never challenged Jim Crow. Despite his liberalism, President Roosevelt didn't either, because his party depended on the "Solid South" to maintain its majorities in Congress and keep the White House. In the absence of popular democratic revival in the Solid South, southern Democrats and Republicans in Congress became a conservative drag on the prolabor and profarmer policies of northern New Dealers.[18]

The New Deal at Retirement Age

Like all party regimes, the New Deal Democrats endured, and we live partly in their shadow even today. After World War II, the coalitions forged in the 1930s created what some called a "normal" politics of Democratic majorities in Congress and—Republican Dwight Eisenhower excepted—Democratic presidents from Harry Truman through John Kennedy and Lyndon Johnson. Government was now responsible for the capitalist economy and for maintaining some level of economic and social support when the capitalist markets didn't provide. New Deal programs and policies—Social Security, disability and unemployment insurance, and the GI Bill—became largely uncontroversial, as Republicans didn't challenge their essentials. By the 1950s, the New Deal Democratic Party had almost rested on its laurels, in the sense that it sought to maintain its majorities and not expand them through new mobilization. An esteemed scholar of the time called it "one of the truly conservative arrangements in the world of politics," while E. E. Schattschneider, a famous political scientist of the period, could see the same New Deal system as embodying "the great moral authority of the majority."[19]

Yet, like previous party systems before it, the New Deal variety became a victim of its own unsolved contradictions in the late 1960s. Because it was both the dominant and governing party and because of its reform traditions, it became the vortex for all the big new issues and contending groups spawned in that decade. Since the 1960s, four central divides in American society broke the Democrats' dominance.

The Democrats and Race. By the 1960s, the Democrats' dependence on southern segregationists for their congressional majorities ran up against the moral force and political power of the civil rights movement. After some foot-dragging, Democratic presidents Kennedy and Johnson and Congress responded to protest with a series of federal civil rights acts dismantling southern segregation and black disenfranchisement. In response to unrest in the northern cities, President Johnson and liberal members of Congress launched the War on Poverty and the

Great Society programs, establishing new commitments to end poverty and provide new assistance for affordable housing, decent schools, medical care for the aged, and income guarantees.[20]

Confronting racist political structures in both the South and North had electoral costs, and a few benefits, for the Democrats. It split off the segregationist southern wing of the party and angered many northern whites, who believed that racial progress should wait for another day. The Democrats gained moral authority and African-American votes. Yet many disgruntled whites, especially in the South, felt betrayed by the national Democrats.

Vietnam, Liberals, and "Communism." In the postwar period, Democrats and Republicans alike pursued a stridently anticommunist foreign policy. The New Deal party system achieved a consensus around "containing" communism through an enormous global military presence. The logical result of the Cold War was the Vietnam War, begun under Republican Eisenhower but greatly expanded into a major conflagration under Democratic presidents Kennedy and Johnson. The war's expense in lives, money, and U.S. credibility gradually spawned a huge antiwar movement. In the Democratic Party, antiwar dissent crystallized in the presidential candidacies of Eugene McCarthy and Robert Kennedy in 1968. The party establishment, including Vice President and 1968 nominee (and LBJ's vice president) Hubert Humphrey, supported the war. Tensions peaked at the party's 1968 Chicago convention, where convention delegates, journalists, and demonstrators were beaten by a police force headed by Mayor Richard J. Daley, himself a prominent old-style Democrat. The war split the nation but sunk the fractious Democrats led by Humphrey. Republican Richard Nixon was narrowly elected in 1968 and then reelected in a landslide against Democratic peace candidate George McGovern in 1972.[21]

Culture Wars. The civil rights and antiwar crusades were the most prominent of many social movements that emerged and grew in the 1960s and 1970s. (See Chapter 10.) Movements among other racial minorities, feminists, environmentalists, civil libertarians, gays and lesbians, and the young questioned the conventions of American life and challenged military, corporate, political, and educational elites. Always a diverse coalition of "outsiders," the Democrats were far more open to these cultural currents than were the Republicans.

Yet each battle over "liberation" produced a backlash of many traditional Democrats, who perceived the new movements as a threat to their beliefs and to their authority. The culture wars were born. The Democrats' ability to gain the support of northern working-class whites was threatened, even as the party was attacked as too conservative by many in the environmental, feminist, and civil rights communities.[22]

Economic Stagnation and the New Economy. The New Deal party system's greatest strength was its ability to provide economic growth and distribute some of the resources to middle- and lower-income voters by means of federal programs and tax policies. Chapter 3 details how the transformation of corporate capitalism since the 1960s made this accommodation more difficult. For the Democrats, the economic stagnation that began in the early 1970s undermined their support among middle- and working-class voters. Elected in 1976, Democratic President Jimmy Carter moved the party's economic policies to the right in the face of business demands for less government spending, regulation, and taxation. In the effort to fight inflation, Carter's policies promoted increased unemployment and the beginning of a downward pressure on working- and middle-class wages. No longer would the Democrats be so clearly identified as the party of the "working person."[23]

REACTION TO THE SIXTIES: A NEW REPUBLICAN ERA?

A substantial debate, both partisan and scholarly, about our current party system has continued ever since Richard Nixon's two presidential victories in 1968 and 1972. Some scholars and many Republican activists—including Karl Rove, George Bush's chief political adviser—have claimed that Nixon's presidency heralded the beginning of a new Republican era. Unlike 1896 and 1932, the electoral realignment has occurred gradually, first with Ronald Reagan's and George H. W. Bush's presidential victories, and second with the "Republican Revolution" of 1994, which ceded Congress to the GOP, and finally culminating in the 2004 election victory of George W. Bush and continuing GOP gains in Congress and the states. Despite the absence of a single critical election, from this perspective the new Republican era is built on the GOP's ability to "change the subject" from the New Deal era's emphasis on economic equality and social justice to a new agenda. Instead of social class, the GOP's gains have been made by dividing the electorate to its favor on the basis of appeals to patriotism, national security, and what some call "traditional" or "moral values" related to abortion, gay marriage, and the role of religion in public life. The aggressive new GOP succeeded in harnessing a backlash against the supposed excesses of the 1960s but also gradually became a party designed to "roll back" the programs of the Great Society and New Deal. The hard edge of this new Republican Party often consists of impugning the patriotism and morality of liberals and Democrats. A new and semi-permanent Republican majority is said to be the result.[24]

Many disagree with this as a description of recent political history and doubt that it is a healthy democratic development even if true. For many of these analysts, there is agreement that the New Deal Democratic Party and its dominance is over. Yet the case for a new Republican era backed by solid popular majorities is far from clear. From this second perspective, although the GOP has occupied the White House and has achieved majorities in Congress, their successes have been sporadic and contingent, and their power in Congress is held up by only razor-thin electoral margins and sustained by gerrymandering and campaign money. From this perspective, the GOP continually overstates its mandate from the voters. Indeed, it has no mandate.

© 2005 Tom Tomorrow.

Until recently, perhaps the dominant argument against the Republican era idea consisted of two words: Bill Clinton. From this perspective, the Democrats under Clinton recouped by building a new, more moderate party that conceded to the Republicans some of their claims about the 1960s. Clinton moved the party to a new center by appealing to the socially tolerant lifestyles of most middle-class and affluent professionals, while maintaining the party's traditional allegiances among African Americans, feminists, environmentalists, and organized labor. Clinton replaced the traditional Democratic language of economic and social justice and rights with the more class-neutral "bridge to the twenty-first century." Rejecting the supposed excesses of sixties' liberalism, Clinton, in this view, delivered an era of limited but effective government. Budget surpluses replaced deficits, excessive regulations and taxation on corporations were replaced by advocacy of a high-tech free-trade global economy, the welfare state was trimmed but maintained, stock markets boomed, and most workers enjoyed modest wage gains. Clinton's "third way" seemed to indicate a bright future for the Democrats, and his survival of the Lewinsky scandal and virulent Republican opposition seemed to confirm his move to the center.[25]

Strong parties are, however, not sustained by individual leaders alone but by widespread loyalties among the electorate. Whatever Clinton's merits as a political leader, he left no apparent heir. His vice president, Al Gore, won the popular vote but lost the 2000 election. In Congress, the Democrats stayed close, but the GOP recaptured their Senate majority in 2002, and continued to hold on to a House majority. In 2004, the Democrats lost the presidency, four seats in the Senate, and six in the House, even though Kerry was considered to be a moderate Democrat. Given the apparent GOP juggernaut, critics began to note that even Clinton's presidential victories had been narrow, and that he'd never won more than 50 percent of the vote.

For these reasons, there is yet a third perspective on our post-New Deal party system. In place of both of these views, this idea stresses that the years since Nixon constitute an era of **electoral dealignment**, not realignment.

Dealignment captures some central tendencies of the last decades by emphasizing that there is a democratic crisis in both parties and in our party system as a whole. Unlike past periods of realignment and strong party regimes, since the sixties there has been broad disillusionment and apathy among many citizens, and exhausted apathy or indifference among millions of others. Why? In part, it is because the debate between the parties doesn't capture the life circumstances and aspirations of many voters and citizens who've lost out in today's economy. Large parts of the citizenry have disengaged from either party, and substantial fluctuation in the voting behavior of many groups has resulted. So too has there been a dramatic rise in the number of independent voters. But the most telling feature of dealignment may be the relatively steady declines in electoral turnout, especially among groups who are the most vulnerable in today's corporate economy: nonunionized wage workers and the young.[26]

This last fact, explored in Chapter 5, captures the essence of a party system in deep crisis, at least if one takes electoral democracy seriously. The reason is simple: Both parties compete, and there are sharp partisan divides and fights among party officeholders about many issues. But the activists of both parties are a tiny minority with priorities far different than many Americans. Giants with feet of clay, both parties compete in elections. Yet they are both vehicles for different versions of upper-class interests and concerns. As such, both parties, with the Republicans in the lead, ignore or distort the growing inequalities created by a ruthless new corporate-based economy. Although the society and economy is increasingly divided by huge inequalities in wealth, income, and power, the partisan debate is over emotional symbols and resentments that have little to do with redressing these disparities.

Republicans appeal to working-class voters on the basis of symbols like the flag and so-called traditional values like prayer in public schools and opposition to gay marriage. But these are wedge issues that disguise the GOP's real policies, which have much more to do with creating a new kind of unbridled and elitist form of capitalism. As Christopher Lasch comments of the Great Communicator, Ronald Reagan, "Reagan made himself the champion of traditional values, but there is no evidence he regarded their restoration as a high priority. What he really cared about was the revival of the unregulated capitalism of the twenties: the repeal of the New Deal." While Republicans talk about moral values, they pass laws that aid the rich and punish everyone else. In turn, Democrats largely ignore class inequalities and blur the party's once strong equalitarian image by appealing to swing voters and affluent new professionals, not to those dropping out of the electorate. The result, according to Thomas Frank, is that "Democrats . . . are dropping the class language that once distinguished them sharply from Republicans. . . . They have left themselves vulnerable to cultural wedge issues like guns and abortion . . . whose hallucinatory appeal would ordinarily be far overshadowed by material concerns."[27]

The partisan implications of each argument are obvious. If you believe in a new Republican era, you are likely to also believe that the parties, and especially the Republicans, are healthily responding to genuine conservative grassroots sentiment. The new Democrat, pro-Bill Clinton argument acknowledges the power of the Republican critique and suggests that the Democrats continue to tack further right to pose as a moderate alternative. The dealignment idea suggests the drifting and undemocratic character of both of our parties, which sets the political agenda in ways that promote low turnout and feeble representation by ordinary people. Which view is best supported? To answer this question, we now examine two key features of parties today.

Two Nations or Three? Democrats, Republicans . . . and Others

In the accompanying map, table, and figure, snapshots of the parties and their strength in the electorate both in 2004 and in recent times are presented. They are worth close examination. Map 7.1 displays "red" and "blue" America in terms of states and the vote margins they provided to either George Bush or John Kerry in 2004. Figure 7.1 tells an important story about **party identification** and how it has changed over time, and Table 7.2 shows a breakdown of social groups and how they have voted in recent presidential elections.

Taken together, these graphics tell several important tales. Table 7.2 shows the evaporation of the New Deal Democrats' once mammoth lead in party identification over the last thirty-five years, falling from a fifteen-point Democratic lead to a near tie in 2004. About one-third of the electorate identify as Democrats, a little fewer with the GOP, and, quite importantly, one-third as independent voters with no party affiliation.

The other stories can be told in terms of shifts and continuities in how the parties divide on the basis of geography, religious affiliation, race, gender and marital status, and social class.

Geography. Although Map 7.1 doesn't tell the whole historical story, what it does show is that something close to a political realignment has taken place in the Deep South (except Florida). In addition to the South, Republicans have a pretty solid but not complete hold on the interior West, the border states, and the Great Plains. Democratic strength has remained and, indeed, has grown in

FIGURE 7.1

Changes in Partisan Identification, 1952–2004

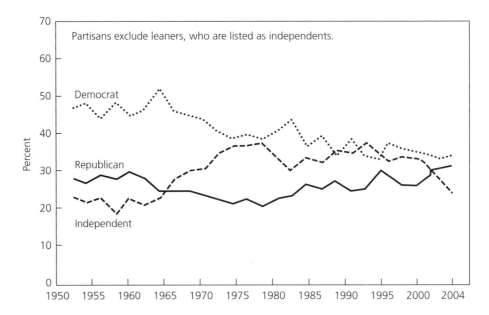

Source: "Changes in Partisan Identification, 1952–2000," from *Vital Statistics on American Politics, 1999–2000* by Harold W. Stanley and Richard G. Niemi (Washington, D.C.: Congressional Quarterly Press, 2000), p. 114. Reprinted by permission of CQ Press. Harris Interactive® telephone poll conducted between January and December 2004 among 10,012 U.S. adults aged 18+. Sampling error is +/– 1 percentage point.

the Northeast, Pacific West, and, to a certain extent, the mid-Atlantic states and upper Midwest.

The defection among southern whites since the 1960s provides the best case for the idea of a new Republican era. Over time, the South has moved from the most solidly Democratic to the most Republican region in the country. From the 1970s until the present, it has resulted in the GOP capture of a solid majority of the South and Mountain West's congressional delegation of House and Senate members.

Yet a simple dichotomy of the nation into "blood red" GOP states and "true-blue" Democratic states, even in some Southern states, is somewhat deceptive. Most of the nation's most populated counties are neither solidly red nor blue but a mixed blend. Repeating age-old patterns, in most states big cities remain strongly Democratic. Suburbs, where a majority of Americans live, are generally split between the two parties, and rural areas and small towns are strongly, although not always overwhelmingly, Republican. Although the regional divide is strong, many states remain competitive for both parties, and within most red and blue states, substantial competition remains. What some call a nation divided into a solid Republican "Jesusland" and Democratic "U.S. of Canada" is really a distortion. Colorado, New Mexico, Nevada, and Montana are hardly homogeneous red states, and Pennsylvania, Michigan, New York, and Wisconsin reveal sharp internal divisions.[28]

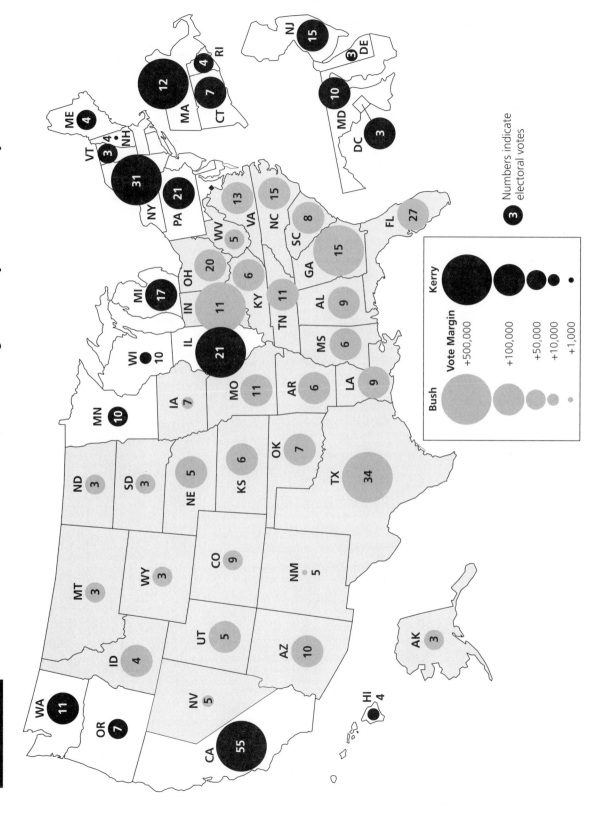

MAP 7.1 The 2004 Presidential Election: States, and the Margin of Victory for Bush and Kerry

TABLE 7.2

How Americans
Voted: A Political
Portrait of the
Party Presidential
Vote

Share of Electorate (2004)			1976	1980	1984	1988	1992	1996	2000	2004
	Overall						Election Year			
100	Total vote	Dem	50	41	40	45	43	49	48	**48**
		Rep	48	51	59	53	38	41	48	**51**
		Ind	—	7	—	—	19	8	2	—
51	Men	Dem	50	36	37	41	41	43	42	**44**
		Rep	48	55	62	57	38	44	53	**55**
		Ind	—	7	—	—	21	10	3	—
49	Women	Dem	50	45	44	49	45	54	54	**51**
		Rep	48	47	56	50	37	38	43	**48**
		Ind	—	7	—	—	17	7	2	—
	Race & Ethnicity									
79	White	Dem	47	36	35	40	39	43	42	41
		Rep	52	56	64	59	40	46	54	58
		Ind	—	7	—	—	20	9	3	—
12	Black	Dem	83	85	90	86	83	84	90	88
		Rep	16	11	9	12	10	12	8	11
		Ind	—	3	—	—	7	4	1	—
6	Hispanic	Dem	76	59	62	69	61	72	67	56
		Rep	24	33	37	30	25	21	31	43
		Ind	—	6	—	—	14	6	2	—
2	Asian	Dem					31	43	54	58
		Rep					55	48	41	44
		Ind					15	8	4	—
	Age									
17	18 to 29	Dem	51	44	40	47	43	53	48	54
		Rep	47	43	59	52	34	34	46	45
		Ind	—	11	—	—	22	10	5	—
29	30 to 44	Dem	49	36	42	45	41	48	48	46
		Rep	49	55	57	54	38	41	49	53
		Ind	—	8	—	—	21	9	2	—
30	45 to 59	Dem	47	39	40	42	41	48	48	48
		Rep	52	55	60	57	40	41	49	51
		Ind	—	5	—	—	19	9	2	—
24	60 or older	Dem	47	41	39	49	50	48	51	46
		Rep	52	54	60	50	38	44	47	54
		Ind	—	4	—	—	12	7	2	—
	Family Status									
63	Married	Dem			36	42	40	44	44	42
		Rep			62	57	41	46	53	57
		Ind			—	—	20	9	2	—
37	Unmarried	Dem			47	53	51	57	57	58
		Rep			52	46	30	31	38	40
		Ind			—	—	19	9	4	—
37	Have children under 18	Dem				44	40	48	45	45
		Rep				55	38	41	52	53
		Ind				—	22	9	2	—
4	Gay, lesbian or bisexual	Dem					72	66	71	77
		Rep					14	22	25	23
		Ind					14	7	4	—
	Political Identification									
37	Republicans	Dem	9	9	7	8	10	13	8	6
		Rep	90	86	92	91	73	80	91	93
		Ind	—	4	—	—	17	6	1	—
26	Independents	Dem	43	30	36	43	38	43	45	49
		Rep	54	55	63	55	32	35	47	48
		Ind	—	12	—	—	30	17	6	—
37	Democrats	Dem	77	67	74	82	77	84	86	89
		Rep	22	26	25	17	10	10	11	11
		Ind	—	6	—	—	13	5	2	—
	Religion									
54	All Protestants	Dem	44	35	32	38	36	41	40	40
		Rep	55	59	67	61	45	50	58	59
		Ind	—	6	—	—	18	8	1	—
41	White Protestants	Dem	41	31	27	33	33	36	34	32
		Rep	58	63	72	66	47	53	63	67
		Ind	—	6	—	—	21	10	2	—

TABLE 7.2

(continued)

Share of Electorate (2004)			1976	1980	1984	1988	1992	1996	2000	2004
							Election Year			
	Religion (continued)									
27	Catholics	Dem	54	42	45	47	44	53	49	47
		Rep	44	50	54	52	35	37	47	52
		Ind	—	7	—	—	20	9	2	—
3	Jews	Dem	64	45	67	64	80	78	79	74
		Rep	34	39	31	35	11	16	19	25
		Ind	—	15	—	—	9	3	1	—
41	Attend church at least once a week	Dem					36		39	39
		Rep					48		59	61
		Ind					15		2	—
	Family Income									
8	Under $15,000	Dem					58	59	57	63
		Rep					23	28	37	36
		Ind					19	11	4	—
15	$15,000 to $29,999	Dem					45	53	54	57
		Rep					35	36	41	42
		Ind					20	9	3	—
22	$30,000 to $49,999	Dem					41	48	49	50
		Rep					38	40	48	49
		Ind					21	10	2	—
23	$50,000 to $74,999	Dem					40	47	46	43
		Rep					41	45	51	56
		Ind					18	7	2	—
14	$75,000 to $99,999	Dem						44	45	45
		Rep						48	52	55
		Ind						7	2	—
18	$100,000 and over	Dem				32		38	43	41
		Rep				65		54	54	58
		Ind				—		6	2	—
	Education									
4	Not a high school graduate	Dem		51	50	56	54	59	59	50
		Rep		46	50	43	28	28	39	49
		Ind		2	—	—	18	11	1	1
22	High school graduate	Dem		43	39	49	43	51	48	47
		Rep		51	60	50	36	35	49	52
		Ind		4	—	—	21	13	1	—
32	Some college education	Dem		35	38	42	41	48	45	46
		Rep		55	61	57	37	40	51	54
		Ind		8	—	—	21	10	3	—
26	College graduate	Dem				37	39	44	45	46
		Rep				62	41	46	51	52
		Ind				—	20	8	3	—
16	Post graduate education	Dem				48	50	52	52	55
		Rep				50	36	40	44	44
		Ind				—	14	5	3	—
	First-Time Voters									
11		Dem			38	47	46	54	52	53
		Rep			61	51	32	34	43	46
		Ind			—	—	22	11	4	—

Figures for 2004 were collected by Edison Media Research/Mitofsky International, based on questionnaires completed by 13,110 voters leaving 250 polling places around the nation on Election Day and on 500 telephone interviews with absentee and early voters. Surveys in 1996 and 2000 were conducted by Voter News Service, in 1992, by Voter Research and Surveys; in earlier years, by The New York Times and CBS News.

"Dem" and "Rep" refer to Democratic and Republican candidates. "Ind" refers to John Anderson in 1980, H. Ross Perot in 1992 and 1996, and Ralph Nader in 2000. Dashes indicate that no third candidate received a significant share of the vote that year (including Mr. Nader in 2004). Blank spaces indicate that the question was not asked or the category not provided that year.

The figures shown for Hispanics are based on respondents who answered "Hispanic" when asked their race. In 1992 and later, "Independents" include those who answered "something else" when asked their party. In 1984, "first-time voters" are those who first registered to vote that year. Figures for Congressional vote in 1976 and 1980 exclude New York and California. In 1976 and 1980, the family financial situation question referred to changes from one year earlier; in 1976 and 1984 figures for that question are from NBC News.

Source: The New York Times Graphic.

Religious Affiliation and Church Attendance. In addition to region, religious affiliation and its intensity have played important roles in Democratic decline. In the 1950s and 1960s, Catholics were heavy New Deal Democratic supporters, and white evangelical Christians split their party allegiances pretty evenly. Weekly churchgoers were just as likely to be Democrats as Republicans. Since the 1990s, that has changed. Basically, the more you attend a Christian church, the more you tend to vote Republican. Among Catholics, party identification is now evenly divided, and Bush narrowly defeated a Catholic candidate, John Kerry, among this group in 2004. Among white evangelical Protestants, whose numbers have slightly expanded in the last two decades, only one-fifth now identify themselves as Democrats, and half declare themselves Republicans. For those who attend church weekly, six in ten voted in 2004 for President Bush.

The flip side of the religious divide is increasing support for the Democrats among people who profess no religion or those who attend church only occasionally, approximately 40 percent of the population. Among Jewish voters, the Democrats have drawn continuous and strong support.[29]

Race and Immigration. Racial divisions have been central in American society and continue to be a big divide in partisan politics. Whites of European origin still constitute about three-quarters of registered voters and eight in ten actual voters. New Deal Democrats used to gain a majority of the white vote, but here the Democrats have lost ground. Since the sixties, the best they've done is a tie with Republicans in the presidential vote. In 2004, Bush defeated Kerry by 17 percent among white voters. Yet as Chapter 5 details, America's racial and ethnic makeup is much more diverse than it was in the 1960s, and even though new immigrants vote in lower proportion than native-born whites, the percentage of people of color in the electorate is steadily growing. As Table 7.2 reveals, Democrats maintain huge advantages among African American voters (9–1), and among a growing Latino and Asian American electorate they roll up sizeable majorities of about 6–4. While the GOP gained a little ground in 2004, their support among people of color remains very weak.

Gender and Marital Status. Besides southerners, there's been no group since the 1970s that has moved to the GOP more than men, especially white, affluent men from all regions. On the other side, women, especially low-income and unmarried women, have moved in symmetrical ways to the Democrats, so much so that the gender gap is about 20 percent in both party identification and presidential voting. In 2004, it was more of a one-sided gap, with Kerry edging Bush by only 3 percent among women, whereas Bush won by nine points among men. The gender gap is exacerbated when marital status is considered: The gap between unmarried women (mostly Democratic) and married men (mostly GOP) was nearly 30 percent in 2004.

Social Class. As class inequalities have increased since the 1980s, the strangest result is the diminishing impact of social class in the partisan divide. To be sure, social class still deeply matters in how people vote, but it matters a lot less than it used to and extraordinarily less than it does in other Western democracies. The wealthiest Americans—the 3 percent of the population with over $200,000 in annual household income—vote over 2–1 Republican, and the poorest Americans, who vote proportionately much less often, give about the same advantage to the Democrats. For most of the New Deal era, the class divide would have been much more pronounced.

Still, however, the old New Deal lives on in some ways. The more household income, the more Republican loyalties increase, and vice-versa. But the differences are surprisingly small in historical terms. Democrats have a minor edge amongst those with a high school diploma or less, while they used to have a massive advantage. Republicans hold a very narrow advantage with people with some college education (the median) and among college graduates, but Democrats recoup slightly among "new professionals"—those with graduate degrees of some kind.

What the graphics can't portray are two important facts. As noted in Chapter 5, the class gap is most reflected not in the partisan divide but between those who vote the most and those who vote the least. Here the differences are as great as ever, if not more so. There is a nearly 40 percent gap in the turnout rates of the poorest and wealthiest Americans. Missing, too, is a sad fact for Democrats: White working- and middle-class voters not only vote less but those who do vote now split their vote between the parties. Insofar as the class gap still exists between the parties, it heavily intersects with the fact that Latino and African-American voters, disproportionately of lower incomes, give huge majorities to the Democrats.[30]

Public Opinion Shifts. What has partly changed is not only the social groups who support the parties but some of the political beliefs of Democrats, Republicans, and independents. The question is, *which* beliefs have changed? And which differences does the partisan debate bring out, and which are ignored or underplayed? If the partisan divide captures some differences in the society but doesn't express others, then it casts doubt on the broad mandates often claimed by newly elected governments. Democratic dominance in the electorate once depended on a wide consensus about the general idea that government ought to be active in addressing questions of social and economic welfare and regulating private business in the public interest. Support for such ideas, from health care to Social Security to public education, was most intense among Democratic adherents but also extended to independent and Republican ranks.

In the current party system, several notable trends are evident.

- Although there is very high support among Democrats and independents for the idea that government should help the poor, even if it means higher taxes, Republican voters are split on this question. Still, since the 1990s there is increasing support for the idea of government responsibility for poverty, even among Republicans. However, only 3 percent of Democrats and Republicans believe that the central differences between the parties concern the "rich-poor" gap. Whatever the class differences between Americans, apparently most people don't see the parties as sharply divided about the policies that might address the gap.

- In surveys since September 11 and the Iraq War, the most pronounced aspect of the partisan divide is instead about national security, including the Iraq War and terrorism. The gap is so important that the Pew Research Center now sees it as the best predictor of one's party affiliation, much more important than differences between partisans over economic and social questions. Republicans tend to believe that terrorism can best be defeated by military action alone, not assertive diplomacy mixed with military strength. Democrats, increasingly, believe the opposite. Republicans believe that people should fight for their country "right or wrong," while the majority of Democrats have doubts. Republicans express high levels of support for the Iraq War, and Democrats don't.

- Republicans and Democrats are now more sharply loyal to their own candidates than they have been in a long time. They vote quite consistently for whomever their party nominates. Dislike and distrust of the "other" party's candidate are intense. Still, one-third of the electorate are independents, and their votes are split about evenly.

- Independents as a whole tend to side with the Democrats on most economic issues, but they are evenly split between the parties when it comes to national security questions.

- Many highly partisan Republican voters feel intensely about so-called moral values—defined as abortion, gay marriage, school prayer, and stem cell research. At the same time, the rest of the public's views—which includes less partisan Republicans and pretty much everyone else—are simply less intense about these questions. In general, Republicans were more supportive than Democrats about the general idea that government should actively protect "morals": Over 40 percent of Republicans said they worried that government was getting too involved, while six out of ten Democrats felt that way. While the idea of two Americas, the red and the blue, signals a nation polarized on a host of issues from religion to Social Security privatization to abortion and gay rights, there are in fact huge areas of general consensus, if not agreement. These range from the high preferences for environmental protection, to the idea that corporate business has too much power and makes too much profit, to the idea that religion is an "important part of my life." Other questions, such as whether or not immigration is good for the United States, don't show much correspondence with the partisan divide.[31]

Parties from the Top Down

Earlier in this chapter, we said that American parties were highly localized and not very well organized nationally compared to major parties in other wealthy democracies. This is one of the oldest truisms in the entire literature of U.S.

political science. Today, however, it may no longer be true—especially for the kind of new Republican Party that has gradually emerged from the 1960s until the present. Before we get to this issue, however, we set out the basics of what parties both do—their formal structure of authority and their means of nominating presidential candidates.

Figure 7.2 shows the pyramid of party organization. The pyramid captures an apparently democratic flow of influence from ordinary voters to the local and state committees of the party and then to the national committees (RNC and DNC) and to the Senate and House party committees that manage campaigns for these offices. Later we'll see how the formal structure may disguise some important issues about just how democratic either political party really is.

Here we describe the formal mechanisms for nominating candidates for president in both parties. Since the Sixties the process has been transformed, ostensibly in a more democratic direction. In most states, voters, rather than party officials or officeholders, choose delegates to the national nominating conventions (although in both parties, some delegate slots are reserved for officeholders). In about four-fifths of the states, voters make their selections during **party primaries**. Primaries come in two varieties, depending on each state and its

FIGURE 7.2

Pyramid of American Party Organization

laws. Closed primaries limit the voting electorate to those who register to vote in one of the parties, whereas in open primary states either any registered voter may participate, or independent voters may. A few states, like Iowa and Alaska, choose delegates through *caucuses*, in which all voters registered in a party are asked to meet in their electoral district to choose a smaller number of delegates to a state convention, which in turn chooses the state's national convention delegates. In a healthy democratic system, the nomination process should draw high voter turnout by the grassroots. But in the last three presidential elections, only a tiny proportion of the electorate decided between the presidential candidates of each party, even in ostensibly very competitive nominating contests. In 1996, only 12 million voters cast ballots in Republican primaries. In 2000, even with the interest sparked by maverick Senator John McCain's challenge to then Governor George W. Bush's candidacy, only 17 million voted. The story is more or less the same for the Democrats: The hotly contested 1992 Democratic primaries drew 25 million voters. In 2000, Al Gore defeated Bill Bradley, but the race drew only 14 million voters. In 2004 a spirited and raucous contest for the nomination that seemed to divide the Democrats still only resulted in a net turnout of 16 million primary and caucus voters.

The principle reason for low turnout in primary elections may be a practice called **frontloading**. From the 1970s through 1992, the delegate selection process was spread out from late January through early June. States that held primaries later in the process were, according to some, shortchanged because the race would be unduly influenced by the states that held the first primaries: New Hampshire, Iowa, and South Carolina. Since 1996, the legislatures of many states, including California, moved their primaries to much earlier dates in the hope of greater influence on the eventual nominee and creating a "unified" party long before the fall campaign season. Whatever its effect on unity, the process has probably backfired in terms of internal party democracy. In the early 2004 Democratic primaries, turnout and voter interest were extraordinarily high, sparked by the contest between Howard Dean, Wesley Clark, John Edwards, and the eventual nominee, John Kerry. Yet once Kerry had won the New Hampshire primary a full nine months before the November election, turnout and voter interest dropped dramatically in the forty-seven states that still hadn't voted. Frontloading may have actually cost Kerry the election, as his candidacy couldn't spark interest and visibility again until the Democratic Convention in August. Worse, frontloading can be undemocratic: Kerry effectively secured the nomination before 90 percent of Democratic party voters had even voted because most of his strong opponents either dropped out or weren't able to raise substantial monies after his early victories.[32]

Primaries and caucuses elect delegates to the **national party conventions**, which in turn decide on a party platform and nominate the presidential and vice-presidential candidates. For most Americans, the party conventions have been the only occasions where the national parties, with all their factions and personalities, display themselves in public. In the olden days, conventions were often rancorous, with dramatic disputes over the most important issues of the day and bare-knuckled battles between presidential contenders. Most of all, the spectacle was covered gavel-to-gavel by the three major networks.

Yet in the new era, the delegates to these conventions decide little, the platform is composed long before the convention begins, and the event is scripted by party operatives to showcase the new presidential and vice-presidential nominees. The conventions do provide an important opportunity for contacts and networks to form. Yet the delegates, supposedly elected to represent the views of voters, are there less to discuss than to ratify choices and cheer for the nominee. Stripped of real power, the delegates wear colorful hats and serve as amusing backdrops for speeches by preordained and scripted speakers.

Worse, not only have conventions become stage-managed, but they are often vehicles for big donors—corporations and economic sectors that hope to influence the parties and their officeholders. The 2004 New York Republican Convention's budget was largely picked up by the banking, pharmaceutical, and telecommunications industries, which used the conclave to showcase its products, lobby for favors like increased tax cuts, and tout their power in the GOP. While the conventions cost millions of dollars, their prescripted quality as well as media greed and indifference mean that they are now hardly even covered by the major networks. Beginning in 1996, their daily proceedings were not broadcast live. In 2004, live coverage was further cut to include only the acceptance speeches of Bush, Cheney, Kerry, and Edwards.[33]

GOP Revolution from Above: The Amway Model

The formal mechanisms and structures of both parties are, on paper, fairly similar. The rules and procedures are pretty much invisible to the average voter, most of whom don't vote in party primaries, contribute to party candidates, or participate in local party committees. These days, even viewership of the conventions is way down, perhaps because its proceedings are hard to find on television.

Yet the formal mechanisms don't capture several trends of enormous, even revolutionary, importance that have strengthened and even transformed the modern Republican Party in particular. Much of this transformation has come from outside the party pyramid, but it has greatly influenced the formal party, what it does, and whom it recruits.

For the Republicans the first big change was in the 1970s, and it came from the responses of a part of corporate America to New Deal and Great Society liberalism. That decade gave birth to ultraconservative foundations, creatures of old family fortunes like the Scaifes and Mellons, and industries from beer (Coors), chemicals (Olin), and Vicks VapoRub (Smith Richardson). The foundations in turn begat conservative **think tanks**, most notably the Heritage Foundation, the American Enterprise Institute, and the Cato Foundation. The role of the new think tanks can't be overstated. Their objectives were to change both elite and popular opinion. Their money was (and is) used to employ intellectuals, "opinion-shapers" and "experts" for promarket, anti–New Deal ideas. And shape the Washington policy agenda they have: Dozens of new policy journals have been produced about matters from foreign policy to Social Security. Position papers and studies are delivered to members of Congress and the executive branch, books and magazine articles are written, supported by generous fellowships for conservative intellectuals. The think tanks and foundations maintain large budgets for expert and prestigious speakers. Paid experts are recruited to speak on news shows and on college campuses and business forums and pen op-ed pieces, as well as serve on congressional staffs and in the executive branch. The conservative speaker's bureaus keep on staff notable conservatives from Robert Bork to Dinesh D'Souza and Stephen Moore. Today, over 500 conservative foundations and think tanks dot the landscape. As of 2000, the top twenty alone spent over $1 billion on such activities.[34]

The conservative movement, led by its business backers, not only sought influence over the established news media but began to buy parts of it as well. In the previous chapter, we outlined some of these developments: the rise of FOX News, run by former Reagan adviser Roger Ailes and Rupert Murdoch, the CEO and chief owner of the News Corporation and a prominent supporter of conservative causes. So too was the effort effective in talk radio, where conservatives lined up funding and advertising supporters first for Rush Limbaugh and later for a whole generation of talk show hosts on local stations. There's also the enormous scope of the Christian Broadcasting Network (CBN), in which prominent GOP evangelicals Pat Robertson and James Dobson have significant influence. In something of a loop, foundations funded think tanks. In turn, think tank intellectuals appeared as experts on conservative news programs. Then the most voluble intellectuals were hired as pundits and finally as journalists in networks like Fox. Conveniently, the new journalists and pundits then used conservative foundations and think tanks as prime sources in their news reports.

Think tanks, foundation money, corporate lobbyists, pundits, and Republican Party and interest group operatives could be unrelated enterprises. But the crucial link between all these activities has been made to party candidates, electoral politics, and campaign consultants through informal coordinating groups in Washington. Their function has been to generate themes, "talking points" and consistent messages that would keep conservative Republicans "on message" in their legislative agenda and before the media and public. More important, they directed money into the party and to the recruitment, training, and media exposure of new candidates in legislative districts throughout the country. Coordinating groups also link policy organizations, officeholders, and candidates with a growing network of professional campaign consultants, who provide polling, advertising, and legal advice and expertise to Republican candidates and their organizations. Among others, there's the Library Group, begun by Christian Right direct-mail guru Paul Weyrich, and the Philanthropy Roundtable, which directs foundation and donor money to needy GOP candidates and causes. Then there's the "K Street Project," Tom DeLay and GOP operative Grover Norquist's innovative effort to ensure lobbying firms in Washington employ exclusively Republican operators, usually supplied by hiring retiring GOP congressional staff as lobbyists for private industry groups. The "Project" extracts campaign contributions from corporate donors by insisting that any corporate donors that give money to the Democrats will have great difficulty getting access to the GOP's bill-writing congressional committees.[35]

The coordinating groups helped create a new generation of political action committees and, all new for 2004, so-called 527s and 501cs, like the Swift Boat Veterans for Truth, ostensibly "independent" of party control. The new groups provided the GOP with independent attack dogs who could go after liberals and Democrats without being traced back directly to the party's officials and officeholders. While forbidden by law to coordinate with the parties or with specific candidates, Swift Boats' legal counsel was also an attorney for the Republican National Committee and worked for the Bush–Cheney campaign in 2004.

Given these developments, the formal Republican National Committee and the Congressional Campaign Committees have been revived as the apexes of a dense and vast network of fundraising, media, research, intellectual, consulting, training, and campaigning functions. Unlike the past model of decentralized parties, the modern GOP can recruit, train, fund, and provide campaign expertise and technology for campaigns throughout the country. It can craft a unified media message and make sure that all the diverse strands of the party's powerful organization are on board. Alternatively, it exerts new power over who gets to run and who doesn't by its control of expertise, technology, and purse strings from the center. More than ever, the party can control any dissent as well, as GOP members of Congress and even state legislators become more and more dependent on party and party-related aid to run their reelection efforts and gain key committee assignments while in office.

So able at fundraising and centralization, the new GOP in 2004 was also able to do something equally rare: coordinate from the center the activities of up to 1 million Bush–Cheney volunteers during the course of the election year. Here, the Bush–Cheney campaign and the Republican National Committee put all these diverse operations to work in what might be the most disciplined and nationally directed party organization in U.S. history. *New York Times* reporter Matt Bai described it in this way.

> In the months leading up to the Republican convention in August, these county organizations will act as a kind of industrial-strength vacuum, gathering up useful information and passing it through the upline to the campaign. Information on every new volunteer is sucked into the campaign's database.
>
> As the fall campaign approaches, someone in Arlington (campaign headquarters) will flip a switch, and the suction will change direction; information will now move primarily from headquarters down to the volunteers. Canvassers in each county will await the message of the day from the campaign, and then, like suburban Paul Reveres, they'll be off to get the word out, by foot or by phone. In the final days of the campaign, the network will be up and running virtually around the clock, making sure Republicans in each precinct show up to vote.[36]

If the object is to win and win alone, the GOP's organization inspires awe. But Bai and many others have noticed one potential problem: Despite the large number of volunteers, the GOP organization is directed utterly from the top, analogous less to a democratic political party than it is to a corporation run along the model of Amway, Tupperware, or Mary Kay Cosmetics. The goals, the methods, the lists, the message, and the money are all directed from Washington and implemented by an army of eager, obedient, but largely uninfluential volunteer salespeople in precincts and counties throughout the country. Bai comments on such multilevel marketing (MLM):

> The notion of translating the MLM concept into politics is visionary—and also a little disquieting. Pyramid-based companies have proved amazingly successful at raising up armies of enterprising Americans. . . . But some MLMs thrive by imposing their own strange and insular cultures on their recruits, and while they offer the illusion of self-employment, those at the top of the pyramid often demand a rigid kind of uniformity and loyalty. When I met with Ken Mehlman, Bush's campaign manager, in suburban Washington, and suggested that the Bush campaign could fairly be compared to Amway in its approach, he agreed without hesitation. "Amway, no question," he said.[37]

The Democrats Respond

By all accounts, one of the causes and results of the Democrats' decline since the 1970s has been their relative inability to match the money, influence, expertise, or coordination of the Republican innovations. That doesn't mean that they haven't tried. After their loss of the White House in 1980, the Democrats at the center have stressed professionalization as well. They built a national headquarters and a media operation, and they gathered enough money in the Democratic National Committee to remain competitive with the Republicans. But if there is one gaping hole in the Democrats' organization, it is that they almost entirely lack the foundation, think tank, and media power of the Republican power structure. Out of power in Congress since 1994 and out of the White House as of 2001, they also lack the ability to extract money and implant operatives in the large lobbying firms, trade associations, and industry interests now centered around the GOP. Most of all, the Democrats are far from unified after their defeats and lack the disciplined message machine of the GOP.

In 2004, this Democratic disadvantage began to change somewhat. In the next chapter, we explore in depth several important trends that simultaneously give pause and hope to the Democratic opposition. These include the rise of Internet fundraising and volunteer groups, typified by Moveon.org, the successful fundraising and volunteer network created by the Howard Dean campaign, and the rise of so-called 527 organizations like Americans Coming Together (ACT) and the Media Fund. In a sharp departure from the Amway model, supporters of the Democrats have largely built structures that remain highly independent from the national and state parties. This may change, as insurgent Howard Dean became chairman of the Democratic National Committee in January 2005. In the next chapter, we will discuss the Democrats' 2004 campaign at length for what it may reveal about their prospects.[38]

CONCLUSION: STRONG PARTIES, UNCERTAIN ELECTORATE

Earlier in this chapter, we set out three different visions of the post–New Deal parties. What do the developments we describe portend? Is it a new Republican era? Or is it an era in which Democrats can win important elections, but only if they move, like Clinton once did, toward the GOP's positions? Or do we live in a party system that is dealigned, mostly because many working-class and poor citizens have dropped out and because the Democrats have largely lost their identity as the party of the ordinary person? There is data to support each of these visions, as well as data which detracts from each argument.

There *have* been serious electoral shifts away from the Democrats and toward the GOP. It is difficult to imagine the Democrats recouping in most southern and mountain states. The partisan division in the electorate has at least partly shifted to questions that most favor Republicans. Moreover, the new Republican Party is a formidable, disciplined, and unified organization that gains greater strength from its dominance of government and its strong presence in the world of culture and the media. Gerrymandering, plus the partisan polarization of much of the existing electorate, has created something of a partisan Republican "lock" on its slender but real majority in the House of Representatives. Very few congressional districts—only 59 in 2004—split their tickets and voted for the presidential candidate of one party and a House member from another. If this trend holds up, it will make it very difficult for either party to gain or lose many House seats in the near future. Under current conditions—a GOP majority in the House—this clearly sustains Republican dominance, and the idea that we do live in a new Republican electoral era.

At the same time, it is far from clear that the GOP has built a semi-permanent electoral majority to match its institutional and financial clout. Despite their prowess and organization, Republicans gain only slim pluralities. Democrats have proven abilities to keep their most loyal groups and remain strong among groups that are growing in the general population, most notably immigrants and professionals. GOP strength seems contingent on the ability to maintain national security as the most prominent divide. It is far from clear whether this will continue, and, as Democratic centrists suggest, Republican failures in the war on terrorism or in Iraq, as well as social trends that favor a less extreme approach to wedge issues like gay marriage and abortion, don't bode well for the GOP.

Last but not least, there is much evidence to support the idea that substantial numbers of citizens remain suspicious of both parties, and that present GOP dominance could vanish as the electorate responds to events and to Democratic party initiatives. Present Democrats could mine rich veins of discontent with the economic and social order built since the Republicans began to make gains. To succeed, Democrats must change the subject, renewing under modern conditions their commitments to social justice and economic equality and security. This means reaching out to the party's new core constituencies and speaking directly and plainly to the needs of wage earners and vulnerable people of all colors and ethnicities who currently don't vote or who don't hear the Democrats address these issues. From this perspective, the rightward drift of the Democrats mistakenly concedes to the GOP the central issue of our time: growing wealth but decreasing social and economic equality. Its relatively weak party organization exacerbates this drift. In Robert Reich's words:

> Had Clinton told Americans the truth—that when the economic boom went bust, we'd have to face the challenges of a country that was concentrating more wealth and power in fewer hands—he could have built a long-term mandate for change. Democrats should pay close attention to what Republicans have learned. . . . It is crucial to build a political movement that will endure beyond a particular electoral contest. In order for a presidency to be effective, it needs a movement that mobilizes Americans behind it.[39]

The future of the party system, elite or popular democratic, will be based on which of these three ideas turns out to be correct.

KEY TERMS

responsible parties
dominant two-party system
single-member (winner-take-all)
    electoral system
proportional representation
Electoral College system
gerrymandering
critical (realigning) election
party regime

system of 1896
Jim Crow laws
New Deal Democratic coalition
electoral dealignment
party identification
party primary
frontloading
national party convention
think tanks

**INTERNET
RESOURCES**

▨ Project Vote Smart
www.vote-smart.org
Targeted to young voters, this site includes highly accessible information on political parties and candidates for public office.

▨ Townhall.com
www.townhall.com
National umbrella site for conservative and GOP-allied groups, foundations, think tanks, and activists of all kinds.

▨ Moving Ideas
www.movingideas.org
A similar site to Townhall, but for liberals. This site contains more nonpartisan groups than Townhall.

The major political parties all maintain extensive websites. The following is a list of their national sites.

▨ GOP
www.rnc.org

▨ Democrats
www.democrats.org

▨ Greens
www.greens.org

▨ Reform Party
www.reformparty.org

**SUGGESTED
READINGS**

Thomas Frank, *What's the Matter with Kansas?* New York: Henry Holt and
Company, 2004. Now a classic, this book explains how the GOP gained the
initiative among heartland voters whose economic status has declined under
the GOP itself.

Michael Nelson, ed. *The Election of 2004.* Washington, D.C.: Congressional
Quarterly Press, 2005. The best overview of this historic contest, with many
essays on its diverse aspects.

Ruy Teixeira and Joel Rogers, *The Emerging Democratic Majority.* New York:
Scribner, 2002. A compelling account of how the Democrats could win elections by appealing to the needs of new professionals, traditional constituencies, and new citizens.

Sidney Verba, Kay Lehman Schlozman, and Henry Brady, *Voice and Equality.*
Cambridge, Mass.: Harvard University Press, 1995. A comprehensive study
of political participation in the United States, with an emphasis on how parties today favor educated and affluent citizens.

Campaigns
Organized Money versus Organized People

Two days after his 2004 election victory, an exultant President Bush proclaimed that he had "earned capital in the campaign—political capital—and now I intend to spend it. It's my style." With a perceived solid mandate from the voters, Bush declared the centerpiece of his second term's domestic agenda: "reforming" Social Security through the introduction of private accounts.

Two month later, Bush's Social Security proposals were floundering. They met not only fierce and united opposition from Democrats but a tepid or hostile reception from many key groups. To the surprise of GOP election strategists, the more Bush traveled the country with carefully choreographed town meetings, the more his proposals met disapproval in the polls. As this is being written—and things could change—even GOP members of Congress were declaring the prospects for Bush's Social Security reforms bleak at best. If President Bush had been reelected after one of the longest, most divisive, most polarized and expensive election campaigns in years, why did his self-proclaimed "mandate" so quickly disappear? If the public was supposed to be neatly divided into red and blue, and red was the victor, why did Bush's plans go haywire?

For 2004, the answer tells us much about contemporary electoral campaigns and their role in the democratic debate. Attentive students of politics and partisans might have known that the think tanks and financial interests attached to the GOP had been talking about privatizing Social Security for years. Yet the public campaign the voters saw and heard couldn't have provided a mandate to transform Social Security. This was due to a simple reason: The issue was largely ignored during the campaign, especially by the Republicans. Of the $177 million spent and 300,000 or so ads run by the Bush campaign and the national GOP, Social Security privatization was never the chief theme of a single advertisement. Attacks on John Kerry for flip-flopping instead led the list. Bush himself had mentioned "reforming" the system in a few of his stump speeches, but he'd provided no details.[1]

For the most part, Bush's chief campaign message was that he was both a strong and consistent leader in the war against terrorism and that his opponent was neither. In the debates between Kerry and Bush, Social Security came up once, but, again, specific plans and extended debate were missing. In voter surveys, privatizing Social Security was not mentioned as a major concern. Majorities of voters in any case weren't aware of Bush's position on privatization of accounts, or they mistakenly believed that he opposed private accounts. Nor did the news media trumpet the issue. Infinitely greater coverage was devoted to a whole host of other matters: war records, gay marriage, and Osama bin Laden's videotaped remarks.[2]

This striking disparity between campaign talk and governing agendas seemed particularly acute in 2004. After all, Bush, by simple virtue of his reelection, had claimed a "mandate" to privatize the best-known, oldest, and most popular government program. Yet the fact that it was almost invisible in the campaign and a central issue thereafter is hardly unique. Similar gaps between campaign themes and governing decisions have been typical in the "dealigned" electoral era since 1968. Bush's father, George H. W. Bush, ran his 1988 campaign by attacking his opponent for his opposition to a constitutional amendment banning flag burning and for furloughing a black Massachusetts convict who later raped a white woman. The amendment was later abandoned, and the black convict, Willie Horton, was forgotten, as Bush began the Persian Gulf War and initiated a series of tax increases. In 2000, the campaign revolved around how to spend projected federal budget surpluses. After the election, the surpluses quickly evaporated, and the agenda moved on to the war on terrorism and in Iraq. The 2000 campaign themes were, after 9/11, ancient history.

In democratic lore, electoral campaigns are supposed to do better than this. After all, they're the one time when competing candidates and parties must actively and directly compete for the people's active approval. During campaigns, voters pay attention, and at the end, they possess the awesome power to elect their leaders. No doubt, in 2004 the vote mattered, and there was a huge difference between the parties and the candidates. But whatever the real differences between the ideas, voters, and people in 2004, the public face of this modern campaign couldn't reveal them.

There are key features of electoral campaigns that serve to distort, disguise, and obscure the actions and policies later proclaimed by the victors. In our view, these features serve elite democracy by narrowing the debate and the agenda of campaigns to issues important to campaign contributors and professional marketers. At the same time, there are also signs of democratic energy that, if they grow, could serve to broaden the democratic debate and enhance popular participation and influence in campaigns. We discuss both developments now.

ELITE DEMOCRACY: CAMPAIGN RULES

In the last chapter, we told the story of how both our parties preserve a duopoly that often serves to limit and constrict voter choice. In recent years, both parties have, especially at the top and with the GOP in the forefront, become much more organized and ideological, at least at the top in Washington and in the state capitals. Parts of the electorate are more sharply partisan in recent years, too.

Elite Campaign Rule 1:
It's the Candidate, Not the Voters

Still, the most casual observer would note that the public face of most electoral campaigns is less about advertising parties than it is about promoting individual candidates. Electoral campaigns are **candidate-centered**. During the course of the electoral campaign, voters learn more about the images, personalities, families, quirks, gaffes, misdeeds, strategies, and tactics of the candidates than anything else. Candidates, not voters and their meetings, or even contributors and their donations, take the public stage. Beyond that, it is the individual candidates who are engaged in a personal struggle to build a campaign organization, raise money, hire strategists, craft a message, contain one's temper, strike a theme. And it is the news media that emphasizes the personal as well. In candidate-centered campaigns, whether Bush wore a wire during the first and second debate is just about as important as whether Kerry's windsurfing vacation sent the wrong message to working-class voters.

Candidate-centered campaigns predominate in recent years in part because of party dealignment. Although many voters are partisans and vote straight party tickets, the deciding margin—perhaps a quarter of the electorate or more—are **undecided and swing voters**, unattached to either party. To influence swing voters, candidates must achieve high **name recognition** and craft consistent and repeatable favorable images that impress them. In these personalized campaigns, swing voters can be turned off by a single gaffe or an unanswered charge of personal corruption or scandal. In an electorate where personality matters but few know the candidates personally, celebrities and mavericks can, with enough money and media attention, emerge from political nowhere to dominate the electoral stage and knock off seasoned political pros. Only in a candidate-centered world could the rise of California actor turned governor Arnold Schwarzenegger or wrestler turned Minnesota governor Jesse Ventura be explained. Or take George W. Bush himself: Would a one-term governor of Texas with a name other than Bush's have gotten so far?[3]

If the candidate-centered world is full of volatility, incumbents seek security amidst the apparent chaos. The response has been what journalist and former Clinton adviser Sidney Blumenthal has called the **permanent campaign**. This term means that campaigns are never really over. Once in office, members of Congress in particular remain opportunistic electoral entrepreneurs, using their positions with an eye to the next electoral contest. They raise money constantly to fend off potential opponents; they make sure that whatever federal money flowing to their districts is identified with their leadership. They use key committee assignments to publicize their power, and they often introduce bills that highlight their performances and power. Highly symbolic "hot button" issues are ready-made for the permanent campaign. Recent examples include the Republicans' seizure of the case of a Florida woman, Terri Schiavo. Republican members were eager to publicize their last-minute effort to keep Florida doctors from removing her feeding tube, even if it meant defying their long-term support for states' rights. In short, the permanent campaign game requires that elected politicians structure their offices, time, activities, and staffs as bulwarks against electoral insecurity.[4]

Elite Campaign Rule 2: The White House Is About You

At first glance, it may seem natural that campaigns are candidate-centered. After all, the ultimate choice on the ballot has always been between individuals. Yet the rules of candidate-centered campaigns favor those with certain kinds of elite credentials or those who can develop them quickly by passing key media and money tests. The contest for party presidential nominations is the candidate-centered campaign in hyper-drive because in these contests people can't vote reflexively on the basis of party label. Here, personalities—or the images of personalities as conveyed through paid and unpaid media—can determine all. So what does it take to be a successful candidate for the White House or Congress? What factors determine who wins and loses?

The presidential nominating process is an inhospitable terrain for the humble, the circumspect, or people with talent but lacking in overarching ambition. It is littered with sad tales of what happens to the worthy, but unlucky and underfunded. First, it's a long race (see Table 8.1). Presidential bids start up to

TABLE 8.1   The Road to the White House: Essential Steps

Two years before the election

Goal: Become a viable candidate.

1. Form a target electoral base among your party's active voters.
2. Establish a distinctive appeal that helps you stand out from the crowd.
3. Visit key states like New Hampshire and Iowa, where convention delegates are first selected.
4. Visit key politicians and get a list together of potential contributors. Help campaign for your party's officeholders in the off-year elections.
5. Establish contacts with national and local news media by appearing before key interest groups and on television programs such as *Larry King Live*, *This Week with George Stephanopoulos*, and *Meet the Press*.

One year before the election (the invisible primary)

Goals: Build a competent campaign team, achieve name recognition, raise enough money to hire a permanent campaign staff and qualify for federal campaign subsidy, save money for early television and radio advertising.

1. Register as an official campaign organization with the Federal Election Commission.
2. Fundraise in at least twenty states to qualify for federal assistance, or opt out of federal help by raising big money (about $40 million required). Establish an Internet site as a way of doing this.
3. Be mentioned by elite news reporters as an up-and-coming presidential candidate with fresh, new ideas and a potentially broad appeal.
4. Assemble a campaign team that includes consultants, managers, pollsters, direct-mail specialists, lawyers, and experts in press relations, media, speechwriting, and issue development.
5. Decide whether to devote lots of resources or little to Iowa and New Hampshire, the first contests. Plan strategy and build organizations in states that hold primaries the first week in March— New York, California, Ohio, and Missouri are expensive media markets. Do you plan on winning all or only on making a strong showing?
6. Announce candidacy.

Primary season, January–June, election year

Goal: Assemble a majority of delegates to your party's national convention in the summer.

1. Win or take a close second in Iowa caucuses and New Hampshire primary in late January.
2. Win at least one really big state like California, Michigan, New York, Ohio, or Georgia in the "frontloaded" primaries, and pick up small states like Vermont and Connecticut as well.
3. Sustain momentum by winning decisively in second round of primaries a week later—most of these are southern state primaries.
4. Win late primaries by decisive margins, forcing other contenders to drop out. Make peace with them.
5. Make sure you've raised the maximum amount of money under federal law so that you receive enough "matching" funds. Or if you're not taking matching funds, make sure that you've raised about $150 million.
6. Dominate rules, procedures, and platform deliberations preceding national convention. Interview and investigate vice-presidential candidates.
7. In your acceptance speech, unite your party while addressing the broader nation. Make sure that you've honed your theme for the fall election.

General election: Convention to November's first Tuesday

Goal: Amass 271 electoral votes and win the presidency.

1. Develop target states where campaign and media spending will be concentrated.
2. Raise lots more money to qualify for matching funds—and help your party raise money from "independent" sources.
3. Stick with your script about why you want to be president, unless focus groups say it is utterly failing. Establish a plan to mobilize core voters.
4. Develop specific appeals to "undecided" voters, and develop a common line of attack against your opponents.
5. Win the presidency, and have a transition team already in place.

three years before the election year and the fifty separate primaries and caucuses that potential candidates must face to win a major party's nomination. Incumbent presidents have it much easier than challengers because their public images are already formed.[5]

Challengers face daunting obstacles, unpleasant surprises, and a filtering process mediated by media elites and big money donors. Take Bill Clinton and his first campaign for the presidency in 1992. His voyage began just after the 1990 congressional elections, as the relatively obscure Arkansas Democrat tried valiantly to make himself known to the **great mentioners** or **gatekeepers**. In those days, elite media columnists and reporters, people like Tim Russert or the *Washington Post*'s David Broder, could make or break a candidate by writing a favorable column or conceding an interview. Clinton impressed many of the mentioners in a crowded field. Being mentioned as a plausible and promising candidate helped Clinton raise money and establish contacts with key Democratic fundraisers.[6]

Next came the so-called **invisible primary**—the struggle to establish a fundraising base from which a plausible candidacy can be launched. Most candidates never pass the test. In 2004, Florida's Democratic Senator Bob Graham and Illinois' Carol Moseley Braun were simply ignored by the mentioners. They never really made it to the second stage, where voters actually matter. The invisible primary is less than a public process: It primarily involves long phone calls and small dinners with potential donors. In these conversations, affluent contributors and partisan groups get to know the candidates' policies and personality in depth.

Passing the invisible primary often means developing a consistent campaign theme that is deemed neither too vague nor too radical to attract continuous donors; it also involves finding campaign professionals whose experience shows that the candidate means business.

Here, though, there are possibilities for mavericks who break the mold by going outside the elite circle of mentioners and big donors. The most recent mold-breaker was Vermont Governor Howard Dean and his campaign for the Democratic presidential nomination. Dean's candidacy tapped into broad anti–Iraq War sentiment among Democratic voters and discontent with the Democrats' tepid response to President Bush's domestic initiatives and aggressively militaristic foreign policy. Unique in modern candidacies, he built a strong grassroots movement of small contributors and through the Internet established a vast network of grassroots supporters, bloggers, small contributors, and volunteers willing to support his long-shot candidacy. Even so, Dean still employed many seasoned campaign veterans, like campaign chief Joe Trippi, in his insurgent candidacy.

Dean's candidacy shows both the possibilities of popular democracy, as well as the limits imposed by the conventional elite-driven norms of candidate-centered campaigns. From the standpoint of his supporters, Dean was representative of a larger political movement and cause. Dean himself ended all his political speeches by shouting, "YOU have the power!" Yet from the perspective of the great mentioners and the Democratic Party's establishment, the campaign was about Dean as a person, and he was seen as an ambitious, too radical, and

© 2005 Tom Tomorrow.

possibly unstable individual who refused to play by the usual rules. The media, who had ignored him when he started, discovered him and his growing organization in the fall of 2003, and he was considered the presumptive nominee by December 2003. Then the proverbial "something" hit the fan. Questions began to appear in the columns of major papers and the comments of TV pundits about his electability. The absence of his doctor wife, Judy, from the campaign trail was seen as inappropriate and inexcusable. Investigations were launched into Dean's behavior as Vermont governor. Pundits queried his electability quotient, even though he was running almost even with Bush in the polls. Now deemed the frontrunner, expectations about his success put pressure on him to make no mistakes. In January 2004, John Kerry's surprise win in Iowa brought down Dean's image as the "frontrunner." It also initiated something of a media frenzy; the famous "Dean Scream" brought Dean more news coverage, all of it unfavorable, in one single day than his entire candidacy had generated in the year before. Two weeks later, his second-place finish in New Hampshire effectively ended his insurgent candidacy for good. Of course, the interesting rise and dramatic fall of Dean led to yet another candidate-centered drama: the rise of John Kerry. Once the presumed choice, he had been branded a loser. But with victory in only two states, he became the Comeback Kid: His coast to the nomination was accompanied, at least for a while, with personal stories of his heroism in Vietnam, told by his battle comrades.[7] On the surface, the candidate-centered campaign seems to be an equal opportunity form of democratic chaos, where only the thick-skinned and savvy survive. But it has other, much more elitist features as well. First, it tends to reward personal style over substance: The criteria by which we judge competing politicians has less to do with the quality of their ideas or even who they represent than with how smoothly and personably they portray themselves on paid media and through the filter of the news media. The personal style and backgrounds of the candidate tend to replace the question of the justice or strength of his or her cause. Or, as in the case of the Bush candidacy, concentration on his "strong" leadership qualities simply buried an important debate on Social Security.

Here, Howard Dean's example is again instructive: It was Dean's Scream that brought him down, not his political views on the Iraq War or the economy. But when he disappeared, a serious reform movement within the Democratic Party was brought down, too, but hardly on its own merits. By replacing causes, issues, and voters with media judgments about personalities, candidate-centered politics devalues the first. Second, voters might be the ultimate judges of candidates, but their ability to see and hear the candidates are heavily mediated. The great mentioners in the press and commentariat are the arbiters of the process. Their thumbs-down signal can easily break a candidacy before voters have even had a chance to judge. And their criteria for judgment are, at best, problematic and biased against disrupters and those who pundits and big donors designate as "losers." Ralph Nader's 2000 crusade is an example of what happens to real mavericks in the candidate-centered world: His message simply never got out. Seen as grumpy and disagreeable, his ideas about corporate power and the two-party system were not so much defeated as they were ignored.[8] Finally, by placing emphasis on the personal characteristics of candidates, the candidates themselves are thrust into a defensive and wary crouch. To hold onto office, to reach voters, to impress the media, to build an image, to create the ads and do the polls, candidates all seek protection in one basic commodity. While it can't buy happiness and doesn't ensure success, raising and spending money becomes the central foundation of candidate-centered campaigns. Next we examine how candidates get it and what its costs are.

Elite Campaign Rule 3: Raise Money, and Lots of It

The biggest hurdle for all candidates is raising enough money to run a viable campaign. In federal elections—races for the House, Senate, and presidency—the amounts spent have risen dramatically in virtually every election since the 1970s, when detailed records began to be required. In the last two decades, what one observer has called "the mighty Mississippi of cash" has reached flood stage.

How much money is spent on elections? Which candidates seem to have an advantage, and which don't?[9] Because of the different funding sources, and depending on what expenses you count, the total amount spent to influence federal elections is a subject of some dispute. The most conservative numbers, though, are astounding enough. In 2004, about $4.8 billion was spent to influence federal elections. That's an increase of nearly $1.8 billion since 2000, which in turn was double the amount spent in 1992. The presidential campaign kicked in at the highest in history, at $880.5 million spent by the Kerry and Bush campaign operations alone. For the 34 Senate races in 2004, $555 million was spent, and for the 435 House races, nearly $700 million, and this amount by the candidates and their official campaign organizations alone.[10] On average, to win a House seat costs about $1.1 million in direct expenditures from the candidates' official organization. A Senate seat was much more expensive: Senate winners spent an average of $6.5 million.[11]

Such costs create a fundraising treadmill, for it means that the average senator has to raise about $6,000 each day of his or her six-year term, whereas victorious House members are stuck with a daily quota of more than $1,500. Two decades ago, the price of victory was less than one-fifth as much. In 2004, the price of the presidential race tripled: Both the Bush and Kerry campaigns refused to limit their spending in order to gain public financing (see below on this) before they were nominated, accounting for the massive increase.

These figures are only a small part of the story because they detail only those monies controlled directly by the candidates. Far more cash was dispensed by the national political parties and their committees and by the "new kids on the block": the **independent issue advocacy** groups named after their tax-code status, the **527s and 501(c)s** (more on these later). The national parties alone dispensed $1.7 billion, while the 527s spent about $620 million. By far the most expensive in the United States, the 2004 election and its multi-billion dollar price tag raises an important question: Who benefits and who is hurt by the money game?

D.C. on $6,000 a Day: Who Money Favors. The permanent campaign doesn't sound like much fun for the participants, as the prospect of waking up every day and raising thousands of dollars does take a lot of time, energy, and moral compromises. For anyone who cares about equitable and fair democratic elections, both the sources and amounts of money involved in campaigns are causes for alarm.[12]

Theoretically, anyone who fits the constitutional qualifications can run for Congress. But modern congressional campaigns are not level playing fields open to any interested or active citizen. While politics is an uncertain art, what is certain is that money is the premier advantage in modern campaigns. Here are the three laws of modern campaign finance.

> *Law 1.* Incumbent members of Congress nearly always receive more money than their challengers. In the House, the 2004 incumbent money advantage was 6–1, and in the Senate 9–1, and this is hardly unusual. As a result, incumbents usually get reelected.

> *Law 2.* Challengers are able to defeat incumbents only when (a) they raise something close to the totals raised by the incumbent, or (b) the incumbent is very unlucky, openly corrupt, or very stupid. While this is rare, it happens often enough to prompt incumbents to defend themselves by raising more and more money.

> *Law 3.* The congressional campaigns that are really unpredictable are the open-seat contests where incumbents have retired. These are usually the most expensive races, and there are more of them than there used to be.

The distribution of campaign cash in recent congressional elections demonstrates why and how these simple laws seem to operate. Although each election featured almost contradictory voter moods and partisan outcomes, the three laws still ruled.

Take the dramatic 1992 and 1994 congressional elections as examples. On the surface, the actual results of these two contests couldn't differ more. In 1992, voters returned a Democratic majority to Congress and elected Democrat Bill Clinton to the White House. Next, 1994 was the year of the "Republican Revolution," when the GOP seized control of both houses of Congress for the first time since 1954. Both elections occurred in a climate of voter anger and even disgust with the performance and record of Congress. In both, challengers ran against incumbents by blaming Congress for scandal, corruption, and policy gridlock. How did the laws work in practice?

Despite the very different outcomes, Laws 1 and 2 held up well in both contests. Despite all the partisan change and voter anger at Congress, the incumbents still did surprisingly well. Given voter moods, how did incumbents win? In both campaigns, successful incumbents beat challengers and fought voter disgust by raising and spending more money. In 1992 and even 1994, Senate and House incumbents compiled something close to three to one spending advantages over challengers.[13]

Still, in 1994 thirty-three Democratic House incumbents were defeated, a record for recent years. What happened? Law 2 held up well; GOP challengers defeated veteran Democrats by coming close to or surpassing incumbent spending totals. Particularly vulnerable were Democratic freshmen—first-termers who couldn't use Law 1 to their full advantage because they hadn't the time or the clout to use their congressional positions to raise much money. Yet even in "revolutionary" 1994, the regular laws applied: The vast bulk of challengers couldn't match incumbent bank accounts, and those that couldn't all lost.[14] Since 1994, the story hasn't changed much, except to benefit incumbents even more. In 2004, House incumbents raised about six times more money on average than challengers did, and only five were defeated in the November election. In the Senate, only one incumbent, South Dakota Democrat Tom Daschle, lost. But his opponent, John Thune, nearly matched Daschle in total expenditures. Table 8.2 details incumbent reelection rates in recent elections.

Law 3—about the expense of "open" seats—has operated with great regularity since the 1990s. In 2004, there were 34 open House seats. Some of these campaigns were remarkably well matched in terms of campaign money, and in a

TABLE 8.2

Incumbent Reelection Rates, 1992, 1994, 2000, 2002, and 2004

Incumbent Reelection Rates in General Elections (percent)

		House	Senate
1992	(Clinton wins: Democrats maintain control of Congress)	90	85
1994	(Republican takeover of Congress; Newt Gingrich becomes Speaker)	90	94
2000	(Bush wins; Republicans retain control)	98	81
2002	(Republicans retain congressional control)	99	90
2004	(Republicans make further gains in Congress)	99	96

Sources: Congressional Weekly Reports for 2000; "Election Results," *CNN*, November 2004, http://www.cnn.com/ELECTION/2004/pages/results/senate/full.list; "Election Results," *CNN*, November 2004, http://www.cnn.com/ELECTION/2004/pages/results/states/WY/; Alan Abramovitz, "The 2004 Congressional Elections," *The American Political Science Association*, 2005, www. aspasanet.org; Results for 1992, 1994, 2000, and 2004 calculated by the author from election data.

few, those who spent a little more still lost. But overall, the winners raised an average of $1.3 million, while the losers on average raised less than half that much. In the six open Senate seats in 2004, three were won by those who spent less than their competitors. But the differences in overall spending were small. The average open Senate seat costs on average about 20 percent more for the winning candidate than for a Senate incumbent.[15]

The iron laws of campaign finance don't mean that only money counts. Yet they do mean that money counts most of the time as the most essential ingredient of a successful campaign. Still, under Law 2, there is still plenty of room for ineptitude, stupidity, and bad luck outpacing money. Take, for example, the rather sad case of former Nevada Republican Senator Chic Hecht back in 1988. The senator, who had plenty of campaign money, had not been able to prevent plans to site a nuclear waste repository in his home state of Nevada. He continually referred to them as "nuclear suppositories." A former Army intelligence officer, he referred frequently to "overt" military operations when he really meant "covert." During a debate, Hecht admitted that he had forgotten what the First Amendment was about. Hecht lost. In 2000, ultraconservative Missouri GOP senator and later Bush Attorney General John Ashcroft lost his seat to a dead man, Missouri Governor Mel Carnahan. When Carnahan died in a plane crash, it was too late to remove his name from the ballot, and his widow, Jean, agreed to serve if people voted for her husband. Ashcroft could hardly campaign against a Carnahan who was hardly in a position to respond. Ashcroft was defeated. And the Democratic Minority Leader of the Senate, South Dakotan Tom Daschle, was narrowly defeated in the most expensive Senate race of 2004. Daschle had been target number one for the GOP, and he hailed from one of the most pro-Bush states in the country. Daschle was unlucky.

Given the three laws, it is natural to think that most incumbents are pretty secure, since most times they far outraise challengers. But the members of Congress who raise the most money don't necessarily feel secure at all. Most of them have to work extremely hard to raise the dough, and they do so precisely because they fear challengers who might come from nowhere, raise several million dollars, and defeat them. The 1994 carnage that defeated so many Democratic House members is a case in point. Since then, every incentive of the campaign game has been to raise more money and take absolutely nothing for granted. The incumbency advantage is preserved only with daunting fundraising work and, as we've already discussed, gerrymandering.

The campaign money game bolsters elite democracy. By making money the indispensable political resource, the formal political equality of citizens is undermined. Those who have the resources to participate in the game can play, while those who don't are generally excluded and are always handicapped. Even many successful candidates and incumbents see burdens and costs to the permanent campaign. Pennsylvania Democratic Congressman Peter Kostmayer raised $1.2 million in a congressional race. Kostmayer still lost to an even-better-funded Republican challenger. He wasn't sad, admitting in a campaign post-mortem that "fundraising became the dominant part of my campaigns—and campaigning came to dominate my life. . . . Members of Congress despise the process but are addicted to it, terrified that change means defeat."[16]

Rules of the Cash Game

There's a profound irony to the permanent campaign and the money game it engenders. The money flows—much of it in large amounts—and most of it from very affluent individuals or, indirectly, from business interests (see below for more on money sources). Yet at the same time, the particular channels through which the money flows and the exact recipients are heavily regulated by a complex web of federal laws, passed with all good intentions. Through a series of political compromises, peculiar Supreme Court and other federal court rulings, curious and lax implementation of the laws, and "creative loopholes," reformers' goals have generally been stymied. The result is that campaign finance regulation is a stunningly elaborate labyrinth negotiated by a new and expensive industry, populated by lawyers and specialized campaign consultants, who interpret, monitor, and find ways around the regulations to keep the money flowing through separate legal channels. We can't hope to explain their full complexity here, but we can try to clarify their basic features.

Campaign Laws: Stage One, 1974–2002

The existing rules were passed by Congress in two waves, in 1974 and in 2002. The first set of laws was the result of revulsion at the tactics of President Richard

Nixon's 1972 campaign and the resulting Watergate scandal. The Nixon campaign took in millions of dollars in unreported cash contributions, often handed over in shopping bags or carry-on luggage. Nixon financed his operation by trading cash for favors or legislation; the dairy industry contributed heavily and received milk price supports; entrepreneurs like H. Ross Perot (later a presidential candidate in 1992 and 1996) gave Nixon $200,000 and got a big federal contract. Others netted ambassadorships, tax breaks, or sub-Cabinet appointments. The 1974 **Federal Election Campaign Act (FECA)**, establishing the **Federal Election Commission (FEC)**, was passed in the hopes of presenting, or at least revealing, such practices.[17]

Among other laudable goals, the FECA requires public disclosure of the names of campaign donors, limits the size of donations to national party organizations and the official campaign organizations of federal candidates, and provides some voluntary provisions for taxpayer funding of presidential candidates in exchange for limits on the amount of money they raise and spend. The FECA also bans direct contributions of corporations and by foreigners to candidates but allows the formation of **political action committees (PACs)** to handle and bundle regulated individual contributions that come from a host of private organizations and their members. The law establishes a regulatory body—the FEC—made up of Democrats and Republicans equally, to monitor the FECA's implementation.

From the law's inception until its revision in 2002, several developments gutted the law's intention of regulating the flow of very big money into electoral politics. Perhaps most important was a 1976 Supreme Court ruling in *Buckley v. Valeo*. This decision upheld the FECA's regulation of the specific amounts that could be given to the official organizations of the candidates and parties. Importantly, though, it struck down any absolute limit on the total amount any organization or individual could spend on federal campaigns. The ability of donors to spend as much as they want was considered "free speech," as was the idea that a rich person could fund his or her campaign without any money limits whatsoever. If they could afford it, any person or PAC could donate the full regulated amount to every single candidate running for Congress or the presidency.

Buckley v. Valeo opened the floodgates to a host of other Court decisions that upheld the legality of a new kind of distinction, and that was between **hard money** and **soft money**. Hard money was defined as all the dough whose amounts were regulated by the FEC, mostly money given to candidates and their organizations or to parties to give specifically to the candidates they wanted. In contrast, soft money was the unregulated and unlimited amounts donated to fund "other," party-building activities. This turned out to be the biggest loophole of all, as "other" soft money was defined so broadly that they soon equaled "hard" money expenditures. At the beginning, soft money was used for "party building" activities of the kind we saw in Chapter 7: If the Republicans wanted to build a new headquarters with state-of-the-art media facilities, then Amway Corporation could write the check for the amount required (which it did). But soon the parties, with the Democrats in the lead but the

GOP close behind, found new loopholes. The Supreme Court was again help-ful. In the 1990s, the Court ruled that the national parties could raise and spend unlimited amounts of money to help their own candidates, as long as these were **"independent expenditures"** of the official campaign organizations of its can-didates. The key in determining "independent" was also the absence of express advocacy for a candidate. At the same time, the parties found new ways of rais-ing soft dollars and then handing them over to state parties, who then spent it to help federal candidates in particular states. The result was a new generation of issue advocacy ads. Pioneered by President Clinton and the Democrats, $25 million in soft money funded an expensive series of ads praising President Clin-ton's record in 1995. The ads never actually asked voters to vote for him. Caught by surprise, the GOP soon raised about the same amount, attacking Clinton without saying "Vote Republican!"[18]

In the "Who Gives" section below, we detail where most of the soft and hard money came from. Here, it is enough to note that the rise of soft money was dramatic and came to nearly outmatch "hard" contributions. From a mere trickle in the 1980s, the parties collected about a half billion in "soft" dollars in the election of 2000.

Campaign Reform, Phase Two: 2002–?

The rise of soft money, and the sheer amount of money in the system, sparked a growing reform movement in the 1990s. The movement was, and is, quite dif-fuse. Pushed by protest, most congressional Democrats supported some reform measures, even though they stood to lose out from any ban on soft money, where their party held a slight edge over the GOP. The GOP, in contrast, held a mammoth edge in all other forms of political donations, especially in "hard" money. Most Republicans defended the existing campaign system and in fact re-sisted some of the existing restrictions in the name of free speech and, more realistically, because their party was the greater beneficiary of existing laws.

Reformers in the 1990s, just as in the 1970s, were concerned about soft money but also about the spiraling costs and generally corporate—and some labor union—sources of most campaign money, both hard and soft. Many sought to replace the entire system with a voluntary system of public financing. Others favored the provision of free media time for candidates and parties on the broadcast media, who'd been making huge profits from the high prices charged for paid political advertising.

In Congress, the impulse for campaign reform of some kind was spearheaded by Republican senator John McCain and Democratic senator Russell Feingold. To attract some GOP support, the McCain–Feingold Bill concentrated on a soft money ban and a ban on independent expenditures financing TV adver-tisements before an election. Most of the other original provisions, requiring cheaper prices for political advertising, were stripped from the bill over time. And to further draw a few Republican votes, reformers in Congress gave the GOP a big plum. They agreed to raise limits on hard individual contributions—

an area where the GOP already had a huge advantage—to candidates and to party committees by almost 100 percent, in exchange for the ban on soft money. The **Bipartisan Campaign Reform Act (BCRA)** passed Congress in 2002 with almost unanimous Democratic support and votes from a few Republicans. A reluctant President Bush, stung by charges of big money bribes in his 2000 race, signed the bill. A loose coalition of big soft money contributors and most Republicans vowed to test the bill in the federal courts, and finally the Supreme Court. To the surprise of many, most of the provisions were judged constitutional, and the bill went into effect just in time for the 2004 election. Its provisions, along with the remaining campaign finance regulations, are summarized in Table 8.3.

Many observers predicted that the BCRA would weaken the parties, especially the soft-money-dependent Democrats. To their surprise, this has hardly been the case, or at least if 2004 is the trendsetter. Riding on the intensity of voter protest against the Bush regime, the Democrats worked hard to expand the numbers of small donors and did so in dramatic fashion. By the end of 2004, the Democrats had over 1 million donors in their Internet database and a mailing list of close to 100 million voters. In 2004, both parties and their congressional committees, as well as the presidential candidates, drew more than twice as many individual contributions as they had in 2000. The Republicans maintained an overall edge of nearly $160 million in donations to the party's national congressional campaign committees, but the numbers and amounts of individual donations to both parties soared, and the Democratic National Committee itself actually outraised its Republican counterpart.[19]

The Return of Big Money: The 501s and 527s

Like floodwater, however, the tide of big money contributions was hardly halted by BCRA in 2004. Instead, it moved into a whole new direction, ostensibly free of control by either of the parties or of specific candidates. Despite the protests of campaign finance reformers like McCain and Feingold, the FEC ruled in 2003 that unlimited "soft money" from corporate groups, rich individuals, or labor unions could flow to so-called "527" organizations. Named after a section of the tax code, the new 527s eventually took in over $600 million in 2004 in contributions. They were barred from coordinating with the party or candidate organizations and from explicitly endorsing any candidate for public office. Although Democratic-affiliated groups had a huge early lead in the 527 money race, the Republicans soon caught up and actually surpassed the Democrats in 527 fundraising in the months before the November election.[20]

While 527s couldn't coordinate with the parties, most of the donors and leaders were nonetheless seasoned party and campaign veterans. On the Democratic side, Americans Coming Together (ACT) and Moveon.org created some of the most impressive grassroots voter registration and get-out-the-vote drives in national history. ACT, much of whose funds came from corporate critic but multibillionaire George Soros and from labor unions, put 45,000 paid workers

TABLE 8.3   Major Contribution Limits, BCRA, 2004 and 2006

	To Any Candidate Committee (per election[1])	To Any National Party Committee (per year)	To Any PAC, State/ Local Party, or Other Political Committee (per year)	Aggregate Total
Individual can give:	*Pre-BCRA*: $1,000	$20,000	$5,000	$25,000 per year
	2004 Cycle: $2,000, subject to aggregate limit[2]	$25,000 per party committee, subject to aggregate limit	$10,000 to each state or local party committee $5,000 to each PAC or other political committee, subject to aggregate limit	$95,000 per two-year election cycle as follows: • $37,500 per cycle to candidates; and • $57,500 per cycle to all national party committees and PACs (of which no more than $37,500 per cycle can go to PACs)
	2006 Cycle[3]: $2,100, subject to aggregate limit	$26,700 per party committee, subject to aggregate limit	$10,000 to each state or local party committee $5,000 to each PAC or other political committee, subject to aggregate limit	$101,400 per two-year election cycle as follows: • $40,000 per cycle to candidates; and • $61,400 per cycle to all national party committees and PACs (of which no more than $40,000 per cycle can go to PACs)
Multi-candidate committee can give[4]:	*Pre-BCRA*: $5,000	$15,000	$5,000	No limit
	BCRA: Same	Same	Same	Same

[1]Primary and general elections count as separate elections.
[2]BCRA's individual contribution limits are higher to candidates facing wealthy opponents financing their own campaigns.
[3]Under BCRA, some individaul contribution limits were indexed for inflation for 2005–2006. They will be indexed again in future cycles.
[4]Multicandidate committees (also known as PACs) are those with more than 50 contributors that have been registered for at least six months and (with the exception of state party committees) have made contributions to five or more federal candidates.
Source: Federal Election Commission via the Center for Responsive Politics.

and volunteers on the street in the battleground states to turn out likely Democratic voters. Moveon.org used its extensive Internet network to bring out the antiwar vote and run ads critical of President Bush. The Media Fund, headed by former Clinton political adviser Harold Ickes, raised soft money for ads that scored President Bush's tax and spending priorities and foreign policy. On the

GOP side, much of the money was raised by the notorious Swift Boat Veterans for Truth, and was given by right-wing corporate raiders like T. Boone Pickens and real estate speculator Bob Perry, who separately contributed huge amounts to the Bush campaign. Swift Boat Veterans ran what turned out to be false ads questioning Senator Kerry's war record and his later antiwar activism. Benjamin Ginsberg, the Swift Boat Veterans lawyer, resigned from his post when it was discovered that he also represented the Republican National Committee. The biggest Republican-oriented 527 was Progress for America, run by two employees of lobbying and political consulting firms that had direct-mail contracts with the Bush Campaign. In short, the 527 organizations, especially the Republican ones, maintained only the fiction of separation from the parties.[21]

527s were not the only new conduits for soft money. Advocacy groups like the National Rifle Association and the Sierra Club also joined the electoral fray as "501(c)s," charities with tax-exempt status. Their official organizations were barred from direct campaign activity, but such groups spent undisclosed millions on voter education and turnout drives in 2004 as well. Most estimates say that the 501s spent between $70 million and $100 million in voter turnout and political education efforts. Like 527s, these groups could accept soft money for advocacy purposes. Unlike them, they couldn't use all their budgets for political advocacy, and the tax code restricted their activities even more than the 527s. 501(c)s, however, were not even obligated to disclose their donors, so the sources of this cash conduit are not known. And many argue that the 501(c)s and their activities are uninvestigated and unregulated.[22]

Who Gives: Taking Care of Business

Especially after the 2004 election, many observers and party officials praised BCRA as something of a model of how democratic politics can be revived by the power of small contributors. With the end of huge soft money contributions flowing to the parties, the authors of BCRA, as well as many other seasoned analysts, proclaimed that the reform had worked: the parties showed they could do without the soft money and still stimulate millions of small donors to give generously.

This assessment contains more than a grain of truth. Especially in 2004, the numbers of individual contributors to parties, the presidential candidates, and members of Congress, as well as some of the 527s, did more than double over previous elections. While the surge of small donors is an achievement, it neglects some obvious facts. Small donations of under $200 surged, but they still made up only a small percentage of the total take. And the number of larger donations rose dramatically as well, in part made possible by BCRA's raising of the allowable limits on hard money donations. Only about 280,000 Americans — one-tenth of 1 percent of U.S. adults — gave $2,000 or more in 2004, but their contributions made up over 80 percent of the take. Only 1.13 million Americans — one-half of 1 percent of U.S. adults — gave enough money to be itemized at all, more than $200.

While detailed studies on the income of donors is not available for 2004, in the recent past almost all campaign money was donated by people in the top

10 percent of American income earners. While no doubt 2004 slightly leveled this incredible class skew toward the affluent, it wasn't by much. As a form of political participation, campaign donations remain the preserve of the affluent and very big donations the preserve of the very rich.[23]

As important is the form in which campaign money is delivered by the affluent and the potential strings attached. We just mentioned George Soros, one of the richest men in the world, who gave $24 million to ACT. Soros, however, is an eccentric critic of the business and corporate system that had helped to make him rich. His contributions to ACT could hardly be seen as an attempt to promote his own business interests or personal wealth, because ACT, also heavily backed by labor unions, was mostly made up of people opposed to the tax and policy advantages enjoyed by large corporations and shareholders like Soros himself.

A far more revealing and self-interested pattern of giving characterizes corporate America. Here, there are many ways to give: PACs and so-called **bundled contributions**. Bundling occurs when leaders of a corporation or an industry get together and pledge a concerted effort to put together a "bundle" of individual contributions to represent their particular interest. Leaders and executives in the finance, banking, health care, military, agribusiness, and a host of other sectors almost all participate in the practice. Here, corporate America and its various industries can speak with a united voice. While every kind of industry, from beer wholesalers to producers of military jets, has a PAC and urges its executives to bundle contributions, the vast number of Americans don't have a PAC and don't bundle. The working poor don't have PACs, nor do they bundle contributions. Neither do college professors, millions of nonunionized workers, Wal-Mart clerks, college students, or dozens of other economic and social groups.

The predominance of corporate donations in politics is overwhelming, even as labor unions and so-called ideological PACs have struggled to keep pace in the campaign finance arms race. Nearly three-quarters of all individual and PAC donations stemmed from business sources, and nearly 70 percent of all PACs donations alone were from so-called trade association and business PACs promoting their interests before Congress and the executive branch. Labor unions have formed some of the biggest PACs, but they are extraordinarily few in number in comparison with the corporate world and contribute only 17 percent of the total PAC and individual donations. So-called "ideological PACs"—organizations promoting pro-life or pro-choice positions, privatization, consumer rights or a host of other causes—contribute about 15 percent of the total PAC take. Of the over 4,100 registered political action committees, business and trade association PACs far outnumber both in numbers and dollar contributions any other category.[24]

Who Gets: The Emerging Republican Advantage

Which of the political parties benefits most from corporate America's contributions? Throughout the 1980s and the early 1990s, the pattern of both individual and PAC giving was mostly bipartisan, with the Republicans in the lead in individual donations, and with PAC donations relatively split between the candidates and organizations of both parties. We just discussed the incumbent advantage in PAC contributions, as donors seek to influence those who are already in office. As we said, corporate and trade association giving has long far outweighed labor donations, and generally speaking, "ideological" PACs split their contributions between the two parties overall. Before 1994, the Republicans were the beneficiaries of corporate largesse more than the Democrats, but the GOP margin in those days was not huge.

However, the pattern of donations did have a profound effect on both parties, pushing the Republicans far rightward and the Democrats away from their working-class roots. Virtually all of the GOP's money then came from business and from right-wing, including Christian Right, sources. In a way, the GOP was pure: Its predictably procorporate, promarket ideology was reflected in its corporate donor base. Its ideology could move rightward without fear of losing donor support; indeed, it thrived. In contrast, the Democrats' sources of money were more mixed and contradictory. The majority came from business and was given to Democratic incumbents, because at that time Democrats controlled both houses of Congress. But the Democrats also depended on labor and liberal ideological support for about 40 percent of their campaign money.

For many observers of that period, one of the central reasons for the Democratic Party's move to center and to the right in the 1980s and 1990s had to do with the growing ties to corporate donors. And, indeed, as we've seen in the previous chapter, the Democrats' message became much more fragmented and more receptive to the kinds of tax cuts, deregulation, and procorporate policies than it had once been, whereas the GOP's rise was unabashedly procorporate in both its message and donor base.

More importantly, these relatively bipartisan giving patterns have altered sharply in the last decade. The Republican takeover of Congress and the White House has led to a notable shift in business giving. Once inclined to hedge its bets by funding the powerful in both parties, corporate America's giving pattern now strikingly benefits the GOP at the expense, and sometimes to the utter exclusion, of the Democrats. In 2004, the Republicans collected over two-thirds of corporate donations in industries like agribusiness, defense, energy, transportation, construction, and health care, and over 60 percent of the dollars of the finance and banking industries. Among wealthy organized interests, Democrats led massively only among trial lawyers—wealthy people whose business is to sue large companies—and in the media and electronics industries, and here only by small amounts. In PAC giving to Senate and House Republicans, corporate donations split over 2–1 for the now dominant Republicans.

In part, the corporate shift to the GOP is a conscious result of GOP strategy and a set of new hardball tactics to expand their majority. GOP House Leader Tom DeLay, nicknamed "The Hammer," launched efforts like the K Street Project along with other conservative operatives. The idea, according to *Washington Post* journalist Thomas Edsall "was to track contribution patterns, with the strong

Making a Difference

Clean Elections Through Public Financing

In Congress and in the national media, campaign financing is seen largely as a problem of eliminating soft money alone. In this battle, the 2002 passage of BCRA was seen as a major victory. But as the 2004 election indicates, big money has flowed through other channels, and candidates spend a good deal of time on the money chase.

Starting in December 2000, a new Maine legislature took office, and most of the people in it weren't beholden to soft *or* hard money donors at all. Instead, Maine elects state officials through a unique system of voluntary public financing. While the federal candidates were awash in a $5 billion wave of private cash, three-quarters of Maine's state senators and 57 percent of State Assembly members in 2004 were free of financial obligations to special-interest contributors.

The Maine Clean Elections Act was passed by a state referendum in 1998. The idea is pretty simple. To conform with U.S. Supreme Court decisions like *Buckley v. Valeo*, the system is entirely voluntary. Candidates for public office of whatever political party can choose to spend private funds for their campaigns, or they can opt into the public system. If they do the latter, they first have to prove popular support by raising a large number of quite small individual campaign contributions from their districts. When they meet the test, "clean elections" candidates pledge not to raise money from private sources. In return they receive state dollars equal to 75 percent of the average amount spent for recent elections to that office. With no money necessary for fundraising, available funds go further. If candidates who take money from private sources outspend their "clean elections" opponents, the latter get more money for their campaign.

How did this system work in Maine? Since 2000, a majority of candidates for the Maine legislature have opted into the public system. The proportion of women in the legislature rose dramatically, and the number of contested party primary races rose by 40 percent. The final vote was more contested and closer for races where publicly financed candidates were running, and over half the "clean elections" candidates won. Witness Chester Chapman, a self-employed Republican machinist who ran for the Maine House of Representatives: "I thought about what would happen if someone gave me $250, then told me how I ought to vote. I figured I'd have to take into account my own conscience, how people in the district feel, and this donor. At least now I've eliminated one." Chapman won. The

suggestion that companies favoring the Republican Party will have better access than those who do not."[25]

If this pattern holds up, the GOP will continue to maintain a substantial advantage in the campaign money chase. So far, corporate enthusiasm for the GOP and the new "pay to play" rules have paid off generously for the main corporate GOP backers. The capital gains and dividend tax cuts passed by the Republicans will cost the federal government $125 billion in lost revenue over six years, "redistributed" to wealthy corporate stockholders. For the banking industry, there's been generous new legislation that gives unprecedented power to credit card companies when people go bankrupt. For military industries, there's legislative results have sometimes been dramatic. Maine passed a law permitting the state to use its size to negotiate lower drug prices for citizens—something the big pharmaceutical companies might have been able to stop if lawmakers were leashed by a need for campaign cash.

How could public financing get going at the national level? Besides Maine, four other states have passed the "clean elections" public financing idea. But due to court challenges, only Arizona has put it fully into effect. There, over half the Clean Elections candidates for the Legislature won, and the percentage of nonwhites and women lawmakers has increased. All statewide offices except one are occupied by candidates who opted into the new system. In Arizona, two public financing candidates defeated incumbents in their race for the State Corporations Commission, charged with regulating corporate practices.

In Congress, public financing doesn't stand much of a chance now because the majority of members see it as impractical and as a threat to their own entrenched incumbency. Still, in the House 59 members have cosponsored clean money and clean election legislation, and the number has grown in recent years. Still, the campaigns of grassroots groups have concentrated on individual states, where the prospects seem brighter. Sensing a grassroots threat, many companies have put big money into opposing it at the state level. In 2000, public financing initiatives were defeated in Missouri and Oregon, due largely to lopsided campaigns by business to defeat it. The basic argument against public financing is that it is "welfare for politicians." But practicing politicians and activists in Maine and Arizona think differently about public financing. Donald Gean, who runs a homeless shelter in York County, Maine, took the plunge and decided to run as a clean elections candidate: "Even if I lose, my enthusiasm won't be dampened. It's just the right thing to do."

All these referenda were put onto state ballots through grassroots activism and enthusiasm—in Maine, it took over a thousand volunteers to collect over 65,000 signatures to get the measure on the state ballot. And that may signal the difference between these state campaigns and the discourse in Washington, where public financing is considered impractical. Sometime soon, "public financing should be the model for a national campaign finance reform program," says the *Portland Press Herald*. Maybe the problem of money isn't so complex after all.

Sources: Public Campaign, "Clean Money in Action," www.Publiccampaign.org/; "Hungry for Good News About the Election? Try This," *USA Today*, December 6, 2000; Clean Elections Institute, Inc. of Arizona. "2004 Election Statistics"; Kate Riley, "Is Washington Ready to Clean Up Its Elections?" *Seattle Times*, November 1, 2004.

the biggest military budget in history, and for thoroughly GOP firms like Halliburton, over $11 billion in federal contracts. For the energy industry, there is an end of drilling regulations in Alaska and on millions of acres of federal land. For public utilities, there's the laxest enforcement of antipollution statutes in history. The drug industry, one of the biggest GOP backers, has perhaps been the biggest beneficiary: the GOP passed prescription drug benefits for seniors in 2003, but its cost has ballooned because it bans the federal government from seeking special bulk buying rates from the drug companies. This ensures billions in additional drug company profits. For the only staunchly Democratic group among donors, trial lawyers, the message from the GOP was clear: Early in 2005, Congress passed a new law limiting the size and scope of liability settlements, a clear hit at the lawyers' financial livelihoods.[26]

The Class Basis of Money Politics

The defenders of the campaign money game argue that there really isn't that much money in politics. After all, the amount spent on federal elections in 2004 was little more than that spent by the drug or auto industry in their TV advertising. A second defense is that money is "free speech" and that regulating and limiting money in politics violates the First Amendment. To the supporters of BCRA, the results in 2004 demonstrated a vast improvement. After all, soft money donations were (kind of) eliminated. A flood of small donors entered the system during the exciting presidential race in both parties.[27]

Both of these positions may miss the most pernicious effect of money in politics. It is that most citizens don't contribute at all and that the biggest source of campaign money remains corporate America. Campaign money may not be bribery in the strict sense, but it does buy access for those who provide it. Most of all, private money is not an equal opportunity resource, and insofar as the U.S. campaign system is full of it, it reduces the equality of citizens in politics and demeans the promise of equality contained in the phrase "one person, one vote." Moreover, it might be asked: Is it a coincidence that as campaigns have become more expensive, voter turnout has generally dropped? Or that fewer people donate time to campaigns, as money buys professionals and television advertising? While the ban on soft money has helped, the general outlines of the campaign finance system have actually become worse in other ways. Wealthy individuals can spend even more, up to $100,000 apiece, in hard money donations. Soft money still flows, if through the indirect paths of 527s. Candidates still spend most of their time in the money chase, and, for the most part, the political system utterly excludes challengers who can't raise $1 million for a House seat and $7 million for a Senate run.

Are there practical alternatives to the money-driven system? There are, and some of them are already in operation in the states. In the Making a Difference box, we summarize the experience of "Clean Money" states that provide voluntary public financing.

WHAT MONEY BUYS: THE RISE OF CAMPAIGN PROFESSIONALS AND MARKETERS

The scramble for money by parties, candidates, and groups as well as the Byzantine rules that govern the whole system are factors largely invisible to most voters who are neither activists nor contributors. The money chase raises a simple question: Why? Why are modern campaigns so fixated on money, and what does it buy?

2004 as a Model

The 2004 Bush campaign provides a good model. Almost immediately after Bush first took office in 2001, the campaign began in earnest, founded on the assumption that campaign dough would be forthcoming. The new president's chief political adviser, Karl Rove, served as a kind of CEO and began to develop a strategic and advertising plan with the president's pollster, media consultants, and fundraising experts. The assumption was risky, but turned out to be prescient: The 2000 election had been too close, they reasoned, because the Republicans hadn't fully mobilized and organized their full base—too many Christian Right voters, and conservatives in the growing exurbs and semirural areas in the battleground states, had sat out the 2000 election. While persuading swing voters would be important, it would take second place to a sophisticated and coordinated battle to identify, register, and get to the polls so-called "soft" Republicans who hadn't voted in 2000.

The strategy led to certain costly decisions and operations. A key component involved hiring a company called TargetPoint Consultants. The goal: Use the massive amount of marketing information on consumer buying preferences and lifestyles and mesh it with the already huge political database of the Republican National Committee. By finding links between, say, bourbon-drinking, SUV-driving, gym-visiting young, married people who used caller IDs and were between twenty-five and thirty-five years old and their likely political opinions, the Bush effort could customize and tailor messages to hundreds of different small groups of voters. Bush's reelection chair Ken Mehlman explained, "We did what Visa did. . . . Based on that, we were able to develop an exact kind of consumer model that corporate America does every day to predict how people will vote—not based on where they live, but how they live."[28]

The second stage was to develop extensive survey data about the "anger points" of up to thirty-two different categories of "consumer"—Republicans. By doing so, the Republicans could customize their direct mail, phone, TV, and grassroots contacts to particular groups of voters. This was a revolutionary model: Instead of just blanketing entire media markets and neighborhoods with the same general Bush brochures or calling possible Republicans with the same taped messages, the operation could use the "anger points" to distinguish likely pro-gun Bush voters from those more concerned with anti-abortion laws, tax cuts, the war on terrorism, or stem-cell research. Voters with particular interests would get a particular taped message on the phone and a visit from a Bush volunteer aware of the "anger point" relevant to each voter.

On the basis of this massive research, the GOP refined its campaign plan to include phone calls, direct mail, TV advertising, radio spots, and volunteer visits. Long before Kerry was nominated, the plan was in place and was test-marketed in two states in the 2002 congressional election. By March 2004, the Bush campaign had already spent millions and had $100 million in the bank. By opting out of the federal public funding provisions for the primary season, the Bush campaign was free to raise unlimited funds and deploy them freely, since Bush faced no opponent in the GOP primaries.

As a result, the Bush campaign had the funding to spend $175 million on its "ground war" (described in Chapter 7). The idea was to coordinate all of the marketing information with the GOP's existing databases and the county and state Bush organizations in the battleground states. The goal: identify, register, and eventually bring to the polls potential Bush voters. In the previous chapter, we described this "Amway" model. Volunteers among targeted groups were recruited and in turn recruited other volunteers. Particular groups—say readers of *Field and Stream* magazine—were recruited and given lists of voters with similar tastes to canvass with progun scripts and brochures. Areas of rapid growth without traditional political organizations—mostly the new exurbs outside cities like Columbus, Ohio, and Jacksonville, Florida—became the focus of advertising buys and volunteer coordination from the Bush headquarters in Virginia. Advertising was bought on cable television channels most likely to be seen by Republican voters. The research indicated that Republicans shunned traditional networks, so the campaign fine-tuned its "media buys," favoring particular channels of communication instead of buying up time in huge markets. TV advertising was bought on the Golf Channel or the QVC network, Christian radio and TV, health club cable channels, country and western stations, or spot buys on talk-radio stations friendly to the GOP. In each venue, the ads and

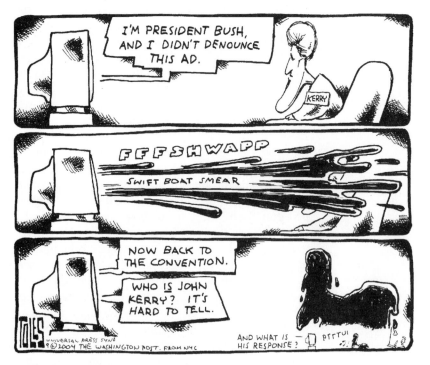

TOLES © 2004 The Washington Post. Reprinted with permission of UNIVERSAL PRESS SYNDICATE. All rights reserved.

direct mail were targeted to particular kinds of voters. Swift Boat Veterans for Truth ads, for instance, initially aired on cable TV in small towns. In other areas, the GOP ran "Ashley's Story," an ad designed for Republican-leaning women about a young child whose mom had been killed at the World Trade Center and her meeting with President Bush. Research showed that *Will and Grace*, a sitcom about gay life in New York, was surprisingly popular among young Republican women. Even as the Bush campaign was touting its opposition to gay marriage, its campaign bought 473 spots on *Will and Grace* to advertise the president's strong leadership on national security.[29]

The total cost of the official Bush campaign, $1.17 billion, was only part of the effort. The key was that common themes emerge in the diverse operations of related Republican efforts by 527 groups, the party committees, the think tanks, and the official Bush–Cheney campaign. It would be the 527s, not the party or the candidate, who'd unleash the most negative and spurious attacks on Kerry, for instance, so that the harsher ads wouldn't be traced back to Bush himself. It would be the Bush–Cheney effort that would coordinate media buys in particular markets with the army of canvassers directed from the Bush headquarters in Arlington, Virginia, and its huge database. And it would be the Republican National Committee and its informal networks that would be important in developing a common campaign message among the think tanks, friendly reporters, and pundits so important in "staying on message."

While the Republicans already had much in place, by the spring of 2004 the Kerry campaign had hardly begun its national campaign. In a preemptive strike against Kerry, the Bush campaign ran a $40 million, six-week assault, attempting to define the prospective nominee as a "flip-flopping," out-of-touch liberal before Kerry had a chance to run his own national ads. The Democratic Party and the Kerry campaign weren't really prepared to respond. For one, the 527 groups couldn't by law support Kerry in their ads, so they limited their response to anti-Bush ads. As a result, Kerry's numbers began to drop slightly, as the GOP had the advantage in defining the agenda, and Kerry's "unfavorable" ratings rose. Like the Republicans, the Democrats and their allied groups had plenty of money, but they'd gotten the money late, and the funds were being used by a host of groups that either couldn't or wouldn't coordinate their strategies. Democrats and some of the 527s built an impressive ground operation, but it was hardly coordinated with the same precision as the GOP campaign machine. Moreover, the Democrats and the 527s and their efforts were based on volunteers, but more often than not the volunteer canvassers were exported into the battleground states from elsewhere. More traditional than the GOP, the Democrats didn't have the marketing research available to the Republicans, either, and tended to buy their TV times on traditional venues like the networks or their local affiliates. Often, because all was not directed by a central office, canvassing efforts overlapped, as workers for ACT duplicated the efforts made by the local Kerry organization. For the most part, Democrats campaigned the old-fashioned way: go over to a neighborhood and talk to people, give them a brochure, and make sure they vote on Election Day.

In the end, the Bush effort was victorious, beating Kerry by about 3 million votes out of 120 million cast. Using Rove's strategy, the GOP increased its vote over 2000 totals by nearly 10.5 million voters, while the Democrats gained 7 million. Thomas Edsall and James Grimaldi comment: "The Bush campaign was run to ensure that every dollar went to fulfill core strategies, that resources were allocated to capitalize on Bush's strengths and Kerry's vulnerabilities, and that the money necessary to finance research, technological advance, television, and the ground war was available when needed."[30]

The 2004 Bush campaign has already become something of a model for the high-tech professionalization of the modern campaign. Rooted as it is in money, media, and marketing with the deployment of volunteers as an instrument of a central headquarters and its strategy, it represents the extreme tendencies of politicking and campaigning in both parties. As we will see below, there are certain offsetting tendencies as well, which rely less on technology and professionalization and more on grassroots organizations in which people and the democratic debate count more. The Bush campaign was successful, but are there costs to democracy? Before addressing this question, we'll first survey the major developments. What else does campaign money buy, and how has it changed over time?

Political Consultants

One big campaign expense is the professional experts themselves. While modern political campaigns have always employed pros, the modern political consultant—personified by the legendary Karl Rove—is a different kind of animal than his party boss predecessors. They're expensive. Back in the 1996 race, Bill Clinton's political consultant, Dick Morris, charged $2 million for his personal advice. A well-run congressional campaign employs consultants for fees of $100,000 or more.

The old party bosses lived in style, too, but their skills were different. The party bosses dealt in votes and as such ran operations where ward heelers, voters, and government jobs came into play along with grassroots contact with ordinary voters through a complex party organization. The old bosses didn't have college educations and were rough-talking, down-to-earth types. Most of them would have died before working for candidates of different parties.

Modern political consultants like Karl Rove tend to be well educated and even fancy themselves to be intellectuals of sorts. Rove himself got his start as a lonely College Republican in the antiwar sixties. His specialty was playing humorous (although sometimes not so funny) tricks on political opponents. Strategic thinkers, modern political consultants are able to manipulate data and design surveys and are likely to feel more comfortable with advertising executives and the press corps than with ordinary voters. Until recently, they were not a particularly ideological bunch, and many consulting firms would work for the highest bidder. Clinton's Dick Morris, for instance, had previously worked for Mississippi Republican senator Trent Lott. In the last decade or so, though, the growing polarization of the parties has produced a solid split in the consulting community between Republican- and Democratic-oriented firms and individuals.

At the same time, consulting has become much more like a science, with a universal toolkit and methodology. In the old days, consultants' origins were often in the worlds of advertising, public relations, and communication. More recently, it has become its own profession. Political consultants have even founded their own graduate school, magazine, and professional association. Unlike party professionals of the past, modern consultants know voters, but only as abstractions and numbers on a survey. The currency of political consultants is high technology applied to politics.[31]

The business of professional political consulting began about four decades ago. Like many innovations, California showed the way, with the two firms of Spencer Roberts and Whitaker & Baxter pioneering the new profession. Today, no serious candidate can afford to be without consultants, if only because all the other candidates have them.

What do consultants offer? According to one lengthy study, since "so much can go wrong . . . professionals are needed to bring order out of chaos, maintain message and strategy discipline, and keep the campaign focused." With the permanent campaign, modern political consultants are not just employed during election years—many firms orchestrate "grassroots" and public relations campaigns for corporate clients in off years and then seek political candidate business during election years. Others, the most successful consultants, become presidential advisers. Dick Morris worked for Clinton for two years, and the Bush campaign's Karl Rove landed a permanent White House job after his boss was inaugurated. However, more typical are specialists of lesser fame who concentrate on polling, website design, TV and radio advertising, direct-mail fundraising, and press relations for congressional and gubernatorial candidates. The rise of political consultants parallels the growth of the permanent and personal campaign.[32]

Polling

Next to consulting, a good pollster is the foundation of the modern campaign. Polling serves as the basis for all other campaign activities. The polls come in many varieties. Just about every reputable congressional campaign conducts a **benchmark survey**, which probes the name recognition, job ratings, and potential strengths and weaknesses of candidates in the race. In tight Senate races and the presidential sweepstakes, polling is much more complex and expensive, since **tracking surveys** recording voter reaction to the campaign's ads and themes are conducted on almost a daily basis. Premier consultants insist on hiring their own favorite firm to do the tracking and trend surveys that trace every nuance and shift in voter opinion and trace the particular groups of swing voters and their concerns. In modern campaigns, pollsters also manage **focus and dial groups**, allowing candidates to "test-market" specific appeals and statements by the candidate before he or she says it. Dial groups are particularly prominent, for they allow each word in a candidate's speech to be tested for negative and positive reactions. This kind of research is expensive; the Clinton campaign spent millions on polls that sometimes asked over 250 questions. In the Bush campaign, it was pollster Michael Dowd who coordinated "TargetPoints" findings with the Bush campaigns tracking, dial, and focus group efforts.

Poll-driven campaigns have been criticized because they change the campaign agenda to adjust to the polls. As such, they can serve to distort and disguise controversial positions and limit debate, replacing both with focus-group tested, feel-good clichés that tell the voters nothing about what the candidate has done or will do. In 2000, many Democrats criticized the Gore campaign for its hyper-reliance on polling, as the Democratic nominee often appeared to change his speech patterns, dress, and personality based on focus group research. At the beginning of this chapter, we already set out another example: President Bush resisted saying much about Social Security during the campaign, substituting instead his declarations about his strong and consistent leadership. But the issue emerged on the top of the agenda literally the day after his reelection.[33]

Media Advertising

Polling is useful only insofar as the candidate's images and opponent's weaknesses are effectively accented in subsequent TV and radio advertising. More than ever, effective ads are important because there's less time devoted to campaigns in both the national and local "free" media. Just how effective ads are is a matter of some dispute. Most studies indicate that few voters change position by watching TV ads alone. But effective ads reinforce existing impressions and motivate people to vote. Ads can highlight existing "positives" among voters. Just as importantly, they can "go negative," defining opponents in the public mind before they have a chance to so themselves. Although people say they don't like negative ads, they seem to work when the subject is rather undefined in many voters' minds, as John Kerry was in early 2004. Most of all, charges against an opponent that would be unseemly to voice in the candidate's own voice can be the most useful function of TV and radio ads. As we said previously, the infamous Swift Boat Veterans for Truth commercials that ran against Senator Kerry in August 2004 helped to shape the overall message, as the ad was picked up by the news media and played again and again. Often, a scurrilous ad to which the victim doesn't respond can shape an entire campaign, as it did in 1988 when George H. W. Bush's campaign successfully labeled Democrat Michael Dukakis a coddler of criminals and a supporter of flag burning. Dukakis believed that it was beneath his dignity to respond, but the ads may have lost many swing voters to the Bush campaign.[34] The overall cost of ads has risen in recent years, mostly because there are more of them, and rates, as well as media profits, have soared. There are also more venues and outlets, from cable TV to radio to traditional networks, on which to advertise. TV ads are usually the greatest portion of expenses for any national or statewide campaign. In 2004, TV ad budgets ran to over $600 million for the presidential race alone.

The importance and expense of campaign media specialists have grown accordingly. They've got to make quick choices about the themes of commercials. (Which "issues" should be presented? Should the candidate talk in the ads? When should positive images be reinforced? When should opponents be attacked?) In contrast to the early days of political advertising, where campaigns tended to produce a couple of ads that were broadcast throughout the country, media "buys" are today a much more complex science. It would be a stupid ad consultant who'd buy any ads at all in deep red or blue states in 2004: in fact, the over 630,000 ads run by the Bush and Kerry campaign were concentrated in 20 states or on particular cable outlets for targeted audiences.[35] We've already seen that media advertising is no longer limited to the days immediately preceding Election Day. In the candidate-centered campaign, name recognition and favorable media images have to be cultivated early, if only because both will allow advertisers to set the agenda for the real campaign season. In both 1996 and 2004, the incumbents started very early—Clinton with "advocacy ads" praising his performance, and Bush with a profoundly negative set of attack ads against his new opponent, John Kerry. Moreover, the ads must be varied to fit into the changing dynamics unearthed by tracking polls and to reach different demographic groups. In 2004, the campaign media team each produced hundreds of separate commercials.

To be sure, media specialists make mistakes. In 2000, Bush nearly lost the election by spending a valuable $11 million on the expensive media markets in California, a state that he eventually lost by double digits.

Media consultants for presidential candidates cannot simply manufacture images completely out of thin air because the major candidates usually have established records. But in the much more numerous congressional and state races, where candidates are often unknown, the potential for consultant creativity and simple invention is enormous. The consultant's dream is a pliable candidate who allows the experts to form images unhindered. A second dream is an opponent with either no ads or whose organization doesn't respond to the attack.

One of the most creative, if now antique, ads lifted Republican Malcolm Wallop, now retired, to a Wyoming Senate seat. A New Yorker by birth, a Yale graduate, and a polo-playing relative of Queen Elizabeth II, Wallop was effectively recast as a simple, lonely, western cowboy more at home on the range than in Buckingham Palace. Here's a transcript of one classic Wallop ad.

VISUAL:
(Wallop, dressed as a cowboy, is saddling and mounting his horse.)
WALLOP SPEAKS:
Everywhere you look these days, the federal government is there, telling you what they think, telling you what they think you ought to think. Telling you how to do things, setting up rules you can't follow. I think the federal government is going too far. Now they say if you don't take a portable facility along with you on a roundup, you can't go.

VISUAL:

(Wallop appears angry and disgusted, as the camera pans to a porta-potty strapped to a donkey tied to Wallop's horse.)

ANNOUNCER:

We need someone to tell 'em about Wyoming. Malcolm Wallop will.

POSTER:

Malcolm Wallop for U.S. Senate.[36]

Internet and Direct Mail

Consultants, polls, and ads are all expensive. The ironic result is that campaigns need a growing number of pricey fundraising consultants to pay for all three. Fundraising specialists aren't cheap. In congressional races, maintaining contacts with PACs and with the national and state parties that dispense money requires trained experts. Fundraisers who deal with ordinary citizens have pioneered the use of direct-mail, toll-free numbers, and websites as ways to raise money. Until recently, the GOP had a distinct advantage in fundraising technology. Before 2004, the Republicans led the Democrats in the amounts of money raised by relatively small contributors; much of the advantage was due to the GOP's honed direct-mail operation. Consultants in direct mail compile names from friendly political organizations, magazine subscription lists, the professions, and interest groups such as the American Medical Association and the National Association of Realtors. They tailor the text of computer-generated letters to accent themes of interest to the addressees.

Like polling and advertising, direct mail features virtually no two-way conversations between the candidate's staff and the voters. Approval or disapproval is measured solely in terms of money gained versus the fundraising costs. A bad direct-mail expert, for instance, might neglect to mention a candidate's anti-estate-tax position to readers of the *Wall Street Journal*.[37]

The new kid on the block and the biggest single innovation in 2004 was the emergence of the Internet as both a campaign communication and a fundraising tool. Here the Democrats have been the pioneers. The Internet has given rise to a whole new generation of Internet consultants, most of them young and intensely committed to particular causes and candidates. First was Howard Dean's legendary primary campaign, run by Joe Trippi, who mobilized many young voters both as volunteers and also as bloggers through an innovative and interactive website. Under Eli Pariser, Moveon.org built support for the anti–Iraq War cause and then turned his e-mail list into a force for Howard Dean. With the innovative use of the Internet, Dean raised a record $20 million. Senator Kerry, the eventual nominee, picked up on Dean's success, netting over $82 million in Internet contributions, most of them small. The total surpassed the $50 million raised by Al Gore from all contributors in the 2000 campaign. Democratic efforts were also buoyed by other informal Internet groups, from the New Democrat Network to the DailyKos. Each site passed on up-to-the-minute news and rumors, and allowed the interested to blog, communicate with others, sign petitions, mount mail campaigns to officeholders, and make contributions.

Online fundraising was generally tied to key events in the campaign. Contributions soared when Kerry won the Iowa caucuses, when he addressed the Democratic Convention, and in the immediate aftermath of the debates with Bush. Internet fundraising was perhaps the one area where the GOP was less efficient: The Bush campaign raised only $14 million from Internet contributions.[38]

Press and Media Relations

The general relationship between campaigns and the news media is discussed in Chapter 6. Here we note some new departures. "Press relations" no longer means just handing out press kits and making the candidate available for chats with the national press.

Today's press relations techniques are much more complex than in the past. In presidential elections, consultants are needed to make it appear that the candidate is accessible but at the same time must be shielded lest he or she wander "off message." They need to leak plausible stories that fit into the general campaign message, as Bush did in 2000 by providing examples of Gore's "overexaggeration" of his achievements. Moreover, consultants today try to find both novel and cheap ways for candidates to communicate directly with voters, thereby avoiding the insider "hardball" questions often posed by the Washington media. Via direct satellite hookups to local TV stations, the campaign strategist decides where and when the candidate's valuable time can be best used in targeted media markets. Press relations can also be expressed through dueling fax machines. In 1992 the "War Room," Clinton's Little Rock, Arkansas, headquarters, successfully countered the Bush team's charges impugning Clinton's record by choreographing "rapid responses" to every news outlet in the country. In 2000 and 2004, the techniques pioneered by the 1992 Clinton campaign had been refined to a science. Keeping the press from "unrehearsed" interactions with the candidates, press relations experts sought other means of influence: since 1992, campaign events have been heavily scripted and have often deluged the press with counterinformation even before the competing campaign had issued a press release or scheduled an event.[39]

MARKETING VERSUS GRASSROOTS CAMPAIGNS: IS THERE A DIFFERENCE?

From expensive campaign consultants through sophisticated media buys and multilevel marketing schemes, the professionalized campaign is built on a foundation of lots of money. In itself, this foundation is also elitist: Raising the money often ties to the parties to corporate elites, and running the professionalized campaign often highlights manufactured images over substance, and hype and clichés over substantive and broad debates. With its emphasis on expensive technology to study and then influence (some would say manipulate) voters, the high-tech campaign also pushes ordinary voters out of participation in campaign decisions and tends to turn them into spectators and judges rather than participants and activists.

In the dealigned electoral system, the professional campaign has certainly come to dominate. Its price is high, and not only in money. One cost is the widespread skepticism and apathy among voters; another is the rise of nonvoting and disinterest in politics as a distant game. Citizens, even when they do vote, often reject the cramped roles assigned to them as spectators, money sources, and laboratory and marketing subjects. When they do, the professional campaign cannot sustain legitimate democratic power, for elections confer neither mandates to govern nor real security to anxious officeholders.

But can campaigns be run differently, where voters and not experts are powerful from the start? Such efforts might be called **grassroots campaigns**. These value volunteer efforts, small monetary donations, and people-based organizations; downplay the role of advertising and money; and make the candidates responsive to organized voters for direction, support, and advice. Rejecting the "hire a campaign" mentality, they make organized people just as important as organized money and consultants.

In recent presidential elections, the campaigns of Senator John McCain and Green Party nominee Ralph Nader in 2000 stand out. Both men relied heavily on "free media" rather than advertising to get their messages across. McCain was famous for his informal, unscripted style on the campaign trail. Nader rejected large contributions and all corporate money, and instead raised money by charging small amounts to people who came to hear him speak (and Ani DiFranco sing!). Typically, these rallies drew thousands. These candidates made a big impact, but they lost.

Below the presidential level, the late Minnesota senator Paul Wellstone showed how grassroots campaigns can actually beat the odds and win. Back in 1990, Wellstone was a well-known liberal-left activist but a political science professor with not a lot of money. In his first race, he took on an incumbent Republican senator who had accumulated over seven times more campaign money than Wellstone had. Wellstone rented an old school bus and used it as a mobile campaign headquarters. He traveled to virtually every town in the state, meeting and recruiting supporters face to face. Instead of hiring professional consultants, he set up volunteer committees in each county and then recruited the most able of them to help manage his statewide effort. To save on ads, the Wellstone campaign stationed enthusiastic supporters at freeway interchanges or in supermarket parking lots. Wellstone never lost an opportunity to speak at the smallest of radio stations. Everywhere, Wellstone's message was the same: He skewered his opponent for accepting big corporate donations and claimed that he'd be an independent senator who looked out after average wage earners. Wellstone won—the only challenger to beat an incumbent senator that year.[40]

There are dozens of other examples of successful grassroots campaigns. Most of them are often launched from necessity, when candidates lack the money that's the essential ingredient of high-tech campaigns. Still, for the most part, the modern professionalized campaign and the candidate-centered campaign have emerged to dominate the current electoral system. Most see this type of campaign as a necessity, a concession to the fact that we live in a country with 300 million citizens with short attention spans and busy lives.

The professionalist evolution of campaigns is, however, neither inevitable nor desirable for a strong democratic debate. The proof is the 2004 election. Here is an election that is both a sharp departure from the norm and in many ways a confirmation of the long-simmering tendencies we've outlined. On the one hand, 2004 was the most expensive in history and deployed all the latest innovations to shape and manipulate voter impressions through advertising and image making. On the other, the 2004 election featured activity of more committed volunteers than any in recent history. While no one knows for sure, most say the 2004 race drew about 2 million volunteers, about evenly split between the two parties. On the Democratic side, legions of eager volunteers commuted to swing states like Pennsylvania, Ohio, and New Mexico. Some even dedicated their entire working lives to political activity, giving up school, taking leave from regular jobs, or postponing retirement activities. Prompted by 527s like ACT and Moveon.org, the volunteers were led by seasoned grassroots activists from the union, environmental, and civil rights movements. These organizations often paid students and young people for their efforts, albeit at the minimum wage. On the GOP side, the effort was built less on traveling volunteers and more on using existing social networks in fundamentalist Protestant and conservative Catholic churches and in pro-GOP businesses and associations. The growing exurbs, and their concerns about taxes and crime, were targeted for special attention.

Most importantly, the parties, the candidates, and the 527s devoted an increased proportion to the "retail" campaign. There were, however, distinctions between the efforts: As we've said, the Democrats and their allies were less organized and coordinated, with the independent 527s doing most of the grassroots activity. Multiple and sometimes contradictory messages and organizational models were targeted at diverse citizen groups by Democratic supporters. The GOP operation was more centralized and worked off a tightly managed hierarchical model that came from direct marketing companies like Amway and Mary Kay Cosmetics. The priorities, strategies, and quotas were set from the center, and the Bush army did its best to implement a nationwide, top-down strategy.[41]

In future elections, we'll see if this level of activism can be sustained without the impetus of an ongoing war and a controversial, polarizing presidency. On the Democratic side, the election of Howard Dean as the new Party Chairman in early 2005 may indicate a turn to further grassroots efforts and an attempt to coordinate the new grassroots energy with activity coordinated by the official Democratic Party. At the same time, "shadow party" groups like ACT and Moveon.org want to continue as independent groups, recruiting, financing, and canvassing for reform Democrats who want to push the party toward a more egalitarian and progressive stance. The Democrats have a big job and enormous possibilities organizing people who've lost ground economically under Republican rule. Yet it remains to be seen whether the party can recover an old identity and forge a new one as the champion of working people. Its fundraising prowess among the affluent may preclude such an effort, as the potential votes and potential donors diverge.

For the GOP, the question is whether activism can be sustained without the existence of a polarizing election, an incumbent president, a war on multiple fronts, and the ability to attract ordinary voters through appeals to "morality" against "liberalism." For the GOP, an important factor making for present success is the separation between its middle-class base and the privileged and monied professionals, officeholders, and lobbyists that decide its strategy in Washington. At bottom, the GOP excites its volunteers through appeals to moral values and patriotism but then succeeds most when it implements a pro-corporate agenda when it governs. That contradiction may not sustain grassroots activism in the long term. In the words of Oregon governor Ted Kulongoski, "They've created those social issues to get the public to stop looking at what's happening to them economically." Another question is the centralization and hierarchy of the Republican operation. It is hardly democratic internally. Volunteers are welcome to help, but not welcome to deliberate or decide. Republican legislative priorities come from its top, and its campaign strategy is based on centralized control of the message and operation. The surge of temporary volunteers for Bush can't be mistaken for popular democracy, in which the volunteers actually decide something about the party's priorities.[42]

CONCLUSION: CAMPAIGNS AND ELITE AND POPULAR DEMOCRACY

In order to sustain and make meaningful the hopeful signs of grassroots activism evident in 2004, the basic rules of the campaign game will need to be changed. Ultimately, the modern high-tech campaign benefits elite democracy by favoring money and experts over grassroots activism and the power of ordinary people to shape the political agenda. Many voters, sensing manipulation, become spectators or army ants and lose interest in campaign politics. "We keep pushing the button, but the public's response is no longer there," complains Democratic consultant Carter Eskew.

To a certain extent, the awesome power of centralized marketing and media manipulation is compelling, at least for anyone who wants to win an election. Yet in terms of the democratic debate, it has its limits. After all, according to a report from an American Political Science Association Standing Committee: "In 2004, the presidential candidates and their supporters launched the most massive and expensive voter-driven ground war in history. Interest groups alone spent $350 million on get-out-the-vote campaigns. Despite these efforts, voter turnout increased from 54 percent in 2000 to just 59 percent in 2004."

Without the crucial element of citizen participation, campaigns become less exercises in popular control of government than political control of the population by existing elites at the expense of citizenship. Deprived of the means to converse and debate among themselves and with politicians, citizens have two choices: to withdraw from their already limited roles in the game or to fight to reshape the game. "The people who are running things," William Greider tells us, "are especially prone to error when they are isolated from the shared ideas and instincts of the larger community." The quests for campaign reform, for grassroots campaigns, and for new ways of bringing politicians into dialogue with voters are healthy signs that the democratic debate may be reviving. Such a revival will depend much more on the organization of citizens than on the goodwill of elites. Our next chapters focus on the interest groups and political movements that dot the landscape of American politics and help organize citizen politics.[43]

KEY TERMS

candidate-centered campaigns
undecided and swing voters
name recognition
permanent campaign
great mentioners (gatekeepers)
invisible primary
independent issue advocacy
527s and 501(c)s
Federal Election Campaign Act (FECA)
Federal Election Commission (FEC)
political action committee (PAC)

Buckley v. Valeo
hard money
soft money
independent expenditures
Bipartisan Campaign Reform Act (BCRA)
bundled contributions
benchmark survey
tracking survey
focus and dial group
grassroots campaign

INTERNET RESOURCES

■ Center for Responsive Politics
www.opensecrets.org
The most comprehensive site for analysis and presentation of FEC data. Extensive breakdowns of donor lists to PACs, 527s, parties, and the presidential campaign.

■ Public Campaign
www.publicampaign.org
News and views from the major advocacy organization for public financing of campaigns.

■ Democracy Network
www.dnet.org
League of Women Voters sponsored site, providing access to state-by-state candidate information and ways to contact and interact with campaign organizations.

SUGGESTED READINGS Dan Clawson, Alan Neustadl, and Mark Weller, *Dollars and Votes: How Business Campaign Contributions Subvert Democracy*. Philadelphia: Temple University Press, 1998. Although written before BCRA's passage, this brilliant study lays bare the subtle and overt ways in which business interests shape campaigns and politicians through campaign contributions.

Dennis Johnson, *No Place for Amateurs: How Political Consultants Are Reshaping American Democracy*. New York: Routledge, 2001. Offers pithy observation about the political consultant's art from the standpoint of an insider.

Michael Nelson, ed., *The Elections of 2004*. Washington, D.C.: Congressional Quarterly Press, 2005. A fascinating compendium of analyses of all aspects of the 2004 race by well-known political scientists.

Joe Trippi, *The Revolution Will Not Be Televised*. New York: Regan Books, 2004. The former Howard Dean campaign manager muses about how to build grassroots interaction by using the Internet and other ways of mobilizing volunteers and support.

Interest Group Politics
Elite Bias

The story of how energy policy was made in the administration of George W. Bush illustrates the tilted playing field of interest group politics. What is extraordinary about the Bush administration is not so much that energy companies had unusual access to lobby the administration but that they actually wrote the president's energy policy. The distinction between lobbyists and government officials basically disappeared. Following the 2000 election, Bush appointed Vice President Dick Cheney to head a task force—the National Energy Development Group—that was given responsibility for drafting the administration's energy plan. Cheney kept the meetings secret, but it was clear that the administration was consulting only with energy companies and excluding environmentalists and consumers from the deliberations. Enron CEO Ken Lay met five times with members of the task force and urged Cheney to reject price caps on electricity being proposed by the governor of California. (See Chapter 3.) The General Accounting Office (now called the Government Accountability Office)

(GAO), an independent watchdog agency set up to ensure the integrity of the federal government, sued the administration to make the records of the task force public—the first time GAO had sued an administration for withholding information in its eighty-one-year history. Under the threat of massive budget cuts, GAO later withdrew its suit, but a freedom of information suit still threatened to make the deliberations public.

The task force report, released on May 17, 2001, almost perfectly reflected the preferences of the big energy companies. In particular, it called for opening up the Arctic National Wildlife Refuge (ANWR) to oil exploration. Bush abandoned his pledge to limit CO_2 emissions and opposed the Kyoto treaty on global warming. Other administration policies friendly to energy companies included aggressively opening up much of the 700 million acres of land owned by the federal government to drilling, mining, and logging; increasing the allowable level of coal dust in mines; and a proposal that would make it easier for mining companies to dump dirt and rubble into streams.[1] The administration proposed a "Clean Skies" initiative that would fundamentally reshape the way the nation regulates air pollution by switching from federal regulation to a system that would allow companies to trade pollution credits with each other for the right to pollute. As we go to press, Congress has balked at passing the Clean Skies initiative.

Copyright 2003, Tribune Media Services. Reprinted with permission.

The way the Bush administration crafted its energy policy is explained by its extraordinarily tight connections to the energy industry. According to the Center for Responsive Politics, 78 cents of every dollar contributed by the oil and gas industry to major party candidates in the decade preceding the 2000 election went to Republicans, with Bush being the number one recipient. In 1999 and 2000 alone the oil and gas industries gave $25.6 million to Republican candidates. Electrical utilities contributed 7:1 to Bush over Gore.[2] According to the Center for Public Integrity, Enron executives, led by Ken Lay, the former head of now bankrupt Enron, whom Bush affectionately called "Kenny boy," were "the singly largest patron of George W. Bush's political career."[3]

Bush was personally acquainted with the energy industry. When his father was president, Bush served as director of the Houston-based energy firm Harken. In 1990, Bush sold his Harken stock for a substantial profit a few weeks before the price plunged.[4] Dick Cheney, Bush's vice president, had even deeper ties to the energy industry. From 1995 to 2000 Cheney served as chairman and CEO of Halliburton, the world's second largest oil services provider. A former congressman and White House chief of staff, Cheney used his contacts to increase government contracts at Halliburton by 60 percent, to approximately $480 million a year. Three months before the 2000 election, Cheney retired from Halliburton, cashing in about $35 million in stock. As Halliburton benefited from huge no-bid contracts for the war in Iraq, Cheney continued to receive bonuses and deferred compensation from Halliburton. The ties of the president and vice president to energy companies shaped high-level appointments, with no less than thirty former executives and lobbyists in the energy industry appointed to powerful posts in the administration.

The key question in the study of interest groups is whether they are broadly representative of the American people. The intimate relationship of the Bush administration with energy interests illustrates a disturbing trend in American politics: the increasing class bias of the interest group system. Interest group politics is usually thought of as the politics that takes place *between* elections, but increasingly the distinction between electoral politics and interest group politics has blurred, giving lobbyists who can mobilize large campaign contributions unusual access. Usually, strong parties are thought to be incompatible with strong interest groups. But the tight relations between the Republican Party and energy interests (or the Democratic Party and lawyers) show that interest groups and parties can reinforce one another.

Although the interest group system is biased toward the rich, determined and well-organized groups representing ordinary citizens can penetrate the system. Indeed, for a time in the 1960s and 1970s, as we will see, the interest group system opened up to a wide range of popular democratic interests. Since then, elites have reconstructed their advantage, but this is not simply because they are better organized or more determined. New communication technologies have given an advantage to moneyed interests, and government policies have favored elite political organizing. Interest groups do not organize spontaneously; new policies are needed to level the playing field of interest group politics.

INTEREST GROUP POLITICS AND THE DEMOCRATIC DEBATE

Interest group politics can be defined as any attempt by an organized group to influence the policies of government through normal extra-electoral channels, such as lobbying, letter writing, testifying before legislative committees, and advertising. Interest groups focus on changing the policies of government in contrast to political parties whose first goal is to change the personnel who run government. Interest group politics cannot be completely separated from electoral politics, however, because interest groups often try to persuade officials that supporting the interest group's policies will enhance their chances for reelection. Also, interest groups often contribute money to campaigns through political action committees (PACs).

Interest groups are held together by the shared interests or goals of their members. The goals of interest groups are varied, stretching from economic goals (limits on foreign car imports) to social goals (the right to family leave) to political goals (campaign finance reform) to humanitarian goals (shelter for the homeless). The shared interests that hold groups together can be as broad as clean air or as narrow as allowing heavier trucks to ride on interstate highways. Generally, narrow economic interests are better represented in the interest group system than are broad moral or political concerns.

Although both elite and popular democrats consider interest groups to be necessary in a democracy, they differ in their evaluations of interest group politics. Interest group politics nicely suits the elite democratic conception of democracy and human nature—that most people are not interested in politics for its own sake but rather view politics as a way of protecting their own private interests. Since most citizens have neither the time nor the inclination to participate directly in politics, the interest group system allows people's wants and desires to be represented by political specialists called lobbyists. Moreover, because policy choices are often highly technical, interest groups hire experts to communicate complex information to decision makers.

According to one variant of elite democratic theory, called pluralism (which we examine later), the interest group system in the United States is open and accessible. Not every group has equal access, but every group can make itself heard at some point in the system.

Finally, we should note that many elite democrats criticize the interest group system as it is practiced in the United States today. Since the upsurge of citizen groups in the 1960s, they argue, the system has become "overheated," with special interests bombarding Washington and steering the policy process to benefit narrow groups at the public's expense. Later in the chapter we will examine the criticism that interest group politics has become too accessible.

Popular democrats are naturally more critical of interest group politics than are elite democrats. By relying on representatives and hired experts, they say, interest group politics asks too little of ordinary citizens, who are given few opportunities for meaningful participation. Interest group politics normally suppresses passionate political participation by requiring that every issue be passed through an elaborate system of political representation, bargaining, and compromise. With decisions made behind closed doors, where industry experts and technocrats dominate the discussions, interest group politics narrows the scope of conflict and excludes the masses of ordinary citizens. In short, interest group politics is easily manipulated by elites—technical experts and political insiders who know how to play the Washington "inside-the-Beltway" game.

Unlike elite democrats, popular democrats view the influx of new citizens' groups into the interest group system beginning in the 1960s as a healthy development. Despite this opening up of interest group politics to new groups, popular democrats charge that the system is still biased in favor of elites with political connections or the money to purchase them. The solution is to mobilize citizens at the grassroots to demand that their interests be represented. The problem with the interest group system is not too much democracy, as elite democrats maintain, but too little.

As we examine the competing claims of elite and popular democrats about interest group politics, keep the democratic debate in mind: Is the playing field of interest group politics level, giving every interest a fair chance to win, or is it tilted in favor of well-connected elites and those who have the money to hire them?

THE GROWTH OF INTEREST GROUP POLITICS

Before the New Deal of the 1930s, Washington, D.C., was a sleepy town with few diversions other than politics. Since then, Washington has become a vibrant cosmopolitan city, the center of one of the fastest-growing metropolitan areas in the country, with highly paid white-collar workers spilling over the boundaries of the District of Columbia to occupy wealthy suburbs in Maryland and Virginia. The metropolitan area surrounding our nation's capital now boasts the best-educated and highest-paid workforce in the nation. This prosperity did not stem solely from the growth in government, but also from a tremendous expansion in the number of people who make a living trying to influence government.

Interest group politics is big business in Washington. Legally, in order to work the halls of Congress as a lobbyist, you must register under the Lobbying Disclosure Act of 1995. In 1999, 12,113 lobbyists registered under the act.[5] But this figure vastly underestimates the number of people working in the lobbying industry because it only includes professional paid lobbyists who directly contact public officials. One study estimated that there were 91,000 lobbyists in Washington trying to influence government policies.[6] Besides trying to influence legislation, interest groups also try to influence the implementation of laws through decisions by executive agencies and the courts. When you include the lawyers, lobbyists, public relations specialists, and trade association and corporate representatives who make a living by keeping track of and attempting to change federal regulations, the number far exceeds 100,000. And this ignores the thousands of public relations specialists and other professionals who manufacture "grassroots" support back in home districts for lobbyists' bills.

	TABLE 9.1		

The Twenty-five Most Powerful Interest Groups in Washington

Rank	Name of Interest Group or Association	Membership	Staff	Budget
1	American Association of Retired Persons (AARP)	32,000,000	1,200	not listed
2	National Rifle Association of America	2,800,000	400	$130,000,000
3	National Federation of Independent Businesses	607,000	225	$65,000,000
4	American Israel Public Affairs Committee	not listed	not listed	not listed
5	American Federation of Labor-Congress of Industrial Organizations (AFL-CIO)	13,300,000	400	not listed
6	Association of Trial Lawyers of America	60,000	165	$19,400,000
7	Chamber of Commerce	219,000	1,200	$70,000,000
8	National Right to Life Committee	50 state groups/3,000 local groups	not listed	not listed
9	National Education Association	2,376,108	600	$200,600,000
10	National Restaurant Association	not listed	not listed	not listed
11	American Bankers Association	2,000	3	not listed
12	National Governors' Association	55	87	$11,000,000
13	American Medical Association	297,000	54 state groups	not listed

The Washington interest group community is large and diverse. It includes powerful business associations, such as the American Bankers Association, and narrow trade associations representing specific industries, such as the U.S. Hide, Skin and Leather Association. It includes organizations with millions of members, such as the AFL-CIO coalition of unions, and organizations with only one member, in particular the Washington offices of national corporations, such as IBM and GM. It includes public associations, such as the National Governors Association and the National League of Cities. It also includes lobbyists hired by foreign governments to represent their interests in Washington, a feature of

TABLE 9.1

(continued)

Rank	Name of Interest Group or Association	Membership	Staff	Budget
14	National Association of Manufacturers	14,000	180	$5,000,000
15	National Association of Realtors	710,000	54 state groups/1,860 local groups	$61,125,000
16	National Association of Homebuilders	208,000	460	not listed
17	Motion Picture Association of America	8	120	not listed
18	Credit Union National Association	9,000	185	not listed
19	National Beer Wholesalers Association	1,835	25	$6,000,000
20	National Association of Broadcasters	7,500	165	not listed
21	American Farm Bureau Federation	4,000	25	$4,000,000
22	American Federation of State, County, and Municipal Employees	1,400,000	not listed	not listed
23	International Brotherhood of Teamsters	1,600,000	596 local groups	$1,400,000
24	United Autoworkers Union	not listed	2	not listed
25	Health Insurance Association of America	1,000	140	$20,000,000

Sources: The most powerful interest groups were selected based on a survey of Washington insiders, including members of Congress, their staffs, and senior White House officials. See Jeffrey H. Birnbaum and Natasha Graves, "How to Buy Clout in the Capital," *Fortune* (December 6, 1999). Information on membership, staff, and budgets was obtained from the *Encyclopedia of Associations*, 40th ed. (Detroit: Gale Group, 2004).

our interest group system that has increasingly come under attack. Two of the best represented foreign governments are Israel and Japan. (Table 9.1 lists the twenty-five most powerful interest groups in Washington, as identified by a survey of Washington insiders.)

Interest groups play a more powerful role in U.S. politics than in most other Western democracies. The main reason is that American political institutions stimulate interest group politics. As we know from Chapter 2, fearing tyranny of the majority in a democratic government, the Federalists wrote a Constitution that fragmented policy-making authority, including the separation of powers into three branches, the bicameral Congress (with decision making further fragmented into committees and subcommittees), the authority of the courts to intervene in administrative decisions, and the division of power among federal, state, and local governments. In this way, the Constitution created a government that provides many access points to interest groups. In addition, interest groups in the United States are able to intervene on the administrative side of government, influencing the implementation of a law after it is passed. Critics of the interest group system charge that in striving to protect the country against tyranny by majorities, the founders may have created a system that allows too much interest group penetration, making it prone to tyranny by privileged minorities.

Money and interest groups

Interest groups are often referred to as lobbies, as in the "gun lobby" or the "steel lobby." (The term *lobbyist* stems from the mid-seventeenth century, when citizens would plead their cases with members of the British Parliament in a large lobby outside the House of Commons.) Interest groups are also referred to as *pressure groups*. Both terms have taken on negative connotations, evoking images of pot-bellied, cigar-smoking influence peddlers prowling the halls of Congress and buying off legislators with bags of money. In fact, lobbying is an essential function in a democracy. Interest group politics is protected by the First Amendment, which guarantees freedom of association, "or the right of the people peaceably to assemble, and to petition the Government for a redress of grievances."

Of course, corruption is a problem in interest group politics. One of the most notorious examples is the California savings and loan company that contributed $1.3 million to the campaigns of five U.S. senators in exchange for their intervention with federal regulators. In 1989, as federal regulators looked the other way, the savings and loan company went bankrupt. The bailout cost the federal taxpayers $2.5 billion. Some perfectly legal practices verge on corruption: Lobbyists frequently purchase large numbers of tickets to congressional fundraisers or pay politicians fat fees for short appearances at association gatherings. In response to abuses, Congress passed tough new lobbying restrictions that took effect on January 1, 1996, banning gifts valued at more than $50, but lobbyists can still pay for expensive trips to exotic locations.

Although a certain amount of corruption and outright bribery goes on, the image of money-toting lobbyists buying votes misrepresents the normal operation of interest group politics in the United States. Nevertheless, interest groups spent $1.56 billion in 2000 on direct lobbying of the federal government.[7] People are not stupid; there must be some reason why interest groups spend all that money. In fact, money does not normally buy a legislator's vote, but it does buy a legislator's time—so you can make the case for your preferred policies. (One study estimated that a legislator's time costs around $10,000 an hour.[8]) Money also buys the ability to frame the issue, to influence the public agenda, to get your story told, and even to manufacture grass-roots support. In short, the corruption of the interest group process by money is more subtle (and pervasive) than the conventional image suggests.

TRADITIONAL LOBBYING: THE INSIDER STRATEGY

In discussing interest group politics it is important to distinguish between an insider strategy and an outsider strategy. The **insider strategy** is what we normally think of as interest group politics: face-to-face discussions in which the lobbyist tries to persuade the decision maker that the interest group's position makes sense.[9] The insider strategy depends on intimate knowledge of how the game is played in Washington and access to what used to be called the "old boy" network. The **outsider strategy**, by contrast, relies on mobilizing forces outside Washington to pressure decision makers. The insider and outsider strategies are often coordinated with each other, but traditional interest group politics is usually associated with the insider strategy. (We examine the rise of the outsider strategy later in the chapter.)

The insider strategy takes place largely behind closed doors and is most effective when applied to issues sufficiently narrow in scope not to have caught the public's attention. Speaking about lobbying regarding the 1986 Tax Reform Act, Representative Pete Stark, Democrat of California, observed that "the fewer the number of taxpayers affected, and the more dull and arcane the subject matter, the longer the line of lobbyists."[10] The effectiveness of the insider strategy stems from the fact that legislation has become so complex that neither legislators nor their staffs are able to keep up with all the relevant information. As we show in Chapter 11, most of the work of Congress now takes place in committees and subcommittees, but even the specialized staffs attached to these committees cannot keep up with the staggering growth of information that pertains to policy making. Lobbyists, therefore, perform an important function in a modern democracy: They provide decision makers with detailed information on the effects of different policies.

The insider lobbying strategy applies to the executive branch as well as Congress. Many political decisions still need to be made *after* a bill is passed. Congress usually formulates broad policies that leave many decisions to the discretion of executive branch employees. For example, the Environmental Protection Agency (EPA) has the power to set standards for particular pollutants. When agencies formulate policies, they usually do so by issuing draft regulations in the *Federal Register*, a publication of all administrative regulations issued by the federal government. Interest groups try to influence the regulations before they are issued in final form.

Whether dealing with Congress or the executive branch, a successful lobbyist must develop relations of trust with key decision makers. Lobbyists who lie or misrepresent the facts will soon be ostracized. Lobbyists are not completely objective, however; they specialize in information that favors their client's cause. Members of Congress are especially interested in how a bill will affect their home districts. In opposing Clinton's 1994 proposal for national health insurance, which would have required businesses to provide health insurance for their employees, lobbyists provided information to members of Congress on the number of businesses in their districts that would have been affected—implying that many businesses would have been harmed by the requirement.

From morning phone calls to afternoon golf dates to evening cocktail parties, lobbyists spend most of their time cultivating personal contacts and seeking out the latest information. Access is the key. A survey of interest groups found that 98 percent contacted government officials directly to express their views, and 95 percent engaged in informal contacts with officials—at conventions, over lunch, and so forth.[11] Skilled lobbyists make decision makers dependent on them. Policy makers begin to call on the lobbyists, who become sources of hard-to-obtain information for overworked political staffs and government officials. As one legislative aide observed,

> My boss demands a speech and a statement for the *Congressional Record* for every bill we introduce or co-sponsor—and we have a lot of bills. I just can't do it all myself. The better lobbyists, when they have a proposal they are pushing, bring it to me along with a couple of speeches, a *Record* insert, and a fact sheet.[12]

A troubling aspect of lobbying is the so-called revolving door. Overall, about 50 percent of Washington lobbyists have prior government experience. When they left government service, they got jobs with lobbying firms or interest groups, usually at much higher pay, exploiting their access and knowledge to the benefit of their clients. James Watt, former Secretary of the Interior under Ronald Reagan, reportedly received $250,000 from a client for a single phone call to a high-level official in the Department of Housing and Urban Development (HUD).

In 1978, Congress passed the Ethics in Government Act to deal with abuses of the revolving door. The act forbids former executive branch employees from lobbying their former agency on any issue for one year (Clinton increased it to five years for top officials) and prohibits all lobbying, with no time limits, on issues in which they were "personally and substantially involved." Former members of Congress are also heavily involved in lobbying, even though the 1989 Ethics in Government Act barred former elected officials from lobbying anywhere on Capitol Hill for one year. In 2004 retiring Louisiana congressman, Billy "the Swamp Fox" Tauzin became head of the pharmaceutical industry's top lobbying group. Watchdog groups criticized Tauzin for taking the job shortly after negotiating the 2003 Medicare prescription drug law that forbid the federal government to negotiate prices with drug companies to save seniors money. Opponents charge the law showered billions on the pharmaceutical industry.

Since the 1960s, interest group activity has exploded in Washington. Lobbyists in Washington now have their own lobbies, including the American League of Lobbyists and the American Society of Association Executives. Part of the reason for the proliferation of interest groups is the growing federal presence in the economy and the mushrooming of federal regulations.

The increase in interest group activity is also attributed to the upsurge of participation in the 1960s and 1970s that created new interest groups representing broad citizens' groups and the poor. Of interest groups that existed in 1981, fully 76 percent of the citizens' groups and 79 percent of the social welfare and poor people's organizations were formed since 1960.[13] In response, corporations countermobilized: The number of corporations with offices in Washington increased tenfold between 1961 and 1982. By 1998, more than 600 corporations had full-time Washington lobbying offices.[14]

The tremendous growth of interest group activity in American national government raises disturbing questions: Have we created an interest group society where every group feels entitled to have its problems solved by government? Are the new interest groups genuine expressions of citizens' needs, or are they the artificial offspring of government programs or elite manipulation? Have some interest groups become so entrenched in government that we can no longer draw the line between public government and private interests? Answers to these questions depend on our understanding of who is represented by the expanded interest group system.

THE CLASS BIAS OF THE INTEREST GROUP SYSTEM

If the U.S. interest group system truly represents the many diverse interests of the citizenry, then it might be one of the most democratic features of our political system. In fact, this argument is the cornerstone of a variant of elite democratic theory called **pluralism**.[15] Pluralist theory views the interest group system as a kind of political marketplace with the following characteristics:

1. *Free competition*. Most people do not participate directly in decision making but, like consumers in the economy, are represented in the system by political entrepreneurs who compete for their support. Competition ensures that all major interests will be heard.

2. *Dispersed power*. Money is an important source of power, but other resources are equally important, including motivation, leadership, organizational skills, knowledge, and expertise. Elites who are influential in one issue arena tend not to be active in others. Power is widely dispersed.

3. *Bargaining*. Success in the interest group system requires bargaining and compromise with other interests, discouraging rigid moralistic or ideological politics that threaten democratic stability.

4. *Balance*. Mobilization on one side of an issue produces countermobilization on the other side; public policies thus reflect a balance of competing interests that approximates the interest of society as a whole.

Pluralism has an element of truth to it. Since the 1960s the interest group system has become more representative of the wide array of interests in American society. Reflecting what Jeffrey Berry calls the "advocacy explosion" that began in the 1960s,[16] the number of national organizations listed in the *Encyclopedia of Associations* increased dramatically, from 10,299 in 1968 to over 22,901 in 1997. (Since then, the number has stabilized.) Many of these new groups represented concerns, such as civil rights and the environment, which had previously been excluded from the interest group system.

Just because more groups are involved, however, does not mean that all active and legitimate interests can make their voices heard in the system. Contrary to pluralism, some groups find it much easier than others to organize and gain power. Three major developments in interest group politics have crippled its ability to serve as a vehicle for popular democratic aspirations.

Decline in National Membership Organizations. National interest groups used to rely upon a large membership base to exert power. Organizations like the American Legion, the Elks, and the PTA were federations of local associations that usually sent representatives to national meetings to elect national leadership. Although often racially segregated and dominated by men, these organizations recruited members across class lines and enjoyed active participation at the grassroots. Since the 1960s, national membership associations have declined. A study of twenty-three national associations that had at least 1 percent of the adult population as members in 1955 found that by 1995 three-fourths of them had experienced sharp membership losses, some as high as 70 percent.[17] The same trend is evident with newer associations. A study of 3,000 "social welfare" and "public affairs" organizations formed from the 1960s to the 1980s found that nearly half claimed no members at all in 1998.[18] The number of Americans who don't belong to any political organization or don't participate in any political activity other than voting has increased significantly.[19] We now have what Theda Skocpol calls "advocates without members."[20]

Dominance by Professionals and Reliance on Technology. From a reliance on members to exert power, interest groups have shifted to a reliance on campaign technologies and public relations experts. The technologies that interest groups use to influence the political process have become more sophisticated and more expensive. These technologies include computerized direct mail solicitations, sophisticated polling and focus groups, advertising campaigns, faxes, e-mails, websites, blogs, and computerized telephone messages. In what is called "warm transfer," individuals dial an 800 number, and their call is automatically transferred to the Washington office of their senator or representative. We examine some of these technologies in greater detail below. However, what they all have in common is that they require money—not just to buy the technology but to hire experts to run it. As a result of interest groups' dependence on expensive technologies, increasingly, money has replaced time as the primary contribution

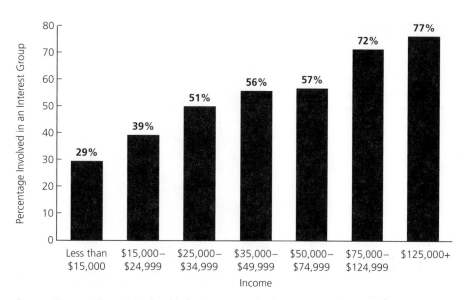

FIGURE 9.1

Interest Group Membership by Income Level

Source: "Interest Group Membership by Income Level," from Kay L. Schlozman, "Voluntary Organizations on Politics: Who Gets Involved," in *Representing Interests and Interest Group Representation*, edited by Crotty, Schwartz and Green (University Press of America, 1994). Reprinted by permission of University Press of America.

most people make. Money is used not just to lobby but to frame issues, generate a nationwide campaign, and even manufacture grass-roots support.[21]

Bias in Favor of Upper Income and Corporate Interests. Increasingly, membership in special interest organizations is skewed by income. A 1989–90 survey found that 77 percent of people from families with incomes over $125,000 were affiliated with a political organization, compared to only 29 percent for those from families making less than $15,000 (Figure 9.1).[22] As political scientist E. E. Schattschneider concluded in a well-known critique of pluralist theory, "The flaw in the pluralist heaven is that the heavenly chorus sings with a strong upper-class accent."[23]

The political bias in interest groups flows from their dependence on expensive technologies. Rich people and poor people have roughly equal amounts of time to contribute to political organizations. But if interest groups are more concerned about raising money than about recruiting volunteers, they will obviously seek out the wealthy. Instead of citizens mobilizing from below to influence the political system, targeted portions of the public are singled out for what Steven Schier calls "activation" by political groups.[24] Advances in technology have enabled interest groups to recruit narrow slices of the population ("niche marketing"). Activation is class-biased. For the most part, poor people are not invited to participate in the interest group system. As Figure 9.2 shows, a near majority of families earning less than $15,000 receive no mass mailings at all.

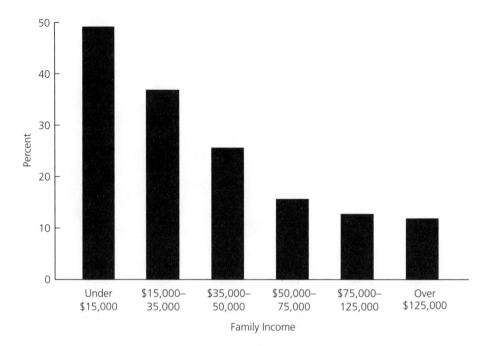

FIGURE 9.2

The Empty Mailbox: People Who Never Receive Mass Mail, by Family Income

Source: "The Empty Mailbox," from Schlozman, Verba, and Brady, "Civic Participation and the Equality Problem," in Theda Skocpol and Morris P. Fiorina, eds., *Civic Engagement in American Democracy* (Washington, D.C.: Brookings Institution Press, 1999), p. 450.

The new public interest associations that began to spring up in the 1960s have tended to focus much more on quality of life issues rather than bread and butter economic issues. As people become more affluent and educated, they become more concerned with what are called "postmaterial" concerns that address issues of culture and lifestyle (gay marriage, abortion), quality of life (environment, consumer safety), and social justice issues (civil rights for minorities and the handicapped). At the same time that liberal groups have moved away from addressing economic inequality, conservative groups have done the same. One of the exceptions to the decline of national membership associations are the evangelical churches, which have been organized into a national network by the Christian Coalition. They have been extraordinarily effective at mobilizing citizens to oppose abortion and gay marriage. As important as all these postmaterial issues are, however, they have the unfortunate effect of pushing the economic concerns of the poor and working class off the national agenda.[25]

What this means is that poor people are not well represented in the interest group system. For example, 35 percent of the recipients of veterans' benefits and 24 percent of those who receive Social Security belonged to an organization that defends the program. By contrast, only 2 percent of AFDC (welfare) recipients and no food-stamp recipients belonged to such organizations.[26] The class bias of the interest group system helps explain rising economic inequality in the

United States (Chapter 3) and why programs for those who need help the most, welfare and food stamps, have been cut back, at the same time that spending on Social Security and veterans' benefits has soared (Chapter 17).

THE RISE OF PUBLIC INTEREST GROUPS

Notwithstanding their limits today, the rise of new public interest groups beginning in the 1960s was basically a victory for popular democracy—in part because these groups reaffirmed the popular democratic view of human nature. Usually, narrow economic interests tend to dominate the interest group system, not just because they have greater resources, but because they find it easier to overcome what political scientists call the **collective action problem**.[27] Assume that each member of a group will benefit from the desired government action and that to provide the common benefit an interest group needs to be formed to pressure the government. The collective action problem is that *everyone* in the group will benefit regardless of his or her contribution to the collective action (and one individual's contribution rarely makes a difference in the outcome). Thus, most people, called "free riders," will try to enjoy the benefits without contributing to the group. As a result, most groups never get off the ground.

Collective action is less of a problem for large corporations, however, when a small number of companies dominate an industry. With fewer members in the interest group, each member recognizes that his or her contribution is necessary for success. Analysis of the problem of collective action helps explain why producer groups dominated by a handful of corporations are more successful in organizing interest groups and obtaining favorable policies than consumer groups, which face the daunting challenge of mobilizing millions of dispersed consumers.

In the 1960s and early 1970s, defying the collective action problem, a distinct species of organized interest, the public interest group, flowered. A **public interest group** can be defined as any group seeking government action that will not principally benefit the members of the group. Special interest groups seek benefits for their members; for example, a steel producers' lobby seeks limits on imported steel to shut out foreign competition. A public interest group, on the other hand, seeks policies that, at least in the minds of the members, will benefit society as a whole. The League of Women Voters, which seeks a better-informed electorate, is a classic example of a public interest group. Environmental groups that advocate for cleaner air, as well as religious groups like the Christian Coalition, are public interest groups because everybody will presumably benefit, not just the members of the group.

Public interest groups would appear to have a difficult time overcoming the collective action problem because their benefits are so widespread. The rise of public interest groups was a confirmation of the popular democratic view of human nature—people will join groups not only to benefit from them materially, but also because they believe in the purposes of the group, whether it be safer cars, cleaner air, or fewer abortions. Environmental groups, such as the Sierra Club (750,000 members in 2005) and the Environmental Defense Fund (450,000 in 2005), have successfully attracted members even though the benefits of the collective action are widely distributed. (We should note that nearly all public interest groups also provide their members with specific benefits for join-ing—all the way from bumper stickers to magazine subscriptions.) People are also attracted to citizens' groups by the companionship that arises from partici-pating with like-minded people in a political cause. Compared to special interest groups, public interest groups are more consistent with the popular democratic view of human nature—that people can transcend their own parochial interests to promote the broader public good. However, the tendency of many of these groups to be dominated by professionals and to have few members or grass-roots chapters cripples their ability to serve as vehicles of popular democracy.

Cultivating the Outsider Strategy

The public interest groups that burst on the scene in the 1960s cultivated an outsider strategy in which they appealed to citizens outside Washington to put pressure on Congress and the executive branch to address their issues. Instead of trying to persuade individual politicians and officials behind closed doors (the insider strategy), they took their issues to the public, dramatizing the effects of inaction and skillfully using the media to communicate their message to the American people. By carefully documenting the facts and exposing problems, often through emotional congressional hearings and published exposés, public interest groups swayed public opinion. Politicians were forced to respond.

Public interest groups opened up the elite-dominated interest group system in Washington to a surge in popular democratic participation. Although the out-sider strategy employed by citizens' groups succeeded in democratizing the sys-tem for a time, elites soon learned how to use the outsider strategy themselves to reassert their dominance. Nevertheless, the rise of public interest groups is instructive because it shows that the American political system is not impervious to popular democratic pressure. One person, even someone lacking wealth and political connections, can make a difference, as Ralph Nader proved.

Ralph Nader: Expanding Democratic Citizenship

Ralph Nader's highly visible and controversial runs for the presidency in 2000 and 2004 have tended to overshadow his accomplishments in opening up the interest group system to more participation. In fact, Nader has had much more influence on interest group politics than on electoral politics.

Little in Ralph Nader's background suggested that he would become the scourge of corporate America.[28] The son of Lebanese immigrant parents, Nader was something of a nerd, often carrying a briefcase to school and reading late into the night. Ironically, his high school yearbook predicted he would become a corporate executive. After graduating from Harvard Law School, Nader practiced law for a number of years in a rather undistinguished fashion.

What set Nader apart from other lawyers was his interest—some called it an obsession—with automobile safety. With lethal protruding fins, dangerous dashboards, and no seat belts, cars in the early 1960s were not designed with safety foremost in mind. Nader's concern with automobile safety stemmed from an incident in 1956 when he "saw a little girl almost decapitated in an accident when the glove compartment door flew open and became a guillotine for the child as she was thrown forward in a 15-mile-an-hour collision."[29] Nader focused on the "second collision"—the collision between the human body and the car. Feeling strongly that cars could be designed much more safely, Nader charged U.S. automakers with designing cars for the sole purpose of increasing sales.

In 1964, Nader moved to Washington, D.C., as a consultant to the U.S. Labor Department, where he wrote a dry 234-page report with 99 pages of footnotes criticizing Detroit automakers on safety issues. Like most government reports, Nader's probably would have gathered dust on a shelf if not for other developments. First, in 1965 Nader published *Unsafe at Any Speed*,[30] an emotional indictment of the auto industry that replaced the dry technical language of the report with vivid accounts of the mayhem caused by unsafe auto design. Singling out GM's Corvair, with its oversteering tendency and vulnerability to "one-car accidents," Nader called it "one of the greatest acts of industrial irresponsibility in the present century." *Unsafe at Any Speed* quickly became a bestseller.

Meanwhile, with over a hundred lawsuits pending against the Corvair, GM began an exhaustive investigation of Nader. As the detective hired to do the job was instructed, "They [GM] want to get something, somewhere, on this guy to get him out of their hair, and to shut him up." This was not a typical background check, as further directions to the detective indicated: "Apparently he's in his early thirties and unmarried. . . . Interesting angle there. . . . They said 'Who is he laying? If it's girls, who are they? If not girls, maybe boys, who?' They want to know this."[31] The exhaustive investigation turned up nothing that could be used against Nader, who led a Spartan lifestyle.

When word of the investigation became public, GM first denied it. At this time, however, Senator Abraham Ribicoff of Connecticut began hearings on auto safety, and Nader became a star witness. Concerned that GM was trying to intimidate a congressional witness, Ribicoff called on GM president John Roche to testify. Unable to deny knowledge of the investigation anymore, Roche was forced to make a public apology to Nader. The image of one of the world's most powerful corporations trying to crush a lone reformer captured the public's imagination. The publicity generated public pressure that resulted in one of the first comprehensive pieces of consumer legislation, the 1966 Traffic and Motor Vehicle Safety Act.

The safety features that we take for granted today—seat belts and shoulder harnesses, head rests, collapsible steering columns, padded dashboards—grew out of the great automobile safety debate in the 1960s that Nader triggered.

MAKING A DIFFERENCE

Defending Children

In her book *The Measure of Our Success: A Letter to My Children and Yours*, Marian Wright Edelman, founder of the Children's Defense Fund (CDF), discusses her role model, Sojourner Truth, an illiterate yet outspoken slave woman: "One day during an antislavery speech she was heckled by an old man. 'Old woman, do you think that your talk about slavery does any good? Why I don't care any more for your talk than I do for the bite of a flea.' 'Perhaps not, but the Lord willing, I'll keep you scratching,' she replied." For more than thirty years, Edelman has followed in her role model's footsteps, trying to "keep them scratching" in her pursuit of "putting children first."

Born in 1939, the daughter of a black Baptist minister, Marian Wright grew up in segregated Bennettsville, South Carolina. Greatly influenced by her father, who taught her the importance of both education and helping others, she graduated first in her class at all-black Spelman College in 1960. Following graduation, she accepted a scholarship to Yale Law School. Active in the civil rights movement, upon completing her law degree she immediately traveled to Mississippi to work for the National Association for the Advancement of Colored People (NAACP) Legal Defense Fund. As the first African-American woman to practice law in the state, she undertook the dangerous work of defending civil rights workers.

Her interests gradually shifted from civil rights to the plight of poor children. In 1967, Senator Robert F. Kennedy visited Mississippi, and Wright was able to show him firsthand the deplorable conditions faced by poor, mostly black, children in that state. It was on this trip that she met her future husband, Peter Edelman, an assistant to Senator Robert Kennedy. The interracial marriage produced three sons, who were given much-publicized "Baptist bar mitzvahs."

In 1968, Marian Wright Edelman, as she was now known, moved to the nation's capital, where she set up a public interest lobbying organization supporting the federal War on Poverty program. Edelman noticed that African Americans had the NAACP (established in 1909) and the elderly had a powerful interest group, the American Association of Retired Persons (AARP, founded in 1958), but children had nothing. In 1973, Edelman formed the Children's Defense Fund (CDF).

Part lobbying organization and part think tank, under Edelman's leadership the CDF, with a budget today of about $13 million, has become an

---

The government-mandated and "voluntary" safety devices that were introduced beginning in the 1960s have saved thousands of lives. Even though Americans drove many more miles each year, automobile-related deaths declined steadily in the 1970s and 1980s, beginning to rise again only in 1993.

Nader sued GM for violation of privacy and after a four-year legal battle settled out of court for $425,000. He used the profits from the lawsuit, book royalties, and speaking fees to start up *public interest research groups* (PIRGs) in states around the country. In 2005 there were PIRG chapters in twenty-eight states and on over ninety college campuses. Supported by student fees, they lobby and conduct research on behalf of students and consumers.

influential and controversial advocate for children. Conservatives argue that Edelman is simply using children to support her liberal causes. The problem, they say, is not just that children are in poverty but that their parents fail to get jobs and become hooked on government handouts.

Edelman's moral approach to the issues has been controversial even for liberals, whom she frequently attacks for being insufficiently attentive to the well-being of children. Senators reportedly hide in the bathroom whenever Edelman is sighted in the Senate Office Building. Clearly, however, her methods are effective; Senator Edward Kennedy has referred to her as the "101st Senator."

With the election of Bill Clinton in 1992, many expected Edelman to become even more influential because Hillary Rodham Clinton was both a long-time friend and former chairperson of the CDF Board of Directors. However, the relationship between Edelman and Clinton was strained by the president's support of welfare reform. In November 1995 the *Washington Post* published her open letter to the president in which she stated that it would be a "tragic irony" for "this regressive attack on children and the poor to occur on your watch." Subsequently, her husband, Peter, resigned a high post in the Department of Health and Human Services to protest Clinton's welfare policies. Edelman's access to the White House ended.

CDF continued its critical ways during the Bush Administration, announcing that it would lead the Leave No Child Behind Movement, a clear reference to Bush's No Child Left Behind school reform. In the midst of Bush's massive tax cuts and cuts in domestic programs that serve the poor, Edelman has faced an uphill battle in advocating for poor children. In an effort to expand her base, CDF has established offices in twelve states and she has reached out aggressively to the faith community to support children's issues. CDF set up the Student Health Outreach Project (SHOUT) in which students work with community-based groups to register children for free health insurance under Medicaid and the Children's Health Insurance Program (CHIP). Unfortunately, facing a looming deficit, Congress is considering major cuts in Medicaid.

Edelman's career illustrates both the accessibility of the interest group system and its tremendous inequalities. Ignoring the fact that children have relatively little power in Washington, Edelman has refused to give up, exemplifying her belief that "enough committed fleas biting strategically can make even the biggest dog uncomfortable."

Sources: Joann J. Burch, *Marian Wright Edelman: Children's Champion* (Brookfield, Conn.: Milbrook Press, 1994); "Children of a Lesser Country," *The New Yorker*, January 15, 1996, pp. 25–26; "Mother Marian," interview, *Psychology Today* (July/August 1993): 26–29; Mark Peyser and Thomas Rosenthal, "She's Taking Her Stand," *Newsweek*, June 10, 1996, p. 32; and childrensdefense.org. This feature was written with the assistance of Paul Goggi.

Nader and his public interest groups are credited with helping to enact key consumer laws, including the Wholesome Meat Act of 1967, the Natural Gas Pipeline Safety Act of 1968, and the Comprehensive Occupational Safety and Health Act of 1970. At the same time, Nader's vision of citizen action is flawed. The consumer issues that Nader has concentrated on benefit the middle class more than the working class and the poor. As we noted earlier, many public interest groups with offices in Washington have become staff dominated, surviving on grants from wealthy patrons and direct mail contributions. Groups in which the staff communicates with members only through direct mail fundraising techniques are more consistent with the values of elite democracy than popular democracy.

THE NEW LOBBYING: ELITE COUNTERMOBILIZATION

In August 1971 Lewis Powell Jr., who would be appointed to the Supreme Court by Richard Nixon a few months later, wrote a confidential memo to the U.S. Chamber of Commerce.[32] Entitled "Attack on the Free Enterprise System," the Powell memorandum depicted American corporations as politically "impotent," the victims of a "massive assault." As a director on eleven corporate boards of director, Powell was especially sensitive to attacks on business. Charging that Ralph Nader and his allies were out to destroy the free enterprise system itself, Powell asserted that "there should be no reluctance to penalize those who oppose [the system]." What is remarkable about the Powell memo is that it lays out a broad strategy focused on four areas—universities, the media, the political establishment, and the courts—that would be implemented over the ensuing decades by big business pretty much as Powell recommended.

Business counterattacked along a broad front—all the way from traditional lobbying to litigation centers, think tanks, and increasingly sophisticated public relations. One of the major outgrowths of the Powell memo was the formation of the Business Roundtable in 1972, an organization made up exclusively of CEOs from the top 200 corporations in the country. The Business Roundtable was able to impose a remarkable degree of "class solidarity" among its members that enabled it to defeat a 1977 attempt by unions to repeal the right-to-work provisions of the Taft-Hartley Act. Inspired by the Powell memorandum, Joseph Coors gave a quarter of a million dollars to found a right-wing think tank known today as the Heritage Foundation.

As business organized, the corporate presence in Washington grew. In 1970, only a small number of Fortune 500 companies had public relations or lobbying offices in Washington; ten years later, 80 percent did.[33] Between 1960 and 1980, business's share of all organizations having representation in Washington increased from 57 percent to 72 percent. Citizens' groups as a proportion of all groups having representation in Washington fell from 9 percent to 5 percent, and the labor union proportion of the total plummeted from 11 percent to 2 percent. Only 2 percent of all interest groups in Washington represented issues concerning civil rights, social welfare, or the poor.[34] According to a Senate study, public interest groups were stretched so thin that they did not even show up at more than half of the formal proceedings on regulatory issues; when they did appear, they were often outnumbered ten to one by industry representatives. Corporations invested fifty to a hundred times more resources than public interest groups on many important issues.[35]

It would be wrong to say that corporate elites were just engaged in a power grab. In classic elite democratic fashion, they argued that elites should filter the emotional demands of the people. Too much democracy, they said, was overloading the system with too many demands.[36] The masses were being manipulated into supporting government regulations by emotional appeals from liberal activists who would benefit from the new jobs in the expanded regulatory state. In the long run, elite democrats argued, regulatory burdens would stifle growth, hurting all Americans' living standards.

Corporate elites portrayed their views not as private interests but as a new version of the public interest: Freeing business from regulatory and tax burdens would, in the long run, benefit all Americans; "a rising tide would lift all boats." Faced with a stagnating economy, ordinary citizens were receptive to the message that excessive regulations and high taxes were choking off economic growth. Using the outsider strategies pioneered by citizen groups, corporate elites mobilized grassroots pressure on Congress, greatly enhancing the power of their insider lobbyists in Washington. Moreover, the development of new communication technologies enabled corporate elites to play the outsider game even more effectively than public interest advocates could.

Think Tanks: Shaping the Agenda

Control over information and ideas is crucial in policy making. One of the best examples is Charles Murray's 1984 book *Losing Ground*, which played a key role in building momentum for welfare reform by arguing that welfare, far from curing poverty, was actually a *cause* of poverty. Welfare rewarded people for not working or marrying, Murray argued, helping to entrench a culture of poverty in urban ghettos. His recommended solution was to scrap "the entire federal welfare and income-support structure."[37] Murray's book had tremendous influence on the 1996 welfare reform (see Chapter 17), for it enabled conservatives to frame cutting welfare spending and limiting recipients to no more than three years of benefits in a row as compassionate, not punitive. Murray successfully framed welfare as more like a dangerous drug than a helping hand to single mothers and their children.

The influence of Murray's thinking was not just due to the persuasiveness of his arguments. Indeed, the evidence suggests that Murray greatly exaggerated the negative effects of welfare on behavior.[38] Besides funding Murray for two years to write the book, the Manhattan Institute, a conservative think tank, hired a public relations specialist who sent out more than 700 free copies and even flew in influential politicians, academics, and journalists, putting them up at an expensive New York hotel so that they could attend a seminar on Murray's book. Most think tank projects are not as influential as Murray's book, but by continuously seeding the ground with ideas and research, think tanks can play a crucial role in setting the policy agenda and framing the policy alternatives. Increasingly, **think tanks**—private, not-for-profit research and advocacy organizations—play the role of evaluating programs and generating new policy ideas. The number of think tanks focused on national issues increased from less than 50 in 1965 to over 200 by 1996.[39] (See Table 9.2 for a list of influential think tanks.)

To maintain their tax-exempt status, think tanks must remain nonpartisan: They cannot support political parties or candidates running for office. Increasingly, however, think tanks have taken on an ideological and partisan edge. Since the 1980s, conservative think tanks, generously funded by corporations and foundations, have been extraordinarily successful at shaping the national agenda. A 2003 survey of major media citations of the top 25 think tanks found that right-leaning think tanks garnered 47 percent of the citations, centrist

TABLE 9.2		Approximate Annual Budget (in millions of $)	Main Goals	Media Hits (2003)
Influential Washington Think Tanks	1. Urban Institute	61	Pro-city and minority; performs objective evaluations of government programs to improve them	892
	2. Heritage Foundation	30	New right; antigovernment; pro–free market; culturally conservative	3,141
	3. Brookings Institution	37	Scholarly policy analysis often with liberal orientation	4,784
	4. American Enterprise Institute	23.6	Advocates private enterprise over government solutions	2,645
	5. Cato Institute	13.8	Libertarian; individual liberty and limited government	1,873
	6. Joint Center for Political and Economic Studies	6.2	Does research to improve the lot of African Americans	NA
	7. Committee for Economic Development	5	Corporate-oriented; favors free market solutions	NA
	8. Economic Policy Institute	5.4	Pro-union; favors more equal distribution of wealth	1,091

Source: National Institute for Research Advancement, *Nira's World Directory of Think Tanks* (Tokyo: National Institute for Research Advancement, 2002). Media citations are from Michael Dolny, "Special Report: Think Tank Coverage," *Fairness in Accuracy and Reporting* (May/June 2004); available at www.fair.org.

institutions received 39 percent, and left-leaning think tanks got only 13 percent of the citations.[40]

Whereas consumer and environmental groups once dominated policy discussions by documenting the costs of private enterprise, conservative think tanks have now succeeded in focusing discussion on the costs of government regulation. Policy debates are now dominated by ideas derived from market economics, such as supply-side economics, privatization, and deregulation. The invasion of Iraq, the policy of preemption, and opposition to the United Nations were ideas hatched in neo-conservative think tanks in Washington and then imported into the Bush administration through figures like Richard Perle and John Bolton (prominent critic of the UN recently appointed by President Bush to be U.S. ambassador to the UN).

Why have conservative think tanks been so much more influential than liberal think tanks? First, they are better funded. But how the funding is used is more important than how much there is. In fact, large foundations that are often considered liberal, such as the Rockefeller and Ford foundations, have much more money than the conservative foundations, like the Lynde and Harry Bradley, Sarah Scaife, and John M. Olin foundations. But the liberal foundations tend to fund direct service projects, such as providing affordable housing or clean water, rather than ideologically driven policy analysis. The liberal think tanks that do exist tend to be less political and more scholarly. The Urban Institute, one of the oldest and biggest, supports government programs for cities and the poor, but it views itself primarily as a scientific evaluator of public policies; its research agenda is driven by government contracts, not by a political vision. The Economic Policy Institute, which receives most of its funding from unions, has a clear political agenda, but it is tiny compared to the large number of pro-corporate think tanks.

The conservative foundations have been much more strategic in their investments, giving conservative think tanks generous open-ended grants that enable them to pursue a long-term, ideologically driven agenda. It often takes many years for new ideas to influence policy. For decades, when it was viewed as politically taboo, the Cato Institute, a libertarian think tank, touted private accounts as an alternative to Social Security. After his 2004 reelection, President Bush began pushing for private accounts.

The most powerful think tank in Washington is the Heritage Foundation, which has a highly partisan, procorporate agenda. Within one year of its founding in 1973 the Heritage Foundation was receiving financial support from eighty-seven corporations. Its budget grew from $1 million in fiscal year 1976–77 to $35 million by 2003. Corporate donors include Mobil Oil, Dow Chemical, Gulf Oil, and the Reader's Digest Association.[41] In 1998–99 the Heritage Foundation raised $105 million to endow its activities, including twenty gifts of $1 million or more. Because of its generous funding, Heritage accepts no government contracts and can concentrate on developing its ideological agenda.

With a permanent staff of about 180, the Heritage Foundation generates over 200 publications per year. Devoting more than one-third of its budget to marketing, Heritage has been especially successful at gaining media attention for its publications. Most of its publications are designed to meet the "briefcase test"— short enough to be read in the time it takes for a taxi to travel from Washington's National Airport to a congressional hearing on Capitol Hill (about twenty minutes).[42] Senior scholars at Heritage are available to produce a paper on a policy issue for a sympathetic member of Congress in a matter of hours.

The Heritage Foundation achieved national prominence in 1980 when it delivered to President Reagan's transition team a 1,000-page volume entitled *Mandate for Leadership* that laid out the detailed steps that would be necessary for conservatives to take over the government. The book soon became a best seller. One reporter characterized it as a "blueprint for grabbing the government by its frayed New Deal lapels and shaking out forty-eight years of liberal policies."[43] After George W. Bush won the 2000 presidential election, the

Heritage Foundation passed on 1,300 names and résumés to the new administration. Former Heritage staffers are sprinkled throughout the Bush administration, including Labor Secretary Elaine Chao. A few days before Bush took office, the foundation issued a 435-page "Budget for America" with detailed program-by-program recommendations for the new president's first budget.

Conservative think tanks and foundations are also making efforts to shape political debates on college campuses, which they maintain have long been dominated by leftist ideas. The Liberation News Service (LNS) provides editorial services for left-wing college papers, but it is not nearly as well funded or organized. Accuracy in Academia (AIA) is an explicit attempt to counter the alleged left-wing bias in American universities. Started by Reed Irvine, also founder of a similar group called Accuracy in Media, AIA recruits students to monitor college classes and report professors who fail to include the conservative point of view or who have "Marxist leanings." The results are published in AIA's monthly newspaper, *Campus Report*, that is distributed online and free to about 1,500 colleges and high schools. The effects of these efforts are uncertain, but they demonstrate a capacity by conservative think tanks and foundations to reach out beyond Washington.

Direct Marketing

Another method used successfully by corporate elites to seize the agenda from citizens' groups is **direct marketing**, the targeted solicitation of individuals for political support, sometimes by phone but more often by mail. The advantage of direct marketing is that, much more than with radio or television, the political appeal can be adapted to specialized audiences. Pioneered by public interest groups, which often relied upon individual membership dues for funding, direct marketing has been greatly enhanced over the years by high-speed computers that maintain huge mailing lists broken down into segments for specialized appeals.

Direct mail marketing begins by contacting a large mailing list. This is an expensive task, and usually only 1 or 2 percent reply to the appeal. Respondents make up the "house list," which can be successfully solicited again and again for support, typically with a 10 percent to 20 percent response rate. Mailing lists are traded and sold between organizations. One enterprising researcher enrolled her four-month-old son in six organizations to trace direct-mail fundraising. Over the next year and a half the infant received 18 pounds of mail—185 solicitations from the original 6 organizations and 63 from 32 other organizations that bought or rented mailing lists.[44]

Direct mail solicitations are cleverly designed so that they will not be thrown in the wastebasket unopened. A licked stamp looks more personal than metered mail. They are often addressed directly to the individual ("Dear Mr. Malone"), are marked "urgent," and contain emotional appeals that evoke an exaggerated threat. A letter from Common Cause talks about "the threat posed by the torrents of special interest campaign cash," which it calls "Alarming. Outrageous. Downright dangerous." A solicitation from the Christian right begins "Just

When You Thought Your Children Were Safe from Homosexual Advances, Congress Introduces House Resolution #427: The 'Gay Bill of Rights.'"[45]

Computers break down mailing lists into niches and specialized appeals. By a simple command, a computer can be ordered to produce letters for all those on the mailing list who live, for example, in the districts of representatives who serve on the House Banking, Finance, and Urban Affairs Committee. Lobbyists increasingly see direct mail as a way to supplement their insider strategy with an outsider strategy that carefully orchestrates grassroots pressure on Congress.

THE NEW INTEREST GROUP POLITICS: ASTROTURF LOBBYING

The new style of lobbying developed by the public interest movement in the 1960s and 1970s tilted the playing field of interest group politics. Previously, lobbying was dominated by **iron triangles**—literally three-pointed relationships between executive branch agencies, committees in Congress, and interest groups. A good example is the strong relationship defense contractors have formed with subcommittees in Congress, and top officials in the Defense Department. Iron triangles still exist but in many areas political scientists believe they have been replaced by looser, more open and decentralized **issue networks**.[46] Complex new regulatory laws helped to make congressional hearings more important, with expert witnesses amassing mountains of information on each issue. In general, many issues have been taken out from behind closed doors in Congress to be decided in more public forums, with public opinion (the outsider strategy) playing a more important role.

It would seem reasonable to conclude that the opening up of the interest group system to broader participation—what political scientists call "expanding the scope of conflict"—would make it more open to popular democratic input. However, this has not been the case. First, the greater emphasis on information in the policy-making process gives an advantage to those who control information. Elected representatives, even presidents, are forced to defer to the issue networks as democratic control passes from elected leaders to unelected technocrats. Few citizens possess the expertise or the free time to track complex regulations on new drugs or the latest scientific knowledge on carcinogens. Corporations do.

More important, corporate elites have devised their own outsider strategy to counter the outsider strategy of the public interest groups. Politicians want to know what the public thinks about an idea before they vote for it. If they think there is a significant grassroots movement that opposes a proposed law, they will vote against it. Corporations now have the ability to create fake grassroots movements—to use the appearance of popular democracy to achieve the objectives of elite democracy. Corporate mergers have spawned a new generation of public relations firms in Washington, D.C., that can, for the right amount of money, generate a grassroots movement for either side on just about any issue. Lloyd Bentsen, a long-time Democratic senator from Texas, coined the term

© 2005 Tom Tomorrow.

"**AstroTurf lobbying**" to describe artificial grassroots campaigns created by public relations firms.[47] By 1995, AstroTurf lobbying was an $800 million a year industry, according to *Campaigns and Elections* magazine.[48]

A good example of the new breed of lobbyists is Bonner & Associates, a small but sophisticated public relations firm located near the Capitol in Washington. Founder Jack "Bombs Away" Bonner emphasizes that corporate grassroots politics was borrowed from the public interest groups that perfected the technique of using factual accusations to generate emotional public responses. "Politics turns on emotion," Bonner says. "That's why industry has lost in the past and that's why we win. We bring emotion to the table."[49] Bonner takes pride in being able to find ordinary citizens who have no financial interest in the policy but are willing to support his corporate clients' positions; "white hat" citizens, he calls them. The offices of Bonner & Associates have a boiler room with three hundred phone lines and a sophisticated computer system. Young people sit in little booths every day, dialing around the country in search of "white hat" citizens who are willing to endorse corporate political objectives. To oppose a law that would have required Detroit automakers to build more fuel-efficient cars, Bonner enlisted seniors and people with disabilities who had concerns about getting in and out of smaller cars. They also got police officers, who feared their police cruisers would be replaced by Toyotas, to speak out against the proposal. The bill was defeated.

The key to astroturf lobbying is deception—the politicians must never know who is really behind the "grassroots" campaign. Bonner, for example, has its callers ask whether the person would be willing to sign a letter of support and then fax it back to them. Bonner then scans the signature onto a computer and puts it on a petition deceiving lawmakers into thinking that people went door-to-door gathering signatures. So-called "stealth campaigns" utilize a series of front organizations to mask the true source of the lobbying.[50] For example, Bonner used the letterhead of Consumer Alliance, a Michigan nonprofit that opposes laws to lower the cost of prescription drugs to low-income consumers, to solicit signatures. In fact, the entire effort was funded by the Pharmaceutical Research and Manufacturers of America.

The newest fad in lobbying is the Internet. Bonner & Associates opened a subsidiary, called NetRoots, which, for a fee, will create sophisticated websites to accompany lobbying campaigns. Its website opposing cutbacks in carbon dioxide emissions provides prewritten e-mail messages from farmers, senior citizens, and small business owners that read as if they were spontaneously written by citizens and can be sent directly to congressional representatives with the click of a mouse.[51]

In a large country like the United States, the increasing sophistication of the mass media and direct marketing has given an advantage to interests with large amounts of money. American politics is approaching "democracy for hire." Researchers found that few corporate interest representatives in Washington expressed a need for more money—only 9 percent. On the other hand, 58 percent of unions and citizens' groups said they needed more money.[52] A chemical company can deduct the cost of flying its executives to Washington to testify against the Clean Air Act; ordinary citizens must pay their own way.

THE BATTLE OVER SOCIAL SECURITY

Created by Franklin Roosevelt in 1935, Social Security is the most popular social welfare program ever enacted in the United States. Every worker must pay Social Security taxes on the first $90,000 in income. (Take a look at your next paycheck; the Social Security tax rate is 6.2 percent; employers also contribute.) When workers reach retirement age, they are entitled to a monthly check based on how much they paid into the system. Although commonly viewed as an insurance system, in fact, workers exhaust what they paid into the system in four to eight years. After that the taxes from current workers pay the benefits for current retirees. Forming a solid safety net, Social Security has been remarkably successful at reducing poverty among the elderly. Benefiting people from all walks of life, Social Security has become so politically popular that pundits dubbed it the "third rail" of American politics: like the third rail on electric railway, politicians touch it only at their peril.

Flush with his reelection victory, in January 2005 President Bush grabbed hold of the third rail in dramatic fashion, proposing to reform Social Security by allowing younger workers to divert their Social Security taxes into private investment accounts that they would personally own. Funding these accounts would require the federal government to borrow trillions of dollars to replace the taxes designed to cover the benefits for current retirees. Bush's proposal set in motion a furious lobbying effort that is reminiscent of the 1993–94 battle over President Clinton's national health insurance proposal. In that case, opponents, using slick ads with misleading claims, succeeded in reversing public opinion from majority support for Clinton's proposal to majority opposition. The two sides spent over $100 million. The battle over private retirement accounts will cost at least twice as much and promises to be even uglier than the fight over national health care. The political tug of war over Social Security demonstrates how a polarized partisan atmosphere mixed with manipulative communications technology can be a toxic brew for democracy, making honest democratic debate difficult, if not impossible.

Leading the fight against Bush's Social Security proposal is the American Association of Retired Persons (AARP), the largest and certainly one of the most powerful interest groups in the nation. Founded in 1958 as a way to use the purchasing power of the elderly to drive down the cost of health insurance, the AARP has grown tremendously as an interest group because it solved the collective action problem by providing individual benefits to its members. Right after their fiftieth birthday, most people receive an invitation to join AARP. It is hard to turn down because there are so many benefits attached to membership, including access to health, auto, and homeowner insurance and discounts on travel, online services, computers, music, and more. You also get a subscription to the AARP magazine whose monthly circulation exceeds *Time*, *Newsweek*, and *US News & World Report* combined. With nearly 36 million members and annual income of $770 million, AARP is a formidable opponent. Indeed, AARP's earlier support of Bush's Medicare drug plan made it nearly impossible for many Democrats to oppose it.

AARP enacted a broad attack on Bush's proposal, portraying it as an effort to dismantle Social Security, not fix it. In one of their radio spots a plumber brings in a wrecking crew to fix a plugged drain. "If you had a problem with the kitchen sink," the announcer says amid sounds of hammers and chain saws, "you wouldn't tear down the entire house. So why dismantle the Social Security system with private accounts when it can be fixed with moderate changes?" Controlling $400 billion in union-sponsored pension plans, the unions are threatening to withdraw their business if major Wall Street firms support the Bush proposal. Several large investment firms pulled out of one of the groups backing the Bush proposal.

To counter AARP the Business Roundtable, U.S. Chamber of Commerce, and Wall Street firms (which stand to reap huge profits if Social Security taxes are diverted to stock purchases) have funded a number of "independent" groups with high sounding names like For Our Grandchildren, Generations Together, and Coalition for the Modernization and Protection of America's Social Security (Compass). Leading the charge is the United Seniors Association, or USA Next. Founded by Richard Viguerie, a pioneer in right-wing direct mail fundraising, USA Next hired the same ad agency and public relations firms that orchestrated the attacks on John Kerry sponsored by the Swift Boat Veterans for Truth. In one ad showing a photograph with two men kissing, USA Next branded AARP as pro-gay marriage. Charlie Jarvis, the head of USA Next, promised that their $10 million campaign would pack a lot of punch. "We're talking about TV, radio, Internet ads, large-scale direct mail and e-mail and telephone alerts. And the telephone alerts, for example, are extraordinarily inexpensive. I can call every household in South Dakota in just four hours. And it would cost only $10,000."[53]

The fight over Social Security has not primarily focused on the facts so that citizens can make up their own minds, but rather upon framing the issue in a way that spins the issue favorable to one side or the other. For example, Bush has stressed that Social Security faces a funding crisis when the baby boomers

"NO WITNESSES, BUT OUR SECURITY CAMERAS CAUGHT KEY REPUBLICAN LEADERS AND SOME KIND OF *USA NEXT* VAN PARKED OUT FRONT OVER THE WEEKEND..."

© R. J. Matson, Roll Call 2005.

retire and the country needs to take action now. Opponents call this a "scare tactic" and argue, correctly, that Bush's proposal won't address the funding crisis anyway. The Bush supporters charge that it is their opponents who are engaging in scare tactics by frightening the elderly with the unsubstantiated claim that giving younger workers more choice will threaten their benefits. Much of the battle is over language. Polling has shown that the term "privatization" is scary to most people, connoting something that is exclusive and not entirely under your control. "Personal accounts" poll much better. Who wins will depend partly on which term prevails.[54]

The battle over Social Security resembles a presidential election, only with issues instead of candidates. As in a political campaign, the two sides tell people what the pollsters say they want to hear. For this reason, neither side has offered any proposal to address the major issue facing Social Security, the long-term shortfall in funding. The reason, of course, is that any solution to this would require either increasing taxes or cutting benefits. The debate, if you can call it that, is dominated by fake grassroots groups, run by associations headquartered in Washington, cynically using sophisticated public relations technology to spin the issue in their favor. As Jack Schnirman, the campaign director of United Leaders, a nonpartisan, nonprofit group trying to mobilize voters twenty-five and under, put it: "It's not being fought about at our level. It's at the grass tops, or Astroturf—big phony 527s against other big phony 527s, like the AARP against USA Next."[55]

CONCLUSION: WHAT CAN BE DONE?

At the present time, interest group politics faces a dilemma: democracy requires that we protect the rights of all groups to organize and "petition the government for a redress of grievances" (in the words of the U.S. Constitution), but this freedom of association has led to an interest group system today that is highly unequal, even undemocratic. In particular, developments in communications technology have enabled interest groups with large sums of money to manipulate public opinion with stealth campaigns and clever sound bites. In what political scientists call "feedback effects," moneyed interests have used their political power to enhance their economic position, setting in motion a vicious circle of widening economic and political inequalities that threatens the very core of our democracy.

The situation cries out for governmental action to level the playing field. However, any attempt by the government to restrict or subsidize interest groups would be abhorrent. Who would pick which groups to stifle or aid? As James Madison said in *Federalist No. 10*, "Liberty is to faction [selfish interest groups] what air is to fire." Thus, it would be foolish to suppress factions, Madison concluded, because to do so would destroy the very atmosphere that breathes life into the democratic process. The cure would be worse than the disease.

With freedom seeming to nurture damaging political inequalities, is there anything we can do? In fact, there are many things we can do. The government cannot directly intervene in interest group politics, but it can help to level the playing field. Here are some suggestions.

1. *Require more disclosure of lobbying activities*: The most effective way to level the playing field is to inform the public about efforts to influence the government. The 1995 Lobbying Disclosure Act (LDA) was a landmark piece of legislation that required any organization employing lobbyists to disclose whom they represent, what they are lobbying for, and how much they are paid. The big flaw in LDA is that it does not require disclosure of so-called grassroots lobbying, the phalanx of public relations specialists, pollsters, and ad companies that wealthy clients hire to shape public opinion, and ultimately influence Congress. If the citizens knew that it was the drug industry that was sponsoring Citizens for Better Medicare, they would be much more skeptical about their ads against the government negotiating lower drug prices for seniors. Requiring lobbyists to disclose these activities would in no way restrict their freedom of association.

2. *Tighten campaign finance laws*: Just as there has been a blurring of the line between the inside and the outside game of lobbying, there has also been a blurring of the distinction between interest group politics and elections. A key way that interest groups achieve power is by giving contributions to elected officials. Wealthy interest groups are not primarily interested in influencing who gets elected because they give overwhelmingly to incumbents who almost always win and when the election is tight, they give to both sides. Election contributions are mostly about buying access for their lobbying. Until we better regulate the flood of money in elections, the wealthy will continue to buy privileged access. (We deal with the issue of campaign finance reform in Chapter 8.)

3. *Improve media oversight*: One of the greatest protections against special political privileges is exposure by the media. It is the duty of journalists to inform the public about who is behind so-called grassroots groups. This will be less likely if the media are controlled by a few giant corporations and there is little competition. (We discuss the importance of the media for popular democracy in Chapter 6.)

4. *Encourage genuine debate*: The problem is not that wealthy corporations are involved in lobbying; clearly, corporations have a valid viewpoint that deserves to be heard in the political system. The problem is the way well-heeled interest groups make their cases, using stealth campaigns, relying upon ten-second sound bites, with misleading claims hitting "hot button" issues. According to two experts on interest group politics, "Electronic smear campaigns have become a key by-product of new communications technologies and typically are filled with misleading, erroneous,

or outright malicious claims."[56] It is difficult for the government to directly regulate these activities, though some states have experimented with "truth in communications" codes or even the banning of false or deceptive ads. Their experiences deserve watching. Codes of ethics in the consulting industry can help. On the positive side, the sponsorship of "deliberative polls" would show that public opinion looks very different when citizens are given a chance to gain information and discuss issues with other citizens—instead of being forced to make snap judgments about fixed alternatives to an anonymous phone call. Some have even called for Deliberation Day, a national holiday in which citizens would be paid to participate in all-day small-group discussions of national issues.[57]

5. *Build real grassroots associations*: It may be tempting for popular democratic groups to fight fire with fire, hiring their own slick consultants to manipulate public opinion. But it won't work: the other side will always have more money and slicker consultants. Ultimately, the only way to counter the Astroturf lobbying of moneyed interests is for ordinary citizens to form real grassroots organizations. The reason why the interest group system became more accessible to ordinary citizens in the 1960s and 1970s is because people were mobilized into mass organizations that went door-to-door and often took the streets to publicize their causes. Landmark laws like the civil rights laws and the Clean Air Act passed because elites felt threatened. Sensing that the alternative was radical change, they became more open to sensible reforms. In the next chapter we turn to protest politics, the ultimate outsider strategy that, under the right circumstances, can give popular democrats a weapon that money cannot buy.

KEY TERMS

interest group politics	public interest group
insider strategy	think tank
outsider strategy	direct marketing
Federal Register	iron triangle
pluralism	issue network
collective action problem	AstroTurf lobbying

INTERNET RESOURCES

■ Center for Responsive Politics
www.opensecrets.org
Enables citizens to follow the money trail in politics.

■ Common Cause
www.commoncause.org
The official site of Common Cause, one of the nation's oldest and largest public affairs interest groups.

■ LaborNet
www.labornet.org
An independent website on labor issues that is both critical of labor unions and sympathetic to them.

■ National Association of Manufacturers
www.nam.org
The National Association of Manufacturers home page contains material similar to that on the AFL-CIO site but from a business point of view.

■ U.S. Public Interest Research Group
www.uspirg.org
The national lobbying office for the public interest research groups organized in states and on college campuses around the nation.

SUGGESTED READINGS

Mancur Olson, *The Logic of Collective Action: Public Goods and the Theory of Groups*. New York: Schocken Books, 1968. A leading statement of rational actor theory that explains why broad public interest groups have trouble organizing.

E. E. Schattschneider, *Semisovereign People: A Realist's View of Democracy in America*. New York: Holt, Rinehart and Winston, 1960. A brief but penetrating analysis of the elitist bias in interest group politics.

Steven E. Schier, *By Invitation Only: The Rise of Exclusive Politics in the United States*. Pittsburgh: University of Pittsburgh Press, 2000. Documents the rise of niche marketing by interest groups to activate highly selective groups in the population—usually ignoring working-class and poor people.

Theda Skocpol, *Diminished Democracy: From Membership to Management in American Civic Life*. Norman: University of Oklahoma Press, 2003. Shows how national membership associations have been replaced by professionally managed interest groups in Washington, D.C.

Darrell M. West and Burdett A. Loomis, *The Sound of Money: How Political Interests Get What They Want*. New York: W. W. Norton, 1998. Shows how in a technological age moneyed interests can dominate interest group politics.

CHAPTER

10

Mass Movement Politics
The Great Equalizer

PROTEST POLITICS: GOALS AND TACTICS
> Mass Movement Goals: Beyond Material Benefits
> Mass Movement Tactics: Protest as a Political Resource

MASS MOVEMENTS IN AMERICAN HISTORY

MASS MOVEMENTS: THE NECESSARY INGREDIENTS

PROTEST TACTICS: WALKING A FINE LINE

THE ELITE RESPONSE TO MASS MOVEMENTS

THE DEMOCRATIC DEBATE OVER MASS MOVEMENTS
> Elite Democratic Criticisms of Mass Movements
> The Popular Democratic Defense of Mass Movements
> Sixties-Style Protest Movements: Elite Backlash
> The Popular Democratic Response: Elite Distemper
> The Achievements of Mass Movements
> Is the Christian Right a Popular Democratic Mass Movement?

CONCLUSION: THE FUTURE OF PROTEST POLITICS

In October 2002, President George W. Bush went to the United Nations and helped persuade the Security Council to pass a resolution calling for Iraq to disarm all weapons of mass destruction (WMDs) within one month or face military action. Bush balked, however, when a second resolution was required before an invasion of Iraq could proceed with UN approval. Key members of the Security Council, including France and Germany, wanted to give the inspections more time to work. Ignoring the UN, Bush began mobilizing for an invasion by what he called a "coalition of the willing." (The only significant ally of the United States was Britain.) Public opinion in the United States was deeply divided. According to a *New York Times* poll, 56 percent of the public favored war only with UN sanction. With Bush seemingly determined to invade regardless of domestic or foreign opposition, the political tension mounted in February and March of 2003. Bumper stickers began appearing on cars and even on yard signs proclaiming "WAR IS NOT THE ANSWER" and "GIVE PEACE A CHANCE."

292

On February 15, 2003, opposition to the invasion burst out in protests spanning five continents. By conservative estimates, 1.5 million demonstrated in Europe, including 750,000 in London, 500,000 in Berlin, 100,000 in Paris, and 70,000 in Amsterdam. Aware that U.S. troops had defeated Nazism and defended Western Europe from communism, the protestors used every opportunity to stress that you could be antiwar and still be pro-American. Protests also occurred in Kashmir, New Zealand, Hong Kong, Istanbul, Prague, Moscow, and Tokyo. No protests at all occurred in China and North Korea, two countries lacking a tradition of civil liberties and free speech.

The U.S. demonstrations that weekend were the largest since Vietnam. A coalition of 120 groups called United for Peace sponsored a demonstration in New York that police estimated at 350,000. Denied a permit to march down First Avenue past the UN, the demonstrators spilled over into the streets, blocking traffic. All in all, more than 800,000 protested that day in the United States. The protestors represented a broad swath of American society, from baby boomers to teens, from veteran demonstrators to those who had never marched in a protest before. The numbers were especially impressive if you consider that protesting is the most demanding form of legal political participation in a democracy. As a commitment, it overshadows the few minutes it takes to vote or sign a petition. Many had to travel hundreds of miles and even pay for overnight accommodations to attend the rallies. Demonstrations are not only time-consuming but they are also frightening to many people—and with good reason. With little provocation, mounted police in Manhattan charged the demonstrators and arrested more than 250 people.

The protests against war with Iraq were organized by an amorphous network of groups lacking any strong central organization or leader. A main reason they were able to turn so many people out so quickly was the Internet.[1] New communication technologies have lowered the threshold for collective action, making it easier to organize protests by communicating with dispersed individuals using e-mail, websites, and cell phones. The protests were hobbled, however, by the lack of a central organization or a charismatic leader. Even though many Democratic politicians harbored doubts about Bush's war plans, they generally shunned the protests, fearing they would be branded as unpatriotic. The message the protestors wanted to send had to be nuanced. They did not want to appear to be supporting Saddam Hussein or opposing efforts to disarm Iraq. Overwhelmingly peaceful, the demonstrators coalesced around the demand that the United States not go to war without UN approval. As is often the case, the central message got diluted as some groups used the demonstration to push their pet issues—all the way from racial justice to the plight of the Palestinians.

Bush was unmoved by the massive protests. During his college days at Yale, Bush had never participated in any of the massive anti–Vietnam War protests, and he seemed proud of this fact. In response to the protests Bush asserted that he knew what was best for the country, and he was not about to listen to the people. "Size of protest—it's like deciding, well, I'm going to decide policy based upon a focus group. The role of the leader is to decide policy based upon the security, in this case, the security of the people."[2] One month later, on the evening of March 19, Bush launched the attack on Iraq, winning a military victory within a few weeks. Two years later, however, the United States was still bogged down in an expensive and bloody occupation.

The massive antiwar protests in 2003 demonstrate both the potential and the limits of protest politics. First, there is no doubt that the protests raised awareness about what was at stake in Bush's war plans and sparked discussion of the issues in the United States and around the globe. Even though the protests broadened the conflict and activated opposition to Bush, the protestors had little leverage inside the administration. Part of the reason is that many Americans believed Bush when he said that Iraq possessed WMDs and was linked directly to Al Qaeda. Still smarting from the 9/11 terrorist attacks, many Americans viewed the invasion as defensive. It didn't matter that, in fact, Iraq had no WMDs and had no link to Al Qaeda. The president implied that he had information that no one else possessed, and many Americans believed him. Throughout Ameri-

© 2005 Tom Tomorrow.

can history elites have charged that protestors are too emotional; policy cannot be made in the streets. Only elites possess the information and expertise necessary to make sound policy. Elite democrats have an advantage in foreign affairs, where the president has tremendous authority to act unilaterally, free of the checks and balances that normally operate in domestic policy.

Although protests are often ineffective (they did not stop the invasion of Iraq), they have become almost a routine part of American politics. The spread of protests is a sign that people feel that the normal operations of representative democracy are failing. Indeed, it is impossible to understand American politics today without understanding protest politics. **Protest politics** can be defined as political actions such as boycotts and demonstrations designed to broaden conflicts and activate third parties to pressure the bargaining situation in ways favorable to the protestors.[3] Because protest politics operates outside of ordinary political institutions, it is sometimes called "extraordinary politics."[4] When protest politics mobilizes large numbers of previously passive bystanders to become active participants, it reaches the stature of a **mass movement**.

Throughout American history, mass movements have enabled outsiders—the poor, minorities, the disabled—to make themselves heard and acquire some power. After examining the goals and tactics that distinguish protest politics from electoral and interest group politics, we will explore the dilemmas that leaders of mass movements face in keeping protests alive—using the civil rights movement as a model of a successful mass movement. After analyzing the ways that elites respond to mass movements, we will examine mass movements in the context of the democratic debate. Finally, we will evaluate modern mass movements, including the Christian Right, which uses protest tactics but whose goals are very different from popular democratic movements of the past. Protest tactics can be misused and abused, but often, when the institutions of representative democracy are failing, they provide a way to level the playing field of politics, helping to fulfill the participatory promise of American democracy.

PROTEST POLITICS: GOALS AND TACTICS

Like interest groups, mass movements are a form of extra-electoral politics; they try to influence government outside of elections. Interest group politics and mass politics often blend into each other. Interest groups sometimes organize demonstrations, and it is common for mass movements to lobby Congress. Over time, mass movements often spawn interest groups that become part of the pressure group system in Washington. Nevertheless, interest group politics and protest politics are distinct phenomena whose primary differences have to do with (1) their goals and (2) the means, or tactics, used to achieve those goals.

In the pages ahead, we illustrate the lessons of protest politics by focusing on the very beginning of the American civil rights movement in the Montgomery bus boycott in 1955–56. Reaching its zenith in the mid-1960s, the civil rights movement was probably the most successful mass movement in American history. Led by a charismatic black preacher by the name of Martin Luther King Jr., the civil rights movement began in 1955 with the Montgomery bus boycott to desegregate the local bus system. The movement reached its highest point of power with the passage of the 1964 Civil Rights Act, which prohibited segregation in public accommodations and discrimination in hiring, and the 1965 Voting Rights Act, which revolutionized politics across the country, and especially in the South, by guaranteeing blacks the right to vote.

Mass Movement Goals: Beyond Material Benefits

Whereas interest groups usually focus on specific economic goals, such as lower taxes or more governmental benefits, mass movements seek broad moral and ideological goals that affect the whole society, such as the "right to life" of the anti-abortion movement or the equal treatment of the civil rights movement. As a result, mass movement goals are not easily subject to bargaining and compromise. The abolitionist movement, for example, refused to compromise on its goal of abolishing slavery. For mass movements, it is not a matter of more or less, but right or wrong. Table 10.1 lists the most important mass movements in American history together with their main goals.

The civil rights movement shows how groups can make the transition from interest groups to mass movements. In the mid-1950s, Montgomery, Alabama, like most southern cities, had laws requiring segregation of nearly all public facilities, including public transportation.[5] Blacks were required to sit in the backs of buses. They could not pass through the white section at the front of a bus, which meant that after a black had bought a ticket, he or she had to get off and reenter through the back door. The ordinance in Montgomery had a special twist: Bus drivers, all of whom were white, were empowered to enforce a floating line between the races. As more whites got on, bus drivers would order a whole row of blacks to stand up and move to the back of the bus to make room. A number of black women could thus be forced to stand to make room for one white man.

On December 1, 1955, Rosa Parks, a dignified, middle-aged African-American woman, boarded a bus in downtown Montgomery. The thirty-six seats on the bus were soon filled with twenty-two blacks and fourteen whites. Seeing a white man standing in the front of the bus, the driver turned around and told the four blacks sitting in the row just behind the whites to get up and move to the back. Rosa Parks refused. The driver threatened to arrest her, but Parks again refused to move. Summoned to the scene, police officers arrested Parks, took her to the police station, booked her, fingerprinted her, and put her in jail.

Word of Parks's arrest spread quickly through the black community, which immediately organized a highly successful boycott of the bus company. Initially, however, the goals of the movement were very cautious, resembling more the goals of an interest group than a militant mass movement. The boycott had three demands: (1) courteous treatment on the buses; (2) seating on a first-come, first-served basis; and (3) the hiring of black drivers for black bus routes.

TABLE 10.1

Mass Movements in American History

Movement	Primary Period of Activism	Major Goal(s)
Abolitionist	Three decades before Civil War (1830–1860)	Abolition of slavery
Nativist	1850s and 1890s–1920s	Restriction of immigration
Populist	1880s and 1890s	Democratic control over railroads, banks, and nation's money supply
Labor	Reached peaks in the 1880s, 1890s, and 1930s	Enhance power of workers to achieve decent wages and benefits, protect jobs, and guarantee safe working environments
Women's suffrage	Late nineteenth and early twentieth centuries	Voting rights for women
Temperance	Late nineteenth and early twentieth centuries	Prohibition of alcohol
Nuclear disarmament	Late 1950s and early 1960s	End of nuclear testing
	Late 1970s and early 1980s	Banning the bomb
Civil rights	1950s and 1960s	Equal rights for black Americans
Anti–Vietnam War	Late 1960s and early 1970s	U.S. out of Vietnam
Student	1960s and 1970s	Student rights and democratic governance of universities
Neighborhood organizing	1960s–present	Community control
Women's liberation or feminist	1970s–present	Equality for women in all aspects of life
Antinuclear	1970s and 1980s	Stopping the construction of nuclear power plants
Environmental	1970s–present	Stop environmental destruction
Pro-life	1970s–present	Outlawing abortion, stem-cell research, euthanasia
Native American rights	1970s–present	Tribal autonomy
Gay rights	1970s–present	Equal rights for homosexuals
Anti-globalization	1990s–present	Controls on multinational corporations
Anti–Iraq War	2002–present	U.S. out of Iraq or UN takeover

The protestors were not calling for an end to segregation but simply for reforms that would make it more humane.

The white establishment in Montgomery refused to compromise. Instead, they tried to suppress the movement by harassing the boycotters and throwing the leaders in jail on trumped-up charges. The refusal of whites to compromise on these issues, King later wrote, caused a shift in people's thinking:

> The experience taught me a lesson. . . . even when we asked for justice within the segregation laws, the "powers that be" were not willing to grant it. Justice and equality, I saw, would never come while segregation remained, because the basic purpose of segregation was to perpetuate injustice and inequality.[6]

At that moment, the goals of the Montgomery boycott shifted from better treatment for blacks within segregation to an end to segregation, or equal rights for all, a goal that could not be compromised. At that point, Montgomery's blacks made the transition from an interest group to a mass movement that could appeal to all Americans on the basis of human dignity, equality, and fairness.

Mass Movement Tactics: Protest as a Political Resource

Mass movements are differentiated from interest groups not only by their goals but also by the political means they use to achieve their goals. Mass movements have a broad array of *protest tactics* to choose from, including petitions, demonstrations, boycotts, strikes, civil disobedience, confrontations and disruptions, riots, and even violent revolution (see Figure 10.1). Unlike interest groups, mass movements do not target their efforts directly at decision makers; protests are a form of political theater designed to educate and mobilize broader publics, who in turn put pressure on decision makers. Mass movements attempt to broaden the scope of conflict in the hope that battles that are lost in the narrow hallways of Congress can be won in the streets or in the broad arena of public opinion. Therefore, mass movement politics has more participatory potential than interest group politics. By relying on mass mobilization and the moral appeal of their cause, people with little money or political clout can use protest tactics to gain power in the political system.

Mass movement tactics vary all the way from the legal to the clearly illegal, with a large gray area in the middle. Protestors often agonize about whether to cross over the line into illegal tactics. In choosing tactics, protesters must go far enough to dramatize their cause but not so far as to alienate potential supporters—a phenomenon known as *political backlash*. Most tactics used by mass movements are legal and protected by the First Amendment guarantees of freedom of speech, press, and "the right of the people peaceably to assemble, and to petition the Government for a redress of grievances" (U.S. Constitution). When legal protests are ignored, protestors become frustrated and sometimes resort to illegal methods, including violence, to dramatize their causes.

In many ways, protest movements are evidence of the failure of our democratic institutions to respond to deeply felt needs and issues.[7] Even if a democ-

FIGURE 10.1 Tactical Options of Protest Movements

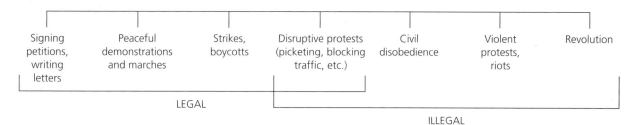

| Signing petitions, writing letters | Peaceful demonstrations and marches | Strikes, boycotts | Disruptive protests (picketing, blocking traffic, etc.) | Civil disobedience | Violent protests, riots | Revolution |

LEGAL

ILLEGAL

racy guaranteed majority rule, it would still need ways for minorities to make themselves heard. For example, blacks in Montgomery could not use electoral politics to achieve their objectives. Representing only 37 percent of the city's population, African Americans lacked the votes to control city government through elections. More important, they were prevented from registering to vote by legal obstacles and outright intimidation. In 1952, only about one in five eligible blacks in the South was registered to vote.[8] Interest group politics was also not a viable option, because whites in Montgomery were unwilling to bargain or compromise; for them, segregation was an all-or-nothing matter.

Following normal political channels, therefore, Montgomery blacks had no chance of success. However, the boycott was a weapon they could use: By withdrawing their fares from the bus company, they could inflict fiscal pain. But it is unlikely that the boycott alone would have brought significant change. The only chance the blacks had was to appeal to a broader audience to put pressure on the entrenched white elite in Montgomery to alter the system of racial segregation. As King said in his speech calling for the boycott, the only weapon they had was the "weapon of protest."

MASS MOVEMENTS IN AMERICAN HISTORY

American politics has been shaken repeatedly by mass movements. About once in a generation, waves of democratic participation, with strong leveling tendencies, sweep the country: the original revolutionary thrust of the 1770s; the Jacksonian era of the 1830s; the culmination of the antislavery movement in the 1850s; the Populist movement of the 1890s; the economic reform movements, including the labor movement, that rose out of the Great Depression of the 1930s; and the social movements that began in the 1960s. Mass movements have probably played a greater role in American politics than in any other Western democracy. Issues that are represented by political parties in Europe are often expressed through protest movements in the United States.

Some mass movements in the United States, such as the nativist movement and one of its offshoots, the Ku Klux Klan, have had antidemocratic goals of excluding certain groups from full citizenship. Today, protest movements against new rights for gays, immigrants, and minorities (e.g., affirmative action) have the same antidemocratic potential. Most mass movements, however, have been popular democratic in character, striving to include previously excluded groups (e.g., blacks, Hispanics, women, workers, students, gays, and Native Americans, and the disabled) in the full benefits of democratic citizenship. In appealing to the American people, popular democratic mass movements have called on two deeply held sets of beliefs—one rooted in politics and the other in religion—that counter Americans' well-known individualism.

First, Americans share a set of core political beliefs in liberty, equality, democracy, and the rule of law. These beliefs are embodied in sacred political texts, including the Declaration of Independence ("all men are created equal"), the Constitution's Bill of Rights (freedom of speech and press), and Lincoln's Gettysburg Address ("government of the people, by the people and for the people"). The American political creed is by its nature inclusive and has frequently been cited by protesting groups to legitimate their causes. Thus, the women's suffrage movement asserted that liberty and equality should apply to all people and not just men. Martin Luther King Jr. repeatedly used the language of equality and rights to legitimate the black cause to the white majority. Being able to tap into a wellspring of egalitarian political beliefs, popular democrats have historically had an ideological advantage over elite democrats. The language of rights has been a powerful tool in the hands of the disadvantaged.

Popular democratic mass movements have also been nurtured by American religious traditions stressing that everyone is equal in the eyes of God, that even the least of us should be treated with dignity and respect, and that morality is a force in the world. King's frequent use of the language of the Old Testament, comparing the liberation struggles of blacks to the struggles of the tribes of Israel to escape from exile in Egypt, is a brilliant example of the political relevance of religion in American politics. The abolitionist and temperance movements were also firmly rooted in religious traditions, as is the modern pro-life, anti-abortion movement, which has adopted many of the direct action tactics of the civil rights movement.

MASS MOVEMENTS: THE NECESSARY INGREDIENTS

Protest is a political resource that can be used by disadvantaged groups lacking traditional sources of political power, such as money or connections, to influence the system. However, protest cannot be used by any disadvantaged group at any time to level the playing field of democratic politics. All the necessary ingredients must be in place before a protest movement can come together and succeed. About half of the eligible voters don't even get to the polls for a presidential election every four years. Protest movements require much deeper levels of commitment than voting, as exemplified by the willingness of blacks in Montgomery to walk to work for thirteen months instead of taking the bus.

Protest movements engage the whole personalities of participants, transcending normal politics. And even when participants are engaged, remarkable leadership is necessary for movements to stay alive and achieve their goals.

For protest movements even to get off the ground, five ingredients are necessary.

1. *Rising expectations.* History has shown that people will endure oppressive conditions for a long time without rebelling. People do not rebel when conditions are at their worst but when conditions have begun to improve and people begin to perceive a gap between the way things are and the way they could be. According to one theory, it is not deprivation itself that drives people to rebel but the feeling that one's group is being deprived of resources and opportunities available to other groups in the society. This is known as the theory of **relative deprivation**.[9]

   In the case of the civil rights movement, blacks had suffered under Jim Crow segregation laws since the nineteenth century, but resistance had been limited. One event that raised black expectations was World War II. Many African-American men died fighting fascism. Those who returned were less willing to accept second-class citizenship, especially after President Truman integrated the armed forces. Urbanization of blacks following the mechanization of southern agriculture also brought many African Americans into contact with new ideas and new opportunities that raised expectations. Most important, the 1954 Supreme Court decision in *Brown v. Board of Topeka* put the power and prestige of the Supreme Court behind the cause of integration. Black people felt they were not alone. As King put it in his speech the night the black community decided to begin the boycott, "If we are wrong, the Supreme Court of this nation is wrong."

2. *Social resources.* Isolated individuals cannot build social movements. Social movements require networks that can spread the word and involve people in the movement.[10] Social movements need what Sara Evans and Harry Boyte call "free spaces"—organizations located between private families and large public organizations where people can learn self-respect, cooperation, group identity, and the leadership skills necessary for democratic participation.[11] Black churches provided spaces for the civil rights movement that were free from white domination, where blacks could express their true feelings and develop confidence in their abilities. Most of the leadership of the civil rights movement came out of the black churches, where traditions of commitment to the congregation and skills in sermonizing nurtured effective leaders. The national organizations of black Baptist churches formed networks that helped the SCLC spread the Montgomery model throughout the South.

   All protest movements in American history have been nurtured in free spaces. Building on earlier organizations like the Grange, the Populist movement of the late nineteenth century built a vast network of Farmers' Alliances that within a few years involved 2 million families. The purpose of the local alliances was to cooperatively market crops and purchase supplies, but they also created free spaces where people could learn the skills of democracy.[12]

The feminist movement grew out of the free spaces created by the civil rights movement in the South and the anti–Vietnam War movement, which was organized mainly on college campuses. Ironically, it was discrimination in these supposedly egalitarian movements that drove women to form their own movement. In the civil rights movement, women, who performed much of the crucial behind-the-scenes work, developed confidence in their abilities and learned the skills of political organizing. At the same time, they were excluded from decision making and public leadership roles. When women in the Student Nonviolent Coordinating Committee (SNCC, known as "snick"), the radical student wing of the civil rights movement, raised the issue of sex roles, one of the leaders, Stokely Carmichael, is reported to have said that "the only position for women in SNCC is prone."[13] Such remarks caused many black women to examine gender, along with race, as a cause of discrimination.

Shortly afterward, the rise of black nationalism forced many white women out of the civil rights movement and into the new left, organizing against the Vietnam War. There they found that their concerns about sex roles were ignored, even ridiculed, by white men as well. The clash between the egalitarian ideas of the movement and the unequal sex roles within it was too much to bear. Women began meeting separately in small "consciousness-raising groups" where they could articulate their concerns in a supportive atmosphere. Spreading across the country, consciousness-raising groups became free spaces where women could recognize their common problems and develop the confidence to bring about change.

3. *An appealing moral cause.* Mass movements in the United States fail unless they can appeal to fundamental American values. For example, animal rights activists have a moral cause, but they have been unable to make the transition to a mass movement because most Americans do not believe that animals deserve the same rights as human beings. The civil rights movement, on the other hand, had an appealing moral cause because the demand for equal rights resonated with all Americans. By wrapping itself in Christian values and the rhetoric of equal rights, the movement was nearly impossible to criticize as un-American. Later, when parts of the civil rights movement shifted from the rhetoric of equal rights to the rhetoric of black nationalism and black power, appealing more to African and Muslim traditions, white majority support for the movement swiftly eroded.

4. *Consciousness raising.* When the necessary ingredients are present for a mass movement, a sudden change of political consciousness occurs and people look at political facts differently. Soon after Rosa Parks was arrested, the leaders of Montgomery's black community called for a meeting to discuss what to do. They asked Martin Luther King to address the crowd. King had barely twenty minutes to prepare his speech. That night

the Holt Street Baptist Church was jammed. Loudspeakers amplified the speeches to the crowd that spread over several acres outside. King began slowly, carefully describing the circumstances of the boycott, including the arrest of Rosa Parks, and praising her integrity and "Christian commitment." Then King paused and intoned in his resonant voice, "And you know, my friends, there comes a time when people get tired of being trampled over by the iron feet of oppression." As if releasing years of frustration, the crowd broke instantly into a flood of yeses, cheers, and applause.

Getting to the heart of the matter—the justice of their cause—King continued: "If we are wrong, the Supreme Court of this nation is wrong. If we are wrong—God Almighty is wrong! And we are determined here in Montgomery," King went on quoting the words of an Old Testament prophet, "to work and fight until justice runs down like water, and righteousness like a mighty stream!" The crowd erupted in a release of pent-up emotion.

King's rhetoric seemed to lift the crowd onto a higher level of unity and resolve. Reflecting on the moment at the Holt Street Baptist Church after King's electrifying speech, when Montgomery's black community voted to continue the boycott, Ralph Abernathy described just such a change in consciousness: "The fear that had shackled us across the years—all left suddenly when we were in that church together."[14]

One of the most remarkable changes in consciousness occurred in the so-called "velvet revolutions" that swept across Eastern Europe in 1989. Before then, democratic social movements were violently repressed by Soviet troops and the secret police. In 1989, encouraged by Mikhail Gorbachev's reform leadership of the Soviet Union, the people of Eastern Europe became bolder in their opposition to Soviet domination. Once they realized that the troops would not fire on peaceful demonstrators, people began to mobilize in massive demonstrations. When the fear disappeared and citizens were able to gather together to feel their collective power, people suddenly realized they had the power to overturn communism and institute democratic regimes. Overnight, the Berlin Wall tumbled and communist regimes across Eastern Europe fell to democratic movements. That same year, however, a similar democratic social movement in Beijing's Tiananmen Square was brutally suppressed by Chinese troops.

5. *Transformational leadership.* The leaders of parties and interest groups are usually **transactional leaders**, who broker mutually beneficial exchanges between their followers and elites, such as votes for patronage jobs or campaign contributions for tax breaks. Mass movements, however, require **transforming leaders**, who engage the full personalities of followers, teaching them to go beyond self-interest and express their commitments in direct political action.[15] Martin Luther King Jr. was such a leader, who challenged his followers to live up to their highest moral

NEW IDEAS

Campus Anti-Sweatshop Movement

Have you ever wondered who makes all the sweat-shirts, mugs, and other things with the university logo that are sold in your college bookshop? Oddly enough, it is mostly highly exploited workers, mainly women and children, in Third World sweatshops. The Union of Needletrades, Industrial & Textile Employees (UNITE) calculated that whereas a major university may receive as much as $1.50 for each $19.95 baseball cap sold, workers in the Dominican Republic producing those caps earn only about 8 cents. This discrepancy has stirred moral outrage.

The anti-sweatshop movement came to life after a series of disclosures in 1995 and 1996 publicized the shocking labor conditions in the apparel industry. Campus action groups have made it clear to the world that Americans do not want to buy clothing that is made in sweatshops. Students on more than 200 campuses have successfully demanded that college and university administrators guarantee that clothing made with college insignias not be made under sweatshop conditions in poor coun-tries. Students have organized demonstrations, engaged in sit-ins, and undertaken hunger strikes.

The anti-sweatshop movement is the largest wave of student activism to hit campuses since students rallied to free Nelson Mandela by calling for a halt to university investments in South Africa more than a decade ago. In a world economy increasingly dominated by giant retailers and manufacturers that control global networks of independently owned factories, organizing consumers may prove to be a precondition for organizing production workers. The student movement is an important by-product of the labor movement's recent efforts to repair the rift between students and unions that dates back to the Vietnam War.

The concern with university-licensed apparel is best understood in the context of the apparel industry that has increasingly relocated production to Third World nations, a pattern of industrial relocation reflecting a search for inexpensive labor. There are many instances of abuse that have made

beliefs. Only twenty-six years old, King was articulate and intelligent, having just received a doctorate from Boston University. But according to some participants, he was chosen because, having lived in Montgomery for only a few months, he was completely independent—the white establishment had not yet "put their hand" on him.

Elizabeth Cady Stanton, the early leader of the women's suffrage movement, was also a transforming leader. In 1848, Stanton adapted the language of the Declaration of Independence to the cause of women's rights by writing the Declaration of Sentiments, a kind of bill of rights for women. By word and by example, Stanton encouraged women to step out of their assigned sphere of family and home and become actors in the public sphere of democratic politics. For more than fifty years she lectured, petitioned, organized, and wrote to encourage women to find their public voices.[16]

headlines. On the U.S. island territory of Saipan, a congressional delegation found Chinese guest workers held in virtual bondage, unable to leave their sub-minimum-wage jobs because they could not repay recruiting fees as high as $7,000. The workers were producing clothing, some of it labeled "Made in the U.S.A.," for more than twenty-five companies, including Champion, The Gap, and The Limited.

Brown University is among the pioneers in the campus anti-sweatshop movement. During the winter of 1999, bed sheets painted with political slogans hung out of windows overlooking Brown University's residence halls. The campus echoed with chants of protests. After negotiations between student groups and Brown product licensing officials, the university agreed to require all manufacturers that supply products with the Brown name or University logo to adhere to a code of conduct that respects labor law, worker rights, environmental preservation, and a high standard of business ethics. There are now 135 colleges and universities that have joined the Workers Rights Consortium (WRC), which monitors manufacturing conditions to make sure that goods sold by universities are not made where workers' rights are not respected.

A recent trend in student activism is support of workers' rights for low-wage workers on university campuses. In April 2005 a nineteen-day sit-in (and six-day hunger strike) at the Chancellor's Office of Washington University in St. Louis won the commitment of $1 million toward improved wages and benefits for campus workers, plus a promise to join the WRC. Similar successful protests have occurred at Harvard, Georgetown, Stanford, and scores of other campuses across the nation. Clearly, campus protests have been effective, but, in order to make a bigger dent in the problem, they will need to be coordinated with an invigorated union movement and laws that respect the right to organize in every nation.

Sources: Peter Dreier and Richard Appelbaum, "The Campus Anti-Sweatshop Movement," *The American Prospect* (Fall 1999); "The Shame of Sweatshops," *Consumer Reports*, August 1999, pp. 18–21; Jay R. Mandle, "The Student Anti-Sweatshop Movement: Limits and Potential," *Annals of the American Academy of Political & Social Science* (July 2000): 92–104; Joel Currier, "WU Hunger Strike Followed Similar Campus Protests Nationwide," *St. Louis Post-Dispatch*, April 17, 2005.

PROTEST TACTICS: WALKING A FINE LINE

Although protest tactics can be a powerful political resource, if not properly handled they can explode like dynamite in the faces of those they are designed to help. By its very nature, protest politics is confrontational and tension producing; protestors deliberately provoke those in power to get a reaction from them. Protest leaders face a tactical dilemma: They must push confrontation far enough to satisfy the needs of the protestors for direct action and dramatize the issues to a broader public. If they push too far, however, they can alienate potential supporters or even create a backlash that strengthens their opponents.

Conflict has two benefits for protest movements: First, it mobilizes the protestors themselves, and it captures the attention of bystanders who are moved to support the cause of the protestors. Saul Alinsky was a master practitioner and theoretician of protest politics. In the 1930s, he organized the Back of the Yards area of Chicago, an area made famous by Upton Sinclair's exposé of the meatpacking industry in his muckraking novel *The Jungle*. Alinsky understood the necessity of conflict if disadvantaged people were to gain power. "A PEOPLE'S ORGANIZATION is a conflict group," Alinsky wrote.[17] A good fight against a common enemy unifies an organization, heightens morale, and mobilizes energies.

Second, conflict has the effect, especially if the protesters are viewed as underdogs, of drawing the broader public into the fray, putting pressure on the elites to negotiate. Protest is a form of political ju jitsu; a movement with few political resources can use the strength of its opponent to its own advantage. In Montgomery the indictment of eighty-nine African Americans, including twenty-five ministers, on trumped-up charges of conspiring to boycott brought national attention to the cause. The protesters celebrated the arrests because they knew the media would paint the white establishment as the aggressors and themselves as the underdogs. Later, SCLC orchestrated Project C—for "confrontation"—in Birmingham, Alabama. "Bull" Connor, Birmingham's commissioner of public safety, played his assigned role perfectly, using powerful fire hoses and vicious police dogs against defenseless children. As the media sent out pictures of police brutality, sympathy for the civil rights movement soared.

Protest tactics can backfire, however, if they go too far. A majority of Americans were opposed to the Vietnam War, but when they saw protestors burning the American flag and destroying property, most people sympathized with the government, not the protestors. Similarly, violence against abortion clinics and doctors did not help the pro-life, anti-abortion cause.

One method for coping with this tactical dilemma of how hard to push confrontation is **civil disobedience**, which can be defined as the deliberate violation of the law to dramatize a cause by activists who are willing to accept the punishment of the law. Civil disobedience is not an attempt to evade the law. An act of civil disobedience, such as being arrested while blocking the shipment of arms during the Vietnam War, is done completely in the open, without any violence, and with a sense of moral seriousness. Civil disobedience provides a middle ground between peaceful demonstrations (which are often ignored) and violent confrontations (which can cause a backlash).

The American tradition of civil disobedience can be traced back to Henry David Thoreau (1817–1862). Passionately opposed to slavery and to the Mexican War, which he saw as a fight for the slave masters, Thoreau refused to pay his poll taxes. As a result, he was thrown in prison. In 1849, Thoreau wrote a powerful essay, later titled "Civil Disobedience," in which he maintained that unjust laws should not be obeyed: "The only obligation which I have a right to assume is to do at any time what I think right."[18] Thoreau acted as an individual; he was not part of a mass movement. However, his writings inspired many leaders to incorporate civil disobedience into their movements.

Mohandas K. Gandhi (1869–1948) read Thoreau and incorporated his ideas about civil disobedience into his successful movement to free India from British rule. Gandhi believed that a careful campaign of civil disobedience could mobilize *satyagraha* (pronounced sa-TYA-gra-ha), or "truth force," to persuade opponents of the justice of a cause. Gandhi stressed that movements of civil disobedience must be willing to negotiate at all times, as long as basic principles are not sacrificed.

As a college student, Martin Luther King Jr. read Thoreau, and later he adapted the ideas of Gandhi to American conditions. King did not begin the Montgomery campaign with a planned strategy of nonviolent resistance. Drawn to nonviolence by his religious training, King reflected on the experiences of the civil rights movement and gradually developed a sophisticated philosophy of nonviolent resistance. King was able to adapt to new conditions and learn from the experiences of others. Dissatisfied with the slow progress being made under the leadership of King and the other ministers in SCLC, college students formed SNCC to push a more aggressive grassroots approach to the struggle. King later praised the student sit-ins at lunch counters across the South for having sought nonviolent confrontations with the segregation laws. His "Letter from Birmingham Jail," originally written in the margins of a newspaper and on scraps of toilet paper, has become a classic defense of nonviolent protest that is read the world over.

Mass movement leaders like King often find it difficult to balance the needs of protestors, who demand more and more radical action to express their moral outrage, with the need to appeal for outside support, which usually requires moderation and patience. In the civil rights movement, young blacks became frustrated watching their brothers and sisters being beaten by racist police. In the mid-1960s, the civil rights movement split, with more radical blacks joining the "black power" movement under the leadership of the Black Panther Party for Self-Defense and the Black Muslims, led by the charismatic Malcolm X. The movement never recovered from the split. The issue of integration versus separatism, or black nationalism, divides the African-American community to this day.

THE ELITE RESPONSE TO MASS MOVEMENTS

Notwithstanding repeated elite democratic warnings that mass movements threaten political order, elites have many resources for controlling mass movements. However, it takes as much leadership skill to deflate a mass movement as it does to build one. Political elites have two basic strategies: repression (forcibly attacking the movement) or cooptation (giving in to some of the demands). Political elites face a strategic dilemma that is similar to that faced by mass movements: If they give in too readily, they risk encouraging more militancy and more demands; on the other hand, if they refuse to give in at all and attack the protestors with force, they risk creating public sympathy for the protesters. Essentially, political elites engage in a complex game of chess with mass movements and their leaders.

The accessibility of American political institutions to interest groups has enabled the demands of mass movements to be incorporated into the system. In this way, mass movements are converted into interest groups. Meeting limited demands of protestors deflates the moral indignation of the movement and splits reformers from the radicals. If the white leadership in Montgomery had given in to the initial demands of the boycott to humanize the system of segregation on the buses, the effect would have been to deflate, or at the very least divide, the movement. By refusing to give an inch, the white leadership in Montgomery made a fatal tactical error. Their intransigence fueled the movement and caused the protestors to shift their goal from reforming segregation to ending it altogether.

Skillfully devised reforms, on the other hand, not only can divide the movement but can also draw parts of the leadership into the system to administer the new reforms. A good example is President Lyndon Johnson's War on Poverty, which was partly a response to the civil rights movement and the urban riots of the 1960s. The War on Poverty gave black activists jobs in federal anti-poverty programs, deflecting their energies away from organizing the movement. Militant black leaders were coopted by federal money.[19] Democracies are supposed to operate this way—making concessions in the face of popular pressure. As we discussed in the previous chapter, mass movements provided the pressure that enabled public interest groups to pass reform legislation in the 1960s and 1970s, including new laws on environmental protection, minority rights, and worker safety. Interest group politics, then, is a safety valve that can deflate mass movements.

In choosing a strategy of concessions or cooptation, those defending the status quo have an advantage: Time is on their side; mass movements cannot maintain a fever pitch of activism for long. Delay is one of the best weapons in the hands of elites. When a problem is brought to public awareness by a mass movement, those in power commonly appoint a commission to find a solution. This strategy gives the impression that something is being done without commitment to specific actions. By the time the commission's report comes out, the movement will have lost its momentum. Even if the report recommends significant reforms, there is no guarantee that they will be enacted. A good example is President Johnson's appointment of the Kerner Commission in 1967 to study the causes of the urban riots. The Kerner Commission recommended significant reforms, but very few were ever enacted.[20]

Another tactic used by elites is *tokenism*, responding with insignificant reforms or symbolic gestures to create the impression that serious action is being taken to solve the problem. These symbolic gestures quiet the protestors, but few tangible benefits are delivered. Political scientist Murray Edelman called this "symbolic reassurance."[21] Appointing members of the aggrieved group—minorities, women, or gays, for example—to commissions or highly visible governmental posts is often used to create the impression of change. The leaders of student movements demanding radical changes in college curriculums in the 1960s were often appointed to committees to study the problems and come up with solutions. The opportunity to serve on committees with professors and top administrators was flattering, but the effect was often to separate student leaders from the movement and involve them in a long process of negotiation. The key to the success of cooptation is calming the confrontational atmosphere that feeds mass movements long enough for protestors to lose interest. Once stalled, mass movements are very difficult to restart.

When mass movements reach a certain momentum, the tactic of concessions loses its effectiveness and elites often turn to repression.[22] Just as protesters feel justified in using confrontation and sometimes even violence to promote their causes, elites sometimes feel justified in using repression when mass movements threaten their power or violate the law. The United States has a proud tradition of upholding the civil rights of dissenters, but as Chapter 16 shows, when elites have felt threatened by mass movements, they often have resorted to repression. American labor history is especially violent. Before passage of the Wagner Act in 1935 (which guaranteed workers the right to organize a union), workers trying to gain recognition turned to strikes and picket lines that often became violent. Governments frequently intervened on the side of owners. In 1877, 60,000 National Guardsmen were mobilized across ten states to defeat the first national railroad strike. In the Pullman strike of 1894, President Grover Cleveland, at the request of the railroads, called in federal troops, who, along with municipal police, put down the strike by railroad workers at a cost of thirty-four deaths and millions of dollars of property damage.

THE DEMOCRATIC DEBATE OVER MASS MOVEMENTS

As the name suggests, mass movements involve large numbers of ordinary citizens in direct political actions. The protest tactics used by mass movements are disruptive and confrontational. Therefore, it is not surprising that mass movements and their protest tactics have been the subjects of heated controversy between elite and popular democrats.

Elite Democratic Criticisms of Mass Movements

From the time of Shays's Rebellion, before the Constitution was written, to the violent demonstrations against globalization, elite democrats have always been suspicious of mass movements. Their attitude is reflected in Alexander Hamilton's statement: "The People! The People is a great beast!"[23] The direct involvement of the masses in political action is dangerous, according to elite democrats, because mass movements can quickly degenerate into lawless mobs that threaten stable democracy. It is safer for political passions to be filtered through representative institutions, where elites can deliberate on the long-term interest of the country as a whole.[24]

Elite democrats maintain that the goals of mass movements in American history have often been utopian and impractical. Critics of those who protested Bush's invasion of Iraq charge that the protestors are naive; they don't understand that the UN is impractical and the United States must engage in preemptive war to kill the terrorists before they kill us. The Populist movement at the turn of the nineteenth century was attacked as an emotional reaction to progress and industrialization, an ill-fated attempt to hold on to a doomed agrarian way of life. (The contemporary environmental movement has been attacked on similar grounds.) According to elite democrats, mass movements lack concrete programs for reform that can benefit the people involved; instead, they seek moral or ideological goals that are unrealizable and threaten to overwhelm democratic institutions. Lacking practical reforms, mass movements traffic in moral absolutes.[25]

Elite democrats criticize not only the goals of mass movements but also their tactics. In stable democracies, participation is channeled through representative institutions and interest group bargaining. Protest politics brings masses of people into direct participation through confrontational tactics that threaten to divide society into warring camps, elite democrats warn, and undermine the norms of tolerance and civility essential to a healthy democracy. Mass movements are not expressions of people's natural desire to participate in politics. Instead, people are enticed into mass movements by demagogues who manipulate emotions, whipping up resentment against the wealthy and the privileged.

Protest tactics can easily get out of hand, elite democrats charge. People in large crowds, or mobs, are incapable of thinking rationally and often do things that, upon reflection, they would never do. Elite democrats favor orderly interest group politics over mass movement politics. One scholar summed up the elite democratic position this way: "Mass politics involve irrationality and chaos; group politics produce sensible and orderly conflict."[26] In short, mass movements are dangerous to democracy.

The Popular Democratic Defense of Mass Movements

The attitude of popular democrats toward mass movements is reflected in a statement by Thomas Jefferson. Remarking on Shays's Rebellion, which Federalists viewed as a sign of impending anarchy, Jefferson wrote to James Madison: "I hold it that a little rebellion now and then is a good thing, and as necessary in the political world as storms in the physical."[27] After all, popular democrats note, the country was born in protest. The Boston Tea Party was an illegal destruction of property intended to dramatize the colonists' opposition to British rule, in particular "taxation without representation."

According to popular democrats, periodic elections and interest group bargaining are inadequate to fulfill the participatory promise of American democracy. Popular democrats see mass movements as ways for the people to communicate directly with the government, unimpeded by experts or elites. Protest tactics enable people to engage their full personality and most deeply held beliefs in the democratic process.

Popular democrats maintain that protest politics is necessary for greater equality in the American political system. Mass movement politics is one arena that is not biased in favor of wealthy elites. Throughout American history, most significant reforms have come about because of pressure from below by mass movements. Protest politics is not only a way to vent emotions but also a way to overcome the inertia of the American system of checks and balances, to bring about much-needed change. Far from threatening democracy, mass movements fulfill it by including more and more groups in the benefits of democratic citizenship. The primary threat to democracy comes not from mass movements but from elites who use repression to block change and hang on to their powers and privileges.

Sixties-Style Protest Movements: Elite Backlash

The democratic debate over the place of protest politics in American democracy became especially heated following the rapid rise of social protest movements beginning in the 1960s. Many of these movements are still active in various forms in the new century, including protests on issues such as the environment, AIDS, homelessness, migrant farm workers, and community opposition to unwanted development. Beginning with the 1970s protests against busing in Boston, conservatives adopted the tactics of the civil rights movement to oppose abortion and taxes. The Montana militia and other far-right groups have used violent tactics to support their antigovernment cause.

According to elite democrats, the spread of political protest since the 1960s threatens American democracy. Elite democrats criticize both the goals and the tactics of the protest movements. The goals, they maintain, are irrational and utopian. For example, business elites criticize the environmental movement for putting environmental goals above everything else. Instead of compromising, opponents charge, environmentalists demand an end to all ecological damage, even at tremendous cost to the American standard of living. According to elite democrats, environmental activists with secure white-collar professional jobs demand sacrifice from blue-collar workers in the name of environmental purity. Like earlier mass movements, the environmental movement is charged with being against progress, with wanting to turn the clock back to a simpler age. In general, social movements encourage every group—from blacks to women, from Native Americans to gays, from students to the disabled—to demand their "rights" with little concern for the general welfare of society.

Elite democrats also criticize the tactics developed by the protest movements beginning in the 1960s. The tactics of protest, elite democrats charge, began to be used by any group that wanted to "shake more benefits from the government money tree." In a biting essay satirizing the 1960s, titled "Mau-Mauing the Flak Catchers," Tom Wolfe described how protest tactics had gotten out of hand:

> Going downtown to mau-mau the bureaucrats got to be routine practice in San Francisco. . . . They sat back and waited for you to come rolling in with your certified angry militants, your guaranteed frustrated ghetto youth, looking like a bunch of wild men. Then you had your test confrontation. If you were outrageous enough, if you could shake up the bureaucrats so bad that their eyes froze into iceballs and their mouths twisted up into smiles of sheer

physical panic, into shit-eating grins, so to speak—then they knew you were the real goods. They knew you were the right studs to give the poverty grants and community organizing jobs to.[28]

According to an editorial in the *Wall Street Journal*, the murder of abortion doctor David Gunn in Pensacola, Florida, on March 10, 1993, by an anti-abortion protestor is evidence that protest politics has gotten out of control. Protest movements have created a new political culture, the elite business publication charged, that encourages every group to express its needs without concern for the overall welfare of society:

> What in the past had been simply illegal became "civil disobedience." If you could claim, and it was never too hard to claim, that your group was engaged in an act of civil disobedience—taking over a building, preventing a government official from speaking, bursting onto the grounds of a nuclear cooling station, destroying animal research, desecrating communion hosts—the shapers of opinion would blow right past the broken rules to seek an understanding of the "dissidents" (in the '60s and '70s) and "activists" (in the '80s and now).[29]

By encouraging people to pressure government, elite democrats maintain, protest movements weaken the authority of government at the same time that the demands on government are multiplying. Political scientist Samuel Huntington said the problem was caused by an excess of democracy, or what he termed the "democratic distemper."[30] In the 1960s and 1970s, as people made more and more demands on government to solve their problems, government responded with massive social programs, "overloading" the system."[31] The result was increasing fiscal deficits and a governmental tendency to cater to minority interests at the expense of the public interest.

At the same time that citizens demanded more from government, however, they were unwilling to sanction governmental authority and thus perversely rendered government less able to satisfy their demands. As a result, the public's trust and confidence in government declined. As Huntington warned, "The surge of participatory democracy and egalitarianism gravely weakened, where it did not demolish, the likelihood that anyone in any institution could give an order to someone else and have it promptly obeyed."[32] In short, as the politics of protest spread, society became ungovernable.

The Popular Democratic Response: Elite Distemper

Although popular democrats acknowledge excesses in social protest movements, they argue that, overall, direct participation by citizens in protests has strengthened American democracy rather than weakened it. Whenever long-suppressed issues are finally addressed by a political system, conflict is bound to result. Conflict is inevitable in a democracy—and healthy. The main threat to democracy comes not from a "democratic distemper"—ordinary people demanding their rights—but from an "elite distemper": elites, fearful of losing their powers and privileges, reacting to protestors with repression and violence.[33]

Ironically, the civil rights movement, which was committed to nonviolence and democratic rights, had its civil liberties repeatedly violated by the government in an attempt to discredit it, and especially its charismatic leader, Martin Luther King Jr. The Federal Bureau of Investigation (FBI) secretly planted newspaper articles alleging that the movement was manipulated by communists. Convincing evidence for this charge has never been made public. Under the direction of FBI Chief J. Edgar Hoover, the FBI treated King as an enemy, employing a campaign of character assassination using wiretaps of King's phone conversations. The FBI fed information on King's sex life and the plans of the civil rights movement to the Kennedy administration, helping it to resist pressures for racial change.[34] The FBI sent King a tape of his extramarital encounters, threatening to make them public if he did not commit suicide.[35]

Another example of elite repression is the campaign of the government under presidents Johnson and Nixon against the anti–Vietnam War movement. Viewing opposition to the war almost as an act of treason, the government harassed antiwar leaders, violated civil liberties, and infiltrated antiwar organizations to spread dissension. In 1968, antiwar protestors organized a demonstration at the Democratic National Convention in Chicago. Denied permission to hold a rally near the convention, the protestors were infiltrated by FBI and Chicago police **agents provocateurs** who spread disinformation and encouraged protestors to violate the law. When demonstrators tried to march on the convention, police attacked, clubbing not just demonstrators but journalists and bystanders as well. As outraged demonstrators chanted, "The whole world is watching!" news cameras recorded the ugly scene for a shocked TV audience.[36] The commission appointed to study the causes of the conflict put most of the blame on the city administration and concluded that the police had rioted.[37]

The Chicago riots polarized public opinion about the war. Some people, especially blacks and younger college-educated whites, sympathized with the demonstrators and felt that the police had used excessive force. However, most Americans were repulsed by what they saw as mobs of long-haired radicals hurling curses at the police and waving communist flags.[38] Gradually, public opinion shifted against the war. Nevertheless, the war continued, frustrating antiwar protestors and shaking their faith in American democracy. In the so-called Days of Rage, antiwar activists launched indiscriminate acts of violence and destruction in American cities to "bring the war home." The cycle of repression and violence precipitated by the Vietnam War deeply divided the country, stretching the fabric of American democracy to the breaking point. According to popular democrats, the fault lay more with the elites responsible for the war and for repressing legitimate dissent than with the protesters.

In the past decade, corporate elites have devised a new way to suppress protest movements that oppose oil drilling and real estate developments such as shopping centers and airports. SLAPPs (Strategic Legal Action Against Public Participation) are lawsuits against protestors designed to chill protests by burdening them with expensive and time-consuming lawsuits. Thousands of protestors have been hit with SLAPPs charging them with harassment and violation of property rights.

The Achievements of Mass Movements

Perhaps the most serious charge against protest movements is that they don't accomplish anything; they simply stir people up and create conflict. Popular democrats maintain that protest movements have not been mere expressions of emotion; they have been the driving force behind reforms that made this country more egalitarian and democratic, including abolishing slavery, winning the vote for women and blacks, and regulating corporations. Pursuing normal channels of electoral and interest group politics, many groups find it difficult even to get their issues onto the agenda for discussion. Protest movements have succeeded in putting previously ignored issues, like equal rights for black Americans, onto the political agenda.

Measuring the effectiveness of protest movements is difficult because their effects are often hidden and indirect. As we noted in the previous chapter, new issues represented by public interest groups never would have made it onto the agenda of interest group politics without the threat of protest movements to goad the system into action. Protest movements have "ripple effects" that extend beyond the initial splash to affect the entire society. These ripple effects include changes in culture and the way we perceive issues.

In the controversy over protest politics, we often lose sight of the wide range of reforms enacted by mass movements. A few of their accomplishments follow.

1. *The civil rights movement.* The civil rights movement began the long process of integrating African Americans into the democratic process. Largely as a result of changes in voting laws, the number of African-American elected officials in the United States increased from 1,469 in 1970 to 9,061 in 2001 (see Figure 10.2). Critics often point out that U.S. race relations are still highly problematic. However, consider what race relations would be like if African Americans were still being denied basic civil rights like the right to vote.

2. *The environmental movement.* As a result of the environmental movement, large construction projects must now issue environmental impact statements (EISs), giving the public a chance to comment. Substantial progress has also been made in cleaning up the nation's polluted waters, with aquatic life returning to many bodies of water, and in communities across the nation, recycling programs are saving energy and reducing the volume of solid waste (see the "Closer Look" box, p. 317).

3. *The neighborhood organizing movement.* Neighborhood protests, including lying down in front of bulldozers, stopped highway engineers and urban renewal planners from ramming their projects through low-income and minority neighborhoods without taking into account the costs to local residents. Many cities in the country now have decentralized policy-making authority to neighborhood governments, expanding the scope of democratic participation.[39]

4. *The antinuclear movement.* The antinuclear movement succeeded in pushing the regulatory agencies to fully consider the dangers of nuclear power

FIGURE 10.2 African-American Elected Officials, 1970–2001

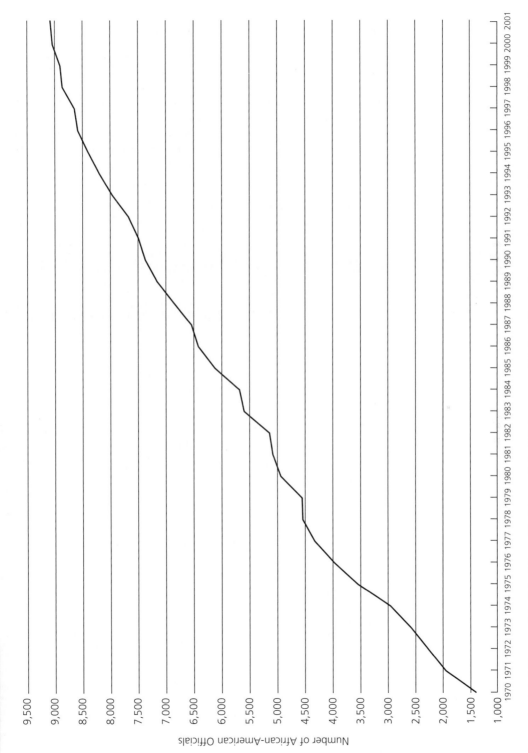

Number of African-American Officials

1970 1971 1972 1973 1974 1975 1976 1977 1978 1979 1980 1981 1982 1983 1984 1985 1986 1987 1988 1989 1990 1991 1992 1993 1994 1995 1996 1997 1998 1999 2000 2001

9,500

9,000

8,500

8,000

7,500

7,000

6,500

6,000

5,500

5,000

4,500

4,000

3,500

3,000

2,500

2,000

1,500

1,000

Source: Statistical Abstract of the United States (Washington, D.C.: U.S. Government Printing Office, various years); and *Black Elected Officials: A National Roster* (Washington, D.C.: Joint Center for Political Studies, annual).

plants. As a result, few new nuclear power plants are constructed in the United States anymore. The chances of a Chernobyl-type disaster are low, and alternatives to nuclear energy, including solar energy and conservation, are being pursued more vigorously.

5. *The gay rights movement.* As a result of years of protests, many state and local governments have passed laws protecting the rights of gays and lesbians, freeing them from employment discrimination, for example, and giving them the right to adopt children. Opposition to recent efforts to give recognition to gay civil unions, so-called "gay marriage," played a significant role in the 2004 election.

6. *The feminist movement.* Probably the most influential of all, the feminist movement transformed American society, opening opportunities for women that were previously unthinkable. As a result, there are now many more women doctors and lawyers, as well as mail carriers, construction workers, and movie directors. Women's wages have steadily gained relative to men. Title IX of the 1972 Higher Education Act opened collegiate sports to women. Thousands of battered women's shelters and rape crisis shelters have opened in communities across the country. The feminist movement even altered our language, introducing new terms such as *Ms.* and *chairperson.*

Is the Christian Right a Popular Democratic Mass Movement?

A new kind of mass movement has arisen in recent years—a movement that uses the tactics of protest but has very different goals than earlier movements. The Christian Right, as it is known, has all the trappings of popular democracy: a deep sense of grievance or even persecution (by what are often referred to as "secular humanists"), broad-based, grassroots networks, and a populist rhetoric of "the people" versus the (liberal) elite. Despite all outward appearances, however, the Christian Right is very different from the democratic mass movements that have struggled over the years to make American democracy more inclusive.

The Christian Right, particularly its anti-abortion movement, has self-consciously modeled itself on the civil rights movement. Operation Rescue trains people in civil disobedience. Protestors block abortion clinic entrances and thousands have been arrested, giving priceless publicity to the cause. Like the civil rights movement, churches are the central resource for the Christian Right. Ministers play key roles in the movement and, like Dr. King, they regularly employ biblical language to legitimate their cause. Finally, like the civil rights movement, the goals of the Christian Right are moral goals that cannot be easily compromised within the political system. This is most true of the primary goal of the Christian Right, banning abortion, but it is also true of their other goals, such as banning stem cell research, gay marriage, and euthanasia; and allowing prayer in schools, alternatives to the teaching of Darwinian evolution, and public display of the Ten Commandments.

A CLOSER LOOK

The Environmental Justice Movement

According to conventional wisdom, the mass movements of the 1960s and 1970s died out in the 1980s and 1990s. Although fewer mass demonstrations in Washington capture media attention, mass movement politics did not die; it simply shifted its focus. A good example is the environmental justice movement, a unique combination of the civil rights and environmental movements.

From its inception, the environmental movement was dominated by white, middle-class activists. In September 1982, however, 500 predominantly black residents of Warren County, North Carolina, were arrested for blocking the path of trucks carrying toxic PCBs to a hazardous landfill in their community. Among those arrested was the Reverend Benjamin Chavis. Suspicious as to why North Carolina would dump its poisons in a black community, Chavis began a nationwide study titled *Toxic Wastes and Race in the United States*. The study concluded that "race was consistently a more prominent factor in the location of commercial hazardous waste facilities than any other factor examined." Chavis coined the term *environmental racism* to describe the phenomenon. (In April 1993 Chavis was appointed executive director of the NAACP; he was removed from the post in August 1994.)

Subsequent studies by the federal government and independent researchers have confirmed that African Americans, even after controlling for income, are exposed to more environmental hazards. According to the data, poor blacks are exposed to neurologically damaging levels of lead at almost twice the rate of the poorest whites, blacks are twice as likely as whites to live in counties with the highest levels of industrial toxins, and blacks are 50 percent more likely to die from acute exposure to hazardous materials outside the home.

A loose coalition of church, civil rights, labor, environmental, and community groups, the environmental justice movement has been led by blacks. Like the early civil rights movement, however, it has not pursued an exclusively black strategy but has articulated goals that appeal to whites as well. As Chavis expressed it, "We're not saying take the incinerators and toxic-waste dumps out of our communities and put them in white communities—we're saying they should not be in anybody's community. You can't get justice by doing an injustice on somebody else."

In fighting environmental racism, the movement has raised basic issues of popular democracy. In Kettleman City, California, residents organized themselves into "People for Clean Air and Water" in opposition to a hazardous waste incinerator. They sued the company building the incinerator, charging that it violated their civil rights by failing to provide notices about the plant in Spanish (40 percent of the residents are monolingual Spanish speakers). A California court ruled in their favor, setting a precedent that communities must be informed and participate meaningfully in environmental decisions that affect them.

Heightened awareness of the issue and the willingness of people to use protest tactics against efforts to "dump" on the communities has made companies think twice when locating hazardous facilities. "Companies now just don't bully in," said Robert Bullard, a prominent researcher on the issue. "When they do, they're in for a rude awakening. There is no path of least resistance any more."

Sources: "A Place at the Table: A Sierra Club Roundtable on Race, Justice, and the Environment," *Sierra* 78 (May/June 1993): 51–58, 90–91; Benjamin A. Goldman, "Polluting the Poor," *Nation*, October 5, 1992, pp. 348–49; Dave Bryan, "Minority Groups Mobilize on Pollution: Alabama Town's Battle for PCB Cleanup Reflects Fight Against 'Environmental Racism,'" Associated Press, April 6, 2003.

Although the goals of the Christian Right are moral in nature, they do not fit easily within the popular democratic tradition. Popular democratic movements like the abolitionist movement, the women's suffrage/feminist movement, and the civil rights movement, all sought to expand democratic participation and citizenship. The Christian Right is basically a "backlash" movement whose goal is to roll back many of the civil and political rights won by the social movements of the 1960s and 1970s. The Christian Right aims to roll back rights for gays, even to the point of making consensual homosexual sex a crime (upholding sodomy laws), and it generally opposes additional rights for immigrants. The goal of the movement is to end women's right to abortion and Christian fundamentalists favor a more traditional role for women focused on, if not confined to, the family. Although the concern with Internet pornography is not exclusionary, laws censoring the Internet could threaten free speech rights. Finally, the Christian Right's support of Bush's aggressive go-it-alone foreign policy, with its emphasis on military force, contradicts popular democracy's long-standing concern with executive power and opposition to an imperial foreign policy.

Just as important as the exclusive cultural issues of the Christian Right is the support the movement has given to elitist economic policies. *Unlike any other mass movement in American history*, the Christian Right has formed a strategic alliance with wealthy elites and large corporations. The Christian Right has consistently supported Bush's tax cuts for the wealthy and the deregulation of the economy favored by big business. The movement is generally anti-union and believes that anyone can succeed in the free market without government help. Pastor Ted Haggard presides over the National Association of Evangelicals (NAE), with 30 million members the nation's most powerful religious lobbying organization. According to Haggard, free market capitalism is "truth" and "globalization is merely a vehicle for the spread of Christianity."[40] This represents a break with the past. Historically, churches have often allied themselves with the labor union and populist movements, supporting the working class and small farmers against large corporations.

Although the Christian Right started out as a fervent movement of outsiders who felt threatened by secular trends in modern culture, it has now become a powerful player in electoral and interest group politics. The pattern is similar to what happened to the labor movement, which became institutionalized in the AFL-CIO, and the civil rights movement that has now faded away leaving behind groups like the NAACP to represent its issues. The Christian Right is a powerful faction within the Republican Party with virtual control over the party platform and veto power over vice presidential nominees. One of the key organizations in the Christian Right is the Christian Coalition, founded by Pat Robertson after his failed 1988 presidential run. In 1999 the Christian Coalition lost its tax-exempt status as a nonpartisan group when the IRS determined that it worked too closely with the Republican Party. In 2004, the Christian Coalition claims to have distributed 70 million voter guides supporting conservative issues and candidates.

The elite connections of the Christian Right became clear in the case of Terri Schiavo, the young woman whose feeding tube was removed after she lived fifteen years in a "persistent vegetative state." Operation Rescue and other Christian Right groups held vigils outside Schiavo's hospice, calling for federal courts to intervene to prevent the feeding tube from being removed. Remarkably, the protestors succeeded in getting Republican Party leaders in Congress to hurriedly pass a law, which President Bush signed, requiring federal courts to once again review the decision of the Florida courts. (The federal courts refused to reverse earlier rulings, Schiavo's feeding tube was removed, and she died thirteen days later.) In this case, a few hundred protestors succeeded even though public opinion polls showed a clear majority of Americans opposed congressional intervention.

CONCLUSION: THE FUTURE OF PROTEST POLITICS

Some argue that protest today has become almost a routine part of American politics and that protestors are more concerned with venting their anger than with achieving important democratic reforms. Instead of enhancing politics, protest has become a substitute for politics.[41] We disagree.

Protest politics provides three important benefits for American democracy. First, on those rare occasions when the proper ingredients come together, mass movements can level the playing field of American politics, offering a way for minorities and the politically disenfranchised to acquire influence. Second, protest movements provide a way to overcome the inertia created by the elaborate system of checks and balances established by the Constitution, enabling political outsiders, especially those with broad political or moral concerns, to get their issues on the agenda. Finally, participation in protest activity creates better citizens. Research shows that compared to nonprotestors, activists who participated in the social movements of the 1960s later participated more in politics, exhibited greater degrees of tolerance, and retained a passionate commitment to their ideals (even those who acquired fortunes).[42]

Popular democratic protests are not dead. Besides opposition to Bush's militaristic foreign policy and rejection of the UN, the most likely candidate for the next mass movement is opposition to corporate-led globalization. The World Trade Organization (WTO) is an elite-dominated organization whose job is to enforce free trade agreements. Meeting in secret with little democratic accountability, gatherings of the WTO have been greeted by large protests, including the infamous 1999 "Battle in Seattle." Globalization protestors are not opposed to free trade, which has many benefits for consumers, but to the way WTO rulings undermine the sovereign powers of nations to protect their environment, consumers, workers, and human rights. The term "free trade" obscures the fact that countries like China are able to export products made with slave labor and keep wages low by outlawing independent unions. Scholars agree that the globalization of the economy is a major cause of rising income inequality in the United States. The issue of corporate-led globalization could produce the first truly global mass movement for democratic rights.

Notwithstanding the many benefits of protest politics, however, lines must be drawn around it. There is some truth to the elite democratic critique that giving protestors complete freedom to disrupt people's lives and to engage in civil disobedience without punishment would enable minorities to dictate terms to society. Violent protestors who injure other people should be swiftly punished. On the other hand, to outlaw nonviolent boycotts, strikes, pickets, and marches and to severely punish civil disobedience would stifle protest politics altogether. Recognizing this, the courts have given special protection to political speech designed to influence public opinion. We believe that if society errs in any direction, it should err in the direction of tolerating more protest activity.

Beyond the courts, the best protection from the destructive effects of protest politics should come from the protestors themselves. Protests should never be carried out simply to vent emotions or shake people up; the purpose should be to enter into negotiations with the powers that be to institute significant reforms. As a well-known book on black political advancement in California cities, *Protest Is Not Enough*,[43] argued, the goal of protests should be to reform the basic structures of democratic governance so that they can respond to the deeply felt issues of every group in the population. Until that time, however, protest politics will be necessary to keep the participatory promise of American democracy alive.

KEY TERMS

protest politics
mass movement
relative deprivation
transactional leader

transforming leader
civil disobedience
satyagraha
agent provocateur

INTERNET RESOURCES

■ AFL-CIO
www.aflcio.org/corporateamerica/stop/
A website sponsored by the AFL-CIO labor federation that contains information on the anti-sweatshop movement on college campuses.

■ Christian Coalition
www.cc.org
Information and links from one of the nation's most powerful Christian Right organizations.

■ NAACP
www.naacp.org
Official website of the NAACP, containing information on issues important to African Americans.

▓ Association of Community Organizations for Reform Now (ACORN)
www.acorn.org
ACORN organizes low-income communities for direct action on issues like housing and banking.

SUGGESTED READINGS

Saul D. Alinsky, *Reveille for Radicals*. New York: Vintage Books, 1969. A classic statement by one of the great theoreticians and practitioners of protest politics in the United States.

Thomas Frank, *What's the Matter with Kansas: How Conservatives Won the Heart of America*. New York: Henry Holt, 2004. Tells how anti-abortion activists took over the Republican Party in Kansas, distracting the electorate from fundamental economic issues.

Samuel Huntington, *American Politics: The Promise of Disharmony*. Cambridge, Mass.: Harvard University Press, 1981. A critique of mass movement politics from an elite democratic viewpoint.

Francis Fox Piven and Richard A. Cloward, *Poor People's Movements: Why They Succeed, How They Fail*. New York: Pantheon, 1977. Argues that when poor people's movements turn into interest groups, they become coopted and cease to represent the interests of the poor.

Juan Williams, *Eyes on the Prize: America's Civil Rights Years 1954–1965*. New York: Penguin Books, 1988. A vivid account of the civil rights movement, produced in conjunction with a riveting television documentary that is available on videotape.

11

Congress
A Vehicle for Popular Democracy?

As the most representative branch of American national government, Congress might be expected to speak for the concerns, grievances, and interests of popular democracy. Popular democrats have often hoped that Congress would live up to its name as the "people's branch"—a branch filled with citizen–lawmakers, accessible to citizens who wished to be heard, open to citizens who wished to hear its deliberations, resistant to arbitrary action and secrecy from the executive.

Yet as we saw in Chapters 5–10, the active and assertive citizenry that might bring out Congress's popular democratic potential is undermined by many contemporary developments. With a mass media dominated by corporate interests and official sources, with parties in decline among the electorate, with "democracy for hire" for wealthy interest groups while a majority of eligible voters fail to turn out for congressional elections, the forces to which Congress responds are as likely to represent elite democracy as popular democracy.

The democratic character of Congress has, in fact, always been a matter of controversy. The Federalists designed the House to be more democratic and the Senate more elitist, but hoped that representatives in both houses would be superior men who would filter out the people's passions and promote their true welfare. The Anti-federalists, worried that legislators of this elite stripe would become arrogant and corrupt, argued for representatives who would closely resemble ordinary people. Some of the Federalists' and Anti-federalists' hopes have been realized—and some of their fears as well. Present-day Congress is a volatile mixture of elite and popular democracy.

Elite democracy, as the Federalists hoped, is reflected in a membership of well-educated political professionals whose lengthy careers produce expertise in the various fields of public policy. Elite democracy, as the Anti-federalists warned, is reflected in a membership whose continuance in office is financed by economic elites and rewarded with aristocratic "perks" of high office. Yet Congress still remains open to the pressure of popular democracy. With members of the House facing reelection every two years and senators facing the voters every six years (as a result of the Seventeenth Amendment, adopted in 1913), representatives need to stay in close touch with their constituents if they hope to enjoy a career in Congress.

To an increasing number of Americans in the late 1980s and early 1990s, congressional elitism was more apparent than congressional populism. But could Congress be cleansed of elitist corruptions and reshaped as a vehicle for popular democratic aspirations? When the Republicans took control of Congress in 1995, after four decades in which the Democrats had always controlled the House and usually controlled the Senate, they promised just such a revolution. The leader of the Republican revolution, Newt Gingrich, claimed that he had a program to take Congress away from Washington elites and return it to the American people. Gingrich and the Republicans delivered on their pledge to bring about changes in Congress. But did these changes result in gains for popular democracy?

This chapter examines Congress through the prism of the Republican revolution. We begin by examining Congress before the revolution. Here, we explain the enduring features of Congress but also emphasize the distinctive ways that Congress operated in the years before 1995—an era in which it was ordinarily under the control of the Democrats. Next, we turn to examine the revolution itself, the dramatic attempt in 1995 by the newly triumphant Republicans to transform how Congress works. This revolution was powerful but short-lived, its limits already apparent by the end of 1995 in the showdown between the congressional Republicans and President Clinton over the budget. "Congress after the Revolution" shows how the changes introduced by the Republicans in 1995 left in their wake a stronger partisan leadership and a deeply polarized

Congress. In the final section of the chapter, we examine executive–legislative relations, as Congress (before, during, and after the revolution) grapples with its sometime partner and more frequent adversary.

CONGRESS BEFORE THE REVOLUTION

Congress has some permanent elements, based in the Constitution, and some near-permanent features, such as the committee system, that go back to the nineteenth century. But much of the landscape of Congress, as unchanging as it may appear to frustrated reformers, is periodically reshaped by socioeconomic, political, and institutional tides. Above all, Congress is susceptible to partisan forces. The congressional revolution of 1995 was a *Republican* revolution. And to understand Congress before this revolution is to understand Congress during the decades when it was mostly under *Democratic* control.[1]

How did Congress work before the revolution of 1995? Four factors, in *descending order of importance*, appeared to be important:

1. Individual members and their districts

2. Committees

3. Parties

4. Leadership

As we will see, the Republican revolutionaries of 1995 attempted no less than a reversal of this order.

Individual Members and Their Districts

Most political scientists' explanations of congressional behavior before 1995 placed the individual members first in importance. Individual members were extensively involved in a permanent quest for reelection that oriented them toward the interests of their own districts or states. Their voting behavior and nonlegislative activities were designed to secure individual success by pleasing the electorate back home. The decentralized structures of Congress also encouraged individualism, with members promoting their favorite policy ideas in entrepreneurial fashion. (While we use the past tense to describe activities before 1995, many of the features of Congress that we describe in this section still persist.)

Getting Elected. At the heart of congressional individualism was the electoral process. In earlier eras of American politics, the parties played a major role in recruiting congressional candidates, financing their campaigns, and mobilizing voters on their behalf. But in an era of party decline, the typical congressional candidate was self-selected. Successful candidates usually shared certain characteristics: First, they were experienced public officials, having gained visibility and stature in such offices as mayors, district attorneys, or state legislators. Second, they were ambitious—running for Congress requires an ego strong enough to overcome attacks and insults and to compensate for loss of privacy, family time, and more lucrative career opportunities. Third, they were willing to work hard—a congressional race required physical and emotional energy. Amazing feats of campaigning were not uncommon. In a successful 1974 bid for a House seat in South Dakota, Larry Pressler shook an estimated 300 to 500 hands a day for 80 days.[2]

Even individuals possessing all of these qualifications faced one daunting barrier: **Incumbents** were almost always reelected in House elections, and in Senate elections challengers had only a slightly better chance. Unless there was an open seat (the incumbent has retired or died), the odds against the aspiring candidate winning a congressional race would scare off all but the hardiest political gamblers. In the House, incumbents regularly won over 90 percent of the contests. Sometimes, as in 1986 and 1988, incumbent reelection rates ran as high as 98 percent. Senate incumbents were often nearly as successful. The aspiring candidate had the greatest chance to win at a moment of political turmoil, such as 1986 or 1992, when incumbents were more vulnerable.[3]

Why did incumbents do so well and challengers so poorly? Many factors favored the incumbent, including money. With years in office to stockpile campaign funds, the incumbent generally had an enormous head start in fundraising. As discussed in Chapter 8, special interests and business PACs, seeking access to legislators (and assuming that those in office are good bets to be reelected), contributed primarily to incumbents. As a result, the typical incumbent had a huge advantage over the typical challenger in campaign funds. However, there was a major drawback for the individual member in this system: the frequently demeaning and seemingly endless process of hitting up wealthy contributors for campaign dough.

Since even fundraising advantages could not guarantee reelection, members of Congress voted themselves further resources to keep their offices. Through the **franking privilege**, they sent mass mailings to constituents without having to pay postage. For example, newsletters publicized their accomplishments and often asked constituents to express their views on major national issues, portraying incumbents skilled in the ways of Washington yet open to the sentiments of the folks back home. Through generous travel allowances, members returned to their districts often, attending group meetings, mingling at ceremonial events, and making their faces as familiar as possible. Benefiting from the growth of personal staff, members could assign staffers in their district offices to help constituents facing problems with federal agencies, a practice known as **casework**. Casework earned the gratitude of individual voters and enhanced the incumbents' reputations among their family and friends.

All of these advantages made it more likely that on election day the voters would recall the names of incumbents while not knowing the people challenging them. Such advantages in fact tended to scare off the kind of politically experienced challengers who might give incumbents a difficult race.

Why was incumbency somewhat less powerful in the Senate than in the House? As a more prestigious institution (and with only two positions per state), the Senate draws more prominent individuals into challenges to incumbents. Such individuals have a better chance of raising the funds to conduct a serious campaign. Statewide constituencies reduce incumbents' opportunities to mingle with them while necessitating more reliance on mass media, through which well-financed challengers can hope to match incumbents in name recognition. Finally, senators' positions on controversial national issues are more visible to constituents than those of House members, leading to greater vulnerability should the incumbent have taken unpopular stands.

The Permanent Campaign. Incumbents would not have won reelection at such impressive rates if they had not devoted so much of their time, energy, and resources to it *between* electoral campaigns. Leading scholars of congressional politics saw the ceaseless pursuit of reelection as the key to congressional behavior. They showed how legislators made themselves familiar "brand names" in their districts through visits home, newsletters, interviews on local TV, and announcements of federal projects bringing jobs and dollars to local folks. They pointed out how members of Congress took credit for creating new programs that inevitably expanded the federal bureaucracy—and then denounced the evils of bureaucracy and took credit again by assisting constituents in their problems with bureaucrats. And they revealed how representatives developed attractive personal images crafted to appeal to constituents and to win their trust.[4]

These scholars suggested that representatives devoted huge amounts of their time and thinking to wooing constituents. An aloof legislator with an aristocratic style, in the classic vein of elite democracy, would not stand a chance today. Yet because representatives had to appear to be just one of the folks did not mean that Congress had become a vehicle for popular democracy. While currying favor with voters through blatant appeals to self-interest and pleasing images, representatives did not appeal to voters' intelligence or speak to them about a larger common good. Nor did they really attempt to encourage meaningful participation in politics, as anyone knows who has filled out a survey in a congressional newsletter. Rather than stimulating a politics that increased citizens' engagement at the local level with major national issues, the politics of Congress before 1995 was the politics of the permanent campaign.

The Individualistic Legislator. Legislators who won and held onto their positions chiefly through their own extensive efforts could not be dictated to by party leaders or presidents. Individualistic motives and practices prevailed in legislative behavior prior to 1995. For example, in deciding how to cast their votes on legislation, members thought first about their own constituents: Could they explain controversial votes to the folks back home? If signals from constituents were weak or divided, members felt free to vote their own policy preferences.[5]

Reforms adopted by House Democrats in the early 1970s also fostered congressional individualism (although this was not the goal of the reforms). With power more widely dispersed under these reforms, even junior legislators became *policy entrepreneurs*, pushing their own individual policy preferences rather than uniting behind a common party program. Skilled at winning reelection, and savvy about capturing media attention, a new generation in Congress competed to see whose ideas could win majority support. Entrepreneurship was even more rampant in the Senate, where a fluid structure encouraged legislators to go their own ways.[6]

Compared to the Congress of the 1950s and 1960s, where a small corps of conservative chairs ruled in hierarchical fashion, the individualistic Congress of the 1980s and early 1990s appeared more egalitarian and open to new ideas. Yet there was a price to be paid for this individualism: Behavior that served the rational self-interest of the members was often harmful to Congress as an institution and to the collective welfare of the American people. A decentralized Congress, fragmented along individual lines, frequently frustrated the popular democratic desire to see majority will at the polls translated into majority rule in the legislature.[7]

Congressional Committees

Second in importance to individual members and their districts in Congress before the revolution was the **committee system**—the system whereby most of the work of Congress is done by smaller groups. There are several kinds of committees in the House and the Senate. *Standing committees*, the most important, are permanent bodies that perform the bulk of the work. They gather information through investigations and hearings, draft legislation (this is called the *markup*), and report it to their parent chambers for a potential vote. The majority of bills proposed by individual members of Congress never get past the standing committee that considers them; these committees thus have great negative power. *Conference committees* meet to reconcile differences when the House and Senate pass alternative versions of the same law. Composed of the members from each chamber of Congress who have been the central actors on the bill in question, they produce the final language of the law. Congress also creates *select committees* for short-term investigations and contains a few *joint committees*, with members from both houses, for the purpose of gathering information.

Because much of an individual member's legislative life is spent in committee work, obtaining an assignment to a standing committee is a matter of great importance. Party committees in each house attempt to place members in accordance with their wishes. In the Senate, with its smaller numbers, every member is assured a spot on one of the most prestigious committees. In the House, however, there is often intense competition for places on the Rules, Appropriations, Ways and Means, and Budget committees. Some legislators are less concerned about winning a spot on one of these powerful committees than on joining a committee that deals with a subject crucial to their constituents. For example, representatives and senators from farm states gravitate toward the agriculture committees.

Once a member has joined a committee, the usual pattern is to remain there, developing expertise and, even more important, **seniority**. Before the revolution of 1995, seniority was crucial to gaining a leadership position. Under the congressional seniority system, the member from the majority party who had the most years of continuous service on a committee became its chair. Reforms initiated by the House Democrats in the early 1970s allowed for occasional breaches in the seniority system to make committee chairs more responsive to the majority of the party, yet seniority still determined committee leadership in all but a handful of cases.

Although the committee system had long been central to the organization and functioning of Congress, its character changed considerably in recent decades. One important trend affecting the system was the growth in committee staff. As the regular workload of committees increased—and as committee leaders sought to gain media attention by initiating new and innovative legislation—large numbers of staff aides were hired. These aides came to perform many of the functions that we associate with committee leaders: developing ideas for legislation, planning hearings to promote them, lining up support for the resulting bills, and negotiating the details they contain. Legislators turned over so much of their work to their staffs that one congressional scholar, Michael Malbin, dubbed these staffs our "unelected representatives."[8]

A second trend affecting committees involved subcommittees—smaller and more specialized units of the parent committee. Although greater reliance on subcommittees, like greater reliance on staff, reflected Congress's expanded workload, the real impetus to the rise of subcommittees came during a wave of congressional reform in the early 1970s. The Democrats in the House strengthened subcommittees at the expense of committees for two reasons: to diminish the power of committee chairs and to allow newer representatives to claim a piece of the legislative "pie." When important legislative provisions were drafted and discussed in subcommittees, it was often the case that only a handful of legislators played any active part.[9]

Through division of labor and specialization, the system of committees and subcommittees provided Congress with *expertise*. Faced with myriad subjects to consider, members of Congress looked for guidance to the experts on its committees and subcommittees, particularly their chairs. Committee expertise was critical in legislative–executive relations as well; without it, Congress would not stand much of a chance in conflicts with policy experts working for the president. The expertise found among long-time members of committees is important evidence for the elite democratic claim that elites bring greater expertise to the art of governance.

While the committee system divided the congressional workload and fostered expertise, it also created some of Congress's most enduring problems. One is a classic problem of elite democracy: Greater expertise is fostered, but this expertise is self-serving. Legislators often join a particular committee because they wish to serve interest groups that are important in their home districts or states. These legislators form alliances with the major interest groups and executive agencies with which their committees interact.

In the **iron triangles** that result, interest groups testify before the committee in favor of existing and potential programs that benefit them. Committee members support such programs in the bills they draft—and gain political support and campaign contributions from the interest groups. The agencies, with their missions and budgets supported by interest group and committee, implement

FIGURE 11.1

The Iron Triangle

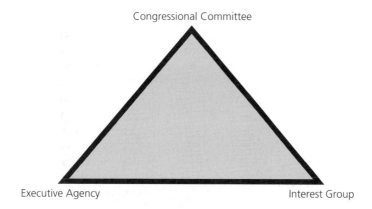

Congressional Committee

Executive Agency   Interest Group

the programs in a way that pleases the interest group and the committee (see Figure 11.1). In recent years, many iron triangles have become less rigid, with outside policy experts, public interest groups, and the press having more input. Some scholars believe that looser *issue networks* with shifting participants are now more common than the old triangular alliances. Yet the narrowly focused expertise that shapes the work of congressional committees and subcommittees remains for the most part the expertise of those whose interests are at stake.

The committee system also tended, like congressional individualism, to make collective action difficult. The more expert and powerful committee chairs were, the more they tended to push their own agendas, even if these agendas conflicted with the objectives of their party and its leaders. Moreover, Congress had few mechanisms to relate or compare the bills produced by its various committees, resulting in inconsistent legislation.

By the early 1990s, committees were not as powerful as in the past. Subcommittees had taken over much of the detailed bill drafting from their parent committees. Enormous deficits had reduced the opportunities for most committees to push new programs. Committees also lost influence to party leaders, and their work was now more susceptible to alteration and rejection once it reached the floor of the House or Senate. Still, as congressional scholars Steven Smith and Christopher Deering wrote in 1990, "committees remain the principal, if not always fully autonomous, players in nearly all policy decisions."[10] (For an overview of how a bill becomes a law, see Figure 11.2.)

Parties in Congress

Third in importance in shaping congressional action before the revolution were the political parties. Independents are occasionally elected to Congress (an independent socialist, Bernard Sanders of Vermont, sits in the 109th Congress), but almost all members belong to one of the two major parties. Party is the vehicle through which the House and Senate are organized. Seats on committees and committee leadership are determined on the basis of party. Party gatherings—called *caucuses* by the House Democrats, and *conferences* by the House

FIGURE 11.2   How a Bill Becomes a Law

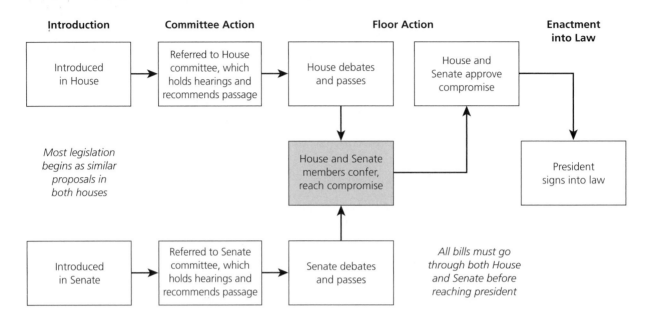

Republicans and both parties in the Senate—choose leaders to run their institutions and sometimes set broad policy directions as well.

Traditionally, congressional parties have been weak, at least when compared to the strong, disciplined parties found in most parliamentary democracies around the world. If legislators gain and retain their offices through their own efforts rather than through their parties, they are going to place the task of pleasing their constituents ahead of the task of cooperating with fellow partisans. Party weakness has also stemmed from the ideological diversity characteristic of America's major parties. A Republican party divided between moderates, pragmatic conservatives, and far-right conservatives, and a Democratic party split between northern liberals and southern conservatives, have had a hard time finding common party ground.

Beginning in the 1980s, however, the parties in Congress became more cohesive and unified. Measures of party unity in voting showed increases in both parties and both chambers. The House provided the most clear-cut example. In 1972, party unity scores (which show how frequently party members vote together) were 70 percent among House Democrats and 76 percent among House Republicans. By 1992, party unity scores were 86 percent among House Democrats and 84 percent among House Republicans. The most dramatic change came in the partisan behavior of southern Democrats, who often voted with Republicans in the past. In 1972 the party unity score for southern Democrats in the House was 44 percent; by 1992, this score had risen to 79 percent.[11]

Why did partisan unity increase if parties had traditionally been weak and were on the decline among the electorate? Several factors came together to spark a resurgence of parties in Congress. Among the Democrats, a key factor was the shrinking ideological difference between northern and southern members. After passage of the Voting Rights Act of 1965, southern Democrats gained large numbers of African-American supporters at the same time they were losing many conservatives to the Republicans; as their electoral base came to resemble that of northern Democrats, so did their voting behavior. Among the Republicans, the electoral successes of Ronald Reagan made the party more conservative; ideological diversity within the party waned. President Reagan's effect on partisanship within Congress was not restricted to his own party. Pursuing a strong conservative legislative agenda, often in an aggressive manner, Reagan forced the Democrats to pull together as a more united opposition party.

The two legislative parties represent distinct coalitions of ideology and interests, and to understand Congress before the revolution it is particularly necessary to understand the ideology and interests represented by the majority party, the Democrats. Reflecting their heritage as the party of Franklin Roosevelt's New Deal and Lyndon Johnson's Great Society, and their electoral strongholds in the urban centers of the Northeast and Midwest, the Democratic Party that controlled Congress for most of the last six decades was a party of government activism. It retained a predominantly liberal character even as the electorate became more ideologically conservative during the Reagan era.[12] Yet its liberal policy priorities in such areas as education, the environment, and Medicare retained substantial majority support.

As a coalition of interests, congressional Democrats were remarkably diverse. Despite their liberal ideology, they did not pose much of a threat to the most powerful and wealthy forces in American politics. In crafting programs for the economy as a whole, Democratic leaders of such committees as Appropriations and Ways and Means were mindful of "the privileged position of business" (see Chapter 3) and generally supported corporate priorities.[13] In crafting programs for more specific sectors of the economy, Democratic chairs and members of the other committees were influenced by the flow of contributions from business and trade association PACs that aided their reelection. Yet the forces that kept the congressional Democrats a party representative of elite democracy were balanced by more popular democratic forces. Minority groups, women's groups, environmentalists, labor unions, senior citizens, and government employees looked primarily to congressional Democrats for representation of their interests and concerns. Further, most minority and female members of Congress were Democrats. Although these groups were often disappointed in the majority party's performance, they did not doubt that they would be worse off should the Republicans become the new congressional majority. (The role that women play in Congress is the subject of the "Making a Difference" box.)

Given the diversity of its coalition, the Democratic majority in Congress was often divided. It was easier to unite in opposition to a Republican president than in support for a Democratic one (witness the case of Clinton's failed health care

MAKING A DIFFERENCE

Women in Congress

Although Congress is supposed to be the "people's branch," it has resembled a men's club that excludes one-half of the people. That women become U.S. representatives and senators in growing numbers is a major goal of popular democrats. Female representatives can provide "substantive representation" for women's interests: They can bring women's distinct experiences and concerns to the legislature and promote measures that foster equality between the sexes. They can also function as symbolic representatives, offering American women role models for political careers and assuring them of the democratic legitimacy of the political process.

Congress did not have any female members until 1917, when Jeannette Rankin of Montana entered the House. The numbers of women in Congress have grown slowly since then. "The Year of the Woman"—1992—produced dramatic gains, as the number of women in the House leaped from twenty-eight to forty-seven and the number of women in the Senate tripled from two to six. In the 109th Congress (2005–2006), there are fourteen female senators and 66 female representatives.

Research on women's membership in the legislatures of twenty-five democracies around the globe shows that even with recent improvements, the United States still ranks in the bottom half.

Discrimination against female candidates appears, according to research by political scientists, to be a thing of the past. Voters no longer prefer male to female candidates; there may even be a small bias in favor of women as more caring and honest. The parties are eager to put forward female candidates. And women seem to do as well as men in raising money for congressional races. What has limited gains for women has not been discrimination but incumbency advantages: With so few male incumbents susceptible to defeat, opportunities for women to replace them have been scarce.

The influence of women in Congress has been limited by more than just the small size of the female contingent. On the average, women enter Congress at a later age (because of child-rearing) and have shorter careers than men; few gain the seniority that many male legislators achieve. Another factor affecting the influence of women in

reform in 1994). The Democrats' lack of cohesion was both cause and effect of the individualism and committee decentralization that characterized Congress before the revolution. Often ineffective in taking action to address the nation's problems, yet complacent after many decades in control of Congress, the majority Democrats made a fat target for public discontent in the 1990s, provided that discontent could be mobilized by a shrewd and skillful Republican leadership.

Congressional Leadership

Fourth—and least powerful—among the factors shaping congressional behavior before the revolution was leadership. Among the top leadership positions in Congress, only one—**Speaker of the House of Representatives**—is specifi-

Congress has been diversity among female representatives. Before the Republican revolution of 1995, most Republican women joined with Democratic women in a Congressional Caucus for Women's Issues. But Newt Gingrich's revolution brought to Congress a new kind of female representative, whose conservative ideology made antifeminism a cardinal principle. In 1995, six of the seven freshman Republican women refused to join the caucus.

Despite limited numbers and ideological divisions, women have made a difference in shaping the agenda of Congress. Recognizing their responsibilities as spokespersons for women in general, Democratic and moderate Republican female legislators have taken the lead in promoting women's rights and fighting for policies of special importance to children and families. They have placed on the legislative agenda such issues as pay equity, child care, women's health, and domestic violence. Women are more likely to sponsor bills on these subjects than men with similar ideological positions.

The hardest realm for congressional women to reach has been legislative leadership. Until 2001, no woman had ever held a top leadership position in either party or chamber. That year, Democrat Nancy Pelosi of California became House minority whip, and two years later she was elected by her party as House minority leader. Most Republicans and some Democrats predicted that Pelosi was too much of a "San Francisco liberal," far to the left of the congressional mainstream, to be an effective legislative leader. Yet she has proven the critics wrong. As minority leader, Pelosi has demonstrated a blend of leadership skills, some conventionally associated with women and others traditionally ascribed to men. She has been an inclusive and supportive leader, bringing harmony to a legislative party famous for its fractiousness. She has also been a sharp critic of the Bush administration and a tough disciplinarian when Democratic members defect to support the Republican leadership on a bill. Under Pelosi's leadership, House Democrats have achieved the highest level of party unity in voting in over four decades.

Sources: Barbara C. Burrell, *A Woman's Place Is in the House: Campaigning for Congress in the Feminist Era* (Ann Arbor: University of Michigan Press, 1994); Karen Foerstel and Herbert N. Foerstel, *Climbing the Hill: Gender Conflict in Congress* (Westport, Conn.: Praeger, 1996); Sue Thomas, *How Women Legislate* (New York: Oxford University Press, 1994); Michele L. Swers, *The Difference Women Make: The Policy Impact of Women in Congress* (Chicago: University of Chicago Press, 2002); and Harold Myerson, "How Nancy Pelosi Took Control," *The American Prospect*, June 7, 2004.

cally mentioned in the U.S. Constitution. The Speaker of the House is the most visible and prestigious congressional leader (and stands second, after the vice president, in the line of presidential succession). Technically chosen by the whole House but in practice selected by a vote of the majority party in that chamber, the Speaker exercises a combination of procedural, policy, and partisan leadership.

The Speaker is the top figure in a complex leadership structure in the House. Beneath the Speaker, on the majority party side, is the **majority leader**. While the Speaker officially presides over the House (more-junior members actually perform this routine function most of the time), the majority leader is responsible for managing party operations on the floor. Along with the Speaker, the majority leader shapes the legislative schedule, confers with members of the party, consults with the president (when he or she is from the same party), and promotes a party perspective through the national media. Underneath the majority leader are whips, who assist the party's top leaders by gathering information and "counting noses" on forthcoming votes, and by encouraging partisan loyalty through persuasion and personal attention. The minority party has a similar leadership structure. The **minority leader** runs party operations on the floor of the House and is also assisted by an elaborate whip system.

There is no equivalent figure to the Speaker in the Senate. Constitutionally, the vice president presides over the Senate, and when he or she is absent, the presiding officer is the *president pro tempore*—usually the most senior senator from the majority party. The most important leaders in the Senate are the majority and minority leaders, assisted by their whips. These Senate leaders perform many of the same functions as their House counterparts.

Before the revolution, congressional leaders were more notable for their weakness than for their strength. Because members won their seats on their own, their "bosses" were their constituents and not their party leaders. Further, congressional leaders did not have a large number of favors to bestow on legislators who provided them support or punishments to exact on legislators who frustrated their objectives. Unable to issue orders, congressional leaders had to be talented at persuasion—at finding the right mix of political and ideological arguments to craft a majority for their party's positions. Coalition builders rather than commanders, they might occasionally twist arms to achieve results but relied mostly on the arts of negotiation, conciliation, and compromise.

Beginning in the 1970s, congressional reformers began to strengthen the hand of the leadership in the hope of fostering more effective collective action. In the House, the Speaker was given several new powers. For example, the Speaker was now able to name the majority members of the Rules Committee, whose decisions determine how much time is devoted to floor debate of a bill and what kinds of amendments can be offered on the floor. Under an *open rule*, any germane, or relevant, amendment can be offered. Under a *closed rule*, no amendments can be introduced. Through their domination of the Rules Committee, Speakers could now restrict amendments offered by the minority party or dissidents from the majority party when priority party legislation faced floor action.[14]

Senate leaders faced a more difficult challenge in pushing party priorities. The Senate, less than one-quarter the size of the House, offers greater freedom of action to individual members. Unlike the House, amendments to most Senate bills do not have to be germane to their subjects. The ability of individual senators to attach *riders* (unrelated provisions) to bills allows them to play complex strategic games on the floor. For example, a senator who favors a measure that has been bottled up in committee can attach it as an amendment to an unrelated bill; a senator opposed to a bill may load it with amendments to draw a presidential veto.

The minority party in the Senate also has weapons to defeat the majority party leadership that are absent in the House. Senators are unrestricted in the time they can talk about a bill. Senate debate can go on as long as senators insist. The practice of trying to talk a bill to death is known as the **filibuster**. Filibusters were most commonly employed by southern opponents of civil rights legislation in the 1950s and 1960s. But in recent decades, filibusters have been often used by the minority party to block many different kinds of legislation. For example, a Republican filibuster killed President Clinton's economic stimulus program in 1993. The Senate does have a procedure, known as **cloture**, whereby debate can be terminated by a vote of three-fifths of the membership. Yet such a large majority is hard to obtain.

Along with differences in official powers between House and Senate leaders there were differences in leadership styles and abilities. Despite their relatively weak institutional position, the top Senate leaders of the late 1980s and early 1990s—George Mitchell for the Democrats and Robert Dole for the Republicans—were both effective coalition builders. Variability was greater in the House. Jim Wright, Democratic Speaker from 1987 to 1989, effectively advanced a partisan legislative agenda. Yet he was forced out of office (and out of Congress) by ethics violations, with the charge against him led by the emerging leader of the House Republicans, Newt Gingrich. Wright's successor in the speakership, Thomas Foley (1989–1994), was a more conciliatory—and weaker—Speaker. Under Foley's loose reign, the tendency of the House Democrats to splinter once more became evident.

CONGRESS DURING THE REVOLUTION

Public anger toward Congress rose sharply during the half-decade before the 1994 elections. Congress was widely blamed for its failure to address the nation's problems, especially the enormous budget deficits. Citizens were irate about the sizable pay raises that members voted themselves and by the practice of widespread check bouncing by members using the House bank.

In 1994, public anger was focused entirely on the Democrats, and their majorities in the House and Senate were swept away by an electoral tidal wave. The GOP takeover culminated a decade of partisan strategizing and guerrilla actions by the new Republican hero, Newt Gingrich. Having seized majority control, Gingrich and his followers aspired to a revolution in the House—and through this a conservative transformation of American society.

As congressional scholars C. Lawrence Evans and Walter J. Oleszek write, "By the end of 1995 (the first session of the GOP-controlled 104th Congress), close observers agreed that the House, if not the Senate, was a remarkably different body compared to the years of Democratic dominance."[15] The difference in the House resulted from a striking reversal in the order of importance for the factors shaping congressional action: The last (leadership) had become first, and the first (individualism) had become last.

Leadership

Speaker Newt Gingrich was at the center of events in 1995. He became the most powerful Speaker since the early years of the twentieth century.[16]

At the start of the 104th Congress, Gingrich took control of the House largely into his own hands. He chose all of the committee chairs, in several cases bypassing senior members in favor of his own loyalists. He also controlled committee assignments and cemented his hold over newly elected Republicans by giving many of them slots on the most prestigious House committees. Republican rules changes reinforced Gingrich's personal assertions of prerogative. Committee chairs were subjected to a three-term limit on tenure, further reducing their independence. Subcommittees were subjected to their parent committees in a reversal of what the Democrats had done two decades earlier, adding to the centralization of power.

Having centralized power in the House leadership, Gingrich and his lieutenants were able to focus the Republican agenda in a way that the Democrats had been unable to do when they ran Congress. The "Contract with America," the electoral platform that the Republicans had adopted for the 1994 elections, supplied the initial unifying agenda.

To advance his vision of conservative change, Gingrich aimed not only to dominate the House but to supplant the president as the nation's premier agenda setter.[17] The Speaker went well beyond his predecessors in seeking the spotlight: televising his daily conferences with the press, delivering a nationally televised address to dramatize House passage of the Contract with America, and orchestrating the Republican campaign to sell the public on the party's radical budget-balancing designs. Yet in his quest for a speaker's "bully pulpit" to overshadow the president's one, Gingrich revealed his greatest weakness as a leader: The more he spoke, the more unpopular he and his agenda became. Polls showed Gingrich to be the least-liked political figure in the nation, viewed by a majority of Americans as abrasive, authoritarian, and mean spirited.[18]

While Gingrich was raising House leadership to new heights of power, Republican leadership in the Senate faced the same limitations as before. The Republican majority leader, Robert Dole, had too narrow a legislative majority (53–47) to overcome Democratic filibusters. Senate individualism also hampered Dole; while Republican moderates were few in number, the prospect that they would side with the Democrats limited Dole's capacity to pass the torrent of conservative legislation gushing out of Gingrich's House.

Party

Newt Gingrich's success as a revolutionary leader of the House depended in the end on an unusual experiment in party government. Under the Democrats, individualism and committee autonomy tended to be stronger than party loyalty and unity; the Republicans promised a new era of congressional government in which the party would take precedence over the committee and the individual.

It was a testament not only to the skills of Gingrich and the other Republican House leaders but to the ideological and electoral appeal of a strong and disciplined party that House Republicans did indeed reach unprecedented levels of party unity during the revolution of 1995. Recall the high levels of party unity scores in 1992: 86 percent for House Democrats and 84 percent for House Republicans. In 1995, House Republicans easily topped these figures with a party unity score of 91 percent.[19]

The Republicans had greater luck with party government than the Democrats because they were a more ideologically cohesive party. Republican moderates in Congress were a dwindling band, drawn mostly from the Northeast; conservatives dominated the party's legislative ranks everywhere else. Newt Gingrich's conservative philosophy—dismantle the federal regulatory and welfare state, turn authority back to state governments and private markets—was widely shared among the Republican majority in the House and also among Senate Republicans (several newly elected senators had been Gingrich allies in the House). The fervor and energy that drove the revolution came largely from conservative ideology, especially among the seventy-three first-term Republicans swept into the House in the elections of 1994.

Republican campaigners in 1994 had capitalized on middle-class and working-class anger at President Clinton and the congressional Democrats. But the core of their party's active constituency was religious conservatives and economic elites. Once the less controversial elements of the Contract with America were out of the way, core Republican groups came to the fore. Republican leaders did not even bother to conceal the extent to which industry lobbyists were actually writing antiregulatory legislation on the environment. Bills passed by the House were designed to gut enforcement of important provisions in the Clean Air, Clean Water, and Endangered Species Acts.

When critics seized upon the role of lobbyists to charge that revolutionary Republicans were just as guilty of selling out to special interests as the status quo Democrats had been, House Republican Whip Tom DeLay replied: "Our pork is freedom. Their pork is projects."[20] But many Americans could not detect a difference. The ties of the House Republicans to elite democratic interests undercut the image of a popular democratic upheaval to purify Washington. As polls showed declining support for Republicans in Congress (and increasing support for President Clinton and the Democrats), it was apparent that the ideology and interests that had brought the Republicans to power commanded less public support than their radical program required.

Committees

The power that had been gained in the Republican revolution in the House by the leadership and the party was in large part power taken away from the committees and their chairs. We have already seen how the Speaker ignored the seniority system and appointed chairs himself while also controlling key committee assignments, and how the Republican Conference adopted term limits for chairs and weakened subcommittees. In addition, committee staffs were slashed by one-third (since the Democrats had lost their majority status, it was their staffers who were fired).

Although the trend toward diminished importance for committees had begun with reforms adopted by the Democrats in the 1970s, the Republicans carried it much further. Committees were sometimes circumvented altogether during the revolution. Speaker Gingrich set up *task forces* to develop priority legislation. Task forces offered him several advantages over committees: They

Bruce Beattie/Copley News Service.

could be stacked with supporters of the leadership, they excluded members of the minority party, and they could operate behind closed doors.[21]

Committee independence was also under assault in the Senate, where the conservative majority in the Republican Conference became frustrated by the persisting power of moderate chairs. Six months after House Republicans had voted to weaken committee chairs, Senate Republicans followed suit, establishing a six-year limit for committee chairs and ranking minority members. Republican members of a committee were given the power to select the chair by secret ballot, to be followed by another secret ballot in the party conference. These reforms made committee chairs more answerable to the party and its leaders.

Individual Members

Revolution in the House required a new type of legislator. If the individualistic pursuit of reelection defined most members during the era of Democratic dominance, the collective pursuit of a partisan and ideological agenda was supposed to define Republicans intent on revolution. The party unity scores achieved in 1995 suggested that members were acting differently, were voting their party and ideology more than their districts.

The typical legislator in the Democratic era had been a self-selected political professional. But many of the new Republican members of the House had been recruited to run, especially by Newt Gingrich's GOPAC. While they still had to raise large sums of money to have a chance at victory, more of this money now came from party sources. Reflecting the antipolitician mood in the country, several of the new Republican members of the House proudly proclaimed that they had no prior political experience. They were coming to Congress, they announced, not to join the corrupt "Washington system" but to purge it.[22] The Senate too had its share of new antipoliticians.

The new class of Republican legislators normally followed the leadership and occasionally bucked it, but in either instance they acted as a group. The individual policy entrepreneurship that characterized the Democrats in power was largely absent during the Republican revolution. Resources for entrepreneurial behavior had been diminished with the reduction in committee staffs and the reining in of subcommittees. But new members had also been socialized differently, to place party unity over individualistic enterprise.[23]

CONGRESS AFTER THE REVOLUTION

At the end of 1995, when congressional Republicans failed to pressure President Clinton into accepting their seven-year plan for balancing the budget and received the bulk of the blame from the public for shutting down the government during the budget showdown, their revolution was stymied. The election results of 1996, continuing Republican control of Congress (but with an even narrower margin in the House) while returning Bill Clinton to the White House, confirmed the basic contours of a post-revolution landscape. The congressional elections of 1998, held as the House worked on the impeachment of President Clinton, dealt another blow to Republicans' lingering revolutionary hopes, as their narrow margin of control shrunk even further.

Gingrich and his followers had made two fundamental errors. First, they had read too much into the election results: A revolution in national policy needed greater public backing than the 20 percent of the eligible electorate who had voted Republican in 1994. Second, in disregard of the constitutional system of checks and balances, they had tried to dominate the government from the House of Representatives; the Senate and especially the President blocked the fulfillment of the Speaker's agenda.

The decline of Republican revolutionary dreams paralleled the fall of the revolution's leader, Speaker Newt Gingrich. His hope to be the nation's premier agenda setter was deflated in the budget showdown at the end of 1995, when he was outfoxed by President Clinton. Gingrich's stature was further tarnished when the House Ethics Committee found him guilty of using tax-exempt money for partisan purposes and ordered him to pay a $300,000 fine. In 1997, Gingrich survived a revolt against his leadership by former conservative loyalists who had become demoralized by his loss of effectiveness. But when House Republicans, performing worse than anyone had anticipated, lost seats in the 1998 elections, Gingrich's image as a leader suffered a mortal blow; accepting the inevitable, he gave up his post and resigned from Congress.[24]

Although he fell from power as dramatically as he had risen, Newt Gingrich left a lasting impact on Congress. His vision of a cohesive legislative majority united behind a conservative policy agenda was carried on by new Republican leaders different in character but equally aggressive and ambitious. Especially after the White House came under Republican control in 2001, congressional Republican leaders revived their hopes for a conservative transformation of American politics. Unlike Congress before the Gingrich revolution, Congress after the revolution continues to place leadership and party above committees and individual members, and ideology above pragmatism.

Leadership

In the House, Republicans are now headed by a pair of leaders: Speaker Dennis Hastert and Majority Leader Tom DeLay. Hastert, a former high school teacher from Illinois known as "Coach" for the wrestling champions he instructed, was chosen as Speaker by House Republicans because his amiable demeanor and calm presence are the opposite of Gingrich's fiery public image. Yet Hastert's goals are little different than Gingrich's; as political scientist Ross Baker has observed, the Speaker is "'a very, very tough partisan who hides behind a kind of cuddly teddy-bear exterior.'"[25] DeLay, a former pest exterminator from Texas, is the more hard-charging and influential of the two House leaders. He has wielded power in the House with a relentless focus on winning at all costs.

DeLay is known as "the Hammer," a nickname suggesting that his dominant role in the House has less to do with public advocacy of a conservative ideology than with hidden mastery of power politics. During Gingrich's speakership, De-Lay was the majority party whip in the House, and he built a large and efficient operation to ensure that Republicans toed the revolutionary line. As whip, De-Lay also established his reputation by putting the fear into Washington lobbying firms: unless they dropped their bipartisan practices and began hiring only Republicans, he warned, they would be frozen out by the House leadership. Through such methods, by the time DeLay became majority leader, no other congressional Republican could match him in raising funds from business interests. The business community provided DeLay with one part of his political base. The other part was the Christian evangelical right, to which the born-again De-Lay was much closer than Gingrich had ever been.[26]

Some analysts believe that the Hastert-DeLay team has centralized power in the House even more effectively than Gingrich did. Picking the leadership of committees (see below), tightly managing the agenda and schedule, manipulating the rules to shut the minority Democrats out from any significant say on legislation, the House Republican leadership has gone a long way toward building a disciplined majority that is rare in modern congressional history. Despite the narrow Republican advantage in seats, conservative legislation has been advanced through the House with consistent success, with the small number of moderate Republicans muscled into line when their votes are crucial.[27]

To avoid losing important votes, Hastert and DeLay have sometimes gone to extraordinary lengths. In 2003, when President Bush pushed a program that provides prescription drugs for seniors under Medicare, some House conservatives, unhappy about establishing a new entitlement program, balked at supporting the legislation. Short of a majority during the customary fifteen-minute period allotted for an electronic vote, House Republican leaders kept the tally open for three hours until they could twist enough arms to eke out a 220–215 victory.[28] Subsequently, one retiring Republican congressman whose vote on the Medicare bill DeLay had tried to change alleged that the Majority Leader had offered financial support for his son's upcoming congressional race to replace his father. The House Ethics Committee agreed with the allegation and reprimanded DeLay for the incident.

Reprimands from the House Ethics Committee were only the start of De-Lay's difficulties. His hardball tactics in fundraising and close ties with a lobbyist under federal investigation drew increasing criticism from Democrats and media commentators. By the spring of 2005, even a few Republicans began to raise doubts about his survival as Majority Leader.[29]

In the Senate, Republican leadership resembles the House model more than in Gingrich's day. Bill Frist, a Tennessee heart surgeon who is a close ally of President Bush, is a soft-spoken Majority Leader, but underneath his courtly demeanor is a determined partisan and fervent ideologue. As *New York Times* journalist David Firestone observes, "While other Republican leaders, including Senators Trent Lott, Bob Dole, and Howard H. Baker Jr., were more independent deal makers who prided themselves on keeping the legislative trains running, Dr. Frist is charting a different path as a committed conservative who says he does not intend to compromise his party's principles . . ."[30] Like previous Republican majority leaders, however, Frist cannot wield power on behalf of a conservative agenda in quite the fashion of Hastert and DeLay, due to the greater independence of individual senators, the prospect of defection by a small but critical bloc of Republican moderates, and the capacity of the minority Democrats to block Republican legislation through the filibuster.

Party

Today, partisanship in Congress is even more intense, and the two parties are even more polarized, than at the peak of the Republican Revolution of 1995. Party unity scores in the House for 2003 were identical to 1995 among Republicans (91 percent) and higher for Democrats (87 percent compared to 80 percent). Influenced by the influx of former House Republicans, the Senate showed an even greater increase in partisan polarization. In 2003, Republican unity in the upper chamber reached a record level of 94 percent, compared to 89 percent in 1995, while Democratic unity grew from 81 percent in 1995 to 85 percent in 2003.[31]

Part of the explanation for the worsening partisan polarization in Congress rests with electoral politics and redistricting maneuvers. Moderates in both parties have retired or been defeated for reelection, and their replacements are typically more to the right or left than the representatives or senators they replace. In redrawing congressional district lines after each national census, parties in the state legislatures have created constituencies that are more staunchly conservative or liberal than in the past. (As a result of this redistricting, fewer House districts are likely to change hands each election, helping the Republicans to maintain their majority but also keeping that majority from growing much larger.) A mounting body of evidence suggests that the American electorate itself is becoming more divided along partisan lines.[32]

Developments inside Congress have also fueled polarization. Feeling slighted and abused by the Democratic majority during their long years in the congressional wilderness, Republicans have retaliated with an even stronger brand of one-party domination since 1995, leaving Democrats marginalized and outraged. Especially in the House, the leaders of the two parties rarely speak to one another, as they generally did in the past, and rank-and-file members no longer tend to form friendships across party lines. Journalist John Cochran notes that there is "a dearth of meaningful cross-party dialogue, . . . one big reason for the mounting incivility [that] undermines the legislative process, erodes public faith in Congress as an institution, and makes the House more difficult than ever to govern."[33]

Legislative battles since 1995 have left partisan scars. Probably no event so dramatically furthered the bitter partisan polarization in Congress after the revolution as did the impeachment and trial of President Clinton in late 1998 and early 1999. Furious with Clinton for his moral transgressions (and perhaps for his political successes in blocking their revolution), House Republicans proceeded to impeach the president even in the face of strong public opposition and electoral losses. Republican moderates who considered opposing impeachment were denied the option of voting for a lesser charge, censure, by Tom DeLay, then the House Republican whip, and were pressured to stick with their party. Meanwhile, congressional Democrats, who had never been enamored of their party's president, rallied behind him when his survival in office was at stake. The votes in the House (on impeachment) and in the Senate (on conviction) told a tale of extreme partisan division: Only four Republicans in the House voted against every one of the four articles of impeachment, and only five Democrats voted for any of them; every Senate Democrat voted for acquittal while 91 percent of Senate Republicans voted that the president was guilty on at least one charge.[34]

Committees

One of the most profound transformations of the House shaped by the Republican revolution was the subordination of committees to party leaders. In today's House, committees are not treated as cavalierly by Republican leaders as they were at the peak of the revolution; unlike Gingrich, Hastert and DeLay refer bills to the standing committees rather than bypassing them with task forces. Nonetheless, the leaders exert dominant influence over the heads of the committees. The seniority system, a basis for committee independence when Democrats were in the majority, is effectively dead in the House. Hastert and DeLay regularly reach past senior committee members to appoint more junior representatives as committee chairs. To become a chair in today's House, the important credentials are conservative ideology, the ability to raise money to help fellow Republicans get elected and maintain the party's majority status, and, above all, loyalty to the leadership.[35]

Through their control over the committee chairs, Hastert and DeLay have sought to build a disciplined partisan and ideological machine in the House. When the chair of the Resources Committee retired at the end of 2002, the two top leaders elevated Rep. Richard Pombo of California to the position in preference to five other Republicans with greater seniority on the committee. The flaw in the five that denied them the chairmanship despite their longer records of service: their past votes were viewed by Hastert and DeLay as too proenvironment.[36] When the Ethics Committee handed down three separate reprimands to DeLay in 2004 for his unethical conduct, the Majority Leader saw to it that the committee's chair, Republican Joel Helfley of Colorado, lost his post at the beginning of the next Congress.[37]

The committee system in the House after the Republican revolution reflects heightened partisanship as well as top-down control. When Democrats were in the majority in the House, greater committee autonomy fostered some measure of bipartisan cooperation on the part of committee members. In today's Republican House, the minority Democrats are largely frozen out from a significant impact on committee outputs. Unable to influence bills as they work their way through the committees, Democrats are further shut out from impacting bills once they reach the floor because the Republican leadership insists on the adoption of "closed rules" that prohibit amendments.[38]

The seniority system for selecting chairs has survived in the Republican Senate. Bill Frist, the Republican Majority Leader, cannot exert the degree of control over committees that Hastert and DeLay enjoy in the House, and his style of leadership is more low-key anyway than DeLay's.[39] Yet even in the Senate, committee chairs do not possess the autonomous power that they used to have. Due to term limits, the tenure of Senate chairs is much shorter than in the past. And there is mounting pressure, especially on more moderate Republican chairs, to support the dominant conservative agenda. In line to become Judiciary Committee chair at the beginning of 2005, Senator Arlen Specter of Pennsylvania came under attack from religious conservatives after he suggested that the Senate was not likely to confirm antiabortion nominees for the Supreme Court. Specter was compelled to pledge that his committee would not block any of Bush's judicial nominees in order to gain the chairmanship.

Individual Members

As the revolutionary Republicans of 1995 aged in office, most of them began to take on some resemblance to the majority Democrats they had supplanted. Shedding the aura of amateurism, House Republicans have become political professionals who court constituents, raise large sums of money, and obtain pork-barrel projects for their districts. Nonetheless, majority Republicans in the House remain distinct from the previous generation of majority Democrats in several crucial respects. Still committed to the revolution that brought them to power, they are, as a group, more ideological than their predecessors. Equally important, they are more attuned than the Democrats, complacent from decades in power,

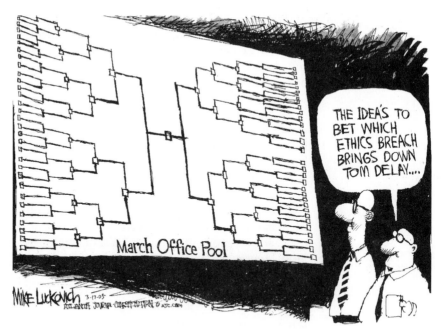

By permission of Mike Luckovich and Creators Syndicate, Inc.

were to the importance of holding onto the majority. As we saw earlier in the chapter, the typical legislator when Democrats ruled the House was an individualistic reelection seeker. Under Republican rule, members concern themselves not only with their own reelections but with the success of their fellow partisans. As political scientists William Connelly Jr., and John J. Pitney Jr. observe, since today only those in the majority have influence over legislation and in committees, it is rational for individuals to be guided by "the majority-status motive" as well as by the motive of perpetuating one's own career through reelection.[40]

Strong partisan leadership, enhanced ideological coherence, and a concern for majority maintenance in the face of narrow margins of control have made the House Republicans less individualistic than most past members of Congress. Yet as the White House and the Republican leadership in Congress pursue an even more far-reaching conservative agenda in President Bush's second term, it is not clear that the remarkable level of party unity achieved during Bush's first term can be sustained. In the first half of 2005, fissures have opened up in the Republican congressional coalition over the president's budget, partial privatization of Social Security, and immigration reform. As these controversial issues come to the fore in Congress, the tension between carrying out a revolution and keeping one's seat is beginning to grow.

For those who want to see the national legislature become a more effective vehicle for popular democracy, Congress after the revolution presents a decidedly mixed picture. On the positive side, both congressional parties have become stronger as instruments for collective action, and their individual members are paying more attention to questions of public policy than to parochial matters pertaining only to their districts. On the negative side, incivility, hostility, and efforts to defeat the "enemy" at all costs too often supplant the dialogue and deliberation that are supposed to characterize a democratic legislature. So long as neither party possesses any better than a narrow control of the House and Senate, we are likely to witness a continuation of the polarized Congress that is probably the principal legacy of the Republican revolution.

CONGRESS AND THE EXECUTIVE

The Constitution places Congress first among the three branches of the federal government, devoting Article 1 to the selection, organization, and powers of the legislature. During the nineteenth century, except for brief periods under strong presidents, Congress was the preeminent branch. But the twentieth century witnessed the rise of "presidential government," with the executive seizing the lead and Congress following.

Although the overall balance of power has shifted from Capitol Hill to the White House, the dynamic of power between the two branches never remains static. From the New Deal of Franklin Roosevelt to the Great Society of Lyndon Johnson, Congress acquiesced in the rise of a strong presidency, particularly in foreign and defense policy. But the Vietnam War prodded Congress to challenge the presidency on international affairs and war making. The sweeping power plays of President Nixon compelled Congress to reassert itself in budget making and domestic policy as well. During the "divided government" of the 1980s and early 1990s, with the Republicans entrenched in the White House and the Democrats controlling Congress, warfare between the two branches was frequent. It grew even more intense when partisan control of the branches was reversed after 1994. Under unified government since 2003, the chief form of conflict between the branches pits the White House, asserting the claims of majority rule, against the Senate Democrats and their defense of minority rights through the filibuster.[41]

Budgetary Politics

One of the primary elements in the rise of presidential government during the middle decades of the twentieth century was presidential capture of a preponderant share of the power of the purse. A legislature dominated by scattered committee power could not produce a coherent budget; a unitary executive, aided by a Bureau of the Budget (renamed the Office of Management and Budget in 1970), could. Congress found itself reduced to snipping budgets framed by the executive. Two developments in the early 1970s, however, propelled Congress to recapture some budgetary power. First, a fragmented congressional budgetary process generated excessive spending. Second (and probably more important), President Nixon usurped Congress's budgetary authority so aggressively that he forced legislators to develop new defensive weapons.

The vehicle Congress chose to reassert its budget-making authority was the **Budget and Impoundment Control Act of 1974**. This act established new budget committees in the House and Senate. It also created a Congressional Budget Office (CBO), a staff of budgetary and economic experts that provided members with information and analysis comparable to those supplied to the president by the Office of Management and Budget. With the assistance of the CBO, House and Senate budget committees were to draft two concurrent budget resolutions. The first, due in May each year, was to set targets for federal spending, thereby constraining other authorizing committees. The second resolution, due in September, was to set final, binding budgetary totals for Congress. Through this new process, Congress hoped to subject the budget to a more coherent review and establish its own priorities against those of the president.

The new budget process did increase congressional power, but it also intensified conflict between Congress and the executive. It was the presidency of Ronald Reagan that turned the budget into the annual battlefield of national politics. In 1981, Reagan dominated Congress, achieving massive tax cuts and increases in defense spending. However, he did not persuade Congress to cut domestic spending as deeply as he wished. The result was mounting federal deficits that loomed over all congressional deliberations.[42]

With Republican presidents and Democratic congresses at an impasse on taxing and spending priorities, the federal deficit ballooned through the 1980s. In desperation, Congress tried an automatic deficit-reduction mechanism, the Gramm–Rudman–Hollings bill (named for its Senate sponsors), but it was a failure. Finally, as massive deficits threatened the health of the economy, two budget agreements that set caps on federal spending and raised taxes began to bring the deficit under control. The first was the product of a compromise between President Bush and congressional Democrats in 1990; the second was proposed by President Clinton and passed by the Democratic majority in Congress (with every congressional Republican in opposition) in 1993.

The Republican revolution of 1995 produced an even more dramatic showdown over the budget. Clinton won the war, but the congressional Republicans forced him in the process to commit his administration to their goal of a balanced budget in seven years. The two sides finally reached agreement on a balanced budget compromise in 1997, with each eager to claim that it had achieved its top priorities in the deal. What permitted the lengthy impasse to end was less a new spirit of cooperation between president and Congress, however, than the booming economy that produced tax revenues abundant enough to give each side a large part of what it wanted.

Deficits finally gave way to surpluses during the last years of the Clinton presidency. However, the era of budget surpluses, projected at the beginning of Bush's presidency in 2001 to last throughout the first decade of the new century, instead ended almost immediately, and by the beginning of Bush's second term the magnitude of annual federal deficits is approaching those of the Reagan years. Bush's massive tax cuts in 2001 and 2003, in conjunction with an economic downturn that began in 2000 and was exacerbated by the September 11 attacks, and the costs of American wars in Afghanistan and Iraq, have brought back the contentious politics of the budget.

Foreign Policy

Foreign policy has been the preferred field of action for most presidents over the last century. Presidents have substantial authority and resources in this policy arena. Preference, authority, and resources have sometimes led presidents and their supporters to claim foreign policy to be almost exclusively executive in character. Yet the Constitution bestows authority and entrusts responsibility to Congress as well as the executive in shaping the relationship of the United States to the rest of the world. Through its appropriations authority, Congress funds American activities abroad. It has the sole power to declare war and is responsible for raising and maintaining military forces. The power "to regulate commerce with foreign nations" draws it into matters of international trade. Moreover, the Senate has the responsibility to deliberate on treaties with other countries.

Despite these constitutional powers, Congress largely accepted presidential dominance over foreign policy from World War II to the Vietnam War, the era of the "Cold War consensus." It was the disaster of Vietnam—a presidential war—that shook Congress out of its compliant stance. Starting in the early 1970s, Congress began to reassert its role in foreign policy issues: war making, covert actions by the CIA, arms sales to foreign nations, and trade strategy. When it engaged in battles with the White House, the presidency still usually enjoyed the upper hand. Yet Congress won some notable victories—for example, instituting economic sanctions, over a veto by President Reagan, against the apartheid government of South Africa in 1986.

The ability of Congress sometimes to prevail over the president in foreign policy was in evidence during the Clinton presidency. Clinton's biggest problem was with the new isolationist mood among conservative Republicans in Congress. Rejecting Clinton's multilateral approach to foreign policy, House Republicans repeatedly refused to appropriate funds to pay the dues and back debt that the U.S. owes to the United Nations. Senate Republicans handed Clinton an even more stinging defeat in 1999 by rejecting the Comprehensive Test-Ban Treaty on nuclear weapons. But Clinton did not have an easy time with congressional Democrats either. Most of them voted against his proposals to expand "free trade" (see Chapter 18), and he was able to win victories in this area only with Republican support. When he sought "fast-track authority" in 1997 that would have increased his ability to negotiate free-trade agreements, congressional Democrats succeeded in denying him this power.

President Bush has had an easier time in dominating Congress on matters of foreign policy. After September 11, 2001, his stature as commander-in-chief gave him the upper hand in obtaining congressional resolutions authorizing him to use force in Afghanistan and Iraq. The tight discipline of Republicans in Congress won Bush the authority over trade negotiations that Clinton was denied.

Many analysts are unhappy when Congress asserts itself in foreign policy. They believe that if the United States is to follow a coherent and prudent foreign policy, Congress should not interfere very often with the president's decisions.

Congress, they allege, moves too slowly, acts too indecisively, deliberates in too much ignorance, is swayed too much by ideological obsessions, and is too pre-occupied with reelection pressures to handle the dilemmas of diplomacy and war. But its inadequacies in foreign policy, congressional scholar Eileen Burgin observes, are exaggerated. Congress can act swiftly if necessary, employing expedited procedures; besides, most foreign policy matters require careful consideration. Although most of its members are inexpert on matters of foreign policy, its foreign affairs and armed services committees boast many impressive students of international affairs. If Congress approaches global events with one eye on the reactions of constituents, the same is often true of the president.[43] And Congress has no monopoly on ideological obsessions in foreign policy, as the presidencies of Ronald Reagan and George W. Bush have demonstrated.

The real question about congressional involvement in foreign affairs is not whether it interferes too much with the presidency but whether it defers too often to presidential initiatives.[44] Perhaps because it is closer to the people, Congress has been more likely than presidents in recent decades to reflect the popular democratic tradition of fearing the engagement of the United States in overt or covert military actions abroad (see Chapter 18). Congressional resistance to President Reagan's Contra war against the Sandinista government of Nicaragua led to a cutoff of funds on several occasions. The Senate fell only five votes short of rejecting President Bush's impending war to drive Iraqi occupiers out of Kuwait. President Clinton's bid to send American troops to Bosnia as peacekeepers courted Senate disapproval until Majority Leader Robert Dole agreed to back the president's plans. The House, on a tie vote, rejected a measure authorizing Clinton to direct air operations and missile strikes against Yugoslavia because of its brutality in Kosovo. President George W. Bush utilized the threat of an upcoming election to overcome substantial congressional opposition to a war in Iraq. In each case, regardless of party, Congress was less keen on the use of armed force. Yet in each case, the executive ultimately prevailed.

Congress is not always prudent about international affairs. In recent years, its involvement has at times been distorted by its ideological rigidity. But the congressional voice is welcome in foreign policy because the alternative is a presidential monologue. When presidents have dominated foreign policy, they have been inclined to secret deliberations, covert actions, and manipulative rhetoric. Congressional participation in foreign policy opens this arena, generating debate, increasing options, and allowing public input. Elite democrats admire a president who is the sole master of foreign policy. Popular democrats turn to Congress to ensure the public's voice in foreign affairs.

Congressional Oversight of the Executive Branch

The most extensive relationship between Congress and the executive involves legislative oversight of the bureaucracy. **Oversight** is the review by congressional committees of the operations of executive branch agencies. In one sense, oversight is simply a logical process—Congress must review what the bureaucracy does to see if laws are being properly implemented. In another sense, oversight is a highly political process—Congress's chief means for contesting the president over guidance of the federal bureaucracy.

Oversight can take many forms. The most visible is the congressional hearing. In an oversight hearing, top agency administrators appear before a congressional committee to report on their implementation of programs and to answer questions. Members of Congress not only elicit useful information but also signal the administrators as to who controls their statutory authority and budget resources. Informal methods of oversight are even more common, and usually less conflictive. Committees may request written reports from agencies, or committee staffers may engage in extensive communications with their agency counterparts.

Oversight hearings can be turned into partisan instruments whose primary objective is to embarrass the president and his administration. Congressional Democrats employed committee hearings to probe the alleged misdeeds of Republican presidents from Nixon through the elder Bush. When Republicans gained control of Congress in 1995, they began to pay the Democrats back with even more frequent hearings. At almost any point during the last six years of the Clinton administration, there was usually at least one congressional committee investigating the White House, whether it was about the Whitewater scandal, the alleged misuse of FBI files, campaign finance shenanigans, or a host of other activities.[45]

Vigorous in their oversight of the Clinton presidency, Republican committee chairs became more relaxed once the White House was in the hands of their own party. Administration failures, such as the blunders that undermined the reconstruction of Iraq after American conquest of the country, produced little oversight activity in either the House or the Senate. Alleging that Republicans were avoiding oversight hearings that risked embarrassment to the Bush administration, Democrats in the Senate tried to attract the press with unofficial hearings of their own; however, their efforts were unsuccessful.[46] Congressional investigations and hearings at the start of Bush's second term are much less noticeable than during the period of divided government.

The majority of oversight hearings are not dramatic or partisan. Nevertheless, some critics still object to extensive oversight on the grounds that by this technique Congress is interfering excessively with the executive branch and trying to "micromanage" its operations. This complaint has been justified in some instances.

Yet an increase in congressional oversight is, on balance, a welcome development, at least from the standpoint of popular democracy. To be sure, some oversight is technical and dull; some is narrowly self-serving advocacy. And, on occasion, oversight is little more than partisan theatrics to humiliate the executive. But oversight is one of the chief means that Congress possesses to hold the presidency and the civil service accountable. Vigorous oversight activities prevent the bureaucracy from becoming a closed world of inaccessible experts. Many oversight hearings have alerted the public to matters that otherwise would have been known only to a small circle of elites.

Conclusion: The Postrevolution Congress and the Democratic Debate

From the standpoint of popular democracy, Congress has critical roles to play in budgeting, foreign policy, and oversight. But how well can Congress perform these and other roles? How well can it give expression to the strengths of popular democracy? Assessing the transformations in Congress brought by the Republican revolution, whose story we tell in this chapter, gives us some clues into the potential for Congress to represent the public's ideas and interests.

There have been elements of genuine popular democracy in the Republican revolution in Congress. The revolution has shaken Congress out of its complacent "inside the Washington Beltway" habits. It has brought a dramatic new emphasis on party responsibility that is essential if Congress is to take collective action and address the nation's problems. Even the centralization of power in the hands of the leadership, disturbing in the authoritarian methods it has spawned, has at least produced a coherent agenda that the public can understand and debate.

But the Republican revolution and its aftermath have fallen far short of popular democratic reform in important respects. Republican leaders from Gingrich to DeLay have sought to enact an ideological agenda by steamrollering over the opposition, short-circuiting the processes of deliberation and debate in Congress.[47] The Republican revolution has also enlisted populist anger for the interests of economic elites. Too often, the popular democratic reforms of the Republicans have served as a cover for an elite agenda—for example, tax cuts that mostly benefit well-to-do investors and deregulation measures that subordinate a clean environment to industry profits.

The polarized and often nasty party conflict that characterizes Congress after the revolution is once again feeding public disenchantment with legislative politics in the nation's capital. But present partisan excesses should not obscure the continuing importance of Congress's democratic revitalization. A strong and effective Congress is indispensable for popular democracy in America. Elite democrats argue that in a complex, dangerous, and technological world, Congress, with its inefficient methods of decision making, has become outdated. They point out that in most other political systems, legislative powers have receded and strong executives have become dominant. Popular democrats respond that unless legislative power balances executive power, democracy is in trouble. Only a vital Congress can ensure that government will be sensitive to the concerns of ordinary citizens and forge genuine compromises among their diverse viewpoints. Above all, whereas the executive branch makes decisions behind closed doors, in the halls of Congress citizens can hear public arguments about the public good.

KEY TERMS

incumbent
franking privilege
casework
committee system
seniority
iron triangle
Speaker of the House of
    Representatives

majority leader
minority leader
filibuster
cloture
Budget and Impoundment Control
    Act of 1974
oversight

**INTERNET
RESOURCES**

▓ Free Congress Foundation
www.freecongress.org
A conservative perspective on Congress, offering numerous publications and
Internet links.

▓ National Committee for an Effective Congress
www.ncec.org
A liberal perspective on Congress, with extensive coverage of liberal challengers to conservative incumbents.

**SUGGESTED
READINGS**

John C. Berg, *Unequal Struggle: Class, Gender, Race, and Power in the U.S. Congress*. Boulder, Colo.: Westview Press, 1994. A radical analysis of power in
Congress, stressing the clout of large and small businesses and the weaknesses of labor, women, and African Americans.

Lawrence C. Dodd and Bruce I. Oppenheimer, eds., *Congress Reconsidered*, 8th
ed. Washington, D.C.: Congressional Quarterly Press, 2005. An anthology
of original, thought-provoking articles on various aspects of congressional
politics.

Richard L. Hall, *Participation in Congress*. New Haven, Conn.: Yale University
Press, 1996. An important study of the ways in which members of Congress
choose to focus their legislative activities.

John R. Hibbing and Elizabeth Theiss-Morse, *Congress as Public Enemy: Public
Attitudes Toward American Political Institutions*. New York: Cambridge University Press, 1995. Through surveys and focus groups, the authors arrive at
an intriguing account of why Congress is the least-respected of American
national institutions.

Gary C. Jacobson, *The Politics of Congressional Elections*, 6th ed. New York:
Longman, 2004. The leading text on how members of Congress convert
their biennial exposure to popular democracy into elite longevity in office.

Nicol C. Rae and Colton C. Campbell, eds., *New Majority or Old Minority? The
Impact of Republicans on Congress*. Lanham, Md.: Rowman & Littlefield, 1999.
Articles by congressional scholars explore the new Republican regime in
Congress.

12

Presidential Leadership and Elite Democracy

Contemporary presidents present themselves to the American people as champions of popular democracy. Aided by a large public relations machine in the White House, they dramatize their status as the sole elected representative of a national majority and their commitment to battle for the public good against selfish special interests. But should we take presidential claims to the title of popular democrat at face value? This chapter suggests that there are circumstances in which popular democracy can indeed be furthered by a leader in the White House. But it also proposes that we be wary of prevailing presidential imagery: Most of the time, we shall see, the presidency is closer to elite democracy than to popular democracy.

In the original debate over presidential power, the most brilliant advocate of strong presidential leadership was an arch elite democrat, Alexander Hamilton. Hamilton believed that the American Revolution had gone too far in placing government directly in the hands of the people and of legislators immediately answerable to the people. A strong executive of uncommon talent and experience was needed to guide public affairs. As Hamilton put it, "Energy in the executive is a leading character in the definition of good government."[1] Only an energetic executive, Hamilton argued, could overcome the tendency of the political system to stalemate and provide creative political direction. Conditions of crisis would make executive leadership even more imperative: "Decision, activity, secrecy, and dispatch will generally characterize the proceedings of one man in a much more eminent degree than the proceedings of any greater number."[2]

To the original popular democrats, the Anti-federalists, the new presidency evoked painful memories of royal governors and British kings. They suspected that Hamilton's lofty executive office would be a breeding ground for elitism. Patrick Henry lamented that "there is to be a great and mighty President, with very extensive powers: the powers of a King. He is to be supported in extravagant magnificence."[3] Another Anti-federalist, George Mason, called upon citizens to look to their own commitment "to their laws, to their freedom, and to their country" rather than depending for their salvation upon a single leader of great power.[4] Anti-federalists placed their political hopes in the people's energies and not the executive's.

Positions in the democratic debate over the executive seemed to be reversed in the twentieth century. First with Theodore Roosevelt and Woodrow Wilson, and even more decisively with Franklin D. Roosevelt, the presidency came to be associated with popular democracy. After FDR's New Deal, which was a genuine outpouring of popular democratic energies, most journalists, political scientists, and historians came to believe that presidents were the principal agents of democratic change in the American political system. Advocates of economic reform, social justice, and racial equality began to rest their hopes on White House leadership.

These hopes were repeatedly disappointed: Presidents after FDR never seemed to bring about as much democratic change as they promised when they ran for office. And while the bond between the presidency and popular democracy was celebrated, presidents were expanding their powers in ways that threatened democratic values. With the Vietnam War, the Watergate scandal, the Iran–Contra affair, the campaign finance scandals of the Clinton presidency, and the assaults on civil liberties by the administration of George W. Bush, the undemocratic potential of executive power was underscored. Anti-federalist warnings, forgotten in the twentieth-century celebration of presidential power, became relevant once more.

This chapter assesses the part that presidents play in the democratic debate. We explain the most important features of the modern presidency and evaluate both its powers and its limitations. We consider presidents as individual leaders who seek to enact their agendas and make their marks upon history. But we give equal weight to the forces that constrain and condition their leadership: Congress, economic elites, the media, the public. It is more the balance of these forces than personality, we suggest, that determines whether the president sides with popular or elite democracy.

THE PERSONALIZED PRESIDENCY

When Americans think or talk about a president, his or her personality is usually the focus of their attention. The man or woman in the White House makes a more engaging subject than the institutional apparatus or policy agenda of his or her administration. Media coverage reinforces this personalization of the presidency. After observing a president's portrayal in the media, citizens are more apt to know trivial details—Gerald Ford bumped his head on helicopter doorframes, Ronald Reagan liked jellybeans, Bill Clinton had a cat named Socks, George W. Bush often naps in the afternoon—than to know the name of the president's chief of staff or the substance of his or her trade policy.

Media coverage of the president also prompts most Americans to assume that how well a president does in office depends almost entirely on his or her strengths and weaknesses. In this light, Ronald Reagan's presidency was viewed through the disparity between his strong communication skills and his weak grasp of his own policies. The elder George Bush was portrayed as an experienced administrator who lacked a vision of where he wanted to lead the nation. Bill Clinton was depicted as a puzzling combination of political talent and moral delinquency. George W. Bush is presented as an incurious and inarticulate leader who nonetheless charts a bold and steadfast course at home and abroad. Political skill, intellect, and character thus seem to matter more than anything else in determining each president's record of successes and failures.

Several political scientists have attempted to provide a more systematic understanding of the contribution of the person to the presidency. James David Barber's famous work on presidential personality places presidents into different categories depending on whether they are active or passive in doing their job and whether they are positive or negative in viewing their office as a source of personal satisfactions. The most desirable type of president, Barber argues, is the active–positive president, who pours considerable energy into the job, has fun in doing so, and possesses sufficient self-esteem to be flexible and adaptable when inevitable roadblocks stand in the way of major presidential goals. In Barber's analysis, active–positive presidents include Franklin D. Roosevelt, Harry Truman, John F. Kennedy, Gerald Ford, Jimmy Carter, and the elder George Bush. The least desirable type of president, according to Barber, is the active–negative president, whose energetic performance is driven by grim self-doubt and who tends to rigidify behind a failing policy at great cost to the nation's welfare. Barber's active–negative presidents are Woodrow Wilson, Herbert Hoover, Lyndon Johnson, and Richard Nixon.[5]

Personality is not the only component of a personalized presidency. Another political scientist, Fred Greenstein, makes "emotional intelligence" (a president's freedom from psychological disturbances) one of six qualities that distinguish presidents from one another, and he finds that the healthiest modern presidents on this measure have been Dwight Eisenhower, Gerald Ford, and George H. W. Bush. Greenstein suggests that in addition to character, we also should assess presidents on how effectively they communicate with the public, how skillfully they forge their White House team, how shrewdly they play the political game with other Washington actors, how thoughtfully they develop a vision of where the country should be going, and how strategically they process the vast flood of information available in the White House. Yet Greenstein, like Barber, ultimately makes personality the most decisive variable: "Beware the presidential contender who lacks emotional intelligence. In its absence all else may turn to ashes."[6]

Raising the media's conventional conclusions to a higher plane of understanding, these scholars make a convincing case that the personal qualities of the president affect his or her performance. But how much can a focus on the personalized presidency really explain? Can Barber's categories, which lump together such diverse presidents as Harry Truman, John F. Kennedy, and George H. W. Bush, tell us much about why their presidencies turned out so differently? Do Dwight Eisenhower, Gerald Ford, and George H. W. Bush, the trio that Greenstein concluded were the freest from personality flaws, stand out in modern history as among the most successful presidents? Character, skill, and intelligence matter in the White House, to be sure, but when we focus on them to the near exclusion of all else, we fail to understand the presidency very well. What tends to be overshadowed by a preoccupation with the personalized presidency are the varying political and historical circumstances in which presidents have to operate. What tends to be obscured when we see only the person who is president is the presidency as an institution.

THE PRESIDENCY AS AN INSTITUTION

In our concern for presidential leadership, we focus on the individual who occupies the White House. Yet the presidency—as distinct from the president—is an institution, and we need to understand its institutional features. The institution of the presidency has expanded dramatically over the last century. Although this expansion has been justified in popular democratic terms—the presidency has had to grow to fulfill public expectations of executive leadership—the consequences have sometimes been unfortunate for popular democracy. Surrounded by a sizable staff and bureaucracy of their own, presidents can become isolated from the people who put them into office. And this staff and bureaucracy can be used to carry out actions that run counter to what Congress has legislated and what the public wants.

White House Staff

The part of the institutional presidency that most directly surrounds the individual president is the **White House staff** (known officially as the White House Office). The White House staff comprises the president's personal aides and advisers along with their numerous assistants, and it has undergone dramatic growth over the last seventy years. Before Franklin D. Roosevelt, presidents had only a handful of personal aides. Abraham Lincoln had to cope with the Civil War with the help of only two personal secretaries. When a telephone was first installed in the White House, Grover Cleveland answered it himself. As late as World War I, Woodrow Wilson typed many of his own speeches.

During the Great Depression of the 1930s, as new responsibilities flooded the White House, Franklin Roosevelt recognized, in the words of the Brownlow Committee that he appointed, that "the president needs help." It was Roosevelt who initiated the dramatic expansion of the White House staff. But later presidents would oversee a staff far larger than Roosevelt had imagined. At its height, FDR's staff numbered around fifty. By Richard Nixon's second term, the staff had grown to over 500 people. Nixon's successors, responding to charges that the presidential staff had become dangerously bloated, cut it back a bit.[7]

The White House staff has not only expanded since the 1930s; it has also taken on important new functions. Before Franklin Roosevelt, presidents tended to turn for advice to cabinet members. Although presidents still consider their cabinet selections important, since the 1930s they have downgraded most cabinet heads, relying instead on their staff for assistance in decision making and even in managing federal policies. Staff members have done more than serve as the president's extra eyes, ears, and hands. Some of them—such as Edwin Meese under Reagan, John Sununu under the first Bush, Leon Panetta under Clinton, and Karl Rove under the second Bush—have become key decision makers in their own right.

The organization and work patterns of the White House staff are shaped, at least in part, by the personality of the president. Bill Clinton's staff was largely youthful, and his White House was notorious for meandering meetings that reflected the president's own lack of discipline. By contrast, the White House of George W. Bush has been designed, according to a report by *New York Times* correspondent Richard Berke, "to function with the crisp efficiency of a blue-chip corporation."[8] In the Bush White House, older staffers with experience in previous Republican administrations predominate. Meetings start and stop on time, briefing memos are restricted to no more than two pages, and staff members must observe a formal dress code in the Oval Office (ties and jackets for men, business attire for women). Since President Bush does not desire the immersion in policy making that President Clinton relished, his corporate-style White House allows him to spend fewer hours on the job than did his predecessor.[9]

Why have recent presidents turned to White House staff rather than cabinet members for advice? To understand this phenomenon, we must consider the differences between cabinet members and White House staffers.

A president may have had little personal contact with most members of the cabinet before assuming office. The cabinet is selected with several criteria in mind: public prestige, managerial ability, interest group or geographic representativeness (e.g., the secretary of the treasury is usually drawn from the business or financial communities, and the secretary of the interior is traditionally a westerner). Potential cabinet heads must pass Senate scrutiny and receive senatorial confirmation. Further, cabinet secretaries can be summoned to appear before congressional committees, where they may be pressed to reveal information that the president would rather keep confidential.

In contrast, top White House staff don't usually come to their jobs from power positions. Rather, many are individuals personally attached to the president—men or women who have worked for the president in the past and whose loyalty is long-standing. Top staff members often reflect the president's roots and political base. Bill Clinton initially drew many of his key aides, including his first chief of staff, from Arkansas; George W. Bush brought several of his top Texas aides with him to Washington. White House staff do not need Senate confirmation. Unlike cabinet heads, they cannot ordinarily be questioned by Congress because of claims of separation of powers and executive privilege.

Considering the differences between cabinet and staff presents clues about why presidents prefer to work with staff. A president has greater flexibility with staff: He or she can hire anyone, move staff members from task to task, and replace ineffective or incompatible staff members with less public notice than with dismissing a cabinet member. A president can also assume greater loyalty from staff. Cabinet members must answer to many forces besides the president who appointed them: congressional committees that control the budget and statutory authority for their departments, the interest groups that are important clienteles for their departments, and the civil servants who work in their departments. But White House staffers answer only to the president.[10]

Offering a president greater flexibility and loyalty than the cabinet, a large and powerful White House staff seems to increase the president's reach and power. But growth of this kind of White House staff has been a mixed blessing for presidents. Members of their staffs have several potential weaknesses. Like presidents themselves, staffers can become isolated from the world outside the White House. David Gergen, who served as a high-level aide to presidents Nixon, Ford, Reagan, and Clinton, observes that "even in the best of times, the White House can be closed off to reality; in the worst of times, it is a bunker."[11]

Isolated from the public, dependent on the president for their jobs, and highly loyal, White House staffers do not necessarily make the best advisers. Desiring to curry favor with a president, staff members have sometimes presented their bosses with distorted pictures of the reality outside the White House. Rather than enhancing presidential power, they have produced a peculiar form of presidential blindness, akin to the monarchical mentality against which Patrick Henry had warned. This blindness is especially evident in the administrations of Johnson, Nixon, Reagan, and the younger Bush.[12]

A contemporary president requires an extensive White House staff. But the tendency of that staff to enhance the illusion of presidential rectitude and wisdom must be avoided.

Executive Office of the President

The White House Office is part of the **Executive Office of the President (EOP),** established under Franklin Roosevelt in 1939. The other most important components of the EOP are the Office of Management and Budget (OMB), Council of Economic Advisers (CEA), and National Security Council (NSC). Whereas the White House staff was designed to provide the president with personal and political assistance, the other EOP units were intended to provide institutional—that is, objective and expert—advice to the president as a policy maker (see Figure 12.1).

The largest and most important institutional unit in the EOP is the **Office of Management and Budget (OMB).** OMB prepares the annual presidential

FIGURE 12.1

Executive Office of the President (EOP)

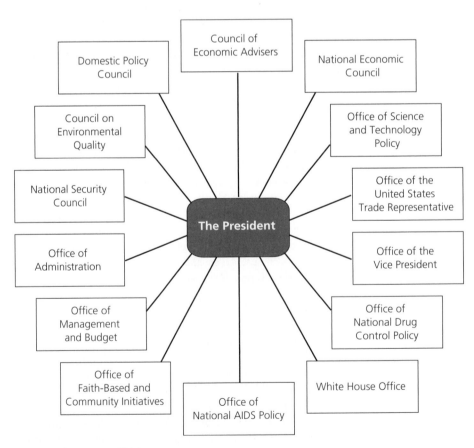

Council of Economic Advisers

Domestic Policy Council

National Economic Council

Council on Environmental Quality

Office of Science and Technology Policy

National Security Council

Office of the United States Trade Representative

Office of Administration

The President

Office of the Vice President

Office of Management and Budget

Office of National Drug Control Policy

Office of Faith-Based and Community Initiatives

Office of National AIDS Policy

White House Office

Source: White House, 2004.

budget. It scrutinizes legislative proposals originating in the agencies of the executive branch to ensure that they accord with the program of the president. It recommends signing or vetoing legislation. In addition, it oversees the management methods of the entire executive establishment.

The **Council of Economic Advisers (CEA)** was established in 1946 to provide regular assistance from professional economists. The CEA has a chair and two other members, along with their staffs. It analyzes economic conditions, projects economic trends, and drafts the president's annual economic report.

The **National Security Council (NSC)** was established in 1947 to coordinate the military and diplomatic aspects of foreign policy in an age of American global involvement. Officially, it brings together the top national security decision makers: the president, vice president, secretary of state, secretary of defense, director of the Central Intelligence Agency, and chair of the Joint Chiefs of Staff. More important than formal meetings of the NSC, however, is the work of its staff, headed by the president's assistant for national security. (See Chapter 18 for a more detailed discussion of the NSC.)

Although the original purpose of the EOP was to provide a president with expert institutional advice to balance the more personal and partisan advice of staff, the distinction has diminished in recent years. The White House has made the institutional components of the EOP more political, more directly responsive to the president's personal views and political needs.[13]

Recent presidents have placed trusted aides at the helm of OMB. OMB head Richard Darman was a prominent adviser to the elder President Bush, and Leon Panetta performed a similar role for President Clinton before becoming White House Chief of Staff in 1994. The NSC was used by President Reagan to implement secret presidential policies involving arms sales to Iran and control of the Contra forces in Nicaragua. The Reagan aide in charge of these projects, Lt. Colonel Oliver North, hardly fit the profile of an objective, neutral institutional aide.

As has been the case with White House staff, the EOP has been turned into a central instrument of presidential views and politics. This extension of personal power, from the president's Oval Office outward, has been justified as an indispensable tool of leadership. But the enhancement of presidential power has not always meant the enhancement of presidential wisdom. A highly politicized OMB under Budget Director David Stockman manipulated the budgetary math to conceal how Reagan's 1981 tax cut would generate a massive deficit. A highly politicized NSC helped Reagan stumble into the disaster of the Iran–Contra affair. Some scholars believe that the EOP might serve the presidency better if it were not so intensely politicized.

The Vice President

An important new political and institutional support for presidents in recent years has been the expanded role of the vice president and his staff. For most of the history of the presidency, vice presidents were obscure figures. Abraham Lincoln is generally regarded as the greatest president, but how many people know the name of his first vice president? (It was Hannibal Hamlin.) Vice presidents were usually chosen because they enhanced the prospects that a party's presidential ticket would win; after the election, they had almost nothing to do with the presidency. The vice presidency seemed dreary and frustrating to most of its occupants—in the words of Franklin Roosevelt's first vice president, John Nance Garner, it was "hardly worth a pitcher of spit."[14] Vice presidents became important leaders only if presidents died and they moved into the White House.

As the burdens placed on the presidency multiplied, however, contemporary chief executives realized that vice presidents and their staffs could provide valuable assistance. The first vice president to play a significant role as a policy and political adviser to the president was Walter Mondale, who brought his years of Senate experience to bear in helping Jimmy Carter, an outsider unfamiliar with the political habits of Washington, D.C. Al Gore played an even more influential role during Bill Clinton's two terms. Until tensions arising from Gore's own bid for the presidency drove them apart, Gore was almost a partner to Clinton. He played a leading role in the meetings where Clinton pondered domestic and foreign policy decisions, and the president gave him special responsibilities for "reinventing government" (see Chapter 13), forging environmental policy, and handling relations with the Russians.

Richard Cheney, George W. Bush's vice president, has surpassed Gore and become the most influential vice president in American history. Cheney's influence on Bush has been felt in staffing, advice, policy making, congressional relations, and public advocacy. The vice president brought his former associates, Donald Rumsfeld and Paul Wolfowitz, into the two top positions in the Pentagon. He is perhaps the president's closest counselor, conferring several times a day with Bush and attending most high-level meetings in the White House. And he is the administration's most important emissary to Congress; his own highly conservative voting record while a member of the House of Representatives gives him a special stature among Republicans on Capitol Hill.

At the outset of the Bush presidency, Cheney was placed in charge of the administration's task force on energy policy (see Chapter 9). As an alumnus of the energy industry (he was CEO of Halliburton Corporation before the 2000 elections), Cheney's task force appears to have conferred with industry executives while largely excluding environmentalists; however, the actual list of participants in task force meetings has been kept secret by Cheney under the claim of executive privilege, a claim ultimately upheld by the Supreme Court. Even more controversial than Cheney's secretive activity in energy policy has been his highly visible role as an advocate for war in Iraq. In the inner circles of the Bush White House, Cheney was a strong advocate for rejecting diplomacy through the United Nations and sending American troops into Iraq. In public, he made the case for war even more hyperbolically than did President Bush. During an August 2002 speech, for example, he said, "Simply stated, there is no doubt that Saddam Hussein now has weapons of mass destruction. There is no doubt he is amassing them to use against our friends, against our allies, and against us. . . ." Cheney's activities in the areas of energy and national security have brought him more criticism than previous vice presidents. By deflecting some of the attacks

by opponents of the administration's policies away from the president and onto himself, the vice president has played the part of lightning rod and performed an important service for Bush.[15]

Cabinet

Beyond the White House staff, the EOP, and the office of the vice president lies the cabinet and the vast expanse of the executive branch. The **president's cabinet** is composed of the appointed heads of the fifteen principal executive agencies, plus a few others, such as the U.S. ambassador to the United Nations. Americans use the term cabinet in two ways. In the first, the cabinet is simply the collection of individuals appointed by the president to head the principal executive agencies. In the second, the cabinet is a collegial body, meeting together with the president to supply its collective advice.

Most presidents talk of using the cabinet as a collective forum. Meetings of the cabinet make excellent TV and photo opportunities, showing off the president surrounded by prestigious and weighty advisers. In actuality, cabinet meetings are routine affairs, useful for little more than symbolism. Not surprisingly, most cabinet members come to meetings to pursue the interests of their own departments. Presidents learn not to expect much from a cabinet meeting and instead solicit advice from individuals directly engaged in policy matters.

Therefore, the cabinet is more accurately described as a collection of individual department heads. In this collection, not all heads are equal. As presidency scholar Thomas E. Cronin has shown, presidents turn most often to their *inner cabinet*, composed of the secretaries of state, defense, and treasury, along with the attorney general.[16] These cabinet secretaries handle the subjects most important to the president. Controversial nominees for inner cabinet posts can provoke intense political conflict, as was evident in the confirmation battle over George W. Bush's first attorney general, John Ashcroft, a Christian conservative.

The *outer cabinet* contains the remainder of the departments, such as agriculture, education, and transportation. The business of these departments is not ordinarily central to a president's program. Members of the outer cabinet often find that the prestige of their title is not matched by their proximity to the president. For example, when President Nixon's secretary of the interior, Walter Hickel, unhappily resigned in 1970, he observed that he had seen the president in private only twice in fifteen months.[17] The administration of George W. Bush is taking a novel approach toward outer cabinet members: rather than neglecting them, it requires them to hold several office hours per week in a building adjacent to the White House so that the White House staff can keep a watchful eye on their activities.[18]

In recent administrations, presidents have been expected by constituency groups and the media alike to have women and minorities in their cabinets. Until President Clinton appointed Janet Reno as attorney general in his first term, women and minorities had only held positions in the outer cabinet. Since Reno's appointment, women and minorities have been moving more frequently into the inner cabinet. Clinton appointed Madeleine Albright as secretary of state during his second term. In his first term, the younger Bush appointed Colin Powell, an African-American, as secretary of state. At the beginning of his second term, Condoleezza Rice, an African-American woman, serves as secretary of state, and Alberto Gonzales, a Hispanic, serves as attorney general.[19]

Managing the Bureaucracy

If presidents are to control the vast federal bureaucracy, they need the assistance of a strong cabinet. But cabinet members are subject to tugs besides the directives of the White House—pressures from Congress, from interest groups, from the staffs of their own agencies. Presidents and their White House staffers have complained about members of the outer cabinet "going native" (that is, taking on the perspectives of the departments they were appointed to head) or building personal empires.

Whatever help they receive from their cabinet appointees, presidents find the management of the federal bureaucracy arduous. Prescribed by the Constitution, it is a task that requires a president to "take Care that the Laws be faithfully executed. . . ." In traditional management theory, the executive branch should be a pyramid, with the president on top, and bureaucrats underneath carrying out decisions. But the modern administrative state diverges from this theory.

A number of factors limit a president's control over the bureaucracy. The vast size of the modern administrative state is itself a limitation, because no president, even with the help of a large White House staff, can keep track of more than a fraction of what is taking place in the bureaucracy. The historical shift from patronage to civil service has also limited presidential control. Civil servants, unlike White House staffers, do not depend on the president for their jobs and are likely to be less concerned about the success of the president than about the mission, budget, and growth of their own agencies. (The perspective of civil servants may seem narrow compared to that of the White House, but civil servants often have more experience and knowledge in their fields than do White House staff.) In addition, Congress has considerable influence over executive agencies through its budgetary and statutory authority.

The capacity of executive agencies to resist directives has frustrated presidents. As President Truman prepared to hand over his office to the newly elected General Eisenhower, he predicted: "He will sit here and he'll say, 'Do this! Do that!' And nothing will happen. Poor Ike—it won't be a bit like the Army!"[20] Frustration with managing the bureaucracy has led presidents to try to shift functions from that bureaucracy into the White House itself. More recently, it has led to determined campaigns to make the bureaucracy serve the president's agenda.

In seeking control over the bureaucracy, an important tool is the **executive order**. An executive order is a presidential directive to subordinates in the executive branch that carries the force of law. Executive orders not only set rules for bureaucrats; they also are binding on individuals and organizations in the private and non-profit sectors if these receive federal funds. Through executive orders, presidents have promulgated major policy changes without needing legislation. President Truman desegregated the armed forces through an executive order. President Johnson instituted the controversial policy of affirmative action for federal contractors with an executive order. President Reagan subjected federal regulations to cost-benefit analysis through an executive order. However, executive orders do not always have the staying power of legislation, for what one president can order another can reverse. Thus, President Reagan ordered a ban on federal funding of international agencies that offer abortion counseling, President Clinton directed that it be lifted, and the younger President Bush reinstated it.[21]

Among recent presidents, none was as successful in reshaping the bureaucracy as Ronald Reagan. Reagan came into office with a strong conservative agenda. His White House deployed several strategies of executive control. Most important was a personnel strategy. Presidential appointees to the bureaucracy were tightly screened by a personnel office in the White House; loyalty to Reagan and his conservative philosophy was a more important criterion for appointment than past experience or professional expertise. Another strategic weapon was the budget. In a period of large deficits, the budget was used as a tool of administrative discipline. Agencies that the Reagan White House regarded as unfriendly to its agenda saw their budgets cut and their staffs reduced. Agencies whose behavior the Reagan White House hoped to change knew that they would be fiscally hurt if they did not satisfy the White House.[22]

Neither the elder Bush nor Clinton was as ideological a leader as Reagan had been. They lacked both the motive and the means to reshape the bureaucracy in the manner of the Reagan White House. But with another ideologue, George W. Bush, in the White House, control over the bureaucracy to advance conservative goals is once again a major presidential priority.

One area where the Bush administration has used its power to alter the bureaucracy has been in the relationship between religious institutions and social services. Although achieving little in promoting a "faith-based initiative" through legislation, the Bush White House has advanced religion's role in welfare through administrative action. By executive order, Bush established a new White House Office of Faith-Based and Community Initiatives. Smaller offices were created in existing cabinet departments, such as Education, Health and Human Services, and Housing and Urban Development, to facilitate greater financial support to religious institutions providing social services. Federal rules were changed to narrow the separation between church and state in this area. For example, reversing a rule established by President Johnson prohibiting organizations receiving federal grants from discrimination on the basis of race, creed, color, or national origin, President Bush announced a new rule whereby religious organizations contracting with the federal government to supply social services may consider religious beliefs in their hiring decisions. In accordance with his own profession of faith, and in service to the Christian conservatives that are a major element of the Republican Party coalition, Bush has thus turned the federal bureaucracy into an ally and financial supporter of religious institutions.[23]

THE PRESIDENCY AND THE CONGRESS

The relationship between the president and Congress is seldom smooth. Conflict is more common than cooperation—as the framers of the Constitution intended. In *The Federalist Papers*, James Madison set down the theory of checks and balances: "Ambition must be made to counteract ambition."[24] The clash of presidential and congressional ambitions is constitutional theory in action.

This clash is often presented by journalists or political scientists as a competition between the national viewpoint of the presidency and the localistic viewpoint of members of Congress—a portrayal that makes the president the unique champion of popular democracy at the national level. But the idea that the presidency is almost always bound to be a better servant of the public interest than Congress is not well founded. Sometimes, presidents do take a national standpoint, while Congress responds with parochial objections. Generally, however, it is more accurate to say that even though presidents speak for a broader coalition of interests than *individual* members of Congress, Congress *as a whole* may speak for an equally broad, or broader, coalition.

Before accepting the claim that Congress is locally oriented and the president alone speaks for the public interest at the national level, we should remember that neither branch has a monopoly on the representation of public ends. Some public ends have been represented better by the White House at one point in time, and by the majority in Congress at another. Social welfare and civil rights legislation drew greater support from Presidents Kennedy and Johnson than from Congress between 1961 and 1969, but from 1969 to 1977 the same kind of legislation had more backing in Congress than in the administrations of Presidents Nixon and Ford. In this case, insisting that what the presidency favors is more in the national interest than what Congress favors would require us to believe that social welfare and civil rights programs ceased to be in the national interest as soon as the White House changed hands.

The image of presidents as champions of popular democracy at the national level draws upon moments when presidents achieved legislative breakthroughs: Franklin Roosevelt in 1933–35, Lyndon Johnson in 1965, Ronald Reagan in 1981. But these were moments when presidents enjoyed electoral mandates and congressional backing—that is, when they could legitimately claim to represent a majoritarian popular democratic coalition. Absent these relatively rare political conditions, presidents and Congress reflect differing coalitions, and it is often hard to tell which institution has the better claim to represent popular democratic goals.

Congressional Roadblocks

Why does Congress so often oppose the president? Perhaps the most important source of conflict is the way they are elected. Elected in districts or states, members of Congress have a different constituency than the president. To keep their jobs, they must satisfy voters who are not necessarily backers of the president. Moreover, members of Congress build their own campaign organizations and raise their own campaign funds. With different constituencies and independent political bases, they must chart their own course.

Presidential efforts to push legislation through Congress may also be frustrated by congressional structure. Prior to 1995, power in Congress was fragmented and decentralized; the legislative process presented the White House with successive barriers, tripping over any of which lost the legislative race. As we saw in the preceding chapter, the triumphant Republicans centralized the legislative process, especially in the House, in 1995. This hardly helped a Democratic president like Clinton, but it has been a godsend to Republican George W. Bush.

Analyses that use the personalized presidency approach suggest that a president's ability to overcome congressional roadblocks hinges mainly on his or her personal skill in legislative matters. But paying attention to historical context suggests that presidents come into office with widely varying opportunities for major legislative achievements. Although skill is never irrelevant, variation in such factors as the public mood or the size of the election victory opens the window for legislative triumphs for some presidents while leaving others facing almost inevitable frustrations at the hands of Congress.[25]

Divided government—in which one party controls the White House and the other party controls one or both houses of Congress—has a large impact on a president's prospects for obtaining passage of legislation. In recent years, the institutional context of divided control between polarized parties has made it even harder for presidents in Congress than in the past. As a consequence, neither the elder George Bush nor Bill Clinton (after his first two years) attempted to push as many large or innovative initiatives through Congress as their predecessors had.[26] On the other hand, polarization in the context of unified control may work to a president's advantage. Although his partisan majorities in the House and Senate have been small, the discipline and cohesiveness of congressional Republicans amid conditions of partisan warfare have been indispensable for George W. Bush's legislative victories in the areas of taxes and Medicare.

In the face of roadblocks from Congress, presidents are hardly helpless. Which factors are most important in determining their success with Congress? Political scientist George C. Edwards has argued that a president's success in securing passage of legislation depends on the partisan composition of Congress and the president's standing with the American public. Examining the years 1953 to 1996, Edwards found that the level of support for a president's program from members of his own party was usually more than 30 percentage points greater than the level of support from members of the other party.[27] A president enjoying a partisan majority in Congress is thus primed for a successful legislative record, whereas a president facing a majority from the other party has dubious legislative prospects. Compare, for example, the legislative situations confronting the two Bushes when each took office. Although George W. Bush had only a narrow Republican majority in the House and a fifty–fifty split in the Senate in 2001, he was still in a far more advantageous position than his father, who faced Democratic majorities of ten in the Senate and eighty-five in the House in 1989.

But unified government, with the president and the congressional majority from the same party, does not guarantee legislative success, as Bill Clinton painfully learned during his first two years in office. A president's public popularity is another important factor with Congress. A popular president is likely to have favorable ratings among constituents. Legislators will not want to appear at odds with a popular president. On the other hand, a president whose popularity is sinking can be opposed by members of Congress with little fear of electoral retribution. To be successful with Congress, a president usually needs both a favorable partisan majority in the legislature and a favorable standing in the public opinion polls. Lacking the latter, President Clinton barely got his deficit reduction plan through Congress in 1993 and failed to get his health care reform bill even to the floor of Congress in 1994.

Presidential Resources

The president does have some resources that improve the prospects that he or she gets congressional approval. The White House legislative program sets the congressional agenda. By establishing a strong, well-timed agenda, a president can shape the terms in which subsequent congressional debate is conducted. Working for that agenda on the president's behalf is the **legislative liaison staff**, a portion of the White House staff that spends its time on Capitol Hill. Members of the liaison staff keep the president informed of the political maneuvering for important bills and provide favors to members of Congress in the hopes that they will later return these favors to the White House with their votes.

The favors that the White House offers are valuable but limited. To win a few swing voters in a tight legislative contest, presidents can promise federal judgeships or positions as U.S. attorneys. Federal grants or contracts can be steered to the district or state of a crucial legislator. Minor provisions of a bill can be altered to favor interest groups. In his uphill 1993 battle to win House approval of the North American Free Trade Agreement (NAFTA), President Clinton successfully wooed several pivotal southern legislators with concessions on citrus and peanut butter imports.[28]

A resource that the White House possesses in somewhat greater abundance is the mystique of the presidency. To be photographed with the president or called to meet with the president at the White House can boost a representative's standing with constituents. Apart from political gain, few members of Congress are immune to the mystique of presidential authority. Ronald Reagan thus bestowed presidential cufflinks on numerous members of Congress and invited legislators to use the presidential box at the Kennedy Center in Washington. George H. W. Bush took members of Congress and their families on personally guided tours of the White House, highlighted by a souvenir snapshot of the visitors in the Lincoln bedroom. George W. Bush tries to cultivate the good will of legislators by bestowing nicknames on them.

If all else fails, a president retains the constitutional weapon of the **veto**. When Congress presents the president with a bill, ten days (Sundays excepted) are given to sign it into law, veto (disapprove) it and return it with a message explaining objections, or do nothing, in which case it becomes law without a signature. Should the president exercise the second option, a two-thirds vote in each legislative branch is necessary to override the veto. If Congress adjourns during the ten-day period and the president does not sign the bill, it is blocked with a *pocket veto*.

Overrides of presidential vetoes are infrequent. The elder Bush had only one veto overridden during his presidency, and only two vetoes were overridden in Clinton's two terms (see Table 12.1). The veto is a particularly important weapon for an administration in which the opposition party controls Congress and is pursuing its own legislative agenda. Thus, Clinton used vetoes—and threats of vetoes—to stop the Republican revolution of 1995 in its tracks, and he continued to block key Republican priorities with his vetoes for the remainder of his presidency. By contrast, enjoying the advantage of Republican dominance in

TABLE 12.1

Presidential Vetoes (1789–2004)

President	Regular Vetoes	Pocket Vetoes	Total Vetoes	Vetoes Overridden
George Washington	2		2	
John Adams			0	
Thomas Jefferson			0	
James Madison	5	2	7	
James Monroe	1		1	
John Q. Adams			0	
Andrew Jackson	5	7	12	
Martin Van Buren		1	1	
W. H. Harrison			0	
John Tyler	6	4	10	1
James K. Polk	2	1	3	
Zachary Taylor			0	
Millard Fillmore			0	
Franklin Pierce	9		9	5
James Buchanan	4	3	7	
Abraham Lincoln	2	5	7	
Andrew Jackson	21	8	29	15
Ulysses S. Grant	45	48	93	4
Rutherford B. Hayes	12	1	13	1
James A. Garfield			0	
Chester A. Arthur	4	8	12	1
Grover Cleveland	304	110	414	2
Benjamin Harrison	19	25	44	1
Grover Cleveland	42	128	170	5
William McKinley	6	36	42	
Theodore Roosevelt	42	40	82	1
William H. Taft	30	9	39	1
Woodrow Wilson	33	11	44	6
Warren G. Harding	5	1	6	
Calvin Coolidge	20	30	50	4
Herbert Hoover	21	16	37	3
Franklin D. Roosevelt	372	263	635	9
Harry S. Truman	180	70	250	12
Dwight D. Eisenhower	73	108	181	2
John F. Kennedy	12	9	21	
Lyndon B. Johnson	16	14	30	
Richard M. Nixon	26	17	43	7
Gerald R. Ford	48	18	66	12
Jimmy Carter	13	18	31	2
Ronald Reagan	39	39	78	9
George Bush	29	17	46	1
Bill Clinton	36	1	37	2
George W. Bush			0	

Source: *Presidential Vetoes, 1789–1991*, Office of the Secretary of the Senate (U.S. Government Printing Office, 1992). Updated by the authors for the Clinton and Bush presidencies.

Congress, the younger Bush did not veto a single bill during his first term. Vetoes and veto threats are not only handy for obstructing the legislation favored by the other party; employed in a strategic fashion, they can compel the congressional majority to modify legislation so that it will be closer to the preferences of the White House.

That presidents cannot regularly dominate Congress has been frustrating to those who assume that the executive is the only champion of popular democracy in national politics. But neither wisdom nor democratic purpose is always on the president's side. Congressional checks on the president fulfill the original constitutional concern to avert a dangerous concentration of power. That Congress represents political constituencies that may not gain a sympathetic hearing from the president can produce legislation that may support narrow special interests, but also legislation that may benefit weak or threatened groups, such as the poor. Rather than expecting presidents to triumph over Congress, we should accept the normality of conflict between the two branches. And we should look closely, in every contest between the president and Congress, to determine which ideologies, interests, and values each one represents.

THE PRESIDENCY AND ECONOMIC POWER

Congress is not the only powerful and independent institution with which a president must come to terms. Numerous centers of private power possess resources presidents want as well as resources to constrain them. Clashes between the White House and Capitol Hill are familiar dramas in American politics. Less visible are the connections between the presidency and the reigning powers of the political economy.

The modern American economy, dominated by multinational corporations and financial enterprises, requires direction to ensure predictability. The presidency, with its Hamiltonian potential for unified will, decisiveness, and swiftness, has long been seen as the only national institution capable of such centralized direction. Presidential responsibility has thus grown with the rise of the corporate economy.

Before the New Deal, the federal government seldom tried to affect overall economic conditions. But once the Great Depression revealed the disastrous consequences of an uncontrolled economy, President Franklin Roosevelt asserted presidential responsibility. His role became a legal responsibility of every president after him, thanks to the **Employment Act of 1946**. It gave the federal government—and especially the president—the duty "to foster and promote free competitive enterprise, to avoid economic fluctuations or to diminish the effects thereof, and to maintain employment, production, and purchasing power." The act also established the Council of Economic Advisers to assist the president and required an annual economic report to Congress.

What can presidents do to promote a healthy economy? Three policy tools are available to the president as an economic manager: fiscal policy, monetary policy, and incomes policy. Fiscal policy involves federal taxation and spending to affect economic conditions. For example, the president can propose a tax cut; such a cut will, predictably, increase economic activity. Monetary policy involves the money supply and the level of interest rates. For example, the president can, with the cooperation of the Federal Reserve, slow down inflationary pressures in the economy through higher interest rates that make borrowing money more expensive. Incomes policy is an effort to deal directly with rising prices. A president can ask the CEA to develop wage–price guideposts and ask business and labor to adhere to them.

All these actions require the president to obtain the agreement of other powerful actors and institutions. A president can propose changes in federal taxation or spending, but Congress has the final authority over them. Presidents can suggest monetary policy, but the Federal Reserve Board has the final say. They can ask business and labor to avoid price and wage decisions that fuel inflation, but short of mandatory wage–price controls (a rarity in peacetime), little can be done.[29]

Presidential power over the economy is limited by the structural power of the corporate sector, which, as we saw in Chapter 3, plays a decisive role in determining the level of private investment in America. This investment is critical to the health of the economy. Although investment decisions are made largely on economic grounds, spokespersons for big business like to attribute lagging investment to the lack of "business confidence" in a president with whom they differ. No president wants to be viewed as undermining business confidence.

Some presidents have smooth sailing with the corporate sector. Republican presidents are more likely to have personal roots in the corporate world: Ronald Reagan had been a spokesperson for General Electric, while both Bushes (and Vice President Dick Cheney) had been executives in the oil industry. Regardless of their résumés, Presidents Eisenhower, Nixon, Ford, Reagan, and the two Bushes have run administrations whose personnel and policies pleased the corporate sector. Reagan's tax cuts and deregulation of business redistributed income from working people to owners of corporate assets. The pro-business policies of George W. Bush have had the same economic effect.

Other presidents, most often Democrats, have had a rockier relationship. Elected in the face of corporate opposition, Presidents Kennedy, Carter, and Clinton struggled against charges that they were hurting business confidence and jeopardizing the health of the American economy.

These presidents have made repeated efforts to convince corporate America of their friendly intentions. After confronting the steel industry in 1962 over price increases that might have wrecked his administration's anti-inflation policy, President Kennedy turned around and actively wooed business executives with both substantive benefits and psychological gestures.[30] President Clinton played up to Wall Street with his initial deficit-reduction program in 1993 and allied himself with corporate lobbyists on several occasions to push free-trade legislation through Congress. Despite his efforts, most business executives continued to favor his Republican opponents. Clinton, like Kennedy, did not get much credit from the business community for the good things he had done for it. Clinton's secretary of labor during his first term, Robert Reich, wrote during the 2000 campaign that "no administration in modern history has been as good for American business as has the Clinton–Gore team; none have been as solicitous of the concerns of business leaders, generated as much profit for business, presided over as buoyant a stock market or as huge a run-up in executive pay."[31]

Whether Republicans or Democrats occupy the White House, corporate power has a major influence on presidential action. The business community does not have to have one of its own in the White House to benefit from presidential policy making. Its weapon of business confidence deters presidents—even ones elected primarily by the votes of ordinary working people—from pursuing a popular democratic economic agenda.

THE PRESIDENCY AND NATIONAL SECURITY

Presidential freedom of action is more extensive in foreign and military policy. Presidents enjoy greater leeway here to protect the national interest, promote democracy around the globe, or act as peacemakers. Yet if presidential dominance in foreign affairs is supposed to serve popular democratic goals, its recent history smacks more of elite democratic methods. Since World War II, presidents have made war upon their own initiative, concealed some of their actions in the deepest secrecy, and employed the agencies under their control to repress opponents. What historian Arthur Schlesinger Jr. has labeled the "imperial presidency" of the Cold War era resembles the dangerous monarch that the Anti-federalists predicted.[32]

Presidents are not free of opposition or constraint in conducting foreign and military policy. Nonetheless, they have exceptional resources when they engage in international relations—resources that cannot be matched by any other national institution.

The Constitution is an important source of these resources. It entrusts the president with making treaties and appointing American ambassadors, although it requires the concurrence of two-thirds of the Senate for the first and a majority of the Senate for the second. The president also receives ambassadors from other governments, and although this power may appear merely ceremonial, it has been interpreted as giving the president a unilateral power of U.S. recognition.

The Supreme Court has upheld a paramount role for the president in the conduct of American foreign policy. In *United States v. Curtiss-Wright Corporation* (1936), the Court gave presidents wide latitude. Writing for the majority, Justice Sutherland proclaimed "the very delicate, plenary, and exclusive power of the president as the sole organ of the federal government in international relations—a power which does not require as a basis for its exercise an act of Congress."[33]

If the Constitution and the Supreme Court have bolstered the president's position in international affairs, so have the institutional resources of the executive branch. The president receives information from American diplomatic and military personnel stationed around the globe, besides secret information from the Central Intelligence Agency (CIA) and the military intelligence services. When foreign policy controversies arise, presidents claim to be the most knowledgeable actors on the scene.

Presidential Dominance in Foreign Affairs

Because the nation needs a coherent foreign policy, a strong case can be made for presidential leadership in this area. Some scholars believe that a weakness in American foreign policy making is that the president does not have enough control.[34] Congress frequently insists on an independent role in foreign policy. Even within the executive branch, different agencies—the State Department, Defense Department, Treasury Department, CIA, National Security Council staff—compete to shape foreign policy. With all the resources in this area, a president may still have a hard time ensuring that the United States speaks with one voice to other countries.

Presidential leadership is necessary in foreign policy but is not without its dangers, as U.S. history since World War II has evidenced. During this era, the United States began to intervene in the affairs of other nations around the globe in the name of anticommunism and freedom. Employing the military machinery and covert capacities of a growing national security state (see Chapter 18), presidents staked out claims of authority that were constitutionally, politically, and morally questionable. In the name of presidential leadership, there were disturbing abuses of power in the areas of war making, secrecy, and repression.

Believing that placing the decision to go to war in the hands of a single individual was dangerous, the drafters of the Constitution entrusted that decision to the assembled representatives of the people. The president was to be the commander in chief of the armed forces once Congress determined the need for armed hostilities. Historically, however, it proved hard to keep presidents in this secondary role. Without any congressional declaration of war, presidents began to use American forces to repulse attacks on American property abroad, to suppress domestic turmoil, or to fight small-scale wars.

The capacity of a president to employ American armed forces became controversial during the Vietnam War. Presidents Johnson and Nixon were determined to carry out their Vietnam policies against rising antiwar protests from American citizens and within Congress. Once the legal authority for their war making was questioned, they asserted that the commander-in-chief clause in the Constitution gave them vast military powers. When Nixon extended the war into neighboring Cambodia in 1970, he justified his action on the grounds that, as commander in chief, he had the right to take any action necessary to protect American troops. With even less justification, he ordered the continued bombing of Cambodia in 1973, even after all American ground forces had been withdrawn. Nixon became precisely what both the framers of the Constitution and their Anti-federalist critics feared: the eighteenth-century British monarch who involved the nation in war on the basis of personal whim.

Congressional Attempts to Rein in the Executive

Congress attempted to reassert its constitutional role in war making by passing, over Nixon's veto, the **War Powers Resolution of 1973**. According to this resolution, the president must, if circumstances permit, consult with Congress before sending American forces into a situation where armed conflict is anticipated. The president must also provide Congress with a written report within forty-eight hours of dispatching American forces into combat. After sixty days, the president must withdraw these forces from combat unless Congress has declared war or otherwise authorized continued engagement. An additional thirty days is granted to remove them from combat if the president claims that this period is needed for their safe withdrawal.

Presidents since Nixon have complained that the War Powers Resolution ties their hands and undercuts American national security. The resolution actually has had little effect. Dramatic military actions since 1973, such as the invasion of Grenada or the war in the Persian Gulf, have not been hampered by the War Powers Resolution. Because the president has enjoyed a near monopoly on information in these situations and the public has supported presidential actions, Congress has been reluctant to insist on the requirements it established in 1973. It will take the assertion of a strong political will on the part of Congress, best expressed at a moment when there is no military crisis that favors the executive, before something closer to constitutional balance in war making can be attained.[35]

The end of the Cold War made only a minor difference in the control over war making. President Clinton was just as insistent as Cold War executives of his right to deploy American troops abroad without needing legal authority from Congress. In March 1999, Clinton, in concert with the United States' NATO allies, began air strikes against Yugoslavia to force the dictator Slobodan Milosevic to call an end to the killing of ethnic Albanians in the Yugoslav province of Kosovo. Legislation authorizing the president to conduct the air war against Yugoslavia passed the Senate, but on a tie vote the House failed to pass the measure. Clinton ignored this rebuff from the House and waged war anyway. As he had previously done in crises in Haiti and Bosnia, Clinton, writes political scientist David Gray Adler, claimed in the Kosovo crisis "an unlimited, unreviewable, unilateral presidential war power."[36]

The shock of the terrorist attacks of September 11, 2001, appears to have restored presidential war-making capacity to a level not seen since the war in Vietnam. Unlike President Clinton, President Bush has had little difficulty with Congress in taking the nation into wars in Afghanistan and Iraq. Bush has asserted sweeping new authority as commander-in-chief to label captured forces as "enemy combatants" and imprison them at the Guantanamo Bay naval base for an indefinite period, and some of these detainees, according to reports by investigative journalists, have been subjected to torture. Civil liberties activists have criticized the president and challenged his authority in the courts, but there has been little outcry from the public over the treatment of the prisoners.

Presidential Secrecy

Inadequate though it may be, the War Powers Resolution at least serves as a statement that we recognize the dangerous potential for abuse in the presidential power to make war. There is similar potential for abuse in the **presidential power of secrecy**. Once the United States became involved in a worldwide Cold War against communism, revolution, and nationalism, new powers of secrecy were assumed by the White House. As we shall see in more detail in Chapter 18, the CIA, created in 1947, became a weapon of presidential policy making in foreign affairs. Through the CIA, presidents could intervene covertly in the politics of other nations, bribing politicians, financing pro-American parties, or encouraging military coups against governments that the president regarded as unfavorable to U.S. interests. Clouded evidence even suggests that the CIA offered presidents means to assassinate foreign leaders.[37]

When presidents' dominant foreign policy role has been challenged, some have resorted to secret repressive tactics. The Nixon administration undertook a notorious covert campaign to destroy its critics. Journalists had their phones wiretapped. A secret White House unit, known as the Plumbers, engaged in illegal break-ins to gather damaging material on foes of Nixon's Vietnam policy. The White House compiled a large list of these critics—the Enemies List—and sought to use the auditing mechanisms of the Internal Revenue Service to harass them. Fundamental American liberties became insignificant when they stood in the way of presidential power.[38]

Secret action is enticing. It offers a president the opportunity to advance foreign policy goals through methods that would raise ethical and constitutional questions if pursued openly. It allows a policy to persist even when it lacks support from majorities in Congress and the American people. Moreover, it is rationalized by the elite democratic argument that presidents have a superior vantage point and greater expertise than Congress and the public in international affairs. But secret action denies the people presidential accountability and undermines the democratic debate.

From the Post–Cold War Era to the Post-9/11 Era

When the Cold War came to an end at the beginning of the 1990s, the presidency lost some of its advantages in foreign policy. There was no longer a feared and despised enemy, communism, against which strong presidential actions could easily be justified. There was no longer a nuclear threat, which called for quick executive decisions in moments of international crisis. There was no longer a consensus on foreign policy goals, which limited partisan disagreements and enhanced popular support.

Popular support seemed increasingly hard to come by for the post–Cold War presidency. In this new era of U.S. foreign policy, the American public appeared little interested in global affairs and less inclined to support presidential activism in foreign policy. Support was especially weak when there was a prospect that a president would use ground troops abroad and risk significant American casualties. Yet presidential ability to define national security had not altogether vanished with the disappearance of Cold War conflict. The first President Bush successfully asserted presidential power during the Gulf War. President Clinton did the same by intervening with American forces in Haiti, Bosnia, and Kosovo.

The terrorist attacks of September 11, 2001, ushered in a quite different era in U.S. foreign policy. With the horrifying crashes of hijacked jetliners into the World Trade Center and the Pentagon, a frightening new international threat stunned Americans, who had turned inward since the collapse of the Soviet Union. National security now regained the status it had held during the Cold War as the most important matter facing Americans.

For the presidency, the consequence of this terrible event was a much more supportive climate for the exercise of executive powers. Once again, there was a public consensus behind the need for assertive presidential actions to combat the terrorists. Once again, there was a despised enemy whose shadowy and sinister threat could be cited each time the president took military action abroad. And

although the threat of surprise attack from a nuclear superpower had vanished with the Cold War, warnings that terrorists or rogue nations might use weapons of mass destruction against the United States played much the same role in centering American security on the single individual in the White House.

After September 11, President Bush proclaimed that the war on terror would be the defining mission of his administration, and the role of commander-in-chief has become the core of his presidential image. Like presidents of the early Cold War era, before the war in Vietnam shattered the Cold War consensus, Bush has been able to dominate the public debate over foreign policy and to count on the willingness of Americans to endure significant military casualties for the sake of the nation's safety. However, the bloody, chaotic occupation and reconstruction of Iraq has evoked opposition from a large number of Americans. The Iraqi elections of January 2005 have raised hopes in the United States for the construction of a democratic state that will allow American troops to come home from Iraq, but if these hopes are not met and the war goes on for a long time, Bush's war power may again be questioned in a democratic debate reminiscent of the challenges to the presidency during the war in Vietnam.

THE PRESIDENT AND THE PUBLIC

Rooted in the assumptions of elite democracy, the framers of the Constitution did not want a president to get too close to the American people. They placed the immediate choice of the chief executive in the hands of electors, who were supposed to be the most distinguished political elite in each state. The framers expected that the dignity of the president's office and the long duration of the president's term would provide insulation from mass passion or popular demand for economic change.[39] Modern presidents, in contrast, claim a close bond with the American people. The voice that originates from the White House purports to be the voice of popular democracy. Cultivating public support has become a central activity of the presidency.

Present-day presidents campaign hard for public support because they believe it boosts their political influence. Congress reacts more favorably to a popular than an unpopular president; bureaucrats and interest group leaders are similarly impressed by high presidential poll ratings. To gain public support, presidents are increasingly, in the words of political scientist Samuel Kernell, "going public." A growing percentage of presidential time is spent on the road, selling White House policies. Kernell suggests that "public speaking, political travel, and appearances before special constituencies outside Washington constitute the repertoire of modern leadership."[40]

A president's effectiveness in "going public" depends in part on his or her communication skills. Among modern presidents, only Franklin Roosevelt, John F. Kennedy, Ronald Reagan, and Bill Clinton were talented at presenting their personalities and programs to the public. Yet even with skilled communicators in the White House, the impact of presidential rhetoric is often exaggerated. Ronald Reagan, labeled "The Great Communicator" by the media, was unable to win support for his anticommunist policy in Central America. Bill Clinton fought a losing public-relations battle on behalf of his health-care plan.[41] Presidential messages are ignored by many inattentive citizens and resisted by others, whose party or ideology makes them skeptical toward what the chief executive is saying. So even when presidents set out to sway public opinion to their side on a priority program, the gains they can make through "going public" are likely to be small and may not last long enough to make a difference with Congress.

Another problem that presidents face in gaining and maintaining public support is the fact that Americans hold high and often contradictory expectations of them. They expect presidents to bring prosperity, peace, and prestige to the nation, while combining the qualities of a statesman and a politician.[42]

Many presidents have not been able to live up to these inflated expectations. Starting with high rates of public approval in the honeymoon period at the beginning of their administrations, they have not been able to prevent declines in popularity over the long term. Such declines are not inevitable, however. President Reagan recovered from huge declines in public approval during the recession of 1981–82 and the Iran–Contra affair to leave office as a popular figure. President Clinton hardly had a honeymoon with the public, but his popularity, approaching record lows for a president's first two years, improved in 1995–96, when he won a budget showdown with congressional Republicans and presided over robust economic growth. Public approval of Clinton's job performance remained at a high level throughout his second term, even rising slightly during the year when he was enmeshed in a sex scandal and was impeached by the House of Representatives!

THE PRESIDENT AND THE MEDIA

The media play a major role in a modern president's relationship with the American people. If we listened only to presidents and their White House staffs, we might conclude that the media function as an impediment to presidential communication with the public. A huge corps of journalists is stationed at the White House to report on a president's every word and deed; when the president travels, the press corps follows. Presidential blunders or White House staff conflicts are often highlighted by the media, while the president's policy proposals are closely scrutinized by reporters and editorial columnists for hidden political motives. Some presidents' political standing has been badly damaged by negative media coverage.

However, White House complaints about the media tell only one side of the story. The media—especially TV—provide a vehicle through which a modern president can cultivate support. The White House staff includes a Press Office and an Office of Communications; if these units are skilled at public relations, the media provide opportunities for dramatic presidential appearances, colorful photo opportunities, and engrossing human interest stories about the "first family." If the president has an attractive personality and is a skilled public speaker, the media can amplify his or her charm, wit, or eloquence in a manner that presidents living before the age of television might well have envied.[43]

Among recent administrations, Ronald Reagan's achieved the greatest mastery over the media. In contrast to Reagan, Bill Clinton had a tumultuous relationship with the media. During the 1992 Democratic primaries, Bill and Hillary Rodham Clinton had resented the press's focus on charges of the candidate's marital infidelity, draft evasion, and marijuana smoking. When Clinton entered the White House in 1993, he struck back at the press by closing staff offices to reporters, making it known that press conferences would be infrequent, and going directly to the public with town hall meetings and cable TV appearances. But Clinton had underestimated the power of the press. Throughout his two terms, he received a great deal of negative coverage, with the press playing a large role in highlighting the various scandals that dogged his presidency.[44]

Presidents differ in their relations with the media, but developments in White House–media relations transcend personalities. With the end of the Cold War, presidents had a diminished capacity for foreign policy drama. Whereas Ronald Reagan could go to the Berlin Wall, Korea, and numerous summits with the Soviets, all of which provided heroic TV, Bill Clinton had to face Bosnia, Somalia, and Haiti, hardly colorful photo opportunities. Changes in technology have also shrunk the audience that watches prime-time presidential speeches. As Matthew Baum and Samuel Kernell note, "What broadcast technology gave the president, cable technology appears to be taking away. In recent years, as the number of television households receiving cable has swelled, as have the programming alternatives it offers, the percentage of viewers who stay tuned to the president has steadily declined."[45]

George W. Bush enjoyed a more favorable press than Clinton did during his early months in the presidency. Bush also benefited when the attacks of 9/11 restored drama to the president's appearances as commander in chief. His administration has emulated Richard Nixon's in trying to manufacture favorable media coverage. It has awarded government contracts to conservative columnists who praise the president's programs in their writing, and it has distributed news videos to local TV stations that neglect to mention that they have been produced by executive agencies, even as they provide a positive depiction of the administration's undertakings.[46]

On the other hand, the shrinking audience for presidential television has made it harder for Bush than for a Kennedy or a Reagan to use the media as his preferred vehicle. This constraint on presidential communication will be unfortunate if a president wants to educate the American people about new problems and policies. But it may also reduce White House manipulation of the public through the media. From the standpoint of popular democracy, the diminishing ability of a president to dominate the media is welcome. A vital democratic debate is not monopolized by the occupant of the White House.[47]

THE PRESIDENCY AND DEMOCRATIC MOVEMENTS

Presidents try to sway public opinion through the media. Can members of the public directly sway the president? What impact can popular democratic movements have on presidential policies?

Some of the finest presidential moments have come when the chief executive responded to citizens and moved the nation closer to fulfillment of its democratic values. When Abraham Lincoln responded to mounting abolitionist pressures by emancipating slaves, when Franklin Roosevelt supported mobilized labor for collective bargaining rights, when Lyndon Johnson endorsed the civil rights movement by voicing its slogan, "We shall overcome," the presidency became an instrument of popular democratic leadership. These presidents were moved in the direction of popular democracy by the force of popular pressures, which compelled them to rethink their previous political calculations. But their popular democratic leadership was not simply a matter of gaining new support or attracting new voters. Mass movements educated these presidents, giving them a new understanding of democratic responsibilities.

Earlier in the chapter, we noted how President Kennedy responded to pressure from big business. But big business was not the only group to influence him; the civil rights movement also changed where Kennedy stood.[48] Kennedy was sympathetic to the movement for racial equality. However, civil rights did not hold a high priority for him. He wished to concentrate on the Cold War struggle against communism. He worried that strong backing for black equality would cost him support among southern members of Congress and southern voters. So he refused to push civil rights legislation or make statements about the immorality of racial discrimination, settling instead for quiet and gradual administrative actions.

The civil rights movement refused to settle for Kennedy's token gestures. The issue of racial equality was too central to democracy to permit the continuance of an unjust status quo. Movement organizations began dramatic campaigns of civil disobedience (see Chapter 10), designed not only to compel action from local white elites but also to pressure the president. In his first two years in office, Kennedy was able to resist this pressure. But in 1963, when civil rights demonstrators led by Martin Luther King Jr. in Birmingham, Alabama, were savagely attacked with dogs and fire hoses, a horrified nation looked to the president.

Kennedy did respond, offering an example of popular democratic leadership. Having been educated himself by the Birmingham demonstrations about the depth of the racial crisis, he was ready to sweep aside his previous caution and take bold action. He proposed a major civil rights law (see Chapter 16). Equally important, he spoke to the nation with words that captured the moral urgency of the civil rights struggle: "We are confronted primarily with a moral issue. It is as old as the Scriptures and is as clear as the American Constitution. . . . This nation, for all of its hopes and all its boasts, will not be fully free until all its citizens are free."[49]

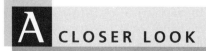

A CLOSER LOOK

Popular or Elite Democrat? The Case of George W. Bush

We have seen that while presidents present themselves as champions of popular democracy, and on occasion live up to this billing, many forces press them in the direction of elite democracy. President George W. Bush has appeared before the American public as a "regular guy" whose plainspoken talk and mainstream ways rebuke the pretensions of "elitist" liberals. So Bush provides an instructive case study for examining the place of the presidency in the debate between elite democracy and popular democracy.

In matters of lifestyle, Bush comes across to Americans as anything but a member of the elite. Despite his education at Yale and Harvard, his language is often ungrammatical and unpolished. His demeanor is cordial and unpretentious; indeed, he likes to tease more solemn officials by bestowing nicknames upon them. His simple professions of faith connect him to the religious values of a majority of Americans. Even his preference for vacations signals his populist bent; unlike Bill Clinton, who favored the company of the rich and famous on fashionable Martha's Vineyard, Bush likes to clear brush on his dusty Texas ranch. In spite of his birth into the wealthy and distinguished Bush clan, most Americans think of "Dubya" as someone to whom they could

relate. During the 2004 campaign, polls showed that far more Americans would like to have a beer with Bush than with his challenger, John Kerry.

Yet like other modern presidents, including Bill Clinton, Bush travels mostly in elite circles. Courting the voters with a popular style, Bush reminds the wealthy of his deeper bonds with them. Speaking at an $800-a-plate dinner in 2000, to an audience attired in formal wear, Bush quipped: "This is an impressive crowd: the haves and the have-mores. Some people call you the elite. I call you my base."

A brief look at some of Bush's policies shows that he was not actually joking. The tax legislation that the president steered through Congress in 2001 and 2003 offered cuts to every tax-paying American—but the bulk of the savings went to a tiny fraction of Americans. Studies of the distribution of Bush's tax cuts vary depending on the methods and assumptions of analysts, but most such studies show that the top 1 percent of earners will receive around 40 percent of the tax savings. According to an analysis by Citizens for Tax Justice, Bush's 2003 bill will bring less than $100 per year in tax relief to half of American earners, whereas those Americans who make $1 million or more a year will average a tax reduction of $93,500.

CONCLUSION: THE ELITE DEMOCRATIC PRESIDENCY

The story of John F. Kennedy and the civil rights movement shows that presidents sometimes act as popular democratic leaders. It also suggests the requirements of the role. If presidents are genuinely concerned about promoting popular democracy, they should respect the capacities and intelligence of the people they claim to lead. Rather than manipulating public opinion, they should engage in a dialogue with citizens. Rather than aiming only to boost their own power, they should recognize their responsibility to empower ordinary citizens.

Popular democrats have long warned of the dangers of extreme economic inequality for a democracy; Bush's tax policy increases such inequality.

Bush's energy and environmental policies have a procorporate thrust that reflects elite interests and ideas. Earlier in the chapter, it was noted that Vice President Cheney, himself an alumnus of the energy industry, headed an administration task force on energy policy that consulted industry representatives while largely shutting out environmentalists. The result was predictable: Bush's legislative proposal on energy adhered so closely to the goals of the energy industry that environmental groups charged that the proposal had actually been written by lobbyists from the oil, gas, and coal companies. Environmental policy, which was redirected to reduce intrusions on private property and open more federal land to logging, mining, and drilling, was in similar hands under Bush. Looking at whom Bush appointed to federal agencies responsible for environmental management, political scientist Mark Peterson writes, "One finds a long list of individuals who previously worked for or lobbied on behalf of the oil, natural gas, coal mining, timber, chemical-manufacturing, pesticide, electric power, and cattle industries or served at libertarian think tanks and advocacy centers."

One of the most influential industries during the Bush presidency has been the pharmaceutical industry. Drug companies were among the largest contributors to Bush's campaigns in 2000 and 2004. When the administration, competing with Democrats for the allegiance of senior citizens, promoted its plan in Congress in 2003 for prescription drug coverage under Medicare, the drug companies put their muscle to work for the plan. According to a report by Public Citizen, the drug industry deployed a battalion of 824 lobbyists, costing over $108 million, to ensure that its interests were protected in the legislation. Bush's successful bill reflected their effort: The new law prohibited Medicare from negotiating with the drug companies for lower prices and forbade the importation of cheaper medicines from Canada.

All politicians look to take care of their base. George W. Bush could not have won and retained the presidency without his base among religious conservatives, most of whom are ordinary people with ordinary incomes. But the money that has financed his rise to power and his reelection, and the personnel that have shaped his policies and staffed his administration, have come from a different part of his base: "the haves and the have-mores." Even more in his second term than in his first, the agenda of President Bush reflects the influence of his corporate backers.

Sources: Colin Campbell and Bert Rockman, eds., *The George W. Bush Presidency: Appraisals and Prospects* (Washington, D.C.: Congressional Quarterly Press, 2004); www.dubyaspeak.com; Chris Hartman and David Martin, "Bush Tax Cuts Unfair," www.faireconomy.org; Public Citizen, "The Medicare Drug War," www.citizen.org; Jim VandeHei, "Business Sees Gain in GOP Takeover," *Washington Post*, March 27, 2005.

Presidents will not play the part of popular democratic leader very frequently. More often, as the case of George W. Bush suggests, the presidency is an instrument of elite democracy. Surrounded by a huge staff and living like monarchs, presidents tend to be cut off from ordinary Americans. Elitist attitudes and secrecy further distance the president, while making accountability difficult. Connections to and pressures from organized private interests, especially from the corporate sector, contradict the presidential claim to represent popular democracy. Presidents may cloak themselves in the symbols of popular democracy, but the modern presidential drama, featuring larger-than-life chief executives and passive citizens, is a far cry from the authentic American tradition of popular democracy.

KEY TERMS

White House staff
Executive Office of the President
    (EOP)
Office of Management and Budget
    (OMB)
Council of Economic Advisers (CEA)
National Security Council (NSC)

president's cabinet
executive order
legislative liaison staff
veto
Employment Act of 1946
War Powers Resolution of 1973
presidential power of secrecy

**INTERNET
RESOURCES**

■ The White House
www.whitehouse.gov

The presidential website, containing speeches, documents, press briefings, and assorted information on the administration; also offers e-mail communication with the White House.

■ Center for the Study of the Presidency
www.cspresidency.org

A nonpartisan organization that holds student conferences and publishes a scholarly journal, *Presidential Studies Quarterly*; its website offers publications and provides links to research sites on the presidency.

**SUGGESTED
READINGS**

Charles Jones, *The Presidency in a Separated System*. Washington, D.C.: The Brookings Institution, 1994. An important argument that we should look less to the success of the president than to the success of the political system.

Sidney M. Milkis and Michael Nelson, *The American Presidency: Origins and Development, 1776–2002*. Washington, D.C.: Congressional Quarterly Press, 2003. A comprehensive history of the presidency.

Bruce Miroff, *Icons of Democracy: American Leaders as Heroes, Aristocrats, Dissenters, and Democrats*. Lawrence: University Press of Kansas, 2000. Portraits of both elite democratic and popular democratic leadership.

Michael Nelson, ed., *The Presidency and the Political System*, 8th ed. Washington, D.C.: Congressional Quarterly Press, 2006. A lively anthology of original articles on the presidency.

Richard E. Neustadt, *Presidential Power and the Modern Presidents*. New York: Free Press, 1990. The classic work on how presidents can gain—or lose—personal power in the White House.

Stephen Skowronek, *The Politics Presidents Make*. Cambridge, Mass.: Harvard University Press, 1997. A pathbreaking historical/structural approach that relates presidential success or failure to the rise and fall of political regimes.

Bureaucracy
Myth and Reality

On March 1, 1995, the U.S. House of Representatives debated "regulatory reform," one of the items in the Republicans' Contract with America. Republican after Republican took the floor to lambaste the evils of bureaucratic regulation. Congressman George Gekas of Pennsylvania leveled a common charge against regulation: "Mr. Chairman, for too long, burdensome and complex rules coming out of Washington have strangled small business. . . . What we are about here today is to slay that dragon, to bring about sanity in the rule-making process of the national bureaucracy." But the most colorful denunciation came from a conservative Democrat, Congressman James Traficant Jr. of Ohio, in a blast at the Environmental Protection Agency: "Mr. Chairman, I am one Democrat who believes regulations have gone too far. . . . It is so bad that if a dog urinates on a side lot, it may be declared a wetlands." March 1, 1995, was a field day for one of America's favorite political sports, bureaucracy bashing.[1]

Bureaucracy comprises the units of the executive branch organized in a hierarchical fashion, governed through formal rules, and distinguished by specialized functions. This chapter concentrates on bureaucracy at the national level. Although all federal bureaus have hierarchy, rule-bound behavior, and specialization, they vary considerably in how they are organized, who staffs them, and what work they do. The employee of the Social Security Administration in Washington processing checks for Social Security recipients and the forest ranger checking on wildlife in the remote reaches of a national park are both bureaucrats. Bureaucracy is not the drab monolith that bureaucracy-bashers condemn.

Bureaucracy is indeed a problem for a democratic political order, but it is also a necessity. It is a problem because bureaucratic hierarchy, expertise, and insulation from direct accountability can produce government operations that ignore the concerns of ordinary citizens. It is a necessity because our modern complex society, including the programs and policies that a democratic majority wants, requires skilled public administration.

This chapter neither bashes nor praises bureaucracy. Rather, it explains the democratic debate over bureaucracy in American politics. Two sets of key questions characterize this debate. First, how much bureaucracy do we need? Can bureaucracy be drastically cut back—for example, by turning to the alternative of economic markets, as some elite democrats now propose? Second, where bureaucracy is necessary, whose influence shapes its behavior? Are bureaucratic agencies predominantly influenced by elites? Or are these agencies responsive to popular democratic forces?

The chapter begins with a short history of the democratic debate over bureaucracy and then examines the size and scope of the modern administrative state in America, clearing away in the process some common myths about bureaucracy. Bureaucracies are inevitably entangled in politics, and the next two sections look at the internal and external political worlds of bureaucracy. Regulation of the economy and society by government—the principal preoccupation of conservative critics of bureaucracy—is the subject of the fifth section of the chapter. Finally, the chapter discusses competing proposals for reforming bureaucracy.

THE DEMOCRATIC DEBATE OVER BUREAUCRACY: A SHORT HISTORY

Bureaucracy has been one of the principal battlegrounds between elite democrats and popular democrats, both of whom have approached the issue with mixed emotions. Elite democrats have usually been the ones building up bureaucratic

capacity in the federal government, but sometimes they have feared that what they have built might be transformed into an instrument of popular democratic control. (This fear is central to the contemporary elite reaction against bureaucracy.) Popular democrats have usually resisted the growth of bureaucracy, but sometimes they have needed it to turn popular democratic objectives into reality.

The Beginnings of American Administration

The Constitution says very little about how the president, as chief executive, will delegate the actual enforcement of the laws. When the first administration was formed under George Washington, there was not much of a bureaucracy. Befitting the aristocratic perspective of the Federalists, national administrators were recruited from the class of "gentlemen," and it was assumed that their personal character and reputation would ensure their good conduct without the need for impersonal rules and institutional checks.

However, Alexander Hamilton saw that a more systematic, impersonal, *bureaucratic* organization of government could achieve some of the central goals of elite democracy. In *The Federalist Papers*, he wrote that the people's "confidence in and obedience to a government will commonly be proportioned to the goodness or badness of its administration."[2] Associating popular democratic politics with disorder, Hamilton thought that efficient administration would pacify the people, turning them from active citizens into satisfied recipients of government services. As secretary of the treasury, he made his own department into a model of bureaucratic organization and efficiency.[3]

The first major challenge to the rule of gentleman administrators came from Jacksonian Democracy. Speaking the language of popular democracy, President Jackson proclaimed that "The duties of all public officers are, or at least admit of being made so plain and simple that men of intelligence may readily qualify themselves for their performance."[4] Although Jackson seemed to be saying that ordinary citizens should fill most of the federal posts, in practice he removed only about 10 percent of the civil servants who had labored under his predecessors and replaced them mostly with well-connected lawyers. However, Jackson's presidency was notable for relying less on trust in the personal character of administrators and more on formal rules and procedures to supervise their behavior. In this regard, political scientist Matthew Crenson writes, "the chief administrative legacy of the Jacksonians was bureaucracy."[5]

The Spoils System and Civil Service Reform

Jackson's successors followed his rhetoric more than his practice, turning out large numbers of officeholders and replacing them with supporters. Under this **spoils system**, the victor in each presidential election considered federal employment mostly as an opportunity for political patronage. In one sense, the nineteenth-century spoils system was democratic: It allowed ordinary people, through their work in a political party, to achieve government positions previously reserved for elites. But the periodic shuffling of civil servants made for inefficient administration, and the close ties of civil servants to local party machines opened the door to corruption.

The system's defects sparked a reform movement after the Civil War that aimed to institute a different basis for selecting national administrators. Reformers demanded that federal employment be based not on party service but on competitive examinations and other measures of competence. Their cause was given a boost when a disappointed office seeker, crazed by his failure to get a patronage position, assassinated President James A. Garfield in 1881. With public attention now fixed on the evils of the spoils system, Congress passed the Pendleton Act in 1883, establishing a civil service commission to administer a merit system for federal employment. Civil service reform, although an important step toward a more efficient and honest federal bureaucracy, was also a victory for elite democrats: Reformers were mainly from the upper class and expected that their class would regain its once-dominant role in administration through examinations that favored the highly educated.

As industrialization transformed American life in the closing decades of the nineteenth century, the problem of regulating the giant business corporations that were emerging gave a further impetus to builders of bureaucracy. Allied with upper-class civil service reformers seeking to expand the administrative capacities of the federal government was a new class of professionals, especially lawyers and social scientists. These state builders were largely elite democrats whose goal was a more rational, expert-dominated administrative order insulated from the partisan strife of popular politics. However, they were stalemated by foes of a federal bureaucracy. Some were genuine popular democrats afraid of new institutions beyond the people's reach. Others, however, were concerned mainly with preserving local party machines and their pork barrel prizes.[6]

It was in the first decades of the twentieth century—the Progressive era— that the bureaucratic state in America first assumed its modern form. The Progressives hoped to combine popular democracy and elite democracy. They sponsored reforms, such as the initiative, referendum, and recall (which allow citizens to vote on legislation and to remove elected officials), that aimed to take power away from party bosses and return it directly to the people. They also proposed to staff an expanded administrative order with scientifically trained and politically neutral experts. As political scientist James Morone has written, "At the heart of the Progressive agenda lay a political paradox: government would simultaneously be returned to the people and placed beyond them, in the hands of the experts."[7] But the Progressives succeeded neither in restoring power to the people nor in achieving scientific administration. The agencies of government they created to regulate an industrial economy generally found it impossible to devise truly scientific standards that furthered the public interest. Even worse, the elite economic interests that were supposed to be the subjects of regulation generally became the most powerful influence on the regulators.

The New Deal and Bureaucracy

The Great Depression led to an expansion of the federal bureaucracy beyond even the hopes of the Progressive reformers, and the New Deal changed the attitudes of popular democrats toward bureaucracy. Just as in the case of federalism (Chapter 15), the need to achieve control over the corporations compelled popular democrats to accept a more powerful and bureaucratic federal government. Yet elite democrats still retained considerable influence within this government. The hastily built administrative apparatus of Franklin Roosevelt contained both popular democratic and elite democratic elements.

Harry Hopkins, a leading administrator, was one example of the New Deal's success in reconciling popular democracy and bureaucracy. President Roosevelt placed Hopkins in charge of federal efforts to aid the unemployed. Hopkins took charge of these efforts in a fashion that led biographer George McJimsey to dub him "democracy's bureaucrat."[8] Putting a public works program for the unemployed into operation with remarkable speed, Hopkins proclaimed that "The only thing that counts is action . . . and we are going to surround [the program] with as few regulations as possible."[9] Determined to avoid bureaucratic red tape, Hopkins was equally determined to avoid the bureaucrat's reliance on a formal hierarchy of superiors and subordinates. He ran his Washington office through group discussion and kept in close touch with administrators in the field who were working with the unemployed.

Hopkins's values, as much as his methods, made him a popular democrat as bureaucrat. When critics complained of waste and confusion in the public works programs that Hopkins headed, he conceded that he had made mistakes. But he would not apologize for them because they had been made "in the interests of the people that were broke."[10] To Hopkins, administration was not primarily a matter of scientific expertise but an opportunity to practice civic virtue. "One of the proudest and finest things that ever happened and ever can happen to me," he said, "is the opportunity to work for this government of ours and the people who make it up. . . . I wouldn't give this last two years of my life for a life work done in another type of endeavor. I have learned, as I never knew before, what it means to love your country."[11]

Unfortunately, much of the bureaucratic machinery created by the New Deal did not reflect either Hopkins's methods or his values. To cope with the emergency conditions of the Depression, the New Deal tied many of the new administrative agencies to the industrial and agricultural interests with which they dealt. Allowing private interests to play a powerful role in public agencies was supposed to be a temporary measure. But when the Depression passed, the tight bonds between private interests and public agencies remained. The bureaucratic state became, to a disturbing degree, a special interest state in which administrative expertise was placed in the service of economic elites.

The next major expansion of American bureaucracy came during the 1960s and early 1970s, with new administrative units established to carry out popular democratic goals such as environmental protection, consumer safety, and the elimination of poverty. Yet while the bureaucracy was becoming a more complicated mixture of elite and popular democratic elements, its image was becoming more simplistic and negative. Bureaucracy—with a capital *B*—became a bogeyman for critics of every political persuasion. Conservatives saw a swollen and monstrous Bureaucracy as the chief threat to individual freedom. Liberals and radicals saw an arrogant and stifling Bureaucracy as the chief barrier to social change. It was the conservatives, with the election of Ronald Reagan in 1980, who had the chance to act on their ideological hostility to bureaucracy.

From Ronald Reagan to George W. Bush: Attack or Reinvent Bureaucracy?

President Reagan entered office as an avowed enemy of bureaucracy, and during his eight years as chief executive he presided over an unprecedented assault on federal administration. Because Congress blunted many of his attacks, Reagan was not able to enact drastic cuts in the federal bureaucracy. But he did manage to heap scorn on bureaucracy and to broadcast negative stereotypes of it to the public.

Big government, the president told Americans, best served the public by "shriveling up and going away."[12] White House chief of staff Edwin Meese showed off a doll he named "the Bureaucrat"; he put the doll on a pile of papers and pointed out how it just sat there and did nothing.[13] In this hostile climate, many civil servants felt undermined and demoralized. The bureaucracy managed to survive Ronald Reagan, but a serious democratic debate over bureaucracy, based on recognition of its true features, had been obscured by scornful stereotypes.

President Clinton and Vice President Al Gore tackled the topic of bureaucratic reform. Even though they hoped, like Reagan, to cut down the size of the bureaucracy, their principal goal was different: They wanted the federal government to work better, not to shrivel up and go away. Meanwhile, the congressional Republican majority after 1994 renewed President Reagan's assault on the bureaucracy.

George W. Bush did not enter the presidency with the overt anti-bureaucratic agenda of Ronald Reagan. Yet Bush has been as determined as Reagan to assert control over federal agencies and to re-direct them to conservative purposes. Political scientist Paul Light observes that under Bush, White House control over the bureaucracy has been "more coordinated and centralized than it has ever been."[14] In approaching the bureaucracy, Bush has enjoyed two political advantages that Reagan lacked. First, legislative opposition to Bush has been weaker, especially since the 2002 elections that brought Republicans control of both houses of Congress. Thus, the kinds of congressional hearings that had embarrassed the Reagan administration over its cutbacks in environmental protection have rarely been conducted in a Congress under the sway of Bush allies. Second, public preoccupation with the war on terror has relegated regulatory issues to the media's back pages. Administrative rule-making that would have erupted in public controversies in Reagan's day barely causes a ripple in the post-9/11 environment. Bush's conservative redirection of the federal bureaucracy is covered in more detail later in this chapter.

THE MODERN ADMINISTRATIVE STATE IN AMERICA

The present-day federal government is largely an **administrative state**. It is involved in regulating or supporting almost every imaginable form of social activity by means of a large, complex, and diverse bureaucracy. In this section, we present a snapshot of the contemporary federal bureaucracy, depicting its most important features. We also set these features against some prevailing myths about bureaucracy.

The Civil Service

About 2.7 million Americans work as civil servants in the federal bureaucracy. (About 1.4 million more serve in the armed forces.) Contrary to the image of a centralized bureaucratic machine, approximately 90 percent of these federal employees work outside Washington, D.C. Most bureaucrats deliver services where the people are—whether as Social Security branch workers, air traffic controllers, or civilian employees at military installations. Although the federal bureaucracy draws the most attention from critics, it is actually smaller in terms of personnel than state and local governments. Moreover, the number of federal civil servants has been declining even as the number of state and local civil servants has been increasing. The states employ about 5.1 million workers, and local governments employ about 13.3 million.[15] When all levels of government are taken into account, about one out of seven employed people in the United States can be called a government bureaucrat![16] (See Table 13.1.)

A majority of federal bureaucrats hold their positions in accordance with the General Schedule, a merit-based personnel system in which there are eighteen pay grades. At the bottom of the General Schedule, GS–1, are the most menial tasks. At the top, GS–18, are executive positions of considerable responsibility and high pay. Competitive examinations and formal education are the two principal determinants of merit in the General Schedule. But other factors may be taken into account, with preference given to armed forces veterans and affirmative action programs for minorities.

At the highest reaches of the bureaucracy are the president's political appointees. Their merits are not necessarily the same as those of career civil servants. Certainly, managerial competence is valued for political appointees, but so are loyalty to the president and agreement with his political program. Presidential appointees are sometimes called "in and outers" because their tenure in public service is usually short; in fact, most do not last for the four years of a president's term.

Although civil servants are supposed to be impartial and to serve whichever party controls the executive branch with equal dedication, the political values and views of federal bureaucrats have been influenced by shifts in political power. From the New Deal through the Great Society, Democrats most often controlled the presidency and a substantial majority of federal bureaucrats identified with the party that had built up the administrative state. Since 1968, however, Republicans have occupied the White House two-thirds of the time and the political coloration of the bureaucracy has been altered. When political scientists Joel Aberbach and Bert Rockman first surveyed federal civil servants in

TABLE 13.1		
Governmental Employment, 2002	Government	Full-time and Part-time Employees (in thousands)
	Federal civilian	2,690
	State	5,072
	Local	(13,277)
	County	2,729
	Municipalities	2,972
	School districts	6,367
	Townships	488
	Special districts	721
	Total	21,039

Source: *Statistical Abstract of the United States 2004–2005* (Washington, D.C.: U.S. Government Printing Office, 2004).

1970, they found that Democrats outnumbered Republicans by a three-to-one ratio. In a similar survey they conducted two decades later, Republicans outnumbered Democrats by 11 percent.[17]

Types of Federal Agencies

The administrative state in America is made up of a bewildering variety of bureaucracies. Federal agencies differ from one another on many scores: form of organization, type of leadership, breadth or narrowness of function, political dependence on or independence from the president, financial dependence on or independence from Congress.

Cabinet departments are the bureaucratic agencies most familiar to Americans. When the federal government was formed, its first agencies were the departments of State, Treasury, and War (along with the individual position of attorney general). Today, there are fifteen cabinet departments, each headed by a secretary appointed by the president: State, Treasury, Defense, Interior, Agriculture, Justice, Commerce, Labor, Health and Human Services, Housing and Urban Development, Transportation, Energy, Education, Veterans Affairs, and Homeland Security. These departments vary enormously in size and complexity. But each is responsible for a broad area of governmental operations whose administration is divided up among specialized bureaus within the department.

Independent agencies stand outside the cabinet departments and generally handle narrower areas of government operation. Examples are the Environmental Protection Agency (EPA), the National Aeronautics and Space Administration (NASA), and the Central Intelligence Agency (CIA). Like cabinet departments, most independent agencies are headed by a single individual appointed by the president. Some, however, like the Merit System Protection Board, which governs federal employment, are multi-headed. Congress sometimes creates independent agencies, rather than simply establishing new bureaus within existing cabinet departments, in the hope that a new agency will be more innovative if it is free of the bureaucratic routines and intraorganizational conflicts that typify existing cabinet departments.

Independent regulatory commissions are designed to regulate various sectors of the economy. Examples are the Nuclear Regulatory Commission, which regulates the nuclear power industry, and the Securities and Exchange Commission (SEC), which regulates the stock market. By creating multimember commissions drawn from both parties and by giving the commissioners long terms and exemption from presidential removal, Congress has tried to distance these agencies from political pressures and make them neutral and expert regulators. In practice, however, the independent regulatory commissions have not been able to separate administration from politics. Presidents are able to exert some influence by their choice of a chair for the commission. The regulated industry itself is a constant source of political pressure as it lobbies the commission for favorable decisions.

Public corporations are government agencies that engage in business activities. The most familiar of these is the Postal Service (until 1971, the Post Office was a cabinet department). Others are the Tennessee Valley Authority (TVA), which generates and sells electric power; Amtrak, which operates passenger railroads; and the Corporation for Public Broadcasting, which sponsors public television and radio. Public corporations have been created largely to carry out economic activities deemed unprofitable by private businesses. The organizational form of public corporations protects them from most political influences. Further, they enjoy far greater financial independence than other kinds of federal agencies, such as the ability to borrow money on their own rather than relying solely on appropriations from Congress.

Federal foundations or endowments allow the government to sponsor scientific and cultural activities that might otherwise languish for lack of funds. The National Science Foundation (NSF) is a major donor to scientific research in the United States. The National Institutes of Health (NIH) funds research on dangerous diseases, such as acquired immune deficiency syndrome (AIDS). The National Endowment for the Humanities (NEH) and the National Endowment for the Arts (NEA) support the creative projects of scholars, writers, and artists.

Myth and Reality in the Administrative State

To its many detractors, the federal bureaucracy is a bastion of elite privilege and irresponsibility. The expertise and power wielded by bureaucrats lend some credence to these criticisms. But myths about bureaucracy exaggerate its elitist character; in reality, the federal bureaucracy is a complex mix of elite and popular democratic features.

Probably the most powerful of the myths about the modern administrative state concerns the identity of the typical bureaucrat. The faceless bureaucrat of myth is inefficient and lazy on one hand, aggressive and hyperactive in meddling in people's lives on the other. But in truth bureaucrats are ordinary people. Compared to presidents and members of Congress, bureaucrats as a group are more representative of the American population.

Even if bureaucrats do resemble other Americans, proponents of the bureaucratic myth contend that the rigid rules of bureaucracy attract people with authoritarian personalities and that the tedious nature of bureaucratic work makes civil servants frustrated and irritable. In this view, bureaucrats, however average they may be with respect to their backgrounds, are afflicted with a "bureaucratic mentality." Yet there is not much evidence that such a mentality is common. On the contrary, public administration scholar Charles T. Goodsell observes, "numerous empirical studies strongly refute the concept of a unified, pervasive bureaucratic personality characterized by inflexibility, conservatism, alienation, timidity, ruthlessness, [or] uncaring haughtiness . . ."[18] These studies demonstrate that on the average, bureaucrats are as open-minded and flexible as employees in the private sector and approach civil service jobs with strong levels of motivation and pride.

But if bureaucrats are ordinary people with regular personalities and a positive attitude toward their work, why do most citizens have a negative attitude toward bureaucracy? Actually, this view has more to do with bureaucracy in the abstract. It reflects constant bureaucracy bashing by politicians and the media.

TABLE 13.2

Size of U.S.
Government
Executive
Departments:
Civilian Personnel,
2003

Department	Personnel
Agriculture	107,204
Commerce	37,330
Defense	669,096
Education	4,593
Energy	15,823
Health and Human Services	67,240
Homeland Security	146,963
Housing and Urban Development	10.660
Interior	74,818
Justice	115,259
Labor	16,296
State	31,402
Transportation	89,262
Treasury	134,202
Veterans Affairs	226,171

Source: Statistical Abstract of the United States 2004–2005 (Washington, D.C.: U.S. Government Printing Office, 2004).

When questioned about contact with civil servants, a large majority report satisfactory experiences.[19]

The myth of bureaucracy rests not only on stereotypes of the individual bureaucrat but also on stereotypes of the organizations that make up the federal bureaucracy. According to these stereotypes, federal agencies are gigantic, aggressively growing larger all the time, and immensely powerful. In reality, federal agencies come in many sizes and shapes. The Department of Defense, with approximately 670,000 civilian employees, supports the image of a gigantic bureaucracy. But most other cabinet departments and independent agencies are much smaller. For instance, the Department of Education has fewer than 5,000 employees (see Table 13.2).

The mythical bureaucratic agency is power hungry, eagerly grasping for ever-larger functions, programs, and budgets. But real bureaucratic agencies are hesitant about growth if it threatens their identity. Most agencies have a **mission**, a central task to which its members are committed. They welcome more authority and money in pursuit of this mission. But they are not eager to take on divergent missions even when these would bring growth to the agency. Thus, the Department of Agriculture, which defines its mission as assisting America's farmers, has been unhappy with—and tried to get rid of—its role in the welfare area as administrator of the food stamp program.[20]

Most bureaucratic agencies are not as large or as imperialistic as believers in the bureaucratic myth presume. Neither are they as powerful. Subject to many constraining forces, federal agencies tend to be defensive rather than offensive, to placate other holders of power rather than assert their own power.[21]

In criticizing the prevalent myth about bureaucracy, we do not mean to claim that all is well with the American administrative state. Many problems of rigidity, inefficiency, and promotion of bureaucratic goals over public needs deserve attention. However, the prevalent myth focuses attention on bureaucracy simply to turn it into a scapegoat. Bureaucracy is a convenient scapegoat for elected politicians who wish to divert attention from their own inability to carry through on the promises they make to voters. It is a convenient scapegoat for citizens who resent both the taxes they pay and the social ills that never seem to get cured by federal spending.

Bureaucrats as Policy Makers

Understanding bureaucracy in a realistic way requires, above all, recognition that bureaucracy is a *political* institution. The scholars who founded the study of public administration in the United States (one of them a future president, Woodrow Wilson) sought to distinguish administration from politics. Bureaucracies existed, they claimed, only to provide the technical means for carrying out ends that political (i.e., elected) officials had decided.[22] Today, few believe in the politics–administration dichotomy. Administrators operate in an intensely political environment, and they must make key political decisions themselves. They are policy makers, not just technicians.

Administrators are politically influential because they possess **expertise**. Bureaucrats tend to know more than anyone else about their particular areas of responsibility. Expertise may come through a combination of specialization and experience. Compare the career civil servant, who has spent many years dealing with a single policy area, to the elected official, who must tackle many different policy areas with a shorter base of experience. An even more formidable ground of expertise is professional training. "A variety of highly trained elites," writes political scientist Francis Rourke, "practice their trade in public organizations— physicists, economists, engineers."[23] The arguments of these elites carry special weight because they are presumed to draw from professional knowledge. Elected officials are the bosses of civil servants but often defer to their expertise.[24]

Bureaucratic expertise is central to the democratic debate over bureaucracy. In the eighteenth and nineteenth centuries, it was elite democrats who were most enthusiastic about bureaucratic expertise. Since the New Deal, however, many elite democrats have come to favor the market mechanisms of the private sector and have grown skeptical about expertise in government.

Popular democrats are also troubled by the claims of expertise. They recognize that when bureaucrats invoke technical criteria to address a problem, the

concerns of ordinary citizens may be shunted aside. For example, highway planners have sometimes ravaged communities in the name of engineering criteria.
Yet popular democrats also recognize that their political agenda requires the help
of experts. How, for example, can we clean up the environment without the
efforts of environmental scientists?

Administrators are also politically influential because they exercise considerable **discretion**. Handed broad and vague policy guidelines by elected officials,
administrators give policy substance through numerous, more concrete decisions. For example, Congress directs the Occupational Safety and Health Administration (OSHA) to protect employees from cancer-causing chemicals in
the workplace. It is up to OSHA to set allowable exposure levels for various carcinogens. In determining these levels, OSHA administrators make decisions
about which companies and unions are likely to disagree; inevitably, the decisions will be political and not just technical.

Legislation can be so precise and detailed that it reduces bureaucratic discretion to a minimum. But for both political and technical reasons, such precision
is usually not possible. In certain cases, a legislative majority can be constructed
only through ambiguous language that leaves contending parties satisfied that
their concerns have been heard. As a result, political conflict in Congress is displaced into the bureaucratic domain. In other cases, Congress may lack the
time, expertise, or foreknowledge to write precise legislation and counts on bureaucratic discretion to fill in the blanks. Extensive discretion is disturbing to
popular democrats, who generally prefer Congress to shape the details.

Expertise and discretion make administrators influential in policy making.
They employ that influence indirectly and directly. Administrators exercise *indirect influence* over policy in their capacity as advisers to elected officials. When a
president, for example, faces a major policy decision, he or she turns to the per-
tinent bureaucratic agency for data, analysis, and recommendations. The agency
cannot determine what the president will decide, but it may be able to shape
how he or she thinks about the decision. Bureaucratic advice may be couched in
the language of technical expertise, but it is seldom neutral and purely technical.
An agency is likely to tell the president to achieve a desired end by giving it,
rather than another agency, the resources and the responsibility to do the job.

Administrators exercise *direct influence* through the **rule-making authority**
that Congress delegates to the bureaucracy. When agencies give specificity to
vague congressional mandates by issuing rules, these rules carry the force of law.
And since they are far more precise than the legislation under which they were
drafted, they shape policy in important ways. Each year, the bureaucracy issues a
far larger number of rules than Congress passes laws, and these rules are published in the *Federal Register*. Limits to arbitrary rule making are established in
the Administrative Procedures Act of 1946, which all agencies must follow.
Before a new rule can be put into effect, for instance, interested citizens and
groups must receive advance notice and be permitted to comment on it.

A common complaint about bureaucrats is that the rules they issue in abundance tie up government in reams of **red tape**. This term refers to restrictions

Making a difference

Dr. Helene Gayle and the Battle Against AIDS

Stereotypes about the kind of people who work in the federal bureaucracy can blind us to the talent and dedication that many civil servants bring to their jobs. One individual who explodes the stereotypes is Dr. Helene Gayle, former director of the HIV program at the U.S. Government's Centers for Disease Control and Prevention (CDC). This African-American woman played an instrumental role in the federal government's domestic and international efforts to combat the horrors of AIDS.

The federal government was slow to adopt measures to cope with the AIDS epidemic, which began in the early 1980s. The Reagan and Bush administrations never placed much of a priority on combating AIDS. Perhaps this was because AIDS in the United States was initially perceived as a disease confined mostly to gay men. But indifference at the top did not lead to inaction among public health professionals in the federal bureaucracy. Government scientists and health officials have been

devoted to finding ways to prevent, treat, and eventually cure AIDS. Dr. Helene Gayle, an epidemiologist, has taken a leading role in these efforts.

Dr. Gayle was born in 1955 in Buffalo, New York. Her parents were activists in the civil rights movement and instilled in her a commitment to seek a better world. She received her medical degree from the University of Pennsylvania and, interested in the social uses to which her training could be put, went on to obtain a master's degree in public health from Johns Hopkins University. At the age of twenty-nine, she joined the CDC and began training as an epidemiologist.

Upon completing this training, Dr. Gayle joined the CDC's Division of HIV/AIDS. She conducted research on how HIV is transmitted from mothers to children and within communities of young people—population groups that have been, contrary to the image of AIDS as a "gay disease," increasingly at risk of contracting it. This research drew her

on individuals, organizations, and even the administrators themselves that delay action without serving any useful purpose. Some bureaucratic rules do add to red tape; for example, rules may be designed to serve the interests of an agency rather than the public or may be inappropriate because the conditions they were meant to influence no longer exist. But what looks to disgruntled citizens like red tape may simply be the requirement that government agencies treat individuals alike, without favoritism. Moreover, government agencies require more rules than private businesses because they are accountable to elected officials for honest performance.[25]

Rule making by administrators is considered *quasilegislative*. The bureaucracy also possesses *quasijudicial* authority in the form of **administrative adjudication**. Whereas rules govern a large number of parties and cover future behavior, adjudications affect only the individual parties in a case and cover past behavior. Adjudication is the province of administrative law judges. Cases in administrative law must follow the rules of due process, but the requirements of due process are not as strict as in the regular courts; thus, there is no right to a jury trial into federal programs aimed at preventing the spread of AIDS. In these programs, her personal and political skills proved to be as valuable as her medical skills. She recognized that given the poor initial record of the federal government in the fight against AIDS, gay and minority groups were understandably suspicious. So she bent her efforts to improving communications between public health officials and community groups in order that the two might become allies instead of adversaries in battling AIDS. She even welcomed the protest campaigns of the gay movement "as extremely important catalysts for pushing the government forward in its response to AIDS."

After her highly successful efforts to bring organizations representing gays, minority communities, and drug addicts into productive involvement in federal programs of AIDS prevention, Dr. Gayle became a leading figure in the international struggle against AIDS. Although most Americans think of AIDS as a disease affecting gay men and drug addicts in the United States, about 80 percent of HIV and AIDS cases globally are found in developing countries, where heterosexual intercourse is the primary source of new infections. Dr. Gayle helped to shape AIDS training programs that enlist doctors and scientists from countries in Africa, Asia, Latin America, and the Caribbean in research and prevention efforts. Through these programs, local expertise on AIDS has been developed and tailored to each country's distinct medical and cultural issues in the fight against AIDS.

Working in the federal bureaucracy, with all of its administrative rules and political conflicts, carried its share of frustrations for a public health activist like Dr. Gayle. Yet she chose to work at CDC for nearly two decades because "the potential within the federal government to have an impact at a very broad level is very compelling." Much honored for her work at CDC, Dr. Gayle accepted a position in 2001 as director of the Bill and Melinda Gates Foundation's HIV, TB, and Reproductive Health Program. In this post, she heads a philanthropic program that makes over a billion dollars in grants for research, prevention, and treatment.

Source: Norma M. Riccucci, *Unsung Heroes: Federal Executrats Making a Difference* (Washington, D.C.: Georgetown University Press, 1995), pp. 201–25; "Helene Gayle, M.D., M.P.H.," www.gatesfoundation.org.

in administrative law. Administrative law judges handle far more cases than federal court judges do.

American citizens most often come into contact with federal authority through rules issued by administrators and decisions handed down by administrative law judges. Indeed, bureaucrats make many of the policy decisions that affect our lives. As Cindy Skrzycki observes, they "shape decisions that influence the quality of the air you breathe, how safe your car is, which immigrants will enter and stay in this country, how airports will be protected from terrorism, what you can expect from your employer in terms of working conditions and pension, and how safe that hamburger is that you just put in your mouth."[26]

Much of this is inevitable, and some of it may even be desirable for the advancement of democratic goals. Yet these people are not elected or necessarily visible in their exercise of power. How to hold administrators, with their expertise and their discretion, their rule making and adjudicatory authority, accountable to the people and their elected representatives is an enduring problem for a democratic society.

THE POLITICAL ENVIRONMENT OF BUREAUCRACY

Bureaucracy is a political institution not only because administrators possess political influence but also because they operate in a highly political environment. A formal, hierarchical, technically focused bureaucracy could wait passively for elected officials to order it into action. But real bureaucratic agencies exist in an environment where policies reflect political, rather than technical, values; where resources are scarce; and where rivals seek to encroach on cherished turf. Thus, agencies actively seek to mobilize political support from others—the public, interest groups, Congress, the White House—and these same political forces seek to shape what agencies do.

Seeking Political Support

Some administrative agencies, such as the Federal Maritime Commission, function largely out of sight of the general public. However, other agencies are highly visible to the public and take steps to ensure favorable citizens' impressions—the more favorable the public is, the better the agency is likely to be treated by Congress and the president. Agencies can inform the public about their work while casting that work in a positive light through free booklets, public service ads on television, and Washington headquarters tours. Agencies can attempt to wrap their activities in the mantle of mysterious expertise and glamorous risk taking—these have been favorite tactics of both the armed forces and NASA. To be visible, however, is to be vulnerable should things go wrong. When the space shuttle *Challenger* exploded after takeoff in 1986, killing all seven crew members, including a schoolteacher, NASA suffered a public relations disaster as well as a human tragedy.

The public is too inattentive, and its backing too fickle, to provide most agencies with all the political support they need. "Hence," Francis Rourke observes,

> It is essential to every agency's power position to have the support of attentive groups whose attachment is grounded on an enduring tie. The groups an agency provides tangible benefits to are the most natural basis of such political support, and it is with these interest groups that agencies ordinarily establish the firmest alliances.[27]

The immediate masters of bureaucratic agencies are Congress and the president, so their political support is indispensable. Congress determines the statutory authority of an agency and holds the purse strings for its annual appropriation. The leadership of an agency must therefore take care to cultivate goodwill on Capitol Hill. Political support is obtained from the key legislative and appropriations committees by respectful, even deferential treatment and by more tangible promises. As political scientist James Q. Wilson notes, "Whenever an agency sends up a budget request it makes certain that there will be projects in it that will serve the districts represented by the members of the appropriations subcommittees (as well as members of certain key legislative committees)."[28]

The goodwill of the president is also a goal of bureaucratic chiefs, who do not want the White House staff or the Office of Management and Budget (OMB) frowning on their legislative and budget requests. Yet presidents, as we saw in Chapter 12, often complain that bureaucrats are insufficiently loyal and take steps to bring the bureaucracy under tighter White House control.

The more successful an agency is in gaining political support from the public, interest groups, Congress, and the president, the greater **autonomy** it will enjoy in the sense of freedom from control by external forces. Autonomy allows a bureaucracy to pursue its mission unhindered. Although this can be desirable, too much autonomy may also prove dangerous.

Probably the extreme case of an autonomous federal agency was the Federal Bureau of Investigation (FBI) under J. Edgar Hoover. By cultivating public support through highly publicized captures of criminals and by courting presidents with inside information on their political rivals, Hoover won extraordinary autonomy for his FBI. This autonomy led to autocratic uses of power. During the early years of the Cold War, Hoover was a fanatical anticommunist who employed the FBI to destroy the careers and lives of numerous individuals suspected of "subversive" activities. When the civil rights movement rose to its zenith in the 1960s, he developed a personal loathing for Martin Luther King Jr. and set out to destroy him.[29] Under Hoover, the FBI became a nightmare bureaucracy.

Constraints on Bureaucracy

Fortunately, the kind of autonomy that Hoover achieved at the FBI is rare. Agencies struggle to mobilize political support not only to increase their autonomy but also to fend off threats to already established autonomy. The political environment that most agencies face is filled with potentially constraining forces: other agencies, Congress, the president, the courts, interest groups, and the public. These checks and constraints are double edged. On one hand, they prevent most agencies from becoming the arbitrary and oppressive bureaucracies that prevailing myths depict (and that occasionally exist, as with Hoover's FBI). On the other hand, the existence of such "potent centrifugal forces," political scientists Charles Levine, B. Guy Peters, and Frank Thompson write, "frequently makes it difficult for officials to design and implement coherent public policies."[30] As is also the case for Congress and the president, checks and balances in the bureaucracy yield greater safety but lesser effectiveness.

An agency seeking to carry out its core mission may be threatened by another agency promoting *its* core mission. A classic illustration of such conflict between agencies, which scholars call **bureaucratic politics**, is the feud between the Air Force and the Navy over bombing. Since the end of World War II, there has been a belief among Navy officers that the Air Force seeks to control all aviation and a conflicting belief among Air Force officers that the Navy, with its aircraft carriers, tries to encroach on the Air Force specialty of strategic bombing. The services have competed to promote their core missions. During the Vietnam War, former NSC official Morton Halperin writes, this competition "probably led each service to exaggerate the effectiveness of its bombing to outshine the other."[31]

In the competitive world of bureaucracy, agencies look for allies on Capitol Hill and in the White House. But friends in high places can sometimes turn into bosses, interested less in supporting the agency's agenda than in advancing their own. Both Congress and the president have in recent years intensified their efforts to shape bureaucratic behavior. Congressional oversight of the bureaucracy has increased, with legislators using formal hearings and informal contacts to signal how they want programs implemented. Presidential efforts to control the bureaucracy through personnel and budgetary strategies have been even more notable, especially during the Reagan presidency. The struggle between Congress and the presidency over the bureaucracy has become more visible, but it is an old struggle rooted in the Constitution. As James Q. Wilson comments, "That document makes the president and Congress rivals for control of the American administrative system. The rivalry leads to struggle and the struggle breeds frustration."[32] This frustration grows out of the requirement that federal agencies serve two different—and often opposed—masters.

A third master has entered the picture in recent decades: the federal courts. For most of American history, judges did not intervene in the actions of bureaucrats, believing that administrative discretion was not subject to the same judicial scrutiny as legislation. But since the New Deal, the federal courts have been more willing to take up cases of agency decision making. The courts have enabled citizens to bring suits against agencies and have required agencies to justify their discretionary actions. Judges have even ordered federal agencies to change how they implement policy. Administrators now must worry not only about how a congressional committee or a White House staff member may respond to their behavior but also about how a district court judge may rule on its legality.

BUREAUCRACY AND THE POLITICAL ECONOMY

How much bureaucracy do Americans need? The initial answer of a popular democrat would be, "Far less." Many citizens complain that the administrative state stifles individual freedom with excessive forms, rules, and personnel. Yet the most influential advocates of bureaucratic downsizing have not been ordinary citizens but members of the business community, and their unhappiness with bureaucracy has less to do with freedom than with profits. In the face of business assaults on bureaucracy since the 1970s, popular democrats have found themselves in the unexpected position of having to defend it.

Popular democrats historically opposed the bureaucratization of American politics and remain worried about the reign of unaccountable elites in the administrative state. Nevertheless, they have also had to acknowledge that their past victories in extending protections to ordinary people against the abuses of private power can be preserved only with the help of administrative agencies. Hence, the historical roles of elite democrats and popular democrats have been reversed: Elite democrats largely built the administrative state but now want to shrink it, while popular democrats defend an administrative state they once feared.

The contemporary debate over bureaucracy has focused primarily on those agencies that regulate the economy. **Regulation** is "a process or activity in which government requires or proscribes certain activities or behavior on the part of individuals and institutions . . . and does so through a continuing administrative process, generally through specially designated regulatory agencies."[33] Understanding the contemporary struggle over regulation means distinguishing two different types. **Economic regulation** is usually conducted by an independent regulatory commission, covers a specific industry, and focuses on matters of prices, quality of services, and ability to enter or leave the industry. **Social regulation** is usually conducted by a single-headed agency answerable to the president, covers all industries, and focuses on such matters as environmental protection, safety, health, and nondiscrimination. It is the latter type that has generated the most controversy.

Economic Regulation

Economic regulation has the longer history in American politics. As industrialization strained the capacities of a weak national state, Congress created independent regulatory commissions to bring the changing economy under some measure of control. The prototype of the new regulatory agency was the Interstate Commerce Commission (ICC), formed in 1887 to regulate the railroad industry. Industrial abuses paved the way for the development of economic regulation, which has often been portrayed as a victory for popular democracy over economic elites. However, revisionist historians have shown that industrialists themselves sometimes pushed for federal regulation, hoping to limit competition or to avert public ownership.[34]

Regardless of whether independent regulatory commissions sprang into existence to serve popular or elite interests, many of them entered into a cozy relationship with the industries they were supposed to oversee. According to the "capture thesis," once a regulatory commission was established and the public and its elected officials turned their attention elsewhere, the only political force exercising constant leverage on the commission was the regulated industry, which captured the commission and made it an ally rather than a check. Although this thesis still has some validity, recent scholarship has pointed out its flaws. In the past few decades, Congress and the presidency have exercised greater influence over the independent regulatory commissions. And public interest groups have turned their attention to the commissions, bringing pressure to bear as a countervailing force against the regulated industries.[35]

Although most economic regulation has not been very burdensome to business, there has been a movement in recent years, promoted by economists and backed by business elites, to scale down the role of the government in the economy. Advocates of such **deregulation** argue that market forces will promote the interests of producers and consumers alike far more efficiently than the intrusive hand of government. Deregulation began during the presidencies of Gerald Ford and Jimmy Carter, and accelerated during the presidency of Ronald Reagan, with the most notable changes in the fields of transportation, communications, and banking. Existing regulatory controls were relaxed, and private economic forces were trusted to serve the public interest by engaging in market competition.

How well has deregulation worked? In the case of the airline industry, the positive effects of deregulation (air fares in general have declined, and the number of passengers has increased) have outweighed the negative.[36] However, the situation is different in the case of savings and loans companies (S&Ls). When Congress and the president took controls off this industry in the early 1980s, savings and loan operators went wild. Poorly conceived real estate loans, financial gimmicks that bilked small investors, and outright looting by operators sent many S&Ls into massive debt. Thanks to government insurance of deposits up to $100,000, the federal government and ultimately the taxpayers have had to pick up the tab of $132 billion. In this case, the assumption that the market automatically promotes the public good has been shown to be mistaken.

Social Regulation

Debates over economic regulation versus deregulation center on which approach has a more beneficial effect on people's pocketbooks. Debates over social regulation versus deregulation tend to pit the physical, moral, and aesthetic well-being of the American people against considerations of economics. Whereas economic regulation goes back to the late nineteenth century, social regulation has largely been a product of the 1960s and 1970s. Examples of social regulation include consumer safety, worker safety and health, antidiscrimination protection, environmental protection, and wildlife protection.

When contemporary foes of bureaucracy rail against "overregulation," it is principally social regulation that they have in mind. Businesses have learned to live with economic regulation, but they are adamant about the ill effects of social regulation. Social regulation draws so much fire from the business community in part because in such areas as worker health and safety, clean air and water, and nondiscrimination, it touches almost all businesses, unlike the more narrowly targeted approach in economic regulation. Social regulation also imposes costs on businesses that cut into profits.

The origins of social regulation hold another clue to business hostility. The social regulation measures of the 1960s and 1970s were supported by Congress and the president in response to the civil rights movement, the environmental movement, and the consumer safety movement. In other words, social regulation has been a potent political vehicle for popular democrats in their struggle against economic elites.

A major assault on social regulation was launched during the presidency of Ronald Reagan. The intellectual justification for this assault was the damage that regulation was supposedly doing to the American economy. Overregulation, opponents charged, was imposing such massive costs on American businesses as to prevent them from investing in productive new technologies, a crippling practice in an era where they faced mounting international competition.

To cut back on social regulation, the Reagan administration adopted a variety of tactics. Budgets for the social regulatory agencies were slashed. Political appointees were selected who were known to be hostile to the missions of the agencies they were to head; Anne Gorsuch Burford, a vehement opponent of environmental regulation, thus became Reagan's first head of the Environmental Protection Agency. New social regulation had to clear the hurdle of a mode of analysis with a built-in bias against such regulation. The Reagan administration claimed that it was using **cost–benefit analysis** as a neutral tool, determining if the dollar benefits of proposed regulation were greater than the dollar costs. The problem was that no clear dollar value could be placed on such intangible benefits as the worth of a human life or the beauty of a natural setting, whereas the costs incurred by an industry were readily quantifiable. Consequently, many new regulations were bound to fail the test of cost–benefit analysis.

However, the success of the Reagan administration's attack on social regulation was limited by the countermobilization of friends of social regulation. They fought with increasing success to preserve their earlier victories. Supporters of social regulation turned to the courts and to Congress to blunt the Reagan administration's efforts.

Reagan's attack on social regulation was revived by Republicans once they took over Congress in 1995, and it took on even stronger momentum in the presidency of George W. Bush. As Joel Brinkley writes in the *New York Times*:

> Allies and critics of the Bush administration agree that the September 11 attacks, the war in Afghanistan, and the war in Iraq have preoccupied the public, overshadowing an important element of the president's agenda: new regulatory initiatives. Health rules, environmental regulations, energy initiatives, worker-safety standards and product-safety disclosure policies have been modified in ways that often please business and industry leaders while dismaying interest groups representing consumers, workers, drivers, medical patients, the elderly, and many others.[37]

Most of the deregulatory measures that the Bush administration has promulgated since September 11, 2001, have flown under the public's radar. In one egregious instance, the administration scrapped new rules, ten years in the making, that would have required testing for tuberculosis for persons at high risk at their workplaces; the administration's decision was announced on New Year's Eve in 2003 and was not noticed by any major newspaper![38] Here are some other decisions made by the Bush administration:

- Authorized U.S. Forest Service managers to expedite logging in federal forests without the standard environmental reviews.
- Proposed a new regulation diluting coal-mining safety rules designed to protect miners from developing black-lung disease.
- Eliminated a rule mandating that employers record their workers' ergonomic (musculoskeletal) injuries.
- Created a new "voluntary" program bringing together OSHA officials and industries, but excluding representatives of unions, to cooperate on issues of workplace safety and health.[39]

On the few occasions when the Bush administration has been pressed to justify such decisions, it has claimed that social regulation is too inflexible and costly. So it is important to ask: How well has social regulation worked? Although the record of social regulation is complicated, popular democrats who champion it can point to the case of occupational safety and health. Because of staffing cuts that were pushed by President Reagan and later by the congressional Republican majority, OSHA had fewer personnel in 2000 than in 1975, even though the job of the agency had grown with the economy.[40] Nonetheless, the death rate at workplaces had been cut in half since the creation of OSHA in 1970.[41] Although some of the improvement in worker safety and health had other causes, it is likely that OSHA regulation has been a significant contributor to this important social purpose.

In the end, the issue of how much bureaucracy Americans need is a matter of what citizens want from government. Certainly, bureaucratic agencies can be too big, inefficient, or wasteful. And agency accountability remains a pressing issue. But much of the present-day administrative state is necessary to protect the public and provide it with services. Popular democrats seek to democratize private corporate bureaucracies, making them more accountable to consumers, workers, and communities. If powerful corporations were limited in these ways, much regulatory bureaucracy would not be needed. Short of such fundamental reforms, however, modern government cannot be "debureaucratized" without major costs to the public.

Bureaucracy, with all of its flaws, is part and parcel of modern American democracy. Thus, the question of whose influence shapes bureaucracy's behavior becomes all the more important. That question lies at the heart of the contemporary debate over bureaucratic reform.

THE DEMOCRATIC DEBATE OVER REFORMING THE BUREAUCRACY

Bureaucratic inefficiency, irrationality, and arrogance are perennial targets for reform. But reformers of bureaucracy do not all necessarily share the same assumptions or seek the same ends. Elite democrats struggle against popular democrats over who will influence the workings of the administrative state.

There are three major prescriptions for reform in this struggle. The technocratic perspective on reform aims to find some rational, comprehensive, technical device for overcoming bureaucratic self-seeking and inefficiency. Developed by academic experts and sponsored by chief executives, technocratic schemes try to control bureaucracy from the top down. They resemble Alexander Hamilton's vision of a wise executive creating a more systematic administrative machine to serve his ends. A second approach to reforming bureaucracy has proposed to measure bureaucratic performance by the yardstick of economic efficiency and to turn to nonbureaucratic alternatives when private economic forces can do better than government agencies. This school of reform believes that markets are superior to governments in securing both individual freedom and economic efficiency. Finally, there is a popular democratic approach to reforming bureaucracy that focuses on citizen understanding and influence—control from the bottom up. This approach assumes that ordinary citizens are individual consumers of government services who can also deliberate intelligently about the public interest.

"Reinventing Government"

The most recent in a long line of efforts to reform the bureaucracy borrowed from all three of these approaches. Vice President Al Gore headed the Clinton administration's National Performance Review (NPR), popularly known as the **"reinventing government" plan**. With great fanfare, the Clinton administration launched this comprehensive plan for a bureaucracy that "works better and costs less" in September 1993. In a classic photo opportunity, Clinton and Gore posed before huge stacks of bureaucratic regulations to dramatize the necessity of transforming the federal bureaucracy. Gore followed up this session with an appearance on the *David Letterman Show*, where he smashed an ashtray for which the government, following outmoded procurement practices, had paid a ridiculously high price.

The technocratic quality of the "reinventing government" plan was evident in its Hamiltonian hope that the White House could reshape the bureaucracy with a comprehensive top-down plan. But the language of the market approach was even more evident in the Clinton–Gore scheme. Government agencies were instructed by the NPR to become more "entrepreneurial" and to begin treating citizens as "customers." They were told that the key to shaking off the hidebound practices of bureaucracy lay in "injecting the dynamics of the marketplace."[42]

Alongside the market ideas in the Clinton–Gore plan were ideas more typical of the popular democratic approach: "All federal agencies will delegate, decentralize, and empower employees to make decisions. This will let front-line and front-office workers use their creative judgment as they offer service to customers and solve problems."[43] By "empowering employees," especially at the lower levels of the bureaucracy, the civil service would be made more participatory and egalitarian. Cutting red tape meant trusting federal workers to have more of a say in how they performed their jobs.

Observers have been divided over how well the "reinventing government" initiative worked. To sympathetic observers, the Clinton–Gore NPR was more ambitious and successful than prior efforts to reform the federal bureaucracy. They were particularly impressed by how well NPR worked with rather than against the career workforce and how it encouraged greater flexibility and good sense in the behavior of bureaucrats.[44] Critics of NPR countered that it represented another attempt by the executive to gain the upper hand with Congress over controlling the bureaucracy and that it failed to address flaws in the working of the federal bureaucracy that stemmed from self-serving directives by the White House itself.[45] They also raised doubts about whether NPR improved public understanding and appreciation of bureaucracy, since in selling the plan to Congress, Clinton and Gore placed the greatest emphasis on their aim of downsizing the federal workforce.

The Market Alternative

To supporters of the market approach, the real flaw in the Clinton–Gore NPR was its continuing reliance on bureaucracy. Government agencies may become more entrepreneurial, say market-oriented reformers, but they still cannot match the efficiencies of private firms subject to the competitive discipline of the market. Supporters of this approach suggest that public purposes can often be served best by replacing programs run by government agencies with vouchers that allow individuals to decide what kind of education or housing they prefer. And where private companies can perform functions more cheaply than government agencies, government should contract out these functions—an idea known as **privatization**.[46]

In the desire to enhance individual freedom of choice, the market approach is compatible with popular democracy. Yet popular democrats are suspicious of claims that markets are the panacea for the problems of bureaucracy. As we have seen, competition in the American market place is imperfect, with large and wealthy corporations often in a dominant position. To substitute private businesses for government agencies is to trust too much in such imperfect markets and to rely for the fulfillment of public needs on those interested only in profit.

What ultimately places advocates of market reforms in the elite democratic camp is the same assumption that guided the Federalists: that self-interest and the acquisition of property are the people's overriding concerns and that the good society results from a proper channeling of self-seeking motives. With this assumption, market forces deserve a larger scope. But popular democrats since the Anti-federalists have also cared about equality and active citizenship, and these values are not fostered by markets.

Privatization has been advocated for most public services, including schools, prisons, fire departments, and social services. But the experience with privatization so far at the state and local levels often has not produced the promised gains in efficiency. And it has revealed difficulties with privatization that have been overlooked by those who believe that competitive markets are the solution to every problem.[47]

Once core functions of government are contracted out to private firms, the performance of those functions can be distorted by the pursuit of profits. A case in point is the rise of corporate-run prisons, which are utilized by a number of states. Analysts have noted that in the drive to lower costs and increase profits, prisons run by private firms cut back on counseling and vocational training, reduce staff and have to rely as a result on manacles and isolation cells when inmates are unruly, and keep prisoners incarcerated for longer periods than public prisons. Some of these firms have even lobbied for longer sentences for criminal offenses, which would ensure higher revenues per inmate.[48]

The terrorist attacks of September 11, 2001, brought home to Americans that some public functions are too important to be left to the profit imperatives of the market. Prior to September 11, airport screening of passengers and baggage had been the responsibility of the airlines. The slack security on September 11 drew attention to the poor quality of screening by the private firms hired by the airlines; concerned primarily to maximize profits, these firms had paid low wages and assembled an inexperienced workforce that included illegal immigrants and ex-convicts. Opposed to expanding the federal bureaucracy, the Bush administration proposed to fix the problem by regulating the private companies in the airport screening business. However, members of the public were reluctant to resume flying without a federal takeover of airport security, so Congress created a new Transportation Security Administration within the Department of Transportation, and screening of passengers and baggage became the responsibility of public employees.[49]

Popular Democratic Reforms

For reasons quite different than those of the market reformers, the popular democratic perspective also perceives inadequacies in the Clinton–Gore approach to bureaucracy. Popular democrats seek to make bureaucratic decisions more open to public scrutiny. Just as the Anti-federalists sought a government that would mirror the people's concerns, so do contemporary popular democrats seek a bureaucracy that is in touch with ordinary citizens.

Government agencies can evade accountability by using secrecy. Therefore, the first requirement for greater citizen influence is greater openness in the bureaucracy. The most positive step in this direction has been the Freedom of Information Act of 1966, amended (and improved) by further legislation in 1974. This act requires government agencies to make available their records (exempting certain sensitive materials) when citizens and citizen groups request them. Thanks to the Freedom of Information Act, citizens have been alerted to such bureaucratic secrets as inspection reports from the Department of Agriculture on the sale of unhealthy meat, Nuclear Regulatory Commission reports on inadequate security at nuclear power plants, and widespread injuries and deaths caused by defective automobiles that the government had refused to recall.[50] Another step toward a more open bureaucracy is the Government in the Sunshine Act of 1976, which requires regulatory commissions to open their meetings to the public.

Once citizens are better informed about federal agency activities, the second requirement for popular influence is greater public input into bureaucratic decision making. In the past four decades, Congress has frequently mandated that administrative agencies hold public hearings before taking action. Lobbyists have always been able to register their views with agencies; public hearings give citizens and citizen groups a chance to do the same. Some critics disparage hearings as symbolic gestures that appease the public but have little real effect. Yet in some areas—especially environmental protection—hearings have had a significant impact on policy.

Popular democratic reforms of bureaucracy have not been a cure-all, but they have made significant strides. As public administration scholar William Gormley Jr. comments, "By broadening and improving public intervention in administrative proceedings, reformers helped to create a more humane, more responsive, and more innovative bureaucracy. This was no small accomplishment."[51]

Greater popular control of bureaucracy also requires involving citizens in policy implementation. Rather than trusting bureaucratic experts to carry out policies alone, citizens directly affected should cooperate in enforcement. (To the extent that citizens have been involved in the past, they have often been locally powerful ones—for example, large farmers and ranchers determining water and grazing rights.) The case of safety and health codes for the workplace illustrates what happens when ordinary people are shut out of the implementation process.

When Congress established OSHA, political scientist Charles Noble points out, the legislation "did not require employers to establish in-plant health and safety committees that might require worker participation."[52] Thus, workers had no part in the implementation of safety and health rules, which was left to factory inspectors from OSHA. The inspectors were far too few in number to provide vigorous enforcement, so the chance that a firm would be inspected in a year was approximately one in one hundred.[53] Matters worsened when Presidents Ronald Reagan and George W. Bush, antagonistic to OSHA's mission, further reduced the agency's efforts. As a result, hostile businesses and an unfriendly administration weakened the workplace protection promised by the legislation.

Although bureaucracy can be reformed from the bottom up, ordinary citizens are limited in the time and resources they can devote to influencing bureaucratic behavior. Furthermore, the narrow, technical nature of many agency decisions shuts out all but the affected interest groups and the bureaucratic experts.

However, popular democratic influence can be furthered without requiring direct, sustained citizen involvement. Here, the role of elected representatives is crucial. When citizens and citizen groups are inattentive, legislators enter into mutually rewarding alliances with agencies and interest groups. When citizens and citizen groups are watching legislators, Congress often prods bureaucratic agencies to be more responsive to the public. The pressures that push Congress toward popular democracy lead it to push the bureaucracy in the same direction.

NEW IDEAS

The New Public Service

In the traditional conception of bureaucracy, public administrators work in centralized, top-down, rule-bound agencies. The individuals and groups whom they serve are considered to be their clients. During the last two decades, the traditional conception has been challenged by a school of thought that seeks to transform public agencies into decentralized units that operate according to entrepreneurial practices learned from private businesses. In this new version of public management, as evident in the Clinton–Gore "reinventing government" program, government employees are instructed to regard those whom they serve as their customers.

Although the new school of thought has helped in many cases to make government agencies more flexible and efficient, it has also placed so much emphasis on the marketplace behavior of self-interested actors that important democratic values, such as equity and community, have been neglected. Now a group of public-administration scholars has suggested an alternative to both traditional bureaucracy and its entrepreneurial challenger: the "new public service."

The central idea behind the "new public service" is to treat the public as neither clients nor customers but rather as citizens. Public administrators, in this view, should be aiming to foster the values of popular democracy. Among the changes proposed are the following:

1. Public administrators should not aim to address issues through regulations or decrees but instead should foster dialogues that encourage conflicting individuals and groups to figure out how they can cooperate on solving their mutual problems.

2. Public administrators should contribute to a search for the public interest rather than emphasize the satisfying of individual and group interests.

3. Once the individuals and groups involved in an issue arrive at a shared vision of what is to be done, public administrators should enlist their continuing efforts in implementing solutions so that they can develop a sense of responsibility and commitment to the common good.

Much like Harry Hopkins, whom we discussed earlier in this chapter, advocates of the "new public service" recognize that the attitudes of public administrators are important in determining whether bureaucracy promotes elite democracy or popular democracy. In the words of Robert B. Denhardt and Janet Vinzant Denhardt, "The actions that public administrators take will differ markedly depending on the types of assumptions and principles upon which those actions are based. If we assume the responsibility of government is to facilitate individual self-interest, we will take one set of actions. If, on the other hand, we assume the responsibility of government is to promote citizenship, public discourse, and the public interest, we will take an entirely different set of actions."

Source: Robert B. Denhardt and Janet Vinzant Denhardt, "The New Public Service: Serving Rather Than Steering," *Public Administration Review* 60 (November/December 2000): 549–59.

Conclusion: Beyond Monster Bureaucracy

In contemporary American political discourse, Bureaucracy—with a capital *B*—is a monster. This Bureaucracy is composed of massive and ponderous organizations staffed by authoritarian drones. It smothers individual freedom under a blanket of unnecessary rules. And it grows more powerful all the time, not in the interest of the American people but in the service of its own voracious appetites. What is wrong with American government today, many people think, is mostly the consequence of Bureaucracy.

Monster Bureaucracy is a mythical creature—a hobbyhorse for irate citizens and a scapegoat for calculating politicians. When we look at real American bureaucracies, we see their diversity: They come in different organizational forms and sizes, and pursue an enormous variety of missions. The people who staff them are not a perverse bureaucratic breed but rather a cross-section of the American people. And the interests that bureaucrats further range from the narrowest and most selfish to the loftiest and most communal. Some agencies are entangled with economic elites in cozy, mutually rewarding alliances. Others try to put into practice the most important legislative victories that popular democrats have won against such elites.

Bureaucracy is one of the most important arenas for political struggle in modern America. The political character of bureaucracy stems in part from the expertise and discretion that administrators possess, which make them key policy makers in their own right. It results from the attempts of federal agencies to mobilize external political support in their search for greater autonomy. And it is underscored by the efforts of every other political force—interest groups, public interest groups, Congress, the president, the courts—to direct these agencies in accordance with their preferred course of action. These political forces recognize that bureaucratic agencies, operating at the point where government directly touches the lives of the American people, are worth fighting over.

Monster Bureaucracy has to be hit with a bludgeon. Real bureaucracies may need reform. But how we approach such reform depends on where we stand in the democratic debate. If we follow the tradition of elite democracy initiated by Alexander Hamilton, we should place our trust in new forms of expertise, deployed by a wise chief executive, that will coordinate and reshape bureaucracy from the top down. If we follow the newer school of elite democracy, which claims the superiority of private markets to public agencies, we should make efficiency our standard and let business do much of what government is accustomed to doing. And if we follow the popular democratic tradition, with its commitments to citizen action, civic virtue, and an egalitarian society, we should open up the world of bureaucracy wherever possible to the grievances, opinions, and democratic hopes of ordinary people.

KEY TERMS

bureaucracy
spoils system
administrative state
cabinet departments
independent agency
independent regulatory commission
public corporation
federal foundation or endowment
mission
expertise
discretion
rule-making authority

red tape
administrative adjudication
autonomy
bureaucratic politics
regulation
economic regulation
social regulation
deregulation
cost–benefit analysis
"reinventing government" plan
privatization

INTERNET RESOURCES

■ American Society for Public Administration
www.aspanet.org
This site provides current news and research tools for those interested in public administration.

■ Center for Progressive Reform
www.progressiveregulation.org
A site that provides extensive accounts of regulatory battles from the liberal perspective.

■ Office of the Federal Register
www.gpoaccess.gov/nara/
A governmental website that lists federal regulations of all types.

SUGGESTED READINGS

Joel D. Aberbach and Bert Rockman, *In the Web of Politics: Three Decades of the U.S. Federal Executive*. Washington, D.C.: Brookings Institution Press, 2000. Two leading political scientists provide an empirical and historical analysis of top-level federal executives.

Charles T. Goodsell, *The Case for Bureaucracy: A Public Administration Polemic*, 4th ed. Washington, D.C.: Congressional Quarterly Press, 2004. A lively polemic that takes on the prevailing myths about a Monster Bureaucracy.

William T. Gormley Jr. and Steven J. Balla, *Bureaucracy and Democracy: Accountability and Performance*. Washington, D.C.: Congressional Quarterly Press, 2004. A study of the administrative state that utilizes four prominent theories of bureaucratic behavior.

James A. Morone, *The Democratic Wish: Popular Participation and the Limits of American Government*. New York: Basic Books, 1990. An ironic argument about how the democratic desire to bring government back to the people results instead in more bureaucracy.

David Osborne and Ted Gaebler, *Reinventing Government*. Boston: Addison-Wesley, 1992. Attacking "bankrupt bureaucracy" and calling for "entrepreneurial government," this book was the chief inspiration for the Clinton administration's National Performance Review.

James Q. Wilson, *Bureaucracy: What Government Agencies Do and Why They Do It*. New York: Basic Books, 1989. A classic treatise on bureaucracy in the United States.

The Judiciary and the Democratic Debate

As a nation with a tradition of transforming myriad issues into legal matters, the United States has an extensive judiciary at both the federal and state levels. The federal courts are organized in a three-tier system, which we describe later in the chapter. But our primary focus in this chapter is on the highest tier, the Supreme Court of the United States.

The nine justices of the Supreme Court form a unique elite. Appointed rather than elected, for tenures that run on "good behavior" until retirement or death, the justices have carved out for themselves the formidable role of serving as final arbiters of the Constitution. Their authority is strengthened by powerful symbolism, as they hand down decisions wearing their black robes in their marble temple, and is protected by the cloak of expertise, as they pronounce their judgments in the esoteric language of the law. In all these ways, the judiciary is the least democratic branch of the federal government. Indeed, it can be said, as political scientist David O'Brien writes, that "the Court wields an antidemocratic power."[1]

Yet the Court's relationship to elite democracy and popular democracy is not this simple. The Supreme Court may be (and has been in its history) a pillar of elite democracy, upholding the interests of the powerful and privileged in the name of authority, expertise, or private property. But the Court also may be (and has been in its history) a champion of the fundamental rules of democratic politics in the face of intolerant and repressive majorities. And the Court may be (and has been in its history) the last hope for the weakest citizens—racial minorities, the poor, persons accused of crimes. Elitist in form and character, the Supreme Court is nonetheless a vital participant in the democratic debate.

This chapter begins with a consideration of contemporary debates over the proper role of the judiciary in a democracy. Next, the chapter looks back at the history of the Supreme Court, noting how the Court's relationship to democracy has changed from one era to the next. Subsequent sections cover judicial selection, the lower federal courts, the processes through which the Supreme Court functions, and the politics that divides it. Finally, the chapter examines the place of the Supreme Court in the broader political system and sums up its role in the democratic debate.

JUDICIAL POWER AND THE DEMOCRATIC DEBATE

What is the place of an unelected judiciary in a democratic republic? Answers to this question begin with a recognition of the Supreme Court's fundamental power: **judicial review**. This is the power of the Court to invalidate the actions of legislatures and executives on the grounds that these actions conflict with the Constitution. This power was first asserted by the Supreme Court in the landmark case of *Marbury v. Madison* (1803). Although the *power* of judicial review remained controversial for much of the nineteenth century, few today would question it. But questions do arise about the proper *extent* of judicial review. How far should the Court go in overturning the actions of the other federal branches or the state governments? In setting these actions against the language of the Constitution, how should the Court interpret the Constitution? Can the Court, despite its elite composition and procedures, advance the goals of popular democracy?

The Judiciary and Democracy

There are several ways in which the Supreme Court is *not* a democratic institution. First, members of the judiciary are not elected; they are nominated by the president and confirmed by the Senate. Second, federal judges serve during good behavior—that is, until they retire, die, or are impeached by the House and convicted by the Senate. No justice of the Supreme Court has ever been removed through impeachment and conviction. Consequently, members of the Court are held accountable only indirectly—by Congress through its power over jurisdiction, by presidents through their appointment power, and by members of the public through their decisions on complying with judicial rulings.

Third, justices wield their power of judicial review by striking down actions taken by elected officials at the federal or state level. The exercise of judicial review is thus *countermajoritarian*, meaning that majority rule has to give way if the Court believes that the actions of the majority conflict with the Constitution.

Fourth, the federal judiciary historically has been even less representative demographically than Congress and the executive branch. Almost all justices have been white, male, and affluent. (Women and minorities have finally won some representation on the federal bench in the past three decades.) Equally important, they have all been lawyers, which means that one of the most powerful branches of the national government is the exclusive domain of the legal profession.[2]

There is, it seems, a potent democratic case to be made against a strong and active judiciary. Yet judicial power in America has sometimes played an essential part in preserving democratic values and rules. Nowhere is this role more apparent than in the areas of individual and minority rights. Majority rule can be used to impose unwelcome beliefs on individuals and to prohibit the expression of unconventional views. Majorities can repress and exploit minorities, whether of race, creed, or color. A democracy with unrestrained majority rule would eventually undermine the very conditions of personal and political freedom that gave it life. It would be like a sports league in which the team that won the first game was able to set the rules for all succeeding games. Therefore, the democratic case for a countermajoritarian judiciary is that it stands as a guardian for the abiding values and conditions that democracy requires.[3]

The Court serves democracy not only when it protects individual and minority rights from infringement by majorities but also when it publicly explains its actions. The Court's impact on public thinking may be limited by its legal language, yet no other branch of government offers such extensive and reasoned accounts of its decisions or elaborates on so many fundamental democratic principles. For example, it was the Supreme Court that explained to Americans why segregated schools denied African Americans the equal protection of the laws and why coerced confessions denied criminal defendants the right to a fair trial.

The Conservative Critique of the Judiciary

Questions about the role of the judiciary in American democracy are not merely of academic interest. A politically important debate has been waged in recent decades about the courts and democracy. What generated this debate was the liberal activism of the Warren Court (discussed later in this chapter and in Chapter 16). There have been three major positions in this debate: the conservative critique of an active judiciary, the liberal defense of an active judiciary, and the progressive (or radical democratic) skepticism toward a democratic judiciary.

The conservative critique has been voiced by such prominent figures as Supreme Court Justices William Rehnquist and Antonin Scalia and failed Supreme Court nominee Robert Bork. But it was given its greatest public visibility by President Reagan's attorney general, Edwin Meese. Unhappy with many of the Supreme Court's liberal decisions of the preceding decades, Meese argued that it was meddling with the affairs of the other federal branches and especially the state governments. This overreaching, he charged, arose not from constitutional duty but from an exaggerated sense of the Court's own powers and a loose reading of the Constitution. Meese believed that the Court conveniently construed the Constitution "as an empty vessel into which each generation may pour its passion and prejudice."[4] As a result, the Court's decisions represented "more policy choices than articulations of constitutional principle."[5] Yet nobody had authorized the justices of the Supreme Court to make policy choices and impose them on elected officials.

According to Meese, the Court could return to its legitimate—and more restrained—role through a **jurisprudence of original intention**.[6] By this, he meant that "the text of the document and the original intention of those who framed it would be the judicial standard in giving effect to the Constitution."[7] The standard of original intention, Meese argued, would make judges into faithful servants of the Constitution. "Any other standard," he warned, "suffers the defect of pouring new meaning into old words, thus creating new powers and new rights totally at odds with the logic of our Constitution and its commitment to the rule of law."[8]

In seeking to restrict the role of the federal judiciary, Meese's case emphasized the Court's nondemocratic aspects. His critique of the judiciary echoed the complaints of popular democrats in the past. One of Meese's allies in the debate, Robert Bork, spells out this argument succinctly: "We are increasingly governed not by law or elected representatives but by an unelected, unrepresentative, unaccountable committee of lawyers applying no will but their own."[9] In Meese's version of democracy, judges should not impede other officials unless their acts clearly violate the original intention of the framers.

The Liberal Defense of the Judiciary

This attack on judicial activism drew a swift retort from Supreme Court Justice William Brennan Jr., one of the most influential figures in crafting the decisions of which Meese was complaining. Brennan's liberal defense of the judiciary presented a dramatically different understanding of the Court's proper role. To Brennan, a jurisprudence of original intention was "arrogance cloaked as humility."[10] It was, he argued, impossible to recover the founders' precise intent for each phrase of the Constitution. The records of their era are incomplete and ambiguous, and what they do reveal is disagreement, rather than consensus, over meaning. Brennan detected a political motive beneath the claim of fidelity to the intentions of the founders: The jurisprudence of original intention was a conservative philosophy that required the Supreme Court to "turn a blind eye to social progress."[11]

Brennan's alternative to original intention gave the judiciary a far broader role in reading the Constitution—and in affecting American life:

> We current Justices read the Constitution in the only way that we can: as Twentieth Century Americans. We look to the history of the time of framing and to the intervening history of interpretation. But the ultimate question must be, what do the words of the text mean in our time? For the genius of the Constitution rests not in any static meaning it might have had in a world that is dead and gone, but in the adaptability of its great principles to cope with current problems and current needs.[12]

To Brennan, the Constitution "embodies the aspiration to social justice, brotherhood, and human dignity that brought this nation into being."[13] His jurisprudence (judicial philosophy) used the means of elite democracy to advance the ends of popular democracy. Judges—indisputably an elite in terms of occupation and expertise—should advance the goals of social justice, brotherhood, and human dignity by serving as forceful advocates for a democracy of inclusion, equality, and fairness. Reading the Constitution as a charter for such popular democratic values, they could not be bound by the fuzzy notion of original intention—especially since the original intenders, the Federalists, were elite democrats! Although popular democrats might naturally mistrust the judicial elite, Brennan wanted them to recognize how this elite might sometimes be their ally.

Progressive Skepticism Toward the Judiciary

Although less publicly visible than the views of a Meese or a Brennan, a third position in this debate—which we label *progressive skepticism*—deserves consideration. According to proponents of this position, the judiciary's role in American democracy has varied enormously, depending on politics—on who nominates and who approves selections to the highest court. The Court's championing of popular democratic values, which Brennan emphasized, has in fact been the exception in its history. As law professor Mark Tushnet observes, "In the long view, the Warren Court was an unusual and brief instance in which the Court happened to come under control of progressive interests."[14] With the departure of Brennan himself from the Court, along with his ally Thurgood Marshall, the last traces of the era of liberal activism have vanished. The conservative majority on the Rehnquist Court reasserted the Court's more traditional role as a pillar of property and order.

We should not be surprised, progressive skeptics argue, when the Court sides with elite democracy over popular democracy. The great nineteenth-century observer of American politics, Alexis de Tocqueville, wrote that lawyers were the one remaining aristocratic class in an otherwise egalitarian society. To progressive skeptics, Tocqueville's argument still holds true for the modern legal profession. They point out how law students are socialized in elite democratic values as they are prepared for lucrative careers in elite democratic institutions. Almost all law schools, writes law professor Duncan Kennedy, provide their students with "ideological training for willing service in the hierarchies of the corporate welfare state."[15]

The progressives' skepticism extends even to the landmark liberal decisions of the Warren Court. Unlike the conservatives, they agree with the substance of what the Warren Court decided. But they argue that the gains for popular democracy were much smaller than liberals like Brennan suggested. Even when the Court called for significant social reform, it lacked the power of implementation that would turn decisions into realities. For example, court orders for school desegregation had almost no impact until the civil rights movement compelled Congress and the presidency to force change on the recalcitrant South.[16]

NEW IDEAS

Populist Constitutional Law

Most observers were surprised when the U.S. Supreme Court agreed to hear George W. Bush's lawsuit seeking to block the Florida recount that might make Al Gore the winner of the 2000 presidential election. When a 5–4 majority on the High Court halted the recount and handed the White House to Bush, critics were quick to denounce the political motives that seemed to lie behind its decision. Yet there was never any doubt that the Court's verdict on the election would be accepted by all parties. Once the Supreme Court interprets the language of the Constitution, its meaning is fixed—at least until the Court speaks again on the same subject.

Must we be so deferential to the Supreme Court when it comes to constitutional interpretation? Law professor Mark Tushnet, a prominent figure among the progressive skeptics we have described, says no. In a provocative book, *Taking the Constitution Away from the Courts*, Tushnet calls for a new approach to interpreting the Constitution. When questions arise about detailed provisions in the Constitution, Tushnet says, the courts are the proper bodies to ascertain constitutional meanings. But when questions arise about fundamental constitutional guarantees of liberty and equality, the courts should not have a monopoly over debate. Disagreements about the application of these guarantees, Tushnet writes, "are best conducted by the people in the ordinary venues for political discussion," assisted by their elected representatives.

This perspective sounds novel, but it is actually rooted in the popular democratic tradition. Larry Kramer, another law professor who shares Tushnet's viewpoint, writes: "Both in its origins and for most of our history, American constitutionalism assigned ordinary citizens a central and pivotal role in implementing their Constitution." Popular democratic leaders such as Thomas Jefferson, Andrew Jackson, and Abraham Lincoln all insisted that the other branches of government and the people had as much right as the courts to interpret the Constitution.

"Populist constitutional law," as Tushnet calls it, does not guarantee any particular outcome. Its basis is the commitment to take democracy seriously, and its assumption is that the American people are capable of making good use of democracy. A number of practical difficulties can be imagined in "taking the Constitution away from the courts," and Tushnet believes that it will require a constitutional amendment to achieve greater public control over constitutional interpretation.

The value in Tushnet's ideas may lie less in their prospects for adoption than in the challenge they pose to public complacency. As he writes, "Neither the people nor their representatives have to take the Constitution seriously because they know—or believe—that the courts will. Political calculations might change if people knew that they were responsible for the Constitution."

Sources: Mark Tushnet, *Taking the Constitution Away from the Courts* (Princeton, N.J.: Princeton University Press, 1999); Larry D. Kramer, *The People Themselves: Popular Constitutionalism and Judicial Review* (New York: Oxford University Press, 2004).

If popular democrats have gained little from Court victories, say these skeptics, they have paid a price for banking their hopes on friends in the judicial elite. As political scientist Gerald Rosenberg points out, when popular democratic movements look to lawsuits to reform society, "there is the danger that litigation by the few will replace political action by the many and reduce the democratic nature of the American polity."[17] Lawsuits siphon off money and other resources that mass movements need for political mobilization. They lead popular democrats to speak in the limited and generally conservative language of lawyers. Even when the litigation is successful, it deludes popular democrats with victories that are more symbolic than substantial. Progressive skeptics make a powerful argument that the struggle for popular democracy must depend on political actions by ordinary citizens rather than legal actions by a sympathetic judicial elite.

THE SUPREME COURT IN HISTORY

For an institution that derives much of its authority from its role as sacred guardian of a timeless text, the Supreme Court has been profoundly shaped by its history. However, the Court's relationship to history is double edged. On one hand, the Court treats history with reverence, claiming to follow past decisions as **precedents** and applying them to new circumstances. On the other hand, the Court has engaged in some dramatic historical shifts. For most of its history, the Supreme Court was a pillar of elite democracy, a champion of national authority and private property against the popular democratic forces struggling for greater equality. Beginning in the 1930s, however, the Court largely abandoned its stance as the protector of economic elites, adopting instead a new focus on civil liberties and civil rights. The 1990s witnessed another shift: the expression (by a narrow majority) of a conservative jurisprudence that favors federalism over national action.

John Marshall and Judicial Power

The Supreme Court did not become a major force in the American political system immediately on ratification of the Constitution. Article III of the Constitution, establishing the judicial branch, was brief and vague, leaving the role of the Court an open question. During its first decade under the Constitution, the Court was relatively weak. Nonetheless, popular democrats feared its potential as a home for a judicial aristocracy. During the ratification debates, Alexander Hamilton, the arch elite democrat, had championed a judicial branch that could invalidate the actions of the other branches or the states as contrary to the Constitution. Anti-federalist writers, such as Brutus, had warned that this judiciary might promote the powers of a remote federal government while diminishing the powers of state governments closer to the people. With the triumph of Jeffersonian democracy over the elitism of the Federalists in 1800, the more radical

Jeffersonians hoped that the power of the federal judiciary could be severely curtailed. As legal historian Kermit Hall observes, "Radicals distrusted lawyers and believed that local democracy in an agrarian society based on 'common sense and common honesty between man and men . . .' offered the surest road to justice."[18]

But it was the fears, not the hopes, of the more radical popular democrats that were to be realized: As Jefferson was assuming the presidency, John Marshall was taking over as chief justice of the Supreme Court. Appointed by President Adams in the waning days of his administration, Marshall, a Federalist, was gifted with great intellectual force, rhetorical grace, and political shrewdness. And he had a vision for the Court: to establish it coequally with the other branches and turn it into a sponsor of national authority and economic development (a vision that he shared with Alexander Hamilton). Marshall dominated the Supreme Court for thirty-four years, serving from 1801 until his death in 1835. The Marshall Court, more than the words of Article III, established the judicial branch as the powerful political force that later generations of Americans came to regard as a key part of the constitutional design.

Marshall's agenda for the Court depended on establishing the power of judicial review. But he wanted to avoid a head-on collision with the Jeffersonian majority that controlled the executive and legislative branches. In a stroke of judicial genius, he found the perfect vehicle for judicial review in the case of ***Marbury v. Madison*** (1803). William Marbury had been appointed by President Adams to a position as justice of the peace for the District of Columbia, but the papers for his commission had not been delivered by the time Jefferson supplanted Adams in the White House. Jefferson's secretary of state, James Madison, refused to hand over the papers. Marbury asked the Supreme Court to order Madison, through a *writ of mandamus* (a court order directing an official to do something), to give him his commission.

Marshall's opinion in *Marbury v. Madison* held that the secretary of state had wrongfully withheld the commission. But the Supreme Court, he went on, could do nothing to rectify this injustice because the authority to issue *writs of mandamus*, mandated by the Judiciary Act of 1789, was unconstitutional—it expanded the original jurisdiction of the Court beyond what was specified in Article III. In bold rhetorical strokes, he crafted the doctrine of judicial review. It was evident, he argued, that "a law repugnant to the constitution is void" and that "it is emphatically the province and duty of the judicial department to say what the law is."[19] Notice how shrewdly Marshall bolstered the power of the Supreme Court. He avoided a confrontation with the Jefferson administration by ruling that the Supreme Court was powerless to reverse the action toward Marbury. But he advanced the Supreme Court's power in the long term by making it, and not the other branches, the final arbiter of constitutionality.

Once Marshall had established the Court's power of judicial review, he moved gradually to further his vision of a powerful national government promoting capitalist economic development. Striking down Maryland's attempt to tax the Bank of the United States in ***McCulloch v. Maryland*** (1819), he emphasized the constitutional supremacy of the federal government over the states (see Chapter 15). And then in ***Gibbons v. Ogden*** (1824), the Marshall Court ruled that the Interstate Commerce Clause, under which Gibbons held a federal coasting license for his steamboat line, was superior to the steamboat monopoly granted to Ogden by the state of New York. As the *Gibbons* case indicates, Marshall was able to advance his goal of economic development in conjunction with his goal of national authority. He read the Constitution, legal historian Robert McCloskey writes, "so as to provide maximum protection to property rights and maximum support for the idea of nationalism."[20]

The Taney Court

When John Marshall died, and Andrew Jackson, a frequent foe of Marshall, appointed Roger Taney as chief justice, supporters of the Court as the champion of nationalism and capitalism shuddered. Surely, they thought, the Court would now become a supporter of states' rights and egalitarian attacks on property. But Marshall had set the Court on a course that was not easily altered. Historians now find more continuity than change between the Marshall and the Taney Courts. Although Taney was more sympathetic to state governments, he upheld national authority and capitalist development. The Taney Court's most important economic decision came in *Charles River Bridge v. Warren Bridge* (1837). In ruling that the Massachusetts legislature could charter a new bridge even when it undercut the profitability of a previously chartered bridge, whose owners claimed that their monopoly rights had been violated, the Taney Court fostered a more competitive capitalist system.

However, Taney's most notorious decision came in ***Dred Scott v. Sandford*** (1857). The *Dred Scott* decision is universally regarded as the worst in the history of the Supreme Court. In a remarkable bit of political miscalculation, Taney thought that the Court could solve with one decision the brewing crisis between North and South over slavery. His solution took the southern side on every burning question of the day: Slaves were held to be a form of property protected by the Constitution, and Congress was told it had no power to forbid or abolish slavery in the western territories. Taney went even further, almost taunting northern champions of the antislavery cause with his vicious racist remark that blacks were regarded by the founders "as beings of an inferior order" who "had no rights which the white man was bound to respect."[21] Taney's ruling and rhetoric incensed the North and increased sectional tensions, helping to lead to a civil war that would obliterate his fateful misuse of judicial power.

From the Civil War to the Roosevelt Revolution

The Civil War confirmed on the battlefield what John Marshall had claimed on the bench: the supremacy of the federal government over the states. After the Civil War, the Supreme Court became preoccupied with Marshall's other major concern: the rights of property. For seventy years, the Court played a critical, activist role in the development of corporate capitalism in America. The Court reread the Constitution, turning the eighteenth-century founders into proponents of the free market capitalism worshiped by business elites of the late nineteenth century. Legal expertise and judicial authority were weapons that elite democrats fired repeatedly—and successfully—to shoot down the cause of popular democracy.

The industrial capitalist order that was growing rapidly in the years after the Civil War imposed heavy costs on workers, farmers, and owners of small businesses. Popular democratic forces, such as the agrarian Granger movement and the Populist movement, gained power in some states and passed legislation to protect ordinary people against capitalist exploitation, especially by the railroads. As the popular democratic forces mobilized, legal historian Michael Benedict writes, "the justices became convinced that the Court must serve as the bulwark of property rights against threatened radical legislation."[22] The Court set up a roadblock against state efforts to regulate the railroads in *Wabash, St. Louis & Pacific Railway Co. v. Illinois* (1886), ruling that states had no power to regulate rail rates for shipments that crossed their borders.

A Court dominated by the doctrine of laissez faire (i.e., government should not interfere in the free market) was not favorably disposed toward federal regulation either. When the government attempted to use the new Sherman Antitrust Act to break up the monopolistic "sugar trust," the Court overturned that action through a narrow interpretation of the Commerce Clause. In *United States v. E. C. Knight Co.* (1895), the Court ruled that manufacturing was a local activity and thus not covered under the Commerce Clause, even when the goods produced were destined for shipment across state lines.

The Court stretched the doctrine of laissez faire the furthest in redefining the meaning of "due process of law." The drafters of the Fourteenth Amendment had included this phrase to protect newly freed African Americans from arbitrary actions by state governments in the South. But the Supreme Court ignored the plight of blacks and turned the Fourteenth Amendment instead into a protective shield for corporations. It was a violation of due process, the Court often ruled, when a state interfered with the contractual freedom of employers and employees to make whatever "bargains" they wished. Thus, in *Lochner v. New York* (1905), the Court struck down a New York law setting maximum hours for bakery workers. "Freedom of contract" was the watchword of the Court, and popular democratic legislation to protect working people from oppressive conditions was declared unconstitutional.

In the face of popular democratic criticism during the Progressive era, the Supreme Court pragmatically allowed some federal and state regulation of the economy. But as Progressivism faded and a new conservative era set in after World War I, the majority of the Court hardened in its laissez faire dogma. It was this majority that fought the most bitter battle in the history of the Court—against Franklin Roosevelt and the New Deal. Once Roosevelt and his Democratic majority in Congress passed far-reaching measures to revive an economy mired in the worst depression in its history, the question of power over the economy was joined by the Court. It invalidated the two linchpins of the New Deal: the National Industrial Recovery Act and the Agricultural Adjustment

Act. The 1936 election gave Roosevelt the largest mandate in presidential history, but the Supreme Court now seemed an impassable barrier to his efforts to improve the economy and reform it in popular democratic fashion.

Early in 1937, Roosevelt unveiled a program to smash through this barrier. He claimed (in deceptive fashion) that he was acting only to enhance the efficiency of a Court dominated by elderly judges. His proposal was that the president be given the authority to add an additional justice each time a sitting justice over the age of seventy refused to retire. (The size of the Supreme Court is not set by the Constitution.) Popular though Roosevelt was, his **court-packing plan** was a political fiasco. Public opinion sided with the Court, and Roosevelt suffered a major defeat in Congress. He lost because the public revered the Supreme Court despite its unpopular recent decisions. He also lost because his plan was viewed as a vehicle to advance his own executive power.

Yet Roosevelt won the larger battle with the Court in the end. While the debate raged over the court-packing plan, the Court narrowly approved two key New Deal measures—the National Labor Relations Act and the Social Security Act—during the spring of 1937. And in the next few years, deaths and resignations of the conservatives who had stymied the president permitted him to name a New Deal majority to the Court. Roosevelt's appointees ended seventy years of laissez faire doctrine. In one of the most important shifts in the history of the Supreme Court—a "Roosevelt revolution"—they took the Court largely out of the business of economic policy.

A signpost of the Roosevelt revolution was the case of *Wickard v. Filburn* (1942), in which a unanimous Court said that the federal government could extend the Interstate Commerce Clause even to regulate wheat consumed on the same farm on which it was grown. A Supreme Court that read federal authority this broadly was a Court that no longer wished to question the economic judgments of the elected branches. It would no longer champion property rights and elite democracy. But what would its new role be?

The Modern Court

Since the Roosevelt revolution, the Court's role has largely centered on civil liberties and civil rights (see Chapter 16). However, this constant preoccupation with questions of civil liberties and civil rights has not meant a consistent pattern of rulings. Responding to changing issues and public moods, and profoundly affected by changing personnel, the Court has gone through several distinct eras in its treatment of civil liberties and civil rights.

Several of the key Court decisions in the fifteen years after 1937 sided with governmental authority over civil liberties and civil rights. Thus, the Court upheld the wartime incarceration of Japanese Americans and the early Cold War conviction of leading American communists. It was only with the emergence of the Warren Court (1953–1969) that it blazed a strong path in support of individual liberties and the rights of racial minorities. But its activism on behalf of the rights of dissenters, criminal defendants, and African Americans won it many vocal enemies, including successful presidential candidate Richard Nixon in 1968.

Nixon had the opportunity to name four new justices, among them Warren Burger as replacement for the retiring Earl Warren. (For membership changes on the Supreme Court since 1960, see Figure 14.1.) Yet the Burger Court (1969–1986) did not carry out the conservative counterrevolution that Nixon had advocated. Holdovers from the Warren Court and Nixon appointees who proved more moderate than expected made the Burger Court a transitional body, cutting back on some of the Warren Court landmarks, especially in matters of criminal procedure, but also announcing a fundamental new right in the area of abortion.

It was only in the era of the Rehnquist Court (1986–2005) that a new conservative jurisprudence, shaped by the appointees of Presidents Reagan and the elder Bush, crystallized. Often by 5–4 votes, a conservative majority, led by Chief Justice Rehnquist, partially shifted the Court's focus from questions of rights back to older questions of authority.

For the first time since the Roosevelt revolution, the ability of the federal government to exercise broad regulatory authority was challenged by the Court. In *United States v. Lopez* (1995), a federal law making it a crime to carry a gun within 1,000 feet of a school was struck down, with the conservative majority arguing that the law was unrelated to interstate commerce and intruded on the police powers of the states. In *Printz v. United States* (1997), a portion of the Brady gun control law was invalidated because it required local law enforcement officers to run background checks on prospective handgun purchasers, with the same conservative majority stating that Washington cannot command state officials to administer a federal regulatory program. A series of Court decisions in 1999, 2000, and 2001 provided immunity to states from lawsuits alleging violations of federal law in such areas as labor rights, violence against women, and discrimination on the basis of age or disability. The states' rights philosophy of the Rehnquist Court majority carried profound implications for both federal regulations and civil rights.[23]

Although Rehnquist and his four allies on the Court made states' rights the central theme of their judicial philosophy, they abandoned states' rights when the presidency of the United States was at stake. In **Bush v. Gore**, decided in December 2000 by the same 5–4 lineup as the federalism cases cited above, the Court's conservative majority overturned the order of the Florida Supreme Court to proceed with a statewide hand recount that would determine who gained Florida's twenty-five electoral votes and thus the presidency. Effectively awarding the White House to Republican George W. Bush, the five justices in the majority argued that hand recounts, by being subject to varying standards in different counties, violated the constitutional guarantee of equal protection of the laws. Moreover, the majority claimed that there was insufficient time to conduct the recounts for Florida's electoral votes to be counted for the Electoral College.

The four dissenters suggested that this was not a situation where the federal courts should have intervened to strike down a state's actions. They pointed out that it was still possible to conduct a hand recount that would meet constitutional standards by the deadline necessary to protect Florida's electoral votes.

FIGURE 14.1 Membership of the Supreme Court, 1960s–September 2005

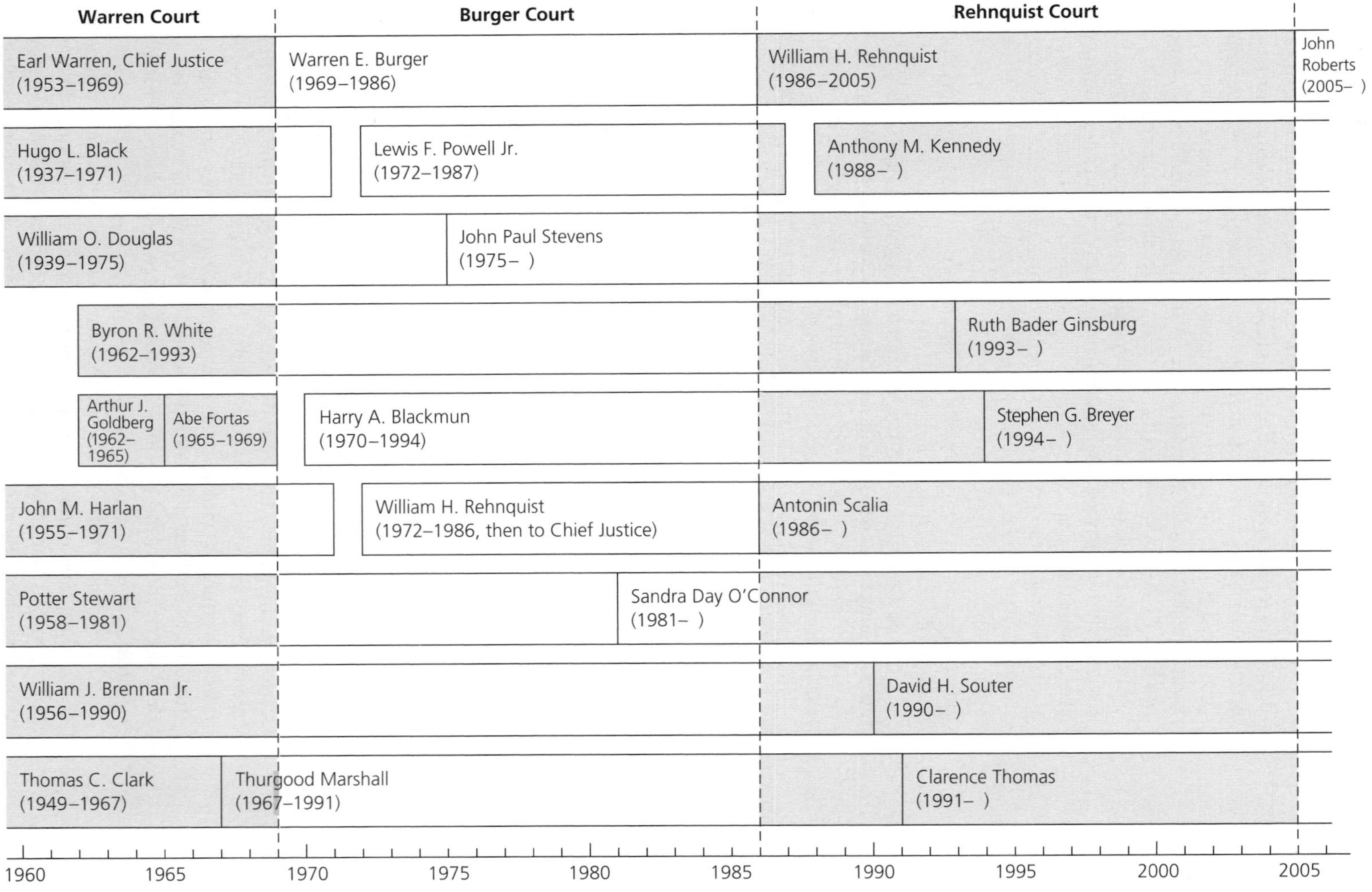

Source: Based on Stephen B. Wasby, *The Supreme Court in the Federal Judicial System*, Fourth Edition. © 1993. Reprinted with permission of Wadsworth, a division of Thomson Learning: www.thomsonrights.com. Fax 800-730-2215. Further updates by the authors.

Behind the dissenters' often biting language was the implication that the majority's decision was based not on constitutional reasoning but on partisan preferences. Five justices, all appointed by Republican presidents, had put another Republican into the White House, where he could be assumed to make future nominations to the Court that would solidify and expand its conservative majority. One of the dissenters in *Bush v. Gore*, Justice John Paul Stevens, phrased the issue in memorable language: "Although we may never know with complete certainty the identity of the winner in this year's presidential election, the identity of the loser is perfectly clear. It is the nation's confidence in the judge as an impartial guardian of the rule of law."[24]

JUDICIAL SELECTION

Article II, Section 2 of the Constitution states that the president "shall nominate, and by and with the advice and consent of the Senate, shall appoint . . . judges of the supreme court." The same clause applies to judges in the lower federal courts, which were created by acts of Congress. These few words did not specify the processes by which a president would pick judicial nominees and the Senate consider them or what advice and consent comprised. Should the Senate defer to the president's judgment, rejecting a nominee only when that individual was found lacking in judicial competence or personal integrity? Or should the Senate's judgment be equal to the president's, allowing the Senate to reject a nominee of unquestioned competence and character on political or ideological grounds? With so little settled by the language of the Constitution, judicial selection has become, for presidents and senators alike, an intensely political affair.

Lower Federal Court Nominations

The politics of judicial selection operates differently for the lower federal courts than for the Supreme Court. Judges of the district courts (described in the next section) serve only in a district within one state, and the senators from that state are closely involved in their selection. According to the tradition of **senatorial courtesy**, if the senior senator from the president's party objects to a district court nominee for his or her state, the Senate as a whole will withhold consent. As a consequence, presidents consult senators on district court nominations and may turn the choice over to them in exchange for future political support on other matters. Senatorial courtesy was weakened under Presidents Reagan and his Republican successors. Individual senators have always had less power—and presidents have had more leeway—in appointing judges to the U.S. courts of appeals (also described in the next section), whose jurisdiction extends over several states.

Although presidents have to share power over lower federal court nominations, they have much to gain by taking a strong interest in judicial selection at this level. Since the Supreme Court hears only a handful of cases, the vast majority of federal court decisions are rendered by the district courts and courts of appeals. Since retirement rates are higher on the lower courts than on the Supreme Court, and since Congress periodically creates new judicial positions to keep up with the expanding workload of a litigious society, a president can exercise more influence through lower court nominations than through Supreme Court nominations. During Reagan's eight years as president, he appointed approximately half of all lower court judges (372 out of 736), giving the lower federal courts a more conservative slant.[25] Rather than countering Reagan (and Bush) conservatives with liberal appointees, Clinton opted for moderates.[26] Because Clinton did not make lower-court nominations a high priority, would not fight for controversial nominees, and faced effective delaying tactics from Senate Republicans, the impact of his two presidential terms on future decisions of the federal courts will be considerably smaller than Reagan's has been.[27]

Clinton's legacy for the lower federal courts is diversity and not ideology. He far surpassed his predecessors in appointing women and people of color to the courts. Jimmy Carter was the first president to respond to the challenge by the civil rights and women's movements to the historic domination of the federal courts by affluent white males; 35 percent of his nominees were women and minorities. Ronald Reagan preferred white males; only 14 percent of his nominees were women and minorities. Seeking a more moderate image, George H. W. Bush raised this figure to 27 percent. Clinton made diversity the centerpiece of his judicial selection strategy, with women and minorities making up 53 percent of his first-term nominees.[28] During his second term, his ability to enhance diversity on the federal bench was restricted because the Senate delayed hearings and confirmations for women and minorities more often than they did for white male nominees.[29]

President George W. Bush has restored the ideological process that President Reagan had introduced for screening prospective judicial nominees. Staffers at the Department of Justice and in the White House who work on judicial nominations are "movement conservatives" and anti-abortion proponents. Virtually all of them have been associated with the Federalist Society, the leading conservative organization on legal matters. Bush's nominees to the lower courts reflect about the same level of racial and gender diversity as those of his father. In his first two years as president, 21 percent of his nominees were women, 7 percent were Hispanic, and 3 percent were African American. In keeping with the ideological slant of his nominations overall, most of the women and minorities he proposed were very conservative.[30]

The conservative character of Bush nominations has fed into the heightened polarization in Congress (see Chapter 11). Recalling how Republicans obstructed many of President Clinton's judicial nominations, Senate Democrats have mobilized to fight Bush's most controversial right-wing choices for the lower courts. Democrats have charged that by nominating extreme ideologues, the president is to blame for the divisiveness and bitterness in the politics of judicial selection. Mounting filibusters, Democrats have effectively blocked a number of Bush's candidates for the bench. In response, Republicans have complained angrily of partisan obstructionism and vengefulness on the part of Senate Democrats. Despite all of the controversy, Democratic opposition has been selective; at the end of his first three years in office, George W. Bush had seen about 70 percent of his nominees confirmed.[31]

Supreme Court Nominations

Most presidents have less of an opportunity in the course of a four-year term to reshape the Supreme Court than to reshape the lower federal courts. George W. Bush did not have a single opportunity to nominate a Supreme Court justice until 2005, his fifth year in office. Nonetheless, any presidential nomination to the Supreme Court today is likely to initiate a high-stakes political drama, for every new member may make a major difference in determining what the Constitution and the laws mean. Some of the Court's landmark decisions, including the one that made George W. Bush president, have come in five–four votes; a replacement of only one justice would have produced a different outcome. And some new appointees influence the Court with more than just their votes. They may prove to be a catalyst for the formation of a firm voting bloc, as was the case with the liberal Justice William Brennan. Or they may bring to the Court a forceful ideological perspective, as is the case with conservative Justice Antonin Scalia.[32]

The appointment process for a new justice of the Supreme Court begins when an existing justice retires or dies. In deliberating over a replacement, contemporary presidents tend to rely heavily on the Justice Department and legal counselors on the White House staff for advice on prospective nominees. Starting with the Eisenhower administration, the elite of the legal profession played a regular role in the selection process: The American Bar Association's Standing Committee on Federal Judiciary rated candidates as "well qualified," "qualified," or "not qualified," and a president was likely to back away from a prospective nominee who had not obtained the highest rating. But conservatives believed that the American Bar Association had a liberal bias, and President George W. Bush put an end to its official role in 2001. Once the Democrats became the majority in the Senate, they restored the ratings procedure. Viewing Supreme Court decisions as critical to the constituencies they represent, many interest groups are involved in the politics of judicial selection as well. Thus, several of the nominees of Presidents Reagan and the elder Bush were vigorously opposed by civil rights and women's groups, which feared that these nominees would roll back the egalitarian gains of recent decades.

The drama of Supreme Court nominations reaches its apex in the hearing room of the Senate Judiciary Committee. In this televised forum, senators are able to question nominees directly about their legal experience and judicial philosophy. Although questions about controversial issues currently before the Court, such as abortion, are supposed to be off limits, senators usually find means to probe these matters. Some recent nominees, such as Robert Bork, have entertained these questions. Others, such as John Roberts, perhaps learning from Bork's rejection, have fended them off with bland generalities.

In announcing the nomination of a new justice, the president is likely to highlight the legal expertise of the nominee. Less will be said about the real criterion that governs most selections: politics. As David O'Brien observes, "The presidential impulse to pack the Court with politically compatible justices is irresistible."[33]

Presidential nominations are influenced by important political forces in the nation. In the past, geographic considerations were significant, as presidents tried to ensure that each region of the country was represented on the Court. Geographic considerations have faded in the face of issues of gender, race, and religion. Thus, when Thurgood Marshall, the only African-American justice in the history of the Supreme Court, retired in 1991, President Bush found an African-American conservative, Clarence Thomas, to replace him. When given his first opportunity to appoint a Supreme Court justice, President Clinton chose a woman, Ruth Bader Ginsburg. An even more important political factor is ideology. Presidents' impacts on public policy depend not only on the legislation they sponsor or the executive actions they take but also on the decisions of the Court that reflect the ideological difference that their nominees have made.

Do presidents get what they want from their appointments to the Supreme Court? Do justices, with the independence of a lifetime tenure, continue to hold to the ideological path that the presidents who appointed them anticipated at the time of nomination? Legal scholar Laurence Tribe says yes. Tribe debunks what he calls "the myth of the surprised president." Presidents who have set out deliberately to alter the ideological direction of the Court, he shows, have generally succeeded in their strategies.[34] Nevertheless, counterexamples suggest that presidents don't always predict the future correctly. For instance, President George H. W. Bush's first appointee, David H. Souter, surprised everyone by becoming one of the Court's more liberal members.

Given the political basis of Court nominations, presidents are sometimes unsuccessful with them in the Senate. About 20 percent of nominees have failed to win confirmation, with rejection rates running particularly high in the mid-nineteenth century and the past forty years (both periods of intense partisan conflict). Four factors seem to explain these defeats. First, the partisan composition of the Senate is crucial: A president is more likely to be defeated if the opposition party has a majority in the Senate. Second, timing is important: A president is less likely to succeed if a vacancy on the Supreme Court occurs during the fourth year of the term, as senators hold off to see what the new election will bring. Third, ideology has become central: Nominees face tougher sledding in the Senate if they are perceived as ideologically extreme or likely to tip a precarious ideological balance on the present Court. Fourth, presidential management is significant: A president can seriously harm the chances of a nominee through political blunders during the selection process.[35]

Even though the process of judicial selection has always been political, politicization has recently intensified as the stakes in controlling the Supreme Court on issues like abortion, affirmative action, and criminal procedure have grown. When President Reagan proposed Robert Bork for the High Court in 1987, political forces on both the left and right mobilized to do battle over the nomination. But it was Bork himself who was the star of the drama. A prominent conservative jurist and an adherent of the same original-intent school of constitutional interpretation as Attorney General Meese, Bork tried to paint himself as more of a moderate during the Senate Judiciary Committee hearings. But a majority of the committee deemed this an unconvincing "confirmation conversion," and Bork was rejected by both the committee and the full Senate. Clarence Thomas narrowly avoided Bork's fate after President Bush nominated him in 1991.

Some recent nominations have drawn little opposition. President Clinton's moderate nominees, Ruth Bader Ginsburg and Stephen G. Breyer, easily won Senate approval. But the acrimonious politics that swirled around the Bork and Thomas nominations has led to widespread complaints that the selection process has become a political circus. Yet would it be better to go back to the quiet, elite proceedings of the past, in which political and legal insiders chose justices of the Supreme Court while the public remained in ignorance until the final outcome? The American people have much at stake in the matter of who will be sitting on the Court for decades to come. From the standpoint of popular democracy, they should welcome a process that, despite its occasional excesses, opens up judicial selection to their scrutiny.

THE FEDERAL COURT SYSTEM

Presidential appointees to the judicial branch serve in a three-tiered federal court system: district courts, courts of appeals, and Supreme Court. (In addition, there are a number of specialized federal courts, such as bankruptcy and tax courts.) The Constitution specified only "one Supreme Court," leaving it to Congress to create "inferior courts" as it deemed necessary. Since the creation of the courts of appeals in 1891, the basic structure of the federal court system has been set. Figure 14.2 outlines the current structure of the federal court system.

U.S. District Courts

On the bottom level of the three-tiered federal court system are the U.S. district courts. The district courts are courts of **original jurisdiction**, meaning the courts where almost all federal cases begin. And they are the trial courts for the federal system, resolving both criminal and civil cases, sometimes with judge and jury and sometimes with judge only. There are currently ninety-four U.S. district courts; each state has at least one, and the larger states have as many as four. As of 2004, there were 665 active district court judges, supplemented by several hundred retired judges who heard cases on a part-time basis.

The caseload of the district courts is large and rapidly expanding. In the great majority of these cases, the district courts have the final say: Decisions are not appealed, are settled before any higher court rulings occur, or are affirmed by the courts of appeals.

FIGURE 14.2 Basic Structure of the Federal Court System

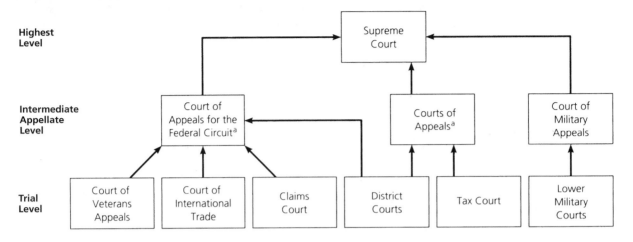

Note: Arrows indicate most common routes of appeals. Some specialized courts of minor importance are excluded.

[a] These courts also hear appeals from administrative agencies.

U.S. Courts of Appeals

The U.S. courts of appeals, the middle tier of the federal court system, hear appeals of decisions rendered by the district courts, specialized courts, and federal regulatory agencies. As **appellate courts**, the courts of appeals bear some resemblance to the Supreme Court and have sometimes been called "mini-Supreme Courts." Yet there are some major differences in the appellate role of the two. Whereas the Supreme Court can choose the cases it hears, courts of appeals must hear every case brought to them. Whereas the Supreme Court is interested in large questions of constitutional and statutory interpretation rather than the fate of the particular parties in a case, courts of appeals seek to correct errors in lower court decisions to ensure that justice is done to the individuals involved. Because the Supreme Court is too busy to consider many types of federal cases, however, the courts of appeals do effectively decide policy in a number of areas of law.

There are twelve courts of appeals with general appellate jurisdiction—one in the District of Columbia and eleven numbered circuits that cover several contiguous states plus associated territories. The circuits vary in size; the First Circuit (Maine, New Hampshire, Massachusetts, Rhode Island, and Puerto Rico) has only six judges, whereas the Ninth Circuit (nine western states plus the territories of Guam and the Northern Marianas) has twenty-eight judges. There are a total of 179 active appeals court judges, plus approximately 80 part-time senior judges, to handle a huge caseload.

Courts of appeals hearings do not retry cases. New factual evidence is not introduced, and no witnesses appear. Lawyers for the two sides in a case make oral arguments and present written briefs to the judges. Ordinarily, a three-judge panel will hear a case (and decisions are sometimes made by 2–1 vote). In especially important cases, a court of appeals may sit *en banc*, with all of its members participating. What makes the courts of appeals so significant a force in the federal court system is that few of their decisions are ever overturned.

U.S. Supreme Court

The highest tier of the federal court system is the Supreme Court of the United States. Not only does it take cases that originate in the lower federal courts; it also hears cases that originate in state courts if these cases raise constitutional issues (see Figure 14.3). That the Supreme Court is "the highest court in the land" invests it with great authority. As Justice Robert Jackson once wryly observed of the Court, "We are not final because we are infallible, we are infallible only because we are final."[36]

The Supreme Court has both original jurisdiction and appellate jurisdiction. The Constitution limits original jurisdiction to "all cases affecting ambassadors, other public ministers and counsels, and those in which a State shall be party." Few cases arise that qualify under these terms. Almost all of what the Supreme Court does falls under its second constitutional role as an appellate court.

Supreme Court decisions are powerful not only because they are the final judicial rulings in a case but also because they establish precedents that bind the lower federal courts and the state courts. Once the Supreme Court has spoken, judges at lower levels are supposed to bring their decisions into line with its interpretation of the Constitution and the laws. But guidance to lower courts is imperfect when the language of Supreme Court decisions is vague or when new circumstances arise that differ from those of the case used to establish a precedent. Consequently, decision making in a complex area such as criminal procedure or affirmative action may shuttle back and forth for years between the lower courts and the Supreme Court.

THE SUPREME COURT: PROCESS

We turn now to a more thorough examination of the Supreme Court as an institution. First, we look at the processes through which the Court hears cases and arrives at its decisions. Second, we look at the politics of those decisions. As shall be seen, the Court is an institution in which the logic and rules of the law genuinely matter, as do the personalities and political beliefs of the human beings who pronounce the law.

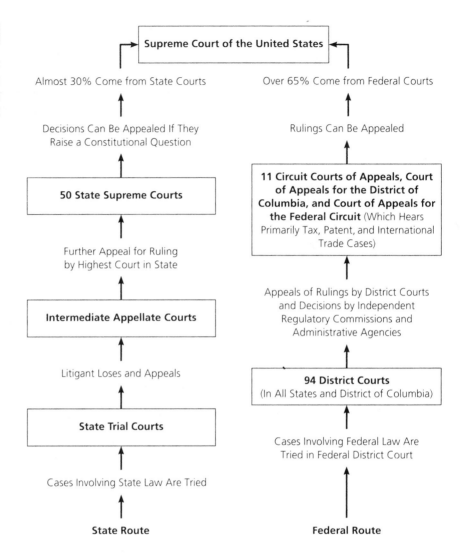

FIGURE 14.3

Avenues of Appeal: The Two Main Routes to the Supreme Court

Note: In addition, some cases come directly to the Supreme Court from trial courts when they involve reapportionment or civil rights disputes. Appeals from the Court of Military Appeals also go directly to the Supreme Court. A few cases come on "original jurisdiction" and involve disputes between state governments.

Choosing Cases

Each session of the Supreme Court begins on the first Monday in October and concludes in late June or early July of the following year. At present, approximately 8,000 cases are filed per year; of these, the Supreme Court will grant a review and produce a written opinion in only 70 to 80 cases (73 in the 2003–04 term)! Disgruntled parties in lawsuits often swear that they will appeal the verdict "all the way to the Supreme Court." Obviously, the chance that the Supreme Court will hear their appeal is minuscule. The only party that has a high rate of success in having its appeals heard before the Supreme Court is the federal government itself. The solicitor general, the third-ranking official in the Department of Justice, determines which cases involving the federal government should be appealed to the Supreme Court, and the Court regards petitions from the solicitor general with a favorable disposition, accepting about three-quarters of them.

In the past, several categories of cases had to be reviewed by the Supreme Court. Since Congress passed the 1988 Act to Improve the Administration of Justice, the Court has been free in all but a few areas to choose the cases it wishes to hear. Today, about 99 percent of the Court's cases arrive through a *writ of certiorari*. The losing party in a lower court proceeding petitions the Supreme Court for this writ; should the Court choose to "grant cert" (shorthand for *certiorari*), it orders the lower court to send the records of the case.

The mountain of cert petitions that arrives at the Supreme Court by the beginning of its fall term has to be sifted to find the few worthy of the Court's full attention. Because the number of petitions has risen, justices have turned over the work of screening them to their law clerks, recent graduates of the nation's elite law schools. Armed with memos from clerks, the justices meet to decide which cases to hear. According to the informal **rule of four**, at least four justices must agree that a case deserves consideration.

Since almost all cases reach the Court through writs of certiorari, the justices have considerable latitude in setting their own agenda. In each year's session, they can accept cases that allow them to grapple with a constitutional or statutory issue that they deem ripe for determination and reject cases if they wish to sidestep some other controversial issue. Even when the Court agrees to take a case, it may choose to decide it without full consideration, a process known as *summary disposition*. After denying the vast majority of petitions for certiorari, and handling some of the remainder through summary dispositions, the Supreme Court leaves itself fewer than a hundred cases each year for full consideration.

Deciding Cases

When a case is granted full treatment, attorneys for the two sides are given several months to prepare briefs—written statements that argue their respective legal positions to the justices. Additional briefs may be filed by individuals or groups that are not parties in a lawsuit but have an interest in the issues it raises; these are known as *amicus curiae* (friend of the court) briefs. Having read these briefs, the justices allow attorneys for the contending litigants to appear in **oral argument**. Each side has only half an hour to present its strongest arguments to the Court. Oral argument often proves to be a battle for the attorney—but less with opposing counsel than with the justices themselves. Lawyers are not allowed to read from prepared texts, and some justices have a habit of asking barbed questions during oral arguments.

The justices meet in conference twice a week (Wednesdays and Fridays) to discuss the cases they have just heard in oral argument. The chief justice begins the discussion by presenting his or her views on how the case should be resolved. The other eight justices follow with their comments in order of their seniority on the High Court. Ordinarily, formal votes are not taken since the positions of the justices have been made clear in their comments. After all nine justices have spoken, one is selected to write a majority opinion for the Court. If the chief justice is in the majority, he or she assigns the opinion. If the chief justice is in the minority, the senior justice on the majority side makes the assignment. The voting alignment at this stage is tentative. Justices may still switch their votes—which makes the next stage, the writing of opinions, all the more crucial.

The crucial test of a majority opinion is not whether it sparkles in style but whether it wins the necessary votes. The justice assigned to write the opinion for the Court must hold on to the votes that constituted the initial majority and, if he or she is persuasive enough, perhaps pick up additional votes. The risk is that an opinion may lose votes along the way. In a closely divided Court, a majority opinion may thus become a minority one as a justice or two switch sides.

The majority opinion announces the position of the Court. Justices who do not want to add their names to this opinion have two options. If they agree with the result announced in the majority opinion but not with the reasoning that justifies this result (or if they simply want to make additional points not found in the majority opinion), they can write a **concurring opinion** that sets out their alternative course of argument. If they disagree with the result, they can write a **dissenting opinion** that challenges the majority's view of what the law should be. Other justices may then sign these concurrences or dissents. In recent years, heated ideological differences and a growing preference for individual expression over institutional loyalty have led to a marked increase in concurrences and dissents.

Once all opinions have been drafted, the justices make their final decisions about whether they will "join" the majority opinion, concurring opinions, or dissents. The Court is now ready for a public announcement of its holding in a case.

THE SUPREME COURT: POLITICS

Throughout the process of decision, from screening cases to announcing opinions, the procedures and precedents of the law are central to the work of the Supreme Court. But the process is political as well as legal. Three political factors influence the Court in this regard: the leadership of the chief justice, the strategic action of other justices, and the central role of ideology in shaping judicial results.

The Chief Justice and Leadership

The chief justice has certain special prerogatives during the decision process, such as speaking first in conference and assigning opinions for the Court when in the majority. The chief justice also has unique administrative responsibilities, both over the Court's own building and personnel and over the federal judicial system as a whole. Nevertheless, the chief justice is only "first among equals"; when it comes to votes, he or she has only one. Whether a chief justice is a leader depends on intellectual talent, interpersonal skills, and ability to manage the business of the Court. A comparison of the three past chief justices shows how widely varying their leadership styles and impact can be.

The most influential chief justice in modern times was Earl Warren, who held the position from 1953 to 1969. Appointed by President Eisenhower, Warren was a former governor of California, and he brought his exceptional political talent to the role of chief justice. Although not a legal scholar, he developed a clear vision of the Court as a champion of individual liberties and equal rights, and he was increasingly effective in marshaling a majority to advance that vision. Warren's personal warmth and moral conviction won him the love and respect of most of his colleagues. Perhaps his greatest feat of leadership came early in his tenure, when he convinced several wavering justices that the Court should speak to the nation with unanimity when it took the historic step of declaring racial segregation to be unconstitutional.[37]

It was one of Warren's sharpest critics, President Nixon, who appointed his successor, Warren Burger. Burger served as chief justice from 1969 to 1986. With a rugged face under a full mane of white hair, he looked every inch the part of a chief justice as a Hollywood movie would portray him. To his fellow justices, however, Burger was distinguished only in appearance. Most found him pompous in personal relations, poorly prepared for cases before the Court, and deficient in legal analysis. When it came to influencing the opinions handed down by the Court, he was a weak leader.[38]

When Burger retired in 1986, President Reagan elevated Associate Justice William Rehnquist to the position of chief justice. Although Rehnquist's views marked him as more extreme than Burger in ideological terms, he proved to be a more effective leader. He had more intellectual firepower, winning him grudging respect even from his liberal adversaries. In personal style, he was unpretentious and good humored, and he ran conferences efficiently. Rehnquist also had a critical advantage in leadership that Burger lacked: A majority on the Court shared his conservative judicial philosophy, especially on matters of federalism.[39]

Despite Chief Justice Rehnquist's achievements in these areas, he and his allies did not move the Court as far to the right on issues of civil liberties and civil rights as conservatives had hoped. On these issues, there was no conservative "counter-revolution" to reverse the results of the Warren Court's liberal "revolution." In 2003, the Court upheld affirmative action in higher education and expanded the right of privacy for gays and lesbians, with Rehnquist dissenting in both cases (see Chapter 16). In 2004, it rebuffed President Bush's assertion that the commander in chief's power to detain alleged enemy combatants indefinitely could not be reviewed by the courts (see Chapter 16). Pragmatism, and not conservative ideology, prevailed in cases involving civil liberties and civil rights, with Justice Sandra Day O'Connor frequently serving as the swing vote in 5–4 decisions.[40]

O'Connor announced her retirement in the summer of 2005, and Rehnquist died a few months later. President George W. Bush's appointee as Chief Justice, John Roberts, may be able to move the Supreme Court farther to the right in the years ahead.

Strategic Action

The chief justice is not the only member of the Court who can exercise leadership. Any of the other eight justices can use *strategic action* to win a majority for a legal doctrine they favor. Justices who engage in strategic action calculate the mix of tactics that will likely win over enough votes to their preferred position. Such tactics may include (1) persuasion on the merits — intellectual arguments to change minds, (2) ingratiation — using personal warmth to woo potential supporters, (3) sanctions — threats to write a stinging concurrence or dissent, and (4) bargaining — negotiation over the argument and language of a decision.[41] (The "Making a Difference" box on pages 440–441 describes a master of strategic action, Justice William Brennan Jr.)

That the Supreme Court is the most elite domain in American politics hardly frees it from internal conflict. Indeed, the Court's elite nature may exacerbate conflict. Protected by lifetime tenure, justices may bring strongly held opinions and large egos to "battles on the bench." However, these battles are ordinarily kept from getting out of hand by prudent calculations (you may need your current adversary's vote in a future case) and considerations of authority (too much visible conflict undermines the legitimacy of the Court).[42]

Copyright 2002, Jimmy Margulies, The Record New Jersey. Reprinted by permission.

Ideology

Although the leadership abilities of a chief justice or the strategic action of other justices may significantly affect the work of the Court, the most powerful political factor is ideology. In deciding how to cast votes and frame opinions, justices are profoundly influenced by their own convictions about society. Changes in the doctrines announced by the Supreme Court stem less from developments internal to the law than from the arrival of new justices with differing ideological perspectives.[43]

The most common ideological distinction among justices is that between liberals and conservatives. Liberal justices tend to favor individual rights (e.g., of political dissenters and criminal defendants) when they clash with governmental authority, to support measures toward greater equality for such previously excluded groups as African Americans and women, and to validate government regulation of the economy. Conservative justices are more inclined to cherish the peace of the existing social order and the authority of the officials (executives, bureaucrats, police, prosecutors) who maintain it, and to look with greater reverence at the rights of property owners. Some justices fall midway between these ideological poles; in a closely divided Court, these "centrists" may hold the balance of power.[44]

Students of the Supreme Court look not only at the ideology of individual justices but also at the formation of **ideological blocs**. An ideological bloc is a group of two or more justices who vote the same way with a high degree of regularity. Thus, we can speak of liberal blocs, conservative blocs, or moderate blocs, such as the bloc of four conservatives who frustrated Roosevelt's New Deal or the bloc of five liberals who spearheaded the expansion of civil liberties in the later years of the Warren Court. Members of an ideological bloc may directly coordinate their actions or may simply vote the same way out of shared beliefs even in the absence of close personal relations.

THE SUPREME COURT AND THE POLITICAL SYSTEM

Ideology is the single most potent force shaping the decisions of the Supreme Court. But other factors enter in, among them concern for how decisions will be received by other political actors. A Supreme Court decision must take into account multiple audiences: the lower courts that must apply the decision to other cases, the government officials who must enforce the decision, and the segment of the public that must abide by the decision. Lacking the power of the purse (financial power) and the power of the sword (executive power, including the use of force if necessary), the Supreme Court is dependent for its power on the reaction to its decisions. As political scientist Stephen Wasby remarks, "The Supreme Court may make law, or the law may be what the Supreme Court says it is, but *only after all others have had their say*."[45] During the process

Making a difference

Justice William J. Brennan Jr.

In a 1990 survey conducted by the *National Law Journal*, only 3 percent of Americans recognized the name William Brennan Jr. Yet few public figures in the last half of the twentieth century had as great an impact on the lives of Americans as this remarkable associate justice of the U.S. Supreme Court.

The son of Irish immigrants, Brennan grew up in Newark, New Jersey. His father began as a coal heaver but quickly rose to become a labor union official and local political leader. Despite his ascent, he never forgot his origins and bequeathed to his son a commitment to activism on behalf of society's have-nots. Brennan maintained this commitment even as he, in turn, ascended into the higher ranks of the judicial elite. Appointed to the U.S. Supreme Court by President Eisenhower in 1956 (an appointment that Eisenhower later regretted), Brennan served until 1990. He died in 1997.

During his thirty-four years on the Court, Brennan was a leading force for judicial activism. No other justice of modern times matched his record for penning landmark decisions. In area after area—reapportionment, the law of libel, obscenity, school prayer, the rights of criminal defendants, equal rights for minorities and women—Brennan crafted decisions that reshaped the rules by which Americans live.

Brennan's influence stemmed as much from his skills at strategic action as from his popular democratic convictions. Unlike his fellow giants of liberal jurisprudence, Hugo Black and William O. Douglas, who were combative and uncompromising, Brennan was adept at building coalitions and molding consensuses. In *New York Times v. Sullivan* (1964), the most conservative members of the Court wanted to retain the existing standard of libel law, by which a newspaper could be sued for an erroneous statement injuring the reputation of a public official, while the most liberal members insisted that the right of free speech barred any judgments

of implementing the Court's decisions, the Court may be checked or held accountable by other institutions or political forces.

When Supreme Court decisions require federal action, the response of the president is most important. Usually, presidents back up the Court's actions, regarding the enforcement of its decisions as a requirement of their oath of office. Sometimes, though, they drag their feet on implementation or repudiate a decision altogether. Believing that the decision in *Brown v. Board of Education* (1954) was forcing racial desegregation too rapidly on the South, President Eisenhower refused, despite repeated requests from others, to encourage southern compliance by placing his enormous prestige behind the Court's ruling. President Bush sharply criticized the Supreme Court's decision in *Texas v. Johnson* (1989), which upheld the right of a protester to burn an American flag as a form of symbolic speech protected under the First Amendment. He proposed a constitutional amendment to ban flag burning—implying that he, and not the Court, stood for patriotism. But Bush failed to get the amendment through Congress.

for libel in such cases. Brennan found a middle ground: To win a libel suit, a plaintiff must show that falsehoods printed about her or him are intentional and motivated by "actual malice." Patiently rewriting his opinion to satisfy colleagues on both sides—it took eight drafts!—Brennan revolutionized libel law and expanded the freedom of the press.

The height of Brennan's influence came during the Warren Court revolution. But he continued to use his intellectual and political talents to shape the law even during the years in which the Burger and Rehnquist Courts sought a counterrevolution. Brennan mounted a powerful defense of the essential achievements of the Warren Court and frequently frustrated conservative ambitions. He was even able to extend Warren Court departures in several areas. Adept as always behind the scenes, he played a major role in shaping the Court's support for abortion rights in *Roe v. Wade* (1973). And he wrote new landmark decisions on women's rights (*Craig v. Boren*, 1976) and symbolic speech (*Texas v. Johnson*, 1989).

Yet the conservative trend on the Court pushed Brennan frequently into the role of dissenter, particularly on the issue of capital punishment. Here, the usually affable and pragmatic Brennan was passionately unyielding. To him, the core of the Constitution and the Bill of Rights was a commitment to human dignity. The death penalty, in his view, was totally inconsistent with this commitment: "The fatal constitutional infirmity of capital punishment is that it treats members of the human race as nonhumans, as objects to be toyed with and discarded." Unlike famous Supreme Court dissenters of the past, Brennan did not relish this role; he much preferred being the strategic actor who could find the common ground upon which a majority could be built. Yet his stance on the death penalty was in keeping with his commitment to justice for the most unpopular and powerless of Americans.

Sources: Kim Isaac Eisler, *A Justice for All: William J. Brennan, Jr., and the Decisions That Transformed America* (New York: Simon & Schuster, 1993); Charles G. Curtis, Jr., and Shirley S. Abrahamson, "William Joseph Brennan, Jr.," in Kermit L. Hall et al., eds., *The Oxford Companion to the Supreme Court of the United States* (New York: Oxford University Press, 1992), pp. 86–89; Owen Fiss, "A Life Lived Twice," *The Yale Law Journal* 100 (March 1991): 1117–29.

(Congress did pass a law against flag burning—and the Court struck it down as well.)

Congress has power to chastise or discipline the Supreme Court since the legislative branch determines the appellate jurisdiction and even the size of the High Court. Congress sometimes altered the size of the Court during the nineteenth century. Since Roosevelt's court-packing fiasco, however, it has been politically unwise to propose adding or subtracting members, and the figure of nine justices has seemingly become sacrosanct. Supreme Court decisions based on the Constitution can be overturned only through the difficult process of constitutional amendment, so the ability of members of Congress to reverse specific decisions is far greater when the Court has been engaged in statutory interpretation. Thus, the Civil Rights Act of 1991, placing the burden of proof on employers in job discrimination lawsuits, overturned a dozen recent Supreme Court holdings.

Even though the justices don't face the public in elections, they know that compliance with their decisions depends ultimately on public opinion. However, public views on the judicial branch tend to be less clear than views on the other two branches. General public support for the Supreme Court is higher than for Congress or the presidency. On the other hand, public knowledge about the Court is lower. For example, surveys indicate that a majority cannot name even one sitting justice. The public is more attuned to controversial Court rulings than to the Court as an institution. Public support for the Court thus fell in response to decisions that favored the rights of criminal defendants. But it rose during the Watergate era, when the Court ordered President Nixon to hand over the tapes that revealed his participation in a criminal cover-up, thereby forcing him to resign.[46]

Respect for law and the Supreme Court inclines most Americans to abide by judicial decisions, even those they disagree with. When the Court treads in the most sensitive areas, however, it may face major problems of evasion or resistance. Its ruling in *Engel v. Vitale* (1962) forbade prayer in the public schools as a violation of the First Amendment, yet decades later many public schools still conduct various forms of religious observance.

Dependent on others for the implementation of its decisions, the Court cannot help but take heed of the political environment. Its conservative critics wish it was even more deferential to elected officials and public opinion. Its liberal defenders praise it for disregarding political pressures when the fundamental values of democracy are at stake. Both, progressive skeptics suggest, tend to exaggerate the boldness of the justices, whose conservative training and cautious legal instincts place them most often on the side of elite democracy.

Conclusion: Law, Politics, and the Democratic Debate

In our examination of the federal judicial system, and especially in our treatment of the Supreme Court, law and politics are separate yet intertwined. The judicial branch is fundamentally different from the other branches in that it is a legal order. Its business is resolving lawsuits or criminal cases. It follows legal procedures and rules for determining how cases are brought to and then handled by the High Court, and gives considerable weight to past decisions as precedents on the grounds that law should be, as much as possible, settled and known. The impressive symbolic power of the Supreme Court—the black robes, the marble temple, and the confidential deliberations—rests on the mystique of the rule of law as something that transcends politics.

Yet politics shapes appointments to the Supreme Court, as presidents try to fill the Court with justices who will carry out the presidents' political and ideological agendas. Politics is found within the internal processes of the Court, as chief justices attempt to exercise leadership and other justices engage in strategic action. Political values influence the Court, with ideology the paramount factor in determining how different justices will vote on cases. Political sensitivity to other institutions and to public opinion characterizes a judicial branch aware of its dependence on others to carry out its decisions. Finally, the Court is political because its decisions set national policy on some of the issues that matter most to Americans.

It is because the judiciary is political, and indeed so important a policy maker, that there has been an intense democratic debate in recent years over its proper role in American life. Popular democrats of the past generally mistrusted the Court as a nondemocratic defender of elite privileges. Their arguments have been taken over by conservatives such as Edwin Meese, whose very different policy agenda also requires a Court that practices self-restraint and does not interfere much with other institutions. In contrast, liberal jurists such as William Brennan Jr., want popular democrats to reexamine their attitude toward the judiciary, arguing that only an activist Court that adapts and modernizes the Constitution can bring out its popular democratic character. Progressive skeptics question both the conservatives' fear of the Court and the liberals' hope for it. In their thinking, the Court can be of only limited value in the struggle for popular democracy. Citizens who seek popular democratic reform must rely on their own political activities rather than looking for salvation from the judicial elite.

KEY TERMS

judicial review
jurisprudence of original intention
precedent
Marbury v. Madison
McCulloch v. Maryland
Gibbons v. Ogden
Dred Scott v. Sandford
court-packing plan
Bush v. Gore

senatorial courtesy
original jurisdiction
appellate court
rule of four
oral argument
concurring opinion
dissenting opinion
ideological bloc

INTERNET RESOURCES

■ University of Pittsburgh School of Law
www.jurist.law.pitt.edu
This website provides Supreme Court opinions and news stories on constitutional law.

■ The American Civil Liberties Union
www.aclu.org
Legal issues and court cases viewed from the perspective of the nation's leading civil libertarian organization.

■ The Federalist Society
www.fed-soc.org
The website of a prominent organization of conservative lawyers, offering perspectives on recent Supreme Court cases and other legal issues.

SUGGESTED READINGS

Robert H. Bork, *The Tempting of America: The Political Seduction of the Law*. New York: Free Press, 1990. A rejected Supreme Court nominee's conservative attack on the judicial selection process and on liberal jurisprudence.

Kermit L. Hall et al., eds., *The Oxford Companion to the Supreme Court of the United States*, 2nd ed. New York: Oxford University Press, 2005. Everything you want to know about the Supreme Court is presented in superb detail.

Peter Irons, *A People's History of the Supreme Court*. New York: Penguin Books, 2000. The history of the Supreme Court is narrated from a popular democratic perspective.

David Kairys, ed., *The Politics of Law: A Progressive Critique*, 3rd ed. New York: Basic Books, 1998. An anthology of articles, most by law professors, expressing the view of progressive skeptics that the courts and the legal profession generally serve elite interests.

Gerald N. Rosenberg, *The Hollow Hope: Can Courts Bring About Social Change?* Chicago: University of Chicago Press, 1991. A provocative argument, with case studies, that casts doubt upon the ability of the courts to advance social reform.

Mark Tushnet, *Taking the Constitution Away from the Courts*. Princeton, N.J.: Princeton University Press, 1999. A provocative critique of judicial review and argument for a "populist constitutional law."

CHAPTER 15

State and Local Politics
The Dilemma of Federalism

The United States has a system of government called *federalism*, which divides power between a central government and state and local governments. Popular democrats have always favored decentralizing power as much as possible, putting policy-making authority in the hands of state, or even better, local governments. Decentralizing power brings government closer to the people, enabling citizens to participate more meaningfully in the decisions that affect their lives. It would seem, then, that the popular democratic position on federalism would be simple: shift as much policy-making authority as possible from the federal government to the states and localities. There are problems, however, with simply moving power down the federal ladder, as we can see by examining the case of homelessness.

When homelessness emerged as a visible problem in the 1980s, homeless policy was handled like a hot potato, shunted from one level of government to another, with no one willing to take full responsibility. The Reagan administration (1981–1989) stressed that homelessness was best addressed by localities, and it was not until 1987 that Congress passed the Stewart B. McKinney Act, providing federal monies for temporary emergency shelters. Funded at less than a billion dollars annually, McKinney Act monies, once spread across the entire country, were stretched paper-thin. A 1988 survey found that 89 percent of the nation's governors thought the federal government was doing an inadequate job on homelessness. The economic boom of the 1990s made the homeless problem even worse. In prosperous metropolitan areas, housing prices and rents soared at the same time that wages for those at the bottom barely budged. By 2000, requests for beds in shelters had reached record highs in many cities.

Almost by default, much of the responsibility for dealing with homelessness has been left to local governments, especially big cities. But the ability of local governments to enact and implement effective homeless policies has varied greatly. Consider the responses of two major American cities, Boston and Miami.

Boston, with a long tradition of active government, probably has done more to help the homeless and near-homeless than any city in the country. Boston's populist mayor Ray Flynn (1983–1993) and his successor, Thomas Menino (1993–present), made affordable housing a top priority. Flynn was one of the few mayors in the country to side openly with the homeless and champion local homeless policies. Under Flynn's leadership, Boston enacted a linkage policy that required downtown developers to contribute to low-income housing, raising over $70 million by 1992. The city also enacted an inclusionary housing ordinance that required housing developers to set aside units for low-income families. The city not only aggressively sought federal grants; it also committed millions of dollars of its own money to fund affordable housing. To prevent people from becoming homeless, condominium conversions were regulated and evictions of renters who could not afford to buy their units were banned. Those who did become homeless were provided with extensive services, and the number of shelter beds was increased.[1]

Miami's response to homelessness has been very different. Until recently, the city spent little money of its own on the homeless. In the mid-1990s, there were only about 400 shelter beds in the city, with another 500 added in the winter — for a homeless population estimated at 15,000. Miami's homeless had few options but the street. But homeless people on the street presented a problem for Miami, which advertises itself as a carefree tourist destination. To address the image problem, Miami implemented aggressive policies to get the homeless off the streets, arresting thousands and harassing others in an effort to persuade them to leave town. Miami, it should be noted, was not the only city to shun the homeless.[2] Los Angeles city officials devised a "bum-proof" park bench; shaped like a barrel, it was so uncomfortable that no one would want to sleep on it. The city also installed sophisticated sprinklers that went off at random times to discourage sleeping in public parks.[3] Some smaller cities simply gave the homeless a one-way bus ticket to the nearest big city and told them never to return.

In 1988 the American Civil Liberties Union filed a suit against Miami on behalf of the homeless. The suit charged that the city discriminated against the homeless: arresting them, harassing them, and destroying their belongings for the purpose of driving the homeless out of the city or otherwise rendering them invisible. In 1992 a Federal District Court judge ruled that Miami's actions violated the Bill of Rights of the U.S. Constitution. Miami appealed the verdict, and it took almost ten years before the case was finally settled. Under the 1997 settlement, Miami agreed to pay $600,000 to those homeless who suffered injury and to train the police to respect the rights of the homeless. As a result of the lawsuit, the treatment of the homeless has improved considerably. A half-cent tax on restaurant meals is dedicated to a fund to help the homeless. Still, Miami has the highest percentage of mentally ill of any metropolitan areas in the country, with many ending up on the streets.

The contrasting responses of Boston and Miami show the problems with simply turning responsibility for social policies over to local governments. Many local governments are dominated by elites that are preoccupied with economic prosperity in a competitive federal system. They deliberately underfund social services in order to discourage the poor and the homeless from moving in. It took a federal lawsuit to force the Miami authorities to stop discriminating against the homeless. Even Boston, which treats its homeless better than most cities, could do little to stop its booming economy from driving up the cost of housing beyond the means of many families.

The problem with giving local governments responsibility for social policies is clear. But if social policies are completely controlled by the federal government, the result is inevitably a great deal of bureaucracy and red tape, and little meaningful participation by ordinary citizens. In short, popular democrats are faced with what we call the *dilemma of federalism*: Either alternative—centralizing power in the hands of federal authorities or decentralizing power into states and localities—presents problems from the viewpoint of democracy.

In this chapter, we explore the dilemma of federalism and look for a popular democratic way out of it. We begin by examining the evolving federal system over the years from the founding to the present, showing how power has moved among the federal, state, and local levels. In the last part of the chapter, we examine the operation of state and local governments today, focusing on the question of their potential for popular democratic participation.

FEDERALISM AND THE CONSTITUTION

The debate over federalism began with the controversy over ratification of the U.S. Constitution. The framers of the Constitution favored moving power from the states to a national government with a strong executive. Under the Articles of Confederation, the state legislatures had great power that the framers feared would be used by envious majorities to confiscate the wealth of the rich. As James Madison maintained in his famous "extended republic" argument in *Federalist No. 10*, a large democracy like the United States would be less vulnerable to majority tyranny than a small democracy because of the greater obstacles to coordination and communication. Moreover, by electing representatives from larger districts, Madison maintained, voters in an extended republic would favor educated and wealthy elites.

Led by Madison and Alexander Hamilton, the framers of the Constitution initially favored a **unitary government** in which all significant powers would rest in the hands of the central government and state and local governments would derive their authority from the central government. (Over 90 percent of all countries in the world today, including France and the United Kingdom, are governed by unitary systems.) However, the founders knew that most citizens, and especially the rank-and-file soldiers who had fought in the Revolution, would not vote for a unitary government that reminded them of their subservience under the British monarchy. To aid in ratification, the Federalists were forced to compromise with Anti-federalist sentiment, creating a mixed system that gave some powers to the federal government and left others to the states. Federalism was born in compromise.

Reluctant to admit that one of the primary characteristics of the new Constitution was the result of a tactical political compromise, the framers put their best "spin" (as we would say today) on the new Constitution in order to boost its chances of ratification. They argued that the federalism of the new Constitution arose not from a compromise but from a general theory of government that carefully balanced the powers of the central government and the state governments. Protection for the states, the Federalists argued, would come from the way that the new Constitution divided power into two spheres, a theory that we have come to call **dual federalism**. Under dual federalism, the national government and the states each have separate spheres of authority, and "within their respective spheres the two centers of government are 'sovereign' and hence 'equal.'"[4] Each level of government relates directly to the citizens, and no level of government can interfere within the legitimate sphere of authority of another level.

Under dual federalism, the federal government has only those powers specifically granted in the Constitution, called **enumerated powers** (see Table 15.1). Seventeen such powers are given to the national government, or Congress, in Article I, Section 8, including the power to "regulate commerce with foreign nations and among the several States," "coin money," and "provide for the common defense." All powers not given to the national government are **reserved** to the states by the Tenth Amendment. (Dual federalism is sometimes called *Tenth Amendment federalism*.) With the powers of the federal government clearly spelled out in the Constitution, Federalists maintained, the Supreme Court would act as a neutral umpire, making sure that the federal government does not go beyond its enumerated powers and invade the powers reserved to the states. In cases where both levels of government possess the power to act—so-called

	Power	Definition	Example
TABLE 15.1 **Principles of Dual Federalism**	Enumerated	Powers specifically granted to Congress	Coin money, national defense
	Concurrent	Powers exercised by both Congress and the states	Taxation
	Reserved	Powers not mentioned in the Constitution and therefore left to the states	Police powers (e.g., land use regulation)

concurrent powers—the **Supremacy Clause** (Article VI) states that national laws supersede state laws.

Anti-federalists opposed the Constitution primarily because it gave too much power to the national government. The Anti-federalists argued that Madison's extended republic was a contradiction in terms; democracy was possible only in small, homogeneous republics. The principal threat to our liberties, they said, came not from tyrannical majorities in the state legislatures but from selfish elites in the national government.

The Anti-federalists did not buy the theory of dual federalism—the idea that the states would be protected because the Supreme Court would prevent the federal government from extending its powers beyond those clearly enumerated in the Constitution. To begin with, they cited the vague language in the Constitution describing the division of powers, which was written in broad terms to encourage agreement. In shaping this compromise, even the framers disagreed about the division of powers between the national and state governments. As a result, the Constitution is full of imprecise language that papers over disagreements, especially on the issue of federalism. In the words of Supreme Court Justice William J. Brennan Jr., the framers "hid their differences in cloaks of generality."[5]

Anti-federalists attacked specific clauses in the Constitution that they felt could be used to expand the power of the federal government. They were suspicious of the so-called **Necessary and Proper**, or **Elastic**, **Clause** (Article I, Section 8) that gave the national Congress the power "to make all Laws which shall be necessary and proper for carrying into Execution the foregoing Powers." In *The Federalist Papers*, Alexander Hamilton maintained that the necessary and proper clause did nothing but state the obvious: "Though it may be chargeable with tautology or redundancy, [it] is at least perfectly harmless."[6] However, the Anti-federalists smelled a rat here: If this were the case, they asked, then why was it included at all? The Anti-federalists also observed that the Supreme Court, itself a federal institution, would tend to interpret the vague language of the Constitution in favor the national government over the states. Appointed by the president for life, with the advice and consent of the Senate, the justices of the Supreme Court would not be democratically accountable.

On the surface, the debate between the Federalists and Anti-federalists was based on principle: Each side claimed it was only trying to create a more perfect representative democracy. In fact, however, both had practical political purposes behind their positions. Fearing the radicalism of the state legislatures, the Federalists thought that they would be able to dominate a national government with a strong executive that could protect their property from radical movements by the poor and propertyless. Conversely, the power base of the Anti-federalists was in the state legislatures, and they feared that the new Constitution would weaken them politically.

In fact, throughout American history federalism has been a political football. Political conflicts over federalism are not surprising because the division of powers between levels of government is not politically neutral. *Where* decisions are made determines the scope of conflict, and the scope of conflict, in turn, helps determine who wins and who loses. From the beginning in American politics, struggles over policy have been transformed into struggles over federalism.

Regardless of whether you favor popular or elite democracy, understanding federalism is essential for understanding American politics. In our political system, disagreements over *what* policies should be enacted are frequently played out as disagreements over *where* policy decisions should be made—at the national, state, or local level. The reason for this is that state and local political systems are not simply miniature versions of the national political system; there are essential differences among the different levels of government.

The Slavery Issue: Reaffirming National Authority

After the Constitution was ratified, elite democrats continued to champion a powerful national government while popular democrats emphasized states' rights. John Marshall, chief justice of the Supreme Court from 1801 to 1835, was a brilliant Federalist advocate of national power. Perhaps his most important decision, *McCulloch v. Maryland* (1819), used the Necessary and Proper Clause to expand the powers of the federal government. In 1836 the popular democrat Andrew Jackson appointed Roger B. Taney, a strong advocate of states' rights, to succeed Marshall as chief justice. Led by Taney until 1864, the Court chipped away at federal powers by upholding state laws that probably would have been struck down by the Marshall Court.

Popular democratic support of states' rights came up against a contradiction with the issue of slavery. Southern states used states' rights to defend the institution of slavery. Led by South Carolina's John C. Calhoun, southern states resisted tariffs that protected northern industries and raised prices for manufactured goods. They also opposed efforts by the federal government to restrict slavery. Calhoun argued for the doctrine of **nullification**—that states have the right to nullify, or refuse to obey, federal laws they consider unconstitutional. In the infamous *Dred Scott* decision (1857), the Supreme Court under Taney ruled that the federal government had no power to prohibit slavery in the territories.[7]

(This case is discussed in more detail in Chapter 14.) By striking down the Missouri Compromise as unconstitutional, the Supreme Court helped precipitate the Civil War. The Civil War finally settled the federalism issues raised by slavery: The federal union is indissoluble, and states do not have the right to declare acts of the federal government unconstitutional or secede from the union.

Federalism and Corporations

During the period of rapid industrialization after the Civil War, a new threat to popular democracy arose: the rise of giant national corporations and the wealthy elites who ran them. Popular democrats had power in many state legislatures, and they used that power to regulate corporations. These efforts were frustrated by the Supreme Court, however, which often ruled against the states when they threatened property rights. Angry about rate discrimination in areas not served by competing railroads, for example, popular democrats in the early 1870s passed laws setting maximum rates. In the celebrated Granger cases of 1877, the Supreme Court upheld the constitutionality of these laws.[8] In 1886, however, the Supreme Court reversed itself and ruled that the Constitution placed power to regulate railroad rates exclusively in the hands of the federal government, even for segments of the journey lying entirely within one state.[9]

The Court's blocking of state action provided an impetus for Congress to create the Interstate Commerce Commission (ICC) in 1887, the first attempt by the national government to regulate the economy through means other than general control over money and credit. Additional support for the ICC came from the railroads, which feared the rising power of popular democrats in the state legislatures. The railroads saw federal railroad regulation "as a safe shield behind which to hide from the consequences of local democracy."[10]

In short, elite and popular democratic forces tried to shift policy-making authority to the federal or state level, depending on where they saw their advantage. In the late nineteenth and early twentieth centuries, the Supreme Court generally acted to protect property rights and was suspicious of governmental efforts, at all levels, to regulate private property. From today's viewpoint, the Court construed the powers of the federal government quite narrowly. For example, it struck down the federal income tax,[11] restricted the powers of the ICC to set railroad rates,[12] and declared federal laws to regulate child labor unconstitutional.[13]

For almost the first 150 years of the U.S. Constitution—until the New Deal in the 1930s—something like dual federalism prevailed in American government. The powers of the federal government were construed narrowly, and Congress did not legislate in many domestic policy areas that we now take for granted. In domestic policy, state and local governments raised more revenues, spent more money, and provided more services than the federal government. There were important exceptions to this pattern of federal reluctance, particularly the assertion of federal power following the Civil War during Reconstruction in the South and federal regulation of corporations during the Progressive era. Nevertheless, until the New Deal the federal government was the junior partner in domestic policy. It was not until the Great Depression of the 1930s that the glaring weaknesses of state and local governments were dramatically exposed.

THE FAILURE OF DUAL FEDERALISM

It is difficult for Americans today to imagine the depth of the economic and political crisis that the nation faced during the Depression. It began with the stock market crash on October 24, 1929—Black Thursday. The effects of the crash rippled out from Wall Street to paralyze the entire nation. The unemployment rate soared from 3 percent in 1929 to over one-quarter of the workforce in 1933. Those who were lucky enough to have jobs saw their average incomes fall 43 percent from 1929 to 1933. The collapse of the economy spread to the financial system; by the end of 1932, more than 5,000 commercial banks had failed. The political situation was tense. Frequent and violent street confrontations broke out between police and communist-led demonstrators as well as workers trying to organize unions.

The initial response of the political system to the Depression was halting and inadequate. Under the system of dual federalism, almost all social welfare functions were left to the states and localities. In 1929–1930, local governments provided 95 percent of the costs of general relief for the destitute.[14] The American welfare state was incredibly fragmented; the state of Ohio, for example, had 1,535 independent poor-relief districts.[15] Burdened by a crazy quilt of jurisdictional responsibilities, welfare was poorly administered and inadequately funded. Local welfare policies had other weaknesses: Able-bodied men were generally excluded from receiving any aid, strict residency requirements excluded many others, and those who did qualify for help were usually required to live in almshouses under wretched conditions and were forced to work at menial jobs with no pay.[16]

Even though donations to private charities increased when the Depression hit, the system was incapable of keeping up with soaring needs. In 1932, less than a quarter of the unemployed got any relief at all. For those who did, relief payments were usually inadequate. In New York City, families received an average grant of $2.39 per week.[17] The cities with the worst problems had the fewest resources to deal with them. With nearly one-third of its industrial workforce unemployed, Detroit made a heroic effort to provide relief, spending more per capita than any other city in the country. However, Detroit's compassion soon surpassed its tax base. Under pressure from the city's creditors, Detroit was forced to cut already inadequate relief appropriations in half in 1931–1932.[18]

Adhering to the principle of dual federalism, President Herbert Hoover refused to expand federal relief efforts. Speaking in 1932, Hoover asserted the following:

> I hold that the maintenance of the sense of individual responsibility of men to their neighbors and the proper separation of the functions of the Federal and local Governments require the maintenance of the fundamental principle that the relief of distress rests upon the individuals, upon the communities and upon the states.[19]

Holding steadfastly to the position that capitalism would right itself, as long as the federal government did not interfere, Hoover remained in office until 1933.

Roosevelt's Dilemma

When Franklin Delano Roosevelt assumed the presidency on March 4, 1933, he faced a difficult dilemma. The situation cried out for decisive federal action, but he knew that any attempt to expand federal power into areas that had previously been reserved for the states would meet crippling opposition in Congress, which strongly represented local interests. More important, the Supreme Court would simply declare such expansions of federal powers unconstitutional. A Supreme Court veto was no idle threat because the Court was dominated by conservative justices who accepted the tenets of dual federalism. In 1935, for example, the Supreme Court struck down the National Industrial Recovery Act, asserting that the regulation of wages and hours fell outside the powers of Congress to regulate interstate commerce.[20] Emboldened by Supreme Court rulings, by late 1935 lower court judges had issued 1,600 orders to prevent federal officials from implementing acts of Congress.[21] In perhaps the biggest blow to the New Deal expansion of federal power, in 1936 the Supreme Court struck down the Agricultural Adjustment Act, which would have enabled the federal government to restrict production in order to increase the prices that farmers received for their crops. Rejecting an expansive definition of the General Welfare Clause, Justice Owen Roberts gave a classic reaffirmation of dual federalism:

> From the accepted doctrine that the United States is a government of delegated powers, it follows that those not expressly granted or reasonably to be implied from such as are conferred, are reserved to the states or to the people. . . . None to regulate agricultural production is given, and therefore legislation by Congress for that purpose is forbidden.[22]

Frustrated by the Supreme Court's opposition, Roosevelt attempted to "pack the court" by adding justices friendly to the New Deal. He failed. Although most Americans opposed Supreme Court limitations on the New Deal, they also opposed tampering with the checks and balances of the Constitution. Roosevelt was caught on the horns of a dilemma: Congress and the Court prevented him from using the federal government to address the problems of the Depression, but if the federal government did nothing, the people would continue to suffer (as would Roosevelt's reelection prospects). How Roosevelt resolved this dilemma would revolutionize federalism in the United States.

Roosevelt's Solution: Grants-in-Aid

Roosevelt gradually embraced a compromise approach that slipped between the horns of the dilemma of federal versus state action; the New Deal used the powers of the federal government to initiate action but gave the states and localities considerable leeway in running the programs. This solution was advocated by Louis Brandeis, a Roosevelt supporter on the Supreme Court. In a famous dissenting opinion in 1932, Brandeis praised the federal system for allowing a state to "serve as a laboratory, and try novel social and economic experiments without risk to the rest of the country."[23] Brandeis recommended to Roosevelt that the federal government encourage the states to assume more active policy roles in addressing the crisis. The Brandeis approach was essentially a "third way" that attempted to slip between the horns of the dilemma of federal domination and state inaction.

Roosevelt implemented the Brandeis approach through **grants-in-aid** that combined federal funding with state administration. Grants-in-aid are funds provided by one level of government to another for specific purposes. Usually, states are required to put up some of their own money (these are called **matching grants**), and they have to meet minimal federal standards for the program. Grants-in-aid had been in existence for many years, and as early as 1923 the Supreme Court had declared them constitutional on the ground that they were not obligatory but simply offered "an option which the state is free to accept or reject."[24] Federal grants-in-aid expanded rapidly during the New Deal, from $217 million in 1932 to $744 million in 1941.[25]

The Death of Dual Federalism

In 1937 the Supreme Court, with no change of membership, approved the New Deal's expansion of the federal government into areas previously reserved for the states. The Anti-federalist fears of federal expansion turned out to be well founded, but in ways they would have found ironical: Vague words in the Constitution, such as the Necessary and Proper Clause and the Interstate Commerce Clause, were used to justify expansions of federal power, but these expansions were opposed by elites and favored by masses of common people who needed help from the federal government against the ravages of the Great Depression. Expanded federal powers were used to redistribute wealth and opportunity from elites to the common people. Supreme Court decisions in 1937 signaled the demise of dual federalism. Within a few years, the federal government was allowed to legislate in almost all areas of domestic policy.

The New Deal revolutionized American federalism, moving the federal government into domestic policy functions previously reserved to the states. At the same time, state and local governments retained a great deal of power over these functions because they controlled the details of policy and who was hired to run the programs. As Figures 15.1 and 15.2 show, although federal spending has soared, most public employees work for state and local governments.

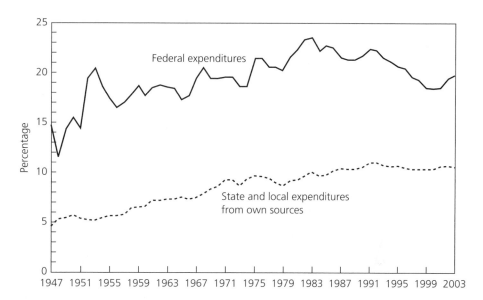

FIGURE 15.1

Federal and State and Local Government Expenditures as a Percentage of GDP, 1930–1995

Source: Budget of the United States Government: Historical Tables, Fiscal Year 2005; available at www.gpoaccess.gov/usbudget/fy05/hist.html.

INTERGOVERNMENTAL RELATIONS

Beginning with the New Deal, dual federalism was replaced with a new federal system called **intergovernmental relations**. Under the new system, relations among federal, state, and local governments are worked out by specific legislation and negotiations, not by judicial rulings establishing separate spheres of authority. Two aspects of the system help preserve a balance of power between the national government and state and local governments: (1) The states remain as separate governments with independent taxing and spending powers, and (2) the states play a crucial role in the selection and orientation of federal officials.[26] Members of Congress are elected from individual states and congressional districts, imparting a "local spirit" to the national government. In addition, state and federal governments lobby the federal government vigorously. Under intergovernmental relations, the powers of states and localities are protected more by political processes than by the courts.

Johnson's Creative Federalism

The system of grants-in-aid put in place by the New Deal expanded slowly until the 1960s. The first Republican president since the New Deal, Dwight Eisenhower, did not roll back the welfare state established by FDR, but, with the

FIGURE 15.2

Number of Government Employees: Federal, State, and Local, 1929–2001

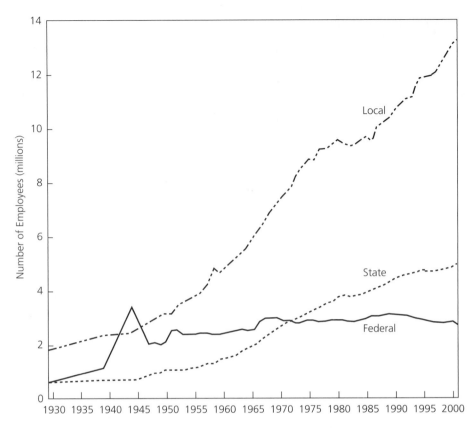

Source: "Number of Government Employees: Federal, State, and Local, 1929–2001," from *Vital Statistics on American Politics, 2003–2004* by Harold W. Stanley and Richard G. Niemi. Copyright © 2005 CQ Press, a division of Congressional Quarterly Inc. Reprinted by permission of CQ Press.

exception of interstate highways, he initiated few major new federal grants. By the end of Eisenhower's presidency in 1960, grants-in-aid totaled only $7 billion.

Massive expansion of the grants-in-aid system occurred in the 1960s under Lyndon Johnson's presidency (1963–1969). By 1970, federal grants had more than tripled, to $24.1 billion, representing about 28 percent of total state and local outlays (see Figure 15.3). Johnson's expansion of the grant system was motivated both by a sincere desire to target social problems and by political considerations. During his presidency, Johnson created hundreds of **categorical grant** programs—which required recipients to apply for funding under specific categories, detailing how the money would be spent and subjecting themselves to strict federal guidelines. The detailed conditions attached to the grants helped ensure that the monies would go to those who needed them the most and not to the most powerful local political interests.

Johnson was also motivated by a desire to tie restive urban blacks to the national Democratic coalition. As part of his War on Poverty, Johnson did an

FIGURE 15.3

Federal Grants-in-
Aid in Relation to
State and Local
Expenditures from
Own Sources and
GNP, 1970–2004

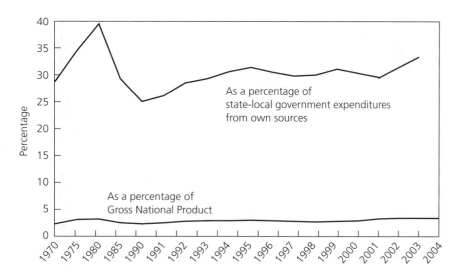

Source: U.S. Bureau of the Census, *Statistical Abstract of the United States 2004–2005* (Washington, D.C.: U.S. Government Printing Office, 2004), p. 266.

end run around white-dominated city governments and gave money directly to community and nonprofit organizations in the inner cities. Johnson called his solution **creative federalism**. For example, the Economic Opportunity Act of 1964 created expensive new categorical grants to fight urban, largely black, poverty and included programs such as Head Start (an early-education program for disadvantaged children), the Job Corps, and community action agencies. Approximately 75 percent of the community action agencies were nongovernmental.[27]

Backlash: Nixon's New Federalism

The huge growth of federal grants during the administration of Lyndon Johnson provoked a backlash among conservatives who thought that the federal grants-in-aid had become intrusive, distorting local decision making and imposing burdensome regulations on state and local governments. Criticisms of the system of federal grants had (and still have) more than a grain of truth. The federal government has funded grants for every conceivable purpose—from rat control to crime control, from urban gardening to home insulation. Every grant requires detailed regulations that can be very burdensome to the recipients. The pages in the *Federal Register*, which prints new regulations for administering grants, increased from 14,479 in 1960 to 71,191 in 1979.[28] Red tape, it was called. Implementation became complicated because each program required the cooperation of different agencies and governments. One study of a federal program in Oakland, California, concluded that it required seventy separate agreements among different agencies, making successful implementation nearly impossible.[29]

The expanding system of federal grants was also criticized for undermining democratic accountability. With hundreds of grants, each involving numerous actors at the federal, state, and local levels, the voters had difficulty pinpointing responsibility. Complex federal grant programs, critics argued, took power away from elected representatives and gave it to staff experts, issue specialists, and bureaucrats. *Grantsmanship*—the ability to write successful grant applications—biased the allocation of funds away from those who needed them the most.

The backlash against federal grants was not just based on issues of federalism but on the purposes those grants were used for. Johnson's creative federalism provoked a backlash among suburban whites, who viewed federal grants as biased toward inner cities and blacks.[30] Welfare became a pivotal issue. The number of families on welfare (AFDC) soared 237 percent from 1965 to 1975.[31] Although most welfare recipients were white, a disproportionate percentage were black, and the public viewed welfare as a black program. The expansion of welfare took place at a time of rising racial tensions worsened by the urban riots of the 1960s. During this period, federal courts began to require busing to achieve integration in the schools and affirmative action to correct historical bias in the workplace. Busing was to the North what the Voting Rights Act had been to the South: It provoked a white backlash against federal intervention.

Republicans took advantage of this backlash, beginning in the 1960s, by appealing to working and lower-middle-class white voters who perceived that their hard-earned tax monies were going, under Democratic-sponsored federal grants, to inner-city poor and minorities. Direct opposition to the objectives of these programs, however, risked alienating traditional Republican voters who would be repelled by any taint of racism. Richard Nixon found a brilliant way out of this dilemma that helped him win the presidency in 1968: He supported the goal of racial equality but opposed federal intervention to achieve it in education, employment, and voting rights. Advocating decentralization of power to states and localities provided a way for Republican (and sometimes Democratic) politicians to appeal to white voters, who felt threatened by racial change, while not explicitly voicing racist views.[32]

Besides appointing judges who opposed policies like busing, Nixon also advocated changes to the grants-in-aid system. In 1969, President Nixon proposed what he called the "first major reversal of the trend toward ever more centralization of government in Washington. . . . It is time for a New Federalism in which power, funds, and responsibility will flow from Washington to the States and to the people."[33] Nixon's **new federalism** shifted the grants-in-aid system from categorical grants to grants giving more discretion to state and local governments. In 1972, Nixon won passage of **general revenue sharing**, which provided for the distribution of about $6 billion per year in federal grants to state and local governments, with few strings attached. The distribution of funds was weighted to give more money to governments that had poor tax bases and were already taxing themselves heavily. General revenue sharing was popular with governors and mayors, who felt that the federal government should share its superior taxing ability. It was not popular with members of Congress, who had little control over how the money was spent compared to traditional categorical grants.

Nixon also proposed a series of **block grants**—grants in which federal involvement is midway between the tight controls of categorical grants and the minimal controls of general revenue sharing. Under this method, a number of related categorical grants are consolidated into one block grant. Instead of competing for the funds, governments are allocated monies according to a formula based on need. The recipients spend the grant as they see fit within the broad purposes of the block grant.

Devolution: The Devil in the Details

Since the Nixon presidency, conservatives, as well as liberals, have attacked the federal government and advocated giving more powers to state and local governments—a process known as **devolution**. The reason is simple—devolution is popular with the voters. Since the 1960s, confidence toward all levels of government has declined, but the drop in confidence has been more severe for the federal government than for state or local governments.[34] By 1995, two-thirds of Americans favored lessening the power of the federal government in a series of domestic programs and giving program funds to the states.[35]

Although politicians give lip service to devolution, for the most part the reality of devolution has fallen far short of the rhetoric. When Republicans were out of power in Washington, it was easy for them to call for returning power to the states. But it was far different once they controlled the presidency and Congress. Once in control of the federal government, they saw that it could be used to pursue conservative goals as well as liberal goals. Liberals, like Bill Clinton, also got on the devolution bandwagon because it was popular with the voters. But Clinton realized that if he wanted to deliver benefits to key constituencies, he needed to use the powers of the federal government. For the most part, both liberals and conservatives practice "situational federalism": their stance on federalism depends on their situation—what their political goals are and where their political strengths lie.

Although Nixon's new federalism represented a significant shift in decision making power from the federal government to states and localities, Nixon did not attempt to dismantle the social welfare policies of the New Deal and Great Society. Nixon's goal was not to shrink government but to make it more flexible by shifting responsibilities within the intergovernmental system. All this changed beginning with Ronald Reagan, who was more concerned with shrinking the size of government than with empowering states and localities.

Reagan had a firm ideological commitment to the market as a better allocator of goods and services than government. He thought that decentralizing power to states and localities would achieve the goal of shrinking government. Three reasons were cited for this belief: (1) Liberal lobbies, which had been centered in Washington, D.C., for a generation, would be less influential at the state and local levels; (2) because they were closer to the voters, state and local governments would be less inclined to increase taxes to pay for social programs; and (3) economic competition among states and localities for mobile investment would force them to cut taxes and limit spending.

Reagan's basic approach to federalism was to cut federal grants, especially grants to state and local governments. Federal spending on payments to individuals, like Social Security, increased 22 percent from 1980 to 1987, after controlling for inflation, at the same time that grants-in-aid to state and local governments declined by 15 percent.[36] The Reagan cuts in intergovernmental grants hurt poor people the most, especially minorities and those living in cities.

When the Reagan administration's new federalism goals came in conflict with its goals of enhancing private decision-making power, however, the federalism goals were sacrificed. Businesses have trouble keeping track of regulations in fifty different states and thousands of local governments. Moreover, states sometimes pass more-restrictive regulations than the federal government. As John Kincaid puts it, "many businesses engaged in interstate commerce would rather be regulated by one 500-pound gorilla in Washington than by 50 monkeys on steroids."[37] To forestall state and local limits on business, the Reagan administration implemented pro-business federal regulatory expansion in many areas, including trucking, nuclear power, offshore oil exploration, and coastal zone management.

Violating his commitment to decentralization, Reagan frequently supported federal preemption of state and local regulatory powers. **Preemption** is the ability of the federal government to assume total or partial control in areas subject to concurrent federal and state responsibility. Under the Supremacy Clause of the Constitution, federal regulations preempt, or supersede, state laws. Reagan signed 106 bills in which the federal government preempted the powers of states or local governments; he vetoed only two preemption statutes.[38]

In contrast to Reagan, Bill Clinton won the presidency in 1992 with a reputation for supporting an expanded federal government, but, in the face of political pressure, Clinton became a supporter of devolution. After President Clinton lost decisively on a health care proposal that opponents smeared as a massive federal intrusion into people's lives, he declared that "the era of big government is over." In fact, during the Clinton administration the number of federal employees fell in absolute numbers to the lowest level since the Kennedy years (see Figure 15.2).

The most controversial federalism issue during the Clinton presidency was welfare reform. Clinton ran for office in 1992 promising to "end welfare as we know it" and in 1996 Clinton signed a bill passed by the Republican Congress that ended the sixty-one-year federal entitlement to welfare. In place of a federal guarantee that everyone who met certain criteria would receive cash assistance under programs administered by the states, the federal government now turns the money over to the states in the form of block grants. Welfare reform was touted as a devolution revolution but in fact it imposed a number of regulatory requirements on the states motivated by conservative values. For example, no person can be on welfare for more than a total of five years. The outcome of welfare reform is mixed. Some states created programs that really supported poor people in the transition to work, while others diverted federal welfare funds to other purposes. As a result, welfare services vary tremendously across the country. (We examine the debate on welfare reform in more detail in Chapter 17.)

© John Branch, San Antonio Express News.

Popular Democracy and Federalism Today

For popular democrats, the standard for judging federalism issues should be what division of powers best enhances democracy. Other things being equal, this will mean that the original Anti-federalist position should prevail: Democracy prospers best in a small setting. In local settings, people more readily see the relationship between their own well-being and the well-being of the group, and they feel their participation can make a difference. Appealing to these popular democratic sentiments, many conservatives have issued a call to return to the era of dual federalism when the courts ruled that the federal government could not legislate on a range of domestic functions. The implication of dual federalism is that if the federal government stands out of the way, state and local governments will be empowered. The reality, however, is not so simple; often, federal action is needed to empower state and local governments.

The most obvious area where federal action is needed to support state and local democracy is in the area of voting rights, where the rhetoric of states rights and local control has often been a cover for racist practices. Southerners criticized the 1965 Voting Rights Act as interference by the federal government in the internal affairs of states. However, the act precipitated a democratic revolution in southern politics, enabling millions of blacks to vote for the first time. In this case, federal "interference" clearly increased freedom and democracy. In fact, federal courts have repeatedly intervened to guarantee citizenship rights against mean-spirited state and local majorities. Although popular democrats believe in empowering local majorities, they also believe in setting limits on what local majorities can do. In a true democracy, basic rights, like the right to vote and speak freely on issues, should not be subject to a vote and should be protected by the courts.

The case of *Bush v. Gore* (2000) represents a particularly embarrassing departure of the Supreme Court from its customary role of protecting voting rights. In this case the Rehnquist court intervened, by a 5–4 majority, to stop the hand-counting of ballots in Florida in the disputed 2000 presidential election. By stopping the count the Supreme Court effectively gave the presidency to George W. Bush, taking the decision out of the hands of the voters (even though a valid recount might have shown Bush the winner anyway). Declaring that a state supreme court could not interpret state election law, the majority seemed to acknowledge the shaky ground on which it stood when it declared that its decision would establish no precedent for future cases. *Bush v. Gore* is a particularly egregious example of "situational federalism," where the five justices knew what outcome they wanted and then created arguments to justify their decision—even if the decision contradicted their loudly proclaimed adherence to states' rights in earlier decisions.[39]

In a series of earlier decisions, a slim majority on the court signaled an intention to restrict the powers of the federal government on the grounds that they are reserved to the states under the Tenth Amendment. In 1995 the Court declared the Gun-Free School Zone Act of 1990 unconstitutional, the first decision in sixty years ruling that Congress had exceeded its authority under the Interstate Commerce Clause of the Constitution.[40] In 1997 the Court struck down a provision of the Brady gun law that required state or local authorities to do background checks on buyers of handguns (*Printz v. United States*). In 2001 the Court limited the ability of state employees to sue for damages for violations of the Americans with Disabilities Act (*Garrett v. Alabama*). Other decisions demonstrated the resolve of the Court, under the leadership of Chief Justice William Rehnquist, to place limits on national power.[41]

As with *Bush v. Gore*, however, there is plenty of evidence that the Court's commitment to states rights is selective. For example, in the case of *Lorillard Tobacco Co. v. Reilly* (2001) the Court overturned a Massachusetts law that regulated the advertising of tobacco products. Generally, the Court has not been respectful of states' rights where states have taken action to regulate business. By declaring that federal laws preempt state laws, the Court has invalidated broad swaths of state consumer law. And the Court has weakened local land use regulations by declaring that they represent "takings" of private property that must be compensated by the government—for example, in *Lucas v. South Carolina Coastal Council* (1992).

Like the Supreme Court, Congress, which declared its commitment to devolution in Gingrich's 1994 Contract with America, has frequently supported expanding federal power when it serves its ends. A good example is the Terri Schiavo case.[42] Terri Schiavo was a young woman who suffered sudden heart failure in 1990 that caused severe brain damage. A feeding tube was inserted to keep her alive, and she remained in a "persistent vegetative state" for fifteen years. Schiavo had left no written instructions about her wishes, but her husband claimed that she had made it clear before her collapse that she would never want to be sustained on life support. Under Florida law the husband has the right to make these decisions, and Schiavo's husband decided to have the feeding tube removed despite strenuous objections by Schiavo's family. The issue was finally settled by the courts after a seven-year legal battle at all levels, approving the husband's decision to remove the feeding tube. Under pressure from the Christian right, Congress took extraordinary action and passed a law that applied only to the Schiavo case (traditionally, only courts decide individual cases), ordering the federal courts to review the decisions of the Florida courts to see if Schiavo's rights had been violated. The federal courts quickly showed their deference for the state court proceedings and refused to intervene. Terri Schiavo died thirteen days after the feeding tube was removed.

How Federal Policies Undermine Democracy in the States

Federal actions have powerful effects on the ability of state governments to meet their financial responsibilities. State revenues are linked to federal tax laws. When the federal government cuts taxes, invariably state revenues go down as well. Unlike the federal government, however, states are required to balance their budget each year. When Congress repealed the estate tax, states suddenly found themselves with less revenue. Federal law currently forbids state and local governments from taxing transactions over the Internet, denying these governments an estimated $45 billion in revenue in 2006. Instead of Revenue Sharing, which Congress ended in 1986, recent actions by Congress would be more accurately termed "revenue shrinking."

On the spending side, the federal government often requires states and localities to provide certain services but does not provide them with the money to cover the cost. These are called **unfunded mandates**. Despite the fact that the Contract with America, which helped the Republicans win control of Congress in 1994, called for an end to unfunded mandates, the National Conference of State Legislatures estimates that they cost state and local governments $25 billion in 2005. A good example is the 2001 No Child Left Behind (NCLB) act that President Bush called "the cornerstone" of his domestic policy. NCLB requires that each school administer annual standardized testing, and if they do not show sufficient improvement in the scores of eight categories of students, including low-income and minority students, the school will be labeled "low performing" and risks losing federal monies or possible reorganization. Besides attacking what they say is an unwarranted intrusion of the federal government into an area traditionally left to the states, critics of NCLB argue that the act does not provide enough monies for implementation.

The greatest pressure for state spending is generated by the federal Medicaid program, which provides medical insurance for the poor with the cost shared by the federal and state governments. In 2002 states and localities spent $112 billion on the program with the federal government spending $147 billion. Between 1991 and 2001 state Medicaid spending grew at an astounding 149 percent, the most rapidly growing part of state budgets. States find themselves in a bind: Federal funds encourage them to provide Medicaid coverage, but constantly increasing costs strain state budgets. As a result, states have begun to shred the social safety net for poor people.

In an earlier period, the federal government provided more direct aid to state and local governments to meet their responsibilities. As we noted earlier, between 1972 and 1986 the federal government shared its revenues with states and localities. Conservatives supported no-strings-attached revenue sharing as a way to end the intrusion of the federal government into state and local affairs. The idea was that the federal government had superior taxing power, partly because it did not have to worry as much as states and localities about investors pulling out if taxes increase. Over the years, the federal government also provided "countercyclical" aid to local governments to help them out during economic downturns.

Cooperative federalism, where the federal, state, and local governments, partnered to address domestic policy needs has been largely replaced by a kind of "fend-for-yourself" federalism in which governments must compete with each other to survive the fiscal pressures.[43] This means that the ability of state and local governments to meet their responsibilities varies tremendously across time and space. In 2001, due to an economic slowdown, states suddenly found themselves in the worst fiscal crisis since the 1930s. California faced a $38 billion deficit. Over a three-year period, states cut spending by $80.9 billion and raised taxes by $26.4 billion.[44] State surplus "rainy day" funds fell 87 percent, from $48.8 billion to only $6.4 billion. States were forced to raise tuition at public universities and slash aid to local governments. Minnesota Governor Tim Pawlenty joked that "the only things we're waiting for are the plagues and the locusts."[45]

The ability to cope with fiscal stress and provide services varies tremendously from state to state because the taxable resources of states vary. As Figure 15.4 shows, per capita incomes vary tremendously across the states. In order to raise the same revenue, states like Arkansas or Mississippi must tax incomes at almost twice the rate of states like New Jersey or Connecticut. Perversely, poor states not only have the fewest resources but also the greatest need for social spending. In the American federal system, resources are divorced from need. Because of their different resources and different political traditions, social policies vary tremendously across the states. In 2000 the amount a working parent with two children could make and still be eligible for Medicaid varied from $3,048 in Alabama to $40,224 in Minnesota.[46]

Nearly all Americans agree that the federal government should guarantee basic rights, like the right to vote and free speech. But Americans disagree when it comes to the question of whether there should be a federal right to health care, even for children, or a minimum income for families. Welfare reform ended the federal entitlement to cash income, leaving it up to the states. With the states under fiscal pressure, the social safety net that had been constructed by the federal government during the New Deal and Great Society is gradually coming unraveled. This will, in turn, undermine civic participation. After all, people cannot be effective citizens if they are worried about where their next

FIGURE 15.4   Personal Income per Capita in Current Dollars, by State, 2003

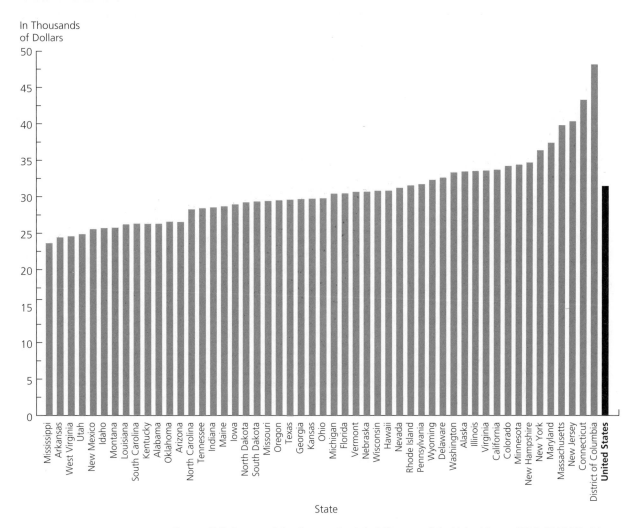

Source: U.S. Bureau of the Census, *Statistical Abstract of the United States 2004–2005* (Washington, D.C.: U.S. Government Printing Office, 2004), p. 434.

meal will come from or where they will sleep that night. Supporters of dual federalism imply that if the federal government would simply step out of the way and stop telling state and local governments what to do, they would be empowered to act on their own, and all the advantages of decentralized decision making would be realized. However, this view that the two levels of government are locked in a zero-sum conflict—that if one level asserts power, the other level loses power—is simplistic and misleading. It ignores what one legal scholar calls the "baseline problem," the idea that state and local governments are shaped by their relations with each other and their ability to act is inextricably linked to the actions of the federal government.[47] As we have seen, state fiscal viability is linked to the policies of the federal government. To realize their democratic potential, state and local governments do not need to just be left alone by the federal government; they need the help of the federal government. The recent actions of the federal government seem less designed to empower states than to drive them to the brink of bankruptcy and force them to shrink the size of government. Local governments face similar pressures.

LOCAL GOVERNMENT AND THE PROBLEM OF UNEVEN DEVELOPMENT[48]

Local governments are not mentioned in the U.S. Constitution. According to what has come to be known as "Dillon's Rule," local governments have no independent powers of their own; they acquire all their powers from the states.[49] In reality, the situation is more complex. The United States has a strong tradition of local control. In colonial times, local governments had a great deal of autonomy; the American Revolution is best understood as a defense of local liberties, not state liberties, against incursions by the British Crown and Parliament. The author of the Declaration of Independence, Thomas Jefferson, defended local self-government as the foundation of American democracy. Notwithstanding Dillon's Rule, many states have granted cities *home rule*, giving citizens the right to organize their local governments as they see fit. Local governments set their own taxing and spending policies, and play a role in the composition of state governments. In many ways, the relations between states and their local governments are similar to the relations between the federal government and the states.

Today, many states have more people than the entire country did in 1789 when the Anti-federalists viewed that nation as too big to nurture popular democracy. For this reason, popular democrats have put a great deal of their hopes in local governments. Writing in the 1830s, Alexis de Tocqueville captured this faith of popular democrats:

> Local institutions are to liberty what primary schools are to science; they put it within the people's reach; they teach people to appreciate its peaceful enjoyment and accustom them to make use of it. Without local institutions a nation may give itself a free government, but it has not the spirit of liberty."[50]

Local governments represent a potentially fertile ground for political leaders in the United States. Nearly 500,000 citizens hold elected office in the 87,525 units of local government in the nation, including 35,933 municipalities and townships and 13,506 school districts.[51]

Local governments are not just training grounds; they are also important political arenas of their own. Spending over $1 trillion a year, about 30 percent of all government outlays, local public goods and services directly affect the quality of our lives. As Robert Lineberry put it, local public services are "vital to the preservation of life (police, fire, sanitation, public health), liberty (police, courts, prosecutors), property (zoning, planning, taxing), and public enlighten-ment (schools, libraries)."[52] The most expensive local service is K–12 public education, followed by police and fire. The federal courts have repeatedly ruled that Americans are not entitled to equal local services; the Fourteenth Amend-ment's guarantee of "equal protection" does not apply to local public services. The provision of local public services is left to the political process. States estab-lish rules for the incorporation of local governments. Once a local government is incorporated, it is responsible for providing the local services assigned to it by the state using local tax revenues, mostly from property and sales taxes.

In many ways, local governments have lived up to their democratic potential. Thanks in part to the passage of the Voting Rights Act in 1965 the number of minority local elected officials has soared. Since 1970, the number of African-American elected officials increased fivefold, reaching 9,016 in 2001.[53] By 2003 almost one-third (twenty-three) of the seventy-six largest cities in the country had African-American or Hispanic mayors.[54] Research also supports the claim that the smaller the unit of government, the greater the level of civic participa-tion.[55] Having greater confidence that your participation could make a differ-ence and getting to know your elected official face-to-face apparently has a pos-itive impact on civic involvements.

The primary obstacles to local governments serving as effective vehicles of popular democracy are the tremendous economic inequalities across units of local governments and the racial segregation that is organized by municipal boundaries. Local governments possess the power over local land use through zoning laws. Zoning maps outline zones within the city where certain types of development are forbidden. The basic idea behind zoning is to forbid certain "incompatible uses," such as building a rendering plant next to single-family homes. Increasingly, however, zoning has been used to exclude "undesirable" people, such as the poor and minorities. Cities cannot directly zone out minori-ties; racial zoning was struck down by the Supreme Court in 1917.[56] In 1926, however, the Supreme Court upheld the right of a suburb of Cleveland to ban apartment buildings from a neighborhood with single-family homes.[57] Essen-tially, this means that municipalities can ban renters from living in the town. Local governments have gone further, restricting single-family homes to the very wealthy by requiring minimum lot sizes of two acres or more. Excluding poor and even middle-class residents results in the exclusion of minorities as well. But the courts have ruled that zoning laws with a discriminatory *effect* do not violate the Constitution as long as plaintiffs cannot prove that there was a racially discriminatory *intent*.

The effects of the politics of exclusion are felt throughout our metropolitan areas. Overall, for example, in 2000 the per capita income of central cities was only 86 percent of that for the suburbs. But this figure masks even greater inequalities in many metropolitan areas: Per capita income in Hartford was only 49 percent of its suburbs, Detroit's only 55 percent, and Milwaukee stood at 58 percent. The gap is not just between central cities and their suburbs; increas-ingly, suburbs are segregated by income. A study of the fifty largest metropoli-tan areas found that the percentage of suburban residents living in middle-class suburbs declined from 74.9 percent in 1980 to 60.8 percent in 2000.[58] Although racial segregation has declined in the past forty years, it still remains stubbornly high: In 2000, about half of blacks would have to move from one census tract, or neighborhood, to another to achieve an equal distribution of the races.[59]

As proud as we should be of the increase in the number of minority elected officials, in many cases they are hobbled by what has been called the "hollow prize" problem: When they are finally elected to office, minority officials often lack the necessary resources to deal with the problems they face. Older central cities with aging infrastructures and concentrations of poverty have higher spending needs, not just for the poor but for all government functions. And the federal government no longer makes a significant effort to help distressed local governments. As a share of city revenues, federal aid to cities fell from 15 percent in 1977 to only 5 percent in 2003.[60] Faced with their own huge deficits, states cut aid to local governments in 2003 for the first time in a decade. In effect, residents of poorer municipalities pay higher tax rates and receive inferior services than residents of more affluent places.

Schools face the same problem. Run by 13,506 independently elected school boards, primary and secondary public education in the United States seems remarkably democratic. However, democratic control can be a hollow prize for very poor school districts. In a landmark case that declared local financing of schools in California unconstitutional, the California Supreme Court called local control of education a "cruel illusion" because poor districts cannot achieve excellence no matter how high they raise taxes.[61] Adjusted for cost-of-living differences, per-pupil spending varied from $4,000 in Mississippi to over $9,000 in New Jersey. In the New York metropolitan area in 1997, per-pupil expenditures varied from $8,171 in New York City to an average of $12,760 in suburban Westchester County. Wealthy schools often have state-of-the-art computer systems and gymnasiums with climbing walls, while poor schools are forced to cope with outdated computers and dilapidated gyms with no equipment.

Even if all schools spent the same amount per pupil, this would not mean that educational opportunity in the United States was equal. Most states provide grants to local school systems that address the unequal taxable resources among districts, but they do not address the extra challenges poor districts face: large numbers of students from broken homes, students with disabilities, and students who speak English as a second language.

Only about 8 percent of state aid is targeted to the socially disadvantaged.[62] Research has shown that schools with a high percentage of students from families below the poverty level face special obstacles in achieving high levels of academic performance. There are many reasons for this, including that poor families tend to move often, disrupting children's schooling. Often they lack quiet places to study and are under constant stress. Many are malnourished or suffer from lead poisoning. Finally, living in areas of concentrated poverty, they lack the networks and role models that would enable them to make the connection between success in school and success in the job market.

The great promise of local democracy in the United States is held back by persistent economic and racial segregation. For the poor and minorities who are left behind in municipalities and school districts that lack the resources to adequately address their needs, the diminished motive to participate in politics is obvious. In neighborhoods of concentrated poverty the poor are surrounded by people who lack the political skills and money to be politically effective, and therefore their ability to petition the state and federal governments for a "redress of grievances" is hampered. As a result, poor and minorities have the same legal rights as everyone else to equal local public services, but, trapped in a kind of American apartheid, their ability to access local services is limited.

Although less obvious, the fragmented system of local government also has negative consequences for the middle and upper classes. Essentially, households with sufficient resources have substituted geographical mobility for local political participation—a process Robert Reich calls "the secession of the successful."[63] By moving into privileged suburbs with other people like themselves, citizens can avoid the kinds of messy, conflictual politics that are present in more diverse places. Suburbs are more like private clubs, or interest groups, than miniature republics. The homogeneity of many suburbs leads to boring politics that disengages the citizenry. Issues concerning race, class, and even religion are simply missing from the agenda. When the biggest issue facing the city council is what color to paint the benches in front of city hall, that is hardly likely to call forth great leaders. Indeed, research has shown that citizens who live in homogeneous places are less likely to vote or to get involved in community affairs.[64] Finally, homogeneous places lack the party competition that draws citizens into politics. One-party rule prevails in many central cities and poor suburbs as well. The loser under one-party rule is always the "have-nots," because political elites, possessing a monopoly, have no incentive to take up their issues.[65]

Finally, local liberty in the United States is frustrated by the fact that local governments are locked in a beggar-thy-neighbor competition for tax ratables and well-off residents. Cities must constantly work to keep service demands down and the tax base up. As a result, the agenda of local politics is tilted toward economic growth, giving business elites an inherent advantage.

Local Growth Machines: Elite Democracy in Action

Popular democrats pin most of their hopes for meaningful participation on local governments. Too often, however, local governments don't live up to their participatory potential. The problem is not that local governments are structured undemocratically. In fact, most city charters are thoroughly democratic, with all citizens over the age of eighteen given the right to vote for the mayor and city council—and sometimes many other offices as well. The problem, for the most part, is not the formal rules, but the way that economic elites are able to dominate local governments.

For many years scholars engaged in a spirited debate about the distribution of power in U.S. cities. The dominant theory of community power in political science was pluralism. The most influential pluralist analysis was Robert Dahl's *Who Governs?*, an examination of community power in New Haven, Connecticut.

According to Dahl, in New Haven many different elites competed for power, with each influential in a different arena. Money was a source of political power, but other resources, like political skills, leadership, and organization, also counted. Most importantly, elections forced elites to be responsive to the wishes of average citizens.[66] Dahl concluded that urban renewal in the 1950s, for example, was guided by Mayor Richard Lee, who pushed business to participate in a program that benefited the city as a whole. Although it was far from perfect, Dahl concluded that New Haven was a democracy, "warts and all." Pluralism salvaged fundamental democratic values.

Over the years, many scholars have challenged the pluralist analysis of local politics. A reexamination of Dahl's study of New Haven, for example, concluded that urban renewal was not initiated by Mayor Lee responding to the needs of the voters but was pushed by businessmen to benefit their commercial interests at the expense of average voters.[67] Shockingly, between 1956 and 1974, nearly one-fifth of the population of New Haven was uprooted by urban renewal. Blacks suffered the most. Besides the disruption of community networks, urban renewal destroyed 5,636 more units of low- and moderate-income housing than it built.[68] Urban renewal benefited mostly business owners, not local residents.

Dahl himself later admitted that pluralism was flawed for failing to note that business is not just another interest group. Because government officials must be concerned about the local economy and business decisions have such an impact on it, they constantly cater to the needs of business even without business lobbying. Dahl and his co-author, Charles Lindblom, called this the "privileged position of business," noting that "the relation between government and business is unlike the relation between government and any other group in society."[69]

Business power takes a different form in cities than in states or the federal government. The distinctive power of local governments is their power over land use—through zoning laws and building codes. Moreover, cities gain a great deal of their revenue from property taxes. For these reasons, as Stephen Elkin has noted, "The battlefield of city politics is not flat but is tilted toward an alliance of public officials and land interests."[70] City officials often do everything in their power to enhance real estate values, contending that what is good for city landowners is good for all citizens. The goal is to attract development that pays more in taxes than it takes back in city services. Usually, that means commercial expansion instead of housing. Many cities spurn housing for low-income families, whose children are expensive to educate in public schools. The tight alliance between local elected officials and real estate interests has been aptly termed a **growth machine**.[71]

The growth machines that dominate many cities pursue what one scholar dubbed the **corporate center strategy**, a focus on development of the downtown service-sector economy with "an orientation toward luxury consumption" that appeals to young educated professionals, convention goers, and tourists.[72] A classic example of the corporate center strategy is Baltimore, Maryland, under the leadership of Mayor William Donald Schaefer (1971–1987), who based a successful run for governor partly on his revitalization of downtown Baltimore. The jewel of Schaefer's string of downtown development projects was the Inner

Harbor. Formerly a bustling port, by the 1960s it was an eyesore of rotting, rat-infested piers, abandoned buildings, and desolate parking lots—perched on a harbor that smelled, in H. L. Mencken's words, "like a million polecats."[73]

Schaefer's audacious idea was to transform the Inner Harbor into a national tourist destination—and he did it. The centerpiece of the $270 million, 240-acre Inner Harbor project was Harborplace, a festival marketplace. Completed in 1980, it attracted 18 million visitors the first year, more than Disneyland.

Even though the Inner Harbor has generated jobs and taxes, it produced surprisingly few benefits for the city's poor black neighborhoods. The fact is, inner-city residents do not qualify for most jobs in the downtown corporate service sector, and those they do qualify for tend to be low wage, with few benefits. Between 1970 and 1990, when the downtown boomed, the percentage of the population living in high-poverty neighborhoods increased 38 percent.[74] As Kurt Schmoke, who succeeded Schaefer as Baltimore's first black mayor in 1987, noted, "If you were revisiting Baltimore today after a twenty-year absence, you would find us much prettier and much much poorer."[75] Despite the booming harbor and downtown, Baltimore lost almost 12 percent of its population between 1990 and 2000.

Downtown-oriented growth machines are also notoriously elite dominated. Schaefer's was no exception. He created a kind of shadow government—twenty-four quasi-public development corporations that contracted with the city to direct downtown development. Because they were not part of government, these development corporations could operate behind closed doors and did not have to provide information to the city council or the public. The rationale was that these entities took the politics out of urban development, speeding up the process and making it more efficient. However, it is impossible to take the politics out of development decisions. Investing in downtown areas is a decision not

The City as a Growth Machine © Lisa Siegel Sullivan.

to invest in small businesses or neighborhood housing. Not surprisingly, many of Mayor Schaefer's biggest campaign contributors received contracts or loans for downtown development.

REFORMERS AND THE ATTACK ON PARTY GOVERNMENT

The effort to "take the politics out" of state and local government has a long lineage. Indeed, state, and especially local, politics have been characterized by a clash between two contrasting philosophies of government—one of which reflects this antipolitical stance. This clash reverberates with many of the same issues that animated the Federalist and Anti-federalist debate.

The popular democratic, or *partisan*, model traces its roots back to Andrew Jackson, president from 1833 to 1841. Jacksonian Democrats were suspicious of strong executives and favored dispersing power among many elected offices. (This belief was tinged with irony, since Jackson substantially enlarged the powers of the presidency at the national level.) Believing in the political adage "to the victor go the spoils," Jackson contended that ordinary citizens could perform most functions of government. By handing out patronage jobs to supporters, the victorious party ensured that the government would be responsive to the needs of common people, not to upper-class elites.

Reformers derided Jackson's idea of party government as the *spoils system*. The reform, or *nonpartisan*, model traces its roots back to the Federalist Alexander Hamilton, who argued that most people did not want more democracy but better services, provided by strong executives and expert administrators.[76] The reform model contrasts the efficient administration of experts with corrupt and inefficient rule by party hacks. The reform movement grew in reaction to the excesses of urban political machines, whose corrupt practices were exposed by muckraking journalists in the late nineteenth century. It wasn't just that the parties hired political supporters but that job recipients were often unqualified for their jobs. The public also lost out when excessive payments were made to politically connected contractors.

In the late nineteenth and early twentieth century, the good government reformers—or "goo goos," as they sometimes are derisively called—aimed to weaken the influence of political parties and their political bosses, and put more power in the hands of well-educated experts. The reform program included the following:

1. Nonpartisan elections (no party label on the ballot).

2. Election to the city council from at-large districts, preferably the entire city, instead of from individual wards. (Remember Madison's extended-republic argument.)

3. Civil service appointment procedures for city workers so that municipal jobs could not be used as patronage by political parties.

4. Switching from party conventions to open primaries, taking the power to nominate out of the hands of party bosses.

5. Making the chief executive in cities an appointed, professional city manager, not an elected mayor.

The reformers were remarkably successful in instituting their reforms (although there has been a movement away from many of these reforms in the past thirty years). Other than civil service systems, which are almost universal (though they vary in coverage), nonpartisan elections are the most widespread reform still in place today, with 72.6 percent of all cities prohibiting party designation on the ballot. The council–manager form of government is used in about half of all cities but in only 20 percent of cities over 500,000. About 60 percent of U.S. cities elect their council members from city-wide districts, although that number has fallen in recent decades.[77]

The nonpartisan reform model is an attempt to take the politics out of government and run it like a business. But it is impossible to take the politics out of governing; no matter how hard you try, politics ends up coming in through the back door. Focusing on efficiency, nonpartisan reformers often overlooked problems of unequal distribution. Reformers are fond of sayings like "There is no Republican or Democratic way to build a sewer—just a right way and a wrong way." This ignores a crucial question, however: *Where* will the sewers be built? San Antonio, Texas, for example, had long been ruled by business-dominated reformers when, on August 7, 1974, large parts of the Mexican-American neighborhoods were flooded by the runoff from Anglo-American highlands. The reason was simple: The Mexican-American neighborhoods lacked storm and sanitary sewers. A coalition of neighborhood organizations, Communities Organized for Public Service, or COPS, protested vigorously, and within months San Antonio passed a $47 million bond issue to implement a drainage plan that had been sitting on the shelf since 1947. In 1977, COPS successfully campaigned for a new city charter with an elected mayor and district elections for city council. The first election under the new charter resulted in the election of five Mexican Americans.[78]

The nonpartisan reform model is biased toward the upper class. This is not surprising given the upper-class background of most reformers.[79] Reformed cities, with nonpartisan elections and/or city manager forms of government, suppress the expression of class, racial, and religious conflicts in the political system, thus reducing turnout, especially among working-class voters. At-large elections give an advantage to middle- and upper-income professionals, who have the money and contacts to successfully wage city-wide campaigns.[80] Perhaps the best-documented finding is that at-large elections underrepresent minorities. Blacks, in particular, feel they have a greater say in cities with district elections. Using 1982 amendments to the 1965 Voting Rights Act, minorities have successfully challenged at-large voting methods, forcing cities to institute district elections, resulting in greater minority representation.[81]

Cities run by strong political parties are seldom paragons of popular democracy. Nevertheless, as we discussed in Chapter 7, parties are necessary institutions for organizing large numbers of people into politics and representing their issues. Parties provide resources, apart from money, for getting elected. The movement to take the politics out of state and local governance is doomed to failure. Reformed governments do not eliminate politics; they simply channel it into new arenas, largely hidden from public view and dominated by elites.

STATES AS LABORATORIES OF DEMOCRACY

Although states are hobbled by fiscal pressures, a survey of state policies shows that there are enough exceptions to elite rule to keep our hopes for popular democracy alive. In the present period, in fact, much like the period before the New Deal, state governments often lead the federal government in experimenting with popular democratic policies.

In the past, states had glaring political weaknesses that limited their ability to innovate. These included antiquated election laws that excluded blacks and systematically underrepresented city dwellers, as well as weak administrative structures. In the past fifty years, states have strengthened their representative and administrative capacities by instituting a number of reforms:

1. Governors now have more control over state bureaucracies, which themselves have been made more representative and professional.[82]

2. Following Supreme Court mandates, beginning with *Baker v. Carr* (1962), state legislatures have been reapportioned to reflect population, making them more responsive to metropolitan and minority interests.

3. Following the Voting Rights Act of 1965, legal barriers to minority voting have been almost eliminated.

4. State legislatures have become more professional. (This is probably the weakest area, as forty-one states still have part-time legislators, and twenty-two states have no paid staff.[83])

Notwithstanding political reforms in the states, we would expect little room for democratic choice if states were tightly constrained by competition for investment. However, research has demonstrated that state policies are not completely constrained by economic forces; there is room for variation. State elections and policies reflect the distinctive political beliefs of their citizens. Based on surveys of 170,000 individuals over thirteen years, researchers classified states according to the liberalism or conservativism of their voters.[84] They found that even after controlling for socioeconomic factors, such as class and race, public opinion made a significant difference in policies: States with liberal voters enacted more liberal policies than did states with conservative voters. For example, Oregon and Oklahoma are similar socially and economically, but Oregon has liberal policies, whereas Oklahoma has conservative ones. States have different political cultures that are expressed through elections. Although states are hardly model popular democracies, public opinion and elections do make a difference.

Political institutions also make a difference. States without party competition tend to be unresponsive to public opinion. For many years the one-party Democratic South enabled a minority of whites, especially wealthy planters, to dominate state politics and kept blacks and many poor whites powerless.[85] The political polarization of the country and the division of the country into "red" (Republican) and "blue" (Democratic) states raises the fear that one-party rule could disable democracy again.

Nevertheless, states have shown a surprising ability to innovate and fill the vacuum created by federal inaction. The federal government has not raised the minimum wage since 1997 and its inflation-adjusted value has plummeted. As of 2004 thirteen states had stepped in to set their minimum wage above the federal level. Voters in Oregon and Washington also passed ballot initiatives that allow the minimum wage to be adjusted annually in response to increases in the cost of living.[86] Many cities have also passed "living wage" laws that exceed the federal minimum wage. By 2004, 117 cities had passed living wage laws but usually these laws only apply to those who work for companies that do business with city government.

States have also gone after corporate abuse. In the 1990s states filed suit against the tobacco companies alleging that they had failed to disclose the ill effects of cigarettes and had caused the states to pay huge amounts through Medicaid and other programs. When the U.S. Congress refused to approve an initial agreement, the state attorneys general settled their lawsuit for an estimated $246 billion over twenty-five years, using some of the money in anti-smoking campaigns. New York Attorney General Eliot Spitzer has acquired national fame by going after the mutual fund industry for boosting fees, suing brokerage firms for recommending stocks they knew were questionable, and stopping an Ohio utility from dumping air pollution on New York State. In each case, one could argue that these were issues that should have been handled by the federal government.

An area where states have been most innovative is health care. States have confronted the federal Food and Drug Administration (FDA) over its ban on importing drugs, with some states setting up websites providing guides to reliable Canadian pharmacies or allowing foreign pharmacies to obtain state licenses. Other states have instituted bulk purchasing to negotiate lower prices. As the federal government failed to come up with a solution to the problem of the uninsured, several states, including Tennessee and Oregon, stepped in with innovative programs to control costs in Medicaid and extend coverage to more people.[87]

States have shown that they can still be laboratories of democracy but their efforts are handicapped by federal fiscal policies that push unfunded mandates on the states. More supportive federal programs would help greatly. Some form of revenue sharing should be reinstituted with the formula favoring states with high levels of poverty and unemployment. In addition, the federal government should have counter-cyclical programs in place to help out states during times of recession. With the massive federal deficit and the continuing war in Iraq,

NEW IDEAS

Metropolitics

The extreme fragmentation of local government in the United States is an obstacle to the flowering of popular democracy. The average metropolitan area has over a hundred local governments, each competing to attract investment and to keep out poor people. One result is that central cities and inner-ring suburbs, possessing the region's older housing stock, become burdened by poor people and face perpetual fiscal stress.

David Rusk, the former mayor of Albuquerque, New Mexico, wrote a book showing that when central cities fail to expand their boundaries to capture suburban growth, the entire region suffers economically and higher levels of economic and racial segregation result. Fragmented local governments compete with each other in a beggar-thy-neighbor competition that moves investments around in the region but does little for the health of the region as a whole. Increasingly, it is becoming clear that success in the global marketplace requires *regional* cooperation.

Two regions have led the country in enacting regional reforms that address these issues: Minneapolis/St. Paul and Portland, Oregon. In 1967 the Minnesota Legislature created a seven-county metropolitan council responsible for land use, housing, transit, sewage, and other issues in the Twin Cities area. In 1971 the state adopted an innovative Fiscal Disparities Act to reduce the destructive competition for investment among local governments. Under the tax-base-sharing scheme, all jurisdictions in the metropolitan area pool 40 percent of their new commercial and industrial tax bases, with the proceeds being distributed back to local governments based on their population and tax base (poorer jurisdictions get more). Tax-base sharing

however, federal efforts to help state and local governments seem unlikely in the near future.

Experiments in Grassroots Democracy

Most people cut their first political teeth in local politics. With almost half a million local elected officials in the United States, there are plenty of opportunities to get involved. If popular democracy is going to be meaningful, however, it must rest on something more than going to the polls every two or four years or even running for office. In the early years of the country, many local governments were run by direct democracies, town meetings in which all citizens gathered together to make the laws.

Elite democrats maintain that direct democracy in the modern world is unrealistic—even dangerous. As an example, they often cite Lyndon Johnson's War on Poverty, which gave federal money directly to community groups with the goal of "maximum feasible participation" by local residents. Daniel Patrick Moynihan, former Democratic senator from New York, skewered the program in a book cleverly titled *Maximum Feasible Misunderstanding* (1969), in which he reduces the incentive for cities to raid their neighbors for investment.

Portland is the only metropolitan area in the country to have a directly elected regional government. Portland's Metro Council is elected from seven districts, each with a population of about 200,000. The chief executive is elected region wide. One of the first tasks of the Metro Council, after it was established in 1978, was to designate an urban growth boundary under Oregon's land use planning law, the strongest in the nation. An urban growth boundary now surrounds Portland, guaranteeing the preservation of open space for recreation and environmental purposes, and pushing development back toward the central city.

All the indications are that regional government in Portland has been a success. Unlike most central cities in the country, Portland gained significant population, according to the 2000 census, and the income gap between the city and its suburbs is one of the smallest in the nation. The repopulation of the city and the building of an extensive light rail system mean that automobile use in Portland is lower than in most metropolitan areas—resulting in less highway congestion and air pollution.

Local governments are naturally suspicious of regional governments, which they view as top-down institutions that will take away their powers of local control. In fact, under the present fragmented system, local governments are locked in a growth competition that undermines local democracy. Many local governments feel they must pursue any commercial or industrial investment they can get—even if that means more pollution and congestion and a lower quality of life. Greater cooperation between governments within regions can dampen the destructive competition for investment and empower local governments to concentrate on the things they do best.

Sources: David Rusk, *Cities Without Suburbs*, 3rd ed. (Baltimore: Johns Hopkins University Press, 2003); Peter Dreier, John Mollenkopf, and Todd Swanstrom, *Place Matters: Metropolitics for the 21st Century*, rev. ed. (Lawrence: University Press of Kansas, 2005).

argued that the poor were simply not ready to govern themselves. In fact, the War on Poverty was not the abysmal failure it is often portrayed as.[88] The program was beset by nasty conflicts, but conflicts must be expected when long-ignored problems such as racial discrimination are finally confronted. Most important, the War on Poverty was not a fair test of participatory democracy because poor people were never really given the power to run their own programs.[89] In many cities, mayors quickly took control of the programs from community groups. Even with all its faults, the War on Poverty had many benefits. It gave many low-income minorities their first experience in politics, which they used to launch their political careers.

The War on Poverty also nurtured the growth of *community-based organizations* (CBOs) that involve low-income people in improving their own neighborhoods. Since the 1960s, there has been a veritable "backyard revolution," with neighborhood organizations springing up in city after city.[90] These organizations have spun off thousands of CBOs that rehabilitate housing and provide services like daycare and job training. One survey found that 60 percent of cities with populations over 100,000 had formally recognized neighborhood councils, many of which integrated CBOs into their systems of neighborhood planning.[91]

In 1999 Los Angeles revised its charter to create over a hundred neighborhood councils that will bring city government much closer to the citizens.

Involving citizens between elections in the implementation of policies, what is called **co-production** of city services, can make government more effective and responsive to citizen needs. A good example is community policing where citizens work directly with police to reduce crime instead of waiting for crimes to occur and then having the police respond. Citizens possess "local knowledge" that can help the police become more effective. As part of its community policing initiative, the City of Chicago funded a community-based organization to increase participation at community policing meetings. Research showed that the usual correlation of civic participation with income, education, and race did not apply. Poor minorities participated at high levels when crime was a major neighborhood concern.[92]

A team of social scientists studied the new forms of participatory grassroots democracy in five cities—Birmingham, Dayton, San Antonio, St. Paul, and Portland, Oregon.[93] The results contradict the fears of elite democrats. Participation did not make people less selfish and more committed to city-wide concerns, but it did make them more knowledgeable about politics, more tolerant of differences, and more willing to believe that participation can make a difference, especially among low-income people. The growth of neighborhood associations and their recognition by city governments are encouraging for popular democrats. But the limits of localism must be recognized. In the five cities with extensive structures of neighborhood participation, business still dominated the economic development agenda with large downtown development projects. Neighborhood organizing is effective at improving housing and protecting communities from unwanted development, but it is much less effective at addressing issues like environmental destruction and rising income inequality.[94]

CONCLUSION: IS THERE A WAY OUT OF THE DILEMMA?

Notwithstanding the many successful examples of local democracy, federalism presents a dilemma for popular democrats today. Ever since the Anti-federalists criticized the Constitution for putting too much power in the hands of a distant central government, popular democrats have favored decentralizing power as much as possible. At the same time, popular democrats recognize the limits of localism. Local communities lack the resources to tackle important issues like economic inequality and environmental pollution, which cross jurisdictional boundaries. All too often, states' rights have been used as a cover-up for racist policies, and growth machines dominate city governments, excluding citizens from meaningful participation.

Which way should popular democrats turn? Is there a way out of the dilemma of federalism? First, popular democrats must understand that concentrations of power in the marketplace require countervailing concentrations of power in government. As we saw in Chapter 3, multinational corporations are not controlled by markets but have acquired huge amounts of power over markets and governments. Until corporations are made more democratically accountable to shareholders, workers, consumers, and especially their communities, we will need powerful federal bureaucracies, such as the Environmental Protection Agency (EPA) and the Securities and Exchange Commission (SEC), to regulate them in the public interest.

For the most part, however, federalism should not be framed as an either/or issue: either give power to the federal government or turn power over to states and communities. An active federal government can bolster democracy at the state and local level. When federal judges ordered southern states to give blacks the right to vote under the 1965 Voting Rights Act, local democracy was enhanced, not undermined. Basic rights, like freedom of speech, press, and assembly, must be protected by a vigilant federal government.

Federal programs to promote greater equality among jurisdictions would also go a long way toward empowering state and local governments to address their own problems. Overall, federal grants do just the opposite, giving more money to wealthier states.[95] Other federal systems, including Germany, Australia, and Canada, have well-funded national laws designed to equalize the tax capacities of subnational governments.[96] A federal program to reduce economic inequalities among regions and between central cities and suburbs would invigorate local democracy. And if local governments ended the practice of exclusionary zoning and provided a mix of housing that met the needs of workers in the area, the experience of politics at the local level would more nearly reflect the full range of issues in the nation and would serve as better training for future national leaders.

Finally, we need to think more creatively about federalism. Some have proposed new regional institutions, modeled on the European Union, that would enable governments to meet together to forge intergovernmental agreements to take into account the effects of their actions on other governments.[97] Others have developed a new theory about how central governments should relate to local governments called "democratic experimentalism."[98] Under this arrangement, state and local governments would be free to set goals and choose the means to attain them so long as they were consistent with national objectives. Instead of a central bureaucracy monitoring adherence to federal goals, the local governments would set the standards of evaluation themselves by pooling information about best practices using local knowledge to solve local problems.

Federalism is the great American contribution to political theory. By holding out the promise of diversity within unity, federalism provides a way for popular democracy to flourish in a large nation like the United States with so much economic and social diversity. In this chapter we have outlined a series of obstacles that hinder our federal system from realizing its democratic potential. But the theory and practice of federalism are still evolving, holding out the promise that our state and local governments will realize their potential as true laboratories of democracy.

KEY TERMS

unitary government
dual federalism
enumerated powers
reserved powers
concurrent powers
Supremacy Clause
Necessary and Proper (Elastic) Clause
nullification
grants-in-aid
matching grant
intergovernmental relations

categorical grant
creative federalism
new federalism
general revenue sharing
block grant
devolution
preemption
unfunded mandates
growth machine
corporate center strategy
co-production

INTERNET RESOURCES

■ James Madison Institute
www.jamesmadison.org

The James Madison Institute is a Florida-based public policy research organization dedicated to promoting economic freedom, limited government, federalism, the rule of law, and individual liberty coupled with individual responsibility. Includes a list of current books and policy studies.

■ Publius
http://ww2.lafayette.edu/~publius/

The website of the leading scholarly journal on federalism.

■ Council of State Governments
www.csg.org

The website of the Council of State Governments, with information on state governments and state-level public policies.

■ National Conference of State Legislatures
www.ncsl.org

Comprehensive information about state governments and their relations to the federal government.

SUGGESTED READINGS

Jeffrey M. Berry, Kent E. Portney, and Ken Thomson, *The Rebirth of Urban Democracy*. Washington, D.C.: The Brookings Institution, 1993. A thorough study of the effects of grassroots participation and neighborhood government.

Timothy Conlan, *From New Federalism to Devolution*. Washington, D.C.: The Brookings Institution, 1998. The best treatment of the new federalism initiatives, arguing that Nixon and Reagan actually had very different goals and politics.

Archon Fung, *Empowered Participation: Reinventing Urban Democracy*. Princeton, N.J.: Princeton University Press, 2004. Shows how citizens can get involved at the local level to improve government performance.

David B. Robertson and Dennis R. Judd, *The Development of American Public Policy*. Glenview, Ill.: Scott, Foresman, 1989. Argues that American federalism biases the policy process in a conservative direction, favoring the status quo.

Thad Williamson, David Imbroscio, and Gar Alperowitz, *Making a Place for Community: Local Democracy in a Global Era*. New York: Routledge, 2002. A synthesis of the latest research on how jobs can be rooted in local communities, building stronger local democracies.

16

Civil Liberties and Civil Rights

Some of the most stirring words in the history of American democracy have been penned by judges in support of the civil liberties and civil rights of unpopular individuals and groups. "If there is any fixed star in our constitutional constellation," wrote Supreme Court Justice Robert Jackson, upholding the right of young Jehovah's Witnesses not to salute the American flag in school, "it is that no official, high or petty, can prescribe what shall be orthodox in politics, nationalism, religion, or other matters of opinion or force citizens to confess by word or act their faith therein."[1] "If there is a bedrock principle underlying the

First Amendment," wrote Justice William Brennan, upholding the right of a citizen to express political dissent by burning an American flag, "it is that Government may not prohibit the expression of any idea simply because society finds the idea itself offensive or disagreeable."[2] Against the grim background of intolerance and repression that has characterized most political systems around the globe, such affirmations of fundamental liberties and rights stand as one of the proudest accomplishments of democracy in the United States.

However, civil liberties and rights have been a focus of bitter conflict, not a subject of comfortable consensus, throughout American history. What strong supporters of civil liberties consider to be basic freedoms have appeared to many other Americans to be threats to order, morality, or community. The right of persons accused of crimes to the multiple protections of due process of law strikes many Americans as favoritism toward criminals at the expense of their victims. The right of authors, photographers, or filmmakers to portray sexual activity with only minimal restrictions strikes many as the protection of filth that corrupts society in general and degrades women in particular. The right of revolutionaries to call for the overthrow of our constitutional order strikes many as a denial of society's right of self-defense against its worst enemies. Struggles over civil liberties and civil rights often pit unpopular minorities or individuals against the popular majority and its elected representatives.

Civil liberties refer to the freedoms that individuals enjoy and that governments cannot invade. **Civil rights** refer to the powers and privileges that belong to us by virtue of our status as citizens. Freedom of speech and the free exercise of religion are liberties that need protection from government; voting and nondiscriminatory treatment in education and employment are rights that need protection by government. Such familiar civil liberties and civil rights are in fact a recent accomplishment. Despite the grand words of the Bill of Rights and despite the historic breakthrough of the Civil War amendments, for most of American history free speech was repressed, individual privacy invaded, and African Americans and women treated as second-class citizens. The flowering of civil liberties and civil rights has taken a long time and required a fierce struggle. And some of the advances that have been made remain precarious, with forces both outside and inside the current Supreme Court striving to roll them back. Civil liberties and civil rights remain one of the central arenas for the continuing democratic debate in America.

The ultimate voice in this debate has been that of the courts. Many social, political, and intellectual forces have battled over the definition of American liberties and rights. Since these liberties and rights are rooted in the Constitution, however, it has largely been the province of the federal judiciary to have the decisive say on their meaning and scope. Consequently, our focus in this chapter is mainly, though not exclusively, on Supreme Court cases.

The chapter begins with a perplexing issue in the democratic debate: how elites and ordinary citizens respond to controversial questions of civil liberties and civil rights. Next, the discussion turns to the historical bases for liberties and rights in America: the Bill of Rights, the Civil War amendments, and the constitutional revolution of the 1930s. The remainder of the chapter examines the major areas of civil liberties and civil rights: the First Amendment rights of expression, a free press, and religion; the rights of persons accused of crimes; the right of privacy; and the right of racial minorities, women, and gays and lesbians to equality in every aspect of American life.

CIVIL LIBERTIES AND CIVIL RIGHTS: FOES AND FRIENDS

It has often been argued that elite democrats are supportive of civil liberties and civil rights, whereas the ordinary citizens in whom popular democrats trust are intolerant and repressive. In our discussion of American political culture, we cited social science surveys indicating that support for civil liberties increases with education and political status. The conclusion frequently drawn from these studies is that civil liberties and civil rights have to be safeguarded from the authoritarian masses by democratically spirited elites.

Unfortunately, elite support for civil liberties and civil rights is less impressive in practice than in theory. The major attacks on civil liberties in recent times were spearheaded by decidedly elite figures: Senator Joseph McCarthy, Director of the FBI J. Edgar Hoover, Attorney General John Ashcroft, President Richard Nixon. Therefore, when it comes to opposition to civil liberties and civil rights, the blame must be shared by elite democrats and popular democrats alike.

Where, then, are the friends of civil liberties and civil rights to be found? Focusing on court cases, as this chapter does, may give the impression that it has been justices of the Supreme Court who have single-handedly advanced liberties and rights out of the depths of their own conscience and democratic faith. This is not the case: Ordinary citizens and democratic social movements have also played a key part in the struggle. Landmark advances in this area have been produced by a collaboration between elites and popular democratic forces. Thus, the credit for progress in civil liberties and civil rights, like the blame for hostility to them, must be shared by elite democrats and popular democrats.

Certainly, any account of progress in civil liberties and civil rights must highlight the beliefs, decisions, and arguments of their judicial champions. An honor roll for civil libertarians on the Supreme Court would include such great figures as Oliver Wendell Holmes, Louis Brandeis, Hugo Black, William O. Douglas, and Earl Warren. Probably the greatest civil libertarian on the High Court in recent years was William Brennan, who retired in 1990. (Recall the profile of Brennan in Chapter 14.)

Whereas the justices who have championed civil liberties and civil rights in landmark cases are famous, the petitioners who brought these cases to the Supreme Court are obscure. Yet these ordinary citizens have made significant contributions to the struggle for civil liberties and civil rights. Popular democratic movements have also been a source of key cases that reached the Supreme Court. The Legal Defense Fund of the National Association for the Advancement of Colored People (NAACP), the pioneer civil rights organization, was the leading force behind the long campaign for desegregated schools. The contemporary women's movement, which sprang up in the 1960s, also played a pivotal role in reshaping the Court's agenda. As women pressed their case for equality with new vigor, the Court responded by considering the issues of abortion and gender discrimination.

The **American Civil Liberties Union (ACLU)**, formed to defend free speech against government repression of dissenters during World War I, has taken the Bill of Rights as its cause ever since. The ACLU has fought for civil liberties and civil rights in many different areas, arguing more cases before the Supreme Court than any other organization save the federal government. The ACLU prides itself on upholding the liberties of the most unpopular and obnoxious groups. Its clients have included not only communists but also Nazis and Ku Klux Klan members.[3]

CIVIL LIBERTIES AND CIVIL RIGHTS: HISTORICAL BASES

Americans regard civil liberties and civil rights as their birthright. After all, the great charter of our freedom, the Bill of Rights, is almost as old as the nation itself. Yet the ringing words of the Bill of Rights took on a powerful meaning *in practice* only through a long struggle waged mainly by popular democratic forces. This section concentrates on three critical moments in this struggle: (1) the establishment of the Bill of Rights, (2) the Civil War amendments to the Constitution, and (3) the constitutional revolution of the 1930s.

The Bill of Rights

The Constitution drafted at Philadelphia in 1787 gave only limited recognition to civil liberties and civil rights. Provisions were incorporated to guarantee individuals the right of *habeas corpus* (persons placed under arrest must be promptly brought before a judge), except under dangerous circumstances of insurrection or invasion, and to prohibit the federal government from passing *bills of attainder* (laws that inflict punishment on individuals without trials) or *ex post facto laws* (laws that make an act committed in the past a punishable offense). But the Constitution left out most of the fundamental rights that had been incorporated in the bills of rights of the revolutionary state constitutions. The Federalist argument was that the Constitution was the charter of a limited government, so written restrictions on nonexistent powers to invade the people's liberty were unnecessary.

Anti-federalists were unpersuaded by this argument. Correctly observing the potential for an enormous concentration of power in the federal government, they insisted that the Constitution be amended to guarantee explicitly the basic liberties and rights of the people. Heeding this protest, the first Congress, sparked by the leadership of James Madison, drafted and passed ten amendments to the Constitution, collectively known as the Bill of Rights.[4] However, this monumental victory for the popular democrats of the founding era was restricted to white males. The Bill of Rights did not address the issue of equality for racial minorities or women.

Civil liberties in America in the decades after passage of the Bill of Rights were much more precarious than its words would suggest. The impact of the Bill of Rights was limited by two factors. First, the meaning of its words would be determined only as specific cases reached the Supreme Court—whose members would not necessarily be civil libertarians. Second, the Supreme Court ruled, in the case of *Barron v. Baltimore* (1833), that the Bill of Rights applied only to the federal government and did not impose any restraints on state governments. Because political activity in nineteenth-century America was mostly at the state and local levels, the Bill of Rights lacked much practical impact in this era.

The Civil War Amendments

Civil liberties and civil rights in America had a second founding: the three constitutional amendments passed during the Civil War and Reconstruction era. The Thirteenth Amendment abolished the institution of slavery. The Fourteenth Amendment protected the freed slaves against discrimination or repression by their former masters. Its key provision stated that "No state shall make or enforce any law which shall abridge the privileges or immunities of citizens of the United States; nor shall any state deprive any person of life, liberty, or property, without due process of law; nor deny to any person within its jurisdiction the equal protection of the laws." The Fifteenth Amendment extended the right of suffrage to the freed slaves—but only if they were male.

The **Civil War amendments**, an accomplishment of popular democratic struggle by abolitionists, radical Republicans, and African Americans, extended the Bill of Rights in two respects. First, to the emphasis of the first ten amendments on liberty, they added a new emphasis on equality. At least one previously excluded group—African Americans—was now promised equality under the Constitution. Second, they aimed to prohibit invasions of rights by state governments rather than by the federal government. Contrary to the decision in *Barron*, the Civil War amendments seemed to safeguard liberty against infringement by government at any level.

But the promises of the Civil War amendments were not kept for several generations. As the passions of the Civil War cooled and as the northern industrial elite made its peace with the southern agricultural elite, the protection of the former slaves ceased to be of importance to persons in positions of power. The Supreme Court validated this change, ruling—in a painful historical irony—that the Fourteenth Amendment protected corporations, but not African Americans, from hostile state actions. Nevertheless, the Civil War amendments remained part of the text of the Constitution, available for a later generation that would reclaim their words and redeem their promises. Indeed, the modern flowering of liberties and rights has been based in large part on the just-quoted words of the Fourteenth Amendment.

The Constitutional Revolution of the 1930s

For most of its history, the Supreme Court was more concerned with questions of property rights than with issues of civil liberties and civil rights. Yet when the Court backed down from further confrontation with President Franklin Roosevelt in 1937, and when Roosevelt had the subsequent opportunity to name a majority of justices, the Court was poised for a profound historical shift. The constitutional revolution of the 1930s, an expression of the popular democratic spirit of the New Deal, made civil liberties and civil rights for the first time the principal business of the Supreme Court.

This constitutional revolution was clearly enunciated in the case of *United States v. Carolene Products Co.* (1938). Writing for the Court, Justice Harlan Fiske Stone upheld congressional authority over commerce in this seemingly routine lawsuit. But Stone added a footnote to his opinion that pointed out how differently the Court might view governmental authority if civil liberties or civil rights, rather than commerce, were at issue.

Probably the most famous footnote in Court history, Stone's **footnote 4** set out three conditions under which the Court would not grant government actions the "presumption of constitutionality." First, government actions would be questioned by the Court if they fell within the prohibitions of the Bill of Rights or the Fourteenth Amendment. Second, they would be questioned if they restricted "those political processes which can ordinarily be expected to bring about repeal of undesirable legislation" (e.g., free elections). Third, they would be questioned if they were directed at "particular religions, or national or racial minorities."[5] With footnote 4, Stone signaled that the Court would now have as its priority the safeguarding of the Bill of Rights, of political freedoms, and of the rights of religious or racial minorities subjected to discriminatory treatment by an intolerant majority.

Footnote 4 articulated what scholars call the "double standard" of the modern Supreme Court. Legislation aimed at regulating the economy is subject only to "ordinary scrutiny" by the Court; the Court presumes that such legislation is constitutional so long as the government can show that the legislation has a "reasonable" basis. In contrast, legislation that might impinge on civil liberties and civil rights must meet the test of **strict scrutiny**, meaning the Court will strike the law down unless the government can demonstrate that a "compelling interest" necessitates such a law. This double standard has been justified on three grounds: that the freedoms protected by strict scrutiny are the basis of all other freedoms, that civil liberties and civil rights are explicitly guaranteed by the Bill of Rights and the Civil War amendments, and that courts themselves are ill equipped to determine economic policy but well equipped to handle the definition of fundamental liberties and rights.[6]

Footnote 4 did not make clear whether the Court intended to apply strict scrutiny to actions by state governments as well as actions by the federal government. In 1925 the Court had announced, in the case of *Gitlow v. New York*, that the right of free speech limited state governments as well as the federal government since free speech was part of the liberty protected from state invasion by the Due Process Clause of the Fourteenth Amendment. In 1937 the Court went further, stating in *Palko v. Connecticut* that several parts of the Bill of Rights applied to the states, through the mechanism of the Fourteenth Amendment, because these rights "represented the very essence of a scheme of ordered liberty."[7]

A CLOSER LOOK

Civil Liberties in Times of War

Throughout American history, civil liberties have been restricted during times of war or warlike crises. In 1798, only seven years after ratification of the Bill of Rights, the Federalists passed the Alien and Sedition Acts to silence Jeffersonian critics of the "quasi-war" with France. During the Civil War, President Abraham Lincoln suspended the writ of habeas corpus and his generals tried civilians under martial law. Using another Sedition Act passed during World War I, President Woodrow Wilson deported or jailed radical critics of his war policies. Soon after the attack at Pearl Harbor brought the United States into World War II, Japanese Americans were forced to leave their homes on the West Coast and relocate to internment camps for the duration of the conflict. The anticommunist crusades led by Senator Joseph McCarthy and his allies marked the early years of the Cold War, damaging the careers and lives of numerous individuals accused of "un-American" activities.

After the wars have ended and the crises have passed, many Americans have had second thoughts, coming to regard these past actions as excessive in boosting the power of government at the expense of basic rights. The same issue has been raised again for Americans by the war on terror that the Bush administration proclaimed in response to the attacks of September 11, 2001.

Six weeks after September 11, Congress passed and President Bush signed the USA Patriot Act, which arms federal authorities with stronger tools of surveillance, detention, and punishment against those involved in terrorist activities. Among its more controversial provisions are: (1) expanding the powers of the federal government to inquire into such private activities as obtaining reading matter from libraries and bookstores or surfing the Internet; (2) permitting the government to detain noncitizens on the basis of suspicion, holding them without trials or immigration hearings for many months while keeping their names secret; and (3) allowing federal officials to wiretap conversations between individuals detained in relation to suspected terrorist activities and their lawyers. In addition to the Patriot Act, President Bush has claimed inherent authority as commander in chief to detain those he labels "enemy combatants" for an indefinite duration and to bring them before military tribunals for trial and punishment without review by civilian courts. Pursuant to presidential orders, hundreds of alleged Al Qaeda fighters seized in Afghanistan were transported to the U.S. naval base at Guantanamo Bay in Cuba; most of them remained incarcerated four years later.

Do the Patriot Act and the executive orders of President Bush resemble earlier wartime excesses that Americans have later regretted, or are they more carefully tailored measures that are invaluable to the U.S. government as it combats an insidious new enemy? The Patriot Act and the president's orders as commander in chief have been touted by the Bush administration as effective weapons in the war on terror. Claiming that critics of these measures have been ill-informed and even hysterical, John Ashcroft, Bush's attorney general during his first term, launched an extensive and vigorous public-relations campaign on their behalf. Ashcroft's former assistant at the Justice Department, Viet Dinh, principal drafter of the Patriot Act, insists that the act's provisions are more carefully limited and less intrusive to liberty than the critics comprehend. More fundamentally, Dinh writes, liberty itself requires order as its precondition; without the kind of security that the Patriot Act is designed to enhance, fearful Americans will have lost some of their most precious freedoms.

To critics, however, the gains to homeland security from the policies of the Bush administration have been small, while the costs to American liberties have been large. Bush policies on homeland security have drawn fire from an unusual coalition, bringing together liberals concerned about a danger to civil liberties and conservatives concerned about an ominous expansion of the federal government. Both kinds of critics see the Patriot Act and Bush's executive orders as tilting the balance between authority and liberty too far toward presidential power. In the view of law professor Stephen Schulhofer, "the domestic security policies of this administration encroach on three principles that are fundamental to the preservation of freedom: accountability, checks and balances, and narrow tailoring of government's power to intrude into the lives of citizens. In each case, the administration has overlooked or dismissed alternative approaches that would strengthen the nation's security at least as effectively without weakening fundamental freedoms."

To this date, the Patriot Act has withstood legal challenges, but Bush's executive orders on "enemy combatants" have not been as successful in the courts. In June 2004, the U.S. Supreme Court rejected Bush's claim that the commander in chief's authority over wartime situations cannot be reviewed by anyone else, ruling that those seized and held as alleged terrorists by the military, whether citizens or noncitizens, must be allowed to challenge their status in civilian courts. In a 6–3 decision, the Court ordered the administration to provide the detainees at Guantanamo Bay with access to lawyers and review by the judicial branch. As Justice Sandra Day O'Connor observed, the Court's message was that "a state of war is not a blank check for the president when it comes to the rights of the nation's citizens."

Even after this rebuff at the hands of the Supreme Court, the Bush administration remains in a strong position to restrict civil liberties in the post–September 11 era. Having proclaimed a war of indefinite duration, amid a climate of fear that it has done much to extend, the Bush administration faces only scattered opposition in its assertions of wartime powers. Opinion surveys show that a majority of Americans believe that President Bush is a strong leader in the war on terror. Opponents of Bush's approach face a difficult struggle in keeping before the public the idea that civil liberties demand greater protection even as we seek to wage an effective battle against the terror networks that wish to do us terrible harm.

Sources: Viet Dinh, "Defending Liberty Against the Tyranny of Terror," in Bruce Miroff, Raymond Seidelman, and Todd Swanstrom, eds., *Debating Democracy: A Reader in American Politics*, 5th edition (Boston: Houghton Mifflin, 2005); Stephen Schulhofer, "No Checks, No Balances: Discarding Bedrock Constitutional Principles," in Richard C. Leone and Greg Anrig Jr., eds., *The War on Our Freedoms: Civil Liberties in an Age of Terrorism* (New York: Public Affairs, 2003); *Hamdi v. Rumsfeld*, 03-6696 (2004); Geoffrey R. Stone, *Perilous Times: Free Speech in Wartime from the Sedition Act of 1798 to the War on Terrorism* (New York: W. W. Norton, 2004).

Since the constitutional revolution of the 1930s, the Supreme Court has often been divided about how much of the Bill of Rights is incorporated in the Fourteenth Amendment and therefore applies to state governments. Some strongly civil libertarian justices have argued for total **incorporation**—that is, every clause in the Bill of Rights applies to the states as well as to the federal government. But the dominant position has been selective incorporation, with the Court deciding one case at a time whether to apply each provision of the Bill of Rights to the states. The practical difference between total incorporation and selective incorporation diminished in the 1960s, however, as the Warren Court separately incorporated almost all of the provisions of the Bill of Rights. Today, the combination of the Bill of Rights and the Fourteenth Amendment protects civil liberties and civil rights from both the federal and state governments.

THE FIRST AMENDMENT

The words of the First Amendment, though few in number, establish the foundation of constitutional liberty in the United States: "Congress shall make no law respecting an establishment of religion, or prohibiting the free exercise thereof; or abridging the freedom of speech, or of the press; or the right of the people peaceably to assemble, and to petition the government for a redress of grievances."

This promise of liberty was more easily set down on paper than fulfilled in practice. For much of American history, the First Amendment was a frail barrier to repression. Consider the guarantee of freedom of speech. Less than a decade after the adoption of the Bill of Rights, the ruling Federalists passed a sedition act and dispatched several of their Jeffersonian opponents to jail for criticizing the administration in power. Later, when socialists and anarchists denounced the new capitalist elite, their meetings were frequently broken up and their publications suppressed. The free speech of which we are so proud is a very recent phenomenon.[8]

Free Speech

The original proponents of a constitutional guarantee of free expression were most concerned with protecting *political speech*, such as criticism of the government or its officials. The prohibition on government interference was thus set down in absolute terms: "Congress shall make *no law* . . ." (emphasis added). But no Supreme Court majority has ever regarded the First Amendment as conferring an absolute protection for speech. The Court has had to grapple repeatedly with where to draw the boundary line dividing free speech from unprotected, and therefore punishable, speech.

The Supreme Court was first moved to draw such a boundary line in response to prosecutions of dissenters during World War I. Charles Schenck, a socialist, was prosecuted under the wartime Espionage Act for a pamphlet that urged young men to resist the draft. In *Schenck v. United States* (1919), the Court upheld the constitutionality of the Espionage Act and thus of Schenck's conviction. In the decision for the Court, Justice Oliver Wendell Holmes explained, in words that became famous, that speech was subject to the **clear and present danger test**:

> The most stringent protection of free speech would not protect a man in falsely shouting fire in a theater and causing a panic. . . . The question in every case is whether the words used are used in such circumstances and are of such a nature as to create a clear and present danger that they will bring about the substantive evils that Congress has a right to prevent.[9]

Fear of political radicalism lay at the heart of the repression of free speech during World War I and its aftermath. This same fear fostered a new repressive climate after World War II, as Americans became obsessed with an external threat from the Soviet Union and an internal threat from domestic communists. Fueling anticommunist hysteria during the early years of the Cold War were demagogic politicians, preeminent among them Senator Joseph McCarthy of Wisconsin. The senator gave his name to the phenomenon of **McCarthyism** by his tactics: waving phony lists of supposed communists in the government before the press, hauling individuals before his congressional committee and tarring their reputation for no other end than publicity, labeling any who opposed him conspirators against American freedom.

Influenced by the sour climate of McCarthyism, the Supreme Court went along with the effort of the executive branch to put the leaders of the American Communist Party in prison. In *Dennis v. United States* (1951), the Court upheld the convictions of eleven top officials of the Communist Party for violating the Smith Act, which made it a crime to advocate the violent overthrow of government in the United States, even though the puny American Communist Party scarcely posed a present danger to the government. It was only after McCarthy and his methods came into disrepute and Cold War hysteria began to ease that the Supreme Court backed away from this repressive stance. The case of *Yates v. United States* (1957) also involved Smith Act prosecution of communist officials, but this time the defendants' convictions were reversed. Abstract advocacy of Communist Party doctrine about revolution, the Court ruled, was protected speech. Only advocacy of immediate action to overthrow the government could be punished.

During the 1960s, radical political dissent was not restricted to communists. Many Americans began to engage in vocal political protests, especially against the war in Vietnam. It was at the end of this turbulent decade that the Warren Court, in *Brandenburg v. Ohio* (1969), finally gave a broad interpretation to the right of free speech. Clarence Brandenburg, a Ku Klux Klan leader, was convicted under an Ohio law for advocating racial conflict at a televised Klan rally. Overturning Brandenburg's conviction, the Court stated that government could punish an individual for advocating an illegal act only if "such advocacy is directed to inciting or producing imminent lawless action, and is likely to incite or produce such action."[10] Under such a test, only a few utterances—such as a speech that called for a riot and actually helped begin it—were still punishable. Political speech in the United States was at last given broad protection—nearly 180 years after the adoption of the Bill of Rights!

In recent decades, the Court has brought **symbolic speech**—political expression that communicates with visual symbols instead of words—under the protection of the First Amendment. Several high school and junior high school students in Des Moines, Iowa, were suspended after they wore black armbands to school as a way of protesting the war in Vietnam. Voiding the suspensions, the Court stated in *Tinker v. Des Moines Independent Community School District* (1969) that wearing an armband as a silent form of protest was "akin to pure speech."[11] More controversial than the *Tinker* decision was the Court's defense of symbolic speech in *Texas v. Johnson* (1989). Johnson had burned an American flag outside the 1984 Republican convention in Dallas, Texas, to protest Reagan's policies. Five justices—an unusual coalition of liberals Brennan, Marshall, and Blackmun and conservatives Scalia and Kennedy—voted to overturn Johnson's conviction on the grounds that the Texas statute against flag burning violated the First Amendment by punishing the communication of a political message.

Should supporters of civil liberties be in a celebrating mood because of these recent decisions? Popular democrats point out that speech can be restricted not only by punishment but by exclusion from the forums where sizable audiences gather. Ordinary citizens or dissenting groups may now be free to say almost anything on the proverbial street corner, law professor Owen Fiss observes, but they are seldom heard in the mass media, where speech reaches large numbers. And what happens when the street corner as local gathering spot has largely been supplanted by the shopping mall? According to several decisions issued by the Burger Court during the 1970s, speakers and pamphleteers can be forbidden in these public spaces because they are private property.[12]

Indeed, even public property can sometimes exclude public speakers. In *United States v. Kokinda* (1990), the Rehnquist Court upheld a ban on political groups distributing literature and soliciting funds on the grounds of a post office in suburban Maryland. The majority argued that when a government agency is operating in a "proprietary capacity," it can prohibit political speech that interferes with business.[13] The space for free speech by those without wealth and power has begun to contract. It will not expand again, Fiss writes, until free speech is guaranteed in public places, even those that are private property, as an essential condition for popular democracy: "a public right—an instrument of collective self-determination."[14]

Unprotected Speech

Not all speech has been granted broad protection by the Supreme Court. Some kinds of expression are considered by the Court to be **unprotected speech**— speech unworthy of full First Amendment protection either because its social value is insignificant or because it verges on conduct that is harmful to others. Commercial speech, unlike political speech, can thus be regulated, as in bans on false advertising. *Fighting words*, such as derogatory names shouted at a police officer, can be punished on the grounds that they do not express any ideas or contribute to any search for truth (*Chaplinsky v. New Hampshire* [1942]). And *libel*—written communication that exposes the person written about to public shame, contempt, or ridicule—is subject to lawsuits for monetary damages. However, the Court ruled in *New York Times Co. v. Sullivan* (1964) that for a public official to win a judgment against a writer, the official must prove not only that the charge in question was false but also that it had been made with malice.

Drawing the line between protected and unprotected speech has been hardest for the Supreme Court in the area of **obscenity**. Probably no other term has been as difficult for the Court to define. The Court first entered the thicket of sexual expression in *Roth v. United States* (1957). In this case, Justice Brennan, declaring obscenity to be unprotected by the First Amendment, defined it as sexual material that appealed to "prurient interest"—that is, excited lust. Confronted by a book, magazine, or film about sex, the Court would decide "whether to the average person, applying contemporary community standards, the dominant theme of the material taken as a whole appeals to the prurient interest." Attempting to protect the free expression of ideas, even about sex, Brennan added that a work should be judged obscene only when it was "utterly without redeeming social importance."[15]

Despite Brennan's valiant effort to define obscenity, observe how many ambiguous terms dot his opinion: "prurient interest," "average person," "contemporary community standards," "redeeming social importance." After the *Roth* decision, obscenity cases became a headache for the Supreme Court. Perhaps their most ludicrous feature was that to study the evidence in a particular obscenity conviction, the mostly elderly justices had to sift through the pages of a sex magazine or sit through the screening of a porno film. It was little wonder that they lost the stomach for these cases.

As sexually explicit material became a booming market for enterprising pornographers, the more conservative justices appointed by Richard Nixon tried to tighten the definition of obscenity in *Miller v. California* (1973). Chief Justice Burger's opinion made two significant changes in obscenity doctrine. First, a sexually explicit work could no longer simply claim minimal social importance (for example, by including a brief scene on some social or political theme); now the work had to possess "serious literary, artistic, political, or scientific value."[16] Second, prurient interest could be measured by local, rather than national, standards, which permitted a bookseller in a small town, for example, to be prosecuted for selling a work that could be legally sold in a more cosmopolitan city. But the *Miller* decision did little to stem the tide of pornography. And the Court soon had to back away from granting local communities a wide latitude to define obscenity after a Georgia town attempted to prosecute *Carnal Knowledge*, a popular Hollywood film, because it contained a simulated sexual act.

Conservative moralists have long decried the scope that the Supreme Court has given to the production of sexually explicit materials. In recent years, they have been joined by some feminists who regard pornography not only as degrading to women but also as contributing to their social subordination.

Freedom of the Press

If the right of free speech promotes an open debate about political matters, the right of a free press provides democratic citizens with the information and analysis they need to enter intelligently into that debate. In authoritarian political systems, the government openly owns or covertly controls the press. In a democracy, the government is expected to keep its hands off the press. (Yet as we saw in Chapter 6, both governmental and economic elites in America possess special influence over the media.)

The landmark case defining freedom of the press was *Near v. Minnesota* (1931). J. M. Near was the publisher of the *Saturday Press*, a Minneapolis weekly that denounced a wide array of targets: corrupt officials, racketeers, Catholics, Jews, blacks, and labor unions. Minneapolis officials obtained a court injunction to close down Near's paper under a Minnesota law that allowed the banning of scandal sheets. The Supreme Court struck down the Minnesota law as a violation of freedom of the press because the law imposed **prior restraint**. A publisher like Near could still be sued for libel, but he could not be blocked from printing whatever he chose in the first place. The Court recognized that prior restraint, by allowing government officials to determine what information could be kept from publication, would effectively destroy freedom of the press.

Prior restraint was also at issue in a case involving the *New York Times*; this time the issue was government secrecy and deception during the Vietnam War. When a disillusioned Defense Department official, Daniel Ellsberg, leaked a copy of a classified department study of the war's history, known as the Pentagon Papers, to the *New York Times*, the Nixon administration obtained a lower court order temporarily halting the paper's publication of excerpts from the study. The Supreme Court's decision in *New York Times Co. v. United States* (1971) voided the order and permitted publication of the Pentagon Papers. But the six justices in the majority were divided in their reasoning. Justices Black, Brennan, and Douglas were opposed to prior restraint under any circumstances. Justices White, Marshall, and Stewart voted to allow publication because the Nixon administration had failed to make a convincing case for the disastrous consequences it claimed would follow once the Pentagon Papers became public. Freedom of the press again won a victory—but a majority of the Court seemed willing to accept prior restraint if the government could make a better case on possible harm to national security.

Even though broadcast media (radio and television) enjoy much the same freedom as print media (newspapers and magazines), they are subject to certain special constraints. Because broadcast frequencies are limited, the federal government regulates broadcast media through the Federal Communications Commission (FCC). And since messages broadcast through the media, unlike messages set in print, often reach audiences for which they were never intended, the FCC may ban words over the air that could not be kept out of print. In *F.C.C. v. Pacifica Foundation* (1978), the Court upheld a ban on further radio broadcasts of a monologue by comic George Carlin about Americans' obsession with "seven dirty words"—which Carlin used freely as part of his routine.[17] The issue here was not obscenity—Carlin's monologue did not excite lust and clearly had artistic value—but the harm done to children who might accidentally hear the seven offensive words.

Is the Internet, the new medium of the computer age, to be treated like print or like broadcast media? In its first major decision about the Internet, *Reno v. American Civil Liberties Union* (1997), the Court struck down the Communications Decency Act of 1996, which criminalized the transmission of "indecent" materials that minors might view, as an infringement of the First Amendment. The Court announced that the Internet, like print media, deserves the highest level of constitutional protection. Congress responded to the decision in 1998 with the more narrowly drawn Child Online Protection Act. Nonetheless, in *Ashcroft v. American Civil Liberties Union* (2004), the Court upheld an injunction against this act on the First Amendment grounds that less restrictive methods than the law required, such as filtering technology, were available to protect minors from exposure to pornographic materials.

Separation of Church and State

The opening words of the First Amendment bar Congress from passing any law "respecting an establishment of religion." At the time the Bill of Rights was adopted, these words were aimed mainly at preventing the federal government from bestowing on any religious denomination the special privileges enjoyed by the official Anglican Church in England. But in modern times, the Supreme Court has given a far broader meaning to the **Establishment Clause**, reading it as requiring an almost complete separation of church and state. Religion and government are kept apart—even though America is one of the most religious nations in the world. Public opinion surveys, notes scholar Garry Wills, show that "eight Americans in ten say they believe they will be called before God on Judgment Day to answer for their sins" and that the same percentage "believe God still works miracles."[18] This religious majority sometimes has difficulty understanding why the Supreme Court believes that government is not supposed to be in the business of supporting God.

School prayer cases illustrate how the Supreme Court, flying in the face of majority sentiments, has insisted that government stay out of religion. The Court has struck down the daily reading of a nondenominational prayer in New York public schools (*Engel v. Vitale* [1962]), Bible reading in Pennsylvania public schools (*Abington School District v. Schempp* [1963]), and even a moment of silence for meditation or prayer in Alabama public schools (*Wallace v. Jaffree* [1985]). School prayer, the Court has reasoned, represents a government endorsement of religion that inflicts psychological injury on students (and their parents) who are not religious believers. The Establishment Clause of the First Amendment mandates government neutrality toward religion.

The Court has not been quite as strict about government approval for religious symbols where school-age children are not involved. For example, in *Lynch v. Donnelly* (1984), the Court approved of a nativity scene erected by the city of Pawtucket, Rhode Island, during the Christmas season—but only because it was accompanied by a Santa's house, a Christmas tree, and colored lights that indicated the city's secular purpose (attracting shoppers to downtown stores).

The Establishment Clause has also been central to the issue of government financial aid to religious schools. However, the Supreme Court's decisions in this area have not been as unpopular as in the area of school prayer because Protestants and Jews do not favor aid that would go mostly to Catholic schools. Beginning in the 1940s, a long series of cases established the principle that government could not financially support religious schools, even in the name of secular educational purposes, although it could provide direct aid to their students (e.g., bus transportation). Chief Justice Burger summed up the Court's approach in *Lemon v. Kurtzman* (1971)—a ruling invalidating state payments for the teaching of secular subjects in parochial schools. According to the **Lemon test**, government aid to religious schools would be constitutional only if (1) it had a secular purpose, (2) its effect was neither to advance nor to inhibit religion, and (3) it did not entangle government and religious institutions in each other's affairs.

The Rehnquist Court's conservative majority eased up somewhat on the criteria for public aid to religious schools. In a 1997 decision, *Agostini v. Felton*, the Court approved a New York program that provided remedial education for parochial school students by teachers from public schools. The decision in *Mitchell v. Helms* (2000) upheld a federal program that placed computers and other instructional equipment in classrooms regardless of whether the schools were public, private, or religious. Since all schools were eligible for this aid, Justice Clarence Thomas argued, it could not be construed as fostering religious indoctrination. Although the Supreme Court has interpreted the Establishment Clause as erecting a "wall between church and state," its recent decisions have made that wall shorter.

A new arena of controversy in church-state relations opened up in 2001, when Alabama's Chief Justice, Roy Moore, had a 2½-ton monument to the Ten Commandments placed in his state's supreme court building. Two years later, the monument was removed from public view upon order of a U.S. District Court judge. Like the school prayer decisions, the removal of the Ten Commandments from a courthouse as a violation of the First Amendment was unpopular; a Gallup Poll reported that 77 percent of Americans disagreed with the District Court judge's order. The importance of religious conservatives in President Bush's reelection ensured that the Ten Commandments issue had not been settled by the Alabama case. A month after the election, in December 2004, the Bush administration urged the U.S. Supreme Court to allow the display of the Ten Commandments in courthouses. In June 2005, the Court said no in a 5–4 decision, ordering two Kentucky courthouses to remove framed copies of the commandments from their walls.

Free Exercise of Religion

The Establishment Clause in the First Amendment is followed by the **Free Exercise Clause**—the right to believe in whatever religion one chooses. The Free Exercise Clause is a legacy of America's colonial past, as many of the original

From *The Huge Book of Hell* © 1997 by Matt Groening. All rights reserved. Reprinted by permission of Penguin Books USA, NY.

white settlers had fled religious oppression and persecution in England and other parts of Europe. It is also a practical necessity in a nation where the diversity of religious faiths is staggering.

The landmark free exercise case is *West Virginia State Board of Education v. Barnette* (1943). At stake was the right of schoolchildren to refuse to salute an American flag because their religious faith—Jehovah's Witnesses—forbade it. Three years earlier, in *Minersville School District v. Gobitis*, the Court had approved of expelling Witness children from school for refusal to salute the flag. But that decision led to brutal physical assaults on the Witnesses in many towns and also became an embarrassment as the United States entered a war against

Nazi tyranny in the name of democratic freedom. With the powerful words of Justice Jackson (quoted at the beginning of this chapter), the Court changed its mind and gave a firm endorsement to the free exercise of religion even when it offended the most cherished sentiments of the majority.

Although the Free Exercise Clause protects any form of religious belief, the matter of religious conduct is more complicated. What happens when a religious order prescribes practices for its adherents that violate local, state, or federal laws having nothing to do with religion? The Court first struggled with this dilemma in *Reynolds v. United States* (1879), when it approved the outlawing of polygamy (where a man takes several wives), a key practice of the Mormon faith. A recent case, *Employment Division v. Smith* (1990), upheld the same distinction between belief and conduct. The Court denied the claim by two followers of the Native American Church that ingesting the drug peyote, for which they had been fired from their job, was a religious sacrament protected by the Free Exercise Clause. However, the position of the Court was different in *Church of Lukumi Babalu Aye v. City of Hialeah* (1993). When the Florida city passed an ordinance to stop the practitioners of Santería, an Afro-Cuban religion, from engaging in animal sacrifice as a ritual, the Court overturned it as a blatant attempt to restrict the free exercise of religion.

THE RIGHTS OF PERSONS ACCUSED OF CRIMES

The constitutional bases for the rights of persons accused of crimes are the Fourth, Fifth, Sixth, and Eighth Amendments, applied to the states through incorporation in the Fourteenth Amendment. Application of these amendments to the criminal justice system at the state and local levels, where the vast majority of criminal proceedings takes place, is a recent phenomenon. The Warren Court of the 1960s set down most of the critical precedents in the area of criminal procedure. The Burger (1969–1986) and Rehnquist (1986–2005) Courts, appointed by "law-and-order" presidents and responsive to the public outcry about crime, carved out numerous exceptions to these precedents.

Criminal Procedure: The Warren Court

Clarence Earl Gideon, a penniless drifter with a criminal record, was convicted for the felony offense of breaking and entering a poolroom and sentenced in a Florida court to five years in prison. Unable to afford an attorney, Gideon had to defend himself after the judge refused to appoint professional counsel for him. The Supreme Court accepted Gideon's petition (appointing a prominent lawyer to argue his case before it) and ruled in *Gideon v. Wainwright* (1963) that the Sixth Amendment right of counsel is so essential to a fair trial that the state must pay for a lawyer for indigent defendants charged with a felony. Gideon won the chance for a second trial, at which he was acquitted after his court-appointed counsel convincingly demonstrated that the prosecution's star witness, who had fingered Gideon for the break-in, was probably the culprit.[19]

Cleveland police officers forced their way into the home of Dolree Mapp without a search warrant in the belief that she was hiding a man wanted for a recent bombing as well as illegal gambling paraphernalia. Their search of the house turned up neither a fugitive nor gambling materials—but they did discover sexual books and pictures. On the basis of this evidence, Mapp was sent to jail for possession of obscene literature. In *Mapp v. Ohio* (1961), the Warren Court reversed her conviction, holding that material seized in an illegal search could not be introduced as evidence in a state court, a doctrine known as the **exclusionary rule**. This rule, based on the Fourth Amendment, had been applied since 1914 to defendants in federal prosecutions. But its extension from the tax evaders and other white-collar defendants typically tried in federal courts to the wider range of defendants tried in state courts, including violent criminals, made the *Mapp* decision controversial.

Ernesto Miranda was arrested by Phoenix police on suspicion of rape and kidnapping. At first, Miranda maintained his innocence, but after two hours of police interrogation he signed a written confession to the crime. At no point had the police advised Miranda that he had a right to have an attorney present during the interrogation. In *Miranda v. Arizona* (1966), the Warren Court ruled the confession to be inadmissible as evidence in court, a violation of Miranda's Fifth Amendment right not to incriminate himself. The Court's majority, in this 5–4 decision, argued that police custody and interrogation tended to create such an intimidating atmosphere that individuals felt pressured to incriminate themselves in the absence of a lawyer's counsel. With the confession thrown out, Arizona retried Miranda for the same crime and convicted him on the basis of other evidence.

The effect of the decision was that police had to change their behavior and provide suspects with what came to be known as the **Miranda warnings**. Criminal suspects must be advised that (1) they have the right to remain silent, (2) anything they say can be used against them, (3) they have the right to speak to an attorney before police questioning and to have him or her present during interrogation, and (4) if they cannot afford to hire an attorney, one will be provided at state expense before any questioning can take place.

The *Mapp* decision, and even more the *Miranda* decision, fueled widespread attacks on the Warren Court for crippling law enforcement at a time of rampant crime. Actually, these Warren Court decisions did not free many criminals. A prominent study of the exclusionary rule later estimated that less than 2.5 percent of felony arrests were undermined by the operation of this rule.[20] After initial grumbling, the police adapted to the requirement of providing *Miranda* warnings. Numerous studies found that criminal confessions continued to be made in large numbers even after suspects were informed of their rights.[21] Nonetheless, critics of the Warren Court convinced many Americans that the justices had in effect taken the handcuffs off criminal suspects and put them on the police.

Presidential candidate Richard Nixon seized on crime as a campaign issue in 1968, lambasting the Warren Court for coddling criminals and promising that his administration would appoint only law-and-order judges. Nixon's success with the issue encouraged other candidates, including his Republican successors in the White House. Supreme Court justices appointed by Nixon, Reagan, and the elder Bush have thus been less likely than were justices of the Warren Court era to emphasize the constitutional rights of criminal suspects or defendants and more likely to emphasize the practical needs of police and prosecutors.

Criminal Procedure: The Burger and Rehnquist Courts

Of the three landmark Warren Court decisions on criminal justice just described, only the *Gideon* decision was received without controversy. No one seemed to doubt the proposition that there could not be a fair trial where the state was represented by a professionally trained prosecutor and the defendant had to represent himself or herself. So it is not surprising that the Burger Court went beyond the *Gideon* ruling in *Argersinger v. Hamlin* (1972), holding that the right of court-appointed counsel for the indigent should be extended from felony defendants to defendants facing misdemeanor charges that carried a jail sentence.

In the more controversial areas of the exclusionary rule and the *Miranda* warnings, however, the Burger and Rehnquist Courts trimmed back the Warren Court precedents—without explicitly disavowing them. Thus, in *United States v. Calandra* (1974), Justice Lewis Powell's majority opinion argued that illegally obtained evidence, although still barred from a trial because of the exclusionary rule, could be admitted before a grand jury considering whether to indict a suspect and thus bring him or her to trial. In *United States v. Leon* (1984), Justice Byron White wrote that if police use a search warrant that later proves to have been invalid, the evidence seized is still admissible during the trial. And in *Pennsylvania Board of Probation v. Scott* (1998), Justice Clarence Thomas wrote that illegally seized evidence could be used in parole revocation hearings because parolees were more likely than other citizens to commit crimes. So many exceptions have been approved by the Burger and Rehnquist Courts that legal scholar Thomas Davies calls the exclusionary rule a "shadow" of its former self.[22]

The Burger and Rehnquist Courts also made it easier for police to obtain confessions by loosening up the requirements for *Miranda* warnings. For example, in emergency situations such as a threat to the safety of the arresting officer, the warnings are not required (*New York v. Quarles* [1984]). Nor do arresting officers have to notify suspects of the specific offense with which they are charged (*Colorado v. Spring* [1987]). However, the Miranda decision survived a frontal challenge in *Dickerson v. United States* (2000). Although a long-time critic of the *Miranda* warnings, Chief Justice Rehnquist, writing the majority opinion in the *Dickerson* case, stated that the warnings were a constitutional rule rather than merely a set of procedural guidelines that Congress was free to change.

The ultimate issue in a criminal justice system—imposition of the death sentence—was not tackled by the Supreme Court until 1972 in the case of *Furman v. Georgia*. With all four of President Nixon's appointees in dissent, the Court struck down existing death penalty laws in every state because the random and arbitrary fashion in which juries decided on capital punishment violated the Cruel and Unusual Punishment Clause of the Eighth Amendment. In response to this decision, state legislatures and the federal government revised their criminal laws to provide juries with explicit sentencing guidelines. The Court ratified this approach in *Gregg v. Georgia* (1976), and prison "death rows" reopened for a new cohort of the condemned.

The criminal procedure decisions of the Burger and Rehnquist Courts were more congenial to public opinion than those of the Warren Court. However, critics of these decisions point out that constitutional rights—even for the most despicable citizens—should not be decided by a popularity test. They argue that the Bill of Rights does not prevent us from putting criminal offenders behind bars, but it does require that we do so in a fair manner. This philosophy is well expressed by Justice Brennan: "The interest of . . . [the government] is not that it shall win a case, but that justice shall be done."[23]

THE RIGHT OF PRIVACY: BIRTH CONTROL AND ABORTION

The controversy surrounding constitutional rights spelled out in the Bill of Rights has been extended to the issue of whether other rights can be legitimately derived from the text of the Constitution even if they are not spelled out there. A **right of privacy** is at the center of this debate. Civil libertarians have long contended for this right. In a 1928 dissent, Justice Louis Brandeis wrote that "The makers of our Constitution conferred, as against the government, the right to be let alone—the most comprehensive of rights and the right most valued by civilized men."[24] But what words in the Bill of Rights established the right to be let alone—the right of privacy?

The Supreme Court finally answered this question in 1965 in *Griswold v. Connecticut*. At issue was a Connecticut law that made it a crime for any person to use a drug or device for birth control. The Court invalidated this law as an invasion of the constitutionally protected right of privacy of married persons. Writing for the majority, Justice William O. Douglas argued that the enumerated guarantees of constitutional rights in the First, Third, Fourth, Fifth, and Ninth Amendments had "penumbras" (shadows) that extended beyond their specific words. These penumbras suggested the existence of "zones of privacy" that the government could not invade. In an important concurring opinion, Justice Arthur Goldberg took a different tack. He based a right of privacy on the words of the Ninth Amendment: "The enumeration in the Constitution, of certain rights, shall not be construed to deny or disparage others retained by the people." To the dissenters in *Griswold*, Justices Hugo Black and Potter Stewart, the right of privacy, whether found among penumbras or read into the Ninth Amendment, was a concoction of the justices lacking any basis in the Constitution.[25]

The *Griswold* case generated a heated controversy on the Court over the idea of a constitutional right of privacy. But few outside the Court paid attention to a decision striking down an antiquated law that even the dissenters in the case considered to be "silly." The right of privacy generated a major public controversy only when it was extended from a couple's freedom to choose contraception and avoid pregnancy to a woman's freedom to choose an abortion and terminate an unwanted pregnancy.

The abortion issue was brought before the Supreme Court by two young lawyers, Sarah Weddington and Linda Coffee, who were inspired by the new feminist movement that had emerged in the 1960s. Their client in *Roe v. Wade* (1973) was Norma McCorvey, a twenty-one-year-old woman who had carried an unwanted pregnancy to term because Texas, like most other states at that time, forbade abortions except to save the life of the mother. (McCorvey's identity was protected from publicity by the pseudonym "Jane Roe.") By a 7–2 vote, the Court struck down anti-abortion statutes in Texas and all other states on the grounds that they violated a woman's right of privacy, located in the Due Process Clause of the Fourteenth Amendment.

Authored by Justice Harry Blackmun, the decision for the Court divided pregnancy into three trimesters. During the first trimester, a state cannot interfere with a woman's right to choose an abortion in consultation with her doctor. During the second trimester, when abortions pose more of a medical risk, states can regulate them to safeguard maternal health. Only during the final trimester, when a fetus may be capable of surviving outside the womb, can a state impose severe restrictions or prohibitions on abortion. To the dissenters in the case, Justices Byron White and William Rehnquist, this trimester scheme was an arbitrary invention of the Court. They argued that the Court was enforcing on the states a right that had neither been enumerated in the Bill of Rights nor envisioned by the drafters of the Fourteenth Amendment.

Hailing the decision on abortion as a great victory for women's rights, the women's movement shifted its attention to other issues. But as supporters of *Roe* grew complacent, opponents of the decision mobilized to fight its results. The initial "right-to-life" movement was spearheaded by Catholic organizations. Later, they were joined by fundamentalist Protestant groups, such as the Reverend Jerry Falwell's Moral Majority. The religious fervor of right-to-life supporters was captured for political purposes by the conservatives of the New Right, whose candidate and hero was Ronald Reagan. Once in the White House, Reagan made abortion a litmus test for his nominees to the federal judiciary. By the end of his two terms, he had named three new justices to the Supreme Court, and *Roe* was at risk of reversal.[26]

Awakening to the peril to *Roe*, the "pro-choice" forces mobilized their supporters at last. After the Court announced early in 1989 that it would consider the restrictive laws on abortion passed by Missouri, a massive Washington rally attempted to show the justices that a majority of Americans wanted to preserve a woman's right to choose. Right-to-life forces girded for battle as well. The Court's decision in *Webster v. Reproductive Health Services* (1989) favored the right-to-life side. Missouri's restrictions on abortion, such as a ban on the use of public hospitals or employees to perform abortions except when the woman's life was in danger, were upheld by a 5–4 majority. But the Court stopped short of overturning *Roe* itself. One member of the majority, Sandra Day O'Connor, the only woman on the Supreme Court at that time, was not willing to go that far.

Closely allied with the right-to-life movement, President Bush replaced two retiring supporters of the original *Roe* decision, Justices William Brennan and Thurgood Marshall, with David Souter and Clarence Thomas. The stage seemed set for the demise of *Roe* when the Court heard the case of *Planned Parenthood of Southeastern Pennsylvania v. Casey* (1992). But in a surprise twist to the historical drama of abortion rights, *Roe* survived. Most of Pennsylvania's restrictions were sustained by the Court, imposing new obstacles to women seeking an abortion. Yet even though four justices wanted to overturn *Roe*, restoring to the states the power to prohibit abortions, the critical fifth vote was still lacking. Justice O'Connor was now joined by Justice Anthony Kennedy (a Reagan appointee) and Justice Souter in a moderate conservative bloc willing to uphold restrictions on abortion but not willing to disclaim the constitutional right of a woman to choose an abortion. In an unusual joint opinion, the three argued that *Roe* was an important precedent deserving of respect and that overturning it would diminish both the legitimacy of the Supreme Court and the public's belief in the rule of law.

For right-to-life supporters, legal disappointment in the *Casey* decision was followed by political disappointment as the first pro-choice president in twelve years, Bill Clinton, was elected in 1992. When Justice Byron White, one of the two original dissenters in *Roe*, retired in 1993, Clinton replaced him with one of the pioneer legal advocates for women's rights, Ruth Bader Ginsburg. For the time being, *Roe v. Wade* was safe from challenge.

During the Clinton presidency, right-to-life advocates focused their efforts on banning a procedure that they called partial-birth abortion. On several occasions, congressional majorities outlawed the procedure, only to be blocked by President Clinton's vetoes. In *Stenberg v. Carhart* (2000), a Nebraska ban on this type of abortion was overturned by the U.S. Supreme Court. A 5–4 majority ruled that the Nebraska law violated *Roe v. Wade* because it contained no exceptions for safeguarding the health of the pregnant woman.

Once George W. Bush replaced Bill Clinton in the White House, prospects brightened for pro-life advocates. A Partial Birth Abortion Act was signed into law by Bush in 2003. During his first term, Bush did not have the opportunity to make any Supreme Court nominations, so *Roe v. Wade* was not threatened. However, the right-to-life movement entertained hopes that new appointments to the Court during Bush's second term might bring foes of abortion the final victory that had eluded them for decades.

Civil Rights

Although this chapter highlights legal and legislative victories in the struggle for civil rights, primary credit for progress in the struggle belongs to the civil rights movement. The decades-long struggle by African Americans and their allies for civil rights not only prodded the white majority to act but also inspired similar

movements for equality among Hispanic Americans, Native Americans, Americans with disabilities, and women. These groups' victories, such as the Americans with Disabilities Act of 1990, have redeemed a basic promise of popular democracy: respect for the dignity of every citizen.

Civil rights achievements of the 1950s and 1960s, establishing the objective of a racially just and equal society, are now applauded even by those who originally opposed them. However, the methods devised to attain that objective have generated intense controversy since the end of the 1960s. As we shall see when we consider the practices of busing and affirmative action, many have come to argue that measures taken in the name of civil rights for racial minorities discriminate against the white majority. To the story of the heroic past of the struggle for civil rights must be appended the story of its painful present.

Fighting Segregation: From *Plessy* to *Brown*

Despite the constitutional amendments drafted during the Civil War and Reconstruction to protect blacks, they soon found themselves in a position of economic, political, and legal subordination. The commitment of the Fourteenth Amendment to equal protection of the laws for former slaves was mocked by a series of Supreme Court decisions refusing to enforce the amendment in the face of the southern states' new system of "Jim Crow" segregation. The last of these decisions, *Plessy v. Ferguson* (1896), established a legal justification for racial segregation that African Americans would have to combat for more than half a century.

The Supreme Court had to consider in the *Plessy* case whether a Louisiana law requiring railroads to provide **separate but equal** facilities for whites and blacks violated the equal protection of the laws. All but one of the justices found the practice legal, arguing that separation of the races did not imply that either race was unequal. If there was a stigma of black inferiority in segregation, the majority said, it was only because blacks viewed it that way. Repudiating this reasoning, the lone dissenter in the case, Justice John Marshall Harlan, offered a powerful and prophetic alternative: "The Constitution is color-blind, and neither knows nor tolerates classes among citizens."[27]

A little more than a decade later, in 1909, the **National Association for the Advancement of Colored People (NAACP)** was founded to take up the battle against racial segregation and discrimination. In the 1930s, its legal arm developed a careful, long-term strategy to demolish the separate but equal doctrine. Rather than a head-on assault on Jim Crow, which the Court was likely to rebuff, NAACP lawyers would chip away at segregation in the area of education, showing in case after case that separate facilities could not possibly be equal.[28]

The NAACP campaign finally reached fruition in ***Brown v. Board of Education of Topeka*** (1954), probably the most famous Supreme Court decision of the twentieth century. Thanks to skillful leadership by the new chief justice, Earl Warren, the Court was unanimous in rejecting the separate but equal doctrine in the field of education. The claim in the *Plessy* decision that segregation did not stamp blacks as inferior was repudiated in Warren's opinion for the Court: "Segregation of white and colored children in public schools has a detrimental effect upon the colored children. . . . A sense of inferiority affects the motivation to learn." The chief justice's concluding words marked a historic watershed for the Court and for the nation: "In the field of public education the doctrine of 'separate but equal' has no place. Separate educational facilities are inherently unequal."[29] Although the case dealt only with public schools, the *Brown* decision, reclaiming the original promise of the Fourteenth Amendment, inflicted a mortal wound on racial segregation in America.

But the death of segregation would not be swift. And the Supreme Court had to share a portion of the blame for its agonizingly slow demise. When the Court considered how to implement its decision in a second *Brown* case a year later, it was fearful of a hostile and potentially violent response by southern whites. So rather than setting a firm timetable for school desegregation, the Court returned the problem to the lower federal courts with the instruction that desegregation proceed "with all deliberate speed." These ambiguous words did not accomplish the goal of heading off southern white hostility and violence; instead, they only seemed to invite southern strategies of delay. The stage for the historic drama of civil rights now shifted from the Supreme Court to the cities and small towns of the South, where the civil rights movement, encouraged by *Brown*, would have to finish off a dying—but still powerful and violent—segregationist system.

Ending Segregation

Up to the *Brown* decision in 1954, the primary focus of the civil rights movement had been litigation, and its leading group had been the NAACP. After *Brown*, new civil rights groups emerged and intensified the pace of the struggle for equality by turning from litigation to direct action. Direct action campaigns began in 1955 with the Montgomery bus boycott, led by Martin Luther King Jr. Subsequent direct action struggles were risky, both in their use of civil disobedience to break unjust segregation laws and in the violence with which they were met by southern mobs and southern police. But these struggles were increasingly effective in riveting the attention of the North on the brutal injustices of southern segregation and in pressuring northern politicians to do something about them.

The legislative triumphs for civil rights in the mid-1960s can be traced directly to the movement campaigns that inspired them. In response to the direct action campaign of King's Southern Christian Leadership Conference in Birmingham, Alabama, President Kennedy proposed major civil rights legislation in 1963 (see Chapter 12). Passed only after his death, the **Civil Rights Act of 1964** struck a powerful blow at segregation in many areas. Its most important provisions outlawed racial discrimination in public accommodations (such as hotels and restaurants) and in employment. In response to another direct action campaign led by King and his organization in Selma, Alabama, President Johnson proposed landmark voting rights legislation early in 1965. Responding more promptly this time, Congress passed the **Voting Rights Act of 1965**. This act, removing the barriers that southern officials had placed in the way of potential black registrants, finally gave effective enforcement to the Fifteenth Amendment.[30]

As the pace of the struggle against segregation picked up in other areas, school desegregation lagged behind. By the end of the 1960s, the Supreme Court had had enough of "all deliberate speed" and was ready to order immediate desegregation. Given residential patterns that separated the races, however, significant desegregation could be accomplished only by busing schoolchildren. In the case of *Swann v. Charlotte–Mecklenburg Board of Education* (1971), a unanimous Court approved a massive busing plan for a sprawling urban/rural school district in North Carolina.

Ironically, court-ordered busing to end the perpetuation of all-white and all-black schools was more controversial in the North than in the South. Angry white parents in the North asked why their children should be bused to remedy patterns of discrimination for which they were not responsible. Despite widespread protests, federal judges ordered busing for such cities as Boston, Denver, and Los Angeles. But the limitations of busing as a remedy for racially separate schools became evident in a case from Detroit.

The phenomenon of "white flight" to the suburbs to escape an increasingly black city, combined with economic changes, left too few white children remaining in Detroit to achieve racial balance in the schools. So a federal judge ordered a busing plan that would have incorporated the city's suburbs as well as the city itself. In *Milliken v. Bradley* (1974), a 5–4 Supreme Court majority rejected the plan, arguing that suburban school districts that had not engaged in segregated practices could not be compelled to participate in a remedy for Detroit's segregation problem. Since only interdistrict desegregation plans like that in Detroit could ever achieve racial balance in the schools, the long-term result has been that African-American children are now more likely to attend an all-black school in a big city in the North than they are in the once-segregated South.

Affirmative Action

As the bitter controversy over busing receded, it was supplanted by an equally bitter debate over affirmative action. **Affirmative action** involves taking positive steps to award educational opportunities or jobs to racial minorities or women because these groups have been the victims of prior discrimination.

Supporters of affirmative action argue that simply adopting a color- or gender-blind approach won't overcome discrimination. Economist Barbara Bergmann observes that "From the 100-member U.S. Senate (92 percent male, 99 percent white, through 1996) to the nearest construction site, it is obvious that white males continue to predominate in the best positions by a wide margin."[31] Only a deliberate policy of preferential treatment for groups victimized by discrimination, supporters of affirmative action insist, can eliminate racial and gender inequities from our society. Affirmative action will open the door of opportunity for those previously excluded, allowing them at last to show what they can do.

Opponents of affirmative action argue that it goes beyond "equal protection of the laws" to promote equal results regardless of merit. Affirmative action, they say, is "reverse discrimination" against white males. Affirmative action is also accused of worsening, not improving, race relations in the United States. Former Reagan administration official Terry Eastland writes that it perpetuates "the very tendency the civil rights movement once condemned: that of regarding and judging people in terms of their racial and ethnic groups."[32] Instead of preferences for anybody, he suggests, we should insist on laws and practices that are blind to a person's color or gender.

The Supreme Court has often seemed as divided and uncertain about affirmative action as the rest of American society. The first and most famous affirmative action case to reach the Court, *Regents of the University of California v. Bakke* (1978), had an inconclusive outcome. The University of California Medical School at Davis set aside 16 of the 100 slots in its entering class for members of racial minorities. Denied admission to the medical school although his grades and test scores were higher than those of the minority students admitted, Alan Bakke sued, claiming a violation of his civil rights. A split Court rejected the idea of a fixed quota of positions for minorities and ordered Bakke's admission to the medical school. Yet the Court also ruled that taking race into consideration as part of a school's admission process was legitimate as a way of enhancing diversity in the student body.

Subsequent decisions sometimes advanced and sometimes cut back affirmative action for African Americans. Affirmative action for women was first considered by the Supreme Court in the 1987 case of *Johnson v. Santa Clara County*.

Two employees of the Santa Clara County Transportation Agency, Diane Joyce and Paul Johnson, sought promotion to a better-paying craft position as a road dispatcher. Both passed an agency test, with Johnson achieving a slightly higher score. Since women held none of the agency's 238 craft positions, Johnson was passed over, and the promotion was given to Joyce on affirmative action grounds. The Court upheld the agency, establishing that voluntary affirmative action plans can operate to end the underrepresentation of women in job categories traditionally dominated by men.

After the *Johnson* decision, affirmative action began to lose ground in the Supreme Court. In *Adarand Constructors v. Peña* (1995), a 5–4 majority ruled that government programs specifying preferential treatment based upon race are unconstitutional unless a pattern of prior discrimination against minorities can be demonstrated. Although the case involved a "set-aside" of 10 percent of Department of Transportation contracts for firms owned by minority businesspeople, the decision cast a legal cloud over most affirmative action programs, announcing that racial classification by government agencies is "inherently suspect and presumptively invalid."[33]

Affirmative action was also challenged outside the Supreme Court. In 1996, voters in California approved Proposition 209, which forbade public agencies and schools in the state from employing racial or gender preferences. A federal appeals court ruled in *Hopwood v. Texas* (1996) that the state university could not continue to admit minority students with lower grades and test scores in the name of promoting diversity.

Although affirmative action programs are increasingly in jeopardy, their goal of opening up greater opportunities for people of color and women still receives substantial support. President Clinton became a defender of affirmative action on the federal level, responding to mounting criticisms of it with the call to "mend it, don't end it." And the states of California and Texas, faced with a plunge in minority enrollments at their most prestigious public universities, have sought remedies that will maintain a diverse student population.

Unlike the Clinton administration, the administration of George W. Bush has opposed affirmative action. But in two important decisions handed down in June 2003, both of which involved affirmative action at the University of Michigan, the Supreme Court refused to endorse the administration's position. By a vote of 6–3, the Court did reject the university's affirmative action program for undergraduate admissions, which awarded extra points to those from minority groups, on the grounds that such a mechanical approach violated the standard set a quarter-century earlier in the *Bakke* decision. More important, however, the university law school's affirmative action program was upheld by a 5–4 vote in *Grutter v. Bollinger*. Writing for the majority, Justice O'Connor praised the law school's "individualized, holistic review" of applicants and harked back to the *Bakke* precedent in validating the consideration of race as one factor in admissions decisions in order to achieve a diverse student body.

Following nearly a decade of defeats for affirmative action, the *Grutter v. Bollinger* decision came as a relief to its supporters even as it angered its opponents. Affirmative action had surmounted another major challenge. Yet its survival seems precarious in view of the prospect that President Bush will fill vacancies on the Supreme Court during his second term with conservative jurists who are not likely to favor the continuance of affirmative action programs.

Equal Rights for Women

The struggle for equal rights for women has taken a different course than the civil rights struggle of African Americans. During Reconstruction, drafters of the Fifteenth Amendment excluded women on the grounds that there was not enough political support to enfranchise both black males and all females, an argument that infuriated pioneer feminist leaders Elizabeth Cady Stanton and Susan B. Anthony. It took several generations of struggle by the women's movement before women won the vote in 1920 with the Nineteenth Amendment. Having attained a goal denied for so long, the women's movement faded in strength for almost half a century.

Energized by the civil rights and New Left movements, a second women's movement sprang up in the 1960s. Modeling its strategy after the NAACP's historic campaign that led to the *Brown* decision, legal advocates from the new women's movement began to press test cases of women's rights on the Supreme Court in the early 1970s. They won some important victories. Yet there was no women's rights equivalent to *Brown*, no landmark case that established full-fledged equality for women. (The most important victory for women in the Supreme Court—*Roe v. Wade*—was decided on the grounds of a right of privacy rather than equal rights for women.)

The first women's rights cases were the easiest. In *Reed v. Reed* (1971), argued before the Court by future justice Ruth Bader Ginsburg, the unanimous justices struck down an Idaho law favoring men over women as executors of estates. In *Frontiero v. Richardson* (1973), all but one justice voted to strike down a federal statute on military pay that discriminated against women. Blatant instances of discrimination against women, the Court was now saying, violated their right to equal protection.

But what test should the Court apply in cases of less blatant gender discrimination? Recall our earlier discussion of the double standard: Most legislation is subject only to ordinary scrutiny, with government merely needing to present a reasonable basis for it, but legislation that infringes upon civil liberties and rights is subject to strict scrutiny, with the Court voiding it unless the government can prove a compelling interest. Women's rights advocates hoped that the Court would apply the same strict scrutiny in cases of discrimination against women that it used in cases of discrimination against racial minorities. But advocates were pressing this argument before the Burger Court, not the Warren Court.

In *Craig v. Boren* (1976), the women's movement fell short of its objective. At issue was an Oklahoma law that allowed women to buy beer at age eighteen but required men to wait until age twenty-one. The Court struck down the law as a violation of equal protection. But Justice Brennan could not get a majority of the Court to base this holding on strict scrutiny toward gender classifications.

The best he could obtain was the creation of a new, intermediate category: *heightened scrutiny*. A statute that classified by gender would pass muster with the Court, according to this new form of scrutiny, only if it aimed at an important government objective and substantially furthered that objective. Women's rights now had more constitutional protection than before but less than the protection enjoyed by racial minorities.

Because the women's movement has shifted its resources to defend the *Roe* decision and abortion rights, fewer sex discrimination cases are now pressed on the Supreme Court. The Rehnquist Court unanimously struck down a "fetal protection policy" through which a business excludes women from certain jobs on the grounds of hazards to pregnancy. And by a 7–1 vote it ordered the all-male Virginia Military Institute, financed by the state, to admit women. But the conservative majority is not inclined to expand the scope of civil rights for women very far.

Equal Rights for Gays and Lesbians

The civil rights movement launched what many have called a "rights revolution" in the United States. Since the 1950s, racial minorities, women, and people with disabilities have won landmark victories in the courts and in Congress. But for Americans who are gay or lesbian, recognition of equal rights has been more problematic. Although public attitudes toward gays and lesbians have been growing more tolerant, legal affirmation of their equal rights has been slow in coming. Congress and the Joint Chiefs of Staff forced President Clinton to back away from an executive order guaranteeing nondiscrimination against gays and lesbians in the military, and Clinton willingly signed a bill denying federal recognition of same-sex marriages. The U.S. Supreme Court has not always championed gay rights either.

The Supreme Court began its consideration of gay and lesbian rights in *Bowers v. Hardwick* (1986). Michael Hardwick was arrested after an Atlanta policeman, entering his bedroom to serve an arrest warrant for not paying a fine, found Hardwick engaged in homosexual conduct. Charges against Hardwick under Georgia's sodomy law were not prosecuted, but he brought a civil suit in federal court challenging the law as an invasion of his constitutionally protected right of privacy. A 5–4 Supreme Court majority rejected his challenge and upheld the sodomy law. What distinguished Hardwick's claim to privacy from those in the *Griswold* contraceptive decision and the *Roe* abortion decision? Justice Byron White, writing for the majority, stated that these decisions involved "family, marriage, or procreation." In other words, the right of privacy belongs to heterosexuals but not to homosexuals.[34]

A decade after the *Bowers* case, the Court issued a ruling more favorable to the rights of gays and lesbians. In *Romer v. Evans* (1996), a 6–3 majority struck down an amendment that voters had added to the Colorado Constitution that nullified existing local ordinances prohibiting discrimination against homosexuals and barred the state or any of its municipalities from enacting any new antidiscrimination measures on behalf of gays and lesbians. Justice Anthony Kennedy's

majority decision argued that the Colorado amendment singled out homosexuals in an unconstitutional fashion: "A state cannot so deem a class of persons a stranger to its laws."[35]

However, the decision in *Romer v. Evans* did not signal a trend toward greater acceptance of gay rights by the Supreme Court, as the case of *Boy Scouts of America v. Dale* (2000) revealed. James Dale had been an Eagle Scout and later became assistant scoutmaster for the same Boy Scout troop he had first joined at the age of eight. When a newspaper photo revealed that he was a gay rights leader at Rutgers University, however, the Boy Scouts of America dropped him from their organization. Dale filed suit and won a ruling from the New Jersey Supreme Court that the Boy Scouts' action violated state law prohibiting discrimination; the Boy Scouts appealed to the U.S. Supreme Court.

By a 5–4 majority, the Supreme Court ruled in favor of the Boy Scouts. Chief Justice William Rehnquist based the ruling on the Boy Scouts' First Amendment right to "freedom of expressive association." The organization had the right to eject Dale from his post as assistant scoutmaster because his sexual orientation clashed with the Boy Scouts' promulgation of values for young people. In his dissent, Justice John Paul Stevens argued that no persuasive evidence had been presented that having gays in the Boy Scouts would undermine the moral teachings of the organization. Dale's exclusion from the Boy Scouts, Stevens wrote, was a denial of his Fourteenth Amendment right to equal protection of the laws.[36]

Catching up a bit with evolving public attitudes, the Supreme Court reconsidered its *Bowers v. Hardwick* precedent in 2003. In a new case with facts similar to those in *Bowers*, police in Houston had arrested two men whom they observed engaging in a sexual act. But this time, in *Lawrence v. Texas*, a 6–3 majority invalidated the Texas sodomy law under which the men had been prosecuted, finally bringing gays and lesbians under the protection of the privacy doctrine. In the majority opinion, Justice Anthony Kennedy wrote that gays and lesbians "are entitled to respect for their private lives. The state cannot demean their existence or control their destiny by making their private sexual conduct a crime."[37]

The struggle for equal rights for gays and lesbians took a dramatic turn a few months after this U.S. Supreme Court decision when the Massachusetts Supreme Court, in a 4–3 decision in November 2003, ruled that same-sex couples have an equal right to marry under the state's constitution. Across the nation, social conservatives were outraged by the court's decision, while supporters of gay rights rushed to build upon it by holding same-sex marriage ceremonies in San Francisco and several other cities and towns outside Massachusetts. Recognizing the electoral potential in the issue of gay and lesbian marriage, President Bush proposed a constitutional amendment that would define marriage as limited to the union of a man and a woman. Although the amendment was defeated in Congress, it appears to have helped Bush win a second term. The lack of public support for same-sex marriage was underscored on Election Day 2004, when measures to ban it passed in all eleven states where they appeared on the ballot. The election results of 2004 make it likely that equal rights for gays and lesbians will not only remain a thorny issue for the courts, but a flash point in the ongoing culture wars between conservatives and liberals as well.

Conclusion: The Struggle over Liberties and Rights

Americans can legitimately take pride in the civil liberties and civil rights they enjoy today. Yet these liberties and rights are the result of long struggles and only recent landmark advances: free speech (1960s), rights of persons accused of crimes (1960s), right of privacy (1960s and 1970s), equal rights for blacks (1950s), and equal rights for women (1970s). The newness of the critical Supreme Court precedents and the political backlash that has trimmed back several and tried to overturn others indicate that the struggle over the definition of American liberties and rights is far from ended.

Both elite democrats and popular democrats have a checkered past in the area of civil liberties and civil rights. Elite democrats in positions of power, while mouthing rhetorical support for American liberties, have moved to limit them in times of crisis and challenge. Popular democrats have often backed and applauded the repressive measures that elites have instituted. Yet some elite democrats and some popular democrats have done better. Judicial champions of civil liberties and civil rights have understood how fundamental these freedoms and powers are to the creation and maintenance of a democratic society. Popular democratic forces (Anti-federalists, abolitionists, New Deal populists, blacks, and feminists) have fought to establish civil liberties and civil rights in the first place as well as to bring before the courts the cases that will broaden their definition and scope.

Given that a majority of ordinary Americans may not support civil liberties and civil rights when they protect unpopular individuals or groups, individuals committed to the values of popular democracy must recognize the responsibilities of democratic education. In the spirit of the tradition initiated by the Anti-federalists, they must remind others of the importance of an open and tolerant society, where new and unconventional ideas can circulate freely, where reigning elites can be challenged, where that spark of protest that launched the American revolutionary experiment can enlighten and revitalize American democracy. And with an emphasis on the importance of citizenship, popular democrats cannot rest content merely with the defense of American liberties and rights. They must also encourage other citizens to make active use of them.

In the aftermath of the terrorist attacks of September 11, 2001, civil liberties in the United States are again a focus for democratic debate. During past national crises, such as the Civil War, World Wars I and II, and the Cold War, the authority of government over citizens was expanded as the rights of individuals and groups deemed dangerous to such authority were curtailed. With the new war on terrorism, the Bush administration has staked a broad claim to greater executive power, and defenders of civil liberties have had only a few successes in countering that claim. With its shadowy foe and indefinite duration, the war on terror will pose a major test of Americans' commitment to their fundamental liberties.

KEY TERMS

civil liberties
civil rights
American Civil Liberties Union
  (ACLU)
Civil War amendments
footnote 4
strict scrutiny
incorporation
clear and present danger test
McCarthyism
symbolic speech
unprotected speech
obscenity
prior restraint
Establishment Clause

Lemon test
Free Exercise Clause
exclusionary rule
Miranda warnings
right of privacy
Roe v. Wade
separate but equal
National Association for the
  Advancement of Colored
  People (NAACP)
*Brown v. Board of Education
  of Topeka*
Civil Rights Act of 1964
Voting Rights Act of 1965
affirmative action

INTERNET RESOURCES

▧ American Civil Liberties Union
www.aclu.org
The ACLU, the nation's oldest civil liberties organization, provides numerous resources and links on issues of civil liberties and civil rights.

▧ The American Center for Law and Justice
www.aclj.org
A Christian legal foundation that provides information and links on school prayer and other issues.

▧ Center for Equal Opportunity
www.ceousa.org
A conservative organization for the promotion of "colorblind" public policies. CEO's website concentrates on issues of racial preferences, immigration, and multicultural education.

SUGGESTED READINGS

Barbara Bergmann, *In Defense of Affirmative Action*. New York: Basic Books, 1996. An economist presents a detailed case for affirmative action.

Terry Eastland, *Ending Affirmative Action: The Case for Colorblind Justice*. New York: Basic Books, 1996. A former official in the Reagan administration presents the arguments against affirmative action.

Peter Irons, *The Courage of Their Convictions: Sixteen Americans Who Fought Their Way to the Supreme Court*. New York: Penguin Books, 1990. Portraits of ordinary Americans who tested the meaning of civil liberties and civil rights.

Richard C. Leone and Greg Anrig Jr., *The War on Our Freedoms: Civil Liberties in an Age of Terrorism*. New York: Public Affairs, 2003. An anthology of essays by prominent critics of the Bush administration's approach to homeland security.

John Witte Jr., *Religion and the American Constitutional Experiment*. Boulder, Colo.: Westview Press, 1999. A comprehensive treatment of religious liberty issues.

17

Economic and Social Policy
The Democratic Connections

Joe considers himself a "self-made" man; personal responsibility is his motto. After putting himself through college by working night jobs, Joe worked for an oil company until he saved enough money to start his own business, a successful truck stop. Within a few years he built a spacious home, much of it with his own hands. Having put aside money for retirement in a successful 401(k) account, Joe wonders why the government does not allow workers to invest their Social Security taxes in personal accounts. Joe often thinks about all the things he could do with the taxes he pays, and he votes for politicians who promise to cut taxes and end welfare.

Although Joe is a fictional character, he reflects the Horatio Alger[1] myth that is so widespread in American society: the idea that through hard work and the right moral values anyone can go from rags to riches. Many Americans believe in the myth of the self-made man, but upon closer inspection, it is just that: a myth.

Consider a typical day in Joe's life. He gets up in the morning and eats a breakfast of bacon and eggs, comfortable in the knowledge that the meat is safe to eat because federal inspectors guarantee it. When he gets into his car, made safer by federal safety standards, he rides on highways paid for by taxpayers. His truck stop would never be profitable if it were not strategically located on an off-ramp of the federal interstate highway that was built through town twenty years ago. On the way home from work, Joe visits his mother, who, to his surprise, has lived to the ripe age of ninety. Joe would never have been able to pay for her nursing care, but fortunately, after spending down her assets, Joe was able to put her on Medicaid, which now pays her medical bills. Her only source of income is Social Security, provided by—you guessed it!—the federal government. On his way back from the retirement home, Joe swings by the local public school, where he picks up his two sons, and then drops off some videos at the public library. As he pulls into the driveway of his spacious new home, made affordable by his ability to deduct the mortgage interest and property taxes on his federal income taxes, Joe is listening to a talk-radio host railing against high taxes and welfare chiselers . . . and Joe's blood begins to boil.

Joe's case may be exaggerated, but it is not far from the truth for many Americans who believe, mistakenly, that they would be much better off if the government would just "leave them alone." Americans celebrate the free market and increasingly view it as the epitome of freedom and democracy. On this view the consumer is sovereign in the private market, but in the public sector citizens are told what to do by elitist planners and social engineers. The idea that taxes are unjust and government is oppressive has gone so far that Daniel Mitchell of the Heritage Foundation compared offshore tax evaders to civil rights protestors, to "Rosa Parks sitting in the back of the bus."[2]

In this chapter we challenge the myth of the self-made man and develop a popular democratic analysis of economic and social policies that recognizes the need for a balance between individual choice in the market and group choices in government. Few Americans want a society where government is all-powerful; markets provide a crucial safety valve in a democracy, a sphere where individuals can express their own tastes and values. But none of us is "self-made." We all depend on government for a high quality of life. Ultimately, democracy is about deliberating with others to make decisions about the things we share. Too often today government is viewed as just another service provider, like private corporations, and public policies are evaluated based on how they make us feel as consumers. Here, we argue, public policies should be evaluated not just on their efficiency or their value to the individual but on whether they impede or enhance democratic participation and inclusiveness.

POLICY DEBATES: THE DEMOCRATIC DIMENSION

Elite democrats view economic and social policy through the lens of free market economics. According to free market economics, consumers drive the marketplace, and corporations must meet consumer demand in the most efficient manner possible or be driven out of business. The implication is that economic policy should be left in the hands of experts, with only broad guidelines coming from ordinary citizens and their political representatives. Like Plato's guardians who rise above private interests through training in philosophy, economic experts are supposedly able, through disciplined study of the laws of economics, to transcend private interests and see what is necessary to make the economy as a whole function effectively. Economics claims to be, like physics, a value-free and objective science. Consistent with the elite democratic view of human nature, it views modern economies as driven by the private interests of consumers and producers whose behavior can be predicted with precision. Economically trained policy makers are like expert watchmakers, who, having studied how all the gears in the market mechanism function, understand what policies are needed to ensure that it runs smoothly.

Elite democrats view social policies very differently from economic policies. With social policies there is more room for democratic input because our values for compassion and equality will vary. Most Americans believe government should help those who cannot help themselves. However, if free market economists are right and economic progress is driven by private interests, then there is an unavoidable trade-off between equality and efficiency. Too much equality lowers the incentive to work and invest, thereby damaging efficiency. Responding to mass pressure, politicians will be tempted to massively redistribute wealth, thus killing the engine of investment, or to spend money on popular programs without raising taxes, resulting in ruinous inflation. Thus, elite democrats conclude, popular control over social, and especially economic, policies should be limited.

Popular democrats view economic policy very differently, and this difference is rooted in how they view markets. They reject the view that economic progress is driven solely by self-interest in the private market. Instead of viewing the economy as a mechanism, which can be guided by nonpolitical experts, popular democrats view it more like a plant, with roots deeply embedded in social and political relations. The mechanistic treatment of the economy, they say, ignores the human factor. Economic policies have profound social and political implications: They determine which investments are profitable and which are not, and they affect the life chances of different groups in the population, the viability of whole communities, and, most important, the prospects for democratic participation and community control.

The popular democratic view implies that in choosing economic policies the experts should be held accountable to ordinary citizens and their political representatives. The trade-offs of economic policy should be debated in an open, democratic fashion — not hidden behind the veil of economic "science." Popular democrats do not believe that expanding democracy into economic policy making will lead to incoherent policies, causing problems for the economy. They believe that people are capable of overcoming their parochial interests through democratic participation. On the contrary, they say, it is the isolation of economic policy in the hands of selfish elites, who are removed from the pain caused by their policies, that results in destructive economic policies. More-democratic economic policy making would be better economic policy making.

Popular democrats also view social policy very differently from elite democrats. Whereas elite democrats blame most poverty on the poor themselves, popular democrats tend to blame poverty on conditions in the environment.

Popular democrats assume that given the proper circumstances, everyone wants to work and contribute to society. If some people are excluded from their fair share in the economy, it must be because of structural defects in the economic system. Popular democrats deny that there is a steep and unavoidable trade-off between equality and growth. In fact, too much inequality can hurt growth by demoralizing those at the bottom and undermining the belief that anybody can get ahead through hard work. Too much inequality also causes social problems which all of us ultimately pay for.

According to popular democrats, the goal of social policies should not just be to provide a minimum standard of living but to provide everyone with the re-sources necessary to become full and equal participants in society. People who are worried about where their next meal will come from are hardly in a position to become active democratic citizens. Poverty is a problem in a democracy not just because some people lack resources, but because the gap between the rich and the poor widens to the point that it undermines political equality. Too much inequality threatens democracy because it gives the rich the resources to domi-nate and demoralize the poor and working classes, thus distorting democracy.

In short, popular democrats aim to subject economic and social policies to democratic standards. The goal should not be just greater GNP per capita or even the alleviation of poverty, but a more inclusive democracy in which no group feels excluded or dominated.

THE DEMOCRATIC DEBATE OVER THE MONEY SUPPLY

Governments are responsible for establishing the basic conditions for smooth-functioning markets; the decisions that establish these conditions are called **macroeconomic policy**. These policies are designed to fine-tune the national economy as a whole while not altering the distribution of economic activity across different sectors, classes, or places. Macroeconomic policies aim to mod-erate the booms and busts of capitalism, making sure that the economy does not grow too fast (causing high inflation) or too slow (causing high unemployment). There are two basic kinds of macroeconomic policies: **Fiscal policy** uses the government's taxing and spending policies to speed up or slow down the econ-omy; **monetary policy** uses government's control over the money supply (the amount of money in circulation) to achieve the same results. We start with monetary policy.

Throughout U.S. history, elite and popular democrats have debated the money supply. Elite democrats have favored *tight money policies*. With fewer dol-lars "chasing" a fixed or expanding supply of goods, prices remain stable or even fall. Falling prices—*deflation*—characterized most of the late nineteenth cen-tury.[3] Deflation is good for those who are owed money (bondholders and bank lenders) because they are paid back in more valuable dollars. Falling prices are not good for those who are in debt because they find it more and more difficult to pay back their debts. For this reason, popular democrats have favored expanding the money supply. In the nineteenth century, farmers found themselves squeezed between falling prices for their crops and rising interest rates for the money they had to borrow to buy land and finance spring planting. Farmers agitated to increase the money supply by having the federal government issue "greenbacks" or use silver, in addition to gold, to back up the currency. To this day, the conflict between wealthy investors and the mass of debtors and businesspeople needing credit remains at the heart of the democratic debate over the money supply.

The main institution responsible for regulating the money supply is the **Federal Reserve**, created in 1913. President Woodrow Wilson compromised with the bankers by creating a unique institution that combined the private powers of bankers with the public powers of government. In 1935, after criticism that contraction of the money supply had contributed to the Great Depression, the Federal Reserve—or "Fed," as it is called—expanded its mission and took full charge of controlling the nation's money supply.

The Federal Reserve is run by a seven-member board of governors appointed by the president for fourteen-year terms with the advice and consent of the Senate. The chair serves a four-year term. To carry out its policies, the Fed relies on twelve regional banks, which are private institutions owned by the approximately 6,000 commercial banks that participate in the Federal Reserve system. The most important policy-making body at the Fed is the *Federal Open Market Committee* (FOMC), which basically determines the nation's money supply and powerfully influences interest rates. The FOMC is made up of the seven members of the Board of Governors, appointed by the president, and the presidents of five regional banks, who are appointed by the commercial banks. The key decision-making body, then, is a mixture of private interests and public authority. As Representative Lee H. Hamilton, an Indiana Democrat, put the matter in 1991, "Nowhere else in the Government are private individuals permitted to participate in decisions which have such an enormous influence over the prosperity and well-being of millions of Americans."[4]

The basic mechanisms by which the Fed controls the money supply are quite simple: The American economy can be thought of as a gigantic plumbing system, with money circulating through the pipes at various rates and pressures. The Fed is the hydraulic engineer, who by turning various valves can either expand or contract the flow of money in the system. Three basic valves control the amount of money in circulation:

1. *The discount rate*: Banks that are members of the Federal Reserve system can borrow money from one of the twelve regional banks when they need additional reserves. The discount rate is the interest rate at which member banks can borrow. Lowering the discount rate makes it less expensive for banks to make new loans, thus increasing the money supply.

2. *Reserve requirements*: The Fed specifies what proportion of a bank's deposits must be held in reserve and cannot be loaned out. Increasing the reserve requirement restricts the ability of banks to make new loans, essentially reducing the money supply.

3. *Open market transactions*: The Fed can buy or sell U.S. government securities, which are Treasury bonds originally sold by the U.S. government to finance the budget deficit. When the Fed buys Treasury bonds, the money is simply credited to the accounts of the former owners of the bonds in one of the Federal Reserve banks. These funds are counted as additions to the reserves of the bank, which is now free to make more loans, increasing the money supply.

Under the Federal Reserve system, the money supply in the United States is firmly under the control of elites, with little democratic accountability. Proponents of this system argue that control over the money supply must be left in the hands of experts who understand how to protect the long-term interests of the American economy. If politicians were in control, elite democrats argue, they would be tempted to increase the money supply to stimulate the economy right before an election to benefit the mass of debtors. The result would be runaway *inflation*, rising prices. Fearing that their returns on investments would be eroded by inflation, people would pull their money out of productive investments and put it into consumption, foreign investments, or speculation in gold or other commodities. Lacking productive investment, economic growth would stagnate, hurting everybody.

Popular democrats reply that the interests of Wall Street are different from the interests of Main Street. The Fed's tight money policies help only a small financial elite. In 2001 the top 10 percent of households held 80 percent of all net financial assets; about half of all households own no stock in any form and close to half have net worth (assets minus debt) of less than $10,000.[5] Tight money, popular democrats argue, acts like a regressive tax, redistributing wealth from debtors to creditors. The shortage of credit curbs business expansion, especially hurting small businesses and farmers, who depend on credit to see them through tough times. Finally, tight money damages sectors of the economy, like home and auto sales, that are dependent on the easy availability of credit.

Popular democrats especially object to keeping unemployment high to fight inflation. Many economists argue that there is a *nonaccelerating inflation rate of unemployment* (NAIRU). If the unemployment rate falls below a certain level — say, 6 percent — tight labor markets will enable workers to demand higher wages, causing inflation. Critics like University of Texas economist James Galbraith argue that no one knows what the NAIRU is. NAIRU simply enables the Fed to shroud its political choices in technical mumbo jumbo.

Reforming the Fed

Because of his leadership position in setting monetary policy, which is crucial to the performance of the economy, the chairman of the Federal Reserve Board has been called "the second most powerful man in the United States" (so far, all have been men). In 1979, President Jimmy Carter, under pressure from Wall Street, appointed Paul Volcker as chairman of the Federal Reserve.[6] During Volcker's tenure, the Federal Reserve came under the influence of an economic doctrine called **monetarism**. Led by Nobel Prize–winning economist Milton Friedman, monetarists argued that if the money supply grows only as fast as the productivity of the economy, the result will be steady growth and stable prices. Using monetarist formulas, the Fed embarked on a series of swift policy shifts that sent the U.S. economy on a roller-coaster ride. The Fed began by severely restricting the growth of the money supply, driving interest rates up to record levels. The prime rate, the rate paid by the best commercial borrowers, peaked at 20 percent. High interest rates were a major factor in Carter's 1980 defeat by Ronald Reagan. The Fed's policies did succeed in licking inflation: The increase in the *Consumer Price Index* (what consumers pay for goods and services) fell from 13.5 percent in 1980 to 1.9 percent in 1986. This victory was acquired at great cost, however; in the early 1980s the country suffered the worst recession since the Great Depression, with unemployment reaching 9.7 percent in 1982.

Even though monetarists claimed that the costs of Fed policies were fairly distributed by free markets, in fact the costs fell unequally on the American people. The manufacturing sector was hit hardest and older industrial cities, like Cleveland and Milwaukee, were devastated. Small businesses and farmers, who depend on debt, were squeezed. Bankruptcies soared. Meanwhile, returns on capital nearly doubled as a proportion of total income, from 11 percent in 1979 to 20 percent in 1984.[7] Inequality soared.

Volcker's successor was Alan Greenspan, who was appointed by President Reagan in 1987 and held the position until late 2005, when President Bush nominated his successor, Ben Bernanke, Princeton University economics professor. Greenspan served under four presidents, including one Democrat, Clinton, and

Mike Ramirez/Copley News Service.

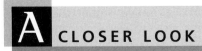

Alan Greenspan: Elite Democrat in Action

On December 5, 1996, the chairman of the Federal Reserve Board, Alan Greenspan, gave a speech in Washington referring to the recent upsurge in stock prices as an instance of "irrational exuberance." Based on fears that this statement signaled the Fed's intention to raise interest rates in order to cool down an overheated economy, stock markets around the world were sent reeling. This incident demonstrates the incredible power of the Fed chair, as well as the problem with putting so much power into one person's hands.

The son of a New York stockbroker, Greenspan was endowed with precocious mathematical abilities; at the age of five, he could reproduce the batting averages of major league ballplayers. After attending graduate school in economics, Greenspan helped found a prosperous economic consulting firm, finally earning his Ph.D. in 1977. He entered government in 1974, when President Nixon nominated him to be chair of the Council of Economic Advisers, a post he assumed the day Nixon left office and continued in under President Ford. In 1987, President Reagan appointed him chair of the Federal Reserve Board.

Greenspan has been a politically shrewd and powerful Fed chair. A close friend and protege of Ayn Rand, the libertarian philosopher and novelist, Greenspan is deeply conservative and hostile to government. "I do not consider the minimum wage a positive force," he told Congress in 1998. In public, however, he rarely discusses his political ideology. Instead, using the classical legitimating device of modern elite democrats, Greenspan stresses his expertise and knowledge of obscure economic statistics that supposedly enable him to predict the economic future. In testimony before Congress, Greenspan drones on about economic statistics in what one journalist called "soporific syntax," leaving committee members drowsy, befuddled, or both.

Greenspan has been frequently attacked for being more concerned about fighting inflation, which is good for banks and stockholders, than about increasing jobs and wages, which is good for ordinary workers. Many argue that Greenspan's slow-growth policies contributed to the defeats of President Ford in 1976 and President Bush in 1992.

Ironically, Republican Greenspan became especially influential under a Democratic president. A

became one of the most powerful Fed chairmen in history. (See the "A Closer Look" box.) Many observers credit Greenspan with engineering the longest continuous economic expansion in American history during the late 1990s. With a reputation as the nation's premier inflation fighter, Greenspan was popular on Wall Street. In classic elite democratic fashion Greenspan's policies frequently sacrificed job growth to fight inflation.

Over time, however, Greenspan became an advocate of what is called the New Economy—the idea that investments in new information technologies have increased productivity so much that the Fed faces a completely different situation than under the old industrial economy. Productivity increases fund noninflationary wage increases, and increased global competition restrains both price increases and wage demands. As a result, NAIRU—the unemployment month after Clinton's 1992 victory, Greenspan met with the president-elect in Little Rock, Arkansas. Taking advantage of Clinton's well-known policy "wonkism," Greenspan spent two and a half hours deploying his incredible knowledge of economic statistics to persuade Clinton that the first priority of his administration should be deficit reduction. Only this way could long-term interest rates be brought down, Greenspan argued, boosting investment and growth. To the disappointment of liberals in his administration like Labor Secretary Robert Reich, Clinton gave up his campaign promise for massive new public investments in areas like job training and infrastructure in favor of a deficit-reduction package that included spending cuts and tax increases.

A month after he assumed office, Clinton announced the plan in a speech before a joint session of Congress. Seated in the audience, right between Hillary Clinton and Tipper Gore, the vice president's wife, was Greenspan. The media widely reported this fact as a symbol that Greenspan, and Wall Street, approved of Clinton's plan. Subsequently, Greenspan testified in Congress in favor of Clinton's deficit-reduction package, which ultimately passed the Senate by one vote. No one was surprised when Clinton reappointed Greenspan to a third term in 1996.

Greenspan angered Democrats by endorsing President George W. Bush's massive tax cuts that sent the deficit soaring, even though Greenspan had earlier been a vigorous proponent of deficit reduction. Later, Greenspan endorsed Bush's proposal for private investment accounts under Social Security. An angry Senate Minority Leader Harry Reid (D.–Nev.) called Greenspan "one of the biggest political hacks in Washington."

Greenspan's career is a classic study of how elite democrats use claims of expertise to insulate decision making from democratic input. Clearly, expertise must play an important role in regulating the money supply. But Greenspan's claim that his decisions are based on nothing but the facts hides the basic fact that they involve unavoidable trade-offs between inflation and unemployment that have no technical solution. In the late 1990s Greenspan presided over one of the longest sustained economic expansions in American history, but it was also a period characterized by ever-widening gaps between the rich and the poor.

Sources: Bob Woodward, *Maestro: Greenspan's Fed and the American Boom* (New York: Simon & Schuster, 2000); Keith Bradsher, "The Art and Science of Alan Greenspan," *New York Times*, January 4, 1996; "Greenspin," *Newsday*, March 13, 2005.

rate the economy can sustain without triggering inflation—is lower. Under Greenspan's leadership, the Fed cut interest rates five times early in 2001 in an effort to sustain the expansion, even though unemployment was still low by historical standards. However, in 2004–2005 the Fed began steadily raising interest rates even though inflation was relatively low.

Controversies over interest rates have prompted many calls for reform of the Fed, which is hardly a democratic institution. First, five of the twelve voting members of the FOMC, which sets monetary policy, represent private banks and have no democratic accountability. Moreover, FOMC's deliberations are secret; only summaries of the meetings are released six weeks later. The independence and power of the Fed depend, in part, on effective political leadership by the chair of the Board of Governors.[8] But Congress and the president have always hesitated to put greater controls on the Fed for fear they will be accused of undermining the confidence of the financial markets.

In 1993, Representative Henry B. Gonzalez (D.–Texas) held hearings to democratize the Federal Reserve. He proposed a bill that would have required the president to appoint the twelve regional bank presidents, forced more timely and detailed records of the meetings, and expanded opportunities for women, minorities, and nonbankers to serve as regional bank directors. Having the president appoint the regional presidents would end the practice of having representatives of the private banks make public policy. Studies have shown that the private bankers on the FOMC vote for tighter money more frequently than do the presidential appointees.[9] Not surprisingly, Greenspan was a vehement opponent of reforming the Fed, arguing that it would then be subject to undue political pressure. With interest rates in 1993 at thirty-year lows, President Clinton had little reason to oppose the Fed and came out against Gonzalez's reforms, which died in committee.

Fiscal Policy: The Rise and Fall of the Keynesian Consensus

Besides regulating the money supply, governments can also use their taxing and spending powers to control the booms and busts of capitalist economies. English economist John Maynard Keynes (1883–1946) promoted the idea of having the government deliberately engineer a deficit by spending more than it received in tax revenues to pull the economy out of a depression. His classic work *The General Theory of Employment, Interest, and Money* (1936) argued that capitalist economies do not have a natural tendency to employ all the nation's workers and achieve full productive capacity because consumers cannot buy all the products that a fully operating economy would produce. At a certain stage of the business cycle, Keynes argued, the savings rate is too high, leaving too little money for consumption. Keynes's solution was for the government to use fiscal policy, its control over taxing and spending, to make the economy perform at maximum capacity. When the economy begins to fall into a recession, the government stimulates consumer demand by spending *more* than it takes in through taxes. Deficit spending heats up the economy, putting people and productive capacity back to work. When demand is too high and an overheated economy begins to cause inflation, the government deliberately spends *less* than it takes in, cooling off the economy. (Keynes did not endorse, as some have attributed to him, a string of budget deficits, even in prosperous times, such as the United States has had in recent years.)

Keynesianism dominated economic policy making in the major industrial countries after World War II. Although Keynes's theory encouraged governments to take an active role in smoothing out the business cycle, it did not require any direct interventions in markets. Keynes called for manipulating the overall level of consumer demand, but he said nothing about how that consumer demand should be distributed. Thus, Keynesianism was a theory that could be embraced by both the left and the right. European governments used Keynes's ideas to justify redistributing wealth through progressive taxes and social spending, a scheme based partly on the notion that giving more resources to those at the bottom would result in immediate increases in consumer demand because poor people save little.

In the United States, Keynesianism was applied in a less egalitarian manner to justify what has been called "military Keynesianism" and "business Keynesianism." Deficits were created by boosting military spending and by cutting taxes on business. The Kennedy tax cuts for investors, passed in 1964, were sold to the public, Congress, and the business community on explicitly Keynesian grounds. With the economy doing well in the 1960s, there was a broad consensus behind Keynesianism and an optimistic feeling that fiscal policy could be used to fine-tune the economy and prevent disastrous economic downturns. In a 1971 *Newsweek* cover story, President Nixon famously proclaimed, "We are all Keynesians now."

SUPPLY-SIDE ECONOMICS AND ITS CRITICS

With the economic troubles of the 1970s, the Keynesian consensus began to crumble. The problems of the U.S. economy did not appear to be the result of too much saving. Indeed, the savings rate was tumbling, and the soaring trade deficit seemed to be caused in part by inadequate savings and investment in the latest production technologies. For the first time, increases in the productivity of American workers lagged behind those of other countries. The problem seemed to lie not in underconsumption but in underinvestment.

Many economists began to move from a demand-side explanation of these economic troubles to a supply-side analysis. **Supply-side economics** argues that the cause of the economic problems is a capital shortage—that we need to reduce consumption and put more of our resources into productive investment. Supply-siders especially stress that we are consuming too much in the way of government services and that a bloated public sector serves as a drag on economic growth. High levels of taxation and government regulation reduce incentives to work hard, innovate, and invest.

Paradoxically, supply-siders stress that the best way to reduce the federal deficit is to *reduce* taxes, not increase them. This idea is based on the **Laffer curve**, which economist Arthur B. Laffer first drew in 1974 on a cocktail napkin in a Washington restaurant. Laffer argued that, above a certain point, increasing tax rates actually decreased total tax revenues because of the disincentive effects on productive effort. Tax rates were so high in the United States, Laffer argued, that by decreasing tax rates the country could move down the Laffer curve, unleashing an explosion of productive effort that would increase tax revenues. Laffer's ideas were popularized by Jude Wanniski, an editorial writer for the *Wall Street Journal*. Wanniski later remarked that after seeing the Laffer curve on the cocktail napkin, "it hit me as a wonderful propaganda device" for persuading policy makers to cut tax rates.[10]

As candidate for president in 1980, Ronald Reagan enthusiastically embraced the tenets of supply-side economics. To illustrate the disincentive effects of high taxes, Reagan was fond of telling the story that when the marginal income tax rate hit 94 percent during World War II, he stopped making movies. Inspired by supply-side economics, Reagan succeeded in enacting massive tax cuts in his **Economic Recovery Tax Act of 1981**. Individual tax rates were cut 23 percent over a three-year period, the marginal tax rate on the highest income group was cut from 70 percent to 50 percent, and a series of tax breaks for investors was written into law.

Reaganomics did not work as expected to decrease the federal budget deficit by reducing tax rates and stimulating the economy. Shortly after taking office, Reagan promised that his economic policies would balance the budget by 1984, but lower tax revenues combined with significant increases in defense spending resulted in the largest budget deficits in history to that point (see Figure 17.1). Most economists believe that the United States was not so far out on the Laffer curve that reducing tax rates would increase total revenue. In fact, as a proportion of the overall economy, taxes in the United States are significantly lower than in almost every other advanced industrial country (see Figure 17.2). There

FIGURE 17.1 **Federal Budget Surpluses and Deficits, 1950–2004**

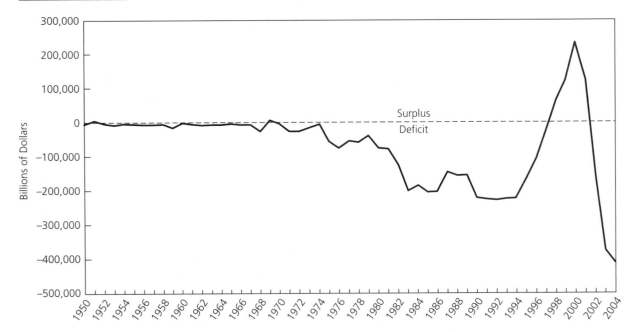

Source: Budget of the United States Government: Historical Tables, Fiscal Year 2006, Executive Office of the President of the United States, 2005 (www.gpoaccess.gov/usbudget/fy06/sheets/hist01z1.xls).

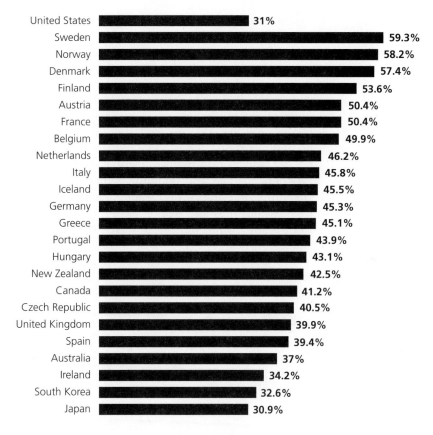

FIGURE 17.2

Tax Receipts as a Percentage of GDP, 2003

Country	Percentage
United States	31%
Sweden	59.3%
Norway	58.2%
Denmark	57.4%
Finland	53.6%
Austria	50.4%
France	50.4%
Belgium	49.9%
Netherlands	46.2%
Italy	45.8%
Iceland	45.5%
Germany	45.3%
Greece	45.1%
Portugal	43.9%
Hungary	43.1%
New Zealand	42.5%
Canada	41.2%
Czech Republic	40.5%
United Kingdom	39.9%
Spain	39.4%
Australia	37%
Ireland	34.2%
South Korea	32.6%
Japan	30.9%

Source: U.S. Bureau of the Census, *Statistical Abstract of the United States, 2004–2005* (Washington, D.C.: U.S. Government Printing Office, 2004), p. 857.

is little evidence that the supply-side tax cuts significantly increased work effort, the savings rate, or investment.[11]

The experience of the Clinton administration casts more doubt on supply-side economics. Bill Clinton ran for president in 1992 promising a middle-class tax cut and an ambitious program of public investments in infrastructure and job training to "put America back to work" that would cost the federal government an additional $50 billion per year.[12] There appeared little prospect of significant progress on the deficit. But under the influence of conservatives in his administration, including Wall Street financier Robert Rubin, who became Clinton's Secretary of the Treasury, Clinton sacrificed most of his domestic agenda in order to reduce the deficit.[13] Giving up his promised middle-class tax cut, in 1993 Clinton increased the top tax rate on high-income earners from 31 percent to 39.6 percent. Supply-siders predicted that the economy would go into a tailspin and tax revenues would shrink. Just the opposite happened: The economy boomed and so did tax revenues. In 1997 Clinton engineered a compromise tax increase, and in 1998 that federal government enjoyed its first budget surplus in almost thirty years. Clinton can take some credit for the dramatic shift from deficits to surpluses, but most of the credit must go to the booming economy spurred by the tremendous productivity gains that resulted from investments in computer technology.

George W. Bush came to office in 2001 facing the pleasant prospect of huge budget surpluses almost as far as the eye could see. The Congressional Budget Office projected they would total almost $10 trillion over ten years. Three developments, however, soon transformed budget surpluses into the largest budget deficits in American history: (1) The 9/11 terrorist attacks, (2) a steep economic decline, and (3) massive tax cuts. The terrorist attacks not only provoked the American invasions of Afghanistan and Iraq that drained the federal treasury, but they also helped push the economy into a recession. The biggest cause of the surging deficits, however, was the huge Bush tax cuts passed in 2001 and 2003.

Bush's first tax cut, signed into law in 2001, is estimated to cost as much as $2.1 trillion over a ten-year period. Tax rates were cut at all levels of income,

TOLES © 2005 The Washington Post. Reprinted with permission of UNIVERSAL PRESS SYNDICATE. All rights reserved.

with the highest bracket falling from 39.6 percent to 35 percent. The most controversial was the repeal of the estate tax, which was phased in over ten years. In 2003, Bush pushed through the Republican Congress another massive tax cut that sharply cut taxes on dividend income and will cost the federal treasury over $100 billion a year. Bush defended his deficits on supply-side grounds, claiming that economic growth stimulated by the tax cuts would cut the budget deficit in half within five years. If present trends continue, however, and the expensive occupation of Iraq drags on, there is every reason to believe that the sea of red ink will continue to grow. The 2003–2004 budget deficit hit a record $413 billion (see Figure 17.1). The prediction of supply-side economics, that cuts in taxes will lead to more tax receipts, has not come true. Concerned that massive government borrowing will drive up interest rates and soak up capital that could be put to productive use in the private economy, business economists in a recent poll ranked deficits as the number one threat to the country—ahead of terrorism.[14]

THE POLITICS OF TAXATION

Supply-side economics suggests that tax cuts can pay for themselves, that choosing to cut taxes is not a political issue because everybody is a winner. In fact, tax cuts always produce losers as well as winners. Tax cuts affect different economic classes differently, and if politicians cut taxes, they will need to cut spending as well or go further into debt. (Politicians rarely make explicit the connection between tax cuts and spending cuts.) Thus, tax policy should be a conscious political choice, and it can favor elite democracy, or it can favor popular democracy.

The popular democratic view of taxes is that they should be **progressive**, meaning that the tax rate should increase as income increases. A tax is called **regressive** if people in lower income brackets pay higher rates. The rationale behind progressive taxation is that the heaviest burden should be borne by those with the greatest ability to pay. Bush's tax cuts are highly regressive. In his first tax cut, 36 percent of the savings went to the richest 1 percent, while only 20 percent of the benefits went to the bottom 60 percent.[15] Overall, the two tax cuts provided an average tax savings for those in the bottom 20 percent of only $61 and an average saving for those in the top 1 percent of $66,601.[16]

One political puzzle is how Bush was able to push through tax cuts that went overwhelmingly to the super-wealthy. The repeal of the estate tax, as part of the 2001 tax cut, is an especially troubling case. The entire tax savings of the repeal, which was phased in so that the tax would disappear completely in 2010, would go to the top 2 percent of estates. Two political scientists charged that "the temporary 2001 estate tax repeal may be the single most regressive change to a tax code passed by a democratic legislature in the history of the world."[17]

Repeal succeeded, against the economic interests of the vast majority of the American people, because a well-funded coalition representing the interests of the wealthy was able to frame repeal as a populist cause representing pro-family farmers and small-business owners against oppressive and insatiable governmental elites. The repeal effort was led by the Family Business Estate Tax Coalition, consisting of over a hundred business associations, which coordinated efforts with wealthy individuals and newspaper publishers. They spent millions on a grassroots lobbying campaign, or what we referred to in Chapter 9 as astroturf lobbying. Recognizing that most Americans would not support repeal on strictly economic terms, the repeal coalition took pains to construct a negative image for estate taxes. The most important move was to label the estate tax the "death tax." The Republican leadership even issued a directive to its members in Congress to only use the term "death tax," and one Republican strategist recommended staging press conferences at the local mortuary. Many Americans supported repeal because they came to view the "death tax" as immoral—as the government taking advantage of families during their time of grief.

The repeal coalition also worked to create the impression that the tax affected many more people than it actually did. They repeatedly claimed that large numbers of small-business owners and farmers would be forced to liquidate the family businesses to pay the tax—leaving nothing to pass on to their children. In fact, the number of such cases is very small. Indeed, a *New York Times* investigative reporter could not find a single instance of a farm that had been sold in order to pay the tax.[18] The disinformation campaign worked: A 2003 poll found that 49 percent of Americans thought that most families would have to pay the estate tax.[19] As a result of sophisticated issue framing that made estate tax repeal both economically and morally appealing, the coalition behind repeal broadened to include many Democrats, including the Congressional Black Caucus, which maintained that the estate tax stood in the way of the accumulation of black wealth.

The estate tax has a proud popular democratic history. First passed in 1916, the estate tax was designed to break up the huge fortunes accumulated by so-called Robber Barons during the age of industrialism and to ensure greater equality of opportunity in each new generation. Modest inheritances do not represent a threat to democracy. But huge accumulations of wealth—what Teddy Roosevelt called in supporting the tax, "fortunes swollen beyond all healthy limits"—threaten to corrupt our political system and beget a hereditary ruling class. Even though a group of over a hundred millionaires, led by Bill Gates Sr., signed a public appeal opposing repeal, opponents had no systematic public relations strategy to counter the Family Business Estate Tax Coalition. In the present period no political force (certainly not the Democratic Party) is able to articulate the popular democratic argument for taxes on huge estates and seize the moral high ground from the well-funded business machine with its pervasive think tanks, slick consultants, and misleading ads.

The main response to critics of Bush's tax cuts is that a majority of the electorate supported them. In fact, polls reported support for "Bush's tax cut proposal" in the 50 percent to 60 percent range. Polls are notoriously difficult to interpret, however. Polls also showed that Americans opposed the distribution of Bush's tax cuts and by strong majorities favored using the budget surplus to bolster Social Security or Medicare rather than cutting taxes.[20] Perhaps the most important point about the tax cuts is that supporters never articulated *where* they would cut spending to make up for the tax cuts. The result of the cuts, quite predictably, has been soaring deficits. Today, the influx of borrowed money is enabling the present generation of Americans to enjoy government services without raising taxes, but young people will be burdened with this debt in the future. According to one estimate, policies in the first Bush term will result in an additional debt of $90,000 per household by 2014.[21]

Some argue that tax cutting is part of a "starve-the-beast" strategy, where huge deficits will finally force Democrats in Congress to cut spending, shrinking government to pre–New Deal size. Such an approach is extremely cynical, assuming as it does that the democratic process is so broken that one side has to resort to subterfuge, risking the financial future of the country, in order to gets its way. It is highly unlikely that the Democrats will roll over and give up their hard-won gains; in fact, history suggests that Democrats are more likely to support additional public spending, regardless of the tax cuts. Moreover, most of the U.S. budget consists of mandatory spending, such as interest on debt and mandated payments to individuals for Social Security and Medicaid. Only about one-quarter of the budget is **discretionary spending** that Congress can control. With terrorism and the occupation of Iraq exempting the military from cuts, Congress will have to look to social programs to address the ballooning deficit. Whether the tax cutters intended it or not, the expanding deficit means that the country is essentially playing a game of chicken with bulging deficits heading toward a collision with growing social programs, especially popular entitlements like Social Security. Irresponsible fiscal policies have transformed the politics of social policy—a topic to which we now turn.

THE CONTOURS OF SOCIAL POLICY

Social policies are designed to protect people against market outcomes that society considers unacceptable. Individuals could take responsibility for insuring against their own risks for illness, disability, or old age, but society has decided that it should guarantee a minimum level of protection against these risks. Social policy also includes efforts to guarantee equal opportunity and provide a social safety net for those who cannot support themselves at an acceptable level in the private market.

In response to these needs, the United States has created a two-tiered welfare state: In the first tier, based on individual contributions into a social insurance fund, people, mostly the elderly, are guaranteed benefits regardless of income; the second tier of programs is targeted at children and the very poor, and requires recipients to apply for benefits and meet a means-test (prove that you make below a certain income and own few assets).

Overall, the United States devotes less of its public spending to social policies than any other developed nation. (See Figure 17.3.) But this overall figure obscures the fact that the United States actually has relatively generous social

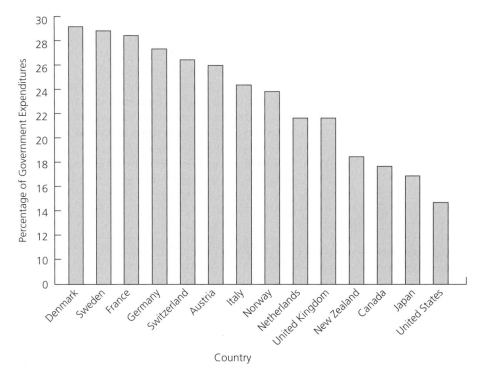

FIGURE 17.3

Total Public Social Expenditures, as Percent of Government Expenditures

Source: OECD (2004), Social Expenditure Database (SOCX, www.oecd.org/els/social/expenditure).

policies for the elderly. Entitlement programs provide almost universal coverage for the elderly, with benefit levels comparable to those in other developed countries. On the other hand, means-tested welfare programs, which mostly benefit children, provide spotty coverage and inadequate benefits. In 2002 all means-tested programs succeeded in reducing the poverty rate for female-headed families with children by about 7 percent (from 32 percent to 24.6 percent).[22]

Most other developed countries have broad entitlement programs to address the needs of the nonelderly poor. The most important of these is health insurance. They also have child allowances in which every family, regardless of income, is entitled to a payment each year from the government for each child. These allowances are politically popular and have played a major role in reducing poverty rates.[23]

The only exception to America's poor showing next to other developed countries is education. The United States provided universal public education at the primary and secondary levels well before Europe and today many more Americans are able to pursue higher education than in Europe. The American tradition of public education played a major role in expanding popular democracy, giving citizens the skills necessary to participate in the democratic process and in the economy.

However, the popular democratic tradition of equal educational opportunity is threatened today by unequal funding. Since funding for primary and secondary schools comes mostly out of local property taxes, children who happen to grow up in poor inner-city school districts suffer from inferior education.[24] Yet many state constitutions do guarantee equal educational opportunity, and lawsuits have successfully forced changes in the unequal funding of schools in many states. With education being the key to good jobs in an information-based economy, inferior schools can doom children to a life of poverty and exclude them from full participation in the democratic process.[25]

Over the years social insurance entitlements have fared much better than means-tested public assistance. In 2004 federal outlays totaled $496 billion on Social Security and $271 billion on Medicare. This represents almost one-third of all federal outlays. By contrast, federal spending on all means-tested programs for the poor totaled $373 billion in 2002.[26] (This includes thirty-three separate programs providing cash and noncash benefits.) But this total overstates aid to the poor. Almost $164 billion of that was for Medicaid, and most of the money spent on Medicaid goes to hospitals and doctors. More important, although you must be poor to qualify for Medicaid, many middle-class households draw down their parents' savings so that they can go on Medicaid to cover nursing home costs. A major part of Medicaid benefits the middle class. Subtracting Medicaid means that in 1998, all federal cash and noncash benefits targeted to the poor totaled $209 billion, less than half the amount going to Social Security alone. Not surprisingly, the poverty rate for the elderly has fallen at the same time that the child poverty rate has risen (Figure 17.4).

The question that arises is why programs targeted on those who need them the most have been cut (with the exception of Medicaid), while other programs that benefit primarily the elderly have fared so well. The reason is that the political dynamics behind these two kinds of programs are completely different.

The Attack on Welfare

The 1935 Social Security Act laid the foundation for our two-tiered welfare state, creating social insurance for the unemployed and the elderly, and public assistance for the blind, disabled, and single mothers with children. The latter program is what came to be known, often pejoratively, as welfare. Designed primarily to help children in families without a male breadwinner, the program was called Aid to Families with Dependent Children (AFDC). Based on a system of matching grants to the states, AFDC created a **means-tested benefit**, which meant that in order to obtain benefits, a person had to prove that he or she lacked adequate means of support. But it was also an **entitlement**, which meant that any family in the nation meeting the federal means test was entitled to get help. Although states could set benefit levels, they could not deny benefits to any eligible person. In the 1960s, welfare was supplemented with other means-tested programs, including food stamps and Medicaid (government health insurance for the poor).

FIGURE 17.4 Poverty Rate of Children (Under 18) and the Elderly (65 and Over) 1996–2002

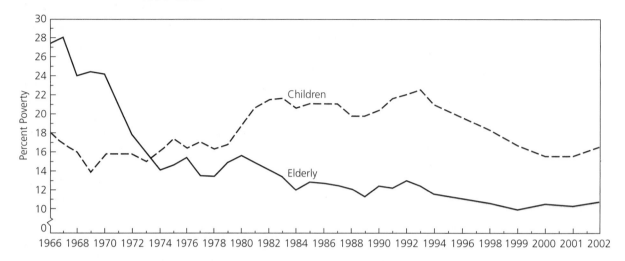

Source: U.S. Bureau of the Census. *Income, Poverty, and Valuation of Noncash Benefits: 1993*. Current Population Reports, Series P60–188. (Washington, D.C.: U.S. Government Printing Office, February); U.S. Bureau of the Census. "Press Briefing on 1994 Income and Poverty Estimates." (Washington, D.C.: U.S. Bureau of the Census, October 5); U.S. Bureau of the Census, *Statistical Abstract of the United States 2004–2005* (Washington, D.C.: U.S. Government Printing Office, 2004), pp. 452–53.

During the 1960s, welfare expenditures grew rapidly, partly because of a militant welfare rights movement that encouraged people to apply for welfare.[27] As expenditures on welfare soared, taxes increased, and industrial jobs declined, a welfare backlash developed, especially among working-class white ethnics. A book on the flight of Jews and Italians of Brooklyn from the Democratic Party to the Republican Party quotes an enraged city worker: "These welfare people get as much as I do, and I work my ass off and come home dead tired. They get up late, and they can shack up all day long and watch the tube. With their welfare and food stamps, they come out better than me. . . . Let them tighten their belts like we have to."[28]

In the late 1960s, politicians began to exploit this resentment against welfare to mobilize votes. Former Alabama governor and segregationist George Wallace led the way in the 1968 presidential election, attracting a surprisingly large number of votes among northern white ethnics. Richard Nixon began to speak out for what he called the "silent majority" against government giveaways like welfare. Ronald Reagan built his political career partly by attacking welfare, saying that we could not solve problems by "throwing money" at them. In 1992, George Bush attacked welfare, promising to "make the able-bodied work," and his opponent, Bill Clinton, put out an ad attacking welfare that boosted his candidacy as a new kind of Democrat: "For so long, Government has failed us, and one of its worst failures has been welfare. I have a plan to end welfare as we know it."[29]

Once he got into office, Clinton was under tremendous pressure to deliver on his campaign promise. Welfare reform was highly popular with the voters. A national survey found that 81 percent of Americans agreed that the welfare system needed "fundamental reform," and 92 percent supported welfare reform that would "require all able-bodied people on welfare to work or learn a job or skill."[30] Clinton, however, put first priority on health care reform which failed in 1994. The Republicans who took over Congress that year and proceeded to pass welfare reform that was more radical than anything Clinton had proposed. With the 1996 presidential election approaching, Clinton saw an opportunity to fulfill his 1992 promise and take an issue away from the Republicans. In August 1996, Clinton signed the **Personal Responsibility and Work Opportunity Act**, ending the federal government's sixty-one-year-old guarantee of aid for the poor.

Known as Temporary Assistance for Needy Families (TANF), the new program converted welfare from a federal entitlement to a state block grant, with wide discretion given to states on who was eligible and how much they would get. Federal spending on welfare was cut $55 billion over six years and federal rules required that states place 50 percent of welfare recipients in private sector jobs within six years. In addition, no person can collect welfare for more than five years in a lifetime or two years in any one stretch. Welfare reform represents one of the biggest social experiments in American history. Riding on welfare reform is not just the economic prospects of the poor but their social and political prospects as well.

By 2001 welfare rolls had fallen 63 percent, and welfare reform was widely hailed as a success by both parties. The drop in welfare rolls had much to do with the booming economy but it also had to do with the new signals sent by TANF that the goal was self-sufficiency. Today, less than 2 percent of the population is on welfare. However, the ultimate goal of welfare reform is not just to get people off welfare but to help them to become self-sufficient by obtaining decent-paying jobs and improving the lives of their children. Here the results are much more mixed.

The primary success of welfare reform is enhanced feelings of self-respect by those who succeed in finding a job. Marla Spencer, a thirty-seven-year-old mother of two in Milwaukee, after spending nineteen years on welfare landed a job folding sheets in a laundry for $5.25 per hour. "My whole family's happy," she said. "Now my son can tell his friends at school that his mother works."[31]

For every success story, however, there is a story of frustration and deprivation. Although we know that two-thirds of those who left welfare have found jobs, half of those earn wages that are insufficient to pull them out of poverty.[32] One-third of those who have left welfare have simply disappeared; we don't know what happened to them. One of the biggest beneficiaries of welfare reform has been fast-food restaurants, low-wage manufacturers, and retailers like Wal-Mart (see Chapter 3) that can keep wages lower because of the influx of millions of poor women desperate to find work. Soup kitchens and homeless shelters are reporting increased demand since welfare reform was enacted, and with many women entering the workforce, the strain on relatives to provide child care is great.[33] Especially when the economy enters a recession, we can expect to see more crime, drug addiction, domestic violence, mental problems, prostitution, and homelessness.

Above all, critics worry about the effect of welfare reform on children, which is largely unknown. Feminists decry the double standard of welfare reform: Society honors middle class women for staying home to take care of children while it vilifies poor women on welfare for doing the same. Many fear that more women will feel pressured to stay in abusive marriages. The number of children in extreme poverty is up since welfare reform. One study found that when the wages of women who left welfare were supplemented with other policies, such as daycare and job training, the children did better in school. Without such supplements, it appears that most children are worse off after their mothers leave welfare.

Despite research showing that people who leave welfare still need help, many states have refused to spend the money that accumulated when welfare rolls dropped precipitously on the poor. By 2000, the states had stashed away $7 billion in federal welfare funds. New York State diverted $1 billion into its budget and Wisconsin channeled $100 million into a property tax cut.[34] Moving control over welfare funds to the states may seem to be the epitome of popular democracy, but motivated by the fear that generous programs would cause them to become "welfare magnets," many states have engaged in a "race to the bottom" to cut benefits.[35]

But the main reason why states have not hesitated to divert welfare monies away from the poor is because of the negative image of means-tested welfare programs. The key transformation in the image of welfare was when conservatives persuaded the public that welfare was not just failing to solve poverty, *it was actually the cause of poverty*. By enabling women to get by without working, getting married, or staying in school, they argued that welfare created a culture of dependency.[36] The claim that welfare was a cause of poverty is highly questionable but it resonated with the American people and it had a wonderful political message: *"The less we spend, the more we care!"*[37]

Because means-tested programs are narrowly targeted on poor, minority, female-headed households, they engender tremendous resentment among groups of the population who do not benefit from them. The fact is, 73 percent of mothers are now employed (59 percent of those with infants), and, unlike forty years ago, it is no longer politically acceptable for women to be supported by the taxpayers to stay home with their children. The working poor also resent welfare. If you are poor enough and wait long enough in line, you may be able to receive a housing voucher, which means that you will never pay more than 30 percent of your income on rent. But many families just above the poverty line pay 50 percent or more of their income on rent, and they receive no public subsidies. Means-tested social policies divide the poor from the working class and make them easy targets for political attack.

Clearly, the resentment against welfare is not based only on economic factors; as we have seen, welfare is a relatively small part of federal and state budgets. This resentment is motivated partly by racism and sexism. Even though blacks are less than a majority of those on welfare, in the mind of the public welfare is a "black" program. Politicians take advantage of this. In 1991, for example, former Ku Klux Klan leader David Duke received a majority of the white vote in his race for governor of Louisiana by, among other things, stoking white resentments against black welfare recipients with such statements as "Middle-class families have difficulty affording children of their own right now, and yet we are financing a very high illegitimate birth rate."[38] In fact, at that time in Louisiana, each baby qualified the mother for only $11 extra per week—hardly a great incentive to have more children.

Another issue in the welfare debate concerns the role of women. When critics say that women on welfare do not work, they are ignoring the fact that raising children *is* work. The disapproving judgments about women on welfare seem to suggest that it is okay to stay home with children only if a woman is part of a traditional family with a male breadwinner. The reason for keeping welfare so unattractive, some feminists say, is to discourage women from leaving bad marriages, even if the husband is abusive.[39] In the public's mind, welfare is wrapped up in the cultural debates that began in the 1960s about permissiveness—allegedly promoting a lifestyle attuned to immediate gratification and sexual promiscuity. In fact, permissive values have spread throughout society in the past forty years, driven more by corporate advertising that uses immediate gratification to stimulate consumption than by welfare policies. Raised with a strong work ethic, hard-working Middle Americans find themselves bombarded by ads stressing pleasure-driven consumption. Fearing a loss of control, they project their own fears onto others, including blacks on welfare.[40]

Although welfare is not nearly as bad as its critics charged, it ultimately fails the popular democratic test of a public policy: Instead of encouraging civic participation, it discourages it. Normally, we think of policies as the result of the political process. But policies also shape the political process, encouraging or discouraging political participation in a process that political scientists call **policy feedback** (Figure 17.5).

Studies have shown that people who receive means-tested benefits vote at lower rates and are less likely to work in a campaign or join a protest than people who receive entitlements, like Social Security.[41] How people experience

FIGURE 17.5

Policy Feedback

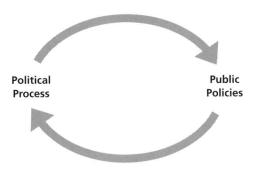

Political
Process

Public
Policies

government is very different for someone on welfare than for someone on Social Security. One former welfare mother described it this way: "Unlike Social Security, AFDC is distributed on a case-by-case basis, with enough strings to hang an elephant. It is meanly administered, hard to qualify for, hard to keep; it provides niggardly benefits and is tough to stomach with all its invasive attempts at behavior modification."[42] Welfare bureaucracies treat clients with disrespect, control their lives, and give them little opportunity for input. Welfare recipients generalize this experience to government as a whole. In the words of another welfare recipient: "The rest of the government mostly works like the AFDC office. I mean, I don't deal with the government when I can."[43] Social Security, on the other hand, has no demeaning application process; anyone who has worked for a number of years is entitled to Social Security. In many ways, Social Security created "senior citizens" as a self-conscious interest group. In short, policies shape citizens as much as citizens shape policies.

In conclusion, welfare reform was needed. The old welfare system provided few incentives for people to get ahead and discouraged them from becoming involved in the political process. But if the goal of welfare reform is simply to get people off welfare, it will fail. There are not enough decent-paying jobs to support families and children at a minimally acceptable level. At $5.15 an hour, taking into account inflation, the federal minimum wage is at its lowest level in sixteen years. Working families need help, but people who receive means-tested benefits are taught to be ashamed that they are "on the dole." The attack on welfare as a form of "dependency" ignores the fact that everyone in society depends on government. Middle- and upper-class Americans depend on a vast array of government benefits that are rarely questioned. Sometimes they are not even acknowledged, such as the benefits hidden in the tax code.

Tax Expenditures: Welfare for the Middle and Upper Classes

Besides government payments to individuals, citizens also benefit from special provisions, known as **tax expenditures**, which enable them avoid paying taxes. Tax expenditures are provisions in the tax code that reduce people's taxes in order to promote worthwhile public objectives. Calling them "tax expenditures" highlights the fact that tax exemptions are essentially the same as spending programs. The government can either exempt certain income from taxes or it can tax income normally and write a check to the recipient for the value of the exemption. Either way, the government is spending resources to subsidize certain taxpayers. In an effort to subject tax expenditures to public scrutiny, the Treasury Department in 1968 published the first budget for the United States that included tax expenditures. The Congressional Budget Act of 1974 made the concept of tax expenditures an integral part of the budget process. Misunderstood by most Americans, tax expenditures disproportionately benefit the middle class and especially the wealthy.

TABLE 17.1		
Major Tax Expenditure Programs, Estimated Cost to the U.S. Treasury in 2005	Homeowner tax breaks	$ 112.8 billion
	Exclusion of employer contributions to health insurance	101.9 billion
	Exclusion of contributions to retirement (employer contributions, 401(k) plans, and individual retirement accounts)	131.1 billion
	Total	$ 345.8 billion

Source: U.S. Bureau of the Census, *Statistical Abstract of the United States, 2004–2005* (Washington, D.C.: U.S. Government Printing Office, 2004), p. 313.

As Table 17.1 shows, tax expenditures are massive, and they have grown at an astounding pace, far outstripping the growth of conventional spending programs. Tax expenditures soared from $36.6 billion in 1967 to $253.5 billion in 1982, rising from 20.5 percent of federal outlays to 34.6 percent.[44] In 2005, all tax expenditures totaled $709 billion.[45]

Tax expenditures go disproportionately to middle-class and wealthy households. A Treasury Department study for 1977 found that the top 1.4 percent of taxpayers received 31.3 percent of the benefits delivered through tax expenditures. Those with the highest annual incomes (above $200,000) received an average tax subsidy of $535,653. At the same time that Congress cut means-tested programs for the poor, tax expenditures for the middle class and upper classes—what one author called "fiscal welfare"—soared.[46] Between 1978 and 2000, for example, the federal government spent $1.7 trillion on homeowner tax breaks compared to only $640 billion on all HUD low-income housing subsidies. The benefits of homeowner tax breaks are skewed to the rich, with 59 percent of the benefits going to the top 10 percent of households with incomes over $100,000.[47] The exclusions of employer contributions to health insurance and retirement benefit mostly higher-income workers. Low-wage workers often get no health insurance or retirement benefits from their companies.

Even though tax expenditures are expensive, they have distinct political advantages over conventional spending programs. First, they are buried in the tax code and therefore have low political visibility. Second, once enacted, they do not require annual congressional appropriations, like conventional spending programs. Third, there are no congressional committees with oversight responsibilities for tax expenditures, and hearings are rarely held to scrutinize their effectiveness—as happens for spending programs.

Defenders of tax expenditures argue that the middle class already pays too much in taxes and they ought to get a break. But this begs the question of why people who rent an apartment or work for a small business should not get a tax break. The people who benefit from these tax breaks still enjoy all of the benefits of U.S. citizenship, but they don't pay their fair share of the costs. Tax expenditures for retirement and health care essentially subsidize a privatized welfare state for the middle and upper classes.

The Battle Over Social Security

Social Security is an example of a program that is consistent with the tenets of popular democracy. Unlike means-tested social policies, Social Security unites people instead of dividing them, encouraging civic participation instead of discouraging it. Recent proposals to reform Social Security, however, threaten to pit the young against the old and the rich against the poor, undermining the broad support for a program that has helped to invigorate the civic commitments of older Americans.

Social Security started out modestly in 1935 as a contributory insurance program designed to guarantee a minimum standard of living in retirement. Over the years, however, it has expanded rapidly, both in benefit levels and in the number of people covered. Coverage was significantly expanded on three occasions: In 1939, widows were included; in 1956, the disabled were added; and in 1965, health insurance for the elderly was enacted. The system is paid for by a payroll tax designated as FICA (Federal Insurance Contributions Act) on your paycheck.

The Social Security tax is *regressive* because it is a flat rate (7.65 percent: 1.45 percent of that is for Medicare) on all income up to $90,000 (2005); above that amount, people pay nothing. However, the benefits paid out for Social Security are mildly *progressive*: Although related to the amount workers pay into the system, formerly low-income workers are given proportionately higher benefits. More important, the benefits far exceed the amount each worker paid into the system. As life expectancy has increased, it became clear that what people paid into the system would not be sufficient to maintain them at a dignified level through retirement. In 1972, Social Security pensions were indexed to inflation, removing the question of future benefits from politics and guaranteeing that future benefits would not be eroded by inflation. Today, most people exhaust the funds they paid into the system within four to eight years. After that, their pension is essentially paid for by the payroll taxes of the present generation of workers. The evolution of Social Security has made it, in the words of Harvard's Theda Skocpol, "America's most effective antipoverty program."[48] As Figure 17.4 shows, the poverty rate among the elderly fell from 28 percent in the late 1960s to only about 10 percent today. Without Social Security, the poverty rate among the elderly would be about 50 percent.[49]

With Social Security now benefiting over 90 percent of the workforce, it has become a classic case of **majoritarian politics**, in which both the costs and the benefits are widely spread. Social Security is supported by a broad coalition uniting the poor and the middle class, blacks and whites, city dwellers and residents of small towns and suburbs. Social Security has also stimulated civic participation among the elderly. In the early 1950s seniors used to participate at a lower rate than nonseniors. Now they participate at a higher rate. Social Security provides the elderly with both the material resources and the leisure time necessary to participate in politics. Research shows that Social Security recipients vote at about twice the rate of those who receive means-tested benefits.

And 31 percent of Social Security recipients belong to an organization that defends their benefits compared to only 2 percent for welfare recipients.[50] What is perhaps most remarkable is that low-income seniors now actually participate at higher rates than high-income seniors in defending the program. Social Security is one of the best examples of what we discussed earlier as policy feedback (see Figure 17.5), the way policies shape citizens.

Despite the popularity of Social Security, after his reelection in 2004, President Bush argued that Social Security faced a crisis and needed to be radically transformed. The main problem he identified is that when baby boomers start to retire in a few years, they will begin draining the Social Security trust fund, which it is now predicted will not be able to pay full benefit levels beginning in 2041. Bush's proposal, allowing younger workers to divert their Social Security taxes into personal investment accounts, however, will not address the long-term fiscal crisis of the system. Indeed, because it will divert taxes presently going to retirees, Bush's proposal will require the government to borrow trillions of dollars to make up the difference. If the stock market does better than treasury bonds, which is where Social Security presently invests its monies, then the young workers will be better off. However, if the stocks they pick do poorly, they could face retirement with little to fall back on. There is also the issue of the costs of administering private accounts and paying stockbrokers. The Social

Security Administration runs the program very efficiently, with overhead costs absorbing less than 1 percent of benefit payments.

Despite all the numbers and the talk of a crisis, the debate over Social Security is fundamentally a political debate. (See Chapter 9 for a discussion of the politics of Social Security.) Bush wants to create what he calls an "Ownership Society." This would mean that each person would be responsible for his or her retirement. By creating private accounts, Bush would begin to pit young against old, and rich against poor, undermining the universal quality of Social Security that has been so effective in maintaining support. By arguing that Social Security will "go broke" and implying that it is a bad deal for middle class Americans, Bush is trying to split apart the cross-generational, cross-class coalition that has supported Social Security for sixty years. By contrast, defenders of Social Security are essentially arguing that we are all in this together and that if Americans band together we can insure each other against the vagaries of old age. In addition, we can build a better democracy by insuring that senior citizens have the dignity, time, and resources to participate in politics.

CONCLUSION: THE FUTURE OF ECONOMIC AND SOCIAL POLICY

Although huge budget and trade deficits threaten our prosperity, the United States still has one of the strongest economies in the world. Measured in terms of buying power, Americans have one of the highest standards of living in the world. But economic policies should not be evaluated only by economic standards. Economic policies have widespread social and political effects. When economic policy is left in the hands of economic experts, they often ignore the social ramifications of their policies. When the Federal Reserve ratchets up interest rates to stop inflation and throws 100,000 people out of work, do they take into account the documented effects of unemployment on suicide, homicide, mental illness, crime, alcoholism, and domestic violence?[51] In the long run, economic policy will be more effective if it has democratic input so that it can balance the complex trade-offs among economic, social, and political outcomes. Although the American economy has performed well in accumulating wealth, it has performed poorly from the standpoint of equality, community, and participation. As we noted in Chapter 3, inequality has widened dangerously in the past thirty years, and large campaign contributions threaten the integrity of the electoral process.

We live in an age when markets are being trumpeted as solutions to all of our problems. Indeed, markets are often portrayed as vehicles of popular democracy, as ways for ordinary citizens to make their voices heard in contrast to the elitism of government. Markets are portrayed as the epitome of freedom whereas government is the realm of coercion. This chapter has challenged the simplistic notions that government is inherently oppressive and the public and private sectors are at war with one another. The idea that markets and government are locked in a zero-sum conflict is contradicted by the facts of history. Since the 1930s, as government has expanded, markets have grown tremendously. Government did not grow at the expense of markets; they prospered together. In fact, healthy markets require a healthy democratic government. If the reader doubts this, examine the case of many former republics of the Soviet Union where, lacking strong governments, "free markets" have enabled the strong to exploit the weak. As the English philosopher Isaiah Berlin once put it: "Freedom for the pike is death for the minnows."[52] We need a strong federal government to check and balance the power of large corporations.

No one is self-made. We all depend on government. Rightly constructed, government policies can enhance individual freedom. Social Security has given seniors freedom from want and the ability to participate in civic life like never before. Critics of government often argue that government social policies push aside the efforts of voluntary associations and nonprofits to help the poor. But in fact government social programs usually work in partnership with nonprofit and voluntary associations.[53] Social Security has freed millions of elderly to volunteer at churches and civic associations.

All of us are dependent on government to achieve a high quality of life and to participate fully in political life. Public education, the most successful entitlement program of all, demonstrates that we do not need to choose between greater economic efficiency and greater equality, because public education promotes both at the same time. Try to imagine what American democracy would be like without the massive system of public education that imparts the skills necessary to debate public policies and organize political associations to defend people's interests.

Not all social policies, however, have strengthened democracy. Means-tested social policies, by treating welfare recipients as undeserving and forcing them to go through a demeaning application process, have stigmatized the poor and made them feel alienated from society, damaging their capacity for independent political action.

But if welfare reform means throwing recipients to the mercy of the private market, then it will fail. Mean-spirited welfare reform is motivated by the fear of "dependency." In fact, in our fast-moving, high-tech society, no one is either independent or dependent; we are interdependent. Popular democracy requires social policies that integrate the poor into mainstream society. But it isn't just poor families that need help; working- and middle-class families are under stress. Instead of dismantling Social Security, popular democrats need to support new family-friendly social policies. Above all, we need a universal system of health care for all Americans.

Beyond education and health care, however, the most effective way of integrating the poor into society would be to guarantee them a job. The vast majority of the American people favor replacing "welfare with a system of guaranteed jobs."[54] The most important entitlement that popular democrats could enact would be the right of every American to a job at a salary that could support a family.

KEY TERMS

macroeconomic policy
fiscal policy
monetary policy
Federal Reserve
monetarism
supply-side economics
Laffer curve
Economic Recovery Tax Act of 1981
progressive and regressive taxes

discretionary spending
means-tested benefit
entitlement
Personal Responsibility and Work
    Opportunity Act of 1996
policy feedback
tax expenditures
majoritarian politics

INTERNET RESOURCES

■ The Federal Reserve Board

www.federalreserve.gov

Comprehensive information about the Federal Reserve.

■ The Economic Policy Institute

www.epinet.org

The Economic Policy Institute provides analysis of economic issues from the viewpoint of low-income and working families.

■ Moving Ideas

http://movingideas.org/

Reports on social welfare issues from a liberal point of view.

■ Federal Government Statistics

www.fedstats.gov

Links to websites of federal government agencies that provide detailed information on economic and social policies.

■ The Urban Institute

www.urban.org

The Urban Institute is a well-respected think tank that has carefully covered the welfare reform issue.

SUGGESTED READINGS

Jason DeParle, *American Dream: Three Women, Ten Kids, and a Nation's Drive to End Welfare*. New York: Viking, 2004. A riveting, evenhanded account of welfare reform that acknowledges the bad choices often made by the poor, while documenting the incredible pressures they face to survive.

William Greider, *Secrets of the Temple: How the Federal Reserve Runs the Country*. New York: Simon & Schuster, 1987. Penetrates the veil of expertise that surrounds the Federal Reserve to expose the politics behind its decisions to regulate the money supply.

Charles Murray, *Losing Ground: American Social Policy 1950–1980*. New York: Basic Books, 1984. A highly influential neo-conservative book that argues that welfare policies not only fail to cure poverty but actually create poverty.

Theda Skocpol, *The Missing Middle: Working Families and the Future of American Social Policy*. New York: W. W. Norton, 2000. A critique of efforts to privatize social policies, Skocpol offers a vision of what popular democratic social policies would look like.

William Julius Wilson, *When Work Disappears: The World of the New Urban Poor*. New York: Alfred A. Knopf, 1996. An update of his influential book *The Truly Disadvantaged*, Wilson argues, contrary to Murray, that the main cause of ghetto poverty is not welfare but the loss of industrial jobs, especially for black males.

Foreign Policy in the National Security State

In the early 1960s, the Central Intelligence Agency (CIA), following the wishes of Presidents Eisenhower and Kennedy, was determined to get rid of Fidel Castro, the communist leader of revolutionary Cuba. Since coming to power in 1959, Castro had seized property in Cuba belonging to American corporations and had drawn his nation closer to the Soviet Union. An invasion force of Cuban exiles organized and trained by the CIA was smashed by Castro's forces at the Bay of Pigs in 1961. But behind the scenes, the CIA was plotting an even more dire fate for Castro: assassination.[1]

The first undercover plot against Castro aimed merely to destroy his popularity. CIA officials were fearful that the charismatic Castro, most famous for his bushy, black beard, would become a hero to the impoverished and the discontented throughout Latin America. So they cooked up a scheme to dust the Cuban leader's shoes with thallium salt, a powerful hair remover that would make his beard fall out. The plot was to be carried out when Castro was on a trip outside Cuba and would leave his shoes to be shined at the hotel in which he was staying. But Castro canceled the trip.

Foiled in this prank, the CIA began to plot murder. It laced a box of Castro's favorite cigars with a botulism toxin, a poison so lethal that Castro would die just from putting the cigar in his mouth. The cigars were delivered to an unknown agent; it is not known what happened to him or to the cigars, but they never reached Castro.

Foiled again, the CIA became even more serious. To kill Castro, it hired experts: the Mafia. Castro had shut down Mafia gambling and prostitution operations in Cuba, so the mob had its own reasons for wanting Castro dead. The CIA paid three Mafia gangsters (two of whom were on the attorney general's list of most wanted criminals) $150,000 in taxpayers' money for the attempt on Castro's life. Mafia agents in Cuba tried to slip poisoned pills, supplied by the CIA, into Castro's drink. But like the previous assassins, they could not get close enough to Castro to carry out the deed.

By now, CIA planners were desperate. They considered the possibility of depositing an exotic seashell rigged with explosives in an area where Castro liked to go skin diving. When this idea proved impractical, they tried to have an unwitting American diplomat offer Castro the gift of a diving suit. The suit was to be dusted with a fungus that would produce a chronic skin disease; its breathing apparatus was to be contaminated with tuberculosis germs. This idea, too, had to be discarded as impractical. Castro survived this—and several further—CIA plots.

What does this bizarre tale of CIA efforts to assassinate Castro, which sounds more like a bad made-for-TV movie than a true story about an agency of the U.S. government, have to do with the democratic debate about American foreign policy? Elite democrats have long claimed that foreign policy, even more than domestic policy, requires the superior expertise and talent of elites. Ordinary citizens, they argue, are generally ignorant about events in other nations and are prone to emotional and fickle responses inconsistent with a realistic and stable foreign policy. Therefore, foreign policy should largely be left in the hands of the president and the diplomatic and military experts who advise him. The tale of the CIA and Castro should lead us to question this conventional wisdom about wise elites and ignorant masses. When foreign policy decisions are made in secret chambers by a handful of elite actors operating free of public scrutiny (and, in the case of the CIA, public accountability), the result can be folly rather than wisdom. And the cost can be great, both to America's true national security and to its most cherished democratic values.

This chapter considers the democratic debate over foreign policy that has been waged since the nation's founding. The discussion begins with the original debate between Federalists and Anti-federalists, with elite democrats arguing for the necessity of expert guidance in a dangerous world of powerful adversaries and popular democrats warning of the threat to the maintenance of republican institutions posed by secret diplomacy and aggressive militarism. Briefly tracing the debate through American history, the chapter focuses on the era of the Cold War, when elite democrats succeeded in building a national security state to run the affairs of a global superpower. Next, the chapter describes the diplomatic, military, intelligence, and economic agencies that conduct American relations with other nations and examines the impact that economic elites and public opinion have on foreign policy. The final sections of the chapter consider the current debate about what American foreign policy should be in a post–Cold War world and examine the foreign and defense policies of the post–Cold War presidents, Bill Clinton and George W. Bush.

Beginnings of the Democratic Debate over Foreign Policy

Elite democrats and popular democrats of the founding generation differed not only on how Americans should govern themselves but also on how the American nation should relate to the rest of the world. The former favored executive control and promoted professional armies, while the latter sought public control and favored citizen militias.

The strongest proponent of the original elite position on foreign policy was Alexander Hamilton. In *The Federalist Papers*, Hamilton called on Americans to recognize that they lived in a dangerous world, where nations would fight regularly over power, territory, and commerce. Hamilton argued that the new United States needed professional armies and navies like those of the great European powers, England and France. These forces would be required for defense and for the establishment of America as a great power, extending its influence throughout the western hemisphere.[2]

In Hamilton's conception of foreign and defense policy, the president was the dominant figure. Members of Congress lacked the information and experience to make wise decisions in foreign policy; furthermore, they could not act swiftly or keep diplomatic secrets. In contrast, the executive had the proper qualities for controlling foreign policy and using military might—in Hamilton's words, "decision, activity, secrecy, and dispatch."[3]

During the war between Great Britain and revolutionary France, Federalists boosted the primacy of the executive in foreign policy, using as their instrument President Washington's Proclamation of Neutrality of 1793. Later in that decade, they seized on the prospect of an American war against the French to create a professional army. It was Hamilton and his faction of Federalists who created the first American military establishment.[4]

The Anti-federalists feared just such an establishment. A standing army might overturn republican institutions and seize power for its commander (the example of Julius Caesar in ancient Rome was frequently cited). Or it might become a dangerous tool for the executive, tempting him to crush his domestic opponents or launch aggressive military adventures abroad. As an alternative to a professional military in times of peace, the Anti-federalists wanted to rely on state militias composed of armed citizens. (The Second Amendment reflects the importance the Anti-federalists gave to militias.) As historian Richard H. Kohn observes, popular democrats of the founding era associated the militia "with liberty, freedom, and colonial virtue — the standing army with European militarism, corruption, and tyranny."[5]

That citizen militias were capable only of defensive military operations reveals a great deal about the Anti-federalist view of foreign policy. The Anti-federalists did not want the new republic to become like the reigning great powers of the day. Rather than playing power politics, America should relate to the rest of the world as an example of how a people could flourish in freedom and self-government. A peaceful, commercial relationship with other nations could be governed as much by the people's representatives in Congress as by the executive. Foreign and defense policy of this kind would, the Anti-federalists believed, provide Americans with genuine security without threatening the republic's institutions and values.

In today's world of massive military forces and awesome technological destructiveness, some of the Anti-federalists' arguments sound old-fashioned. Yet the fundamental questions of the original democratic debate endure: Should American foreign and military policy be determined largely by a small elite acting often in secret and be directed toward the projection of American power abroad? Or should American foreign and defense policy be subject to greater popular democratic control and seek a form of national security that violates as little as possible the nation's professed values as a democratic society?

ISOLATION AND EXPANSION

For much of American history, elite democrats who shared Hamilton's vision of the United States as a great power were frustrated. **Isolationism**, not power politics, was the core principle of American foreign and defense policy. Apart from commercial relations, the United States sought to stay isolated from the political and military quarrels of the rest of the world. Protected by two vast oceans, the young republic concentrated on its internal development. Since military threats were remote, the standing army remained small. Only when the United States actually became engaged in a war did the military swell in size; once war was over, the citizen–soldiers who composed the bulk of the forces were rapidly demobilized.

Even though isolationism characterized American relations with other nations until well into the twentieth century, American foreign policy was neither as defensive nor as passive as the term seems to imply. The American republic from its inception was engaged in a process of **expansion**, first on a continental scale and later into Latin America and even Asia. American expansion drove the European powers from their remaining holdings on the continent. But it had a

© 2005 Tom Tomorrow.

dark side: Expansion also drove Native Americans from their ancestral lands, often in brutal fashion. And later it extended American power over Latin Americans and Filipinos, speaking the language of benevolence but employing the instrument of armed force. The responsibility for this dark side of American expansion belonged both to elite democrats and popular democrats.

Removal of indigenous peoples, the initial pillar of American expansion, was the work of popular democrats. The central figure in this removal was popular democratic hero Andrew Jackson. He understood that many ordinary Americans hungered for the fertile lands that the Native American tribes occupied—and he shared their incomprehension at Indians' refusal to give up their way of life and adopt the white man's economic and social practices. Under Jackson's leadership, Native Americans were driven from their homes in the southeastern states. As historian Richard Barnet notes, "In 1820, 125,000 Indians lived east of the Mississippi; by 1844 there were fewer than 30,000 left. Most had been forcibly relocated to the west. About a third had been wiped out."[6]

If popular democrats had their shameful moments in the history of American expansion, so, too, did elite democrats. Consider, for example, the clique of elite expansionists in the 1890s, led by such avowed admirers of Hamilton as Massachusetts Senator Henry Cabot Lodge and Assistant Secretary of the Navy Theodore Roosevelt. It was these elite expansionists, eager to project American power abroad, who prodded a wavering President William McKinley to fight a Spanish-American war and to extend the war from its ostensible focus, Cuba, halfway around the world to the Philippine Islands. The same men guided the subsequent American military campaign to crush Filipino nationalists, who wanted independence rather than American rule. A forerunner to the Vietnam conflict, the American war in the Philippines caused as many as 200,000 Filipino deaths.[7]

Although expansion drew support from both elites and masses, it always had its critics, who echoed the original Anti-federalist fear that America could become a great power only by violating its republican principles. America's role in the Mexican War, the war in the Philippines, and World War I was denounced by those who wanted the nation not to follow the path of European militarism and imperialism. These critics, among them Abraham Lincoln, were especially outraged by claims that American expansion was motivated by a desire to spread liberty to other lands; they detected the real desire for wealth and power that such rhetoric disguised.[8]

Even as the United States expanded across the continent (and into Latin America and the Philippines), even as it became the greatest industrial power in the world, the doctrine of isolationism remained strong. America came late to World War I—and recoiled after the war from the slaughter on the battlefield and the power politics of the victorious allies. Only with World War II did the nation begin to change its traditional foreign and defense policy, and it was in the immediate postwar years that the great transformation in American international relations occurred. Then, in the Cold War era, some of Hamilton's dreams were finally fulfilled, and some of the Anti-federalists' fears finally came true.

THE DEMOCRATIC DEBATE OVER THE COLD WAR

The **Cold War** was a forty-year struggle (lasting from the late 1940s to the late 1980s) between the United States and its allies, championing the cause of democracy and capitalism, and the Soviet Union (USSR) and its allies, championing the cause of communism. It was called a "cold" war because the two principal adversaries, the United States and the Soviet Union, armed themselves to the teeth yet never actually engaged in direct combat with each other. But the Cold War became a "hot" war in many places, with major armed conflicts in Korea and Vietnam, and numerous smaller armed conflicts around the globe. It was also waged with nonmilitary weapons ranging from political manipulation and economic pressure to propaganda and espionage.

The Cold War remains essential to study because it fundamentally transformed American foreign policy. With the Cold War, the United States became an active and interventionist global superpower. It developed an enormous peacetime military establishment, armed with weaponry of previously unthinkable destructiveness. Presidents became the overwhelmingly dominant factors in policy making and came to possess, among other resources, the capacity to operate in secret, employing new agencies of covert action like the CIA. Meanwhile, Congress and the public were reduced to a marginal role, expected to support but not to question American actions abroad. These developments gave rise to a **national security state**, a complex of executive, military, and secret powers previously unknown in the American republic. Even though the Cold War has now come to an end, this national security state remains.

For roughly the first half of the Cold War, almost all Americans believed in its ideas and institutions. But this "Cold War consensus" cracked during the Vietnam War of the 1960s and early 1970s. It was during the protests against American policy in Vietnam that the popular democratic tradition of opposing a foreign and defense policy based on unchecked executive power, militarism, and secret, unaccountable institutions was revived. This opposition was expressed chiefly through mass movements, first against the war in Vietnam and later against President Reagan's policy in Central America and his nuclear arms build-up. These movements were supported by some sympathetic political elites, such as Senators George McGovern (the Democrats' 1972 presidential candidate) and Edward Kennedy. During the last half of the Cold War, the debate over foreign policy was intense. In the following sections, we consider more fully the perspectives of both sides in the democratic debate over the Cold War.

The Elite Democratic View of the Cold War

Most elite democrats admitted that the Cold War contained some unpleasant features and unfortunate episodes, but they insisted that it was a necessary, even heroic struggle. The advance of international communism had to be halted, they believed, if freedom and democracy were to survive in the world. And only a prudent and tough-minded elite could guide the complex and often nasty enterprise of containing communism until it collapsed of its own contradictions. Secretary of State Dean Acheson, one of the original architects of American Cold War policy, remarked that "the limitation imposed by democratic political practices makes it difficult to conduct our foreign affairs in the national interest."[9] For Acheson and other elite democratic managers of the new national security state, deviations from democracy were acceptable if needed to win the Cold War.

The elite case for the Cold War argued, first, that American policy had to have as its priority an opposition to aggression. The mistake of the Western allies before World War II—appeasing Adolf Hitler at Munich in 1938—must never again be repeated. The United States organized a European alliance, the **North Atlantic Treaty Organization (NATO)**, to block any Soviet expansion in Europe. Aggression by Soviet allies and clients in the Third World also had to be halted, a rationale that involved the United States in wars in Korea and Vietnam. In this view, the United States had built a national security state not to secure military supremacy but to keep peace in the world.

Second, elite democrats saw the American effort in the Cold War as a defense of freedom around the globe. In advocating a global American struggle for the **containment** of communism, President Truman declared that "I believe that it must be the policy of the United States to support free peoples who are resisting attempted subjugation by armed minorities or by outside pressures."[10] The strategy of containment, proclaimed in what came to be known as the Truman Doctrine, formed the basis of American policy throughout the Cold War.

Third, the American Cold War policy was a prudent combination of force and diplomacy. The presidents who shaped this policy had to engage in a frightening arms race, but they always kept one eye on peace. President Eisenhower sought "peaceful coexistence" with the Russians, President Kennedy negotiated a ban on the testing of nuclear weapons in the atmosphere, President Nixon restored American ties to the People's Republic of China, and even President Reagan, the harshest critic of the Soviet Union among Cold War executives, agreed to an intermediate nuclear forces treaty with Soviet leader Mikhail Gorbachev.[11]

Fourth, the Cold War had the support of the American people. The Cold War necessitated a shift of power from Congress to the president, a huge and expensive military establishment, and agencies of secret action outside the constitutional system of public accountability. Yet, elite democrats argued, Americans understood that they were in a difficult struggle with a dangerous, undemocratic enemy, and they accepted the fact that this struggle could not always be conducted in accordance with democratic political practices.

The Popular Democratic View of the Cold War

Popular democrats agreed with elite democrats that communism had to be opposed. But they believed that the threat posed by the communists to the freedom of other nations and to the United States itself was often exaggerated by elite democrats in the presidency, the military, and the CIA because such exaggerations increased their own power and resources. Further, popular democrats favored more peaceful and open methods to block communism, methods more in keeping with democratic practices and values. In the eyes of popular democrats, American Cold War policy as run by elite democrats purchased whatever successes it achieved at a high price.

The most haunting price of Cold War policy, in the eyes of popular democrats, was the war in Vietnam. In the name of containing the aggressive expansionism of the Soviet and Chinese communists, elite democratic managers of the national security state plunged the United States into what was actually a Vietnamese civil war. By the time the United States pulled all of its troops out of Vietnam, almost 60,000 Americans had died, along with hundreds of thousands of Vietnamese soldiers and civilians. The Vietnamese countryside bore terrible ecological scars, as did Vietnamese society and economy. Americans, too, were scarred by the war, especially in psychological traumas that persist to this day.[12]

Vietnam was an unparalleled disaster for America, but it was not, popular democrats insisted, an aberration for American foreign policy. A second price of Cold War policy was American backing of dictators and military regimes that repressed their own people in the name of anticommunism. Although President Truman had promised to assist "free peoples" resisting communism, the policy of containment he initiated led the United States to support some rather dubious representatives of freedom. Thus, the CIA overthrew a nationalist government in Iran in 1953 and restored the autocratic shah to power. For the next twenty-five years, the shah was the recipient of lavish American aid, including CIA training of his ruthless secret police, SAVAK. When he was overthrown in 1979—by Islamic fundamentalists rather than communists—Iran became a bitter foe of the United States.[13]

A third price of Cold War policy was that the United States, the global sponsor of democracy, schemed to overthrow democracies abroad if they infringed on American political and economic interests and to replace them with authoritarian governments that would do what the national security managers wanted. The most important case of this type was Chile in the early 1970s. Employing the CIA, President Nixon and his national security adviser, Henry Kissinger, tried to block the election of socialist Salvador Allende as president of Chile. When this failed, they worked secretly to disrupt Chile's economy and to foment political opposition to the Allende government. They also courted the Chilean military, which finally undertook a coup in 1973 in which Allende was killed and his supporters were arrested.[14]

Claiming to champion democracy in a global campaign against communism, American Cold War policy damaged democracy at home as well as abroad. In the popular democratic view, a fourth price paid for the Cold War was the damage done to the constitutional values of open debate and checks and balances. With the emergence of a national security state, a government that was supposed to be open and accountable to the people began to classify massive amounts of information as secret and to hide numerous operations from public view. As facts were concealed, democratic debate was also stifled by Cold War taboos. No political figure who aspired to high office dared question fundamental Cold War premises lest he or she appear "soft on communism." Meanwhile, executive power swelled to previously unknown proportions in international relations, taking on the character of an "imperial presidency." Two major threats to the Constitution, the Watergate affair under Nixon and the Iran–Contra affair under Reagan, could be traced to the mentality of the imperial presidency during the Cold War.

A final price paid for American Cold War policy, in the eyes of popular democrats, was the damage done to economic progress and social justice in America. The Cold War arms race introduced distortions into the economy, leaving the United States at a disadvantage in many areas of civilian production compared to the nonmilitarized economies of West Germany and Japan. Equally damaging was the impact on spending for social needs. The arms race was often used to justify the country's failure to address adequately the needs of its own poor and disadvantaged. The one extensive effort to meet these needs, President Johnson's War on Poverty and Great Society programs, was cut back because of the mushrooming costs of the war in Vietnam. President Eisenhower, the Cold War president who best understood the tragic cost of the arms race, eloquently made the popular democrats' point: "Every gun that is made, every warship launched, every rocket fired signifies, in the final sense, a theft from those who hunger and are not fed, those who are cold and are not clothed."[15]

The End of the Cold War

The Cold War came to a sudden and surprising end in the late 1980s. In an attempt to reform the decrepit structure of the Soviet state, Gorbachev managed only to expose its fatal weaknesses. The global power of the Soviet Union slipped away in 1989, when Gorbachev refused to respond with force as popular upheavals toppled communist regimes in Eastern Europe. The Soviet Union itself crumbled in 1991 after a botched coup against Gorbachev by hard-line communists. Soon Gorbachev himself was swept from power in peaceful fashion, and the Soviet state was dismantled, with Boris Yeltsin and other leaders of the Soviet republics proclaiming their independence in a loosely knit federation.

The United States and its allies exulted in the Cold War's demise. Indeed, the whole world breathed easier now that the frightening prospect of a third world war and a nuclear holocaust had been removed. Yet celebration was bound to be brief, for the post–Cold War world already contained new problems and violent conflicts. Nonetheless, there were new opportunities as well, new openings to address fundamental issues of economic progress, human rights, and environmental protection. At the same time, the institutions of the national security state groped to redefine their roles in an era that lacked the simplifying assumption of a global communist enemy.

FOREIGN AND DEFENSE POLICY: INSTITUTIONS

The presidency is the dominant institution in the making of foreign and defense policy, and in the first half of the Cold War era it controlled this area with few checks from anywhere else. But the disastrous presidential war in Vietnam sparked Congress to reassert its constitutional role in shaping American policy abroad. Since Vietnam, foreign and defense policy has often been the subject of struggle between presidents and Congress (see Chapters 11 and 12).

Agencies of the executive branch are central to the formulation and implementation of national security policy. Presidents have considerable latitude to use these agencies as they see fit, so the role of each agency and the structure of the foreign policy process itself have varied from one administration to the next. National security agencies are subordinate units that advise and assist the president, yet they shape how the United States understands and operates in international affairs.

The National Security Council

The **National Security Council (NSC)** was created in 1947, at the dawn of the Cold War, to serve as a coordinating mechanism for foreign and defense policy at the highest level. The president, vice president, secretary of state, and secretary of defense are statutory members of the NSC; the director of Central Intelligence and the chair of the Joint Chiefs of Staff are statutory advisers (see Table 18.1).

TABLE 18.1	**Statutory Members of the NSC** President Vice president Secretary of state Secretary of defense
Composition of the National Security Council	**Statutory Advisers to the NSC** Director of Central Intelligence Chairman, Joint Chiefs of Staff
	Other Attendees Chief of staff to the president Assistant to the president for national security affairs Secretary of the treasury Attorney general Others as invited
	Source: U.S. Army War College, Carlisle Barracks, Pennsylvania, December 1989, and "National Security Council Organization," National Security Council mimeo, April 17, 1989, as reprinted in James M. McCormick, *American Foreign Policy and Process*, 2nd ed. (Itasca, Ill.: Peacock, 1992), p. 371.

Presidents have found NSC meetings to be a ponderous instrument. The importance of the NSC has come to reside, instead, in the head of its staff, the president's **national security adviser**. President Kennedy was the first to transform this position from bureaucratic assistant to the council to personal adviser to the president; his national security adviser, McGeorge Bundy, came to overshadow his secretary of state, Dean Rusk, in influence. Subsequent national security advisers expanded on Bundy's role. None dominated American foreign policy so thoroughly as Henry Kissinger. Under Presidents Nixon and Ford, Kissinger was the basic architect of American foreign policy and its most celebrated spokesperson in the media.

National security advisers are in a strong position to exert influence. They have an advantage over secretaries of state in physical proximity to the president, working in the White House and briefing the president frequently on developments around the globe. National security advisers and their small staffs filter the massive amounts of information flowing into the White House from American diplomatic, military, and intelligence personnel throughout the world and can tailor what they report to fit the president's interests more effectively than the larger and more bureaucratic State Department can.[16]

However, criticism in the media and among foreign policy experts that NSC advisers had grown too powerful has led recent presidents to downgrade the adviser's role somewhat. Occupants of the position are now expected to act mainly as coordinators and facilitators and not to compete with the secretary of state for public attention. Brent Scowcroft, national security adviser to President George H. W. Bush, and Anthony Lake and Samuel Berger, national security advisers to President Bill Clinton, operated in this manner. The national security adviser for President George W. Bush, Condoleezza Rice, had unusual visibility as an African-American woman, and her personal closeness to the president also enhanced her influence. She was elevated to the position of secretary of state at the start of Bush's second term, with her assistant, Stephen Hadley, becoming the new NSC adviser.

Department of State

The **Department of State** is the oldest department in the president's cabinet and the traditional organ of American diplomacy. For most of American history, the secretary of state was the president's principal foreign policy adviser. State Department personnel, stationed in embassies and consulates in nations with which the United States maintained diplomatic relations, were America's principal point of contact with the rest of the world.

During the Cold War, however, the Department of State was eclipsed in influence by other institutions. The national security adviser often had greater influence with the president than did the secretary of state. The Department of Defense grew vastly larger than the Department of State in budget and personnel, and played a more central role in overseas conflicts. The Department of State also suffered from its reputation as a rigidly bureaucratic institution whose recommendations to the president were overly cautious and uncreative.[17]

With the end of the Cold War, the Department of State made a comeback. President George H. W. Bush selected his closest political friend and counselor, James Baker, as secretary of state. President Clinton employed his first secretary of state, Warren Christopher, as his principal foreign policy adviser. As Christopher's successor, Clinton selected the first female secretary of state, Madeleine Albright, and she quickly made a splash as a global diplomat. President George W. Bush's selection of Colin Powell, the first African-American secretary of state, continued the trend toward reviving the prestige of the State Department.[18]

With the initiation of President Bush's war on terror, however, the State Department fell back into the secondary role it had played during the Cold War. As the sole voice of moderate multilateralism at the highest levels of a conservative administration inclined to a unilateral foreign policy, Secretary of State Powell was at a disadvantage in Bush's "war cabinet"; his influence with the president declined as the power of the secretary of defense, Donald Rumsfeld, rose. The State Department's more realistic appreciation of the situation in Iraq, although validated by subsequent events, left it largely on the sidelines of Iraq policy. The stature of the department may rise again in Bush's second term, but only because the new secretary of state, Condoleezza Rice, is a Bush loyalist who is unlikely to question the White House perspective on the world.

Below the top echelon of State Department officials, who are appointed by the president, the department is staffed by a unique government elite: the Foreign Service. The Foreign Service is highly selective: Rigorous written tests weed out the vast majority of applicants, and subsequent interviews and group simulations eliminate most of the remaining pool, leaving only 1–2 percent able to gain admission to the service. Yet, although the exclusivity of the Foreign

Service bestows prestige, its members are not necessarily as influential as other actors in foreign and defense policy bureaucracies. Their rivals in the National Security Council, Defense Department, or the Central Intelligence Agency often possess the specialized academic expertise or the important political contacts that Foreign Service officers normally lack.[19]

Department of Defense

The end of the Cold War was more beneficial to the State Department than to the **Department of Defense**. During the Cold War, this umbrella organization for the armed forces, symbolized by its massive headquarters, the Pentagon, had been the most powerful agency of the national security state.

The Department of Defense has a dual leadership structure: civilian and military. The secretary of defense heads the department and maintains the American tradition of civilian control of the military. Below the secretary on the civilian side are several assistant secretaries for specialized functions, along with civilian secretaries for the army, navy, and air force. Secretaries of defense have varied considerably in their approaches to the military. Some, such as President Kennedy's secretary, Robert McNamara, have seen their role as imposing organizational rationality on the military, especially by setting limits to the services' unceasing request for costly new weapons systems. Others, such as President Reagan's secretary, Caspar Weinberger, have been zealous advocates for rapid increases in defense spending.

Each of the military services also has a commanding officer from among its ranks. The top uniformed leaders come together in the **Joint Chiefs of Staff (JCS)**, headed by a chair. The JCS conveys the military's point of view to the president and to the secretary of defense. The JCS's influence with civilian officials has often been diminished by the perception that its advice is biased toward military priorities. But it did reach a peak of prestige after the elder President George Bush appointed as its chair General Colin Powell, the highest-ranking African American in the history of the armed forces.

The enormous expansion of the American military during the Cold War was built on claims, at times deliberately exaggerated, of a communist campaign to take over the planet. Concealed beneath the rhetoric about the communist threat was a different fuel for military expansion: inter-service rivalry. Each branch of the services was eager to grow larger, more powerful, and better armed; each was fearful that the others would encroach on its central missions (see Chapter 13 for an example). Each service pushed for its own preferred new weapons system, even when the result was overlap and duplication in weaponry. Every time the Air Force developed a new model fighter plane, for instance, the Navy had to have a new fighter plane to match, and vice versa.

Cold War expansion of the military was furthered by the growth of the *military–industrial complex*. Coined by President Eisenhower, the term refers to the potentially dangerous influence of the political alliance between the Pentagon and the corporations that manufacture its arms. Expensive new weapons systems are mutually rewarding to the armed forces and to companies, especially in such fields as aircraft, electronics, and shipbuilding, for which defense contracts can bring in several billion dollars a year in guaranteed sales. Defense contractors thus place their financial muscle and lobbying resources behind Pentagon budget requests.

The terrorist attacks of September 11, 2001, restored the Pentagon to its dominant place in the national security state. Even before September 11, Secretary of Defense Rumsfeld had announced that his mission was to transform American armed forces into a "leaner and meaner" military machine adapted to fighting the wars of the twenty-first century. Rumsfeld's mobile military was effective in the invasion of Saddam Hussein's Iraq. However, the size and ferocity of the subsequent Iraqi insurgency surprised American military planners, and as the number of American dead and wounded mounted, critics argued that Rumsfeld's strategy of a "leaner and meaner" military had put too few troops on the ground in Iraq to subdue the enemy. Despite mounting criticisms of Rumsfeld and his Defense Department, President Bush retained confidence in him and kept him at the Pentagon at the beginning of his second term.

The Intelligence Community

One of the central features of the national security state is a large and diverse *intelligence community*. A number of U.S. agencies gather intelligence (information) about military, political, and economic developments in other countries. Some of the institutions in this community specialize in high-tech intelligence gathering. Among these is the National Security Agency, which employs the most advanced computer technology and spy satellites to monitor communications around the world. Each branch of the armed forces maintains its own intelligence unit. But the preeminent force in the intelligence community has been the **Central Intelligence Agency (CIA)**.

When Congress created the CIA, it thought it was establishing an agency to gather intelligence by various means ranging from analyses of foreign newspapers to espionage. Yet a vague phrase in the 1947 law referring to "other functions and duties" was seized on by the CIA to establish a unit that had little to do with intelligence gathering.[20] This was the **covert action** wing of the CIA, which specialized in clandestine operations that could not be traced to the U.S. government. Covert action became a secret weapon for presidents, allowing them to conduct a hidden foreign policy by, for example, bribing foreign politicians, stirring up economic unrest in other nations, or pushing for military coups to overthrow governments considered unfriendly.

Covert action became the hallmark of the CIA and was usually supported by the argument that the nation's communist enemies were employing the same kinds of "dirty tricks" to advance their sinister objectives. Few covert operations, as it turned out, actually hurt the communists or furthered American national security. Many backfired, making more enemies than friends in the long run; the Iranian people's continuing hostility to America is a prime example.[21]

However, it is not the ineffectiveness of covert action that has made the CIA the national security agency that most disturbs popular democrats. They are even more worried about the incompatibility of covert action with American democracy. Political scientist Loch Johnson notes that whereas democracy requires open government, public debate, the rule of law, and ethical behavior, covert action requires "the use of tactics or 'dirty tricks' that are far removed from the accepted philosophical tenets of democratic theory—lying, sabotage, even clandestine warfare and assassination in times of peace."[22]

Revelations in the mid-1970s of CIA abuses, including spying on American citizens as well as assassination plots, led to the formation of intelligence committees in the House and Senate to monitor and occasionally veto covert operations. Through these congressional committees, there is now at least some measure of CIA public accountability.[23] Yet the CIA has found ways to evade accountability. President Reagan's director of the CIA, William Casey, misled the congressional committees about the agency's covert actions against the government of Nicaragua. When Congress later prohibited the Reagan administration from using the CIA to fund and direct the Contras, who were fighting to overthrow that government, Casey turned to the NSC staff and Lieutenant Colonel Oliver North to carry out this mission—a covert action that led to the Iran–Contra scandal.

The post–Cold War CIA was shaken by a new crop of embarrassing revelations. Two CIA officials were arrested for selling U.S. secrets to the Russians. And the agency's habit of collaborating with the most unsavory of foreign allies survived the end of the Cold War, as an exposé of its activities in Guatemala documented. The CIA kept on its payroll Guatemalan military officers known to be engaged in kidnapping, torture, and assassination. When these officers covered up the murders of an American citizen and a guerrilla leader married to an American lawyer, the CIA hid the information from the congressional intelligence committees.[24]

The CIA has been subjected to even harsher criticism in the new era of U.S. foreign policy that began on September 11, 2001. Failure to anticipate and prevent the terrorist attacks that destroyed the World Trade Center and damaged the Pentagon represents one of the greatest intelligence disasters in American history. Top CIA officials were more attuned to the threat posed by Al Qaeda than were others in the federal government, but they were unable to mobilize their organization to respond to it effectively. As the 9/11 Commission Report put it: "The intelligence community struggled throughout the 1990s and up to 9/11 to collect intelligence on and analyze the phenomenon of transnational terrorism. The combination of an overwhelming number of priorities, flat budgets, an outmoded structure, and bureaucratic rivalries resulted in an insufficient response to this new challenge."[25]

CIA officials and analysts did not do much better in the aftermath of September 11 than they had done in the period prior to the terrorist strikes. In selling the American public on the need to invade Saddam Hussein's Iraq, President Bush, Vice President Cheney, and Secretary of State Powell claimed that the CIA had uncovered persuasive evidence that Saddam possessed weapons of mass destruction (WMD) which could be used to threaten the security of the United States and its allies. Some CIA career personnel told reporters that they felt pressure from the administration to shape their intelligence analyses in accordance with the White House view. But at the top of the CIA, officials were vigorous in promoting the idea of Saddam as a menace to the world. The CIA's director, George Tenet, told the president that it was a "slam dunk" conclusion that the Iraqi regime possessed WMD.[26] Tenet was completely wrong: After the United States invaded and occupied Iraq, no WMD were ever found.

The CIA, along with the military intelligence services, has also been implicated in some of the more seamy episodes of the war on terrorism. Some CIA agents stand accused of involvement in the torture of detainees at prisons in Iraq and Afghanistan. The CIA operates a secret "rendition" program whereby individuals suspected of having information on terrorist activities are transported for interrogation to other countries, such as Egypt, Saudi Arabia, and Pakistan, where torture is commonly employed. Released later, without ever being charged with an offense, a number of these individuals have told tales of being drugged, beaten, or subjected to electric shocks by their captors.[27]

In response to its glaring failures, two major changes were made to the U.S. intelligence community in 2004. After initial resistance, President Bush accepted the recommendation of the special 9/11 Commission and signed a law establishing a new position of National Intelligence Director. This official is responsible for compelling the CIA and the other fourteen intelligence agencies of the U.S. government to coordinate their activities. Even as Bush moved to reorganize the intelligence community in response to outside pressure, however, he also moved to tighten White House control of the CIA. Bush picked a Republican congressman, Porter Goss, to become the new director of the CIA, prompting a number of veteran CIA officials, who had been skeptical of the Bush administration's conduct in Iraq, to resign their positions.[28] These changes at the CIA leave it unclear whether the agency will improve the quality of its advice about threats to American security or simply echo the ideological perspective of its boss in the White House.

International Economics Agencies

As national security threats declined with the end of the Cold War, American foreign policy makers began to direct greater attention to the globalized economy (see Chapter 3). Officials with responsibilities for international economics have become more prominent on the global stage than previously, sometimes coming to rival diplomats, generals, and intelligence chiefs in their impact on American foreign policy.

Created in 1974, the *Office of the United States Trade Representative* was upgraded and raised to cabinet status under President Clinton. The head of this office leads the American team that participates in multilateral trade negotiations. The U.S. trade representative also negotiates bilateral agreements with important trading partners. President Clinton's special interest in international economics was also evident in his creation of the National Economic Council (NEC). Designed to parallel the National Security Council, this new coordinating instrument for foreign and domestic economic policy brings together the top economic policy makers in a council headed by a special assistant to the president.

The new focus on international economics also brought greater influence and visibility to cabinet agencies previously associated primarily with domestic affairs. President Clinton's second secretary of the treasury, Robert Rubin, was arguably the most important American official in international affairs during the last half of the 1990s. When an Asian financial crisis threatened the global economy, it was Treasury Secretary Rubin and not Secretary of State Albright who shaped and led the American effort to stabilize the situation. Clinton's Commerce secretaries, Ronald Brown and William Daley, also became prominent international actors, taking an aggressive role in promoting American business interests abroad.

President George W. Bush's appointment of his close friend, the businessman and fundraiser Donald Evans, as Commerce secretary for his first term continued the Clinton policy of choosing well-connected power brokers as cheerleaders and champions of American exports. Overall, however, Bush is far less interested in international economics than his predecessor had been.

FOREIGN POLICY AND ECONOMIC POWER

Although military concerns were uppermost for American foreign policy makers during the Cold War, economic concerns were by no means forgotten. The United States emerged from World War II as an unchallenged economic giant, its superiority all the greater because its rivals had been physically or economically devastated by the war. To restore the shattered economies of Europe as trading partners (and to prevent European nations from falling prey to communist subversion), the United States undertook a massive program of economic aid, the Marshall Plan. During the first several decades of the Cold War, the United States was the hegemonic (predominant) power in the capitalist part of the world, setting the rules on international economic relations. American overseas investments and trade boomed during these decades.

But this hegemonic power weakened, eroded both by the economic resurgence of Western Europe and Japan and by the heavy burden of the arms race against the Soviet Union (a burden that America's capitalist competitors largely escaped). Starting in 1971, the United States began to run up a trade deficit, importing more from other countries than it sold to them. This deficit grew to huge proportions, and by the mid-1980s the United States had become the world's largest debtor. Rather than being able to set the rules, America now had to engage in extended—and frequently frustrating—multinational negotiations to bring down tariff barriers or open up foreign markets.[29]

The 1990s saw a partial restoration of American dominance. As the United States regained the technological edge from Japan, and as the economic boom during the Clinton years surpassed the rates of growth among capitalist competitors who had been doing better than the United States in the previous decades, Americans again began to talk—and act—as a hegemonic player in the international economy. And despite many foreign voices expressing resentment of American arrogance, most other nations accepted American economic leadership. Nonetheless, the global economy at the beginning of the new century is far more complex than it was after World War II, so America's economic power in the world is now more difficult to deploy and more susceptible to challenge.

Private interests have always played a significant role in American foreign economic policy. Labor unions are active, especially in seeking to restrict imports from low-wage nations because they eliminate American jobs. Farm groups press for greater government efforts to promote agricultural exports. But the most influential private force is the corporate sector. Empirical research by political scientists Lawrence R. Jacobs and Benjamin I. Page finds that "internationally oriented business leaders exercise strong, consistent, and perhaps lopsided influence on the makers of U.S. foreign policy."[30]

Individuals in the top decision-making echelon of the national security state have often been recruited into temporary government service from large corporations, investment banks, and corporate law firms.[31] Regardless of economic background, American foreign policy makers have generally subscribed to the proposition that what advances the interests of American corporations and banks abroad advances the American national interest. In the globalized economy of the post–Cold War era, business interests have become even more important players in American foreign policy than before.

It is difficult at times to disentangle economic interests from political interests in the history of U.S. foreign policy. Consider two cases concerning the CIA: Iran and Chile. In Iran, the CIA's role in putting the shah in power not only established an anticommunist bastion in the Middle East; it also opened up Iran as a profitable field of operations for American oil companies. In Chile, American-owned corporations were just as zealous as Nixon and Kissinger in getting rid of President Allende. Fearful that Allende might nationalize their properties, the International Telephone and Telegraph Corporation and other American businesses offered the CIA $1.5 million for its covert campaign against him.[32]

That American foreign policy has often served corporate interests abroad leads critics to look for economic motives underneath the national security rationales advanced by government officials. Some opponents of President Bush's war in Iraq believe that it was not undertaken to protect the United States or to advance the cause of democracy in the Middle East, but rather was a war for oil.

FOREIGN POLICY AND PUBLIC OPINION

Until recently, scholars presented a picture of American public opinion in foreign policy that was closely in line with the perspective of elite democracy. Their studies suggested that the mass of Americans lacked interest in or knowledge of foreign affairs, were subject to emotional reactions to foreign events, and tended to defer to elites, especially presidents, in the determination of foreign policies. This view implied that it was fortunate for U.S. foreign policy that elites had the upper hand and that ordinary citizens had relatively little influence.

A CLOSER LOOK

Selling Wars

Survey research suggests that ordinary citizens are more cautious than are foreign policy elites in sending American forces to fight in wars overseas. Perhaps this is because it is the elite managers of the national security state who plan the wars, while it is ordinary citizens who pay for them with their money and their blood. The American public quickly rallies behind the government when the nation comes under attack, as happened after Pearl Harbor and September 11, 2001. But when the threat appears distant and the connection to vital American interests is murky, war has to be sold to the public.

In the Gulf War of 1991, the first President Bush mobilized Americans for war by pointing to the demonic nature of the enemy. Saddam Hussein, the Iraqi dictator, was a brutal leader who had committed an act of naked aggression against his neighbor, tiny but oil-rich Kuwait. However, the danger that Saddam posed to American national interests was unclear. To convince Americans that this was a righteous as well as a necessary war, the Bush administration stoked the public's sense of moral outrage. For this task, nothing was as useful as babies.

A shocking story of Iraqi brutality helped persuade many Americans that the nation had to go to war to rescue the suffering people of Kuwait. A fifteen-year-old Kuwaiti girl, identified only by her first name, Nayirah, appeared before a congressional caucus and related in a tearful voice how she had witnessed Iraqi soldiers take Kuwaiti babies out of their hospital incubators and leave them on the floor to die. The incubator story was widely repeated by President Bush and other advocates of war. After the war, it was revealed that Nayirah was in fact the daughter of Kuwait's ambassador to the United States and that the incubator story had been devised by an American public-relations firm in the pay of the Kuwaiti government. Reporters seeking evidence of the incubator tragedy found none and concluded that this notorious Iraqi atrocity had never happened.

Eleven years later, the second President Bush confronted the same evil dictator. Having come under attack on September 11, Americans were now more receptive to fighting a large-scale war abroad. On the other hand, there was no obvious act of aggression to charge against Saddam this time; weakened by United Nations sanctions, his military forces had not threatened anyone in a decade. To mobilize the American public for a second war against Saddam, the second President

Further research by political scientists has altered this picture substantially.[33] The view of public opinion that has emerged is more favorable to the perspective of popular democracy. Although public knowledge of foreign affairs may fall short of the standard held by foreign policy experts, the newest research shows public opinion about foreign policy to be sensible and stable. The public responds rationally to the information it receives. It rallies behind a president who monopolizes the dissemination of information in a foreign crisis. But it may turn against the White House when alternative sources of information become available.

According to the new research, the public seldom has a direct impact on *specific* foreign policy decisions. But it can establish a climate of opinion that policy makers have to take into account. During the era of Cold War consensus, elites

Bush needed stronger medicine than moral outrage; he needed to sell this war with fear.

The Bush administration's principal argument for war was that Saddam's regime already possessed terrible biological and chemical weapons and was frantically attempting to obtain nuclear weapons. These weapons of mass destruction (WMD), the administration claimed, must not be permitted to be distributed to terrorist groups or used by Saddam against the United States or its friends. To back up this argument, Bush and his aides made a number of dubious claims. For example, the president told the public that according to a report by the International Atomic Energy Agency (IAEA), Iraq was six months away from developing nuclear weapons, and then said, "'I don't know what more evidence we need.'" What IAEA actually reported was that there was *no* evidence that Iraq was currently manufacturing such weapons or even had the physical capability or materials to produce them. The president also told the nation that Iraq was developing unmanned aircraft that could deliver chemical or biological weapons against U.S. targets. He neglected to mention that the unmanned aircraft did not have the range to reach Europe, much less cross the Atlantic Ocean.

The Bush administration also tried to link Saddam, a secular leader, to Al Qaeda, the fanatical religious organization that had carried out the September 11 attacks. If these two evil forces were in cahoots, eliminating Saddam would be a major victory in the war on terror. The administration's prime piece of evidence for a connection was the allegation that Mohammed Atta, the ringleader for the September 11 plot, had met with an Iraqi intelligence officer in Prague, Czech Republic, in April 2001. However, when the FBI investigated the story, it found that Atta had been in Virginia at the time of the supposed meeting. Further, the president of the Czech Republic informed the U.S. government that his intelligence agents had also discredited the story. Nevertheless, Bush officials continued to use the allegation to suggest a link between Saddam and September 11, while carefully hedging their remarks with the claim that the veracity of the story had not yet been conclusively determined.

There is an old saying: "In war, truth is the first casualty." The same seems to be the case for selling the public on the war in the first place. No decision is as critical for a democracy as a decision on war or peace. Unless the military threat to the nation is imminent, no occasion so demands a genuine democratic debate. Instead, what Americans usually get from their leaders in this situation is more akin to false advertising.

Sources: John R. MacArthur, *Second Front: Censorship and Propaganda in the Gulf War* (New York: Hill and Wang, 1992); Sheldon Rampton and John Stauber, *Weapons of Mass Deception: The Uses of Propaganda in Bush's War on Iraq* (New York: Tarcher/Penguin, 2003); Louis Fisher, *Presidential War Power*, 2nd ed. revised (Lawrence: University Press of Kansas, 2004).

enjoyed a permissive climate for dispatching American troops to overseas conflicts. In the 1970s and 1980s, however, the majority of Americans were affected by a "Vietnam syndrome," an apprehension about sending troops abroad that constrained decision makers. President Reagan tried to overcome this syndrome with a guaranteed military victory in Grenada. Yet his efforts were not very successful: Public opinion constrained the Reagan administration from sending troops to attack the Sandinista government of Nicaragua and pressured the president to resume arms control negotiations with the Soviet Union.[34] The first President Bush claimed that he had finally vanquished the Vietnam syndrome in the Persian Gulf War of 1991. Yet public fears about sending American forces "in harm's way" continued to restrict President Clinton's options abroad. For example, his decision to rely exclusively on air power in the Kosovo crisis of 1999 reflected his concern that public opinion would turn sharply against U.S. involvement should there be a significant number of American casualties.

Rather than always deferring to foreign policy elites, public opinion can, if it becomes strong and intense, compel elites to change their policies. Neither the president nor Congress is likely to hold out long once public opinion moves sharply in a new direction. Political scientists Robert Shapiro and Benjamin Page found that when public opinion changed significantly, American foreign policy subsequently changed with it about two-thirds of the time. The more that public unhappiness over American casualties in the war in Vietnam mounted, for example, the faster the president withdrew American forces from the conflict.[35]

POST–COLD WAR FOREIGN POLICY

In one form or another, *containment* of communism was the U.S. strategy during the Cold War era. What should U.S. strategy be for a post–Cold War period in which no single adversary or problem towered over everything else? Many foreign policy elites and academic specialists proposed new doctrines, but no contender for the position of successor to containment managed to capture a dominant place. The post–Cold War world seemed too complex to be addressed through a single approach. Consequently, U.S. foreign and defense policies after the collapse of the Soviet Union emerged not in accordance with a "blueprint," but rather in piecemeal fashion, in response to diverse diplomatic, military, economic, environmental, and humanitarian problems.

Compared to the Cold War era, foreign policy in its immediate aftermath seemed far less urgent to the majority of Americans. There was no longer a despised enemy against whom a president could easily rally Americans. There was no longer the threat of attack from a nuclear superpower that had given the subject of national security a life-and-death quality during the Cold War. Most Americans were now reluctant to commit American troops or resources abroad and preferred that the president concentrate instead on making life at home more prosperous and harmonious. The lack of an overarching national security strategy and the diminished public support for presidential activism in international relations were especially evident in the administration of Bill Clinton.

Bill Clinton and the Post–Cold War World

From the moment he took office, President Clinton's foreign and defense policies were subjected to vigorous criticisms by international relations experts. One common complaint was that Clinton was preoccupied with domestic policies and politics, and gave international affairs only fitful attention. Another was that his foreign policy was ad hoc and incoherent, devoid of any strategic vision.[36] Yet by the end of his presidency Clinton could claim that he had achieved several successes and avoided any major disasters in foreign policy. After the terrorist attacks of September 11, 2001, it became evident that the Clinton administration had failed to counter effectively the mounting threat from Al Qaeda. However, his administration had taken the threat more seriously than the Bush administration did before September 11, 2001.

Although many Clinton foreign policy decisions seemed ad hoc, two consistent commitments characterized his approach to the world. First, Clinton sought to shift the emphasis of U.S. foreign policy from military power to economic power. Believing that the new measuring stick of national power in an age of globalization is economics, and that America's new rivals are market competitors rather than military adversaries, Clinton was a dedicated apostle of free trade as the key to American economic primacy. Second, Clinton went further than Cold War predecessors in shaping a foreign policy of **multilateralism**, in which the United States prefers to work in combination with partners in its international endeavors. To Clinton, multilateralism was a matter of genuine belief in growing international interdependence, but it was also a political necessity: in the post–Cold War world, he recognized, the American people were increasingly eager to share with our allies the military and financial burdens of ensuring a peaceful world.

However Clinton is evaluated, the foreign and defense issues that his administration faced were characteristic of the post–Cold War era. We consider four of these issues: (1) international trade and finance, (2) the size and role of the U.S. military, (3) the uses of force in the post–Cold War world, and (4) peacemaking and peacekeeping.

International Trade and Finance. The most distinctive feature of Bill Clinton's foreign policy was its emphasis on international economics. Recognizing the importance of the international economy for his domestic agenda as much as for his international goals, Bill Clinton promised a new activism in foreign economic policy. This was one campaign pledge that even his critics had to admit he fulfilled.

The promotion of free trade was a constant in Clinton's foreign policy. His most prominent achievements in this area came in his first and last years in office. In 1993, Clinton waged an uphill battle to obtain congressional passage of the North American Free Trade Agreement (NAFTA). Allying himself with large corporations, Clinton overcame opposition spearheaded by labor and environmental groups which argued that NAFTA would keep wages low and environmental regulations impotent on both sides of the border with Mexico. In 2000, Clinton reached another landmark in his free trade strategy: congressional approval of "permanent normal trade relations" with the People's Republic of China. Highlighting China's continuing abuse of civil and religious liberties, an unusual coalition of liberals and conservatives fought against welcoming it into the camp of free traders. But Clinton, who had promised in 1992 to condition U.S. trade with China on its human-rights improvements, now insisted that a policy of "constructive engagement" with China through free trade was the best way to encourage its democratic progress.

Along with championing free trade, the Clinton administration was especially active in managing the international financial system. Circumventing Congress in 1995, it provided $50 billion in loans to bail out a Mexican financial system in danger of collapse. In 1998, Treasury Secretary Robert Rubin took the lead in coordinating a successful international response to a financial crisis that had engulfed Asia. With all economies vulnerable, through their interdependencies, to currency disorders anywhere in the world, the Clinton administration successfully asserted American leadership in international finances.

The Size and Role of the Military. Many of those who supported Bill Clinton in 1992 anticipated that with the disappearance of the communist threat there would be a "peace dividend": Military spending could be substantially slashed, and the funds freed up could be redirected to domestic needs. But from the start of his presidency, Clinton, embarrassed by campaign revelations of his efforts to avoid the draft during the war in Vietnam, and then assailed by armed forces members when he tried to end discrimination against gays and lesbians, was on the defensive in military matters. Moreover, the military–industrial complex could not be cut back rapidly without threatening large numbers of jobs, especially in the state richest in electoral votes, California. So Clinton's proposed cuts from a Cold War–era defense budget were modest during his first term. During the last two years of his second term, the president began to advocate new increases in defense spending.

Initially, Clinton was reluctant to use this military might. Public opinion was opposed to the dispatch of American troops to global hot spots, and Congress, where the new isolationists in the Republican Party were increasingly noisy, repeatedly threatened to block American engagements abroad. But with Haiti in 1994, Bosnia in 1995, and Kosovo in 1999, Clinton overrode objections—some of them constitutional—and sent in American forces. These uses of the military reflected a paradox of post–Cold War foreign policy: Presidents still had considerable latitude for unilateral deployments of armed forces, but they had to restrict the use of ground forces out of fear that the public would not put up with any significant number of American casualties.

Military interventions in the Clinton style did not blow up in the president's face, especially because there were no American combat deaths in Haiti, Bosnia, or Kosovo. Neither, however, did their successes bring Clinton boosts in popularity either, as had been the case with Cold War–era presidential uses of the military (and as would again be the case with Bush's war in Afghanistan and invasion of Iraq).

Military Action: Bosnia and Kosovo. The two principal tests for Bill Clinton in military affairs came in the Balkans and involved the violent breakup of the former Yugoslavia. First in Bosnia, and later in Kosovo, Clinton had to cope with Yugoslav dictator Slobodan Milosevic, a type of regional aggressor who had become more prominent with the decline of the old Cold War power blocs.

No foreign policy issue so bedeviled Clinton's national-security team as Bosnia—the "problem from hell," in the words of Secretary of State Warren Christopher.[37] The civil war in Bosnia, which began early in 1992, reflected the new post–Cold War landscape in which nationalist and ethnic hatreds exploded once the old superpower conflict had vanished. In the former Yugoslav republic of Bosnia-Herzegovina, ethnic Serbs battled ethnic Muslims for control. Aided by neighboring Serbia, led by Milosevic, the Bosnian Serbs had the upper hand militarily and followed their victories with "ethnic cleansing" (driving Muslims from their villages) and the mass rape of Muslim women.

As a presidential candidate, Bill Clinton had blasted President Bush for standing by while human rights and democracy were violated on a massive scale in Bosnia. But once he took office, Clinton found himself standing by as well, even as the horror of Bosnia deepened. After 2½ years of vacillation, Clinton finally seized an opening in the summer of 1995 and took strong action. A new American diplomatic mission, backed up by large-scale bombing of Serb positions, brought the warring parties to a peace conference in Dayton, Ohio. The agreement hammered out by American diplomats at Dayton maintained the legal integrity of Bosnia but effectively partitioned the country between a Muslim–Croat Federation and a Serb Republic. A NATO peacekeeping force, including 20,000 American troops, took military control of Bosnia, separating the warring ethnic factions while the political and economic reconstruction of the nation began. With a quarter of a million dead and 2 million driven from their homes, a fragile peace came to Bosnia.[38]

Blocked in Bosnia, Milosevic began a new campaign of ethnic cleansing and mass murder against the ethnic Albanian population that constituted the majority in the Yugoslav province of Kosovo. This time, having learned a bitter lesson in Bosnia, Clinton and America's NATO allies acted more swiftly. To stop the rampage by Milosevic's forces, NATO began a massive air war against his government and military in March 1999. Uncertain of winning public and congressional support, Clinton limited America's military options by foreswearing the use of ground troops. The success of the air campaign remained in doubt until Clinton and his allies began to discuss sending in forces on the ground. In June 1999, the Serbian dictator heeded the threat and ordered the withdrawal of his forces from Kosovo. Milosevic fell from power in the fall of 2000 after losing an election and subsequently was tried by an international court as a war criminal.

Peacemaking. President Clinton used U.S. forces as peacekeepers after the fighting ceased in Bosnia and Kosovo. But he also played a major diplomatic role as a peacemaker, especially in Northern Ireland and the Middle East.

One of Clinton's signal foreign policy achievements was his role in fostering a peace agreement between the Catholic and Protestant militants who had long been warring with each other in Northern Ireland. He was the first president to venture into this thorny conflict. Once he had the collaboration of a friendly British prime minister, Tony Blair, and the negotiating talent of a former senator, George Mitchell, Clinton was able to bring the two sides together in the Easter Sunday pact of 1998.

Clinton's peacemaking in the Middle East was more familiar, building on the efforts of his predecessors, especially Jimmy Carter. His administration devoted extensive efforts to finding a formula for a final settlement between Israel and the Palestinians, and the president was repeatedly engaged on a personal level in marathon negotiating sessions with Israeli and Palestinian leaders. Despite some successes, his final attempt at a definitive solution collapsed in the summer of 2000, and a terrible new cycle of violence between Palestinians and Israelis brought the peace process to a crashing halt as George W. Bush assumed office.

U.S. FOREIGN POLICY AFTER SEPTEMBER 11

The post–Cold War period proved to be brief, lasting only from the collapse of the Soviet Union in 1991 to the terrorist attacks on the World Trade Center and Pentagon on September 11, 2001. The horrific events of 9/11 catapulted national security back to the primacy in U.S. politics it had held during the Cold War period. Once again, Americans had a despised enemy in the world. Once again, international affairs took on a life-and-death quality for Americans.

Yet if in the post–September 11 period international affairs have taken on the same kind of urgency as during the Cold War era, U.S. foreign policy after 9/11 has not been marked by the consensus that prevailed during the early years of the Cold War. All sides in the developing democratic debate over foreign policy agree on the need for an aggressive global campaign to defeat the terrorist threat. How to combat Al Qaeda and other terrorist groups, however, is a question that inspires major political divisions.

The Bush administration has approached the war on terror as, primarily, a matter of the effective application of America's overwhelming military superiority in the world. The United States must strike aggressively at terrorist groups or rogue nations *well before* they can threaten American lives, and it should not be constrained in its actions by more cautious allies. In the wake of military action, as terror groups are destroyed and tyrants are toppled, the United States can foster democracy as the long-term antidote to terrorism.

To its critics, however, the foreign policy of the Bush administration is a mistaken, and even dangerous, response to the events of September 11. They argue that Bush's **unilateralism** (in which the United States looks to its own interests and often goes its own way regardless of the concerns of other countries) and preference for military action over diplomacy represent an arrogant, reckless policy that alienates the rest of the world and generates unsustainable costs for American armed forces and the federal budget. Instead, U.S. foreign policy must revive the institutions and policies of multilateralism that served us well during the Cold War period to fight the new global foe.[39] Most critics of Bush agree that the United States must be an active force for the promotion of democracy in the world. The flaw in his approach, as Benjamin Barber puts it, is that "democracy cannot be imposed at the muzzle of a well-wishing outsider's rifle."[40]

George W. Bush and American Foreign Policy

George W. Bush entered the White House without much experience or expertise in international affairs. Unlike his father, who had been an envoy to China, ambassador to the United Nations, and director of the Central Intelligence Agency, the younger Bush was basically a homebody, having made only three trips abroad in his adult life. Inexperience—and a lack of curiosity about the world—made Bush highly dependent on his top foreign policy advisers. Bush's foreign policy team during his first term was very different from Clinton's: Its members' backgrounds lay not in diplomacy or trade relations but in military affairs. Vice President Cheney and Secretary of State Colin Powell served under the first Bush as secretary of defense and chair of the Joint Chiefs of Staff, respectively. Secretary of Defense Donald Rumsfeld held the same post under President Ford. Only Condoleezza Rice, national security adviser during Bush's first term and secretary of state in his second, lacked a Pentagon background.

Prior to September 11, 2001, foreign policy took a back seat to the conservative domestic agenda of the new Bush presidency. During the 2000 campaign, Bush criticized the Clinton administration for allowing American military power to decline. However, instead of proposing to use renewed American military strength to take a more active role in global affairs, Bush actually complained that Clinton had intervened too often in regions of the world peripheral to American security interests. Rejecting Clinton-style "nation-building" in countries such as Bosnia, candidate Bush argued that the United States would have more influence in the world if it appeared to others as a "humble nation."[41]

Repudiating the multilateral approach that Clinton had favored, Bush in office at first pursued an approach to foreign policy that most observers characterized as unilateralist. The most controversial early foreign policy actions of the Bush administration were its rejection of international agreements. President Bush rejected the Kyoto Protocol on global warming, the Comprehensive Test Ban Treaty on nuclear weapons, and a Biological Weapons Protocol that enforces compliance with a treaty banning biological weapons. His administration also withdrew the United States from the Antiballistic Missile Treaty in order to develop a national missile defense program. This go-it-alone approach drew international protests. As *New York Times* reporter Thom Shanker wrote, "By knocking off several of the hard-earned, high-profile treaties on arms control and the environment, Mr. Bush has been subjected to outrage from some of America's closest friends—who wonder what will replace a world ordered by treaties—as well as its adversaries who see arrogance in Mr. Bush's actions."[42]

September 11 and the War on Terror. The focus of Bush's foreign policy was dramatically altered by the horrifying attacks on the American homeland on September 11, 2001. National security issues that had preoccupied the administration up to that date were shelved as Bush proclaimed a global war against terrorism as the defining purpose of his presidency.

An administration whose dominant national security actors had favored unilateral American actions quickly had to shift gears and adopt a multilateral approach as it sought to construct an international coalition against terrorism. Cooperation from other nations was essential in the war that Bush began to wage, especially because American military force was, in the eyes of foreign policy analysts, only one component of a campaign to defeat the terrorists. The

events of September 11 brought the United States some unexpected allies: Pakistan, previously the main supporter of the Taliban regime in Afghanistan that harbored the terror network of Osama bin Laden, and Russia, which gained greater American sympathy for its harsh war against its own Islamic foes in Chechnya. But Bush had strong backing as well from traditional American allies, such as Great Britain and Germany.

Ensured of overwhelming support at home and around the globe, President Bush launched a military campaign that swiftly shattered the Taliban regime in Afghanistan. However, relying primarily on Afghan fighters rather than American troops, Bush's Pentagon failed to capture the top leadership of Al Qaeda, including its chief, Osama bin Laden. The outcome in Afghanistan appeared to demonstrate that a multilateral coalition could wage an effective campaign against a terror network that threatened many nations. However, President Bush was soon to disrupt this coalition, as he announced a broader and more controversial definition of the war on terror.

The "Axis of Evil" and the New National-Security Strategy. In his State of the Union address in January 2002, Bush called for an expansion of the war on ter-

ror beyond the fight against the Al Qaeda terror network, focusing on three nation-states—North Korea, Iran, and Iraq—that he depicted as "an axis of evil." This dramatic phrase, recalling American enemies from World War II and the Cold War, signaled that the United States under President Bush, far from accepting the limits of a "humble nation," would now take on the mission of ridding the world of its most immoral and dangerous regimes. Apart from Great Britain, most of America's traditional allies were disturbed by President Bush's return to unilateralism. Their unease would only grow once the Bush administration prepared to turn its rhetoric into reality.

As the Bush administration made it increasingly clear that the first target for its war against evil would be Saddam Hussein's Iraq, it introduced a new national-security doctrine in September 2002. During the Cold War, American foreign policy was based on the doctrines of *containment* of communism and *deterrence* against attacks on the United States by building up such powerful armed forces that any aggressor would pay a terrible price from American military retaliation. Bush's new foreign policy strategy abandons containment and deterrence, arguing that terrorist groups or the rogue nations that might assist them or use weapons of mass destruction (WMD) on their own accord cannot be constrained in the old way.[43] Instead, according to the Bush administration's statement of its new doctrine, the United States must be prepared to wage **preventive war**: "The greater the threat, the greater is the risk of inaction—and the more compelling the case for taking anticipatory action to defend ourselves—even if uncertainty remains as to the time and place of the enemy's attack. To forestall or prevent such hostile acts by our adversaries, the United States will, if necessary, act preemptively."[44]

War in Iraq. Al Qaeda had struck the United States on September 11, 2001, but it was Iraq that was to become the centerpiece of President Bush's war on terror. From September 2002 to March 2003, Bush and his foreign policy team concentrated their efforts on convincing the American people of the necessity of a preventive war against Saddam Hussein's Iraqi regime. (The selling of the Iraq War is a subject of this chapter's "A Closer Look" box.)

Around the world, many governments and the vast majority of ordinary citizens responded to the claims of the Bush administration about Iraq with skepticism. Bush failed to win United Nations support for a war, and while he had the steadfast support of British Prime Minister Tony Blair, the president's Iraq policy was opposed by Germany, France, and Russia, among others. Within the United States, an antiwar movement sprang to life and mounted massive demonstrations in major cities. Nonetheless, like his Cold War predecessors, Bush was able to evoke the "rally-round-the-flag" effect, winning majority support at home with the argument that the president stands for the nation's vital interests at times of crisis. The president began the war in March 2003, and within a month American forces were in Baghdad and Saddam Hussein had gone into hiding. On May 1, 2003, a triumphant commander in chief, dressed in flight gear, appeared on the aircraft carrier USS *Lincoln* to proclaim, "Mission accomplished!"

However, the proclamation was premature, and the mission was far from accomplished. The first major problem that Bush faced in the occupation of Iraq was that his premises for this preventive war proved to be false. Despite extensive efforts by American search teams, no WMD were found in Iraq. Increasing evidence emerged in the United States that the Bush administration had exaggerated ambiguous intelligence data about WMD before the war in order to convince the American public that it was in danger.[45] The Bush administration also had to backtrack on its claims of a tie between Saddam's Iraq and Al Qaeda when its evidence proved to be faulty. Increasingly, the president had to rely on what had been a minor part of his prewar case: that an invasion of Iraq was necessary for democratic "nation-building."

A second—and even larger—problem was that the occupation and reconstruction of Iraq proved far more difficult than the invasion had been. Contrary to the prediction of Vice President Cheney, American armed forces were not welcomed by Iraqis as liberators. On the contrary, former supporters of Saddam's secular regime joined with Islamic fundamentalists and nationalists in an insurgency whose size and ferocity stunned Americans. As insurgents turned to increasingly brutal tactics, including car bombings and beheadings, both Iraqi civilians and soldiers and American troops suffered heavy casualties. American efforts to persuade Iraqis that U.S. motives were benign were further undercut by revelations that American military personnel at the Abu Ghraib prison had sexually humiliated and tortured detainees. Iraq under American occupation was not quite the democratic showplace that the Bush administration promised, although the Iraqi elections of January 2005 generated hopes that Iraq was on a track to democratic self-government.

The War on Terror as Politics. During the brief post–Cold War period, President Clinton did not enjoy any boosts to his presidential popularity when he sent American troops into overseas conflicts. After 9/11, however, as Americans turned to the presidency to keep the nation safe, the role of commander in chief regained its former luster. The Bush presidency was genuinely committed to its new global strategy in the war on terror—but it was also prepared to capitalize on the president's wartime prestige to score political gains.

Although the Democrats tried to keep the focus on economic and social issues, where they held an advantage, in the elections of 2002 and 2004, the Republicans succeeded in centering both of these elections around the president's leadership in the war on terror. In the 2002 congressional elections, Bush and the Republicans played up Democratic resistance to the president's proposal for a Department of Homeland Security because it eliminated civil service protections for federal employees, and this issue was pivotal in contests that restored control of the Senate to Bush's party. In the 2004 presidential campaign, the president's trump card was his appeal to voters that he was more capable than Democratic candidate John Kerry of defending the nation. Republican dominance in Washington at the beginning of Bush's second term owed more to the politics of the war on terror than to any other factor.

CONCLUSION: A MORE DEMOCRATIC FOREIGN POLICY?

The political climate in the United States after the terrorist attacks of 9/11 has not been favorable to a democratic debate over American foreign policy. Frightened by the unprecedented vulnerability of the homeland to terrorist violence, most Americans have looked to the White House for safety and security. Congress has largely acquiesced in the president's renewed dominance of foreign policy, although the federal courts have stepped in to restrain excessive presidential claims for the indefinite detention of enemy combatants. Although criticism of the Bush administration's war in Iraq has been widespread, it has not prompted the president or his advisers to rethink or to scale back their assertive, unilateral approach to the world. At times, the Bush administration has even suggested that vigorous political debate may jeopardize American security. Attacking critics who warned that Bush security measures posed a threat to civil liberties, Attorney General Ashcroft testified to a Senate committee that their "tactics only aid terrorists for they erode our national unity and diminish our resolve. . . ."[46]

At a moment of danger like the present, it is all the more important that the popular democratic tradition, which questions elite dominance over foreign policy, be maintained. Popular democrats have long argued that American strength in the world depends on a healthy economy and society and on the vigor of democratic life. They have believed that America should seek peaceful relations with other nations and support democratic progress around the globe. They have warned of a large, expensive, and aggressive military and emphasized the distortions it can introduce into the conduct of America's international relations.

Popular democrats seek to widen the democratic debate over foreign policy. To open up this debate, the secretive habits of the national security state, including excessive classification of information and covert action, must be challenged. Foreign policy experts in the executive branch and the Pentagon must not monopolize the discussion; voices in Congress and in citizen groups also must be heard. Because the United States must speak to the rest of the world in a clear fashion and must defeat the threat of terrorism, presidential leadership in foreign policy will remain necessary. But in the post–September 11 world, presidents should not be the sole masters of foreign policy. Their approach to the world should emerge from a democratic dialogue over the goals and instruments of American foreign policy.

KEY TERMS

isolationism
expansion
Cold War
national security state
North Atlantic Treaty Organization (NATO)
containment
National Security Council (NSC)
national security adviser

Department of State
Department of Defense
Joint Chiefs of Staff (JCS)
Central Intelligence Agency (CIA)
covert action
multilateralism
unilateralism
preventive war

<table>
<tr><td>

**INTERNET
RESOURCES**

</td><td>

■ Center for Defense Information

www.cdi.org

The Center for Defense Information's website offers critical perspectives on issues involving the military–industrial complex.

■ Global Exchange

www.globalexchange.org

A website for labor, environmental, and other activists who seek links to international groups concerned with the harmful consequences of unchecked economic globalization.

■ World Trade Organization (WTO)

www.wto.org

Official site of the World Trade Organization, with links to government and business sites that favor free trade in the global economy.

</td></tr>
</table>

**SUGGESTED
READINGS**

Benjamin R. Barber, *Fear's Empire: War, Terrorism, and Democracy*. New York: W. W. Norton, 2003. A popular democratic argument that "preventive democracy" is a more effective response to the threat of terror than "preventive war."

Max Boot, *The Savage Wars of Peace: Small Wars and the Rise of American Power*. New York: Basic Books, 2003. A leading neoconservative provides support for the Bush strategy by showing how the United States has been successful in fighting "small wars" in the past.

Ivo H. Daalder and James M. Lindsay, *America Unbound: The Bush Revolution in Foreign Policy*. Washington, D.C.: Brookings Institution Press, 2003. A critical account of George W. Bush's "revolutionary" approach to American foreign policy.

Chalmers Johnson, *Blowback: The Costs and Consequences of American Empire*. New York: Henry Holt and Company, 2004. A leading scholar on Asian politics argues that America's imperial overreaching produces unforeseen retaliation from those who have suffered from American actions abroad.

Joseph S. Nye Jr., *The Paradox of American Power: Why the World's Only Superpower Can't Go It Alone*. New York: Oxford University Press, 2002. A prominent scholar in international relations presents the case for a more multilateral orientation in U.S. foreign policy.

APPENDIX

For additional primary sources, log on to the text's ONLINE STUDY CENTER at http://college.hmco.com/pic/TheDemocraticDebate4e.

THE DECLARATION OF INDEPENDENCE IN CONGRESS   JULY 4, 1776

The unanimous declaration of the thirteen United States of America

When, in the course of human events, it becomes necessary for one people to dissolve the political bonds which have connected them with another, and to assume, among the powers of the earth, the separate and equal station to which the laws of nature and nature's God entitle them, a decent respect to the opinions of mankind requires that they should declare the causes which impel them to the separation.

We hold these truths to be self-evident: That all men are created equal; that they are endowed by their Creator with certain unalienable rights; that among these are life, liberty, and the pursuit of happiness; that, to secure these rights, governments are instituted among men, deriving their just powers from the consent of the governed; that whenever any form of government becomes destructive of these ends, it is the right of the people to alter or to abolish it, and to institute new government, laying its foundation on such principles, and organizing its powers in such form, as to

them shall seem most likely to effect their safety and happiness. Prudence, indeed, will dictate that government long established should not be changed for light and transient causes; and accordingly all experience hath shown that mankind are more disposed to suffer, while evils are sufferable, than to right themselves by abolishing the forms to which they are accustomed. But when a long train of abuses and usurpations, pursuing invariably the same object, evinces a design to reduce them under absolute despotism, it is their right, it is their duty, to throw off such government, and to provide new guards for their future security. Such has been the patient sufferance of these colonies; and such is now the necessity which constrains them to alter their former systems of government. The history of the present King of Great Britain is a history of repeated injuries and usurpations, all having in direct object the establishment of an absolute tyranny over these states. To prove this, let facts be submitted to a candid world.

He has refused his assent to laws, the most wholesome and necessary for the public good.

He has forbidden his governors to pass laws of immediate and pressing importance, unless suspended in their operation till his assent should be obtained; and, when so suspended, he has utterly neglected to attend to them.

He has refused to pass other laws for the accommodation of large districts of people, unless those people would relinquish the right of representation in the legislature, a right inestimable to them, and formidable to tyrants only.

He has called together legislative bodies at places unusual, uncomfortable, and distant from the depository of their public records, for the sole purpose of fatiguing them into compliance with his measures.

He has dissolved representative houses repeatedly, for opposing, with manly firmness, his invasions on the rights of the people.

He has refused for a long time, after such dissolutions, to cause others to be elected; whereby the legislative

A-1

powers, incapable of annihilation, have returned to the people at large for their exercise; the state remaining, in the mean time, exposed to all the dangers of invasions from without and convulsions within.

He has endeavored to prevent the population of these states; for that purpose obstructing the laws for naturalization of foreigners; refusing to pass others to encourage their migration hither, and raising the conditions of new appropriations of lands.

He has obstructed the administration of justice, by refusing his assent to laws for establishing judiciary powers.

He has made judges dependent on his will alone, for the tenure of their offiices, and the amount and payment of their salaries.

He has erected a multitude of new offices, and sent hither swarms of officers to harass our people and eat out their substance.

He has kept among us, in times of peace, standing armies, without the consent of our legislatures.

He has affected to render the military independent of, and superior to, the civil power.

He has combined with others to subject us to a jurisdiction foreign to our constitution, and unacknowledged by our laws, giving his assent to their acts of pretended legislation:

For quartering large bodies of armed troops among us;

For protecting them, by a mock trial, from punishment for any murders which they should commit on the inhabitants of these states;

For cutting off our trade with all parts of the world;

For imposing taxes on us without our consent;

For depriving us, in many cases, of the benefits of trial by jury;

For transporting us beyond seas, to be tried for pretended offenses;

For abolishing the free system of English laws in a neighboring province, establishing therein an arbitrary government, and enlarging its boundaries, so as to render it at once an example and fit instrument for introducing the same absolute rule into these colonies;

For taking away our charters, abolishing our most valuable laws, and altering fundamentally the forms of our governments;

For suspending our own legislatures, and declaring themselves invested with power to legislate for us in all cases whatsoever.

He has abdicated government here, by declaring us out of his protection and waging war against us.

He has plundered our seas, ravaged out coasts, burned our towns, and destroyed the lives of our people.

He is at this time transporting large armies of foreign mercenaries to complete the works of death, desolation, and tyranny already begun with circumstances of cruelty and perfidy scarcely paralleled in the most barbarous ages, and totally unworthy the head of a civilized nation.

He has constrained our fellow-citizens, taken captive on the high seas, to bear arms against their country, to become the executioners of their friends and brethren, or to fall themselves by their hands.

He has excited domestic insurrection among us, and has endeavored to bring on the inhabitants of our frontiers the merciless Indian savages, whose known rule of warfare is an undistinguished destruction of all ages, sexes, and conditions.

In every stage of these oppressions we have petitioned for redress in the most humble terms; our repeated petitions have been answered only by repeated injury. A prince, whose character is thus marked by every act which may define a tyrant, is unfit to be the ruler of a free people.

Nor have we been wanting in our attentions to our British brethren. We have warned them, from time to time, of attempts by their legislature to extend an unwarrantable jurisdiction over us. We have reminded them of the circumstances of our emigration and settlement here. We have appealed to their native justice and magnanimity; and we have conjured them, by the ties of our common kindred, to disavow these usurpations, which would inevitably interrupt our connections and correspondence. They too, have been deaf to the voice of justice and of consanguinity. We must, therefore, acquiesce in the necessity which denounces our separation, and hold them, as we hold the rest of mankind, enemies in war, in peace friends.

We, therefore, the representatives of the United States of America, in General Congress assembled, appealing to the Supreme Judge of the world for the rectitude of our intentions, do, in the name and by the authority of the good people of these colonies, solemnly publish and declare, that these United Colonies are, and of right ought to be, FREE AND INDEPENDENT STATES; that they are absolved from all allegiance to the British crown, and that all political connection between them and the state of Great Britain is, and ought to be, totally dissolved; and that, as free and independent states, they have full power to levy war, conclude peace, contract alliances, establish commerce, and do all other acts and things which independent states may of right do. And for the support of this declaration, with a firm reliance on the protection of Divine Providence, we mutually pledge to each other our lives, our fortunes, and our sacred honor.

JOHN HANCOCK
and fifty-five others

THE CONSTITUTION OF THE UNITED STATES OF AMERICA*

Preamble

We the people of the United States, in order to form a more perfect union, establish justice, insure domestic tranquillity, provide for the common defense, promote the general welfare, and secure the blessings of liberty to ourselves and our posterity, do ordain and establish this Constitution for the United States of America.

Article I

Section 1 All legislative powers herein granted shall be vested in a Congress of the United States, which shall consist of a Senate and a House of Representatives.

Section 2 The House of Representatives shall be composed of members chosen every second year by the people of the several States, and the electors in each State shall have the qualifications requisite for electors of the most numerous branch of the State Legislature.

No person shall be a Representative who shall not have attained to the age of twenty-five years, and been seven years a citizen of the United States, and who shall not, when elected, be an inhabitant of that State in which he shall be chosen.

Representatives and direct taxes shall be apportioned among the several States which may be included within this Union, according to their respective numbers, *which shall be determined by adding to the whole number of free persons, including those bound to service for a term of years and excluding Indians not taxed, three-fifths of all other persons.* The actual enumeration shall be made within three years after the first meeting of the

Congress of the United States, and within every subsequent term of ten years, in such manner as they shall by law direct. The number of Representatives shall not exceed one for every thirty thousand, but each State shall have at least one Representative; *and until such enumeration shall be made, the State of New Hampshire shall be entitled to choose three, Massachusetts eight, Rhode Island and Providence Plantations one, Connecticut five, New York six, New Jersey four, Pennsylvania eight, Delaware one, Maryland six, Virginia ten, North Carolina five, South Carolina five, and Georgia three.*

When vacancies happen in the representation from any State, the Executive authority thereof shall issue writs of elections to fill such vacancies.

The House of Representatives shall choose their Speaker and other officers; and shall have the sole power of impeachment.

Section 3 The Senate of the United States shall be composed of two Senators from each State, *chosen by the legislature thereof,* for six years; and each Senator shall have one vote.

Immediately after they shall be assembled in consequence of the first election, they shall be divided as equally as may be into three classes. The seats of the Senators of the first class shall be vacated at the expiration of the second year, of the second class at the expiration of the fourth year, and of the third class at the expiration of the sixth year, so that one-third may be chosen every second year; and if vacancies happen by resignation or otherwise, during the recess of the legislature of any State, the Executive thereof may make temporary appointments until the next meeting of the legislature, which shall then fill such vacancies.

No person shall be a Senator who shall not have attained to the age of thirty years, and been nine years a citizen of the United States, and who shall not, when elected, be an inhabitant of that State for which he shall be chosen.

The Vice-President of the United States shall be President of the Senate, but shall have no vote, unless they be equally divided.

The Senate shall choose their other officers, and also a President *pro tempore,* in the absence of the Vice-President, or when he shall exercise the office of President of the United States.

The Senate shall have the sole power to try all impeachments. When sitting for that purpose, they shall be on oath or affirmation. When the President of the United States is tried, the Chief Justice shall preside: and no person shall be convicted without the concurrence of two-thirds of the members present.

* Passages no longer in effect are printed in italic type.

Judgment in cases of impeachment shall not extend further than to removal from the office, and disqualification to hold and enjoy any office of honor, trust or profit under the United States: but the party convicted shall nevertheless be liable and subject to indictment, trial, judgment and punishment, according to law.

Section 4   The times, places and manner of holding elections for Senators and Representatives shall be prescribed in each State by the legislature thereof; but the Congress may at any time by law make or alter such regulations, except as to the places of choosing Senators.

The Congress shall assemble at least once in every year, and such meeting *shall be on the first Monday in December, unless they shall by law appoint a different day.*

Section 5   Each house shall be the judge of the elections, returns and qualifications of its own members, and a majority of each shall constitute a quorum to do business; but a smaller number may adjourn from day to day, and may be authorized to compel the attendance of absent members, in such manner, and under such penalties, as each house may provide.

Each house may determine the rules of its proceedings, punish its members for disorderly behavior, and with the concurrence of two-thirds, expel a member.

Each house shall keep a journal of its proceedings, and from time to time publish the same, excepting such parts as may in their judgment require secrecy; and the yeas and nays of the members of either house on any question shall, at the desire of one-fifth of those present, be entered on the journal.

Neither house, during the session of Congress, shall, without the consent of the other, adjourn for more than three days, nor to any other place than that in which the two houses shall be sitting.

Section 6   The Senators and Representatives shall receive a compensation for their services, to be ascertained by law and paid out of the treasury of the United States. They shall in all cases except treason, felony and breach of the peace, be privileged from arrest during their attendance at the session of their respective houses, and in going to and returning from the same; and for any speech or debate in either house, they shall not be questioned in any other place.

No Senator or Representative shall, during the time for which he was elected, be appointed to any civil office under the authority of the United States, which shall have been created, or the emoluments whereof shall have been increased, during such time; and no person holding any office under the United States shall be a member of either house during his continuance in office.

Section 7   All bills for raising revenue shall originate in the House of Representatives; but the Senate may propose or concur with amendments as on other bills.

Every bill which shall have passed the House of Representatives and the Senate, shall, before it become a law, be presented to the President of the United States; if he approve he shall sign it, but if not he shall return it with objections to that house in which it originated, who shall enter the objections at large on their journal, and proceed to reconsider it. If after such reconsideration two-thirds of that house shall agree to pass the bill, it shall be sent, together with the objections, to the other house, by which it shall likewise be reconsidered, and, if approved by two-thirds of that house, it shall become a law. But in all such cases the votes of both houses shall be determined by yeas and nays, and the names of the persons voting for and against the bill shall be entered on the journal of each house respectively. If any bill shall not be returned by the President within ten days (Sundays excepted) after it shall have been presented to him, the same shall be a law, in like manner as if he had signed it, unless the Congress by their adjournment prevent its return, in which case it shall not be a law.

Every order, resolution, or vote to which the concurrence of the Senate and House of Representatives may be necessary (except on a question of adjournment) shall be presented to the President of the United States; and before the same shall take effect, shall be approved by him, or being disapproved by him, shall be repassed by two-thirds of the Senate and House of Representatives, according to the rules and limitations prescribed in the case of a bill.

Section 8   The Congress shall have power

To lay and collect taxes, duties, imposts, and excises, to pay the debts and provide for the common defense and general welfare of the United States; but all duties, imposts and excises shall be uniform throughout the United States;

To borrow money on the credit of the United States;

To regulate commerce with foreign nations, and among the several States, and with the Indian tribes;

To establish an uniform rule of naturalization, and uniform laws on the subject of bankruptcies throughout the United States;

To coin money, regulate the value thereof, and of foreign coin, and fix the standard of weights and measures;

To provide for the punishment of counterfeiting the securities and current coin of the United States.

To establish post offices and post roads;

To promote the progress of science and useful arts by securing for limited times to authors and inventors the exclusive right to their respective writings and discoveries;

To constitute tribunals inferior to the Supreme Court;

To define and punish piracies and felonies committed on the high seas and offenses against the law of nations;

To declare war, grant letters of marque and reprisal, and make rules concerning captures on land and water;

To raise and support armies, but no appropriation of money to that use shall be for a longer term than two years;

To provide and maintain a navy;

To make rules for the government and regulation of the land and naval forces;

To provide for calling forth the militia to execute the laws of the Union, suppress insurrections, and repel invasions;

To provide for organizing, arming, and disciplining the militia, and for governing such part of them as may be employed in the service of the United States, reserving to the States respectively the appointment of the officers, and the authority of training the militia according to the discipline prescribed by Congress;

To exercise exclusive legislation in all cases whatsoever, over such district (not exceeding ten miles square) as may, by cession of particular States, and the acceptance of Congress, become the seat of government of the United States, and to exercise like authority over all places purchased by the consent of the legislature of the State, in which the same shall be, for erection of forts, magazines, arsenals, dockyards, and other needful buildings;—and

To make all laws which shall be necessary and proper for carrying into execution the foregoing powers, and all other powers vested by this Constitution in the government of the United States, or in any department or officer thereof.

Section 9 *The migration or importation of such persons as any of the States now existing shall think proper to admit shall not be prohibited by the Congress prior to the year 1808; but a tax or duty may be imposed on such importation, not exceeding $10 for each person.*

The privilege of the writ of habeas corpus shall not be suspended, unless when in case of rebellion or invasion the public safety may require it.

No bill of attainder or ex post facto law shall be passed.

No capitation, or other direct, tax shall be laid, unless in proportion to the census or enumeration herein before directed to be taken.

No tax or duty shall be laid on articles exported from any State.

No preference shall be given by any regulation of commerce or revenue to the ports of one State over those of another; nor shall vessels bound to, or from, one State, be obligated to enter, clear, or pay duties in another.

No money shall be drawn from the treasury, but in consequence of appropriations made by law; and a regular statement and account of the receipts and expenditures of all public money shall be published from time to time.

No title of nobility shall be granted by the United States: and no person holding any office of profit or trust under them, shall, without the consent of the Congress, accept of any present, emolument, office, or title, of any kind whatever, from any king, prince, or foreign state.

Section 10 No State shall enter into any treaty, alliance, or confederation; grant letters of marque and reprisal; coin money; emit bills of credit; make anything but gold and silver coin a tender in payment of debts; pass any bill of attainder, ex post facto law, or law impairing the obligation of contracts, or grant any title of nobility.

No State shall, without the consent of Congress, lay any imposts or duties on imports or exports, except what may be absolutely necessary for executing its inspection laws: and the net produce of all duties and imposts, laid by any State on imports or exports, shall be for the use of the treasury of the United States; and all such laws shall be subject to the revision and control of the Congress.

No State shall, without the consent of Congress, lay any duty of tonnage, keep troops or ships of war in time of peace, enter into any agreement or compact with another State, or with a foreign power, or engage in war, unless actually invaded, or in such imminent danger as will not admit of delay.

Article II

Section 1   The executive power shall be vested in a President of the United States of America. He shall hold his office during the term of four years, and, together with the Vice-President, chosen for the same term, be elected as follows:

Each State shall appoint, in such manner as the legislature thereof may direct, a number of electors, equal to the whole number of Senators and Representatives to which the State may be entitled in the Congress; but no Senator or Representative, or person holding an office of trust or profit under the United States, shall be appointed an elector.

The electors shall meet in their respective States, and vote by ballot for two persons, of whom one at least shall not be an inhabitant of the same State with themselves. And they shall make a list of all the persons voted for, and of the number of votes for each; which list they shall sign and certify, and transmit sealed to the seat of government of the United States, directed to the President of the Senate. The President of the Senate shall, in the presence of the Senate and House of Representatives, open all the certificates, and the votes shall then be counted. The person having the greatest number of votes shall be the President, if such number be a majority of the whole number of electors appointed; and if there be more than one who have such majority, and have an equal number of votes, then the House of Representatives shall immediately choose by ballot one of them for President; and if no person have a majority, then from the five highest on the list said house shall in like manner choose the President. But in choosing the President the votes shall be taken by States, the representation from each State having one vote; a quorum for this purpose shall consist of a member of members from two-thirds of the States, and a majority of all the States shall be necessary to a choice. In every case, after the choice of the President, the person having the greatest number of votes of the electors shall be the Vice-President. But if there should remain two or more who have equal votes, the Senate shall choose from them by ballot the Vice-President.

The Congress may determine the time of choosing the electors and the day on which they shall give their votes; which day shall be the same throughout the United States.

No person except a natural-born citizen, *or a citizen of the United States at the time of the adoption of this Constitution,* shall be eligible to the office of President; neither shall any person be eligible to that office who shall not have attained to the age of thirty-five years, and been fourteen years a resident within the United States.

In cases of the removal of the President from office or of his death, resignation, or inability to discharge the powers and duties of the said office, the same shall devolve on the Vice-President, and the Congress may by law provide for the case of removal, death, resignation, or inability, both of the President and Vice-President, declaring what officer shall then act as President, and such officer shall act accordingly, until the disability be removed, or a President shall be elected.

The President shall, at stated time, receive for his services a compensation, which shall neither be increased nor diminished during the period for which he shall have been elected, and he shall not receive within that period any other emolument from the United States, or any of them.

Before he enter on the execution of his office, he shall take the following oath or affirmation:—"I do solemnly swear (or affirm) that I will faithfully execute the office of the President of the United States, and will to the best of my ability preserve, protect and defend the Constitution of the United States."

Section 2   The President shall be commander in chief of the army and navy of the United States, and of the militia of the several States, when called into the actual service of the United States; he may require the opinion, in writing, of the principal officer in each of the executive departments, upon any subject relating to the duties of their respective offices, and he shall have power to grant reprieves and pardons for offenses against the United States, except in cases of impeachment.

He shall have power, by and with the advice and consent of the Senate, to make treaties, provided two-thirds of the Senators present concur; and he shall nominate, and by and with the advice and consent of the Senate, shall appoint ambassadors, other public ministers and consuls, judges of the Supreme Court, and all other officers of the United States, whose appointments are not herein otherwise provided for, and which shall be established by law: but Congress may by law vest the appointment of such inferior officers, as they think proper, in the President alone, in the courts of law, or in the heads of departments.

The President shall have power to fill up all vacancies that may happen during the recess of the Senate, by granting commissions which shall expire at the end of their next session.

Section 3   He shall from time to time give to the Congress information of the state of the Union, and recommend to their consideration such measures as he shall judge necessary and expedient; he may, on extraordinary occasions, convene both houses, or either of them, and in case of disagreement between them, with respect to the time of adjournment, he may adjourn them to such time as he shall think proper; he shall receive ambassadors and other public ministers; he shall take care that the laws be faithfully executed, and shall commission all the officers of the United States.

Section 4   The President, Vice-President and all civil officers of the United States shall be removed from office on impeachment for, and on conviction of, treason, bribery, or other high crimes and misdemeanors.

Article III

Section 1   The judicial power of the United States shall be vested in one Supreme Court, and in such inferior courts as the Congress may from time to time ordain and establish. The judges, both of the Supreme and inferior courts, shall hold their offices during good behavior, and shall, at stated times, receive for their services a compensation which shall not be diminished during their continuance in office.

Section 2   The judicial power shall extend to all cases, in law and equity, arising under this Constitution, the laws of the United States, and treaties made, or which shall be made, under their authority;—to all cases affecting ambassadors, other public ministers and consuls;—to all cases of admiralty and maritime jurisdiction;—to controversies to which the United States shall be a party;—to controversies between two or more States;—*between a State and a citizens of another State;*—between citizens of different States;—between citizens of the same State claiming lands under grants of different States, and between a State, or the citizens thereof, and foreign states, citizens or subjects.

In all cases affecting ambassadors, other public ministers and consuls, and those in which a State shall be party, the Supreme Court shall have original jurisdiction. In all the other cases before mentioned, the Supreme Court shall have appellate jurisdiction, both as to law and fact, with such exceptions, and under such regulations, as the Congress shall make.

The trial of all crimes, except in cases of impeachment, shall be by jury; and such trial shall be held in the State where said crimes shall have been committed; but when not committed within any State, the trial shall be at such place or places as the Congress may by law have directed.

Section 3   Treason against the United States shall consist only in levying war against them, or in adhering to their enemies, giving them aid and comfort. No person shall be convicted of treason unless on the testimony of two witnesses to the same overt act, or on confession in open court.

The Congress shall have power to declare the punishment of treason, but no attainder of treason shall work corruption of blood, or forfeiture except during the life of the person attainted.

Article IV

Section 1   Full faith and credit shall be given in each State to the public acts, records, and judicial proceedings of every other State. And the Congress may by general laws prescribe the manner in which such acts, records, and proceedings shall be proved, and the effect thereof.

Section 2   The citizens of each State shall be entitled to all privileges and immunities of citizens in the several States.

A person charged in any State with treason, felony, or other crime, who shall flee from justice, and be found in another State, shall on demand of the executive authority of the State from which he fled, be delivered up, to be removed to the State having jurisdiction of the crime.

No person held to service or labor in one State, under the laws thereof, escaping into another, shall, in consequence of any law or regulation therein, be discharged from such service or labor, but shall be delivered up on claim of the party to whom such service or labor may be due.

Section 3   New States may be admitted by the Congress into this Union; but no new State shall be formed or erected within the jurisdiction of any other State; nor any State be formed by the junction of two or more States, or parts of States, without the consent of the legislatures of the States concerned as well as of the Congress.

The Congress shall have power to dispose of and make all needful rules and regulations respecting the territory or other property belonging to the United States; and nothing in this Constitution shall be so construed as to prejudice any claims of the United States, or of any particular State.

Section 4   The United States shall guarantee to every State in this Union a republican form of government, and shall protect each of them against invasion; and on application of the legislature, or of the executive (when the legislature cannot be convened), against domestic violence.

Article V

The Congress, whenever two-thirds of both houses shall deem it necessary, shall propose amendments to this Constitution, or, on the application of the legislatures of two-thirds of the several States, shall call a convention for proposing amendments, which, in either case, shall be valid to all intents and purposes, as part of this Constitution, when ratified by the legislatures of three-fourths of the several States, or by conventions in three-fourths thereof, as the one or the other mode of ratification may be proposed by the Congress; provided *that no amendments which may be made prior to the year one thousand eight hundred and eight shall in any manner affect the first and fourth clauses in the ninth section of the first article;* and that no State, without its consent, shall be deprived of its equal suffrage in the Senate.

Article VI

All debts contracted and engagements entered into, before the adoption of this Constitution, shall be as valid against the United States under this Constitution, as under the Confederation.

This Constitution, and the laws of the United States which shall be made in pursuance thereof; and all treaties made, or which shall be made, under the authority of the United States, shall be the supreme law of the land; and the judges in every State shall be bound thereby, anything in the Constitution or laws of any State to the contrary notwithstanding.

The Senators and Representatives before mentioned, and the members of the several State legislatures, and all executive and judicial officers, both of the United States and of the several States, shall be bound by oath or affirmation to support this Constitution; but no religious test shall ever be required as a qualification to any office or public trust under the United States.

Article VII

The ratification of the conventions of nine States shall be sufficient for the establishment of this Constitution between the States so ratifying the same.

Done in Convention by the unanimous consent of the States present, the seventeenth day of September in the year of our Lord one thousand seven hundred and eighty-seven and of the Independence of the United States of America the twelfth. In witness whereof we have hereunto subscribed our names.

GEORGE WASHINGTON
and thirty-seven others

AMENDMENTS TO THE CONSTITUTION*

Amendment I

Congress shall make no law respecting an establishment of religion, or prohibiting the free exercise thereof; or abridging the freedom of speech, or of the press; or the right of the people peaceably to assemble, and to petition the government for a redress of grievances.

Amendment II

A well-regulated militia being necessary to the security of a free State, the right of the people to keep and bear arms shall not be infringed.

Amendment III

No soldier shall, in time of peace, be quartered in any house without the consent of the owner, nor in time of war, but in a manner to be prescribed by law.

Amendment IV

The right of the people to be secure in their persons, houses, papers, and effects, against unreasonable searches and seizures, shall not be violated, and no warrants shall issue but upon probable cause, supported by oath or affirmation, and particularly describing the place to be searched, and the persons or things to be seized.

Amendment V

No person shall be held to answer for a capital, or otherwise infamous crime, unless on a presentment or indictment of a grand jury, except in cases arising in the land or naval forces, or in the militia, when in actual service in time of war or public danger; nor shall any person be subject for the same offense to be twice

*The first ten amendments (the Bill of Rights) were adopted in 1791.

put in jeopardy or life or limb; nor shall be compelled in any criminal case to be a witness against himself, nor be deprived of life, liberty, or property, without due process of law; nor shall private property be taken for public use without just compensation.

Amendment VI

In all criminal prosecutions, the accused shall enjoy the right to a speedy and public trial, by an impartial jury of the State and district wherein the crime shall have been committed, which district shall have been previously ascertained by law, and to be informed of the nature and cause of the accusation; to be confronted with the witnesses against him; to have compulsory process for obtaining witnesses in his favor, and to have the assistance of counsel for his defense.

Amendment VII

In suits at common law, where the value in controversy shall exceed twenty dollars, the right of trial by jury shall be preserved, and no fact tried by jury shall be otherwise reexamined in any court of the United States, than according to the rules of the common law.

Amendment VIII

Excessive bail shall not be required, nor excessive fines imposed, nor cruel and unusual punishments inflicted.

Amendment IX

The enumeration in the Constitution, of certain rights, shall not be construed to deny or disparage others retained by the people.

Amendment X

The powers not delegated to the United States by the Constitution, nor prohibited by it to the States, are reserved to the States respectively, or to the people.

Amendment XI   *[Adopted 1798]*

The judicial power of the United States shall not be construed to extend to any suit in law or equity, commenced or prosecuted against one of the United States by citizens of another State, or by citizens or subjects of any foreign state.

Amendment XII   *[Adopted 1804]*

The electors shall meet in their respective States, and vote by ballot for President and Vice-President, one of whom, at least, shall not be an inhabitant of the same State with themselves; they shall name in their ballots the person voted for as President, and in distinct ballots the person voted for as Vice-President, and they shall make distinct lists of all persons voted for as President, and of all persons voted for as Vice-President, and of the number of votes for each, which lists they shall sign and certify, and transmit sealed to the seat of government of the United States, directed to the President of the Senate;—the President of the Senate shall, in the presence of the Senate and House of Representatives, open all the certificates and the votes shall then be counted;—the person having the greatest number of votes for President shall be the President, if such number be a majority of the whole number of electors appointed; and if no person have such majority, then from the persons having the highest numbers not exceeding three on the list of those voted for as President, the House of Representatives shall choose immediately, by ballot, the President. But in choosing the President, the votes shall be taken by States, the representation from each State having one vote; a quorum for this purpose shall consist of a member or members from two-thirds of the States, and a majority of all the States shall be necessary to a choice. And if the House of Representatives shall not choose a President whenever the right of choice shall devolve upon them, before *the fourth day of March* next following, then the Vice-President shall act as President, as in the case of the death or other constitutional disability of the President.

The person having the greatest number of votes as Vice-President shall be the Vice-President, if such number be a majority of the whole number of electors appointed; and if no person have a majority, then from the two highest numbers on the list the Senate shall choose the Vice-President; a quorum for the purpose shall consist of two-thirds of the whole number of Senators, and a majority of the whole number shall be necessary to a choice. But no person constitutionally ineligible to the office of President shall be eligible to that of Vice-President of the United States.

Amendment XIII   *[Adopted 1865]*

Section 1   Neither slavery nor involuntary servitude, except as a punishment for crime whereof the party shall have been duly convicted, shall exist within the United States, or any place subject to their jurisdiction.

Section 2   Congress shall have power to enforce this article by appropriate legislation.

Amendment XIV   *[Adopted 1868]*

Section 1   All persons born or naturalized in the United States, and subject to the jurisdiction thereof, are citizens of the United States and of the State wherein they reside. No State shall make or enforce any law which shall abridge the privileges or immunities of citizens of the United States; nor shall any State deprive any person of life, liberty, or property, without due process of law; nor deny to any person within its jurisdiction the equal protection of the laws.

Section 2   Representatives shall be apportioned among the several States according to their respective numbers, counting the whole number of persons in each State, excluding Indians not taxed. But when the right to vote at any election for the choice of Electors for President and Vice-President of the United States, Representatives in Congress, the executive and judicial officers of a State, or the members of the legislature thereof, is denied to any of the male inhabitants of such State, being twenty-one years of age and citizens of the United States, or in any way abridged, except for participation in rebellion, or other crime, the basis of representation therein shall be reduced in the proportion which the number of such male citizens shall bear to the whole number of male citizens twenty-one years of age in such State.

Section 3   No person shall be a Senator or Representative in Congress, or Elector of President and Vice-President, or hold any office, civil or military, under the United States, or under any State, who, having previously taken an oath, as a member of Congress, or as an officer of the United States, or as a member of any State legislature, or as an executive or judicial officer of any State, to support the Constitution of the United States, shall have engaged in insurrection or rebellion against the same, or given aid or comfort to the enemies thereof. Congress may, by a vote of two-thirds of each house, remove such disability.

Section 4   The validity of the public debt of the United States, authorized by law, including debts incurred for payment of pensions and bounties for services in suppressing insurrection or rebellion, shall not be questioned. But neither the United States nor any State shall assume or pay any debt or obligation incurred in aid of insurrection or rebellion against the United States, or any claim for the loss of emancipation of any slave; but all such debts, obligations, and claims shall be held illegal and void.

Section 5   The Congress shall have power to enforce, by appropriate legislation, the provisions of this article.

Amendment XV   *[Adopted 1870]*

Section 1   The right of citizens of the United States to vote shall not be denied or abridged by the United States or by any State on account of race, color, or previous condition of servitude.

Section 2   The Congress shall have power to enforce this article by appropriate legislation.

Amendment XVI   *[Adopted 1913]*

The Congress shall have power to lay and collect taxes on incomes, from whatever source derived, without apportionment among the several States, and without regard to any census or enumeration.

Amendment XVII   *[Adopted 1913]*

Section 1   The Senate of the United States shall be composed of two Senators from each State, elected by the people thereof, for six years; and each Senator shall have one vote. The electors in each State shall have the qualifications requisite for electors of [voters for] the most numerous branch of the State legislatures.

Section 2   When vacancies happen in the representation of any State in the Senate, the executive authority of such State shall issue writs of election to fill such vacancies: Provided, that the Legislature of any State may empower the executive thereof to make temporary appointments until the people fill the vacancies by election as the Legislature may direct.

Section 3   This amendment shall not be so construed as to affect the election or term of any Senator chosen before it becomes valid as part of the Constitution.

Amendment XVIII   *[Adopted 1919; Repealed 1933]*

Section 1   After one year from the ratification of this article the manufacture, sale, or transportation of intoxicating liquors within, the importation thereof into, or the exportation thereof from the United States and all territory subject to the jurisdiction thereof, for beverage purposes, is hereby prohibited.

Section 2   The Congress and the several States shall have concurrent power to enforce this article by appropriate legislation.

Section 3   This article shall be inoperative unless it shall have been ratified as an amendment to the Constitution by the legislatures of the several States, as provided by the Constitution, within seven years from the date of the submission thereof to the States by the Congress.

Amendment XIX   *[Adopted 1920]*

Section 1   The right of citizens of the United States to vote shall not be denied or abridged by the United States or by any State on account of sex.

Section 2   The Congress shall have power to enforce this article by appropriate legislation.

Amendment XX   *[Adopted 1933]*

Section 1   The terms of the President and Vice-President shall end at noon on the 20th day of January, and the terms of Senators and Representatives at noon on the 3rd day of January, of the years in which such terms would have ended if this article had not been ratified; and the terms of their successors shall then begin.

Section 2   The Congress shall assemble at least once in every year, and such meeting shall begin at noon on the 3d day of January, unless they shall by law appoint a different day.

Section 3   If, at any time fixed for the beginning of the term of the President, the President-elect shall have died, the Vice-President-elect shall become President. If a President shall not have been chosen before the time fixed for the beginning of his term, or if the President-elect shall have failed to qualify, then the Vice-President-elect shall act as President until a President shall have qualified; and the Congress may by law provide for the case wherein neither a President-elect nor a Vice-President-elect shall have qualified, declaring who shall then act as President, or the manner in which one who is to act shall be selected, and such persons shall act accordingly until a President or Vice-President shall have qualified.

Section 4   The Congress may by law provide for the case of the death of any of the persons from whom the House of Representatives may choose a President whenever the right of choice shall have devolved upon them, and for the case of the death of any of the persons from whom the Senate may choose a Vice-President whenever the right of choice shall have devolved upon them.

Section 5   Sections 1 and 2 shall take effect on the 15th day of October following the ratification of this article.

Section 6   This article shall be inoperative unless it shall have been ratified as an amendment to the Constitution by the Legislatures of three-fourth of the several States within seven years from the date of its submission.

Amendment XXI   *[Adopted 1933]*

Section 1   The eighteenth article of amendment to the Constitution of the United States is hereby repealed.

Section 2   The transportation or importation into any State, Territory, or Possession of the United States for delivery or use therein of intoxicating liquors, in violation of the laws thereof, is hereby prohibited.

Section 3   This article shall be inoperative unless it shall have been ratified as an amendment to the Constitution by conventions in the several States, as provided in the Constitution, within seven years from the date of submission thereof to the States by the Congress.

Amendment XXII   *[Adopted 1951]*

Section 1   No person shall be elected to the office of President more than twice, and no person who has held the office of President, or acted as President, for more than two years of a term to which some other person was elected President shall be elected to the office of President more than once. But this article shall not apply to any person holding the office of President when this article was proposed by the Congress, and shall not prevent any person who may be holding the office of President, or acting as President, during the term within which this article becomes operative from holding the office of President or acting as President during the remainder of such term.

Section 2   This article shall be inoperative unless it shall have been ratified as an amendment to the Constitution by the legislatures of three-fourths of the several States within seven years from the date of its submission to the States by the Congress.

Amendment XXIII   *[Adopted 1961]*

Section 1   The District constituting the seat of Government of the United States shall appoint in such manner as the Congress may direct:

A number of electors of President and Vice-President equal to the whole number of Senators and Representatives in Congress to which the District would be entitled if it were a State, but in no event more than the least populous State; they shall be in addition to those appointed by the States, but they shall be considered for the purposes of the election of President and Vice-President, to be electors appointed by a State; and they shall meet in the District and perform such duties as provided by the twelfth article of amendment.

Section 2 The Congress shall have the power to enforce this article by appropriate legislation.

Amendment XXIV *[Adopted 1964]*

Section 1 The right of citizens of the United States to vote in any primary or other election for President or Vice-President, for electors for President or Vice-President, or for Senator or Representative in Congress, shall not be denied or abridged by the United States or any State by reason of failure to pay any poll tax or other tax.

Section 2 The Congress shall have the power to enforce this article by appropriate legislation.

Amendment XXV *[Adopted 1967]*

Section 1 In case of the removal of the President from office or of his death or resignation, the Vice-President shall become President.

Section 2 Whenever there is a vacancy in the office of the Vice-President, the President shall nominate a Vice-President who shall take office upon confirmation by a majority vote of both Houses of Congress.

Section 3 Whenever the President transmits to the President pro tempore of the Senate and the Speaker of the House of Representatives his written declaration that he is unable to discharge the powers and duties of his office, and until he transmits to them a written declaration to the contrary, such powers and duties shall be discharged by the Vice-President as Acting President.

Section 4 Whenever the Vice-President and a majority of either the principal officers of the executive departments or of such other body as Congress may by law provide, transmit to the President pro tempore of the Senate and the Speaker of the House of Representatives their written declaration that the President is unable to discharge the powers and duties of his office, the Vice-President shall immediately assume the powers and duties of the office as Acting President.

Thereafter, when the President transmits to the President pro tempore of the Senate and the Speaker of the House of Representatives his written declaration that no inability exists, he shall resume the powers and duties of his office unless the Vice-President and a majority of either the principal officers of the executive department[s] or of such other body as Congress may by law provide, transmit within four days to the President pro tempore of the Senate and the Speaker of the House of Representatives their written declaration that the President is unable to discharge the powers and duties of his office. Thereupon Congress shall decide the issue, assembling within forty-eight hours for that purpose if not in session. If the Congress, within twenty-one days after receipt of the latter written declaration, or, if Congress is not in session, within twenty-one days after Congress is required to assemble, determines by two-thirds vote of both Houses that the President is unable to discharge the powers and duties of his office, the Vice-President shall continue to discharge the same as Acting President; otherwise, the President shall resume the powers and duties of his office.

Amendment XXVI *[Adopted 1971]*

Section 1 The right of citizens of the United States, who are eighteen years of age or older, to vote shall not be denied or abridged by the United States or by any State on account of age.

Section 2 The Congress shall have power to enforce this article by appropriate legislation.

Amendment XXVII *[Adopted 1992]*

No law, varying the compensation for the services of the Senators and Representatives, shall take effect, until an election of Representatives shall have intervened.

FEDERALIST NO. 10 1787

To the People of the State of New York: Among the numerous advantages promised by a well-constructed union, none deserves to be more accurately developed than its tendency to break and control the violence of faction. The friend of popular governments, never finds himself so much alarmed for their character and fate, as when he contemplates their propensity to this dangerous vice. He will not fail, therefore, to set a due value on any plan which, without violating the principles to which he is attached, provides a proper cure for it. The instability, injustice, and confusion introduced into the public councils, have, in truth, been the mortal diseases under which popular governments have everywhere perished; as they continue to be the favorite and fruitful topics from which the adversaries to liberty derive their most specious declamations. The valuable improvements made by the American constitutions on the popular models, both ancient and modern, cannot certainly be too much admired; but it would be an unwarrantable partiality, to contend that they have as effectually obviated the danger on this side, as was wished and expected. Complaints are everywhere heard from our most considerate and virtuous citizens, equally the friends of public and private faith, and of public and personal liberty, that our governments are too unstable; that the public good is disregarded in the conflicts of rival parties; and that measures are too often decided, not according to the rules of justice, and the rights of the minor party, but by the superior force of an interested and overbearing majority. However anxiously we may wish that these complaints had no foundation, the evidence of known facts will not permit us to deny that they are in some degree true. It will be found, indeed, on a candid review of our situation, that some of the distresses under which we labour have been erroneously charged on the operation of our governments; but it will be found, at the same time, that other causes will not alone account for many of our heaviest misfortunes; and, particularly, for that prevailing and increasing distrust of public engagements, and alarm for private rights, which are echoed from one end of the continent to the other. These must be chiefly, if not wholly, effects of the unsteadiness and injustice, with which a factious spirit has tainted our public administrations.

By a faction, I understand a number of citizens, whether amounting to a majority or minority of the whole, who are united and actuated by some common impulse of passion, or of interest, adverse to the rights of other citizens, or to the permanent and aggregate interests of the community.

There are two methods of curing the mischiefs of faction: The one, by removing its causes; the other, by controlling its effects.

There are again two methods of removing the causes of faction: The one, by destroying the liberty which is essential to its existence; the other, by giving to every citizen the same opinions, the same passions, and the same interests.

It could never be more truly said, than of the first remedy, that it was worse than the disease. Liberty is to faction what air is to fire, an ailment without which it instantly expires. But it could not be a less folly to abolish liberty, which is essential to political life, because it nourishes faction, than it would be to wish the annihilation of air, which is essential to animal life, because it imparts to fire its destructive agency.

The second expedient is as impracticable, as the first would be unwise. As long as the reason of man continues fallible, and he is at liberty to exercise it, different opinions will be formed. As long as the connection subsists between his reason and his self-love, his opinions and his passions will have a reciprocal influence on each other; and the former will be objects to which the latter will attach themselves. The diversity in the faculties of men, from which the rights of property originate, is not less an insuperable obstacle to an uniformity of interests. The protection of these faculties is the first object of government. From the protection of different and unequal faculties of acquiring property, the possession of different degrees and kinds of property immediately results; and from the influence of these on the sentiments and views of the respective proprietors, ensues a division of the society into different interests and parties.

The latent causes of action are thus sown in the nature of man; and we see them everywhere brought into different degrees of activity, according to the different circumstances of civil society. A zeal for different opinions concerning religion, concerning government, and many other points, as well as of speculation as of practice; an attachment to different leaders ambitiously contending for preeminence and power; or to persons of other descriptions whose fortunes have been interesting to the human passions, have, in turn, divided mankind into parties, inflamed them with mutual animosity, and rendered them much more disposed to vex and oppress each other, than to cooperate of their common good. So strong is this propensity of mankind, to fall into mutual animosities, that where no substantial occasion presents itself, the most frivolous and fanciful distinctions have been sufficient to kindle their unfriendly passions and excite their most violent conflicts. But the most common and durable source of factions, has been the various and unequal distribution of property. Those who hold, and those who are without property, have ever formed distinct interests in society. Those who are creditors, and those who are debtors, fall under a like discrimination. A landed interest, a manufacturing interest, a mercantile interest, a moneyed interest, with many lesser interests, grow up of necessity in civilized nations, and divide them into different classes, actuated by different sentiments and views. The regulation of these various and interfering interests forms the principal task of modern legislation, and involves the spirit of the party and faction in the necessary and ordinary operations of the government.

No man is allowed to be a judge in his own cause; because his interest will certainly bias his judgment, and, not improbably, corrupt his integrity. With equal, nay, with greater reason, a body of men are unfit to be both judges and parties at the same time; yet what are many of the most important acts of legislation, but so many judicial determinations, not indeed concerning the right of single persons, but concerning the rights of large bodies of citizens? And what are the different classes of legislators, but advocates and parties to the causes which they determine? Is a law proposed concerning private debts? It is a question to which the creditors are parties on one side, and the debtors on the other. Justice ought to hold the balance between them. Yet the parties are, and must be, themselves the judges; and the most numerous party, or, in other words, the most powerful faction, must be expected to prevail. Shall domestic manufactures be encouraged, and in what degree, by restrictions on foreign manufactures? are questions which would be differently decided by the landed and the manufacturing classes; and probably by neither with a sole regard to justice and the public good. The apportionment of taxes, on the various descriptions of property, is an act which seems to require the most exact impartiality; yet there is, perhaps, no legislative act, in which greater opportunity and temptation are given to a predominant party to trample on the rules of justice. Every shilling, with which they overburden the inferior number, is a shilling saved to their own pockets.

It is in vain to say, that enlightened statements will be able to adjust these clashing interests, and render them all subservient to the public good. Enlightened statesmen will not always be at the helm: nor, in many cases, can such an adjustment be made at all, without taking into view indirect and remote considerations, which will rarely prevail over the immediate interest which one party may find in disregarding the rights of another, or the good of the whole.

The inference to which we are brought is, that the *causes* of faction cannot be removed; and that relief is only to be sought in the means of controlling its *effects*.

If a faction consists of less than a majority, relief is supplied by the republican principle, which enables the majority to defeat its sinister views, by regular vote. It may clog the administration, it may convulse the society; but it will be unable to execute and mask its violence under the forms of the constitution. When a majority is included in a faction, the form of popular government, on the other hand, enables it to sacrifice to its ruling passion or interest, both the public good and the rights of other citizens. To secure the public good, and private rights, against the danger of such a faction, and at the same time to preserve the spirit and the form of popular government, is then the great object to which our inquiries are directed. Let me add, that it is the great desideratum, by which alone this form of government can be rescued from the opprobrium under which it has so long laboured, and be recommended to the esteem and adoption of mankind.

By what means is this object attainable? Evidently by one of two only. Either the existence of the same passion or interest in a majority, at the same time, must be prevented; or the majority, having such coexistent passion or interest, must be rendered, by their number and local situation, unable to concert and carry into effect schemes of oppression. If the impulse and the opportunity be suffered to coincide, we well know that neither moral nor religious motives can be relied on as an adequate control. They are not found to be such on the injustice violence of individuals, and lose their efficacy in proportion to the number combined together; that is, in proportion as their efficacy becomes needful.

From this view of the subject, it may be concluded, that a pure democracy, by which I mean a society consisting of a small number of citizens, who assemble and administer the government in person, can admit of no cure for the mischiefs of faction. A common passion or interest will, in almost every case, be felt by a majority of the whole; a communication and concert, results from the form of government itself; and there is nothing to check the inducements to sacrifice the weaker parts, or an obnoxious individual. Hence, it is, that such democracies have ever been spectacles of turbulence and contention; have ever been found incompatible with personal security, or the rights of property; and have in general been as short in their lives, as they have been violent in their deaths. Theoretic politicians, who have patronized this species of government, have erroneously supposed, that by reducing mankind to a perfect equality in their political rights, they would, at the same time, be perfectly equalized and assimilated in their possessions, their opinions, and their passions.

A republic, by which I mean a government in which the scheme of representation takes place, opens a different prospect, and promises the cure for which we are seeking. Let us examine the points in which it varies from pure democracy, and we shall comprehend both the nature of the cure and the efficacy which it must derive from the union.

The two great points of difference, between a democracy and a republic, are, first, the delegation of the government, in the latter, to a small number of citizens, elected by the rest; secondly, the greatest number of citizens, and greater sphere of country, over which the latter may be extended.

The effect of the first difference is, on the one hand, to refine and enlarge the public views, by passing them through the medium of a chosen body of citizens, whose wisdom may best discern the true interest of their country, and whose patriotism and love of justice, will be least likely to sacrifice it to temporary or partial considerations. Under such a regulation, it may well happen, that the public voice, pronounced by the representatives of the people, will be more consonant to the public good, than if pronounced by the people themselves, convened for the purpose. On the other hand the effect may be inverted. Men of factious tempers, of local prejudices, or of sinister designs, may by intrigue, by corruption, or by other means, first obtain the suffrages, and then betray the interest of the people. The question resulting is, whether small or extensive republics are most favourable to the election of proper guardians of the public weal; and it is clearly decided in favour of the latter by two obvious considerations.

In the first place, it is to be remarked that, however small the republic may be, the representatives must be raised to a certain number, in order to guard against the cabals of a few; and that however large it may be, they must be limited to a certain number, in order to guard against the confusion of a multitude. Hence, the number of representatives in the two cases not being in proportion to that of the constituents, and being proportionally greatest in the small republic, it follows, that if the proportion of fit characters be not less in the large than in the small republic, the former will present a greater option, and consequently a greater probability of a fit choice.

In the next place, as each representative will be chosen by a greater number of citizens in the large than in the small republic, it will be more difficult for unworthy candidates to practice with success the vicious arts, by which elections are too often carried; and the suffrages of the people being more free, will be more likely to centre in men who possess the most attractive merit, and the most diffusive and established characters.

It must be confessed, that in this, as in most other cases, there is a mean, on both sides of which inconveniences will be found to lie. By enlarging too much the number of electors, you render the representatives too little acquainted with all their local circumstances and lesser interests; as by reducing it too much, you render him unduly attached to these, and too little fit to comprehend and pursue great and national objects. The federal constitution forms a happy combination in this respect; the great and aggregate interests being referred to the national, the local and particular to the state legislatures.

The other point of difference is, the greater number of citizens, and extent of territory, which may be brought within the compass of republican, than of democratic government; and it is this circumstance principally which renders factious combinations less to be dreaded in the former, than in the latter. The smaller the society, the fewer probably will be the distinct parties and interests composing it; the fewer the distinct parties and interests, the more frequently will a majority be found of the same party; and the smaller the number of individuals composing a majority, and the smaller the compass within which they are placed, the more easily will they concert and execute their plans of oppression. Extend the sphere, and you take in a greater variety of parties and interests; you make it less probable that a majority of the whole will have a common motive to invade the rights of other citizens; or if such a common motive exists, it will be more difficult for all who feel it to discover their own strength, and to act in unison with each other. Besides other impediments, it may be remarked, that where there is a consciousness of unjust or dishonorable purposes, communication is always checked by distrust, in proportion to the number whose concurrence is necessary.

Hence, it clearly appears, that the same advantage, which a republic has over a democracy, in controlling the effects of faction, is enjoyed by a large over a small republic,—is enjoyed by the union over the states composing it. Does this advantage consist in the substitution of representatives, whose enlightened views and virtuous sentiments render them superior to local prejudices, and to schemes of injustice? It will not be denied that the representation of the union will be most likely to possess these requisite endowments. Does it consist in the greater security afforded by a greater variety of parties, against the event of any one party being able to outnumber and oppress the rest? In an equal degree does the increased variety of parties, comprised within the union, increase the security? Does it, in fine, consist in the greater obstacles opposed to the concert and accomplishment of the secret wishes of an unjust and interested majority? Here, again, the extent of the union gives it the most palpable advantage.

The influence of factious leaders may kindle a flame within their particular states, but will be unable to spread a general conflagration through the other states; a religious sect may degenerate into a political faction in a part of the confederacy; but the variety of sects dispersed over the entire face of it, must secure the national councils against any danger from that source: a rage for paper money, for an abolition of debts, for an equal division of property, or for any other improper or wicked project, will be less apt to pervade the whole body of the union than a particular member of it; in the same proportion as such a malady is more likely to taint a particular county or district, than an entire state.

In the extent and proper structure of the union, therefore, we behold a republican remedy for the diseases most incident to republican government. And according to the degree of pleasure and pride we feel in being republicans, ought to be our zeal in cherishing the spirit, and supporting the character of federalists.

JAMES MADISON

ANTI-FEDERALIST PAPER OCTOBER 18, 1787

To the Citizens of the State of New-York.
When the public is called to investigate and decide upon a question in which not only the present members of the community are deeply interested, but upon which the happiness and misery of generations yet unborn is in great measure suspended, the benevolent mind cannot help feeling itself peculiarly interested in the result.

In this situation, I trust the feeble efforts of an individual, to lead the minds of the people to a wise and prudent determination, cannot fail of being acceptable to the candid and dispassionate part of the community. Encouraged by this consideration, I have been induced to offer my thoughts upon the present important crisis of our public affairs.

Perhaps this country never saw so critical a period in their political concerns. We have felt the feebleness of the ties by which these United-States are held together, and the want of sufficient energy in our present confederation, to manage, in some instances, our general concerns. Various expedients have been proposed to remedy these evils, but none have succeeded. At length a Convention of the states has been assembled, they have formed a constitution which will now, probably, be submitted to the people to ratify or reject, who are the fountain of all power, to whom alone it of right belongs to make or unmake constitutions, or forms of government, at their pleasure. The most important question that was ever proposed to your decision, or to the decision of any people under heaven, is before you, and you are to decide upon it by men of your own election, chosen specially for this purpose. If the constitution, offered to your acceptance, be a wise one, calculated to preserve the invaluable blessings of liberty, to secure the inestimable rights of mankind, and promote human happiness, then, if you accept it, you will lay a lasting foundation of happiness for millions yet unborn; generations to come will rise up and call you blessed. You may rejoice in the prospects of this vast extended continent becoming filled with freemen, who will assert the dignity of human nature. You may solace yourselves with the idea, that society, in this favored land, will fast advance to the highest point of perfection; the human mind will expand in knowledge and virtue, and the golden age be, in some measure, realized. But if, on the other hand, this form of government contains principles that will lead to the subversion of liberty—if it tends to establish a despotism, or, what is worse, a tyrannic aristocracy; then, if you adopt it, this only remaining asylum for liberty will be shut up, and posterity will execrate your memory.

Momentous then is the question you have to determine, and you are called upon by every motive which should influence a noble and virtuous mind, to examine it well, and to make up a wise judgment. It is insisted, indeed, that this constitution must be received, be it ever so imperfect. If it has its defects, it is said, they can be best amended when they are experienced. But remember, when the people once part with power, they can seldom or never resume it again but by force. Many instances can be produced in which the people have voluntarily increased the powers of their rulers; but few, if any, in which rulers have willingly abridged their authority. This is a sufficient reason to induce you to be careful, in the first instance, how you deposit the powers of government.

With these few introductory remarks, I shall proceed to a consideration of this constitution:

The first question that presents itself on the subject is, whether a confederated government be the best for the United States or not? Or in other words, whether the thirteen United States should be reduced to one great republic, governed by one legislature, and under the direction of one executive and judicial; or whether they should continue thirteen confederated republics, under the direction and control of a supreme federal head for certain defined national purposes only?

This enquiry is important, because, although the government reported by the convention does not go to a perfect and entire consolidation, yet it approaches so near to it, that it must, if executed, certainly and infallibly terminate in it.

This government is to possess absolute and uncontrollable power, legislative, executive and judicial, with respect to every object to which it extends, for by the last clause of section 8th, article 1st, it is declared "that the Congress shall have power to make all laws which shall be necessary and proper for carrying into execution the foregoing powers, and all other powers vested by this constitution, in the government of the United States; or in any department or office thereof." And by the 6th article, it is declared "that this constitution, and the laws of the United States, which shall be made in pursuance thereof, and the treaties made, or which shall be made, under the authority of the United States, shall be the supreme law of the land; and the judges in every state shall be bound thereby, any thing in the constitution, or law of any state to the contrary notwithstanding." It appears from these articles that there is no need of any intervention of the state governments, between the Congress and the people, to execute any one power vested in the general government, and that the constitution and laws of every state are nullified and declared void, so far as they are or shall be inconsistent with this constitution, or the laws made in pursuance of it, or with treaties made under the authority of the United States.—The government

then, so far as it extends, is a complete one, and not a confederation. It is as much one complete government as that of New York or Massachusetts, has as absolute and perfect powers to make and execute all laws, to appoint officers, institute courts, declare offenses, and annex penalties, with respect to every object to which it extends, as any other in the world. So far therefore as its powers reach, all ideas of confederation are given up and lost. It is true this government is limited to certain objects, or to speak more properly, some small degree of power is still left to the states, but a little attention to the powers vested in the general government, will convince every candid man, that if it is capable of being executed, all that is reserved for the individual states must very soon be annihilated, except so far as they are barely necessary to the organization of the general government. The powers of the general legislature extend to every case that is of the least importance—there is nothing valuable to human nature, nothing dear to freemen, but what is within its power. It has authority to make laws which will affect the lives, the liberty, and property of every man in the United States; nor can the constitution or laws of any state, in any way prevent or impede the full and complete execution of every power given. The legislative power is competent to lay taxes, duties, imposts, and excises;—there is no limitation to this power, unless it be said that the clause which directs the use to which those taxes, and duties shall be applied, may be said to be limitation: but this is no restriction of the power at all, for by this clause they are to be applied to pay the debts and provide for the common defence and general welfare of the United States; but the legislature have authority to contract debts at their discretion; they are the sole judges of what is necessary to provide for the common defence, and they only are to determine what is for the general welfare; this power therefore is neither more nor less, than a power to lay and collect taxes, imposts, and excises, at their pleasure; not only [is] the power to lay taxes unlimited, as to the amount they may require, but it is perfect and absolute to raise them in any mode they please. No state legislature, or any power in the state governments, have any more to do in carrying this into effect, than the authority of one state has to do with that of another. In the business therefore of laying and collecting taxes, the idea of confederation is totally lost, and that of one entire republic is embraced. It is proper here to remark, that the authority to lay and collect taxes is the most important of any power that can be granted; it connects with it almost all other powers, or at least will in process of time draw all other after it; it is the great mean of protection, security, and defence, in a good government, and the great engine of oppression and tyranny in a bad one. This cannot fail of being the case, if we consider the contracted limits which are set by this constitution, to the late [state?] governments, on this article of raising money. No state can emit paper money—lay any duties, or imposts, on imports, or exports, but by consent of the Congress; and then the net produce shall be for the benefit of the United States: the only mean therefore left, for any state to support its government and discharge its debts, is by direct taxation; and the United States have also power to lay and collect taxes, in any way they please. Every one who has thought on the subject, must be convinced that but small sums of money can be collected in any country, by direct taxe[s], when the federal government begins to exercise the right of taxation in all its parts, the legislatures of the several states will find it impossible to raise monies to support their governments. Without money they cannot be supported, and they must dwindle away, and, as before observed, their powers absorbed in that of the general government.

It might be here shewn, that the power in the federal legislative, to raise and support armies at pleasure, as well in peace as in war, and their controul over the militia, tend, not only to a consolidation of the government, but the destruction of liberty.—I shall not, however, dwell upon these, as a few observations upon the judicial power of this government, in addition to the preceding, will fully evince the truth of the position.

The judicial power of the United States is to be vested in a supreme court, and in such inferior courts as Congress may from time to time ordain and establish. The powers of these courts are very extensive; their jurisdiction comprehends all civil causes, except such as arise between citizens of the same state; and it extends to all cases in law and equity arising under the constitution. One inferior court must be established, I presume, in each state, at least, with the necessary executive officers appendant thereto. It is easy to see, that in the common course of things, these courts will eclipse the dignity, and take away from the respectability, of the state courts. These courts will be, in themselves, totally independent of the states, deriving their authority from the United States, and receiving from them fixed salaries; and in the course of human events it is to be expected, that they will swallow up all the powers of the courts in the respective states.

How far the clause in the 8th section of the 1st article may operate to do away all ideas of confederated states, and to effect an entire consolidation of the whole into one general government, it is impossible to say. The powers given by this article are very general and comprehensive, and it may receive a construction to justify the passing almost any law. A power to make all laws, which shall be *necessary and proper*, for carrying into execution, all powers vested by the constitution in the government of the United States, or any department or officer thereof, is a power very comprehensive and definite [indefinite?], and may, for ought I know, be exercised in a such manner as entirely to abolish the state legislatures. Suppose the legislature of a state should pass a law to raise money to support their government and pay the state debt, may the Congress repeal this law, because it may prevent the collection of a tax which they may think proper and necessary to lay, to provide for the general welfare of the United States? For all laws made, in pursuance of this constitution, are the supreme law of the land, and the judges in every state shall be bound thereby, any thing in the constitution or laws of the different states to the contrary notwithstanding—By such a law, the government of a particular state might be overturned at one stroke, and thereby be deprived of every means of its support.

It is not meant, by stating this case, to insinuate that the constitution would warrant a law of this kind; or unnecessarily to alarm the fears of the people, by suggesting, that the federal legislature would be more likely to pass the limits assigned them by the constitution, than that of an individual state, further than they are less responsible to the people. But what is meant is, that the legislature of the United States are vested with the great and uncontrollable powers, of laying and collecting taxes, duties, imposts, and excises; of regulating trade, raising and supporting armies, organizing, arming, and disciplining the militia, instituting courts, and other general powers. And are by this clause invested with the power of making all laws, *proper and necessary*, for carrying all these into execution; and they may so exercise this power as entirely to annihilate all the state governments, and reduce this country to one single government. And if they may do it, it is pretty certain they will; for it will be found that the power retained by individual states, small as it is, will be a clog upon the wheels of the government of the United States; the latter therefore will be naturally inclined to remove it out of the way. Besides, it is a truth confirmed by the unerring experience of ages, that every man, and every body of men, invested with power, are ever disposed to increase it, and to acquire a superiority over every thing that stands in their way. This disposition, which is implanted in human nature, will operate in the federal legislature to lessen and ultimately to subvert the state authority, and having such advantages, will most certainly succeed, if the federal government succeeds at all. It must be very evident then, that what this constitution wants of being a complete consolidation of the several parts of the union into one complete government, possessed of perfect legislative, judicial, and executive powers, to all intents and purposes, it will necessarily acquire in its exercise and operation.

Let us now proceed to enquire, as I at first proposed, whether it be best the thirteen United States should be reduced to one great republic, or not? It is here taken for granted, that all agree in this, that whatever government we adopt, it ought to be a free one; that it should be so framed as to secure the liberty of the citizens of America, and such an one as to admit of a full, fair, and equal representation of the people, The question then will be, whether a government thus constituted, and founded on such principles, is practicable, and can be exercised over the whole United States, reduced into one state?

If respect is to be paid to the opinion of the greatest and wisest men who have ever thought or wrote on the science of government, we shall be constrained to conclude, that a free republic cannot succeed over a country of such immense extent, containing such a number of inhabitants, and these encreasing in such rapid progression as that of the whole United States. Among the many illustrious authorities which might be produced to this point, I shall content myself with quoting only two. The one is the baron de Montesquieu, spirit of laws, chap. xvi. vol. I [book VIII]. "It is natural to a republic to have only a small territory, otherwise it cannot long subsist. In a large republic there are men of large fortunes, and consequently of less moderation; there are trusts too great to be placed in any single subject; he has interest of his own; he soon begins to think that he may be happy, great and glorious, by oppressing his fellow citizens; and that he may raise himself to grandeur on the ruins of his country. In a large republic, the public good is sacrificed to a thousand views; it is subordinate to exceptions, and depends on accidents. In a small one, the interest of the public is easier perceived, better understood, and more within the reach of every citizen; abuses are of less

extent, and of course are less protected." Of the same opinion is the marquis Beccarari.

History furnishes no example of a free republic, any thing like the extent of the United States. The Grecian republics were of small extent; so also was that of the Romans. Both of these, it is true, in process of time, extended their conquests over large territories of country; and the consequence was, that their governments were changed from that of free governments to those of the most tyrannical that ever existed in the world.

Not only the opinion of the greatest men, and the experience of mankind, are against the idea of an extensive republic, but a variety of reasons may be drawn from the reason and nature of things, against it. In every government, the will of the sovereign is the law. In despotic governments, the supreme authority being lodged in one, his will is law, and can be as easily expressed to a large extensive territory as to a small one. In a pure democracy the people are the sovereign, and their will is declared by themselves; for this purpose they must all come together to deliberate, and decide. This kind of government cannot be exercised, therefore, over a country of any considerable extent; it must be confined to a single city, or at least limited to such bounds as that the people can conveniently assemble, be able to debate, understand the subject submitted to them, and declare their opinion concerning it.

In a free republic, although all laws are derived from the consent of the people, yet the people do not declare their consent by themselves in person, but by representatives, chosen by them, who are supposed to know the minds of their constituents, and to be possessed of integrity to declare this mind.

In every free government, the people must give their assent to the laws by which they are governed. This is the true criterion between a free government and an arbitrary one. The former are ruled by the will of the whole, expressed in any manner they may agree upon; the latter by the will of one, or a few. If the people are to give their assent to the laws, by persons chosen and appointed by them, the manner of the choice and the number chosen, must be such, as to possess, be disposed, and consequently qualified to declare the sentiments of the people; for if they do not know, or are not disposed to speak the sentiments of the people, the people do not govern, but the sovereignty is in a few. Now, in a large extended country, it is impossible to have a representation, possessing the sentiments, and of integrity, to declare the minds of the people, without having it so numerous and unwieldy, as to be subject in great measure to the inconveniency of a democratic government.

The territory of the United States is of vast extent; it now contains near three millions of souls, and is capable of containing much more than ten times that number. Is it practicable for a country, so large and so numerous as they will soon become, to elect a representation, that will speak their sentiments, without their becoming so numerous as to be incapable of transacting public business? It certainly is not.

In a republic, the manners, sentiments, and interests of the people should be similar. If this be not the case, there will be a constant clashing of opinions; and the representatives of one part will be continually striving against those of the other. This will retard the operations of government, and prevent such conclusions as will promote the public good. If we apply this remark to the condition of the United States, we shall be convinced that it forbids that we should be one government. The United States includes a variety of climates. The productions of the different parts of the union are very variant, and their interests, of consequence, diverse. Their manners and habits differ as much as their climates and productions; and their sentiments are by no means coincident. The laws and customs of the several states are, in many respects, very diverse, and in some opposite; each would be in favor of its own interests and customs, and, of consequence, a legislature, formed of representatives from the perspective parts, would not only be too numerous to act with any care or decision, but would be composed of such heterogenous and discordant principles, as would constantly be contending with each other.

The laws cannot be executed in a republic, of an extent equal to that of the United States, with promptitude.

The magistrates in every government must be supported in the execution of the laws, either by an armed force, maintained at the public expense for that purpose; or by the people turning out to aid the magistrate upon his command, in case of resistance.

In despotic governments, as well as in all the monarchies of Europe, standing armies are kept up to execute the commands of the prince or the magistrate, and are employed for this purpose when occasion requires: But they have always proved the destruction of liberty, and [are] abhorrent to the spirit of a free republic. In England, where they depend upon the parliament for their annual support, they have always been complained of as oppressive and unconstitutional, and are seldom employed in executing of the laws; never except on extraordinary occasions, and then under the direction of a civil magistrate.

A free republic will never keep a standing army to execute its laws. It must depend upon the support of its citizens. But when a government is to receive its support from the aid of the citizens, it must be so constructed as to have the confidence, respect, and affection of the people. Men who, upon the call of the magistrate, offer themselves to execute the laws, are influenced to do it either by affection to the government, or from fear; where a standing army is at hand to punish offenders, everyman is actuated by the latter principle, and therefore, when the magistrate calls, will obey: but, where this is not the case, the government must rest for its support upon the confidence and respect which the people have for their government and laws. The body of the people being attached, the government will always be sufficient to support and execute its laws, and to operate upon the fears of any faction which may be opposed to it, not only to prevent an opposition to the execution of the laws themselves, but also to compel the most of them to aid the magistrate; but the people will not be likely to have such confidence in their rulers, in a republic so extensive as the United States, as necessary for these purposes. The confidence which the people have in their rulers, in a free republic, arises from their knowing them, from their being responsible to them for their conduct, and from the power they have of displacing them when they misbehave: but in a republic of the extent of this continent, the people in general would be acquainted with very few of their rulers: the people at large would know little of their proceedings, and it would be extremely difficult to change them. The people in Georgia and New Hampshire would not know one another's mind, and therefore could not act in concert to enable them to effect a general change of representatives. The different parts of so extensive a country could not possibly be made acquainted with the conduct of their representatives, nor be informed of the reasons upon which measures were founded. The consequence will be, they will have no confidence in their legislature, suspect them of ambitious views, be jealous of every measure they adopt, and will not support the laws they pass. Hence the government will be nerveless and inefficient, and no way will be left to render it otherwise, but by establishing an armed force to execute the laws at the point of the bayonet—a government of all others the most to be dreaded.

In a republic of such vast extent as the United States, the legislature cannot attend to the various concerns and wants of its different parts. It cannot be sufficiently numerous to be acquainted with the local condition and wants of the different districts, and if it could, it is impossible it should have sufficient time to attend to and provide for all the variety of cases of this nature, that would be continually arising.

In so extensive a republic, the great officers of government would soon become above the controul of the people, and abuse their power to the purpose of aggrandizing themselves, and oppressing them. The trust committed to the executive offices, in a country of the extent of the United States, must be various and of magnitude. The command of all the troops and navy of the republic, the appointment of officers, the power of pardoning offenses, the collecting of all the public revenues, and the power of expanding them, with a number of other powers, must be lodged and exercised in every state, in the hands of a few. When these are attended with great honor and emolument, as they always will be in large states, so as greatly to interest men to pursue them, and to be proper objects for ambitious and designing men, such men will be ever restless in their pursuit after them. They will use the power, when they have acquired it, to the purposes of gratifying their own interest and ambition, and it is scarcely possible, in a very large republic, to call them to account for their misconduct, or to prevent their abuse of power.

These are some of the reasons by which it appears, that a free republic cannot long subsist over a country of the great extent of these states. If then this new constitution is calculated to consolidate the thirteen states into one, as it evidently is, it ought not to be adopted.

Though I am of opinion, that it is a sufficient objection to this government, to reject it, that it creates the whole union into one government, under the form of a republic, yet if this objection was obviated, there are exceptions to it, which are so material and fundamental, that they ought to determine every man, who is a friend to the liberty and happiness of mankind, not to adopt it. I beg the candid and dispassionate attention of my countrymen while I state these objections—they are such as have obtruded themselves upon my mind upon a careful attention to the matter, and such as I sincerely believe are well founded. There are many objections, of small moment, of which I shall take no notice—perfection is not to be expected in any thing that is the production of man—and if I did not in my conscience believe that this scheme was defective in the fundamental principles—in the foundation upon which a free and equal government must rest—I would hold my peace.

Brutus.

Presidents of the United States

	Party	Term
1. George Washington (1732–1799)	Federalist	1789–1797
2. John Adams (1735–1826)	Federalist	1797–1801
3. Thomas Jefferson (1743–1826)	Democratic-Republican	1801–1809
4. James Madison (1751–1836)	Democratic Republican	1809–1817
5. James Monroe (1758–1831)	Democratic-Republican	1817–1825
6. John Quincy Adams (1767–1848)	Democratic-Republican	1825–1829
7. Andrew Jackson (1767–1845)	Democratic	1829–1837
8. Martin Van Buren (1782–1862)	Democratic	1837–1841
9. William Henry Harrison (1773–1841)	Whig	1841
10. John Tyler (1790–1862)	Whig	1841–1845
11. James K. Polk (1795–1849)	Democratic	1845–1849
12. Zachary Taylor (1784–1850)	Whig	1849–1850
13. Millard Fillmore (1800–1874)	Whig	1850–1853
14. Franklin Pierce (1804–1869)	Democratic	1853–1857
15. James Buchanan (1791–1868)	Democratic	1857–1861
16. Abraham Lincoln (1809–1865)	Republican	1861–1865
17. Andrew Johnson (1808–1875)	Union	1865–1869
18. Ulysses S. Grant (1822–1885)	Republican	1869–1877
19. Rutherford B. Hayes (1822–1893)	Republican	1877–1881
20. James A. Garfield (1831–1881)	Republican	1881
21. Chester A. Arthur (1830–1886)	Republican	1881–1885
22. Grover Cleveland (1837–1908)	Democratic	1885–1889
23. Benjamin Harrison (1833–1901)	Republican	1889–1893
24. Grover Cleveland (1837–1908)	Democratic	1893–1897
25. William McKinley (1843–1901)	Republican	1897–1901
26. Theodore Roosevelt (1858–1919)	Republican	1901–1909
27. William Howard Taft (1857–1930)	Republican	1909–1913
28. Woodrow Wilson (1856–1924)	Democratic	1913–1921
29. Warren G. Harding (1865–1923)	Republican	1921–1923
30. Calvin Coolidge (1871–1933)	Republican	1923–1929
31. Herbert Hoover (1874–1964)	Republican	1929–1933
32. Franklin Delano Roosevelt (1882–1945)	Democratic	1933–1945
33. Harry S. Truman (1884–1972)	Democratic	1945–1953
34. Dwight D. Eisenhower (1890–1969)	Republican	1953–1961
35. John F. Kennedy (1917–1963)	Democratic	1961–1963
36. Lyndon B. Johnson (1908–1973)	Democratic	1963–1969
37. Richard M. Nixon (1913–1994)	Republican	1969–1974
38. Gerald R. Ford (b. 1913)	Republican	1974–1977
39. Jimmy Carter (b. 1924)	Democratic	1977–1981
40. Ronald Reagan (1911–2004)	Republican	1981–1989
41. George Bush (b. 1924)	Republican	1989–1993
42. Bill Clinton (b. 1946)	Democratic	1993–2001
43. George W. Bush (b. 1946)	Republican	2001–

GLOSSARY

527s and 501(c)s   Named after provisions of the Internal Revenue code, new political advocacy and political education groups formed after the passage of the Bipartisan Campaign Reform Act to promote the raising and spending of unlimited money to influence public opinion. Both types of organizations are prohibited from direct advocacy for particular candidates or parties, and from coordination with particular campaigns or political parties. In 2004, prominent groups include the liberally oriented Americans Coming Together (ACT) and MoveOn.org; on the right, the Swift Boat Veterans for Truth.

administrative adjudication   The quasijudicial powers delegated to executive agencies to try individuals or organizations that have violated legally binding agency rules.

administrative state   A national government involved in regulating or supporting almost every form of social activity by means of a large, complex, and diverse bureaucracy.

affirmative action   Positive steps taken to award educational opportunities or jobs to racial minorities or women because these groups have been the victims of prior discrimination.

agenda setters   The media and their ability to determine what issues are considered legitimate, or even worthy of discussion, within the political arena.

agent provocateur   A person employed, usually by the government, to incite other people to break the law and thus make them liable to punishment.

American Civil Liberties Union (ACLU)   An organization that defends the civil liberties and civil rights of many individuals and groups in court challenges.

Anti-federalist   Opponent of the Constitution during the ratification debates of 1787–1788.

appellate court   A court that possesses the power to review the decisions of lower courts.

Articles of Confederation   The first written U.S. Constitution, ratified by the states in 1781, establishing a loose confederation among the former colonies under a weak national government.

AstroTurf lobbying   A lobbying campaign that appears to be a spontaneous expression of citizens at the grassroots but in fact is purchased through consultants and public relations firms.

autonomy   Greater freedom on the part of executive agencies from control by external forces.

benchmark survey   A poll conducted by professional campaign consultants that investigates a potential candidate's name recognition and reputation among voters; one of the preliminary steps for all potential candidates in large electoral districts and states.

Bipartisan Campaign Reform Act (BCRA)   Also known as the McCain-Feingold Law, the BCRA was passed by Congress and signed by President Bush in 2003. In 2004, its basic provisions were held constitutional by the U.S. Supreme Court. The BCRA bans "soft money" contributions to the political parties, doubles the allowable individual contributions to federal candidates and the congressional campaign committees of the national political parties, and regulates direct advocacy for candidates by independent advocacy groups in television and radio advertisements in the weeks preceding a federal election.

block grant   The consolidation of a number of related categorical grants into one larger grant that provides recipients with the ability to spend the money as they see fit within the broad purposes of the grant.

Brown v. Board of Education of Topeka   The 1954 case in which the Supreme Court rejected the separate but equal doctrine in the field of education and thereby began the end of legal racial segregation.

Buckley v. Valeo   A 1976 U.S. Supreme Court ruling that struck down federal limits on overall campaign contributions by individuals. The decision also allowed interested citizens to spend unlimited amounts of money to support candidates independently of a campaign organization.

Budget and Impoundment Control Act of 1974 A law that reasserted congressional authority in budget making by creating new budget committees and the Congressional Budget Office, and requiring annual timelines for the budgetary process.

bundled contributions A practice, most often employed by business and trade association groups, to gather together legal individual contributions to candidates or political parties and to deliver them in a "bundle" to parties and candidates. The idea is to magnify the influence of a particular interest by demonstrating its fundraising prowess and power.

bureaucracy Units of the executive branch, organized in a hierarchical fashion, governed through formal rules and distinguished by their specialized functions.

bureaucratic politics The conflict that arises when an agency seeking to carry out its core mission is threatened by another agency promoting its core mission.

Bush v. Gore A five-four Supreme Court decision in December 2000, which halted Florida's hand recount of ballots, ensuring that George W. Bush would become president.

cabinet departments The fifteen major divisions of the executive branch, each responsible for a broad area of governmental operations.

candidate-centered campaigns Election contests in which candidates base their support on their personality, distinctive record, and self-developed organization rather than on their party affiliations.

casework The help given individual constituents by congressional staffs.

casino economy An economy prevalent since the 1980s, characterized by a high number of speculative sales, purchases, and mergers of corporations.

categorical grant Federal money to state and local governments that requires recipients to apply for funding under specific categories, detailing exactly how the money will be spent, and subject themselves to strict monitoring.

Central Intelligence Agency (CIA) The chief government intelligence-gathering agency, which has two primary functions: espionage and covert action.

chief executive officer (CEO) The person, hired by the board of directors, who runs the day-to-day affairs of a private corporation.

civil disobedience The deliberate violation of the law by persons willing to accept the law's punishment in order to dramatize a cause.

civil liberties The basic freedoms embodied in the Bill of Rights, such as speech and religion, which individuals enjoy and government cannot invade.

civil rights Constitutional guarantees, such as the right to vote and equal treatment under the law, that belong to people because of their status as citizens.

Civil Rights Act of 1964 A law that made racial discrimination in public accommodations (hotels and restaurants) and employment illegal.

civil society The public space between the formal realm of government and the private realm of the family in which people form voluntary ties to each other.

Civil War amendments The Thirteenth, Fourteenth, and Fifteenth Amendments to the Constitution, which extended the Bill of Rights to and emphasized equality in the treatment of the former slaves.

clear and present danger test A Supreme Court standard stating that the government can prohibit political speech only if it can bring about an immediate evil that Congress has a right to prevent.

cloture A Senate procedure for terminating debate and ending a filibuster, which requires a three-fifths vote of the membership.

Cold War A worldwide political, economic, and ideological struggle between the United States and the Soviet Union that lasted from 1945 to 1989.

collective action problem The difficulty in getting individuals to act collectively to obtain a common good when everyone in a group will benefit regardless of whether she or he contributes to the collective action.

committee system The division of the legislative workload among several congressional bodies assigned specific issues.

communitarianism A political doctrine emphasizing the mutual obligations between individuals, society, economy, and government. Communitarianism limits individual rights to property and to non-conformity in the name of the larger collective good, emphasizing instead government and society's duty to regulate individual behavior and to impose a minimal standard of social and economic well-being on the capitalist economy.

concentration of ownership   The tendency of corporate capitalism toward bigger and more coordinated ownership of capital, assets, and information technology. In the mass media, concentration has resulted in the emergence of media corporations who own across diverse enterprises, from cable television to book and movie production.

concurrent powers   The constitutional authority granted to both the federal and state governments, such as the authority to tax.

concurring opinion   A written statement by a Supreme Court justice about why he or she agrees with the decision reached in a case by the majority of the Court but not with the majority reasoning.

conservatism   A political ideology emphasizing streamlined government, low taxes, and a business sector generally free from government regulation and interference. Conservative ideology also stresses traditional social values, such as a father-centered family, and a priority for military spending over social spending.

containment   A Cold War policy, also known as the Truman Doctrine, of a global American struggle to restrict the spread of communism.

co-production   A system in which the recipients of government services contribute to their production or delivery, rather than having government employees solely responsible.

corporate capitalism   The developed or advanced stage of capitalism in which large corporations dominate the means of production and often the political system as well.

corporate center strategy   An urban development strategy that focuses on downtown, transforming the industrial city into a center of high-level, corporate, professional service functions.

corporate welfare   Government subsidies, tax breaks, and tax expenditures that directly aid corporations.

cost–benefit analysis   A method of determining if the dollar benefits of proposed government regulation are greater than the dollar costs.

Council of Economic Advisers (CEA)   A body of professional economists who provide the president with regular assistance.

court-packing plan   A failed attempt by President Franklin Roosevelt in 1937 to change the direction of the Supreme Court, by giving the president the power to name one new justice to the Court for each current justice over the age of seventy.

covert action   Secret CIA activities that cannot be traced to the U.S. government.

creative federalism   The attempt by President Lyndon Johnson to solve the problems of urban poverty by having the federal government bypass state and city governments and give grants directly to community and nonprofit organizations in the ghettos.

critical (realigning) election   An election that shapes entire electoral eras; it features increased voter turnout and a reshuffling of the social groups that support each party, resulting in the domination of one party in succeeding elections.

Declaration of Independence   The document written by Thomas Jefferson and adopted by the Continental Congress on July 4, 1776, in which the American colonies announced themselves to be free and independent from Great Britain and set forth the revolutionary principle of democracy.

deliberative poll   A new type of survey in which a representative selection of the population is brought together, presented with objective information about certain public questions, discusses the issues, and is then surveyed for its opinions.

democratic elitism   The idea that responsible, well-educated, and experienced political, cultural, and economic elites protect democratic values and institutions more than ordinary citizens do.

Department of Defense   The cabinet department that coordinates and controls American military activities and is headed by a civilian secretary.

Department of State   The cabinet department that is the traditional organ of American diplomacy and is headed by a secretary.

deregulation   The reduction or elimination of government control of the conduct or activities of private citizens and organizations.

devolution   The movement of decision-making authority down the federal ladder from the federal government to state and local governments.

direct democracy   The face-to-face meeting of all citizens in one place to vote on all important issues.

direct marketing   The direct solicitation of individuals for political support, by phone or more frequently by mail.

discretion   The latitude that administrators have in carrying out their agency's mission.

discretionary spending   That part of the federal budget that is not committed and can be controlled by Congress each year. Discretionary spending is contrasted with mandatory spending, such as interest on debt and payments committed to individuals, such as Social Security.

dissenting opinion   A written statement by a Supreme Court justice about why he or she disagrees with the decision reached in a case by the majority of the Court.

dominant two-party system   The idea that Democrats and Republicans together control the electoral machinery and legal frameworks that promote their near monopoly on most political offices. While third parties are not prohibited in the U.S., the two-party system tends to perpetuate itself through single-member electoral districts, the Electoral College, and control of ballot access.

downsizing   Reducing the numbers of employees of a company by a conscious strategy of layoffs, firings, and retirements.

Dred Scott v. Sandford   The infamous 1857 case in which the Supreme Court decided that blacks were not citizens and that slaves were property protected by the Constitution.

dual federalism   The system created at the founding of the Constitution in which the national and state governments each have separate spheres of authority and are supreme within their own sphere.

economic planning   Long-term decisions by either government or corporations about what and how much to produce.

Economic Recovery Tax Act of 1981   Reagan administration legislation that dramatically cut taxes to encourage capital investment and economic growth.

economic regulation   Control by an independent regulatory commission of a specific industry that focuses on prices, quality of services, and the ability to enter or leave the industry.

Electoral College system   The body of electors, whose composition is determined by the results of the general election in each state, that chooses the president and vice president of the United States. Winning candidates must garner a majority of the 540 electoral votes.

electoral dealignment   The weakening of the party system caused by growing popular indifference to the parties themselves.

elite democracy   A political system in which the privileged classes acquire the power to decide by a competition for the people's votes and have substantial freedom between elections to rule as they see fit.

Employment Act of 1946   A law giving the federal government responsibility to promote free enterprise, avoid economic fluctuations, and maintain jobs, production, and purchasing power.

entitlement   A social benefit, such as Social Security, in which all who pay into it have a right to the benefits; you do not have to apply for the program or prove that you deserve help.

enumerated powers   The authority specifically granted to the federal government in the Constitution under Article I, section 8.

equality of condition   The idea that income and wealth should be leveled so that nobody is either very rich or very poor.

equality of opportunity   The idea that there should be no discriminatory barriers placed on an individual's access to economic success.

Establishment Clause   That part of the First Amendment that forbids Congress to make any law instituting a religion; the central component of the separation of church and state.

exclusionary rule   A doctrine, based on the Fourth Amendment's guarantee against unreasonable searches and seizures, in which the Supreme Court established that material seized in an illegal search cannot be introduced as evidence in a criminal case.

Executive Office of the President (EOP)   The complex of support agencies designed to assist the chief executive, including the White House staff, the Office of Management and Budget, the Council of Economic Advisers, and the National Security Council.

executive order   A presidential directive to subordinates in the executive branch that carries the force of law and may alter public policies.

expansion   Nineteenth-century activities by the United States to extend the nation to the Pacific

Ocean and to gain territorial acquisitions in Latin America and Asia.

expertise   The specialized knowledge of administrators about their particular areas of responsibility.

Federal Election Campaign Act (FECA)   A series of federal laws regulating the size of campaign donations to federal candidates for office, administered by the Federal Election Commission.

Federal Election Commission (FEC)   The federal regulatory body in charge of regulating and enforcing the Federal Elections Campaign Act of 1974 and its successor, the Bipartisan Campaign Reform Act of 2003. The Commission is composed of an equal membership of Democrats and Republicans.

federal foundation or endowment   Organization that enables the federal government to sponsor scientific and cultural activities.

Federal Register   The daily government publication of all national administrative regulations.

Federal Reserve   The main institution responsible for monetary policy in the United States. Created in 1913 to regulate banks and adjust the money supply, thus controlling inflation, its seven-member board of governors is appointed by the president with the consent of the Senate.

federalism   A system in which power is divided between the central government and the states.

Federalist   Supporter of the Constitution during the Constitutional Convention of 1787 and the ratification debates of 1787–1788.

filibuster   The Senate tradition whereby a senator can try to delay or defeat a vote on legislation by talking the bill to death.

fiscal policy   The manipulation of components of the national budget, taxes, and spending to regulate the economy.

focus and dial group   A selected sample of voters intensively interviewed by campaign consultants to gain knowledge about reactions to particular candidates and their campaign messages and themes.

footnote 4   A footnote in a 1938 Supreme Court decision that sets out three conditions under which the Court will not grant government action the presumption of constitutionality: when the action falls under the prohibitions of the Bill of Rights or Fourteenth Amendment, when the action restricts the democratic process, or when the action is harmful to particular religions or national or racial minorities.

fortunate fifth   The top 20 percent of income earners.

franking privilege   The benefit enjoyed by members of Congress of free postage to send mass mailings to their constituents.

Free Exercise Clause   The part of the First Amendment that states that Congress shall make no law prohibiting the practice of religion.

frontloading   The decisions made by state governments to move their presidential primaries to dates earlier in the election year in order to increase their influence on presidential candidates.

gender gap   Distinctions between the attitudes, voting behavior, and political outlooks of men and women.

general revenue sharing   Federal grants to states and localities without the stringent requirements associated with categorical grants.

generational effects   The idea that public opinion is shaped primarily by the collective experience of particular generations in their early adulthood; advocates argue for distinctive ideas of politics that came from the generation that fought World War II, that lived through the Vietnam War, and that experienced the "postmodern" politics of the 1980s.

gerrymandering   The practice of drawing electoral districts to favor one outcome over another, named after eighteenth-century Massachusetts politician Elbridge Gerry. In recent years, gerrymandering has been used in most states to ensure the reelection of incumbents of both parties. More controversial is the recent use of gerrymandering in Texas and elsewhere by Republicans to unseat incumbent Democrats.

Gibbons v. Ogden   The 1824 case in which the Supreme Court broadly defined the congressional power to "regulate commerce among the states," thereby establishing the supremacy of the federal government over the states in matters involving interstate commerce.

grants-in-aid   Money provided by one level of government to another to perform certain functions.

grassroots campaign   A run for office that emphasizes volunteer efforts, person-to-person contact, and voter organization over paid advertising, extensive polling, and other costly activities managed by a central staff.

Great Compromise   An agreement, also known as the Connecticut Compromise, in which the Constitutional Convention of 1787 resolved that Congress would be bicameral, with the Senate composed of two members from each state and the House of Representatives apportioned according to each state's population.

great mentioners (gatekeepers)   Prominent media pundits and reporters who can make or break presidential candidacies early on by giving or withholding credibility to particular candidates. These include CNN's Larry King, the *Washington Post*'s David Broder, and ABC's Cokie Roberts, Sam Donaldson, and George Will.

growth machine   A local political coalition, centered on urban real estate interests, that pushes public policies designed to maximize economic growth that supposedly benefits all elements of the population.

hard money   In federal elections, the contributions by individuals and PACs to specific candidates whose campaigns are regulated by the FECA.

horse race journalism   The tendency of the media to report election campaigns in terms of who is winning and losing rather than in terms of what issues are at stake.

ideological bloc   A group of two or more Supreme Court justices who vote the same way with a high degree of regularity on the basis of a shared legal philosophy.

ideology   A specific set of beliefs for making sense of issues and actions; a consistent pattern of opinion used to justify political behavior.

incorporation   The doctrine that the Supreme Court used to apply the Bill of Rights to the states under the 14th Amendment Due Process Clause.

incumbent   The person who currently holds an office.

independent agency   An executive branch organization that stands outside of and generally handles more narrow areas of governmental operation than the cabinet departments.

independent expenditures and independent issue advocacy   Campaign expenditures by advocacy groups like 527s and 501(c)s which occur independently of the formal organizations of candidates and

political parties. Generally, contributions are unregulated, but independent expenditures cannot be coordinated with parties and candidate organizations and cannot expressly advocate election of particular candidates for federal office.

independent regulatory commision   A governmental body that controls a sector of the economy and is directed by commissioners who are appointed by the president, have long terms, and are exempt from presidential removal so that the agency is distanced from political pressures.

insider strategy   The use by an interest group of face-to-face, one-on-one persuasion to convince decision makers in Washington that the interest group's position makes sense.

interest group politics   Any attempt by an organization to influence the policies of government through normal extra electoral channels, such as lobbying, writing letters, testifying before legislative committees, or advertising.

intergovernmental relations   The modern system of federalism in which relations between the different levels of government are worked out by specific legislation and negotiations, rather than through the formal distinction of separate spheres of authority that characterized dual federalism.

invisible primary   The pre-election year competition for money, support, and media attention among potential presidential candidates.

iron triangle   An alliance between a congressional committee, an interest group, and an executive agency that serves each one's interest, often at the expense of the general public.

isolationism   The idea that apart from commercial relations, the United States should stay out of the political and military quarrels of the rest of the world; the core principle of American foreign and defense policy from the founding until World War II.

issue network   Loose networks of experts and advocates that are active in particular issue areas.

Jim Crow laws   A series of measures, instituted by Southern state governments around the turn of the century, enforcing strict racial segregation as well as exclusion of African Americans from political participation by means of literacy tests, poll taxes, and "whites only" party primary contests. "Jim Crow" was struck down by a series of Federal civil rights acts in the 1960s.

Joint Chiefs of Staff (JCS)   A body composed of the commanding officer of each military service, and headed by a chair, that conveys the military's point of view to the president and the secretary of defense.

judicial review   The power of the courts to invalidate legislative or executive actions because they conflict with the Constitution.

jurisprudence of original intention   The argument that Supreme Court justices should restrict their constitutional interpretation to the precise words of the Constitution and the known intentions of the men who drafted it.

Laffer curve   The representational graph that argues that decreasing tax rates below a certain point will actually increase total tax revenues.

legislative liaison staff   The group of people responsible for keeping the president informed of the political maneuvering and likely vote lineup in Congress for important bills and for providing small favors to members of Congress in the hopes that they will later return these favors to the president with their votes.

Lemon test   The standard used by the Supreme Court in cases involving government aid to religion, which states that government assistance is constitutional only if it has a secular purpose, its effect does not advance or inhibit religion, and it does not entangle government and religious institutions in each other's affairs.

liberalism   A political ideology stressing the necessity of active government for the achievement of some measure of social and economic equality within the corporate capitalist system. Liberalism stresses the preservation of individual and group rights and liberties, and toleration for social change and ethnic and religious diversity. Historically, American liberals have usually placed a priority on social over military spending.

macroeconomic policy   Economic policy that influences the performance of the economy as a whole and is not designed to have direct effects on different sectors or on the distribution of economic opportunities among different groups in the population.

mail order politics   The modern tendency for some to participate in politics through monetary contributions to Washington lobbying groups.

majoritarian politics   The politics of policy making in which all, or nearly all, citizens receive some benefits of the policy and pay the costs.

majority leader   The head of the majority party in the House of Representatives or Senate.

Marbury v. Madison   The 1803 case in which the Supreme Court established that it had the right to exercise judicial review even though that power was not stated in the Constitution.

market competition   The process in which markets become decentralized arenas where many producers and consumers make free choices among a wide range of products and services.

mass movement   The participation of large numbers of previously passive bystanders in a political protest action.

matching grant   Money given by the federal government to lower levels of government to fulfill certain functions, requiring that the recipients put up some of their own money and meet minimal federal standards for the program.

McCarthyism   The practice, named after Senator Joseph McCarthy, of falsely accusing individuals of being disloyal or subversive in order to gain publicity or suppress opposition.

McCulloch v. Maryland   The 1819 case in which Justice Marshall emphasized the constitutional supremacy of the federal government in striking down Maryland's attempt to tax the Bank of the United States.

means-tested benefit   The method of granting public assistance that forces people to prove their inability to support themselves in order to secure that assistance.

media frames   The ways in which the news media establishes routine ways of defining and reporting on a news story. Frames create a uniformity in modes of determining what is, and what isn't, important in a news story. In electoral campaigns, such frames often mean a concentration on strategy, tactics, and candidate personality.

minority leader   The head of the minority party in the House of Representatives or Senate.

Miranda warnings   The requirement that police inform all criminal suspects of their rights before taking them into custody.

mission   The central task to which the members of a government agency are committed.

monetarism An economic philosophy that believes steady growth can be achieved if the money supply grows only as fast as the economy's productivity.

monetary policy A method of economic management that regulates the supply of money in the economy.

multilateralism An approach to foreign policy in which the U.S. prefers to work in partnership with allies in its international endeavors.

name recognition The extent to which a candidate's or potential candidate's name is known by voters.

National Association for the Advancement of Colored People (NAACP) An organization that fights for the rights of black Americans.

national entertainment state Term used to describe the increasing concentration of ownership and control of new and old media by a few media conglomerates.

national party convention Meetings held every four years to determine a political party's national platform and presidential and vice presidential candidates. Generally, convention delegates are selected through primaries and caucuses held in every state during election years.

national security adviser The personal counselor to the president in foreign policy and defense matters.

National Security Council (NSC) A governmental body created in 1947 to advise the president and coordinate foreign and defense policy.

national security state A complex of executive, military, and secret powers that shaped American international relations in the Cold War and largely excluded Congress and the public from decisions about the country's security.

Necessary and Proper (Elastic) Clause The clause in the U.S. Constitution at the end of Article I, Section 8, that says that Congress has all powers that are required for it to execute its other powers. The Elastic Clause has been used by the Supreme Court to expand the powers of the federal government.

New Deal Democratic coalition The Democrats' alliance of the Solid South, organized labor, Catholics, and urban ethnic groups stemming from Franklin Roosevelt's policies of the 1930s.

new federalism The attempt by President Richard Nixon to weaken the power of liberal political lobbies in Washington and reverse the trend toward centralization of authority and control in Washington by placing more power, monies, and responsibility for government programs in the hands of the states.

New Jersey Plan The proposal submitted by the New Jersey delegation at the Constitutional Convention of 1787 to reform the Articles of Confederation but maintain most governmental power in the states.

new working class Those who make wages and labor in subordinate positions in the service industries that have grown rapidly in the past two decades.

North Atlantic Treaty Organization (NATO) The military alliance among the United States, Canada, and the Western European states, created to oppose Soviet aggression in the Cold War period.

nullification The doctrine that the states have the right to declare invalid any federal legislation that they believe violates the Constitution.

obscenity Sexually explicit material that lacks serious literary, artistic, political, or scientific value and that appeals to a "prurient" interest; one of the categories of unprotected speech.

Office of Management and Budget (OMB) The agency responsible for preparing the annual presidential budget and for scrutinizing legislative proposals originating in the agencies of the executive branch to ensure that these proposals are in accord with the president's legislative program.

oligopoly A system of domination in which power is concentrated in the hands of a few unaccountable people and institutions. In this book, the term *media oligopoly* is used to express the growing concentration of private ownership of the U.S. information system. A situation where a few firms control a market and have power over production and prices.

oral argument The spoken presentation of each side of a case to the justices of the Supreme Court.

original jurisdiction The power of a court to hear a case at its inception.

outsider strategy The mobilization by an interest group of forces outside Washington to put pressure on decision makers to act in ways favorable to the interest group.

outsourcing The ability of large companies to avoid wage and benefit costs by contracting out many of their operations to smaller companies that hire cheaper, often part-time labor.

oversight Congressional attempts to exercise control over the activities of executive branch agencies through a variety of techniques, including hearings and investigations.

pack journalism The development by a group of reporters of similar views after receiving the same information and insights from the same sources.

paper entrepreneur A person who makes his or her fortune by managing mergers or speculating in stocks.

party identification A person's psychological identification with or tie to a particular political party.

party primary An election in which voters decide which of a party's candidates will be nominated to run for office in the general election. Closed primaries permit only those requested in a particular party to participate. Open primaries leave the balloting open to nonparty registrants.

party regime The long-term domination of one party of most of the political agenda and offices, following a critical or realigning election.

permanent campaign The process by which incumbent officeholders are constantly gearing their official actions toward their reelection prospects.

personal registration The practice, introduced in the Progressive era of the early twentieth century, whereby individual citizens are given the responsibility to register to vote. In most countries, the government itself assumes the responsibility of registering citizens.

Personal Responsibility and Work Opportunity Act of 1996 The act passed by Congress and signed into law by President Clinton in August 1996 that did away with the federal entitlement to welfare and replaced it with a block grant to the states that required the states to move half of the people on welfare into jobs by 2002. The new program, called Temporary Assistance to Needy Families (TANF), replaced Aid for Families with Dependent Children (AFDC).

pluralism The elite democratic theory that views the interest group system as a political marketplace in which power is dispersed among many interest groups competing for influence through a process of bargaining and compromising.

policy feedback A situation where policies, after they are passed, influence future political participation and influence, either undermining or reinforcing the coalition behind the original policies.

political action committee (PAC) A voluntary organization that funnels monies from individuals in corporations, trade associations, labor unions, and other groups into political campaigns under Federal Election Commission laws.

political culture The political values shared by the vast majority of citizens in a nation despite disagreements about their precise meanings.

political efficacy The extent to which citizens believe that their participation in politics makes a difference for what government does.

political socialization The ways in which individuals obtain their ideas about human nature, politics, and political institutions.

popular democracy A political system in which the citizens are involved as much as possible in making the decisions that affect their lives.

populism A political doctrine advocating the regulation of excessive concentration of economic and political power, and the redistribution of power and wealth towards ordinary people. Populism stresses the importance of a common social morality over the claims of social and cultural minorities.

precedent A previous decision by a court that is treated as a rule for future cases.

preemption The ability of the federal government to assume total or partial responsibility for a function where there is concurrent authority for both the federal government and the states to act.

presidential power of secrecy The ability of the chief executive to make foreign policy and national security decisions that are not subject to public scrutiny.

president's cabinet The executive body composed of the appointed heads of the fifteen major executive departments, plus any others designated by the chief executive.

preventive war A military conflict initiated against a potential future enemy in the absence of any immediate threat.

prior restraint The First Amendment prohibition against government officials preventing information from being published.

privatization The turning over of governmental functions to the private sector when it can perform functions more cheaply than government agencies.

privileged position of business   The idea that business has the advantage in most political disputes because of its power to threaten "disinvestment" when government proposes regulations and/or taxation.

progressive and regressive taxes   Progressive taxes take a higher proportion of income as income rises, whereas regressive taxes take a higher proportion of income from lower income earners.

proportional representation (PR)   An electoral system in which legislators are elected at large and in which parties receive electoral representation in proportion to the percentage of total votes they receive.

protest politics   Political actions designed to broaden conflicts and activate outside parties to pressure the bargaining process in ways favorable to the protestors.

public corporation   A government agency that engages in business activities.

public interest group   Any association seeking government action, the achievement of which will not principally benefit the members of the association.

public opinion   The average person's ideas and views on political issues.

red tape   Unnecessary bureaucratic rules that delay or obstruct action.

regulation   A process by which the government imposes restrictions on the conduct of private citizens and organizations.

"reinventing government" plan   An initiative of President Clinton and Vice President Gore to reform the federal bureaucracy by making executive agencies more entrepreneurial and by empowering civil servants.

relative deprivation   The theory that people mobilize politically not when they are worst off, but when they perceive that they are deprived unjustly, relative to other groups in the population.

republicanism   The eighteenth-century body of political thought, based on the ideas of liberty versus power, legislatures versus executives, civic virtue, and the small republic, that shaped the political activities of colonial Americans and infused them with the revolutionary "Spirit of '76."

reserved powers   The authority not given to the federal government and left to the states by the Tenth Amendment.

responsible parties   A scholarly ideal in which parties fulfill their democratic character by forming consistent and meaningful ideologies and programs that become well known to the voters and in which the winning party is held accountable by voters for implementation of programs and their consequences.

revolving door   The phenomenon whereby people working in Congress or in an executive branch agency become lobbyists or journalists once they leave government service, using their experience and knowledge for the benefit of their clients.

right of privacy   The freedom to be left alone implied in the Constitution.

Roe v. Wade   The 1973 Supreme Court case that established a woman's right to choose abortion and rendered unconstitutional all state laws that made abortion a crime.

Rolodex syndrome   The journalistic practice of relying on the same, very limited sources for quotes and information. The practice tends to exclude voices from outside the elite circles of think-tank opinion.

rule-making authority   The power of an executive agency to issue regulations that carry the force of law.

rule of four   An informal Supreme Court standard whereby if any four justices vote that a case deserves consideration, the Court will grant certiorari.

satyagraha   "Truth force," or the belief of the Indian pacifist Mahatma Gandhi that a carefully orchestrated civil disobedience plan can persuade one's opponents of the justice of one's cause.

senatorial courtesy   The Senate's withholding of consent to the nomination of a district court judge if the senior senator of the president's party from the nominee's state objects to that nomination.

seniority   The congressional norm that dictates that the member from the majority party who has the most years of continuous service on a committee becomes its chair.

separate but equal   The doctrine established by the Supreme Court in the 1896 case of *Plessy v. Ferguson*, that separate equivalent facilities for whites and blacks did not violate the Fourteenth Amendment's guarantee of equal protection of the laws, thereby providing the legal basis for segregation of the races.

shareholder democracy   The idea that corporations are held accountable to the public through the power of shareholders over corporate policies.

Shays's Rebellion   A 1786 upheaval by desperate small farmers in Massachusetts that alarmed conservative republicans and thereby set the stage for the Constitutional Convention of 1787.

single-member (winner take all) electoral system The principle and practice of electing only one representative for a given electoral district. Typically, the winner receives a plurality of the votes cast. Ubiquitous in the U.S., single-member districts contrast with other forms of representation such as multimember districts in which representation is shared in a given electoral district based on the proportion of votes received. Single-member districts help to sustain the two-party system, and some say white domination of the House of Representatives and state legislatures, by depriving third-party challengers or candidates of color of any representation unless candidates receive a plurality.

social regulation Executive agency rules that cover all industries and focus on such matters as environmental protection, safety, health, and nondiscrimination.

soft money Campaign funds raised legally by national political parties and used to influence federal elections, while often circumventing federal restrictions on campaign spending.

source bias The tendency of modern journalists to seek a limited range of opinions and views from certain groups and institutions as they report the news.

Speaker of the House of Representatives The presiding officer of the House of Representatives, who is chosen by the majority party in the House and is second, after the vice president, in the line of presidential succession.

spoils system The awarding of political jobs to political supporters and friends.

strict scrutiny A Supreme Court standard in civil liberties or civil rights cases of striking down a law unless the government can demonstrate a "compelling interest" that necessitates such a law.

structural obstacles A nexus of laws, institutions, and practices that enforces systematic advantages for some over others. In U.S. electoral practices, a complex of practices prevents high voter turnout and the mobilization of many new voters.

supply-side economics The economic theory used by the Reagan administration to justify reducing taxes on investment, profits, and income and reducing government regulation of industry to promote economic prosperity.

Supremacy Clause Article VI of the Constitution, which states that when the national and state governments conflict, the national laws shall supersede the state laws.

symbolic speech Protected political expression that communicates with visual symbols instead of words.

system of 1896 The electoral era initiated by Republican William McKinley's defeat of Democrat/Populist William Jennings Bryan in 1896. The system featured Democratic control of southern state governments, Republican control of the big states and the national government, as well as low voter turnout and the initiation of restrictions on voter registration based on race.

tax expenditure Defined in the 1974 Budget Act as "revenue losses attributable to provisions of the federal tax laws which allow a special exemption, exclusion, or deduction." Tax expenditures are calculated by subtracting what the government actually collects in taxes from what it would have collected had the special exemptions not been in place.

Telecommunications Act of 1996 Sweeping federal legislation that abolishes many of the Federal Communications Commission's previous restrictions on radio and television ownership by individuals and corporations. The Telecommunications Act ostensibly promotes competition between different parts of the telecommunications and media industries, but has instead prompted new corporate mergers and concentration.

think tank A nonprofit institution, funded primarily by foundations and corporate grants, that conducts public policy research.

tracking survey Polls conducted on a frequent, sometimes daily basis that gauge voter changes in opinion and mood. Tracking surveys are most used by campaigns to measure the influence of campaign themes and propaganda on voters.

transactional leader A party or interest group leader whose leadership is based on brokering beneficial exchanges with followers, such as patronage jobs for votes.

transforming leader A mass movement leader who engages the full personalities of followers, helping them to go beyond self-interest and participate in direct political action.

undecided and swing voters Voters who tend to lack firm party loyalties whose allegiances can shift during electoral campaigns, depending on the strategies and tactics of campaign organizations. In recent years, the proportion of swing voters in presidential elections has dropped, but their importance has grown because the "swing" will determine the electoral outcome.

unfunded mandates Laws passed by higher levels of government that force lower levels of government to spend more money without providing them with additional resources.

unilateralism An approach to foreign policy in which the U.S. goes its own way and looks to its own interests regardless of the concerns of other countries.

unitary government A system in which all significant powers rest in the hands of the central government.

unprotected speech Communication that is not protected by the First Amendment either because its social value is insignificant or because it verges on conduct that is harmful to others.

upscale demographics The tendency of advertisers and media outlets to appeal to high-income, big-spending consumers.

vertical integration For corporate media organizations, the tendency toward single corporate ownership of a chain of production, distribution, and marketing arrangements across diverse media. The idea is to create a synergy that promotes the sale of diverse media products, from theme parks to films, books, and TV and radio stations, across a wide spectrum.

veto The constitutional power of the president to reject legislation passed by Congress, subject to a two-thirds override by both houses.

Virginia Plan The proposal submitted by the Virginia delegation at the Constitutional Convention of 1787, to create a strong national government.

virtual democracy The idea that the information superhighway created by the Internet and the World Wide Web will initiate new debates and discussions between citizens and officeholders.

Voting Rights Act of 1965 The law that removed the barriers that southern officials had placed in the way of African Americans who sought to register to vote, and involved federal supervision of the voting process.

Wagner Act Also known as the National Labor Relations Act of 1935 and named for its sponsor, New York Senator Robert Wagner; legislation affirming the rights of workers to form unions and bargain with employers. The act established the National Labor Relations Board (NLRB).

War Powers Resolution of 1973 An attempt by Congress to reassert its constitutional authority in the area of war making.

wealth inequality The gap in net money worth among various population groups.

White House staff The president's personal aides and advisers along with their numerous assistants.

yellow journalism A form of reporting pioneered in the late nineteenth century by the Hearst and Pulitzer newspaper chains, emphasizing entertaining and often lurid scandals as news.

ENDNOTES

CHAPTER 1

1. The surprisingly contentious history of voting rights in the United States from the founding up to the present is told in Alexander Keyssar, *The Right to Vote: The Contested History of Democracy in the United States* (New York: Basic Books, 2000). Our account of the 2000 election is based on *36 Days: The Complete Chronicle of the 2000 Presidential Election Crisis*, correspondents of the *New York Times* (New York: Times Books, 2001); and Gerald M. Pomper et al., eds., *The Election of 2000* (New York: Chatham House, 2001).

2. The following facts are drawn from Stephen Macedo et al., *Democracy at Risk: How Political Choices Undermine Citizen Participation and What We Can Do About It* (Washington, D.C.: Brookings Institution Press, 2005), chap. 3.

3. Joseph A. Schumpeter, *Capitalism, Socialism and Democracy*, 3rd ed. (New York: Harper & Row, 1950), p. 269. In Part IV Schumpeter makes one of the classic defenses of elite democracy. For critiques of the elite theory of democracy from a popular democratic viewpoint, see Jack L. Walker, "A Critique of the Elitist Theory of Democracy," *American Political Science Review*, 60 (1966): 285–95; and Peter Bachrach, *The Theory of Democratic Elitism: A Critique* (Boston: Little, Brown, 1967).

4. The most influential political scientist who has written on the ideas of elite and popular democracy is Robert Dahl. Dahl began his career by defending a version of elite democracy in *A Preface to Democratic Theory* (Chicago: University of Chicago Press, 1956) and in *Who Governs? Democracy and Power in an American City* (New Haven, Conn.: Yale University Press, 1961). In his later works, Dahl shifted dramatically to a more popular democratic position. See *A Preface to Economic Democracy* (Berkeley: University of California Press, 1985) and *Democracy and Its Critics* (New Haven, Conn.: Yale University Press, 1989).

5. See Ralph Ketcham, ed., *The Anti-Federalist Papers and the Constitutional Convention Debates* (New York: New American Library, 1986), p. 213.

6. We are not the first to present a cyclical view of American politics in which participatory upsurges are followed by periods of elite consolidation. See Arthur M. Schlesinger Jr., *Paths to the Present* (New York: Macmillan, 1949); Arthur M. Schlesinger Jr., *The Cycles of American History* (Boston: Houghton Mifflin, 1986); and Albert O. Hirschman, *Shifting Involvements: Private Interest and Public Action* (Princeton, N.J.: Princeton University Press, 1982).

7. George Will, "In Defense of Nonvoting," *Newsweek*, October 10, 1983, p. 96.

CHAPTER 2

1. Gordon S. Wood, *The Radicalism of the American Revolution* (New York: Alfred A. Knopf, 1992), pp. 11–92.

2. Jon Butler, *Becoming America: The Revolution Before 1776* (Cambridge, Mass.: Harvard University Press, 2000).

3. For an excellent account of this political dynamic, see Pauline Maier, *From Resistance to Revolution: Colonial Radicals and the Development of American Opposition to Britain, 1765–1776* (New York: Vintage, 1974).

4. Sidney Hook, ed., *The Essential Thomas Paine* (New York: New American Library, 1969), pp. 48, 33.

5. On republicanism and the origins of the American Revolution, see Bernard Bailyn, *The Ideological Origins of the American Revolution* (Cambridge, Mass.: Harvard University Press, 1967); and Gordon S. Wood, *The Creation of the American Republic: 1776–1787* (New York: W. W. Norton, 1972), pp. 3–124.

6. On the place of the Declaration of Independence in American political thought, see especially two books by Garry Wills: *Inventing America: Jefferson's Declaration of Independence* (New York: Vintage, 1978); and *Lincoln at Gettysburg: The Words That Remade America* (New York: Simon & Schuster, 1992).

7. Roy P. Basler, ed., *The Collected Works of Abraham Lincoln*, vol. 3 (New Brunswick, N.J.: Rutgers University Press, 1953), p. 375.

8. The Declaration of Independence was creatively used by Elizabeth Cady Stanton to advance the cause of women and by Frederick Douglass, W. E. B. Du Bois, and Martin Luther King Jr. to promote equality for African Americans.

9. On the state constitutions of 1776, see Wood, *Creation of the American Republic*, pp. 127–255.

10. On the economic legislation of the 1780s, see Merrill Jensen, *The New Nation: A History of the United States During the Confederation, 1781–1789* (New York: Vintage, 1950), pp. 302–26.

11. Jackson Turner Main, "Government by the People: The American Revolution and the Democratization of the Legislatures," in Jack P. Greene, ed., *The Reinterpretation of the American Revolution, 1763–1789* (New York: Harper & Row, 1968), pp. 322–38.

12. Marvin Meyers, ed., *The Mind of the Founder: Sources of the Political Thought of James Madison*, rev. ed. (Hanover, N.H.: University Press of New England, 1981), p. 62. For a penetrating analysis of Madison as an elite democratic thinker, see Richard K. Matthews, *If Men Were Angels: James Madison and the Heartless Empire of Reason* (Lawrence: University Press of Kansas, 1995). For an impressive presentation of the opposing position that Madison was something of a popular democrat, see Lance Banning, *The Sacred Fire of Liberty: James Madison and the Founding of the Federal Republic* (Ithaca, N.Y.: Cornell University Press, 1995).

13. Among the many treatments of the Constitutional Convention and the political system it shaped, one of the richest in insights is Jack N. Rakove, *Original Meanings: Politics and Ideas in the Making of the Constitution* (New York: Alfred A. Knopf, 1996).

14. Alfred A. Young, "Conservatives, the Constitution, and the 'Spirit of Accommodation,'" in Robert A. Goldwin and William A. Schambra, eds., *How Democratic Is the Constitution?* (Washington, D.C.: American Enterprise Institute, 1980), pp. 118, 138.

15. Max Farrand, ed., *The Records of the Federal Convention of 1787*, vol. 1 (New Haven, Conn.: Yale University Press, 1937), pp. 65, 66.

16. Charles A. Beard, *An Economic Interpretation of the Constitution* (New York: Macmillan, 1913).

17. Farrand, ed., *Records of the Federal Convention*, vol. 2, p. 370.

18. See Michael Allen Gillespie and Michael Lienesch, eds., *Ratifying the Constitution* (Lawrence: University Press of Kansas, 1989).

19. Saul Cornell, *The Other Founders: Anti-Federalism and the Dissenting Tradition in America: 1788–1828* (Chapel Hill: University of North Carolina Press, 1999), p. 81.

20. Herbert J. Storing, *What the Anti-Federalists Were For* (Chicago: University of Chicago Press, 1981), p. 72.

21. Clinton Rossiter, ed., *The Federalist Papers* (New York: New American Library, 1961), p. 79.

22. Ibid., p. 54.

23. Ibid., p. 346.

24. Ibid., p. 414.

25. On the Anti-federalist conception of virtue, see Storing, *What the Anti-Federalists Were For*, pp. 19–23.

26. Ralph Ketcham, ed., *The Anti-Federalist Papers and the Constitutional Convention Debates* (New York: New American Library, 1986), p. 202.

27. Rossiter, ed., *Federalist Papers*, p. 83.

28. See Storing, *What the Anti-Federalists Were For*, pp. 16–23.

29. Herbert J. Storing, ed., *The Anti-Federalist* (Chicago: University of Chicago Press, 1985), p. 116.

30. Rossiter, ed., *Federalist Papers*, p. 82.

31. Storing, ed., *The Anti-Federalist*, p. 340.

32. Rossiter, ed., *Federalist Papers*, p. 322.

33. Ibid., p. 423.

34. Ketcham, ed., *Anti-Federalist Papers*, p. 213.

35. Rossiter, ed., *Federalist Papers*, p. 78.

36. Ibid., p. 88.

37. Ketcham, ed., *Anti-Federalist Papers*, pp. 207–8.

38. Rossiter, ed., *Federalist Papers*, p. 314.

39. Merrill D. Peterson, ed., *The Portable Thomas Jefferson* (New York: Penguin, 1975), p. 417.

40. Jackson Turner Main, *The Anti-Federalists: Critics of the Constitution, 1781–1788* (New York: W. W. Norton, 1974), p. 133.

41. On Madison and the Bill of Rights, see Robert A. Rutland, *James Madison: The Founding Father* (New York: Macmillan, 1987), pp. 59–65.

42. Cornell, *The Other Founders*, p. 307.

CHAPTER 3

1. Ehrenreich's experiences in the underbelly of the American labor market are detailed in *Nickel and Dimed: On (Not) Getting By in America* (New York: Metropolitan Books, 2001).

2. The Jobs Now Coalition estimated that a "living wage" for a single parent with one child living in the Twin Cities metropolitan area in 1977 would have to be at least $11.77 an hour. With rapid inflation in housing, it would have been considerably higher by 2000. Ehrenreich, *Nickel and Dimed*, p. 127.

3. Rebecca Blumenstein and Louis Lee, "The Changing Lot of the Hourly Worker," *Wall Street Journal*, August 28, 1997.

4. Liza Featherstone, *Selling Women Short: The Landmark Battle for Workers' Rights at Wal-Mart* (New York: Basic Books, 2004), p. 218.

5. Bob Ortega, *In Sam We Trust: The Untold Story of Sam Walton and How Wal-Mart Is Devouring America* (New York: Random House, 1998), p. 349.

6. Featherstone, *Selling Women Short*, pp. 7 and 128–29.

7. Sam Walton with John Huey, *Made in America: My Story* (New York: Bantam, 1992).

8. Featherstone, *Selling Women Short*, p. 10.

9. Ortega, *In Sam We Trust*, pp. 236–40.

10. Featherstone, *Selling Women Short*, p. 147.

11. Ortega, *In Sam We Trust*, pp. 195–96.

12. For information and advice on how to fight Wal-Mart, go to the website www.sprawl-busters.org.

13. Charles Lindblom, *Politics and Markets: The World's Political and Economic Systems* (New York: Basic Books, 1977), chap. 13.

14. The classic defense of free markets is Milton Friedman, *Capitalism and Democracy* (Chicago: University of Chicago Press, 1964).

15. Mickey Kaus, *The End of Equality* (New York: Basic Books, 1992); Charles Murray and Richard Herrnstein, *The Bell Curve* (New York: Free Press, 1994).

16. See Bill Gates, *The Road Ahead* (New York: Penguin, 1995). For a provocative account of how Americans increasingly view their relationship with government in market terms, see Lizabeth Cohen, *A Consumers' Republic: The Politics of Mass Consumption in Postwar America* (New York: Random House, 2003).

17. See Kenneth Dolbeare, *Democracy at Risk* (Chatham, N.J.: Chatham House, 1988).

18. Dale Kasler, "Enron, Lay Blamed for California Energy Crisis," *Sacramento Bee*, July 11, 2004; Jonathan Peterson, "Tapes Reveal Enron's Power Plant Rigging," *Los Angeles Times*, February 4, 2005.

19. Our account of the gutting of state incorporation laws is based on Ralph Nader, Mark Green, and Joel Seligman, *Taming the Giant Corporation* (New York: W. W. Norton, 1976).

20. Michael Sandel, *Democracy and Its Discontents* (Cambridge, Mass.: Harvard University Press, 1996), chap. 5. For a history of the emergence of the modern corporation, see Martin Sklar, *The Corporate Reconstruction of American Capitalism, 1890–1916* (Cambridge: Cambridge University Press, 1988); R. Jeff Lustig, *Corporate Liberalism: The Origins of Modern American Political Theory 1890–1920* (Berkeley: University of California Press, 1982); Alfred Chandler, *The Visible Hand: The Managerial Revolution in American Business* (Cambridge, Mass.: Belknap Press, 1977).

21. Ted Nace, *Gangs of America: The Rise of Corporate Power and the Disabling of Democracy* (San Francisco: Berrett-Koehler, 2003), pp. 16–17.

22. Ehrenreich, *Nickel and Dimed*, p. 210.

23. Charles Lindblom, *Politics and Markets* (New York: Basic Books, 1977), p. 356.

24. Lawrence Mishel, Jared Bernstein, and Sylvia Allegretto, *The State of Working America 2004/2005* (Ithaca, N.Y.: Cornell University Press, 2005), pp. 289–90.

25. See Jeremy Rifkin and Randy Barber, *The North Will Rise Again: Pensions, Power and Politics in the 1980s* (Boston: Beacon, 1979); Richard Ippolito, *Pensions, Economics and Public Policy* (Homewood, Ill.: Dow Jones–Irwin, 1986).

26. Quoted in Leslie Wayne, "Shareholders Who Answer to a Higher C.E.O.," *New York Times*, February 19, 2005.

27. For a survey of popular democratic ideas on corporate governance, see Lee Drutman and Charlie Cray, *The People's Business: Controlling Corporations and Restoring Democracy* (San Francisco: Berrett-Koehler, 2004), chap. 3.

28. Two of the most important works on the function of the modern corporation are Gardiner Means and Adolph Berle, *The Corporation and Private Property* (New York: Macmillan, 1948); and John Kenneth Galbraith, *The New Industrial State* (Boston: Houghton Mifflin, 1985).

29. Lindblom, *Politics and Markets*, pp. 154–55.

30. Drutman and Cray, *The People's Business*, p. 264.

31. Juliet B. Schor, *The Overspent American: Upscaling, Downshifting, and the New Consumer* (New York: Basic Books, 1998), p. 78. For a provocative critical analysis of our consumer culture, go to www.adbusters.org, or buy a copy of the magazine *Adbusters* (with no ads of course).

32. For accounts of postwar American oligopoly, see Robert Reich, *The Work of Nations* (New York: Random House, 1991); Jeremy Rifkin, *The End of Work* (New York: Tarcher/Putnam, 1995); Donald Barlett and James Steele, *America: What Went Wrong?* (Kansas City: McMeel and Andrews, 1993).

33. Richard J. Barnet, *Global Reach: The Power of Multinational Corporations* (New York: Simon & Schuster, 1974).

34. William Greider, *One World, Ready or Not: The Manic Logic of Global Capitalism* (New York: Touchstone, 1997), p. 22.

35. See Louis Uchitelle and N. R. Kleinfield, "On the Battlefields of Business, Millions of Casualties," *New York Times*, March 3, 1996, p. A1; Rifkin, *The End of Work*, part II.

36. David Korten, *When Corporations Rule the World* (New York: Kumarian, 1995), pp. 216–18; Uchitelle and Kleinfield, "On the Battlefields," p. 27.

37. David Sanger and Steve Lohr, "A Search for Answers to Avoid Layoffs," *New York Times*, March 9, 1996, p. A1; Alan Downs, *Corporate Executions* (New York: American Management Association, 1996).

38. Korten, *When Corporations Rule*, p. 223.

39. Susan Strange, *The Casino Society* (London: Basil Blackwell, 1984).

40. U.S. Bureau of the Census, *Statistical Abstract of the United States 2003* (Washington, D.C.: U.S. Government Printing Office, 2003), p. 511.

41. Aaron Elstein, "Bankers Bask in Glow of New Merger Boom," *Crain's New York Business*, February 7, 2005.

42. For a vivid account of union decline, see Thomas Geoghegan, *Which Side Are You On?* (New York: Plume, 1991). See also Michael Goldfield, *The Decline of Organized Labor in the United States* (Chicago: University of Chicago Press, 1987).

43. According to a poll by Hart Research Associates, 2002, as reported in Margaret Levi, "Organizing Power: The Prospects for an American Labor Movement," *Perspectives on Politics*, 1, no. 1 (March 2003): 51.

44. For a recent update, see Steven Greenhouse, "Labor Board's Detractors See a Bias Against Workers," *New York Times*, January 2, 2005.

45. Steven Greenhouse, "Report Faults Laws for Slowing Growth of Unions," *New York Times*, October 24, 2000.

46. Robert B. Reich, *Locked in the Cabinet* (New York: Alfred A. Knopf, 1997), pp. 280–81. For articles about the revival of unions, see David Moberg, "Can Labor Change?" *Dissent* (Winter 1996): 16. See also Steven Greenhouse, "A Union

Comeback? Tell It to Sweeney," *New York Times*, June 6, 1997, p. 4; Roger Waldinger et al., "Justice for Janitors: Organizing in Difficult Times," *Dissent* (Winter 1997): 37–47.

47. Robert B. Reich, *The Work of Nations* (New York: Random House, 1991). Unless otherwise noted, all data on inequality are from Lawrence Mishel, Jared Bernstein, and Sylvia Allegretto, *The State of Working America 2004/2005* (Ithaca, N.Y.: Cornell University Press, 2005).

48. Deborah Lutterbeck, "Falling Wages," *Common Cause Magazine* (Winter 1995): 14; Herbert Stein and Murray Foss, *The New Illustrated Guide to the American Economy* (Washington, D.C.: American Enterprise Institute, 1995), pp. 126, 130, 132; Steven Greenhouse, "Minimum Wage Maximum Debate," *New York Times*, March 31, 1996, p. 3.

49. Reported in Paul Krugman, "For Richer," in Bruce Miroff, Raymond Seidelman, and Todd Swanstrom, eds., *Debating Democracy: A Reader in American Politics*, 5th ed. (Boston: Houghton Mifflin, 2005), p. 346.

50. Drutman and Cray, *The People's Business*, p. 102.

51. Ibid., p. 98.

52. Mishel, Bernstein, and Allegretto, *The State of Working America 2004/2005*, p. 216.

53. Originally, the government has set the poverty level by determining how much it costs to feed a family at a basic minimum level and then multiplying that by three (on the assumption that food represents about one-third of the typical family's budget). Over the years, however, the cost of food has gone down while the cost of other basic necessities has gone up. This means that the cost of a basic bundle of groceries should be multiplied by about seven and thus a realistic poverty threshold today would be much higher and many more families should be classified as poor.

54. Nina Bernstein, "Family Needs Far Exceed the Official Poverty Line," *New York Times*, September 13, 2000.

55. See Michael W. Cox and Richard Alm, *Myths of Rich and Poor* (New York: Basic Books, 1999).

56. For these reasons, even middle-class families often have trouble making ends meet. See Elizabeth Warren and Amilia Warren Tyagi, *The Two-Income Trap: Why Middle-Class Mothers and Fathers Are Going Broke* (New York: Basic Books, 2003).

57. For the connection between inequality and health, see Ichiro Kawachi, Bruce P. Kennedy, and Richard J. Wilkinson, eds., *The Society and Population Health Reader: Income Inequality and Health* (New York: New Press, 1999).

58. Larry Bartels, "Economic Inequality and Political Representation." Paper presented at the 2002 meeting of the American Political Science Association, Boston, and winner of the Association's "Best Paper" award.

59. Task Force on Inequality and American Democracy, American Political Science Association (APSA), *American Democracy in an Age of Rising Inequality*, APSA, 2004; available at www.apsanet.org.

60. The political philosopher Michael Walzer calls this the "art of separation." See his *Spheres of Justice: A Defense of Pluralism and Equality* (New York: Basic Books, 1983).

61. See Peter Dreier, John Mollenkopf, and Todd Swanstrom, *Place Matters: Metropolitics for the 21st Century*, rev. ed. (Lawrence: University Press of Kansas, 2005).

62. In 1973 the U.S. Supreme Court ruled that there is no right to equal education under the Constitution (*San Antonio v. Rodriquez*, 1973). Since then, however, state courts have intervened in many states to order more equal funding of local schools. Kenneth K. Wong, *Funding Public Schools: Politics and Policies* (Lawrence: University Press of Kansas, 1999).

63. Sidney Verba, Kay Lehman Schlozman, and Henry E. Brady, *Voice and Equality: Civic Voluntarism in American Politics* (Cambridge, Mass.: Harvard University Press, 1995).

64. Louis Uchitelle, "Gaining Ground on the Wage Front," *New York Times*, December 31, 2004.

65. Mishel, Bernstein, and Schmitt, *State of Working America 2000–01*, p. 103.

66. Randy Albelda, *Real World Macro*, 12th ed. (Somerville, Mass.: Dollars and Sense, 1995); Margery Turner et al., *Opportunities Denied, Opportunities Diminished: Racial Discrimination in Hiring* (Washington, D.C.: Urban Institute, 1992).

67. Folbre, *Field Guide*, table 3.7; U.S. Department of Labor, Employment and Earnings Report, 40 (January 1993): 231.

68. Two recent works argue persuasively that strong civil societies are necessary for effective democratic participation: Robert D. Putnam, *Bowling Alone: The Collapse and Revival of American Community* (New York: Simon & Schuster, 2000); and Verba, Schlozman, and Brady, *Voice and Equality*.

69. Verba, Schlozman, and Brady, *Voice and Equality*, chap. 3.

70. Putnam, *Bowling Alone*, p. 438.

71. Ibid., p. 46.

72. Ibid., pp. 360–61.

73. William Julius Wilson, *The Truly Disadvantaged: The Inner City, the Underclass, and Public Policy* (Chicago: University of Chicago Press, 1987); and *When Work Disappears: The World of the New Urban Poor* (New York: Alfred A. Knopf, 1996).

74. Verba, Schlozman, and Brady, *Voice and Equality*, p. 315. The poor are defined as having family incomes below $15,000, the rich at $125,000 and over.

75. Uchitelle and Kleinfield, "On the Battlefields," p. A1.

76. Putnam, *Bowling Alone*, pp. 198–201.

77. John Cassidy, "Who Killed the Middle Class?" *The New Yorker*, October 16, 1995, pp. 113–26.

78. Mishel, Bernstein, and Schmitt, *State of Working America, 2000–01*, p. 34.

79. Juliet B. Schor, *The Overworked American: The Unexpected Decline of Leisure* (New York: Basic Books, 1992), pp. 34–38.

80. Quoted in ibid., pp. 123–24.

81. Higher Education Research Institute (HERI), *The American Freshman: National Norms for Fall 2004* (Los Angeles: HERI, 2005).

82. Wendy M. Rahm and John E. Transue, "Social Trust and Value Change: The Decline of Social Capital in American Youth, 1976–1995," *Political Psychology* 19, no. 3 (1998): 545–65.

83. Vincent P. Bzdek, "The Ad Subtractors, Making a Difference," *Washington Post*, July 29, 2003; as reported in Drutman and Cray, *The People's Business*, p. 264.

84. Schor, *The Overspent American*, p. 107.

85. Cornel West, *Democracy Matters: Winning the Fight Against Imperialism* (New York: Penguin, 2004), p. 5.

86. See Theda Skocpol, "Unraveling from Above," *The American Prospect* (March–April 1996): 22–23.

CHAPTER 4

1. Robert Nisbet, "Public Opinion versus Popular Opinion," in Bruce Miroff, Raymond Seidelman, and Todd Swanstrom, eds., *Debating Democracy* (Boston: Houghton Mifflin, 2001), p. 117; Phillip Converse, "The Nature of Belief Systems in Mass Publics," in David Apter, ed., *Ideology and Discontent* (New York: Free Press, 1964), pp. 243–45. Hamilton is quoted in Clinton Rossiter, ed., *The Federalist Papers* (New York: New American Library, 1961), p. 432.

2. Robert Erikson and Kent Tedin, *American Public Opinion* (New York: Longman, 2000), p. 54; PIPA/Knowledge Networks poll, July 22, 2004 (www.pipa.org).

3. Benjamin Ginsberg, *The Captive Public* (New York: Basic Books, 1986). See also Walter Lippmann, *The Phantom Public* (New York: Harcourt Brace Jovanovich, 1925), pp. 15, 155; Thomas Dye and Harmon Ziegler, *The Irony of Democracy* (Monterey, Calif.: Brooks/Cole, 1987), p. 145; Anthony King, *Running Scared* (Cambridge, Mass.: Harvard University Press, 1997); Michael Delli Carpini and Scott Keeter, "The Public's Knowledge of Politics," in David Kennamer, ed., *Public Opinion, the Press, and Public Policy* (Westport, Conn.: Praeger, 1992).

4. C. Wright Mills, *The Power Elite* (New York: Oxford University Press, 1956), pp. 298–304; John Dewey, *The Public and Its Problems* (Athens, Ohio: Swallow Press, 1954). For a discussion of Dewey's views on public opinion, see Robert Westerbrook, *John Dewey and American Democracy* (Ithaca, N.Y.: Cornell University Press, 1991).

5. Robert Cirino, *Don't Blame the People* (New York: Basic Books, 1971). For a brilliant account of public opinion during the Vietnam War, see Godfrey Hodgson, *America in Our Time* (New York: Pantheon, 1976).

6. Erikson and Tedin, *American Public Opinion*, p. 153; National Election Study, University of Michigan, 1988.

7. Kenneth Dolbeare and Linda Medcalf, *American Political Ideas in the 1980s* (New York: Random House, 1985); John Sullivan, James Pierson, and George Marcus, *Political Tolerance and American Democracy* (Chicago: University of Chicago Press, 1982).

8. See Robert Bellah et al., *Habits of the Heart* (New York: HarperCollins, 1995), chaps. 1, 10, 11; James Kluegel and Eliot Smith, *Beliefs About Inequality* (New York: Aldine De Gruyter, 1986), pp. 135–43; Roper Center for Public Opinion Research, "Change and Persistence in American Ideas," *The Public Perspective* (April/May 1995): 14; Robert Putnam, "The Strange Disappearance of Civic America," *The American Prospect* (May 1996); Andrew Greeley, "The Other Civic America: Religion and Social Capital," *The American Prospect* (May/June 1997).

9. See Jennifer Hochschild, *What's Fair: American Beliefs About Distributive Justice* (Cambridge, Mass.: Harvard University Press, 1981). See also William Jacoby, "Public Opinion and Economic Policy in 1992," in Barbara Norrander and Clyde Wilcox, *Understanding Public Opinion* (Washington, D.C.: Congressional Quarterly Press, 1997); Leslie McCall and Julian Brash, "What Do Americans Think About Economic Inequality?" Demos—A Network of Ideals and Action, May 2004 (www.demos.org).

10. See Gallup Poll, November 13, 2000 (www.gallup.com); FAIR, Action Alert of December 22, 2000 (www.fair.org).

11. See John Zaller and Stanley Feldman, "A Simple Theory of the Survey Response: Answering Questions and Revealing Preferences," *American Journal of Political Science* 36 (1992): 579–616. See also John Zaller, *The Nature and Origins of Mass Opinion* (Cambridge: Cambridge University Press, 1992). See also Paul Sniderman et al., "Principle Tolerance and the American Mass Public," *British Journal of Political Science* (February 1989): 25–45; Herbert McClosky and Alida Brill, *Dimensions of Political Tolerance* (New York: Russell Sage, 1983); Dye and Ziegler, *The Irony of Democracy*, pp. 137–43; Samuel Stouffer, *Communism, Conformity, and Civil Liberties* (New York: Doubleday, 1955).

12. Erikson and Tedin, *American Public Opinion*, 3rd ed., pp. 144–54; Robert Weissberg, *Political Tolerance: Balancing Community and Diversity* (Thousand Oaks, Calif.: Sage, 1998); James Gibson, "Political Intolerance During the McCarthy Red Scare," *American Political Science Review* (June 1988): 512–19; Michael Rogin, *The Intellectuals and McCarthy* (Cambridge, Mass.: MIT Press, 1970).

13. Weissberg, *Political Tolerance*, Conclusion.

14. "Americans on Detention, Torture and the War on Terrorism," PIPA/Knowledge Networks, July 22, 2004, p. 3 (www.pipa.org); "War on Terrorism Has Not Made Public Feel Safer," PIPA/Knowledge Networks, September 9, 2004 (www.pipa.org); Reg Whitaker, "After 9/11: A Surveillance State?" in Cynthia Brown and Aryeh Neier, eds., *Lost Liberties: Ashcroft and the Assault on Personal Freedom* (New York: The New Press, 2003), pp. 52–71.

15. Benjamin Page and Robert Shapiro, *The Rational Public* (Chicago: University of Chicago Press, 1992); Ted Halstead, "The Politics of Generation X," *Atlantic Monthly* (April 1999); Pew Research Center for the People and the Press, "2004 Political Landscape," Part 9 (www.people-press.org).

16. Polling data from PIPA/Knowledge Networks poll, "Americans and Iraq on the Eve of the Presidential Elections,"

October 28, 2004, and "The Separate Realities of Bush and Kerry Supporters," October 21, 2004 (www.pipa.org).

17. Pew Research Center for the People and the Press, "Retropolitics: The Political Typology Version 3.0," 1999 (www.people-press.org/archives.html); Program on International Policy Attitudes, "Americans on Globalization: A Summary of U.S. Findings," School of Public Affairs, University of Maryland, 1999 (www.pipa.org); Pew Research Center for the People and the Press, "2004 Political Landscape," Part 4, "Success, Poverty and Government Responsibility" (www.people-press.org/reports).

18. Kluegel and Smith, *Beliefs*, chaps. 3–4; Pew Research Center for the People and the Press, "Updates of Social Survey," April 1999 (www.people-press.org/archives); PIPA/Knowledge Networks, "Globalization," 2002 (www.pipa.org); Ruy Teixeira and Joel Rogers, *America's Forgotten Majority: Why the White Working Class Still Matters* (New York: Basic Books, 2002), pp. 147–60; Andrew Kohut, "Globalization and the Wage Gap," *New York Times*, December 3, 1999, p. A31.

19. Leon Baradat, *Political Ideologies: Their Origins and Impact* (Englewood Cliffs, N.J.: Prentice Hall, 1979), pp. 30–37.

20. Kathleen Knight and Robert Erikson, "Ideology in the 1990s," in Norrander and Wilcox, *Understanding Public Opinion*, p. 107.

21. This is particularly true of both the 2000 and 2004 elections, where the issue advantages were clearly with the Democrats, even though Bush won both elections. Pew Research Center for the People and the Press, "2004 Electoral Landscape, Part I" (www.people-press.org). See also Pamela Conover and Stanley Feldman, "The Origins and Meanings of Liberal and Conservative Self-Identification," *American Journal of Political Science* (November 1981): 617–45; Knight and Erickson, "Ideology," in Norrander and Wilcox, *Understanding Public Opinion*, pp. 107–10.

22. For the blurring of ideology in the 1980s, see Sidney Blumenthal, *Pledging Allegiance: The Last Campaign of the Cold War* (New York: HarperCollins, 1989). For the 1990s, see the master of ideological blur himself, Dick Morris, *Behind the Oval Office* (New York: Random House, 1997). See also Teixeira and Rogers, *America's Forgotten Majority*, chaps. 2 and 3. For 2004, see Pew Research Center for the People and the Press, "The 2004 Political Landscape—An Overview" (www.people-press.org).

23. E. J. Dionne, *Why Americans Hate Politics* (New York: Simon & Schuster, 1993), p. 14

24. See Robert Putnam, *Bowling Alone: The Collapse and Revival of American Community* (New York: Simon & Schuster, 2000), chap. 6; Alan Wolfe, *One Nation, After All* (New York: Penguin, 1999), and Alan Wolfe, *The Transformation of American Religion* (New York: Free Press, 2003).

25. For an unconventional but important account, see Thomas Hine, *Rise and Fall of the American Teenager* (New York: Bard Books, 1999); William Finnegan, *Cold New World* (New York: Modern Library, 1999).

26. M. Kent Jennings, "Residuals of a Movement: The Aging of the American Protest Generation," *American Political Science Review* 81 (June 1987): 365–82.

27. Putnam, *Bowling Alone*, p. 259; Halstead, "The Politics of Gen X"; Daniel Yankelovich, "How Changes in the Economy Are Reshaping American Values," in Henry Aaron, Thomas Mann, and Timothy Taylor, eds., *Values and Public Policy* (Washington, D.C.: Brookings Institution Press, 1994).

28. See M. R. Jackman and R. W. Jackman, *Class Awareness in the United States* (Berkeley: University of California Press, 1983); Jared Bernstein et al., *The State of Working America 2003* (White Plains, N.Y.: M. E. Sharpe, 2003).

29. General Social Survey, 1998; AFL-CIO Survey of Young Workers, Peter Hart Associates, 1999 (www.afl-cio.org).

30. See David Croteau, *Politics and the Class Divide* (Philadelphia: Temple University Press, 1995).

31. Michael Goldfield, *The Color of Politics* (New York: New Press, 1998); David Roediger, *The Wages of Whiteness* (London: Verso, 1991); Pew Research Center for the People and the Press, "2004 Political Landscape: Race" (www.people-press.org).

32. Edward Carmines and James Stimson, *Issue Evolution: Race and the Transformation of American Politics* (Princeton, N.J.: Princeton University Press, 1989); David Shipler, *A Country of Strangers* (New York: Alfred A. Knopf, 1997).

33. Howard Schuman, Charlotte Steeh, Lawrence Bobo, and Maria Krysan, *Racial Attitudes in America* (Cambridge, Mass.: Harvard University Press, 1997); Steven Tuch and Lee Sigelman, "Race, Class, and Black-White Differences in Social Views," in Norrander and Wilcox, *Understanding Public Opinion*, pp. 48–49. See also "Whites Retain Negative Views of Minorities," New York Ties, January 14, 1991; David Bositis, Joint Center for Political Studies, "2004 National Opinion Poll" (www.jointcenter.org).

34. Kluegel and Smith, *Beliefs*, pp. 135–43; Lee Sigelman and Susan Welch, *Black Americans' Views of Racial Inequality* (Cambridge, Mass.: Harvard University Press, 1991), p. 589; Jennifer Hochschild, *Facing Up to the American Dream* (Princeton, N.J.: Princeton University Press, 1995).

35. See Kristi Anderson, "Gender and Public Opinion," in Barbara Norrander and Clyde Wilcox, eds., *Understanding Public Opinion* (Washington, D.C.: Congressional Quarterly Press, 1997); John Judis and Ruy Teixeira, *The Emerging Democratic Majority* (New York: Scribners, 2002); James Ceasar and Andrew Busch, *Red Over Blue* (New York: Rowman and Littlefield, 2005).

36. Sara Diamond, *Not By Politics Alone* (New York: Guilford, 1999); Kenneth Wald, *Religion and Politics in the United States*, 3rd ed. (Washington, D.C.: Congressional Quarterly Press, 1997). See also Ted Jelen, "Religion and Public Opinion in the 1990s," in Norrander and Wilcox, *Understanding Public Opinion*, pp. 19–36. For 2004, see Pew Center for the People and the Press, "2004 Political Landscape, Religion, Public Life," (www.people-press.org). See also Wolfe, *The Transformation*; Jim Wallis, *God's Politics* (San Francisco: HarperCollins, 2005).

37. Pew Center for the People and the Press, "2004 Political Landscape: Religion" (www.people-press.org).

38. Gallup quoted in Christopher Hitchens, "Voting in the Passive Voice," *Harpers* (April 1992), p. 46; Susan Herbst, *Numbered Voices* (Chicago: University of Chicago Press, 1993), p. 2; Michael Traugott and Paul Lavrakas, *The Voter's Guide to Election Polls*, 2nd ed. (New York: Chatham House, 2000), pp. 129–30; Bruce Miroff, Raymond Seidelman, and Todd Swanstrom, *The Election of 1994: Revolution or Reaction?* (Boston: Houghton Mifflin, 1995).

CHAPTER 5

1. For primary figures, see "The Republican Primary Vote," *Congressional Quarterly Weekly Report*, August 3, 1996; August 7, 2000, pp. 63–64. For 2004, see David Leip's Presidential Atlas (www.uselectionatlas.org). See for U.S. voter statistics Dave Leip's Presidential Atlas, "Voter Turnout by State as Percentage of VAP," www.uselectionatlas.org.

2. See Todd Swanstrom and Edward Sauerzopf, "Urban Electorates," unpublished paper, Rockefeller College of Public Policy, State University of New York, Albany, 1995; *The Almanac of American Politics, 2002* (Washington, D.C.: National Journal, 2003).

3. "The Race for the House," *New York Times*, November 4, 2004, Section P12; Robert Wiebe, *Self-Rule* (Chicago: University of Chicago Press, 1996); Paul Kleppner, *Who Voted? The Dynamics of Electoral Turnout* (New York Harper & Row, 1983).

4. George F. Will, "In Defense of Nonvoting" *Newsweek* (October 10, 1996), p. 96.

5. Two founding studies in this tradition are Anthony Downs, *An Economic Theory of Democracy* (New York: Harper & Row, 1978); V. O. Key, *The Responsible Electorate* (New York: Cambridge University Press, 1966). One of the most well-known works is Morris Fiorina, *Retrospective Voting in American National Elections* (New Haven, Conn.: Yale University Press, 1981). See also Ruy Teixeira, *The Disappearing Voter* (Washington, D.C.: The Brookings Institution, 1992).

6. See Michael Barone, "The Road Back to Tocqueville," *Washington Post*, January 7, 1996, pp. C1–C2.

7. George F. Will, *Statecraft as Soulcraft* (New York: Simon & Schuster, 1983).

8. Alexander Keyssar, *The Right to Vote: The Contested History of Democracy in the United States* (New York: Basic Books, 2000); Anthony King, *Running Scared* (Cambridge, Mass.: Harvard University Press, 1997). For a refutation, see Theda Skocpol, "Unravelling from Above," *The American Prospect* (March 1996): 20–24.

9. Keyssar, *The Right to Vote*, chap. 5; Stephen Hill, *Fixing Elections* (New York: Routledge, 2002).

10. Keyssar, *The Right to Vote*, chap. 4.

11. See Frances Fox Piven and Richard Cloward, *Why Americans Don't Vote* (New York: Pantheon, 1987); see also Steven Rosenstone and John Mark Hansen, *Mobilization, Participation, and Democracy in America* (New York: Macmillan, 1993).

12. See G. Bingham Powell, "Voter Turnout in Comparative Perspective," *American Political Science Review* (March 1986): 1; Raymond Wolfinger and Steven Rosenstone, *Who Votes?* (New Haven, Conn.: Yale University Press, 1978), pp. 61–88; Walter Dean Burnham, "The Appearance and Disappearance of the American Voter," in Burnham, *The Current Crisis in American Politics* (New York: Oxford University Press, 1982). See also "Vanishing Voter Project" press release, November 4, 2004 (www.vanishingvoter.org). See also Ruy Teixeira, "Voter Turnout: Ten Myths," in Bruce Miroff, Raymond Seidelman, and Todd Swanstrom, eds., *Debating Democracy: A Reader in American Politics* (Boston: Houghton Mifflin, 1999), pp. 164–69.

13. Keyssar, *The Right to Vote*, pp. 311–14; Frances Fox Piven, personal communication with the author, July 17, 1996; Frances Fox Piven and Richard Cloward, "Northern Bourbons: A Preliminary Report on the National Voter Registration Act," *PS* (March 1996): 39–41; Committee for the Study of the American Electorate, "2004 Election Report" (www.fairvote.org).

14. See "Voting Irregularities in Florida During the 2000 Presidential Election," U.S. Commission on Civil Rights, July 2001.

15. Joann Wypijewski, "The Party's Over," *The Nation*, November 2004; "Ground War, 2004," *The Nation*, November 2004; Greg Palast, *The Best Democracy Money Can Buy* (New York: Plume Books, 2004).

16. Ronald Dworkin, "A Badly Flawed Election," *New York Review of Books*, January 11, 2001, pp. 54–55.

17. Committee for the Study of the American Electorate, November 4, 2004, p. 2.

18. "Democracy Denied," *Demos*, April 2004 (www.demos.org); Steven Hill, *Fixing Elections* (New York: Routledge, 2002); Roberto Suro, Richard Fry, and Jeffrey Passel, "Hispanics and the 2004 Election," Pew Hispanic Center, 2005 (pewhispanic.org).

19. Michael Goldfield, *The Color of Politics* (New York: New Press, 1998); John Dittmer, *Local People* (Champaign-Urbana: University of Illinois Press, 1995), chaps. 10–12.

20. Roman Hedges and Carl Carlucci, "The Implementation of the Voting Rights Act," unpublished paper, State University of New York, Albany; Jim Sleeper, *The Closest of Strangers* (New York: W. W. Norton, 1990).

21. Robert Putnam, "Bowling Alone: America's Declining Social Capital," *Journal of Democracy* (January 1995): 34–35. Putnam's larger and monumental study is *Bowling Alone: The Collapse and Revival of American Community* (New York: Simon & Schuster, 2000). A refutation of Putnam's general thesis can be found in Everett Carll Ladd's article in *Public Perspective* (June/July 1996). See also Jason Kaufman, *For the Common Good* (New York: Oxford University Press, 2002).

22. See Sidney Verba, Kay Scholzman, and Henry Brady, *Voice and Equality: Civic Voluntarism in American Politics* (Cambridge, Mass.: Harvard University Press, 1995), p. 532. See also Theda Skocpol and Morris Fiorina, eds., *Civic Engagement in American Democracy* (Washington, D.C.: Brookings Institution Press, 1999).

23. See Robert Reich, "Secession of the Successful," *New York Times Magazine*, January 20, 1992. See also Robert Kaplan, *An Empire Wilderness* (New York: Vintage, 1999).

24. See Verba, Schlozman, and Brady, "Civic Participation and the Equality Problem" in Skocpol and Fiorina, *Civic Engagement*, pp. 427–60; Burnham, "The Appearance and Disappearance," in *Current Crisis*, p. 86.

25. See Ruy Teixeira and Joel Rogers, *America's Forgotten Majority* (New York: Basic Books, 2000).

26. See League of Women Voters, "Mellman Group and Wirthlin Group Worldwide Survey of Nonvoters," Press Release, May 29, 1996; Campaign Study Group, *No-Show '96: Americans Who Don't Vote* (Evanston, Ill.: Northwestern University Press, 1966); Thomas Paterson, "Vanishing Voter Project News Release," February 2, 2005, Rockthevote blog, November 4, 2004 at www.rockthevote.org; "Major National Survey Snows Emerging Electorate of Young Voters," *PR Newswire*, November 16, 2004.

27. See David Croteau, *Politics and the Class Divide* (Philadelphia: Temple University Press, 1994); Nina Eliasoph, *Avoiding Politics* (New York: Cambridge University Press, 1998).

28. Ruy Teixeira, "What the Election Told Us," *Challenge* (March/April 1999): 83. For other data, see William Maddox and Stuart Lilie, *Beyond Liberal and Conservative* (Washington, D.C.: Cato Institute, 1984); Campaign Study Group, *No-Show '96*, pp. 1–8.

29. Pew Research Center for the People and the Press, "Religion and the Presidential Vote," December 6, 2004; Alan Cooperman and Thomas Edsall, "Evangelicals Say They Led Charge for GOP," *Washington Post*, November 8, 2004; Thomas Frank, *What's the Matter with Kansas* (New York: Metropolitan Books, 2004).

30. Harold Meyerson, "A Tale of Two Cities," *The American Prospect*, June 6, 2004; Beth Shuster, "Latinos May Give Labor Key to City Hall Control," *Los Angeles Times*, December 29, 1998, p. A1; Harold Meyerson, "Voters," *The American Prospect*, July 2000; Frank Swoboda, "Labor Targets 71 House Districts in Watershed Year," *Washington Post*, February 16, 2000, p. A14.

31. Matt Bai, "Who Lost Ohio?" *New York Times Magazine*, November 21, 2004; Mark Gruenberg, "The 2004 Election: Sweeney, After Kerry Loss," *Public Affairs International*, November 4, 2004; Harold Meyerson, "The Tsunami," *LA Weekly*, October 29, 2004; Peter Hart Research Associates, "Survey on Labor Participation in 2000 General Election," November 9, 2000; Harold Meyerson, "A Tale of Two Cities"; Meyerson, "Voters," *American Prospect*, July 2000. Frank Swoboda, "Labor Targets 71 House Districts in Watershed Year," *Washington Post*, February 16, 2000, p. A14.

32. Paterson, "Vanishing Voter Project," chaps. 3–6.

33. Rosenstone and Hansen, *Mobilization*, p. 229.

CHAPTER 6

1. PIPA/Knowledge Networks Poll, "Americans and Iraq on the Eve of the Presidential Election," October 28, 2004; PIPA/Knowledge Networks Poll, "The Separate Realities of Bush and Kerry Supporters," October 21, 2004 (www.pipa.org). For TV ads, see Marian Currinder, "Campaign Finance: Funding the Presidential and Congressional Election," in Michael Nelson, ed., *The Election of 2004* (Washington, D.C.: Congressional Quarterly Press, 2005), p. 3.

2. Pew Center for the People and the Press, "Trends 2005: Media: More Voices, Less Credibility," January 2005 (www.people-press.org).

3. *Bacon's Magazine Directory*, 2004; *Bacon's Newspaper Directory*, 2004; *Benn's Media 2004*, 152nd edition.

4. Pew Internet and Daily Life Project, August 11, 2004, "The Internet and Daily Life" (www.pewinternet.org).

5. Thomas Leonard, *The Power of the Press* (New York: Oxford University Press, 1986).

6. Michael Schudson, *Discovering the News* (New York: Basic Books, 1978).

7. Frank Luther Mott, *American Journalism 1660–1960* (New York: Macmillan, 1962), p. 529. For an account of Hearst's life, see W. A. Swanberg, *Citizen Hearst* (New York: Scribners, 1961).

8. Richard Niemi and Harold Stanley, *Vital Statistics on American Politics, 2003–2004* (Washington, D.C.: Congressional Quarterly Press, 2004); Pew Research Center for the People and the Press, "Media," January 2005 (www.people-press.org).

9. See the account in Ronald Berkman and Laura Kitch, *The Politics of Mass Media* (New York: St. Martin's Press, 1990), p. 42.

10. On TV coverage of the 1960s, see Edward Epstein, *News from Nowhere* (New York: Random House, 1973); Michael Arlen, *The Living Room War* (New York: Viking, 1969).

11. National Annenberg Election Survey, "Daily Show Viewers Knowledgeable About Presidential Campaign," September 21, 2004 (www.naes04.org); Edward Wong, "Hard Times for TV Documentaries," *New York Times*, January 4, 2001, p. E1.

12. Pew Research Center for the People and the Press, "Trends 2005: Media," January 2005 (www.people-press.org).

13. Pew Research Center for the People and the Press, "Internet Sapping Broadcast News Audience," Media Report 2000 (www.people-press.org/media00rept.htm); Nicholas Negroponte, *Being Digital* (New York: Alfred A. Knopf, 1995).

14. Cass Sunstein, "The Daily We," *Boston Review*, Summer 2001; Cass Sunstein, *Republic.com* (Princeton, N.J.: Princeton University Press, 2002).

15. For 1940s media studies, see Paul Lazarsfeld, Bernard Berelson, and Hazel Gaudet, *The People's Choice* (New York: Columbia University Press, 1948). For the 1970s, see Thomas Paterson and Robert McClure, *The Unseeing Eye* (New York: G. P. Putnam, 1976), p. 90.

16. Shanto Iyengar and Donald Kinder, *News That Matters: The Agenda Setting Functions of the Press* (Chicago: University of Chicago Press, 1987); S. Iyengar, M. Peters, and D. Kinder, "Experimental Demonstrations of the Not-So-Minimal Consequences of Television News Programs," *American Political Science Review* (Winter 1980).

17. Robert McChesney, *The Problem of the Media: U.S. Communications Politics in the 21st Century* (New York: Monthly Review Press, 2004), chap. 5.

18. Robert McChesney, *Rich Media, Poor Democracy* (New York: The New Press, 2001), chap. 2; Peter Golding and Phil Harris, eds., *Beyond Cultural Imperialism: Globalization, Communication and the New International Order* (London: Sage, 1997); McChesney, *Problem of the Media*, p. 178. See also Mark Crispin Miller, "Big Media, Bad News," *The Nation*, January 7, 2002.

19. "Who Owns What," *Columbia Journalism Review*, 2004 (www.cjr.org/tools.owners).

20. Peter Philips, *Censored 2000* (New York: Seven Stories Press, 2001); "Project Censored 2005," Sonoma State University (www.projectcensored.org).

21. Todd Gitlin, "What Was Gained at WTO," *Los Angeles Times*, December 7, 1999, p. 9; Janet Thomas, *The Battle in Seattle* (Eugene, Ore.: Fulcrum, 2001). See also "Protesting the Piece," NPR, *On the Media*, November 1, 2002; Michael Frome, The 21st Century Economy," *The American Writer* (Winter 2000), p. 14.

22. McChesney, *Rich Media*, chap. 2; Golding and Harris, *Beyond Cultural Imperialism*.

23. McChesney, *Problem of the Media*, p. 82 and chap. 5. See Ken Auletta, "Sign Off," *The New Yorker*, March 2, 2005; Doug Underwood, *When MBAs Rule the Newsroom* (New York: Columbia University Press, 1996).

24. McChesney, *Problem of the Media*, p. 84; Joe Strupp, "New Advertorials Raise Old Ethical Questions," *Editor and Publishers*, November 17, 2003; Mark Jurkowitz, "When Journalists Become Pitchmen," *Boston Globe*, February 10, 2000; Lance Bennett, *News: The Politics of Illusion* (New York: Longman, 2004).

25. Douglas Rushkoff, "The Internet: Coercion in Cyberspace?" in Miroff, Seidelman, and Swanstrom, *Debating Democracy: A Reader in American Politics*, 3rd ed. (Boston: Houghton Mifflin, 2001), p. 205.

26. Lawrence Lessig, "Will AOL Own Everything?" *Time*, June 19, 2000, p. 160.

27. See Martha Honey, "Contra Coverage: Paid for by the CIA," *Columbia Journalism Review* (March/April 1987).

28. Michael Massing, "Now They Tell Us," *New York Review of Books*, February 26, 2004; Michael Massing, "The Unseen War," *New York Review of Books*, May 29, 2003; Sheldon Rampton and John Stauber, *Weapons of Mass Deception* (Boston: Common Courage Press, 2004); David Barstow and Robin Stein, "Under Bush, Prepackaged News," *New York Times*, March 13, 2005, p. A1. "Judith Miller Goes to Jail," *New York Times*, July 7, 2005, p. A22.

29. For excellent accounts of the corrosive effects of celebrity journalism on the political agenda, see James Fallows, *Breaking the News: How the Media Undermine American Democracy* (New York: Pantheon, 1995). See also Martin Lee and Norman Solomon, *Unreliable Sources* (New York: Carol Publishing Group, 1991). Jim Drinkard, "President Criticizes Education Dept.'s Payout to Williams," *USA Today*, January 14, 2005.

30. See also Robert McChesney, *Telecommunications, Mass Media, and Democracy* (New York: Oxford University Press, 1993), chaps. 1, 6; Joshua Rosenkranz, "Free TV Speech for Candidates," *The Nation*, June 8, 1998, p. 31; Christopher Stern, "Broadcast Loan Has Xmas Wrapping," *Variety*, April 4, 1997, p. 24; Robert McChesney, "The Digital TV Scandal: How a Powerful Lobby Stole Billions in Public Property," *Public Citizen News* (Fall 1997).

31. McChesney, *Problem of the Media*, final chapter; Robert Siegel, "Federal Appeals Court Tosses Out Set of FCC Regulations Regarding the Number of Media Properties That a Single Company Can Own," NPR *All Things Considered*, June 24, 2004.

32. Daniel Weaver and C. Cleveland Wilhoit, *The American Journalist in the 1990s: U.S. News People at the End of an Era* (Mahwah, N.J.: Erlbaum, 1996), p. 7; David Croteau, "Examining the Liberal Media Claim: Journalists' Views on Politics, Economic Policy, and Media Coverage," Fairness and Accuracy in Reporting (FAIR), June 1998 (www.fair.org/reports); Pew Center for the People and the Press and Project for Excellence in Journalism, *State of the Media, 2004*, Journalists' Survey (www.journalism.org).

33. Fallows, *Breaking the News*, pp. 33, 80.

34. Robert Entman, *Democracy Without Citizens: Media and the Decay of American Politics* (New York: Oxford University Press, 1989).

35. Bennett, *News*, chap. 4.

36. Michael Massing, "The Unseen War," *New York Review of Books*, May 29, 2003, pp. 16–19.

37. See David Okrent, "Weapons of Mass Destruction? Or Mass Distraction?" *New York Times*, May 30, 2004, Opinion-Editorial section; Judith Miller, "Illicit Arms Kept Till Eve of War," *New York Times*, April 23, 2003, p. A1; John R. MacArthur, "The Lies We Bought," *Columbia Journalism Review*, 2003.

38. Massing, "The Unseen War," p. 16; Bennett, *News*, pp. 37, 120; Sally Covington, *Moving a Public Agenda: The Strategic*

Philanthropy of Conservative Foundations (Washington, D.C.: The National Committee for Responsive Philanthropy, 1997).

39. See Jarol Manheim, *All of the People, All of the Time* (Armonk, N.Y.: M. E. Sharpe, 1991), chap. 3; W. Lance Bennett and Timothy Cook, "Journalism Norms and News Construction," *Political Communication* (Winter 1996); Doris Graber, *The Mass Media in American Politics* (Washington, D.C.: Congressional Quarterly Press, 1996), pp. 44–45; Ray Suarez, *Talk of the Nation*, National Public Radio, March 13, 1997; Bennett, *News*, pp. 173–77.

40. Timothy Crouse, *The Boys on the Bus* (New York: Random House, 1973), p. 44.

41. Peter Hart, "Re-Establishing the Establishment," *Extra!* April 2004; Eric Boehlert, "Dean," *Salon*, January 6, 2004 (www.salon.com); Bryan Keefer, "Spin Buster," *Columbia Journalism Review Daily Campaign Desk* (www.campaigndesk.org/archives); Dana Milbank, *Smashmouth* (New York: Basic Books, 2001). See also, for material on framing, Shanto Iyengar, *Is Anyone Responsible? How Television Frames Political Issues* (Chicago: University of Chicago Press, 1991).

42. "Protesting the Piece," *On the Media*, NPR, November 1, 2002 (www.onthemedia.org).

43. Jim Rutenberg, "Fox Portrays a War of Good and Evil, and Many Applaud," *New York Times*, December 3, 2001. See for this general point Tom Rosenstiel and Bill Kovach, *Warp Speed: America in the Age of Mixed Media* (New York: The Century Foundation, 1999).

44. Manheim, *All of the People*, chap. 3.

45. Bennett, *News*, pp. 43–44; Christina Alsina, Philip John Davies, and Bruce Gronbeck, "Preference Poll Stories in the Last Two Weeks of Campaign 2000," *American Behavioral Scientist*, August 2001; Project for Excellence in Journalism, "The Debate Effect," October 27, 2004 (www.journalism.org).

46. Bill Kovach, *Talk of the Nation*, National Public Radio, December 7, 2000; Marjorie Randon Hershey, "The Campaign and the Media," in Gerald Pomper, ed., *The Election of 2000* (New York: Chatham House, 2001), pp. 46–72; Erika Falk and Sean Aday, "Candidate Discourse on Network Evening News Programs," Annenberg Public Policy Center, University of Pennsylvania; Stephen Hess, "Hess Report on How Television Networks Covered the 2000 Presidential Campaign," Brookings Institution, November 13, 2000; Project on Excellence, "The Debate" (www.journalism.org).

47. James Boylan, "Where Have All the People Gone?" *Columbia Journalism Review* (May/June 1991): 31–38.

48. Project for Excellence in Journalism, "E-Politics 2004," October 2004 (www.journalism.org); Cass Sunstein, "The Daily We," *Boston Review*, Summer 2001. For data on Jon Stewart's *Daily Show* viewers, see "No Joke: Daily Show Viewers Follow Presidential Race," *Business Journal*, September 21, 2004.

CHAPTER 7

1. Lawrence Goodwyn, *The Populist Moment in America* (New York: Oxford University Press, 1976; Thomas B. Edsall and Mike Allen, "Bush Fundraisers," *Washington Post*, July 14, 2003.

2. There are a number of classic works on political parties. They include Maurice Duverger's *Political Parties* (New York: Wiley and Sons, 1954); and Max Weber, "Politics as a Vocation," in Hans Gerth and C. Wright Mills, eds., *From Max Weber* (New York: Oxford University Press, 1958), pp. 77–128. See also E. E. Schattschneider, *Party Government* (New York: Holt, Rinehart and Winston, 1942).

3. See Walter Dean Burnham, "The End of American Party Politics," *Transaction* (December 1969): 16–36. Samuel Huntington, "The Visions of the Democratic Party," *Public Interest* (Spring 1985): 64.

4. See Burnham, "The End of American Party Politics."

5. Huntington, "The Visions of the Democratic Party."

6. Walter Dean Burnham and William Nisbet Chambers, *The American Party Systems* (New York: Oxford University Press, 1976); Paul Kleppner, *Who Voted? The Dynamics of Electoral Turnout 1870–1950* (New York: Harper & Row, 1983).

7. This is now somewhat less true of European parties, as there are "Americanizing" tendencies. See Joel Krieger and Mark Kesselman, *European Politics in Transition* (Boston: Houghton Mifflin, 1983).

8. See the discussion in Walter Dean Burnham, *The Current Crisis in American Politics* (New York: Oxford University Press, 1983).

9. See Ted Lowi, "Toward a Responsible Three Party System," in Theodore Lowi and Joseph Romance, eds., *A Republic of Parties?* (Lanham, Md.: Rowman and Littlefield, 1998).

10. See Stephen Hill, *Fixing Elections: The Failure of America's Winner Take All Politics* (New York: Routledge, 2002), p. 82.

11. Dan Cantor and J. W. Mason, "Inside, Outside, or Somewhere in Between?: Fusion Voting," Working Families Party paper, 2003 (www.wfp.org). See also L. Sandy Maisel and John Bibby, *Two Parties or More?* (Boulder: Westview Press, 1998); and Micah Sifry, *Spoiling for a Fight: Third Party Politics in America* (New York: Routledge, 2002).

12. See George Edwards III, *Why the Electoral College Is Bad for America* (New Haven, Conn.: Yale University Press, 2004); and Alexander Keyssar, "The Electoral College Flunks," *New York Review of Books*, March 24, 2005.

13. See Hill, *Fixing Elections*; Jeffrey Toobin, "The Great Election Grab," *The New Yorker*, December 8, 2003; "Drawing Lines: A Public Interest Real Redistricting Reform," *Demos* (www.demos-usa.org), 2005.

14. For the Reform Party, see Lowi, "Toward a Responsible Three Party System"; for the Greens, see Ruth Conniff, "On the Road with Ralph Nader," *The Nation*, July 17, 2000; Ralph Nader, "Parties to Injustice; Democrats Will Do Anything to Keep Me Off the Ballot," *Washington Post*, September 5, 2004.

15. Giovanni Sartori, *Parties and Party Systems* (Cambridge: Cambridge University Press, 1976), p. 42.

16. Walter Dean Burnham, *Critical Elections and the Mainsprings of American Politics* (New York: W. W. Norton, 1967). See also John Aldrich, *Why Parties?* (Chicago: University of Chicago Press, 1995).

17. See Jerome Clubb, Nancy Zingale, and William Flanigan, *Partisan Realignment: Voters, Party, and Government in American History* (Beverly Hills, Calif.: Sage, 1980). See Richard Jensen, *The Winning of the Midwest: Social and Political Conflict 1888–1896* (Chicago: University of Chicago Press, 1971). See also Walter Dean Burnham, "The Appearance and Disappearance of the American Voter," in Walter Dean Burnham, ed., *The Current Crisis*, pp. 142–60. There are many outstanding accounts of this period. See Michael McGerr, *The Decline of Popular Politics* (New York: Oxford University Press, 1986); Robert Wiebe, *The Search for Order* (New York: Hill and Wang, 1967); V. O. Key, *Southern Politics* (New York: Alfred A. Knopf, 1967); Michael Goldfield, *The Color of Politics* (New York: New Press, 1998).

18. See Steve Fraser and Gary Gerstle, eds., *The Rise and Fall of the New Deal Order* (Princeton, N.J.: Princeton University Press, 1989); Stephen Skowronek, *The Politics Presidents Make* (Cambridge, Mass.: Harvard University Press, 1993); Sidney Milkis, *The Modern Presidency and the Transformation of the American Party System* (New York: Oxford University Press, 1993).

19. E. E. Schattschneider, quoted in Leon Epstein, *Political Parties in the American Mold* (Madison: University of Wisconsin Press, 1986).

20. One account of racial and cultural divides is Thomas and Mary Edsall, *Chain Reaction* (New York: W. W. Norton, 1991). See also James Davison Hunter, *Culture Wars: The Struggle to Define America* (New York: Basic Books, 1990).

21. Two good accounts of this are to be found in Goldfield, *The Color*, chap. 8; and Godfrey Hodgson, *America in Our Time* (New York: Pantheon, 1976). See the classic account by Norman Mailer, *Miami and the Siege of Chicago* (New York: Harper & Row, 1970); and Garry Wills, *Nixon Agonistes* (New York: Pantheon, 1970). See also Terry Anderson, *The Movement and the Sixties* (New York: Oxford University Press, 1995); and Rick Perlstein, *Before the Storm* (New York: Hill and Wang, 2002).

22. See Hodgson, *America in Our Time*.

23. A good account of Democratic economic policy is Barry Bluestone and Bennett Harrison, *The Great U-turn* (New York: Basic Books, 1985).

24. Nicole Mellow, "Voter Behavior: The 2004 Election and the Roots of Republican Success," in Michael Nelson, ed., *The Election of 2004* (Washington, D.C.: Congressional Quarterly Press, 2005), chap. 4; David Greene, "Architect of a Re-Election," *Newsday*, November 8, 2004; Todd Purdum and David Kirkpatrick, "Campaign Strategist Is in Position to Consolidate Republican Majority," *New York Times*, November 5, 2004.

25. This is best articulated in Sidney Blumenthal, *The Clinton Wars* (New York: Farrar, Straus, & Giroux, 2003); Kenneth Baer, *Reinventing Democrats* (Lawrence: University Press of Kansas, 2000); Morris Fiorina, *Culture War: Myth of a Polarized America* (New York: Longman, 2004).

26. Walter Dean Burnham, "Critical Realignment, Dead or Alive?" in Byron Shafer, ed., *The End of Realignment* (Madison: University of Wisconsin Press, 1991). See also Benjamin Ginsberg and Martin Shefter, *Politics by Other Means*, 3rd ed. (New York: W. W. Norton, 2002); John Aldrich, *Why Parties? The Origin and Transformation of Political Parties in America* (Chicago: University of Chicago Press, 1995).

27. Christopher Lasch, *The True and Only Heaven* (New York: W. W. Norton, 1991), p. 515; Thomas Frank, *What's the Matter with Kansas?* (New York: Metropolitan Books, 2004), pp. 6–7, 245. For more on dealignment characteristics, see also Shafer, *The End of Realignment*; and Martin Wattenberg, *The Decline of American Political Parties* (Chicago: University of Chicago Press, 1990).

28. Phillip Klinkner, "Red and Blue Scare," *The Forum*, 2:1 (2004); Pomper, "The Presidential Election," and Mellow, "Voting Behavior," in Nelson, ed., *The Election*, chap. 3.

29. See Pomper, "The Presidential Election," in Nelson, ed., *The Election*, chap. 3. Edison Mitosky Exit Polls, "The 2004 Election Exit Poll" (www.cnn.com), 2004; Pew Research Center, "Public Opinion Little Changed by Presidential Election," December 20, 2004 (www.people-press.org).

30. Ruy Teixeira and John Judis, *The Emerging Democratic Majority* (New York: Scribner, 2002). These points are discussed at length in Rick Perlstein et al., "Symposium on the Democrats," *Boston Review*, June 2004.

31. Pew Research Center, "Trends 2005" (www.people-press .org); Mellow, "Voting Behavior," in Nelson, ed., *The Election*, chap. 4; Gerald Pomper, "The Presidential Election," in Nelson, ed., *The Election*, chap. 3; and Morris Fiorina, *Culture War: Myth of a Polarized Electorate* (New York: Longman, 2004).

32. William Mayer, "The Presidential Nominations," in Gerald Pomper, ed., *The Election of 2000* (Chatham, N.J.: Chatham House, 2001), pp. 12–45. For 2004, see Barry Burden, "The Nominations," in Nelson, ed., *The Election*, chap. 8; and Ron Nessen, "Frontloading: The Wrong Approach to Presidential Politics," a forum at The Brookings Institution, January 14, 2004, Ron Nessen, moderator (www.brookings .edu/).

33. Ben White, "Wall Street Bankers, Reelection Backers," *Washington Post*, January 22, 2004, p. E1; Glen Justice, "Young Bush Fundraisers Are Courted by the GOP," *New York Times*, January 22, 2005, p. A11.

34. David Brock, *Republican Noise Machine* (New York: Crown Publishers, 2004), chap. 2; Trudy Lieberman, *Slanting* *the Story: The Forces That Shape the News* (New York: New Press, 2000); and "Buying a Movement: Right Wing Foundations," People for the American Way (www.pfaw.org).

35. Brock, *Republican Noise Machine*, chap. 2.

36. Matt Bai, "The Multilevel Marketing of the President," *New York Times Magazine*, April 25, 2004, p. 43. See also James Rainey and Sam Howe Verhovek, "Thousands Are Deployed," *Los Angeles Times*, October 31, 2004, p. A27.

37. Matt Kerbel, "Media in the 2004 Election," in Nelson, *The Election*; and Harold Meyerson, "Whither the Ward Heelers," *The American Prospect*, January 2005.

38. Charles Cook Political Report, "Off to the Races," March 29, 2005; and Robert Reich, "Movement Politics," *Boston Review*, Summer 2004.

CHAPTER 8

1. "The Great Ad Wars," *New York Times*, November 1, 2004, p. A19; Thomas Edsall and James Grimaldi, "On November 2, GOP Got More Bang for Its Billion," *Washington Post*, December 30, 2004.

2. John Tierney, "Know Where He Stands?" *New York Times*, October 26, 2004.

3. See Martin Wattenberg, *The Rise of Candidate-Centered Politics* (Cambridge: Harvard University Press, 1991); David Meneffee-Libey, *The Triumph of Campaign Centered Politics* (Chatham, N.J.: Chatham House, 2000).

4. Sidney Blumenthal, *The Permanent Campaign* (New York: Harper & Row, 1981). See also David Mayhew, *Congress: The Electoral Connection* (New Haven, Conn.: Yale University Press, 1974).

5. William Mayer, ed., *In Pursuit of the White House* (Chatham, N.J.: Chatham House, 2000). See also Michael Nelson, ed., *The Elections of 2004* (Washington, D.C.: Congressional Quarterly Press, 2005).

6. William Mayer, "The Presidential Nominations," in Gerald Pomper, ed., *The Election of 1996* (Chatham, N.J.: Chatham House, 1997).

7. Evan Thomas and the staff of *Newsweek*, *Election 2004* (New York: Public Affairs, 2005); Howard Dean with Judith Warner, *You Have the Power: How to Bring Back Our Country* (New York: Simon & Schuster, 2004); Matthew Kerbel, "Media in the Presidential Election," in Nelson, ed., *The Elections of 2004*.

8. Norman Solomon, "Dean and the Corporate Media Machine," *Common Dreams*, FAIR, December 5, 2003; Simon Hooper, "Media Screws a Social Democrat," *The New Statesman*, February 2, 2004. See also Matt Taibbi, *Spanking the Donkey: Dispatches from the Dumb Season* (New York: The New Press, 2005).

9. Anthony Corrado, "Financing the 2000 Election," in Gerald Pomper, ed., *The Election of 2000* (Chatham, N.J.: Chatham House, 2001).

10. "Political Money Line Guide to Presidential Races," Political Money Line, 2005; "2004 Elections," Center for Responsive Politics, "Open Secrets," October 2004 (www.open secrets.org).

11. Campaign Finance Institute, "House Winners," Press release, November 5, 2004. Other data compiled from Center for Responsive Politics, "527 Committee Activity" (www.open secrets.org), July 2005.

12. Alan Neustadl, Dan Clawson, and Mark Weller, *Dollars and Votes* (Philadelphia: Temple University Press, 1998); Darrell West, *Checkbook Democracy* (Boston: Northeastern University Press, 2000).

13. Herbert Alexander and Anthony Corrado, *Financing the 1992 Election* (Armonk, N.Y.: M. E. Sharpe, 1995); Clyde Wilcox, *The Revolution of 1994* (New York: St. Martin's Press, 1995).

14. Calculated from Federal Elections Commission data, press release, November 4, 1994.

15. Campaign Finance Institute, press release, November 4, 2005 (www.cfi.org).

16. Peter Kostmayer, "The Price of Politics," *The Korea Herald*, May 31, 1993.

17. For an exhaustive review of the early period of the FECA, see Anthony Corrado, Thomas Mann, and Frank Sorauf, eds., *Campaign Finance Reform: A Sourcebook* (Washington, D.C.: The Brookings Institution, 1997).

18. Jennifer Keen and John Daly, *Beyond the Limits: Soft Money in the 1996 Elections* (Washington, D.C.: Center for Responsive Politics, 1997); see also Anthony Corrado, "Financing," in Pomper, ed., *Election of 2000*, pp. 152–57. For general accounts, see Elizabeth Drew, *The Corruption of American Politics* (Secaucus, N.J.: Carol Publishing, 1999); and Michael Malbin and Thomas Gais, *The Day After Reform* (Albany, N.Y.: Rockefeller Institute Press, 1998).

19. David Broder, "A Win for Campaign Reform," *Washington Post*, February 3, 2005.

20. Center for Responsive Politics, "Election 2004 Overview" (www.opensecrets.org/527s); Thomas Edsall, "After Late Start, Republican Groups Jump into the Lead," *Washington Post*, October 17, 2004.

21. Edsall, "After Late Start"; Edsall and Grimaldi, "On November 2," p. A1.

22. Thomas Edsall, "New Routes for Money to Sway Voters," *Washington Post*, September 27, 2004.

23. Center for Responsive Politics, "2004 Election Overview, Donor Demographics"; and CRP, "Election 2002 Overview," both at www.opensecrets.org. See also, for a more comprehensive study of this subject, Sidney Verba, Kay Schlozman, and Henry Brady, *Voice and Equality: Civic Voluntarism in American Politics* (Cambridge, Mass.: Harvard University Press, 1995), pp. 49–87. For survey data on contributors, see "Banners for a Survey of 200 Political Contributors," Lake Research Paper, July 1997; Robert Borosage and Ruy Teixeira, "The Politics of Money," *The Nation*, October 21, 1996.

24. Center for Responsive Politics, "2004 Election Overview: Business-Labor-Ideology Split" (www.opensecrets.org).

25. Thomas Edsall, "Study: Corporate PACs Favor GOP," *Washington Post*, November 25, 2004; Politicalmoney line.org, November 2004.

26. Public Campaign, "Who Gets What," March 2005 (www.publiccampaign.org).

27. Neustadl et al., *Dollars and Votes*, final chapter; Jeffrey Birnbaum and Thomas Edsall, "Wall Street Plays Party Host," *Washington Post*, August 30, 2004; David Cay Johnston, *Perfectly Legal* (New York: Portfolio Penguin, 2003).

28. Adam Nagourney, "Bush Campaign Manager Views the Electoral Divide," *New York Times*, November 19, 2004; Katherine Seelye, "How to Sell a Candidate to a Porsche-Driving Leno-Loving Nascar Fan," *New York Times*, December 6, 2004.

29. Edsall and Grimaldi, "On November 2"; Edsall, "After Late Start," p. A15.

30. Edsall and Grimaldi, "On November 2"; Matt Bai, "The Multi-Level Marketing of the President," *New York Times Magazine*, April 25, 2004; Matt Bai, "Who Lost Ohio," *New York Times Magazine*, November 21, 2004; Nicole Mellow, "Republicans," in Nelson, ed., *The Elections of 2004*; Ronald Brownstein and Richard Rainey, "GOP Plants Flag on New Voting Frontier," *Los Angeles Times*, November 22, 2004, p. A1.

31. See James Moore and Wayne Slater, *Bush's Brain* (New York: Wiley, 2003); Dennis Johnson, *No Place for Amateurs* (New York: Routledge, 2001); Dick Morris, *Behind the Oval Office* (New York: Random House, 1997).

32. Larry Sabato, *The Rise of Political Consultants* (New York: Basic Books, 1981); Lou DuBose, *Boy Genius* (New York: Public Affairs, 2003).

33. "What Kind of Party for the Democrats," Editorial, *New York Times*, February 25, 2001; Johnson, *No Place*, p. 107; Christopher Hitchens, "Voting in the Passive Voice," *Harper's*, April 1992; Edsall and Grimaldi, "GOP and More Bang."

34. "Cable and Talk Radio Boost Public Awareness," National Annenberg Election Survey, August 20, 2004 (www.naes.org); Fair Media Advisory, "Swift Boat Smears," August 30, 2004 (www.fair.org); Sidney Blumenthal, *Pledging Allegiance: The Last Campaign of the Cold War* (New York: HarperCollins, 1990).

35. "The Great Ad Wars," *New York Times*, November 1, 2004; Thomas Edsall and Derek Willis, "Fundraising Records Broken," *Washington Post*, December 3, 2004.

36. Recorded in Sabato, *The Rise of Political Consultants*, p. 149. For 2004, see Edsall and Grimaldi, "On November 2"; National Annenberg Election Survey Studies (www.naes04.org) for surveys of voter response to ads; Glen Justice, "Frantic Presidential Campaign," *New York Times*, November 1, 2004. See also Stephen Ansolabehere and Shanto Iyengar, *Going Negative* (New York: The Free Press, 1995); Darrell West, *Air Wars: Television Advertisements in Election Campaigns* (Washington, D.C.: Congressional Quarterly Press, 1997). For Bush media buys, see Marjorie Randon Hershey, "The Campaign and the Media," in Michael Nelson, ed., *The Election of 2004* (Washington, D.C.: Congressional Quarterly Press, 2005).

37. Richard Viguerie, *America's Right Turn: How Conservatives Used New and Alternative Media* (Santa Monica, Calif.: Bonus Books, 2004).

38. Glen Justice, "Kerry Kept Money Coming with Internet," *New York Times*, November 6, 2004. See Joe Trippi, *The Revolution Will Not Be Televised* (New York: Regan Books, 2004); Michael Cornfield, *Politics Moves Online* (New York: Century Foundation, 2004).

39. For an early defense of these practices, see James Carville and Mary Matalin, *All's Fair* (New York: Random House, 1994). For the Bush campaign and administration's rapport with the press, see the "Campaign Watch" website of the *Columbia Journalism Review* (www.cjr.org). Timothy Cook, Marion Just, and Ann Crigler, *Crosstalk: Campaigns, Candidates, Citizens, and the Press* (Chicago: University of Chicago Press, 1996).

40. Dennis J. McGrath and Dane Smith, *Professor Wellstone Goes to Washington: The Inside Story of a Grassroots U.S. Senate Campaign* (Minneapolis: University of Minnesota Press, 1995); Richard Berke, "Several Won Big by Spending Less," *New York Times*, November 2, 1990.

41. James Rainey and Sam Howe Verhovek, "Thousands Are Deployed," *Los Angeles Times*, October 31, 2004; Dan Balz and Thomas Edsall, "Unprecedented Efforts to Mobilize Voters Begins," *Washington Post*, November 1, 2004; Harold Meyerson, "The Tsunami," *LA Weekly*, October 29–November 4, 2004.

42. John Nichols, "Deciding What's Next," *The Nation*, December 6, 2004; Katherine Seelye, "Money Rich Advocacy Groups Look Far Beyond Election Day," *New York Times*, October 17, 2004; Abby Goodnough and Don Van Natta, "Bush Secured Victory in Florida by Veering from Beaten Path," *New York Times*, November 7, 2004; Michael Moss and Ford Fessenden, "Interest Groups Mounting Costly Effort," *New York Times*, October 20, 2004.

43. Eskew quote from "60 Seconds to Victory," *Harper's*, July 1992, pp. 36–38. Greider cite from William Greider, *Who Will Tell the People?* (New York: Simon & Schuster, 1991). See also American Political Science Association Standing Committee on Civic Education and Engagement, "Democracy at Risk," Electoral Processes chapter, 2005 (www.apsa.org).

CHAPTER 9

1. Joel Brinkley, "Out of Spotlight, Bush Overhauls U.S. Regulations," *New York Times*, August 4, 2004.

2. Mark A. Peterson, "Bush and Interest Groups: A Government of Chums," in Colin Campbell and Bert A. Rockman, eds., *The George W. Bush Presidency: Appraisal and Prospects* (Washington, D.C.: Congressional Quarterly Press, 2004).

3. As reported in Peterson, "Bush and Interest Groups," p. 235. See also "Political Campaigns—Who Gives? 2000 election cycle, www.opensecrets.org; as reported in Nomi Prins, *Other People's Money: The Corporate Mugging of America* (New York: The New Press, 2004), p. 150.

4. The SEC investigated the transaction for possible insider trading violations, but the case was closed by Richard Breedan, head of the SEC appointed by President Bush's father.

5. "Influence, Inc.: Lobbyists Spending in Washington" (2000 edition), available at www.opensecrets.org.

6. Kevin Phillips, *Arrogant Capital: Washington, Wall Street, and the Frustration of American Politics* (Boston: Little, Brown, 1994), p. 43.

7. "Influence, Inc.: Lobbyists Spending in Washington" (2000 edition), available at www.opensecrets.org.

8. Laura Langbein, "Money and Access: Some Empirical Evidence," *Journal of Politics* 48 (1986): 1052–62.

9. The distinction between insider and outsider lobbying strategies is discussed in Jack L. Walker, *Mobilizing Interest Groups in America: Patrons, Professions and Social Movements* (Ann Arbor: University of Michigan Press, 1991).

10. Quoted in Jeffrey H. Birnbaum and Alan S. Murray, *Showdown at Gucci Gulch: Lawmakers, Lobbyists, and the Unlikely Triumph of Tax Reform* (New York: Random House, 1987), pp. 178–79.

11. Kay Lehman Schlozman and John T. Tierney, "More of the Same: Washington Pressure Group Activity in a Decade of Change," *Journal of Politics* 45 (1988): 351–75.

12. Quoted in Kay Lehman Schlozman and John T. Tierney, *Organized Interests and American Society* (New York: Harper & Row, 1986), p. 85.

13. Schlozman and Tierney, *Organized Interests*, p. 75.

14. Allen J. Cigler and Burdett A. Loomis, "The Changing Nature of Interest Group Politics," in William Lasser, ed., *Perspectives on American Government: A Comprehensive Reader* (Lexington, Mass.: D. C. Heath, 1992), pp. 305–06; Ronald G. Shaiko, "Lobbying in Washington: A Contemporary Perspective," in Paul S. Hernnson and Ronald G. Shaiko, eds., *The Interest Group Connection: Electioneering, Lobbying, and Policymaking in Washington* (Chatham, N.J.: Chatham House, 1998), p. 6.

15. See David Truman, *The Governmental Process* (New York: Alfred A. Knopf, 1951); Robert Dahl, *A Preface to Democratic Theory* (Chicago: University of Chicago Press, 1956); and Dahl, *Who Governs? Democracy and Power in an American City* (New Haven, Conn.: Yale University Press, 1961). Since *Who Governs?* Dahl has shifted from an elite democratic to a more popular democratic analysis of American politics. See his *A Preface to Economic Democracy* (Berkeley: University of California Press, 1985).

16. Jeffrey Berry, *The Interest Group Society*, 2nd ed. (Glenview, Ill.: Scott, Foresman, 1989), p. 16.

17. Theda Skocpol, *Diminished Democracy: From Membership to Management in American Life* (Norman: University of Oklahoma Press, 2003), p. 153.

18. Ibid., pp. 162–63.

19. Robert Putnam, *Bowling Alone: The Collapse and Revival of American Community* (New York: Simon & Schuster, 2000), p. 49.

20. Theda Skocpol, "Advocates Without Members: The Recent Transformation of American Civic Life," in Theda Skocpol and Morris P. Fiorina, eds., *Civic Engagement in American Democracy* (Washington, D.C.: Brookings Institution Press, 1999), pp. 461–509.

21. Darrell M. West and Burdett A. Loomis, *The Sound of Money: How Political Interests Get What They Want* (New York: W. W. Norton, 1998).

22. Sidney Verba, Kay Lehman Schlozman, and Henry E. Brady, *Voice and Equality: Civic Voluntarism in American Life* (Cambridge, Mass.: Harvard University Press, 1995), p. 190.

23. E. E. Schattschneider, *The Semi-Sovereign People: A Realist's View of Democracy in America* (New York: Holt, Rinehart and Winston, 1960), p. 35. For critiques of pluralist theory as a form of democratic elitism, see Jack Walker, "A Critique of the Elitist Theory of Democracy," *American Political Science Review* 60 (1966): 285–95; and Peter Bachrach, *The Theory of Democratic Elitism: A Critique* (Boston: Little, Brown, 1967).

24. Steven E. Schier, *By Invitation Only: The Rise of Exclusive Politics in the United States* (Pittsburgh, Pa.: University of Pittsburgh Press, 2000).

25. For a provocative account of how cultural issues have displaced basic economic issues in one state, see Thomas Frank, *What's the Matter with Kansas?: How Conservatives Won the Heart of America* (New York: Henry Holt and Company, 2004).

26. Kay Lehman Schlozman, Sidney Verba, and Henry E. Brady, "Civic Participation and the Equality Problem," in Skocpol and Fiorina, eds., *Civic Engagement in American Democracy*, p. 440.

27. See Mancur Olson Jr., *The Logic of Collective Action: Public Goods and the Theory of Groups* (New York: Schocken Books, 1968).

28. The following account of Nader's life and accomplishments relies on Robert F. Buckhorn, *Nader: The People's Lawyer* (Englewood Cliffs, N.J.: Prentice-Hall, 1972); Jay Acton and Alan LeMond, *Ralph Nader: A Man and a Movement* (New York: Warner Books, 1972); and Charles McCarry, *Citizen Nader* (New York: Saturday Review Press, 1972).

29. Buckhorn, *Nader*, p. 36.

30. Ralph Nader, *Unsafe at Any Speed: The Designed-in Dangers of the American Automobile* (New York: Grossman, 1966).

31. From court documents filed when Nader sued GM. Quoted in Nader, *Unsafe*, p. 14.

32. Our discussion of the Powell memo is based on Jerry M. Landay, "The Powell Manifesto: How a Prominent Lawyer's Attack Memo Changed America," August 20, 2002; available at www.mediatransparency.org/storeis/powell.htm.

33. William Greider, *Who Will Tell the People: The Betrayal of American Democracy* (New York: Simon & Schuster, 1992), p. 48.

34. Schlozman and Tierney, *Organized Interests*, pp. 77–78.

35. Greider, *Who Will Tell*, p. 50.

36. Samuel Huntington called this the "democratic distemper." See his article "The United States" in Michel J. Crozier, Samuel Huntington, and Joji Watanuki, eds., *The Crisis of Democracy: Report on the Governability of Democracies to the Trilateral Commission* (New York: New York University Press, 1975), pp. 59–118.

37. Charles Murray, *Losing Ground: American Social Policy, 1950–1980* (New York: Basic Books, 1984), p. 227.

38. For a critique of Murray's analysis, see William Julius Wilson, *The Truly Disadvantaged: The Inner City, the Underclass, and Public Policy* (Chicago: University of Chicago Press, 1987), chap. 4.

39. Andrew Rich and R. Kent Weaver, "Advocates and Analysts: Think Tanks and the Politicization of Expertise," in Allan J. Cigler and Burdett A. Loomis, eds., *Interest Group Politics* (Washington, D.C.: Congressional Quarterly Press, 1998), p. 244. See also James A. Smith, *The Idea Brokers: Think Tanks and the Rise of the New Policy Elite* (New York: Free Press, 1991), and Andrew Rich, *Think Tanks, Public Policy, and the Politics of Expertise* (New York: Cambridge University Press, 2004).

40. Michael Dolny, "Special Report: Think Tank Coverage: More Attention but Not More Balance," Fairness & Accuracy in Reporting (FAIR); available at www.fair.org.

41. Thomas Byrne Edsall, *The New Politics of Inequality* (New York: W. W. Norton, 1984), p. 117.

42. Jean Stefancic and Richard Delgado, *No Mercy: How Conservative Think Tanks and Foundations Changed America's Social Agenda* (Philadelphia: Temple University Press, 1996), p. 53.

43. Quoted in Smith, *Idea Brokers*, p. 195.

44. Schlozman and Tierney, *Organized Interests*, pp. 94–95.

45. Cited in ibid., p. 22.

46. Hugh Heclo, "Issue Networks and the Executive Establishment," in Anthony King, ed., *The New American Political System* (Washington, D.C.: American Enterprise Institute, 1978), pp. 87–124.

47. John C. Stauber and Sheldon Rampton, *Toxic Sludge Is Good for You: Lies, Damn Lies, and the Public Relations Industry* (Monroe, Maine: Common Courage Press, 1995), p. 79.

48. As reported in Ken Silverstein, "Hello. I'm Calling this Evening to Mislead You," *Mother Jones* (November/December 1997).

49. Quoted in Greider, *Who Will Tell*, p. 38.

50. See West and Loomis, *The Sound of Money*.

51. Jeffrey H. Birnbaum, "Washington's Power 25," *Fortune*, December 8, 1997.

52. Schlozman and Tierney, *Organized Interests*, p. 115.

53. Quoted in an interview with Deborah Solomon in *New York Times Magazine*, March 13, 2005, p. 23.

54. Robin Toner, "On Bush Plan, It's 'Private' vs. 'Personal,'" *New York Times*, March 22, 2005.

55. Damien Cave, "How to Get Young People to Care About Old Age," *New York Times*, March 20, 2005.

56. West and Loomis, *The Sound of Money*, p. 240.

57. Bruce Ackerman and James Fishkin, *Deliberation Day* (New Haven, Conn.: Yale University Press, 2004). For a discussion of deliberative polling, see Bruce Ackerman, *We the People*, Vol. 2 (Cambridge, Mass.: Beklnap Press, 1998).

CHAPTER 10

1. Jennifer Lee, "How Protestors Mobilized So Many and So Nimbly," *New York Times*, February 23, 2003.

2. Quoted in Richard W. Stevenson, "Threats and Responses; The White House; Antiwar Protests Fail to Sway Bush on Plans for Iraq," *New York Times*, February 19, 2005.

3. Michael Lipsky, *Protest in City Politics: Rent Strikes, Housing and the Power of the Poor* (Chicago: Rand McNally, 1970), p. 2. We draw freely in this chapter on Lipsky's analysis of protest as a political resource.

4. Charles C. Euchner, *Extraordinary Politics: How Protest and Dissent Are Changing American Democracy* (Boulder, Colo.: Westview Press, 1996).

5. The following account of the Montgomery bus boycott is based on Taylor Branch, *Parting the Waters: America in the King Years 1954–63* (New York: Simon & Schuster, 1988); and Juan Williams, *Eyes on the Prize: America's Civil Rights Years 1954–1965* (New York: Penguin, 1987).

6. Quoted in Williams, *Eyes on the Prize*, p. 78.

7. Euchner, *Extraordinary Politics*; Craig A. Rimmerman, *The New Citizenship: Unconventional Politics, Activism, and Service* (Boulder, Colo.: Westview Press, 1997).

8. Paul Kleppner, *Who Voted? The Dynamics of Electoral Turnout* (New York: Praeger, 1982), p. 116, as cited in Frances Fox Piven and Richard A. Cloward, *Why Americans Don't Vote* (New York: Pantheon, 1989), p. 144.

9. T. R. Gurr, *Why Men Rebel* (Princeton, N.J.: Princeton University Press, 1970).

10. John D. McCarthy and Mayer N. Zald, "Resource Mobilization and Social Movements: A Partial Theory," *American Journal of Sociology* 82, no. 6 (1977): 1212–41.

11. Sara M. Evans and Harry C. Boyte, *Free Spaces: The Sources of Democratic Change in America* (Chicago: University of Chicago Press, 1992).

12. For an insightful account of the Populist movement that stresses the formation of a movement culture, see Lawrence Goodwyn, *The Populist Moment* (New York: Oxford University Press, 1978).

13. Quoted in Sara Evans, *Personal Politics: The Roots of Women's Liberation in the Civil Rights Movement and the New Left* (New York: Vintage, 1980), p. 87.

14. Quoted in Williams, *Eyes on the Prize*, p. 76.

15. The concepts of transactional and transformational leaders are developed in James MacGregor Burns, *Leadership* (New York: Harper & Row, 1978).

16. For an analysis of Stanton as a dissenting movement leader, see Bruce Miroff, *Icons of Democracy: American Leaders as*

Heroes, Aristocrats, Dissenters, & Democrats (New York: Basic Books, 1993), chap. 4.

17. Saul D. Alinsky, *Reveille for Radicals* (New York: Random House, 1969), p. 132.

18. Henry David Thoreau, "Civil Disobedience," in Milton Meltzer, ed., *Thoreau: People, Principles, and Politics* (New York: Hill and Wang, 1963), p. 38.

19. Frances Fox Piven and Richard A. Cloward, *Poor People's Movements: Why They Succeed, How They Fail* (New York: Pantheon, 1977).

20. *Report of the National Advisory Commission on Civil Disorders* (New York: Bantam Books, 1968).

21. Murray Edelman, *The Symbolic Uses of Politics* (Urbana: University of Illinois Press, 1967); see also Edelman's *Constructing the Political Spectacle* (Chicago: University of Chicago Press, 1988).

22. See Alan Wolfe, *The Seamy Side of Democracy* (New York: David McKay, 1978); David Caute, *The Great Fear* (New York: Simon & Schuster, 1978); and Robert Justin Goldstein, *Political Repression in Modern America* (Cambridge, Mass.: Schenkman, 1978).

23. Quoted in William Greider, *Who Will Tell the People? The Betrayal of American Democracy* (New York: Simon & Schuster, 1992), p. 17.

24. For an elite democratic critique of mass politics, see Samuel P. Huntington, *American Politics: The Promise of Disharmony* (Cambridge, Mass.: Harvard University Press, 1981).

25. For a critique of the Populist/Progressive movements along these lines, see Richard Hofstadter, *The Age of Reform: From Bryan to F.D.R.* (New York: Vintage, 1955).

26. Michael Paul Rogin, *The Intellectuals and McCarthy: The Radical Specter* (Cambridge, Mass.: M.I.T. Press, 1967).

27. Merrill D. Peterson, ed., *The Portable Thomas Jefferson* (New York: Penguin, 1975), p. 417.

28. Tom Wolfe, *Radical Chic and Mau-Mauing the Flak Catchers* (New York: Bantam, 1971), pp. 117–18.

29. "No Guardrails," editorial, *Wall Street Journal*, March 18, 1993.

30. Samuel P. Huntington, "The United States," in Michael J. Crozier, Samuel P. Huntington, and Joji Watanuki, eds., *The Crisis of Democracy: Report on the Governability of Democracies to the Trilateral Commission* (New York: New York University Press, 1975), pp. 59–118.

31. See Richard Rose, ed., *Challenge to Governance: Studies in Overloaded Politics* (Beverly Hills, Calif.: Sage, 1980).

32. Samuel P. Huntington, *American Politics: The Promise of Disharmony* (Cambridge, Mass.: Harvard University Press, 1981), p. 219.

33. Thomas R. Dye and Harmon Ziegler, *The Irony of Democracy: An Uncommon Introduction to American Politics*, 9th ed. (Belmont, Calif.: Wadsworth, 1993), p. 17.

34. In 1977 a federal district court ordered all tapes, transcripts, and other FBI information on King's private life to be impounded for fifty years under the seal of secrecy. Branch, *Parting the Waters*, p. 872.

35. Euchner, *Extraordinary Politics*, p. 221.

36. For a gripping account of the events in Chicago, see James Miller, *"Democracy Is in the Streets": From Port Huron to the Siege of Chicago* (New York: Simon & Schuster, 1987), chap. 12.

37. *Rights in Conflict: The Violent Confrontation of Demonstrators and Police in the Parks and Streets of Chicago During the Week of the Democratic National Convention of 1968*, report submitted by Daniel Walker, director of the Chicago Study Team, to the National Commission on the Causes and Prevention of Violence, 1968.

38. Most Americans—57 percent, according to one poll—felt that the police had used the right amount of force or too little. John P. Robinson, "Public Reaction to Political Protest: Chicago 1968," *Public Opinion Quarterly* 34 (Spring 1970): 1–9.

39. Jeffrey M. Berry, Kent E. Portney, and Ken Thomson, *The Rebirth of Urban Democracy* (Washington, D.C.: The Brookings Institution, 1993).

40. Jeff Sharlet, "Soldiers of Christ," *Harper's*, May 2005, p. 48.

41. See Kevin Mattson, "Goodbye to All That," *The American Prospect*, April 5, 2005, pp. 32–37; and Christina Larson, "Postmodern Protests," *Washington Monthly*, March 2005, pp. 12–14.

42. For evidence on the personal effects of participation in protests, see Euchner, *Extraordinary Politics*, pp. 232–33.

43. Rufus P. Browning, Dale Rogers Marshall, and David H. Tabb, *Protest Is Not Enough: The Struggle of Blacks and Hispanics for Equality in Urban Politics* (Berkeley: University of California Press, 1984).

CHAPTER 11

1. Ronald M. Peters Jr., "The Republican Speakership," paper delivered at the Annual Meeting of the American Political Science Association, San Francisco, August–September 1996, p. 20.

2. Gary C. Jacobson, *The Politics of Congressional Elections*, 4th ed. (New York: Longman, 1997), p. 69.

3. Ibid., pp. 19–28.

4. David R. Mayhew, *Congress: The Electoral Connection* (New Haven, Conn.: Yale University Press, 1974); Morris P. Fiorina, *Congress: Keystone of the Washington Establishment*, 2nd ed. (New Haven, Conn.: Yale University Press, 1989); Richard E. Fenno Jr., *Home Style: House Members in Their Districts* (Boston: Little, Brown, 1978).

5. John W. Kingdon, *Congressmen's Voting Decisions*, 3rd ed. (Ann Arbor: University of Michigan Press, 1989).

6. See Burdett Loomis, *The New American Politician: Ambition, Entrepreneurship, and the Changing Face of Political Life* (New York: Basic Books, 1988).

7. For a rational-choice explanation of this problem, see Kenneth R. Mayer and David T. Canon, *The Dysfunctional Congress? The Individual Roots of an Institutional Dilemma* (Boulder, Colo.: Westview, 1999).

8. Michael J. Malbin, *Unelected Representatives: Congressional Staff and the Future of Representative Government* (New York: Basic Books, 1980).

9. Richard L. Hall, *Participation in Congress* (New Haven, Conn.: Yale University Press, 1996), pp. 37–48.

10. Steven S. Smith and Christopher J. Deering, *Committees in Congress*, 2nd ed. (Washington, D.C.: Congressional Quarterly Press, 1990), p. 216.

11. Norman J. Ornstein, Thomas E. Mann, and Michael J. Malbin, *Vital Statistics on Congress, 1993–1994* (Washington, D.C.: Congressional Quarterly Press, 1994), pp. 201–2.

12. John R. Hibbing and Elizabeth Theiss-Morse, *Congress as Public Enemy: Public Attitudes Toward American Political Institutions* (New York: Cambridge University Press, 1995), p. 49.

13. John C. Berg, *Unequal Struggle: Class, Gender, Race, and Power in the U.S. Congress* (Boulder, Colo.: Westview, 1994), pp. 37–47.

14. See Barbara Sinclair, "The Emergence of Strong Leadership in the 1980s House of Representatives," *Journal of Politics* 54 (August 1992): 657–84.

15. C. Lawrence Evans and Walter J. Oleszek, *Congress Under Fire: Reform Politics and the Republican Majority* (Boston: Houghton Mifflin, 1997), pp. 2–3.

16. Peters, "The Republican Speakership."

17. David S. Cloud, "Speaker Wants His Platform to Rival the Presidency," *Congressional Quarterly* (February 4, 1995): 331–35.

18. Katharine Q. Seelye, "He's Top Man in the House, But Not in the Nation," *New York Times*, March 19, 1995.

19. For the party unity scores, see *CQ Weekly*, January 3, 2004.

20. Quoted in Evans and Oleszek, *Congress Under Fire*, p. 134.

21. Steven S. Smith and Eric D. Lawrence, "Party Control of Committees in the Republican Congress," in Lawrence C. Dodd and Bruce I. Oppenheimer, eds., *Congress Reconsidered*, 6th ed. (Washington, D.C.: Congressional Quarterly Press, 1997), p. 163.

22. Janet Hook, "Conservative Freshman Class Eager to Seize the Moment," *Congressional Quarterly* (January 7, 1995): 47–49.

23. Chester B. Rogers, "The Decline of the Entrepreneurial Culture in Congress," paper delivered at the Annual Meeting of the American Political Science Association, San Francisco, August–September 1996.

24. Ronald M. Peters Jr., "Institutional Context and Leadership Style: The Case of Newt Gingrich," in Nicol C. Rae and Colton C. Campbell, eds., *New Majority or Old Minority? The Impact of Republicans on Congress* (Lanham, Md.: Rowman & Littlefield, 1999), pp. 43–65.

25. Quoted in Sheryl Gay Stolberg, "Quietly but Firmly, Hastert Asserts His Power," *New York Times*, January 3, 2005.

26. Lou Dubose and Jan Reid, *The Hammer: Tom DeLay, God, Money, and the Rise of the Republican Congress* (New York: Public Affairs, 2004).

27. Jonathan Allen, "Effective House Leadership Makes the Most of Majority," *CQ Weekly*, March 29, 2003.

28. John Cochran, "Disorder in the House—And No End in Sight," *CQ Weekly*, April 3, 2004.

29. Mary Curtius, "2 in GOP Take Aim at DeLay," *Los Angeles Times*, April 11, 2005.

30. David Firestone, "Frist Forsakes Deal-Making to Focus on Party Principles," *New York Times*, March 13, 2003.

31. See *CQ Weekly*, January 3, 2004.

32. Gary C. Jacobson, "Partisan Polarization in Presidential Support: The Electoral Connection," *Congress & the Presidency* 30 (Spring 2003): 1–36; Dan Balz, "Partisan Polarization Intensified in 2004 Election," *Washington Post*, March 29, 2005.

33. Cochran, "Disorder in the House."

34. Gary C. Jacobson, "Party Polarization in National Politics: The Electoral Connection," in Jon R. Bond and Richard Fleisher, eds., *Polarized Politics: Congress and the President in a Partisan Era* (Washington, D.C: Congressional Quarterly Press, 2000), p. 10.

35. Derek Willis, "Republicans Mix It Up When Assigning House Chairmen for the 108th," *CQ Weekly*, January 11, 2003; Allen, "Effective House Leadership."

36. Willis, "Republicans Mix It Up."

37. Mike Allen, "GOP Leaders Tighten Their Grip on House," *Washington Post*, January 9, 2005.

38. Allen, "Effective House Leadership."

39. John Cochran, "Two Years In, Frist Struggles to Tame an Unruly Senate," *CQ Weekly*, October 16, 2004.

40. William F. Connolly Jr. and John J. Pitney Jr., "The House Republicans: Lessons for Political Science," in Bruce Miroff, Raymond Seidelman, and Todd Swanstrom, eds., *Debating Democracy: A Reader in American Politics*, 5th ed. (Boston: Houghton Mifflin, 2005), pp. 284–86.

41. On heightened warfare between the branches under Reagan, Bush, and Clinton, see Benjamin Ginsberg and Martin Shefter, *Politics by Other Means: Politicians, Prosecutors, and the Press from Watergate to Whitewater* (New York: W. W. Norton, 1999). For a contrary view, see David Mayhew, *Divided We Govern: Party Control, Lawmaking, and Investigations, 1946–2002*, 2nd ed. (New Haven, Conn.: Yale University Press, 2005).

42. James A. Thurber, "The Impact of Budget Reform on Presidential and Congressional Governance," in James A. Thurber, ed., *Divided Democracy: Cooperation and Conflict Between the President and Congress* (Washington, D.C.: Congressional Quarterly Press, 1991).

43. Eileen Burgin, "Assessing Congress's Role in the Making of Foreign Policy," in Dodd and Oppenheimer, eds., *Congress Reconsidered*, pp. 293–324. Also see James M. Lindsay,

Congress and the Politics of U.S. Foreign Policy (Baltimore: Johns Hopkins University Press, 1994).

44. See Stephen R. Weissman, *A Culture of Deference: Congress's Failure of Leadership in Foreign Policy* (New York: Basic Books, 1995).

45. See Ginsberg and Shefter, *Politics by Other Means*, pp. 39–46.

46. Dana Milbank, "Frustrated Democrats Find a Voice," *Washington Post*, February 15, 2005.

47. Evans and Oleszek, *Congress Under Fire*, pp. 176–79.

CHAPTER 12

1. Alexander Hamilton et al., *The Federalist Papers* (New York: New American Library, 1961), p. 423.

2. Ibid., p. 424.

3. Ralph Ketcham, ed., *The Anti-Federalist Papers* (New York: New American Library, 1986), p. 211. Support for Henry's suspicions can be found in William E. Scheuerman, "American Kingship? Monarchical Origins of Modern Presidentialism," *Polity* 37 (January 2005): 24–53.

4. Max Farrand, ed., *The Records of the Federal Convention of 1787*, vol. 1 (New Haven, Conn.: Yale University Press, 1937), p. 112.

5. James David Barber, *The Presidential Character: Predicting Performance in the White House*, 4th ed. (Englewood Cliffs, N.J.: Prentice Hall, 1992).

6. Fred I. Greenstein, *The Presidential Difference: Leadership Style from FDR to Clinton* (New York: Free Press, 2000), p. 200.

7. Precise numbers for the White House staff are difficult to determine. See John Hart, *The Presidential Branch: From Washington to Clinton* (Chatham, N.J.: Chatham House, 1995), pp. 112–25.

8. Richard L. Berke, "Bush Is Providing Corporate Model for White House," *New York Times*, March 11, 2001.

9. Ibid.

10. See Thomas E. Cronin, *The State of the Presidency*, 2nd ed. (Boston: Little, Brown, 1980), pp. 223–51.

11. David Gergen, *Eyewitness to Power: The Essence of Leadership* (New York: Simon & Schuster, 2000), p. 85.

12. See George E. Reedy, *The Twilight of the Presidency* (New York: New American Library, 1971).

13. See Hugh Heclo, "OMB and the Presidency: The Problem of 'Neutral Competence,'" *The Public Interest* 11 (1975): 80–98.

14. Quoted in George C. Edwards III and Stephen J. Wayne, *Presidential Leadership: Politics and Policy Making*, 5th ed. (New York: St. Martin's Press, 1999), p. 208.

15. Liz Harper, "Dick Cheney," www.pbs.org/newshour/vote2004/candidates.

16. Cronin, *State of the Presidency*, pp. 276–78.

17. For a hilarious and insightful view of life in President Clinton's outer cabinet, see Robert B. Reich, *Locked in the Cabinet* (New York: Alfred A. Knopf, 1997).

18. Michael A. Fletcher, "Bush Is Keeping Cabinet Secretaries Close to Home," *Washington Post*, March 31, 2005.

19. See MaryAnne Borrelli, *The President's Cabinet: Gender, Power, and Representation* (Boulder, Colo.: Lynne Rienner Publishers, 2002) and Janet M. Martin, *The Presidency and Women: Promise, Performance, and Illusion* (College Station: Texas A&M University Press, 2003).

20. Quoted in Richard E. Neustadt, *Presidential Power and the Modern Presidents* (New York: Free Press, 1990), p. 10.

21. See Kenneth Mayer, *With the Stroke of a Pen: Executive Orders and Presidential Power* (Princeton, N.J.: Princeton University Press, 2001) and William G. Howell, *Power Without Persuasion: The Politics of Direct Presidential Action* (Princeton, N.J.: Princeton University Press, 2003).

22. Richard P. Nathan, *The Administrative Presidency* (New York: Wiley, 1983). Also see Terry M. Moe, "The Politicized Presidency," in James P. Pfiffner, ed., *The Managerial Presidency*, 2nd ed. (College Station: Texas A&M University Press, 1999), pp. 144–61.

23. Anne Farris, Richard P. Nathan, and David J. Wright, *The Expanding Administrative Presidency: George W. Bush and the Faith-Based Initiative* (Albany, N.Y.: Rockefeller Institute of Government, 2004).

24. Hamilton et al., *Federalist Papers*, p. 322. For a view of legislative–executive relations that stresses cooperation as well as conflict, see Mark A. Peterson, *Legislating Together: The White House and Capitol Hill from Eisenhower to Reagan* (Cambridge, Mass.: Harvard University Press, 1990).

25. See William W. Lammers and Michael A. Genovese, *The Presidency and Domestic Policy: Comparing Leadership Styles from FDR to Clinton* (Washington, D.C.: Congressional Quarterly Press, 2000).

26. Paul C. Light, "Domestic Policy Making," *Presidential Studies Quarterly* 30 (March 2000): 109–32.

27. Edwards and Wayne, *Presidential Leadership*, pp. 330–31.

28. *Washington Post*, November 18, 1993.

29. On presidential resources and constraints in economic policy making, see M. Stephen Weatherford and Lorraine M. McDonnell, "Clinton and the Economy: The Paradox of Policy Success and Political Mishap," *Political Science Quarterly* 111 (Fall 1996): 403–36.

30. See Bruce Miroff, *Icons of Democracy: American Leaders as Heroes, Aristocrats, Dissenters, and Democrats* (Lawrence: University Press of Kansas, 2000), pp. 294–300.

31. Robert Reich, "Why Business Should Love Gore," *The American Prospect* (July 31, 2000): 56.

32. Arthur Schlesinger Jr., *The Imperial Presidency* (Boston: Houghton Mifflin, 1973).

33. *United States v. Curtiss-Wright Corp.*, 299 U.S. 304 (1936).

34. For an example, see Theodore Lowi, *The End of Liberalism*, 2nd ed. (New York: W. W. Norton, 1979), pp. 127–63.

35. See Victoria Farrar-Myers, "Transference of Authority: The Institutional Struggle Over the Control of the War Power," *Congress & the Presidency* 25 (Autumn 1998): 183–97.

36. David Gray Adler, "The Clinton Theory of the War Power," *Presidential Studies Quarterly* 30 (March 2000): 163.

37. See Christopher Andrew, *For the President's Eyes Only: Secret Intelligence and the American Presidency from Washington to Bush* (New York: HarperCollins, 1996).

38. For a vivid account of repression in the Nixon administration, see Jonathan Schell, *The Time of Illusion* (New York: Vintage, 1976).

39. For a good analysis of the framers' view of the president, see Jeffrey K. Tulis, *The Rhetorical Presidency* (Princeton, N.J.: Princeton University Press, 1987), pp. 25–45.

40. Samuel Kernell, *Going Public: New Strategies of Presidential Leadership*, 2nd ed. (Washington, D.C.: Congressional Quarterly Press, 1993), pp. 90–91.

41. See George C. Edwards III, *On Deaf Ears: The Limits of the Bully Pulpit* (New Haven, Conn.: Yale University Press, 2003).

42. See Stephen J. Wayne, "Great Expectations: What People Want from Presidents," in Thomas E. Cronin, ed., *Rethinking the Presidency* (Boston: Little, Brown, 1982), pp. 185–99.

43. See John Anthony Maltese, *Spin Control: The White House Office of Communications and the Management of Presidential News*, 2nd ed. (Chapel Hill: University of North Carolina Press, 1994).

44. Howard Kurtz, *Spin Cycle: Inside the Clinton Propaganda Machine* (New York: Free Press, 1998).

45. Matthew A. Baum and Samuel Kernell, "Has Cable Ended the Golden Age of Presidential Television?" *American Political Science Review* 93 (March 1999): 110.

46. David Barstow and Robin Stein, "News or Public Relations? For Bush It's a Blur," *New York Times*, March 13, 2005.

47. Bruce Miroff, "Monopolizing the Public Space: The President as a Problem for Democratic Politics," in Cronin, ed., *Rethinking the Presidency*, pp. 218–32.

48. Material in the following paragraphs is adapted from Miroff, *Icons*, pp. 300–305.

49. Quoted in ibid., p. 304.

CHAPTER 13

1. *The Congressional Record—House*, March 1, 1995, pp. H2402, H2407.

2. Clinton Rossiter, ed., *The Federalist Papers* (New York: New American Library, 1961), p. 174.

3. On the administrative apparatus under Washington and Hamilton, see Leonard D. White, *The Federalists: A Study in Administrative History, 1789–1801* (New York: Free Press, 1948).

4. Quoted in James A. Morone, *The Democratic Wish: Popular Participation and the Limits of American Government* (New York: Basic Books, 1990), p. 87.

5. Matthew A. Crenson, *The Federal Machine: Beginnings of Bureaucracy in Jacksonian America* (Baltimore: Johns Hopkins University Press, 1975), p. 4.

6. On late nineteenth-century state builders, see Stephen Skowronek, *Building a New American State: The Expansion of National Administrative Capacities, 1877–1920* (New York: Cambridge University Press, 1982), esp. pp. 42–45.

7. Morone, *Democratic Wish*, p. 98.

8. George McJimsey, *Harry Hopkins* (Cambridge, Mass.: Harvard University Press, 1987), p. 114.

9. Quoted in ibid., p. 63.

10. Quoted in ibid., p. 97.

11. Quoted in ibid., p. 66.

12. Quoted in Charles T. Goodsell, *The Case for Bureaucracy*, 2nd ed. (Chatham, N.J.: Chatham House, 1985), p. 166.

13. Ibid., p. 166.

14. Quoted in Paul Singer, "By the Horns," *National Journal*, March 26, 2005, p. 899.

15. Data on government employment are taken from *Statistical Abstract of the United States 2004–2005* (Washington, D.C.: U.S. Government Printing Office, 2004).

16. In 2002, there were roughly 21 million government employees (federal, state, and local) in a civilian workforce of 145 million.

17. Joel D. Aberbach and Bert Rockman, *In the Web of Politics: Three Decades of the U.S. Federal Executive* (Washington, D.C.: Brookings Institution Press, 2000), pp. 101–7.

18. Charles T. Goodsell, *The Case for Bureaucracy: A Public Administration Polemic*, 4th ed. (Washington, D.C.: Congressional Quarterly Press, 2004), p. 101.

19. Ibid., pp. 24–41.

20. See James Q. Wilson, *Bureaucracy: What Government Agencies Do and Why They Do It* (New York: Basic Books, 1989), pp. 179–95.

21. Ibid., pp. 113–36.

22. See John A. Rohr, *To Run a Constitution: The Legitimacy of the Administrative State* (Lawrence: University Press of Kansas, 1986), pp. 59–89.

23. Francis E. Rourke, *Bureaucracy, Politics, and Public Policy*, 2nd ed. (Boston: Little, Brown, 1976), p. 16.

24. Kenneth J. Meier, *Politics and the Bureaucracy: Policymaking in the Fourth Branch of Government*, 3rd ed. (Pacific Grove, Calif.: Brooks/Cole, 1993), pp. 68–72.

25. Barry Bozeman, *Bureaucracy and Red Tape* (Upper Saddle River, N.J.: Prentice Hall, 2000).

26. Quoted in William T. Gormley Jr. and Steven J. Balla, *Bureaucracy and Democracy: Accountability and Performance* (Washington, D.C.: Congressional Quarterly Press, 2004), p. 164.

27. Rourke, *Bureaucracy, Politics, and Public Policy*, p. 46.

28. Wilson, *Bureaucracy*, p. 251.

29. David J. Garrow, *The FBI and Martin Luther King, Jr.* (New York: Penguin, 1983), pp. 125–34.

30. Charles H. Levine, B. Guy Peters, and Frank J. Thompson, *Public Administration* (Glenview, Ill.: Scott, Foresman, 1990), pp. 52–53.

31. Morton H. Halperin, *Bureaucratic Politics and Foreign Policy* (Washington, D.C.: The Brookings Institution, 1974), p. 43.

32. Wilson, *Bureaucracy*, p. 257. For a historical account of this rivalry, see Skowronek, *Building a New American State*, pp. 165–292.

33. Michael D. Reagan, *Regulation: The Politics of Policy* (Boston: Little, Brown, 1987), p. 15.

34. See Gabriel Kolko, *The Triumph of Conservatism* (Chicago: Quadrangle Books, 1967).

35. For a critique of the capture thesis, see Wilson, *Bureaucracy*, pp. 83–88.

36. Adam Bryant, "On a Wing and a Fare," *New York Times*, November 5, 1995.

37. Joel Brinkley, "Out of Spotlight, Bush Overhauls U.S. Regulations," *New York Times*, August 14, 2004.

38. Amy Goldstein and Sarah Cohen, "Bush Forces a Shift in Regulatory Thrust," *Washington Post*, August 15, 2004.

39. Brinkley, "Out of Spotlight," and Goldstein and Cohen, "Bush Forces a Shift."

40. John B. Judis, "It's the EPA and OSHA, Stupid!" *The American Prospect* (September 25, 2000): 12.

41. Bozeman, *Bureaucracy and Red Tape*, p. 98.

42. Al Gore, *Report of the National Performance Review* (New York: Times Books, 1994), p. 43.

43. Ibid., p. 71.

44. See Peri E. Arnold, "The Managerial Presidency's Changing Focus, Theodore Roosevelt to Bill Clinton," and Steven Kelman, "White-House Initiated Management Change: Implementing Federal Procurement Reform," in James P. Pfiffner, ed., *The Managerial Presidency*, 2nd ed. (College Station: Texas A & M University Press, 1999), pp. 217–64.

45. David Lowery, "The Presidency, the Bureaucracy, and Reinvention: A Gentle Plea for Chaos," *Presidential Studies Quarterly* 30 (March 2000): 79–108.

46. See E. S. Savas, *Privatizing the Public Sector: How to Shrink Government* (Chatham, N.J.: Chatham House, 1982).

47. See Elliott D. Sclar, *You Don't Always Get What You Pay For: The Economics of Privatization* (Ithaca, N.Y.: Cornell University Press, 2000).

48. Matthew A. Crenson and Benjamin Ginsberg, *Downsizing Democracy: How America Sidelined Its Citizens and Privatized Its Public* (Baltimore: The Johns Hopkins University Press, 2004), pp. 210–11.

49. Donald F. Kettl, *System Under Stress: Homeland Security and American Politics* (Washington, D.C.: Congressional Quarterly Press, 2004), pp. 45–47.

50. William T. Gormley Jr., *Taming the Bureaucracy: Muscles, Prayers, and Other Strategies* (Princeton, N.J.: Princeton University Press, 1989), p. 71.

51. Ibid., p. 89.

52. Charles Noble, *Liberalism at Work: The Rise and Fall of OSHA* (Philadelphia: Temple University Press, 1986), p. 34.

53. Ibid., p. 201.

CHAPTER 14

1. David M. O'Brien, *Storm Center: The Supreme Court in American Politics*, 3rd ed. (New York: W. W. Norton, 1993), p. 14.

2. The Constitution, ostensibly an expression of the will of the people, has become a lawyers' document. See John Brigham, *The Cult of the Court* (Philadelphia: Temple University Press, 1987).

3. For an illuminating treatment of the conflicting theories of democracy that have been used by different justices on the modern Supreme Court, see Martin Edelman, *Democratic Theories and the Constitution* (Albany: State University of New York Press, 1984).

4. Edwin Meese, address to the D.C. Chapter of the Federalist Society Lawyers Division, November 15, 1985, in Paul G. Cassell, ed., *The Great Debate: Interpreting Our Written Constitution* (Washington, D.C.: Federalist Society, 1986), p. 37.

5. Edwin Meese, address to the American Bar Association, July 9, 1985, in Cassell, ed., *Great Debate*, p. 9.

6. Ibid.

7. Ibid., p. 1.

8. Ibid., p. 10.

9. Robert H. Bork, *The Tempting of America: The Political Seduction of the Law* (New York: Free Press, 1990), p. 130.

10. Justice William Brennan Jr., address to the Text and Teaching Symposium, Georgetown University, October 12, 1985, in Cassell, ed., *Great Debate*, p. 14.

11. Ibid., p. 15.

12. Ibid., p. 17.

13. Ibid., p. 11.

14. Mark Tushnet, "The Politics of Constitutional Law," in David Kairys, ed., *The Politics of Law: A Progressive Critique* (New York: Pantheon, 1990), p. 230.

15. Duncan Kennedy, "Legal Education as Training for Hierarchy," in David Kairys, ed., *The Politics of Law: A Progressive Critique*, 3rd ed. (New York: Basic Books, 1998), p. 54.

16. Gerald N. Rosenberg, *The Hollow Hope: Can Courts Bring About Social Change?* (Chicago: University of Chicago Press, 1991).

17. Ibid., p. 12.

18. Kermit L. Hall, *The Magic Mirror: Law in American History* (New York: Oxford University Press, 1989), pp. 78–79.

19. *Marbury v. Madison*, 1 Cranch 137 (1803).

20. Robert G. McCloskey, *The American Supreme Court* (Chicago: University of Chicago Press, 1960), p. 57.

21. *Dred Scott v. Sandford*, 19 How. (60 U.S.) 393 (1857).

22. Michael Les Benedict, "History of the Court: Reconstruction, Federalism, and Economic Rights," in Kermit L. Hall et al., eds., *The Oxford Companion to the Supreme Court of the United States* (New York: Oxford University Press, 1992), p. 388.

23. Linda Greenhouse, "The Court Rules, America Changes," *New York Times*, July 2, 2000.

24. *Bush v. Gore*, 531 U.S. 98 (2000).

25. O'Brien, *Storm Center*, p. 107.

26. Ronald Stidham, Robert A. Carp, and Donald R. Songer, "The Voting Behavior of President Clinton's Judicial Nominees," *Judicature* 80, no. 1 (July–August 1996): 16–20.

27. David M. O'Brien, "Judicial Legacies: The Clinton Presidency and the Courts," in Colin Campbell and Bert A. Rockman, eds., *The Clinton Legacy* (New York: Chatham House, 2000), pp. 96–117.

28. Joan Biskupic, "Making a Mark on the Bench," *Washington Post National Weekly Edition*, December 2–8, 1996, p. 31.

29. O'Brien, "Judicial Legacies," p. 113.

30. David M. O'Brien, "Ironies and Disappointments: Bush and Federal Judgeships," in Colin Campbell and Bert A. Rockman, eds., *The George W. Bush Presidency: Appraisals and Prospects* (Washington, D.C.: Congressional Quarterly Press, 2004), pp. 146–47.

31. Ibid., p. 154.

32. See Laurence H. Tribe, *God Save This Honorable Court: How the Choice of Supreme Court Justices Shapes Our History* (New York: New American Library, 1986), pp. 36–48.

33. David M. O'Brien, *Storm Center: The Supreme Court in American Politics*, 5th ed. (New York: W. W. Norton, 2000), p. 55.

34. See Tribe, *God Save This Honorable Court*, pp. 60–92.

35. See John Massaro, *Supremely Political: The Role of Ideology and Presidential Management in Unsuccessful Supreme Court Nominations* (Albany: State University of New York Press, 1990).

36. *Brown v. Allen*, 344 U.S. 443 (1953).

37. Bernard Schwartz, *Super Chief: Earl Warren and His Supreme Court* (New York: New York University Press, 1983).

38. For a scathing portrayal of Chief Justice Burger, see Bob Woodward and Scott Armstrong, *The Brethren: Inside the Supreme Court* (New York: Avon, 1981), esp. pp. 27–29, 179–81, 199–201, 220–23, 303–4, 372–73.

39. Bernard Schwartz, *A History of the Supreme Court* (New York: Oxford University Press, 1993), pp. 364–76.

40. Linda Greenhouse, "Same Justices, New Court," *New York Times*, July 3, 2004.

41. See Walter Murphy, *Elements of Judicial Strategy* (Chicago: University of Chicago Press, 1964).

42. See Phillip J. Cooper, *Battles on the Bench: Conflict Inside the Supreme Court* (Lawrence: University Press of Kansas, 1995).

43. Lawrence Baum, "Membership Change and Collective Voting Change in the United States Supreme Court," *Journal of Politics* 54, no. 1 (February 1992): 3–24.

44. Lawrence Baum, *The Supreme Court*, 4th ed. (Washington, D.C.: Congressional Quarterly Press, 1992), pp. 144–56.

45. Stephen L. Wasby, *The Supreme Court in the Federal Judicial System*, 4th ed. (Chicago: Nelson-Hall, 1993), p. 349.

46. See Gregory A. Caldeira, "Neither the Purse Nor the Sword: Dynamics of Public Confidence in the Supreme Court," *American Political Science Review* 80, no. 4 (December 1986): 1209–26.

CHAPTER 15

1. Joel Blau, *The Visible Poor: Homelessness in the United States* (New York: Oxford University Press, 1992), pp. 129–31; Peter Dreier and W. Dennis Keating, "The Limits of Localism: Progressive Housing Policies in Boston, 1984–1989," in Roger W. Caves, ed., *Exploring Urban America: An Introductory Reader* (Thousand Oaks, Calif.: Sage, 1995), pp. 360–81.

2. Blau, *Visible Poor*, pp. 117–18.

3. Mike Davis, *City of Quartz: Excavating the Future of Los Angeles* (New York: Verso, 1990), p. 233.

4. Edward S. Corwin, "The Passing of Dual Federalism," *Virginia Law Review* 36, no. 1 (1950): 4.

5. Justice William J. Brennan Jr., "Reading the Constitution as Twentieth Century Americans," in Bruce Miroff, Raymond Seidelman, and Todd Swanstrom, eds., *Debating Democracy* (Boston: Houghton Mifflin, 2001), p. 335.

6. Clinton Rossiter, ed., *The Federalist Papers* (New York: New American Library, 1961), no. 33.

7. *Dred Scott v. Sandford*, 19 How. 393 (1857).

8. *Munn v. Illinois*, 94 U.S. 113 (1877).

9. *Wabash, St. Louis and Pac. Ry. v. Illinois*, 118 U.S. 557 (1886).

10. Gabriel Kolko, *Railroads and Regulation: 1877–1916* (Princeton, N.J.: Princeton University Press, 1965), p. 232.

11. *Pollock v. Farmers' Loan and Trust Co.*, 157 U.S. 429 (1895).

12. *Cincinnati N.O. & T.P. Railway Co. v. Interstate Commerce Commission*, 162 U.S. 184 (1896).

13. *Hammer v. Dagenhart*, 247 U.S. 251 (1918).

14. James A. Maxwell, *The Fiscal Impact of Federalism in the United States* (Cambridge, Mass.: Harvard University Press, 1946), p. 135.

15. Josephine Chapin Brown, *Public Relief 1929–1939* (New York: Henry Holt, 1940), pp. 14–15, as cited in Frances Fox Piven and Richard A. Cloward, *Regulating the Poor: The Functions of Public Welfare* (New York: Random House, 1971), p. 47.

16. In fact, in 1929 ten states authorized no outdoor relief at all. (Outdoor relief allows people to stay in their homes while they receive aid, like the present welfare system.) Advisory

Commission on Intergovernmental Relations (ACIR), *The Federal Role in the Federal System: The Dynamics of Growth, Public Assistance: The Growth of a Federal Function* (Washington, D.C.: ACIR, 1980), p. 7.

17. Piven and Cloward, *Regulating the Poor*, p. 60.

18. Mark I. Gelfand, *A Nation of Cities: The Federal Government and Urban America 1933–1965* (New York: Oxford University Press, 1975), pp. 32–33.

19. *Congressional Record*, vol. 75, p. 11597, as quoted in Maxwell, *Fiscal Impact*, p. 138.

20. *Schechter Poultry Corp. v. United States*, 295 U.S. 495 (1935).

21. David B. Robertson and Dennis R. Judd, *The Development of American Public Policy: The Structure of Policy Restraint* (Glenview, Ill.: Scott, Foresman, 1989), p. 105.

22. *The United States v. Butler et al.*, 297 U.S. 1 (1936).

23. *New State Ice Company v. Liebmann*, 285 U.S. 262 (1932).

24. *Massachusetts v. Mellon* (1923), as quoted in Robertson and Judd, *American Public Policy*, p. 138.

25. Maxwell, *Fiscal Impact*, p. 26.

26. The classic statement of American federalism as regulated by political processes is Herbert Wechsler, "The Political Safeguards of Federalism: The Role of the States in the Selection of the National Government," *Columbia Law Review* 54 (1954): 543–60.

27. Piven and Cloward, *Regulating the Poor*, p. 295.

28. David B. Walker, *Toward a Functioning Federalism* (Cambridge, Mass.: Winthrop, 1981), p. 193.

29. Jeffrey L. Pressman and Aaron Wildavsky, *Implementation*, 3rd ed. (Berkeley: University of California Press, 1984).

30. Not all federal grant programs targeted the poor. Many large federal grants, such as those for interstate highways and the construction of sewer and water systems, primarily benefited the suburban middle class.

31. Thomas Byrne Edsall and Mary D. Edsall, *Chain Reaction: The Impact of Race, Rights, and Taxes on American Politics* (New York: W. W. Norton, 1991), p. 106.

32. Ibid., pp. 75–76.

33. Quoted in Timothy Conlan, *New Federalism: Intergovernmental Reform from Nixon to Reagan* (Washington, D.C.: The Brookings Institution, 1988), p. 31.

34. U.S. Advisory Commission on Intergovernmental Relations (ACIR), *ACIR News: Negative Opinions of Federal Government Increase in 1992 ACIR Poll* (Washington, D.C.: ACIR, 1992), as reported in Frank J. Thompson, ed., *Revitalizing State and Local Public Service: Strengthening Performance, Accountability, and Citizen Confidence* (San Francisco: Jossey-Bass, 1993), p. 11.

35. "Opinion Outlook," *National Journal* (March 4, 1995); as reported in Ann O'M. Bowman, "American Federalism on the Horizon," *Publius: The Journal of Federalism* 32, no. 2 (Spring 2002): 10–11.

36. Conlan, *New Federalism*, p. 154.

37. John Kincaid, "The Devolution Tortoise and the Centralization Hare," *New England Economic Review* (May–June 1998): 34.

38. Joseph F. Zimmerman, *Contemporary American Federalism: The Growth of National Power* (New York: Praeger, 1992), p. 67.

39. For a critical analysis of *Bush v. Gore*, see Alan M. Dershowitz, *Supreme Injustice: How the High Court Hijacked Election 2000* (New York: Oxford University Press, 2001).

40. *United States v. Lopez*, 115 S. Ct. 1624 (1995).

41. *U.S. Term Limits v. Thornton* (1995) and *Seminole Tribe v. Florida* (1996), U.S. Lexis 2165.

42. Charles Fried, "Federalism as a Right to Life, Too," *New York Times*, March 24, 2005.

43. Christopher W. Hoene and Michael A. Pagano, "Fend-for-Yourself Federalism: The Impact of Federal and State Deficits on America's Cities," *Government Finance Review* (October 2003): 36–42.

44. Dale Krane, "The State of American Federalism, 2003–2004: The States," paper prepared for delivery at the American Political Science Association Meeting in Chicago, Illinois, September 2–5, 2004.

45. Krane, "The State of American Federalism, 2003–2004," p. 24.

46. Kevin B. Smith, Alan Greenblatt, and John Buntin, *Governing States and Localities* (Washington, D.C.: Congressional Quarterly Press, 2005), p. 476.

47. David J. Barron, "A Localist Critique of the New Federalism," *Duke Law Journal* 51 (2001): 377–433.

48. This section draws heavily from Stephen Macedo et al., *Democracy at Risk: How Political Choices Undermine Citizen Participation, and What We Can Do About It* (Washington, D.C.: Brookings Institution Press, 2005), chap. 3.

49. Judge John F. Dillon was chief justice of the Iowa Supreme Court and wrote the influential *Treatise on the Law of Municipal Corporations*, stressing that cities derived all their powers from states.

50. Alexis de Tocqueville, *Democracy in America*, edited by J. P. Mayer (New York: Anchor Books, 1969), p. 63.

51. Census Bureau, *2002 Census of Governments*, vol. 1, no. 1: *Government Organization* (Washington, D.C.: U.S. Government Printing Office, 2002).

52. Robert L. Lineberry, *Equality and Urban Policy: The Distribution of Municipal Public Services* (Beverly Hills, Calif.: Sage, 1977), p. 10.

53. U.S. Bureau of the Census, *Statistical Abstract of the United States: 2004–2005* (Washington, D.C.: U.S. Government Printing Office, 2004), p. 255.

54. Neil Kraus and Todd Swanstrom, "The Continuing Significance of Race: African American and Hispanic Mayors, 1968–2003," *National Political Science Review* 10 (2005): 54.

55. Eric Oliver, *Democracy in Suburbia* (Princeton, N.J.: Princeton University Press, 2001); and Frank Bryan, *Real De-*

mocracy: The New England Town Meeting and How It Works (Chicago: University of Chicago Press, 2004).

56. *Buchanan v. Warley*, 245 U.S. 60 (1917).

57. *Village of Euclid v. Ambler Realty Co.*, 272 U.S. 365 (1926).

58. Middle-class suburbs are defined as suburbs with per capita incomes between 75 and 125 percent of the regional per capita income. Todd Swanstrom, Colleen Casey, Robert Flack, and Peter Dreier, *Pulling Apart: Economic Segregation in the Top Fifty Metropolitan Areas, 1980–2000* (Brookings Center on Urban and Metropolitan Policy, October 2004).

59. Edward L. Glaeser and Jacob L. Vigdor, "Racial Segregation: Promising News," in Bruce Katz and Robert E. Lang, eds., *Redefining Urban and Suburban America: Evidence for Census 2000* (Washington, D.C.: Brookings Institution Press, 2003), pp. 211–34.

60. Hoene and Pagano, "Fend-for-Yourself Federalism."

61. *Serrano v. Priest*, 5 Cal.3d 584 (1971).

62. Kenneth B. Wong, *Funding Public Schools: Politics and Policies* (Lawrence: University Press of Kansas, 1992), p. 12.

63. Robert B. Reich, *The Work of Nations* (New York: Random House, 1992).

64. Eric Oliver, *Democracy in Suburbia* (Princeton, N.J.: Princeton University Press, 2001).

65. V. O. Key Jr., *Southern Politics in State and Nation* (New York: Alfred A. Knopf, 1949), chap. 14.

66. Robert Dahl, *Who Governs? Democracy and Power in an American City* (New Haven, Conn.: Yale University Press, 1961).

67. G. William Domhoff, *Who Really Rules: New Haven and Community Power Reexamined* (Santa Monica, Calif.: Goodyear Publishing Company, 1978).

68. Norman I. Fainstein and Susan S. Fainstein, "New Haven: The Limits of the Local State," in Susan S. Fainstein et al., eds., *Restructuring the City*, rev. ed. (New York: Longman, 1986), pp. 47–49.

69. Robert Dahl and Charles E. Lindblom, *Politics and Economics: Planning and the Politico–Economic Systems Resolved into Basic Social Processes* (Chicago: University of Chicago Press, 1976), preface, xxxvii.

70. Stephen Elkin, *City and Regime in the American Republic* (Chicago: University of Chicago Press, 1987), p. 100.

71. The term was coined in Harvey Molotch, "The City as a Growth Machine," *American Journal of Sociology* (September 1976): 309–32. See also John R. Logan and Harvey Molotch, *Urban Fortunes: The Political Economy of Place* (Berkeley: University of California Press, 1987).

72. Richard Child Hill, "Crisis in the Motor City: The Politics of Economic Development in Detroit," in Fainstein et al., eds., *Restructuring the City*, p. 105.

73. Quoted in Tony Hiss, "Annals of Place: Reinventing Baltimore," *New Yorker* (April 29, 1991), p. 62. The following account of Baltimore is based on Dennis Judd and Todd Swan-

strom, *City Politics: The Political Economy of Urban America* (New York: Longman, 2006), pp. 365–68.

74. Paul A. Jargowsky, *Poverty and Place: Ghettos, Barrios, and the American City* (New York: Russell Sage Foundation, 1997), p. 227.

75. Quoted in Hiss, "Annals of Place," p. 41.

76. For Hamilton's arguments for a strong executive with expert administration, see James Madison, Alexander Hamilton, and John Jay, *The Federalist Papers*, ed. Isaac Kramnick (New York: Penguin, 1987), Nos. 67–77.

77. Figures on the extent of structural reforms are taken from Terry Christenson, *Local Politics: Governing at the Grassroots* (Belmont, Calif.: Wadsworth, 1994), chap. 6.

78. Carl Abbott, *The New Urban America: Growth and Politics in Sunbelt Cities* (Chapel Hill: University of North Carolina Press, 1987).

79. Dennis R. Judd and Todd Swanstrom, *City Politics: Private Power and Public Policy*, 4th ed. (New York: Longman, 2004), chap. 4.

80. See Robert R. Alford and Eugene C. Lee, "Voter Turnout in American Cities," *American Political Science Review* 62 (September 1968): 796–813; and Albert R. Karnig and B. Oliver Walter, "Decline in Municipal Voter Turnout: A Function of Changing Structure," *American Politics Quarterly* 11, no. 4 (October 1983): 491–505.

81. Judd and Swanstrom, *City Politics*, pp. 97–98.

82. Ann O'M. Bowman and Richard C. Kearney, *State and Local Government*, 2nd ed. (Boston: Houghton Mifflin, 1993), pp. 12–13.

83. Center for Policy Alternatives, *Progress in the States: A Report on Proactive, Progressive Victories in 2004* (Washington, D.C.: author, July 2004), p. 2, as cited in Krane, "The State of American Federalism, 2003–2004," p. 3.

84. Robert S. Erickson, Gerald C. Wright, and John P. McIver, *Statehouse Democracy Public Opinion and Policy in the American States* (New York: Cambridge University Press, 1993).

85. V. O. Key Jr., *Southern Politics in State and Nation*, new ed. (Knoxville: University of Tennessee Press, 1984).

86. Mishel, Bernstein, and Allegretto, *The State of Working America 2004–2005*, p. 378.

87. Smith, Greenblatt, and Buntin, *Governing States & Localities*, pp. 482–83.

88. John E. Schwarz, *America's Hidden Success: A Reassessment of Public Policy from Kennedy to Reagan*, rev. ed. (New York: W. W. Norton, 1988).

89. This point is made in Jeffrey M. Berry, Kent E. Portney, and Ken Thomson, *The Rebirth of Urban Democracy* (Washington, D.C.: The Brookings Institution, 1993), chap. 2.

90. For an early account of this movement, see Harry C. Boyte, *The Backyard Revolution: Understanding the New Citizen Movement* (Philadelphia: Temple University Press, 1980).

91. Carmine Scavo, "Use of Participative Mechanisms by Large U.S. Cities," *Journal of Urban Affairs* 15 (1993): 93–109.

92. Archon Fung, *Empowered Participation: Reinventing Urban Democracy* (Princeton, N.J.: Princeton University Press, 2004).

93. Berry, Portney, and Thomson, *Rebirth of Urban Democracy*.

94. Barbara Ferman, *Challenging the Growth Machine: Neighborhood Politics in Chicago and Pittsburgh* (Lawrence: University Press of Kansas, 1996), p. 151.

95. Paul Peterson, *The Price of Federalism* (Washington, D.C.: The Brookings Institution, 1995), p. 144.

96. David B. Robertson and Dennis R. Judd, *The Development of American Public Policy* (Glenview, Ill.: Scott, Foresman, 1989), p. 380.

97. Frug, "Beyond Regional Government," *Harvard Law Review* 115 (2002): 1763–836.

98. Michael C. Dorf and Charles F. Sabel, "A Constitution of Democratic Experimentalism," *Columbia Law Review* 98, no. 2 (March 1998): 267–473.

CHAPTER 16

1. *West Virginia State Board of Education v. Barnette*, 319 U.S. 624 (1943).

2. *Texas v. Johnson*, 491 U.S. 397 (1989).

3. See Samuel Walker, *In Defense of American Liberties: A History of the ACLU* (New York: Oxford University Press, 1990).

4. Actually, twelve amendments passed Congress. One was rejected by the states; the other, which required that congressional pay raises not take effect until after an election, was not ratified by enough states. Resurrected in the early 1980s, this amendment finally became the Twenty-seventh Amendment in 1992—over two hundred years after it was originally proposed!

5. *United States v. Carolene Products Co.*, 304 U.S. 144 (1938).

6. On the double standard, see Henry J. Abraham and Barbara A. Perry, *Freedom and the Court: Civil Rights and Liberties in the United States*, 6th ed. (New York: Oxford University Press, 1994), pp. 9–29.

7. *Palko v. Connecticut*, 302 U.S. 319 (1937).

8. See Alan Wolfe, *The Seamy Side of Democracy: Repression in America* (New York: David McKay, 1973).

9. *Schenck v. United States*, 249 U.S. 47 (1919).

10. *Brandenburg v. Ohio*, 395 U.S. 444 (1969).

11. *Tinker v. Des Moines Independent Community School District*, 393 U.S. 503 (1969).

12. Owen M. Fiss, *Liberalism Divided: Freedom of Speech and the Many Uses of State Power* (Boulder, Colo.: Westview, 1996), pp. 9–30, 49–66.

13. *United States v. Kokinda*, 497 U.S. 720 (1990).

14. Fiss, *Liberalism Divided*, p. 5.

15. *Roth v. United States*, 354 U.S. 476 (1957).

16. *Miller v. California*, 413 U.S. 15 (1973).

17. *F.C.C. v. Pacifica Foundation*, 438 U.S. 726 (1978).

18. Garry Wills, *Under God: Religion and American Politics* (New York: Simon & Schuster, 1990), p. 16.

19. See the classic account by Anthony Lewis, *Gideon's Trumpet* (New York: Vintage, 1964).

20. See Thomas Y. Davies, "Exclusionary Rule," in Kermit L. Hall et al., eds., *The Oxford Companion to the Supreme Court of the United States* (New York: Oxford University Press, 1992), pp. 264–66.

21. See Yale Kamisar, "*Miranda v. Arizona*," in Hall et al., *Oxford Companion to the Supreme Court*, pp. 552–55.

22. Davies, "Exclusionary Rule," p. 266.

23. *Jencks v. United States*, 353 U.S. 657 (1957).

24. *Olmstead v. United States*, 277 U.S. 438 (1928).

25. *Griswold v. Connecticut*, 381 U.S. 479 (1965).

26. See Barbara Hinkson Craig and David M. O'Brien, *Abortion and American Politics* (Chatham, N.J.: Chatham House, 1993), pp. 35–68.

27. *Plessy v. Ferguson*, 163 U.S. 537 (1896).

28. For the story of the NAACP campaign against school segregation, see Richard Kluger, *Simple Justice* (New York: Alfred A. Knopf, 1976).

29. *Brown v. Board of Education of Topeka*, 347 U.S. 483 (1954).

30. See Juan Williams, *Eyes on the Prize: America's Civil Rights Years, 1954–1965* (New York: Penguin, 1988).

31. Barbara Bergmann, *In Defense of Affirmative Action* (New York: Basic Books, 1996), p. 16.

32. Terry Eastland, *Ending Affirmative Action: The Case for Colorblind Justice* (New York: Basic Books, 1996), p. 8.

33. *Adarand Constructors v. Peña*, 515 U.S. 200 (1995).

34. *Bowers v. Hardwick*, 478 U.S. 186 (1986).

35. *Romer v. Evans*, 517 U.S. 620 (1996).

36. *Boy Scouts of America v. Dale*, 520 U.S. 640 (2000).

37. *Lawrence v. Texas*, 539 U.S. 558 (2003).

CHAPTER 17

1. Horatio Alger was a Unitarian minister who, by 1904, had published 107 books under his name about poor boys who rose from rags to riches.

2. Quoted in Peter G. Peterson, *Running on Empty: How the Democratic and Republican Parties Are Bankrupting Our Future and What American Can Do About It* (New York: Farrar, Straus and Giroux, 2004), p. 143.

3. The wholesale price index dropped an astonishing 65 percent between 1864 and 1890. Robert B. Reich, *The Work of Nations* (New York: Vintage, 1992), p. 27.

4. Quoted in David E. Rosenbaum, "Critics Want Fed's Power Under More Accountability," *New York Times*, November 14, 1991.

5. Lawrence Mishel, Jared Bernstein, and Sylvia Allegretto, *The State of Working America 2004/2005* (Ithaca, N.Y.: Cornell University Press, 2005), chap. 4.

6. Our account of Volcker's experiment with monetarism is based on William Greider, *Secrets of the Temple: How the Federal Reserve Runs the Country* (New York: Simon & Schuster, 1987).

7. Greider, *Secrets of the Temple*, p. 579.

8. Donald F. Kettl, *Leadership at the Fed* (New Haven, Conn.: Yale University Press, 1986).

9. Greider, *Secrets of the Temple*, p. 313.

10. Quoted in Alfred L. Malabre, *Lost Prophets: An Insider's History of the Modern Economists* (Boston: Harvard Business School Press, 1994), p. 183. See Jude Wanniski, *The Way the World Works* (New York: Basic Books, 1978).

11. See Barry Bosworth, *Tax Incentives and Economic Growth* (Washington, D.C.: The Brookings Institution, 1984); and Charles R. Hulten and Isabel V. Sawhill, eds., *The Legacy of Reaganomics: Prospects for Long-Term Growth* (Washington, D.C.: Urban Institute Press, 1984).

12. For a detailed discussion of the 1992 Clinton plan for public investments, see Bill Clinton and Al Gore, *Putting People First: How We Can All Change America* (New York: Random House, 1992).

13. See Bryan Snyder, "Pop Austerity: Clinton Talks Populism But His Program Thrills Wall Street," in Randy Albeda et al., eds., *Real World Macro*, 12th ed. (Somerville, Mass.: Dollars and Sense, 1995), pp. 63–65.

14. For a summary of the damage that large deficits could inflict on the economy, see Peterson, *Running on Empty*.

15. Citizens for Tax Justice, "Year-by-Year Analysis of the Bush Tax Cuts Shows Growing Tilt to the Very Rich," June 12, 2002.

16. Mishel, Bernstein, and Allegretto, *The State of Working America 2004/2005*, p. 85.

17. Mayling Birney and Ian Shapiro, "Death and Taxes: The Estate Tax Repeal and American Democracy," Department of Political Science, Yale University, October 5, 2003. Our account of estate tax repeal relies heavily on this article.

18. David Cay Johnson, "Focus on Farmers Masks Estate Tax Confusion," *New York Times*, April 8, 2001.

19. Reported in Paul Krugman, "The Tax-Cut Con," *New York Times Magazine*, September 14, 2003, p. 59.

20. See Jacob S. Hacker and Paul Pierson, "Abandoning the Middle: The Revealing Case of the Bush Tax Cuts." Prepared for delivery at the 2003 Annual Meeting of the American Political Science Association, August 28–31, 2003.

21. Peterson, *Running on Empty*, pp. 9–10.

22. Mishel, Bernstein, and Allegretto, *The State of Working America 2004/2005*, p. 338.

23. Arnold J. Heidenheimer, Hugh Heclo, and Carolyn Teich Adams, *Comparative Public Policy: The Politics of Social Choice in America, Europe, and Japan*, 3rd ed. (New York: St. Martin's, 1990), p. 249.

24. In 1973 the Supreme Court ruled that education is not a right guaranteed equal protection under the U.S. Constitu-tion. See *Rodriguez v. San Antonio Independent School District*, 411 U.S. 1 (1973).

25. Jonathan Kozol, *Savage Inequalities: Children in America's Schools* (New York: HarperCollins, 1991).

26. U.S. Bureau of the Census, *Statistical Abstract of the United States 2000* (Washington, D.C.: U.S. Government Printing Office, 2000), pp. 113, 382, 385.

27. See Frances Fox Piven and Richard A. Cloward, *Regulating the Poor: The Functions of Public Welfare* (New York: Random House, 1971).

28. Quoted in Jonathan Rieder, *Canarsie: The Jews and Italians of Brooklyn Against Liberalism* (Cambridge, Mass.: Harvard University Press, 1985), p. 102.

29. Quoted in Gwen Ifill, "Clinton Offers Plan for Overhaul of Welfare, with Stress on Work," *New York Times*, September 10, 1992.

30. *Time*/CNN poll of 600 adults conducted by Yankelovich Partners, Inc., with a sampling error of plus or minus 4 percent. Reported in Nancy Gibbs, "The Vicious Cycle," *Time*, June 20, 1994, p. 26.

31. Quoted in Jason DeParle, "Cutting Welfare Rolls But Raising Questions," *New York Times*, May 7, 1997.

32. Sharon Hays, *Flat Broke with Children: Women in the Age of Welfare Reform* (New York: Oxford University Press, 2003), p. 8.

33. Andrew C. Revkin, "Welfare Policies Alter the Face of Food Lines," *New York Times*, February 26, 1999; Jason De Parle, "As Welfare Rolls Shrink, Load on Relatives Grows," *New York Times*, February 21, 1999.

34. Jason DeParle, *American Dream: Three Women, Ten Kids, and a Nation's Drive to End Welfare* (New York: Viking, 2004), p. 216.

35. Paul E. Peterson and Mark C. Rom, *Welfare Magnets: A New Case for a National Standard* (Washington, D.C.: The Brookings Institution, 1990); Sanford F. Schram and Samuel H. Beer, eds., *Welfare Reform: A Race to the Bottom?* (Washington, D.C.: Woodrow Wilson Center Press, 1999).

36. The most influential statement that welfare is a cause of poverty is Charles Murray's *Losing Ground: American Social Policy, 1950–1980* (New York: Basic Books, 1984). For an effective critique of Murray, see William Julius Wilson, *The Truly Disadvantaged: The Inner City, the Underclass, and Public Policy* (Chicago: University of Chicago Press, 1987).

37. DeParle, *American Dream*, p. 131.

38. Quoted in Roberto Suro, "Duke Campaigns on Distorted Facts Despite Rebuttals and Clarifications," *New York Times*, November 12, 1991.

39. See Theresa Funiciello, *Tyranny of Kindness: Dismantling the Welfare System to End Poverty in America* (New York: Atlantic Monthly Press, 1993), p. 268.

40. See Barbara Ehrenreich, "The New Right Attack on Social Welfare," in Fred Block et al., eds., *The Mean Season: The Attack on the Welfare State* (New York: Pantheon, 1987), pp. 161–95.

41. Andrea Louise Campbell, *How Policies Make Citizens: Senior Political Activism and the American Welfare State* (Princeton, N.J.: Princeton University Press, 2003), p. 128.

42. Ibid., p. 268.

43. Quoted in Joe Soss, "Lessons of Welfare: Policy Design, Political Learning, and Political Action," *American Political Science Review* 93, no. 2 (June 1999): 367.

44. Stanley S. Surrey and Paul R. McDaniel, *Tax Expenditures* (Cambridge, Mass.: Harvard University Press, 1985), p. 34.

45. U.S. Bureau of the Census, *Statistical Abstract of the United States 2004–2005* (Washington, D.C.: U.S. Government Printing Office, 2004), p. 313.

46. Michael Peter Smith, *City, State, and Market: The Political Economy of Urban Society* (Cambridge: Basil Blackwell, 1988).

47. Peter Dreier, John Mollenkopf, and Todd Swanstrom, *Place Matters: Metropolitics for the Twenty-first Century*, rev. ed. (Lawrence: University Press of Kansas, 2005), p. 122.

48. Theda Skocpol, "Targeting Within Universalism: Politically Viable Policies to Combat Poverty in the United States," in Christopher Jencks and Paul E. Peterson, eds., *The Urban Underclass* (Washington, D.C.: The Brookings Institution, 1991), p. 425.

49. Theda Skocpol, *The Missing Middle: Working Families and the Future of American Social Policy* (New York: W. W. Norton, 2000), p. 76.

50. Andrea Louise Campbell, *How Policies Make Citizens: Senior Political Activism and the American Welfare State* (Princeton, N.J.: Princeton University Press), pp. 129–30.

51. See the studies cited in Barry Bluestone and Bennett Harrison, *The Deindustrialization of America: Plant Closings, Community Abandonment, and the Dismantling of Basic Industry* (New York: Basic Books, 1982), chap. 3.

52. Isaiah Berlin, *Four Essays on Liberty* (London: Oxford University Press, 1969).

53. Lester M. Salamon, *Partners in Public Service: Government-Nonprofit Relations in the Modern Welfare State* (Baltimore: Johns Hopkins University Press, 1995).

54. Yankelovich poll, as reported in *U.S. News & World Report*, October 5, 1992, p. 40.

CHAPTER 18

1. The story of CIA plots against Castro is drawn from U.S. Senate, Select Committee to Study Governmental Operations with Regard to Intelligence Activities, *Alleged Assassination Plots Involving Foreign Leaders* (Washington, D.C.: U.S. Government Printing Office, 1975).

2. See especially Hamilton's arguments in *Federalist No. 6* and *No. 11*.

3. Clinton Rossiter, ed., *The Federalist Papers* (New York: New American Library, 1961), p. 424.

4. Richard H. Kohn, *Eagle and Sword: The Federalists and the Creation of the Military Establishment in America, 1783–1802* (New York: Free Press, 1975).

5. Ibid., p. 9.

6. Richard J. Barnet, *The Rockets' Red Glare: When America Goes to War—The Presidents and the People* (New York: Simon & Schuster, 1990), p. 82.

7. Ibid., pp. 111–15, 125–38; Bruce Miroff, *Icons of Democracy: American Leaders as Heroes, Aristocrats, Dissenters, and Democrats* (Lawrence: University Press of Kansas, 2000), pp. 182–87.

8. Roy P. Basler, ed., *The Collected Works of Abraham Lincoln* (New Brunswick, N.J.: Rutgers University Press, 1953–55), vol. 3, p. 357.

9. Quoted in Barnet, *Rockets' Red Glare*, p. 15.

10. Quoted in Ralph B. Levering, *The Cold War, 1945–1987* (Arlington Heights, Ill.: Harlan Davidson, 1988), p. 30.

11. Of all the Cold War presidents, Eisenhower probably had the deepest interest in peace. See Robert A. Divine, *Eisenhower and the Cold War* (New York: Oxford University Press, 1981), pp. 105–55.

12. George C. Herring, *America's Longest War: The United States and Vietnam, 1950–1975*, 2nd ed. (New York: Alfred A. Knopf, 1986).

13. John Prados, *Presidents' Secret Wars: CIA and Pentagon Covert Operations Since World War II* (New York: William Morrow, 1986), pp. 91–98.

14. Seymour M. Hersh, *The Price of Power: Kissinger in the Nixon White House* (New York: Summit, 1983), pp. 258–96.

15. Quoted in Divine, *Eisenhower and the Cold War*, p. 108.

16. James M. McCormick, *American Foreign Policy and Process*, 2nd ed. (Itasca, Ill.: Peacock, 1992), pp. 377–80.

17. Ibid., pp. 361–69.

18. Donald M. Snow and Eugene Brown, *United States Foreign Policy: Politics Beyond the Water's Edge*, 2nd ed. (Boston: Bedford/St. Martin's, 2000), p. 151.

19. Ibid., pp. 152–54.

20. Loch K. Johnson, *America's Secret Power: The CIA in a Democratic Society* (New York: Oxford University Press, 1989), pp. 16–17.

21. Prados, *Presidents' Secret Wars*, pp. 402–13.

22. Johnson, *America's Secret Power*, p. 10.

23. Ibid., pp. 107–10, 118–29, 207–33.

24. Tim Weiner, "CIA Hired Suspected Assassins, Panel Says," *New York Times*, June 29, 1996.

25. The 9/11 Commission Report, Executive Summary, p. 12 (www.9-11commission.gov/report).

26. Mark Leibovich, "George Tenet's 'Slam Dunk' into the History Books," *Washington Post*, June 4, 2004.

27. Douglas Jehl and David Johnston, "Rules Change Lets C.I.A. Freely Send Suspects Abroad to Jails," *New York Times*, March 6, 2005.

28. John Diamond, "CIA Shake-up Continues: Two Veteran Spies to Step Down," *USA Today*, November 15, 2004.

29. Charles W. Kegley Jr., and Eugene R. Wittkopf, *World Politics*, 4th ed. (New York: St. Martin's, 1993), pp. 214–50.

30. Lawrence R. Jacobs and Benjamin I. Page, "Who Influences U.S. Foreign Policy?" *American Political Science Review* 99 (February 2005): 120.

31. Richard J. Barnet, *Roots of War* (New York: Penguin, 1973), pp. 179–82.

32. Johnson, *America's Secret Power*, p. 22.

33. See Thomas W. Graham, "Public Opinion and U.S. Foreign Policy Decision Making," in David A. Deese, ed., *The New Politics of American Foreign Policy* (New York: St. Martin's, 1994), pp. 190–215.

34. McCormick, *American Foreign Policy and Process*, pp. 498–505.

35. Robert Y. Shapiro and Benjamin I. Page, "Foreign Policy and Public Opinion," in Deese, *New Politics*, pp. 229–33.

36. Emily O. Goldman and Larry Berman, "Engaging the World: First Impressions of the Clinton Foreign Policy Legacy," in Colin Campbell and Bert A. Rockman, eds., *The Clinton Legacy* (New York: Chatham House, 2000), pp. 226–30.

37. Quoted in Elizabeth Drew, *On the Edge: The Clinton Presidency* (New York: Simon & Schuster, 1994), p. 162.

38. *New York Times*, November 22, 1995.

39. See Joseph S. Nye Jr., *The Paradox of American Power: Why the World's Only Superpower Can't Go It Alone* (New York: Oxford University Press, 2002).

40. Benjamin R. Barber, *Fear's Empire: War, Terrorism, and Democracy* (New York: W. W. Norton, 2003), p. 147.

41. Quoted in Nye, *The Paradox of American Power*, p. 156.

42. Thom Shanker, "White House Says the U.S. Is Not a Loner, Just Choosy," *New York Times*, July 31, 2001.

43. Ivo H. Daalder and James M. Lindsay, "Bush's Foreign Policy Revolution," in Fred I. Greenstein, ed., *The George W. Bush Presidency: An Early Assessment* (Baltimore: Johns Hopkins University Press, 2003), pp. 125–29.

44. Quoted in Barber, *Fear's Empire*, p. 79.

45. See Juan Cole, "The Lies That Led to War," www.salon.com, May 19, 2005.

46. Quoted in CNN.com, "Ashcroft: Critics of New Terror Measures Undermine Effort," December 7, 2001.

INDEX